C A N A D I A N
INDUSTRIAL ORGANIZATION
—— AND POLICY ——

D0943138

C A N A D I A N

INDUSTRIAL ORGANIZATION ———— AND POLICY ————

Second Edition

CHRISTOPHER GREEN
Professor of Economics
McGill University

McGRAW-HILL RYERSON LIMITED

Toronto Montreal New York Auckland Bogotá Cairo Guatemala Hamburg
Johannesburg Lisbon London Madrid Mexico New Delhi Panama Paris
San Juan São Paulo Singapore Sydney Tokyo

CANADIAN INDUSTRIAL ORGANIZATION AND POLICY,
Second Edition

ISBN 0-07-548906-6

2 3 4 5 6 7 8 9 0   AP   4 3 2 1 0 9 8 7 6

Printed and bound in Canada

Care has been taken to trace ownership of copyright material contained in this text. The publishers will gladly take any information that will enable them to rectify any reference or credit in subsequent editions.

Canadian Cataloguing in Publication Data

Green, Christopher, date
   Canadian industrial organization and policy

Includes bibliographical references and index.
ISBN 0-07-548906-8.

1. Industrial organization–Canada.   2. Industry and state–Canada.
3. Canada–Economic policy.   I. Title.

HD70.C2G74 1985   338.6′0971   C85-098233-2

To Lenore, and to
Andrea, Kirsten, and Peter

Table of Contents

List of Tables

List of Illustrations

Foreword

In its first edition, this book was a distinguished addition to the literature of industrial organization and public policy. It was both a pioneering and a comprehensive treatment of Canada's industrial economics and policies. Since then, and especially with the advent of this second edition, the book has become a major feature of the field: thorough, balanced, and authoritative.

The field of industrial organization itself has two parts. First is *diagnosis*: the nature of industrial competition and monopoly, their determinants, and their influence on industrial performance. Second is *treatment*: public policies which may cure (or often, alas, worsen!) the deviations from good economic performance.

The issues are ancient and urgent, though the field has emerged in full technical splendour only since the 1930s. The old truths have been affirmed by the new concepts and tests: competition applies healthy pressure to produce cheaply, to sell at cost, and to try new methods. Comparative studies have also shown that the basic laws do not change at national borders.

Yet there are national differences, which are important but often misunderstood. This book about Canadian industries and public policies is not only the first of its kind. It is also especially valuable because it shows the distinctive Canadian features clearly and fairly. Canada is different, on three planes. First, certain industrial *facts* differ. For example, the country has a large area but low population density. It is like the United States in resources and technology, but at one tenth the market size. Climate, language division, and other conditions make Canada unusual among all modern economies.

Second, there are certain special *issues*. With the United States as neighbours, Canadians are unusually sensitive to foreign ownership. Foreign trade is also of special importance, especially for farm and mining products. On the third plane, Canada has evolved an unusual variety of *public policies*, toward price fixing, monopolizing, utilities, foreign ownership, and other industrial issues. Its public enterprises are also of special interest for their unique features.

Professor Green's task has been to convey both the body of mainstream concepts and the distinctive Canadian attributes, all within the covers of one book. The task is much harder than it seems. More than I had thought possible for such a complex field and such a special country, he has done so with great skill and thoroughness. And this revised edition has incorporated new ideas and events, fitting them in the larger picture. The reader will come away knowing not only Canada's own features but also the basic concepts for comparing them with those of other countries.

The book is packed with technical content and details, as it must be for such a booming, varied economy. Yet Professor Green always sees the whole and connects the parts. That is your challenge too, to absorb the parts within a balanced perspective.

The book is also a critique of the policies, showing unsparingly those that are silly or bad, as well as those that work pretty well. Your second challenge is to do the same, to develop an independent cast of mind about these all-too-human policies. The conditions and debates are lively and changing, and some of them occasionally are argued at white heat. But you will now see them objectively and in good humour. Again and again, as years go by, you will be pondering which policies should be dropped, which should be revised, and which new ones should be started. This book gives you an expert, balanced start.

With these merits, this book has become the standard gateway by which each new generation of students comes to learn about Canada's industries and policies. That makes it especially valuable as a critique. For some of the readers will soon be filling positions of influence over just these policies. If you and the other readers will acquire this book's fair and rigorous habits of mind along with its technical content, there is hope that Canada's policies will in time become even better than they already are.

WILLIAM G. SHEPHERD

Preface

Canadian Industrial Organization and Policy was written to fill an obvious gap: until its appearance no systematic treatment of Canadian industrial organization and public policies toward business was available to teachers and their students. Canadian teachers and students of industrial organization had to rely on U.S. textbooks supplemented by copious and expensive "handouts" and government reports to cover distinctively Canadian material. The first edition of *Canadian Industrial Organization and Policy* provided an alternative to these less efficient methods of covering Canadian facts and institutions. The book was clearly designed to present the facts of Canadian market structure, behaviour, performance and public policies toward business, with just enough theory to meet the student's basic needs. It made no attempt to survey all of industrial organization theory and evidence.

The second edition of *Canadian Industrial Organization and Policy* both updates and expands upon the coverage in the first edition. While the focus of the second edition continues to be on (updated) Canadian facts, policies and institutions, and the distinctive aspects of Canadian industrial organization, there are some changes. The second edition includes more theoretical material, particularly at the beginning of chapters 2 and 10 and in a new third chapter, than did the first edition. The second edition also gives considerable space to an analysis of the underlying assumptions and the predictions of an alternative to the standard (structure-conduct-performance) industrial organization paradigm, and suggests a synthesis of the two. It also gives more attention to foreign ownership and control at three levels: the descriptive level (in chapter 1), analytical level (in chapter 4) and policy level (in chapter 12). There are now two chapters on Canadian competition policy instead of the single one in the first edition. As did its predecessor, this edition includes subject matter that one does not usually find in U.S. textbooks. Chapter 4, "The Tariff, Foreign Ownership and Canadian Industrial Organization" and chapter 11, "Public Enterprise in Canada" cover institutions (tariffs, foreign ownership, and public enterprise) which, in a relative sense at least, are much more important to Canadian industrial organization than to that of the U.S. In chapter 5, "Collusive and Competitive Behaviour in Canadian Industry," I have followed the example of the first edition in attempting to illustrate the richness and variety of industrial behaviour mainly through a series of (now nine) industrial vignettes or case studies, rather than through the presentation of a series of oligopoly models. However, this edition does give some attention to oligopoly theory by distinguishing the assumptions and results of some of the leading models. Nevertheless, this is one subject for which many industrial organization teachers may want to provide supplementary theoretical material to that contained in the book.

As was the case with the first edition, *Canadian Industrial Organization and Policy*, Second Edition, is essentially divided into two parts. The first six chapters cover industrial organization proper. Following an introductory chapter describing the Canadian economic landscape, the outline of the structure-conduct-performance paradigm is evident in the titles to chapters 2 through 6. The second six chapters cover public policies toward business. They might be thought of as an abbreviated Canadian counterpart to the well-known encyclopedic U.S. text, W.G. Shepherd and C. Wilcox, *Public Policies Toward Business*, 6th edition (Irwin: 1979). Chapter 7 provides a theoretical and philosophical introduction to the public policy issue. Chapters 8 and 11 successively cover Canadian competition policy, regulation, and public ownership. Chapter 12 deals with Canadian government intervention in "atomistic" industries (particularly agriculture), and "industrial policies" designed to foster industry growth and regional economic development.

Canadian Industrial Organization and Policy is primarily designed for either a full-year course, more or less equally divided between Industrial Organization and Public Policies Toward Business, or for a one-term course combining the two subject matters, although not necessarily in equal parts. In a full-year course the instructor may want to supplement *Canadian Industrial Organization and Policy*, Second Edition, with (or use the book as a supplement to) a standard U.S. text which gives more attention to industrial organization theory. Excellent examples are F.M. Scherer, *Industrial Market Structure and Economic Performance* (Rand-McNally, 1980) and William G. Shepherd, *The Economics of Industrial Organization* (Prentice-Hall, 1985). For those who agree with Professor Stigler that there is no such field as Industrial Organization, only applied price theory, *Canadian Industrial Organization and Policy* can be used alongside a standard price theory textbook.

In a one-term course, the book can probably stand alone, or be combined with "outside" readings. It is hoped that instructors in either one term or full-year courses in intermediate microeconomic theory will find *Canadian Industrial Organization and Policy* a useful supplement to a standard micro theory textbook. The public policy material in chapters 7-12 should also be of use to students in political science and law courses which have an important economics interface.

I wish to acknowledge help of various kinds from a number of people. In the preface to the first edition, I made clear that were it not for Professor W.G. Shepherd of the University of Michigan I would not have written *Canadian Industrial Organization and Policy*. He suggested the project, secured a publisher, provided constant encouragement, and read the total manuscript, making invaluable comments and suggestions. He has honoured me and the book by contributing a Foreword to each of the editions.

I am also indebted to two former teachers, Professors Leonard Weiss and Joel B. Dirlam who, more than twenty years ago, kindled my interest in the fields of industrial organization and regulation. They have left an indelible mark on my approach to the subject. A more recent, but no less influential, "teacher" was Professor Almarin Phillips who was, for a year, a colleague of mine at McGill University's Centre for the Study of Regulated Industries.

There are many persons whose comments and suggestions contributed to the revision of *Canadian Industrial Organization and Policy*. Memory and space permit mentioning only a few. I am particularly indebted to Professor Richard Schwindt who read the manuscript and made many valuable suggestions for improvement. Professor John Palmer made available his "annotated" copy of the book, which proved useful in discerning gaps and correcting mistakes, typographical and otherwise, which appeared in the first edition. I received helpful suggestions, in correspondence and conversation, from Professor Gideon Rosenbluth, whose review of the first edition of the book has provided lasting moral support. Professor Richard Schultz, who succeeded me as Director of McGill's Centre for the Study of Regulated Industries, made valuable comments on the content and organization of chapter 10. Among the numerous persons who sent me material, made suggestions, or provided encouragement were Bernie Wolf, Andrew Muller, Bill Jordan, W.T. Stanbury, Klaus Stegemann, Ron Saunders, Paul Gorecki, Shmuel Shamir, D.G. McFetridge, Steven Globerman, Andrew Judson, Leonard Waverman, Chris Maule and Robert Cairns. Edward P. Neufeld granted permission to reprint two tables from his study of the Canadian financial system. The assistance and editorial help of Edie Franks, Brian Dunster, Wendy Thomas, Gail Johnstone, and Christopher Blackburn are gratefully acknowledged. My deepest debt is to Cathy Duggan for her typing wizardry, and her sustaining help and interest in the project since its inception almost eight years ago.

In addition, I should like to thank the countless students who, during the past decade and a half, have enrolled in my full-year course, "Government and Business" (Industrial Organization and Public Policies Toward Business). Their interest in the subject, their questions, and their exams and term papers, contributed to my enthusiasm for and knowledge of the subject—both ultimately invaluable in bringing the original edition and now its revision to fruition. I have also found invaluable my long contact with McGill Law School where I have successfully co-taught "Legal Problems in Government Control of Business" and "The Law of Competition" with Professors Maxwell Cohen, David Jones, and Julius Grey, and Mr. David Henry.

Finally, to my wife Lenore, and to my children, Andrea, Kirsten and Peter, to all of whom this book is dedicated, my deepest affection for your patience and love.

C.G.

1

The Canadian Economic Setting

The development of the Canadian economy has been strongly influenced by two characters of geography and one of policy. First, Canada's land area is exceeded only by that of the U.S.S.R., whose population is eleven times that of Canada. Second, Canada has a 3000 mile border with the United States, the world's leading industrial nation. To "protect" herself economically Canada has historically employed high tariffs as part of a "National Policy," ostensibly designed to promote the industrialization of Canada. These three factors, two geographic and one legislative, have played very important roles in the evolution of Canada's economic structure. Thus, Canada's resource-based economy is reflected in its geographic extent; the unique extent to which Canadian industry is foreign owned is related to our proximity to the United States; and the relative inefficiency of our manufacturing sector is related to our small and tariff-protected domestic markets. No study of Canadian industrial reorganization can ignore these elements of geography and policy, and no application of a Canadian "industrial policy" can escape their force.

As noted, Canada is the world's second largest nation, measured in terms of square miles. Canada is also one of the smaller industrialized nations measured by population. While much of Canada is virtually uninhabited, and its population is largely concentrated in a few "corridors" near the U.S. border, the population-land ratio is an important part of Canada's economic story. Since the earliest explorations by Europeans the "Dominion of the North" has been recognized as a land-rich, resource-abundant nation. Fish and furs were the earliest in demand. Next came timber. Later, cereal production in the West held the spotlight. Today petroleum and natural gas, mineral ores, and water power are the most important natural resource industries. In the 19th century

1

Canada's resource base gave credence to the jibe that we are a nation of "hewers of wood and drawers of water." In the last two decades of the twentieth century such a statement hardly describes a nation 75 percent urban and largely employed in nonresource industries and white-collar occupations. Nevertheless, Canada's comparative advantage still largely resides in her resource sector. This fact remains important in understanding the development and evolution of the Canadian economy and related public policies.[1]

Canada's long border with the United States has had an important influence on economic and social affairs in Canada. There have been demographic movements beginning with the settlement of Loyalists fleeing from the American revolution. In the early 19th century, chiefly before the War of 1812, southwestern Ontario was heavily settled by American pioneers searching for new lands as western New York, Pennsylvania and the Ohio valley began to fill up. In the latter half of the 19th century there was a constant drain of Canadian settlers south and westward into the United States seeking better land and job opportunities. In the twentieth century, the sharp limits on immigration legislated in the 1920s by the United States undoubtedly propelled into Canada many persons fleeing their European homelands. In the 1960s there was a substantial migration of Americans to Canada in response to economic opportunities here and political events at home.

Of more economic importance than the movement of people has been the movement of goods and capital across the Canadian-U.S. border. Economists have long pointed to the tendency for trade patterns to be of a north-south rather than of an east-west variety.[2] In fact, in its formative years there was genuine concern whether a Canada from Atlantic to Pacific could survive. Thus, the ostensible motive for the building of the Canadian Pacific Railway in the 1870s-'80s was to indissolubly link the West with the Eastern provinces, and thereby forestall an extension of American "manifest destiny" into the Canadian North West.[3] While Canada's geographic integrity was thus assured its economic ties

---

1. Two classic discussions of Canada's early economic development are H.A. Innis, *The Fur Trade in Canada* (Yale University Press, New Haven, 1930), and W.A. MacKintosh, *The Economic Background of Dominion Provincial Relations*, Appendix III of the Report of the Rowell-Sirois Commission (Ottawa, King's Printer, 1939, republished by McClelland and Stewart, 1964). Also useful is a collection of Innis' papers, *Essays in Canadian Economic History* (University of Toronto Press, 1967).

2. Actually this greatly oversimplifies. In the 19th century much Canadian trade was "triangular" between U.K., U.S. and Canada. Moreover, semifinished goods imported from the U.S. for finishing were often "reexported" to other parts of Canada, suggesting that north-south and east-west were sometimes complementary rather than mutually exclusive.

3. Another view is that the railroad was built to facilitate an alternative route for the British-East India-China Trade in the event the Suez Canal route was blocked. Keep in mind that most of the financial capital required to build the CPR came from Great Britain. See Tom Naylor, *The History of Canadian Business 1867-1914*, Vol. II, pp. 235-36.

with the United States have grown with increased trade and financial links. By the end of the 19th century, the United States had replaced Great Britain as the chief external economic influence upon Canada.

The Canadian tariff has been a bulwark against genuine North American economic integration. Although it has not isolated Canada from the U.S. business cycle and the impact here of U.S. monetary and fiscal policies, the Canadian tariff has limited imports of manufactured goods to Canada. At its inception the "National Policy" almost surely contributed to the growth of manufacturing employment opportunities in Canada. However, the tariff has also dampened the growth of efficient manufacturing plant capacity, as we shall see in chapter 4, thereby hampering the ability of the manufacturing sector to grow via export capabilities. Moreover, the tariff, now in decline, has contributed to the high levels of foreign (chiefly U.S.) ownership and control of the Canadian manufacturing sector. Since Canada is a "natural" market for the sales of U.S. firms, trade barriers are overcome or "jumped" by the establishment of Canadian subsidiaries of U.S. parent firms. Apparently Canadians place greater weight on whatever employment the tariff protects than upon the external control over our resources that the tariff induces.

The Industrial Structure of the Canadian Economy

The chief role of this chapter is to paint a picture of the Canadian economic landscape—or in more mundane terms to describe the industrial structure of the Canadian economy. In describing a nation's economic structure, it is usual to classify economic activities into three broadly defined groups or sectors:

1. The *primary* sector: includes agriculture, forestry, fishing and hunting, and mining, including oil and gas wells.
2. The *secondary* sector: includes manufacturing, construction, and utilities in the transportation, communication and energy fields.
3. The *tertiary* sector: includes wholesale and retail trade, finance, insurance and real estate, community, business, and personal services and public administration.

In all industrial nations the share of total production or total employment accounted for by the primary, secondary, and tertiary sectors has changed markedly over time. In the pre-industrial age the primary sector accounted for most economic activity chiefly because of the predominance of agriculture. During the 19th century the process of industrialization in Europe and North America caused the share of activity accounted for by the secondary sector, chiefly manufacturing and transportation activities, to rise at the expense of the primary sector. The first half of the twentieth century witnessed the strong relative growth of the tertiary sector as technology, rising incomes, and greater leisure time generated increasing demands for all sorts of services, including those which are publicly financed and provided. The growth in the tertiary sector's share has been mainly at the expense of a continuing decline in the primary sector's share, while the share accounted for by the secondary sector has in recent decades ceased to grow. These trends, typical of the experience of

Table 1-1

Production Shares by Sector, Selected Years 1870-1980

	% of Gross Domestic Product at Factor Cost					
	1870	1911	1926	1960	1970	1980
Primary	46.2	39.4	23.4	10.4	8.3	10.9
Agriculture	34.3	30.8	18.1	4.9	3.3	3.3
Forestry	9.9	4.6	1.3	1.3	.8	.9
Fishing & trapping	1.1	1.5	.8	.2	.2	.2
Mining, quarrying, oil wells	.9	2.5	3.2	4.0	4.0	6.5
Secondary	22.6	29.7	38.7	44.8	41.4	39.4
Manufacturing	NA	18.8	21.7	26.4	23.3	21.6
Construction	NA	10.3	4.1	6.0	6.3	5.8
Transportation & communication	NA	NA	} 12.9	9.6	8.9	8.5
Electric power, gas & water utilities	NA	.6		2.8	2.9	3.5
Tertiary	31.2[a]	30.8[a]	37.9	44.8	50.2	49.1
Wholesale-retail trade	NA	NA	11.6	12.8	12.4	11.0
Finance, insurance, real estate	NA	NA	10.0	11.6	11.3	10.6
Public administration, defence	NA	NA	3.4	6.9	7.3	7.5
Service	NA	NA	12.9	13.5	19.2	20.6
Total	100.0	100.0	100.0	100.0	100.0	100.0

[a]Includes income generated by the railway and telephone industries.
Sources: M.C. Urquhart and K.A.H. Buckley, *Historical Statistics of Canada* (Cambridge: Macmillan, 1965), Series E 46-45, E 202-213; E 214-44 for 1870, 1911, and 1926; second edition, 1983, series F56-75 for 1960 and 1970; Statistics Canada *National Income and Expenditure Accounts* Cat. 31-201, Ottawa, Dec. 1981, Table III, p. 97, for 1980.

economies which have passed through the industrialization process, generally apply to Canada as well. Table 1-1 tells the story. As Canada entered the last two decades of the twentieth century the production shares of the primary, secondary, and tertiary sectors in Canada were approximately 10, 40, and 50 percent respectively.[4]

The detail in Table 1-1 establishes the following: in terms of relative shares of gross domestic output (GDP) the biggest decline is in agriculture, followed by forestry. Offsetting this decline is the rise in the share of services. Except for fishing and trapping, and perhaps construction, the shares of the remaining industry groups have remained constant or increased slightly in the last half century or so. It is of some interest that the share of GDP accounted for by public administration has grown very little since 1960, and that the share of the service sector has grown dramatically, accounting for the characterization of post-industrial economies as "service economies."

The time trends of the output shares mask even more dramatic developments in employment trends. When employment rather than output is the measure, as in Table 1-2, the dramatic decline of the primary sector is now matched, and more, by the dramatic rise of the tertiary sector. By 1980, almost 60 percent of the work force was employed in tertiary industries and only 7 percent in primary industries. Since 1960, employment shares in secondary industries have declined, particularly in manufacturing. These trends will probably continue into the 1990s, and beyond. In contrast, Table 1-2 indicates the tremendous increase in the utilization of human resources by the service sector of the economy, which presently absorbs almost a third of all employed persons. Compare these figures with the respective output shares shown in Table 1-1.

Measuring the relative economic importance of the different sectors of the economy using employment data tends to overstate the relative importance of the tertiary and understate the relative importance of the secondary sector. This is so to the extent that it is more meaningful to measure economic contributions in terms of outputs instead of inputs. Thus the shares of GDP presented in Table 1-1 are a more accurate reflection of the relative economic importance of the various sectors and subsectors of the Canadian economy than are the employment share figures in Table 1-2.

But even the figures in Table 1-1 are somewhat misleading, if what we want is a measure of the share of actual output accounted for by each sector. (They are presented here because they are the only ones that are available in historical time series extending back to the last century.) The problem with measuring output at factor cost, the basis for the numbers in Table 1-1, is that they are

4. For reasons elaborated on below, the figures in Table 1-1 tend to overstate the decline (rise) in the secondary (tertiary) sectors' share of actual (real) output.

Table 1-2

Employment Shares (%) by Economic Sector and Industry

	1891[a]	1921[a]	1947	1960	1970	1975	1980	1982
Primary	49	36	27.5	14.3	9.3	7.8	7.3	6.9
Agriculture			24.1	11.3	6.5	5.2	4.5	4.4
Forestry			1.2	1.1	.9	.9	.7	.6
Fishing & trapping			.7	.4	.3	.3	.3	.3
Mining, quarrying, oil wells			1.5	1.5	1.6	1.4	1.8	1.6
Secondary	31	34	40.3	40.7	37.5	37.3	34.0	32.0
Manufacturing			26.7	24.9	22.7	22.1	19.7	18.2
Construction			5.2	7.2	6.0	6.5	5.8	5.6
Transportation & communication			7.7	7.5	7.7	7.6	7.3	7.1
Public utilities			.7	1.1	1.1	1.1	1.2	1.1
Tertiary	20	30	32.1	45.0	53.2	54.9	58.7	61.1
Trade (wholesale, retail)			12.3	16.2	16.7	17.2	17.2	17.4
Finance, insurance, real estate			2.7	3.8	4.6	4.9	5.7	5.7
Community, business, personal services (incl. health, education)			17.1	25.0	25.7	26.1	28.9	30.8
Public administration					6.2	6.7	6.9	7.2
Total	100.0	100.0	100.0	100.0	100.0	100.0	100.0	100.0

[a]Based on occupational data in which all clerical workers are allocated to the tertiary sector and all non-primary sector labourers are allocated to the secondary sector.

Sources: M.C. Urquhart and H.Buckley, *Historical Statistics of Canada*, Series C8-35 for 1891 and 1921; C 130-151 for 1947, 1960: Statistics Canada, *The Labour Force* Cat. 71-001 for 1970, 1975, 1980 and 1982.

sensitive to (a) intersectoral differences in the rate of growth of productivity, measured as output per unit of input, and (b) differential increases in factor input prices over time. Thus in Table 1-1 the decline in the GDP (at factor cost) share of the secondary sector, and in particular the manufacturing sector, during the 1960s, was due primarily to the fact that the rate of growth of productivity in manufacturing was both absolutely and relatively high. Measuring GDP at factor cost tends to understate output share in sectors which by virtue of rapid productivity growth require relatively less input to produce a given amount of output. At the same time, in the employment-intensive service sector, which experienced little or no *measured* productivity growth, but had to absorb substantial wage increases, the share of GDP, measured as the factor cost of producing that output, increased sharply in the 1960s.

When GDP is measured in "real" terms (the value of output deflated for price increases), the broad sectoral shares are as follows:

	1960	1970	1980
	%	%	%
Primary sector	8.8	8.0	5.9
Secondary sector	36.2	40.4	41.3
Tertiary sector	55.0	51.6	52.8
Total	100.0	100.0	100.0

Instead of declining as indicated in Table 1-1, the share of the secondary sector actually rose during the 1960s, as did the real GDP share of its main component, manufacturing (not shown). In contrast, the share of real GDP accounted for by the tertiary sector actually fell during the 1960s. Sectoral shares remained more or less constant during the 1970s, a period which saw the growth rate of productivity in manufacturing fall dramatically. Of course, the real GDP shares must be treated with care because of difficulties in constructing accurate price deflators and in measuring productivity growth in the service sector. Nevertheless, they imply that forecasts of the demise of the manufacturing sector in Canada, based on trends in the share of employment or GDP (measured at factor cost) are probably inaccurate and certainly premature.[5]

When the preceding tables are taken together they suggest a certain paradox: the Canadian economy is still heavily reliant on the production of tangible goods, while increasingly its work force is engaged in providing services either

5. Much of the discussion about an "industrial strategy" for Canada is based on the view that Canadians have overemphasized the importance of the resource sector to Canada's prosperity and have given too little attention to promoting an allegedly deteriorating manufacturing sector. However, Watson has shown that all but 2 of 16 indicators of Canadian manufacturing performance improved between 1963 and 1980. See W.G. Watson, *A Primer on the Economics of Industrial Policy* (Toronto: Ontario Economic Council, 1983), p. 52.

unrelated or only loosely related to goods production. Looked at in another way, by 1981, 65 percent of the employed work force were engaged in occupations classified as "white collar," 35 percent in "blue collar" (see Table 1-3).

The differences between the trends in industry output and employment shares are reflected in inter-industry differences in productivity growth rates. Table 1-4 indicates how the average rates of growth of real domestic product (RDP) per employed person have varied among economic sectors in the postwar period. (Ideally, labour productivity should be measured as output per man-hour rather than output per person employed, in order to take account of potential differences in the relative importance of part-time work between different industries.) For the period 1948-70 the four industry groups with the lowest average annual rates of growth of productivity were found in the tertiary sector. Except for electric, gas, and water utilities, the three industry groups included in the primary sector were the productivity growth leaders. The same story is told by the productivity estimates for 1969-73. Similar results were forecast for the period 1977-82 but, as column 5 shows, matters turned out very differently. We will have more to say about the great "productivity slowdown" below, after some caveats regarding the measurement of productivity.

Table 1-3

The Employed by Occupation, 1981

Occupations	Persons Employed (000)	%
Blue collar (35.0% of all)		
Primary	672	6.2
Processing, machining, fabricating, assembling	1 664	15.2
Construction	658	6.0
Transportation	409	3.8
Materials handling	417	3.8
White collar (65.0% of all)		
Service	1 468	13.4
Sales	1 125	10.3
Clerical	1 934	17.7
Managerial, professional, administrative	2 585	23.6
All occupations	10 933	100.0

Source: Statistics Canada, *The Labour Force* (Cat. 71–001). Reproduced by permission of the Minister of Supply and Services Canada.

There are difficulties in measuring productivity in service industries. Often the output (or service) is identified with the input (i.e. with the person providing the service, as, e.g., nurses, lawyers, doctors, accountants), so that an increase in the former only appears when there is an increase in the latter. Here, increases in productivity are likely to take the form of improvements of quality of service provided. Moreover, for many services there is typically little potential for increasing output per unit of labour via substitution of capital for labour, at least over the short and medium runs. For all these reasons the productivity estimates in Table 1-4 should be treated carefully and in any event should not be considered as indicating anything about the value that society places on the services provided by the tertiary sector.

The fourth column of Table 1-4 indicates the contributions of the various sectors to the 2.63 average annual productivity growth experienced by Canada from 1961 to 1971. Although the primary sector accounted for only about 10 percent of GDP in the 1960s, increases in output per employed person in the primary industries accounted for an estimated 25 percent or more of the overall growth in productivity. The secondary sector's relative contribution to productivity growth also exceeded its output share. In contrast, the tertiary sector's stagnant output share and its rapidly increasing employment share combined to eliminate any net contribution by that sector to productivity growth during the period, according to estimates made by the Economic Council of Canada. That is, quality improvement aside, output per employed person did not, on the average, increase in the tertiary sector as a whole. At a more detailed level one discovers that there was positive productivity growth per employed worker in the trade and finance sectors offset by estimated productivity declines in services and public administration. From the vantage point of the early 1970s, the low productivity growth in the sectors where employment growth had been, and would continue to be, most rapid, might have led one to the conclusion that the prospect for maintaining postwar levels of productivity growth were dim. The conclusion, however, did not necessarily follow. So long as the tertiary sector's share of real GDP did not rise and if productivity growth rates in the primary and secondary sectors had not declined, average productivity growth could have been maintained.

In fact, the latter half of the 1970s and the early 1980s witnessed a substantial slowdown in productivity growth, centred particularly in the manufacturing and mining sectors where productivity growth had been above average during the first two and a half decades of the postwar era. Overall, average annual productivity growth fell to about a quarter of its 1969-73 rate, and became negative in the first years of the 1980s (not shown). The causes of the productivity slowdown remain something of a mystery. The sharp fall in productivity growth was coincidental with the rapid rise in energy prices in the

Table 1-4

Productivity Growth Rates by Industrial Sector

Annual Rates of Growth of Real Domestic Product per Person Employed

	(1) Rank 1948-70	(2) 1948-70	(3) 1969-73	(4) Contribution[b] to Growth in Productivity 1961-71 (percentage pts.)	(5) 1973-79[a]	(6) Percentage Contribution to Productivity Slowdown 1974-79
Primary				.78		19.2
Agriculture	3	4.6	5.3	.48	.23	7.0
Forestry	4	4.2	2.1	.06	.73	1.5
Mining, quarrying, oil wells	2	4.9	6.6	.24	−2.13	10.7
Secondary				1.89		47.8
Manufacturing	6	3.3	3.1	1.13	1.95	29.1
Construction	7	2.6	.9	.12	.08	9.8
Transportation and storage	5	3.7	3.8	.64	1.80	8.4
Communication					5.76	−2.2
Utilities	1	5.1	6.4		.64	2.7

Tertiary				-.03		3.8
Wholesale, retail trade	8	2.0	1.6	.28	.2	7.2
Finance	9	.7	1.1	.15	.9	-3.0
Community, business, personal services	11	-1.1	-.2	-.42	-.11	-.4
Public administration and defence	10	.1	-.6	-.04		NA
Total economy[c]		2.6	2.1	2.63	.55[d]	70.8[d]

[a]Gross output per man year

[b]Includes the impact of changes in industry structure.

[c]Includes fishing.

[d]Excludes government sector.

Sources: Economic Council of Canada, *Eleventh Annual Review*, 1974, Table 8-1 pp. 178-9; Economic Council of Canada, *Twelfth Annual Review* 1975, Appendix, Table D-4, pp. 164-5; A. Sharpe, "The Causes of the Productivity Slowdown in Canada" (paper presented to the annual meeting of the Canadian Economics Association, June 3, 1983) Table 4 and Appendix Table 1.

mid-1970s—and there seems little doubt that the rise in oil prices has played a role.[6] But how much? Productivity growth also tends to decline when recessions reduce the rate of growth of aggregate demand and output. The 1970s were certainly more recession-prone than the 1960s or 1950s, but to what extent this is cause or effect, so far as productivity growth is concerned, is more debatable.

In any event, compared to the first two postwar decades output growth in the last decade was due more to increasing employment than to increased output per employed person. In part, this reflects the operation of diminishing returns in conditions where labour inputs have increased more rapidly (due to the coming of age of the postwar "baby boom" and the rise in the labour force participation rates of married women) than the capital stock. As we approach the latter half of the 1980s with predicted declines in labour force growth, productivity growth rates will have to be raised, if real income is to resume growing at post World War II rates.

The Continued Importance of Canada's Natural Resource Base

The small share of GDP accounted for by the primary sector and its even smaller share of total employment may prompt one to question the importance of the resource sector to the Canadian economy. However, the output and employment shares of the primary sector actually understate the importance of natural resources to the Canadian economy. We may note, to begin with, that an important part of the rapidly growing (energy) utility sector really relates directly to our resource base: the harnessing of our rivers to generate vast amounts of hydroelectric power. More to the point is the role of natural resources in Canadian foreign trade. As all beginning students of economics learn, nations with differing resource endowments can mutually gain from specializing production in those activities for which one has a "comparative advantage," then exchanging this output in return for goods and services for which the trading partner has a comparative advantage in production. It is instructive, then, to look at the distribution of Canada's exports and imports with an eye to pinpointing where our "advantage" lies.[7]

6. The higher price of energy reduced the net return from employing energy-using machinery. If this led to a tendency to substitute labour for capital at the margin, labour productivity (the measure used in Table 1-4) could be expected to fall. However, this would not appear to explain the decline in total factor productivity that also took place during this period.
7. For a discussion of Canada's comparative advantage and evidence that it lies in our natural resource sector, see Donald J. Daly, "Theory and Evidence on Canada's Comparative Advantage," in *International Business: A Canadian Perspective* (Toronto: Addison-Wesley, 1981), pp. 32-47.

Table 1-5

Distribution of Merchandise Exports and Imports in 1982

	Exports (%)[a]	Imports (%)
Farm and fish products	12.6	7.4
Crude materials	18.1	13.0
Fabricated materials	34.2	17.6
Auto products	20.2	22.6
Other highly manufactured products	14.9	39.4
Total	100.0	100.0

[a]Domestic exports. Does not include re-exports.
Source: Statistics Canada, *Canadian Statistical Review* Cat 11-003.

Table 1-5 breaks merchandise exports and imports into five broad groups of products. The first two groups, farm and fish products and crude materials, accounting for a little more than one third of our exports, are obviously outputs of the primary sector. Another quarter of our exports are fabricated materials, the processed and crudely fabricated outputs of the resource-oriented part of our manufacturing sector.[8] Thus more than three-fifths of our exports are raw produce and materials, or one stage removed. Most of our highly manufactured exports are automobile products. In contrast, 60 percent of our merchandise imports are highly manufactured products, including autos. Based on what is traded internationally, Canada's comparative advantage clearly appears to lie in its resource-based and related industries.[9]

Within the manufacturing sector the resource processing and fabricating

8. One resource processing industry that depends wholly on imports for its raw material is aluminum. Canada does not have bauxite deposits. However, because aluminum production is highly electricity intensive, bauxite valued in excess of $100 million is imported to take advantage of our unequalled supplies of hydro-electric power. In turn, much of the aluminum produced is "re-exported."

9. This statement must be qualified in three respects. Analysis of comparative advantage cannot ignore the effect of a nation's legislation, including tax and subsidy, on production and trade patterns. Also because of the high degree of foreign control of Canadian industry, some non-negligible portion of our exports and imports are not "arms length" but represent intracorporate transactions, on which it is difficult to base judgements about comparative advantage. Finally, and perhaps most important, a comparative advantage in the production of natural resources does not preclude gains from specialization and trade in the production of manufactured goods. In fact the importance of *intra*-industry trade cannot be explained in comparative advantage terms. See R.G. Harris and D. Cox, *Trade, Industrial Policy, and Canadian Manufacturing* (Toronto: Ontario Economic Council, 1984).

Table 1-6

Percent Distribution of Manufacturing Value Added and Employment by Industry Group, 1978

Industry Group	Value Added %	Total Employees %
Food and fibres group	21.6	25.2
1. Food and beverages industries	13.4	12.8
2. Tobacco products industries	.8	.5
3. Leather industries	.8	1.4
4. Textile industries	2.9	3.8
5. Knitting mills	.7	1.1
6. Clothing industries	3.0	5.6
Resource processing and fabricating group	27.6	23.7
7. Wood industries	6.8	6.7
8. Paper and allied products	8.8	7.1
9. Primary metal industries	8.3	6.8
10. Non-metallic mineral products industries	3.7	3.1
Secondary manufacturing: fabricating & assembling	38.9	41.9
11. Furniture and fixture industries	1.7	2.6
12. Metal fabricating industries	8.1	8.7
13. Machinery industries (except electrical)	4.6	5.1
14. Transportation equipment industries	11.4	10.0
15. Electrical products industries	5.5	6.4
16. Printing, publishing & allied industries	5.0	5.5
17. Miscellaneous manufacturing industries	2.6	3.6
Petrochemicals, plastics and related	11.9	9.2
18. Chemicals & chemical products	6.7	4.7
19. Rubber and plastics products industries	2.8	3.4
20. Petroleum and coal products industries	2.4	1.1
Total	100.0	100.0

Source: Canada Year Book, 1980-81, Table 18.11, p. 684. Reproduced by permission of the Minister of Supply and Services Canada.

industries account for about a quarter of manufacturing value added and of employment (see Table 1-6). Included in this group of industries are wood products, pulp and paper, primary metals, and non-metallic mineral products such as glass, cement, and asbestos. Despite the important role played by these industries, there are many who would argue that Canada does not do enough of the processing and fabricating prior to export. The argument is that employment could be boosted by using our comparative advantage in resource-related industries to further develop the somewhat more labour-intensive manufacturing sector. This proposition encounters, however, another fact. A substantial proportion of the mining industry in Canada is owned by vertically integrated American and European firms seeking to fulfil their raw material requirements. The processing and fabricating plants are, in numerous cases, located in the United States and in Europe (e.g., iron and steel plants which rely heavily on Quebec and Labrador iron ore). The plants cannot be moved to Canada, and would presumably seek elsewhere if Canadian raw materials were no longer available.

One final set of statistics: Canada has led the world in mineral exports and ranks third behind the U.S. and the U.S.S.R. in non-fuel mineral production. In 1969 Canada was the world leader in the production of nickel, zinc, and asbestos, the second largest producer of molybdenum, the third largest producer of natural gas and gold and the fourth largest producer of iron ore and copper. In the late 1970s, Canada was still the world's largest producer of zinc and nickel, the second largest producer of molybdenum, the third largest producer of silver, and the fourth largest copper producer. Canada is also a world leader in the production of sulphur and uranium. In a world which is more conscious of resource scarcities that it was two decades ago, these rankings are more than simply a matter of national pride in leadership.[10]

Intra-Industry Group Structure

To this point we have described the evolution of sectoral shares within the Canadian economy. In this section we briefly summarize the structure *within* each sector or broad industry group. The subject of industrial organization focuses on the structure, behaviour and performance of more narrowly defined industries, particularly in the manufacturing sector of the economy. Much of the remainder of this book probes issues arising at the industry level, being neither as "macro" as the preceding section on sectoral shares, nor as "micro" as the individual firm of standard economic theory.

Table 1-7 summarizes for the major sectors of the economy, the number of establishments contained therein, the number of specific industries or trades within each sector, the typical range of industry "concentration ratios," and

10. *Canada Year Book*, 1972, p. 646; *Canada Year Books* 1978-79; 1980-81, Chapter 12.

Table 1-7

Summary of Typical Market Structures Within Nine Industrial Sectors

Sector	Number of Establishments	Number of Industries or Trades	Typical Industry Concentration (CR_4) Ratio	Comment
Agriculture	318 000	—	Very low	Competitive market structures, but cartelized where marketing boards employ supply management.
Forestry (logging)	3 241[b]	1	$CR_4 = 20\%$	Most firms are of single establishment type. Each industry has a large no. of firms, the largest 50 of which account for most shipments.
Mining	507[b]	15	2/3 of $CR_4 > 75\%$	Canada is a world leader in nickel, zinc, asbestos, and among the leaders in iron ore, copper, gold, uranium. Each of these industries is dominated by a few large firms.
Manufacturing	35 495[b]	172	Varies from very high to very low. Approx. 1/2 have $CR_4 > 50\%$	Oligopoly predominates—but this term covers a wide variety of actual market structures and market behaviour.
Transportation, communication, and energy utilities	—	—	Very high	Duopoly in rail transportation, duopoly with a fringe of competitors in air transport and television networks. Franchised monopoly and/or publicly owned firms in telecommunications, electric energy, water, and natural gas pipelines.

Wholesale trade	31 899	87	Low to moderate	An important form of competition comes from sales by manufacturers direct to retailers.
Retail trade	134 480	91	Low to high	Monopolistically competitive, a chief differentiating factor being location. Chains play an important role in some trades (e.g. grocery, department stores); results in moderate to high concentration in small cities and towns.
Community, business, and personal services	107 996	103	Low in most cities	Monopolistically competitive chiefly due to quality differences (actual and perceived). Professional services often characterized by fee setting and indirect impediments to entry (licences, certification, etc).
Finance, insurance, and real estate	—	—	Moderate to high in finance and insurance, moderate in real estate	A wide variety of financial intermediaries in Canada; to the extent they provide closely substitutable services there is adequate competition. However, as Table 1-18 suggests, intra-intermediary market structures are typically concentrated.

[a]The number of "firms" is somewhat less than the number of "establishments" (places of production or business) because of the existence of multi-establishment or multi-plant firms. Figures for wholesale trade, retail trade, and services are 1971 data.
[b]1980
Source: 1971 Censuses of Wholesale Trade, Retail Trade, Services; 1981 Census of Agriculture; Statistics Canada, *Industrial Organization and Concentration in the Manufacturing, Mining and Logging Industries*, 1980. Cat. 31-402.

some salient characteristics of each sector in the Canadian setting. Perhaps the key descriptive statistic at the industry level is the "concentration ratio"—the share of a specific (relatively narrowly defined) industry's output accounted for by a small number (4, 8, 12) of the largest firms in the industry. In Canadian mining and manufacturing industries, concentration ratios are typically "high"—the four largest firms accounting for more than 50 percent of industry shipments or value added in most mining and almost half of all manufacturing industries. Industry structure within the mining and manufacturing sectors and the meaning and measurement of industry concentration, will be discussed in detail in chapter 2.

In agricultural and community services, firm sizes and market shares are usually small so that the typical market structure could be described as "atomistic." However, we must be careful in interpreting the term "atomism," for it is not necessarily synonymous with "competition." Where agricultural industries (e.g. eggs, broilers, turkeys, milk) have been effectively "cartelized" (see chapter 12), atomism does not necessarily imply competitive behaviour on the supply side of the market. In villages and towns, local service and retail firms may be small, but they may nevertheless have substantial monopoly power where the population is too sparse to support more than one or two enterprises of a particular sort within the relevant geographic market.

At the other extreme are public utilities where "natural monopoly" conditions exist in electric energy, and natural gas transmission and distribution and local telephone service (these are discussed in chapter 10). In rail and air transportation and in network broadcasting Canada is unique in having duopolistic market structures consisting of a large private and a large public firm in competition with each other.

The trade sector, particularly retail trade, is more difficult to characterize. On the one hand there are numerous small units. In 1971, there were over 134 000 retail establishments, most of them with gross sales of less than $100 000. On the other hand, a not insubstantial number of establishments are part of chains with gross sales running into the billions of dollars. Table 1-8 shows the leading merchandising firms in Canada. Not surprisingly, the leading merchandisers are grocery chains and department store chains. These chains have establishments in numerous cities and towns. In all but the largest population centres it is customary to find that two or three grocery chains dominate food retailing. In addition there are numerous "Ma and Pa" stores and specialty shops but these usually (Montreal is, perhaps, an exception) do not provide much head-on competition with the multi-faceted chain-owned supermarkets. The department stores, however, are more apt to feel competition from specialty shops and variety stores.

While some monopoly elements exist in retailing, the monopsony power of

Table 1-8

Canada's Leading Merchandisers

Company[11]	Rank Among Financial Post 500	Sales 1983 ($ 000)
1. George Weston Ltd (includes Loblaw Co, and Kelly, Douglas & Co)	6	7 799 600
2. Hudson's Bay	13	4 370 528
3. Provigo	16	3 891 151
4. Canada Safeway	23	3 437 683
5. Steinberg	25	3 352 851
6. Simpsons-Sears	26	3 314 113
7. Oshawa Group	33	2 434 985
8. Dominion Stores	34	2 409 232
9. Canadian Tire	44	1 903 378
10. F. W. Woolworth	48	1 738 821

Source: *Financial Post 500*, June 1984, p. 112.

the large retailer may be of more consequence.[12] Because large retailers are big buyers of the goods they resell, they are in a position to threaten integration backwards into manufacture as well as wholesaling. They therefore provide a credible form of "countervailing power" against oligopolistic manufacturers. So long as the large merchandiser faces vigorous competition in resale to final consumers, some of the benefits of the retailer's exercise of monopsony power may be passed on to the consumer. Even two large merchandisers may be enough for vigorous competition at the retail level because collusion is made difficult by the existence of thousands of branded items sold at varying gross margins over invoice cost. One of the lessons from the study of industrial

11. Of the ten leading merchandisers only two, Canada Safeway and F.W. Woolworth, are 100 percent foreign owned. Simpsons-Sears is 61 percent foreign owned. All the other leading merchandisers are Canadian owned. Incidentally the T. Eaton Company, which is wholly-owned by the Eaton family, and does not make its financial data available, probably would be among the top 10. In 1982, it was estimated to have had $2 billion in sales revenue.

12. However, Hudson's Bay's purchase of Zeller's Ltd., its takeover of Simpson's, and the subsequent takeover of Hudson's Bay by the Thomson (of newspaper, but also North Sea oil and gas fame) empire, has resulted in increased concentration at the retail department store level, a structural change which at the time was feared would have potentially important implications for effective competition in the Canadian economy.

organization is that numbers of firms by themselves are often an inadequate predictor of monopolistic or competitive behaviour and performance.

Corporate Size, Ownership and Control

In describing the structure of the Canadian economy we have to this point concentrated on sectoral shares and broad industry groupings. Now we go to the opposite extreme and say something about the largest firms in Canada. The firm is, of course, the basic entrepreneurial unit, making the production decisions in a decentralized private enterprise economy.[13] There are several hundred thousand firms in Canada and over 30 000 alone in the manufacturing sector. However, firm sizes vary tremendously, with a relatively few large firms accounting for a substantial share of total assets or sales. For example, in 1980, the 25 largest nonfinancial enterprises (including four government-owned corporations such as Hydro Quebec and Ontario Hydro) accounted for 30 percent of corporate assets; the largest 100 for almost half of corporate assets. Within the manufacturing sector, the largest 4 firms accounted for almost 9 percent of manufacturing assets—the 100 largest 48 percent.[14] Table 1-9 shows the 40 largest industrial firms in Canada ranked by sales. The table also includes their assets, employees and owner if foreign owned. The top 40 includes the "big three" automakers, the big five integrated petroleum firms, 2 steelmakers, 3 pulp and paper companies, and several "utilities."

Some well-known firms actually are engaged in several very different types of production activities. Conglomerate firms are those firms whose production activities are truly diverse. Among the 20 largest industrial firms, Canadian Pacific Ltd. is a truly conglomerate enterprise. In addition to operating one of the world's largest and most famous railways, CP Ltd. owns the important firms shown in Figure 1-1. Many other of the largest industrial firms are diversified (see chapter 2), although not nearly to the extent of CP Limited.

The existence of very large, often diversified, firms in Canada was the subject of investigation by the Royal Commission on Corporate Concentration.[15] The

---

13. In some cases multi-plant firms may decentralize production decisions so that they are made at the plant rather than the firm level.

14. Statistics Canada, *Corporations and Labour Unions Returns Act*, Part I, Cat. 61-210. C. Marfels, *Concentration Levels and Trade in the Canadian Economy, 1965-1973*, Study No. 31, Royal Commission on Corporate Concentration (Ottawa, 1977) pp. 45, 49. In 1980, the 25 largest manufacturing firms accounted for 25 percent of manufacturing value added; the 100 largest accounted for 46 percent of manufacturing value added.

15. See *Report of the Royal Commission on Corporate Concentration*, March 1978 (Ottawa: Minister of Supply and Services, 1978). In addition to the main report the Commission issued 33 background and technical reports which provide extensive information for the student of industrial organization and Canada's corporate structure.

establishment of the Commission, which issued its report in 1978, was prompted by the attempt by the Montreal-based Power Corporation to take over Toronto-based Argus Corporation in 1975. Power and Argus, and somewhat similar enterprises such as Genstar, are different from conglomerates such as CP Ltd. in that they are not known for the goods they produce. Rather these firms are "holding companies" engaged in the essentially financial role of holding securities in a wide variety of operating companies.[16] Their influence on the decision making of the firms is exercised via representation on the Boards of Directors and Executive Committees of the operating firms, and is exerted mainly in matters financial. Power and Argus hold majority or substantial minority (and thereby controlling) shares in numerous firms, many of which are separately ranked among the largest 200 industrials in Canada. Figure 1-2 shows the holdings of Power and Argus at the time of Power's attempted takeover. Also shown are some of the important holdings of the operating companies in other major firms.

Who controls the largest corporations? Their owners? Those who manage the enterprises? More than fifty years ago, Berle and Means postulated that the growth of large firms was separating ownership of the firm from its control, as stock ownership became more widely distributed, with no individual shareholder likely to own more than a small percentage of a given firm's common stock.[17] Thirty years later Larner confirmed that the process that Berle and Means observed in its early stages was virtually complete. Among the largest 200 U.S. corporations, in 1963, less than twenty percent had a single owner or family who controlled more than 10 percent of the firm's common (voting) stock.[18] For Berle and Means, Larner, and many other students of the modern corporation, these findings implied managerial control, a broadening of firm goals, and a weakening of single-minded profit maximization as the overriding objective of the firm, with implications for the theory of the firm. Although in recent years some doubts have been cast on the importance of the separation phenomenon for firm behaviour, few doubt that on paper at least, ownership and control are separated in almost all large U.S. firms.

What about Canada? Is the same phenomenon observable here? To begin with, it is important to note that many large Canadian firms are foreign-owned (see below) by an American parent holding a majority, if not 100 percent, of the Canadian subsidiary's stock. Clearly, in the case of foreign-controlled firms

16. Power tends to hold majority interests (the main exception being its 38 percent interest in Consolidated-Bathurst), while Argus, consistent with its goal of long-term growth, holds only minority (yet sufficient for control) interests in its several companies.

17. A.A. Berle and G.C. Means, *The Modern Corporation and Private Property* (New York: Harcourt, Brace and World, 1932).

18. R.J. Larner, "Ownership and Control in the 200 Largest Nonfinancial Corporations, 1929 and 1963," *American Economic Review*, 56 (September 1966), pp. 777-787.

Table 1-9

The Top 40 Industrials

Rank by Sales		Sales or Operating Revenue	Company	Assets		Foreign Ownership	
1983	1982	$'000	(Head Office)	$'000	Employees	%	Major Shareholders
1	2	13 805 450	General Motors of Canada Ltd. (Oshawa, Ont.)	3 027 638	43 410	100	General Motors Corp. Detroit
2	1	12 759 297	Canadian Pacific Ltd. (Montreal)	17 601 949	121 000		Power Corp. of Canada 12%
3	3	8 919 000	Imperial Oil Ltd. (Toronto)	8 049 000	14 732	70	Exxon Corp., New York
4	4	8 874 700	Bell Canada Enterprises Inc. (Montreal)	14 940 400	100 874		Wide distribution
5	5	8 580 600	Ford Motor Co. of Canada (Oakville, Ont.)	2 256 600	33 500	90	Ford Motor Co., Dearborn, Mich.
6	6	6 418 339	Alcan Aluminium Ltd. (Montreal)	8 213 040	70 000		Wide distribution
7	8	5 652 000	Texaco Canada Inc. (Toronto)	3 288 000	3 904	90	Texaco Inc. 68%, Texaco International N.Y., 22%
8	7	5 300 000	Shell Canada Ltd. (Toronto)	5 240 000	7 975	79	Shell Investments Ltd. Netherlands/Britain

9	9	Gulf Canada Ltd. (Toronto)	5 078 000	5 112 000	9 700	60	Gulf Oil Corp. Pittsburgh
10	10	Canadian National Railway (Mtl.)	4 625 100	6 789 765	63 496		Federal government, 100%
11	12	Chrysler Canada Ltd. (Windsor, Ont.)	4 325 500	980 300	12 028	100	Chrysler Corp., Detroit
12	18	PetroCanada (Calgary)	4 123 817	8 239 025	6 601		Federal government 100%
13	11	Canada Development Corp. (Vancouver)	3 834 700	7 558 600	18 605		Federal government 48%
14	13	Nova Corp. (Calgary)	3 823 005	6 796 056	8 600		Wide distribution
15	17	Ontario Hydro (Toronto)	3 805 131	23 193 894	31 233		Ontario government 100%
16	19	Hydro-Quebec (Montreal)	3 656 000	25 199 000	18 975		Quebec government 100%
17	15	Brascan Ltd. (Toronto)	3 555 000	3 284 900	28		Brascan Holdings Corp. 44%
18	14	TransCanada PipeLines Ltd. (Calgary)	3 470 700	5 034 500	1 915		Bell Canada Enterprises Inc. 42%
19	16	Hiram Walker Resources Ltd. (Toronto)	3 402 826	4 839 576	10 200		Interprovincial Pipe Line Ltd. 16%
20	22	Noranda Mines Ltd. (Toronto)	3 094 292	6 130 970	51 700		Brascade Resources 35% Zinor Holdings 16%

Table 1-9 Continued

Rank by Sales 1983	1982	Company (Head Office)	Sales or Operating Revenue $'000	Assets $'000	Employees	Foreign Ownership %	Major Shareholders
21	20	Canada Packers Ltd. (Toronto)	3 001 447	558 941	14 000		Wide distribution
22	21	Dome Petroleum Ltd. (Calgary)	2 594 600	8 178 000	6 500		Dome Mines Ltd. 26%
23	23	Total Petroleum (North America) Ltd. (Calgary)	2 553 480	1 180 866	4 500	44	Compagnie français des petroles, France
24	28	IBM Canada Ltd. (Toronto)	2 462 000	1 391 000	11 068	100	IBM Corp. Armonk, N.Y.
25	26	Air Canada (Montreal)	2 298 485	2 190 567	21 584		Federal government 100%
26	27	Moore Corp. (Toronto)	2 235 047	1 433 468	26 100		Wide distribution
27	25	Seagram Co. (Waterloo, Ont.)	2 222 934	6 621 788	14 000		Bronfman family trusts 39%
28	36	Imasco Ltd. (Montreal)	2 121 466	1 530 063	31 000	45	B.A.T. Industries, Britain
29	31	MacMillan Bloedel Ltd. (Vancouver)	2 044 100	2 118 800	15 472		Noranda Group 49%
30	29	Stelco Inc. (Toronto)	2 033 169	2 769 494	19 519		Wide distribution

31	32	1 928 712	John Labatt Ltd. (London, Ont.)	953 337	11 000		Brascan Ltd. 40%
32	24	1 894 344	Massey-Ferguson Ltd. (Toronto)	1 973 562	27 609		Wide distribution
33	33	1 826 700	Genstar Corp. (Vancouver)	2 348 836	15 000		Wide distribution
34	35	1 820 000	Domtar Inc. (Montreal)	1 350 200	15 151		Dofor Inc. 21%, Caisse de depot 24%
35	37	1 722 985	Atco Ltd. (Calgary)	2 779 529	6 800		Southern family 51%
36	34	1 663 932	Mitsui & Co. (Canada) (Toronto)	NA	140	100	Mitsui & Co., Japan
37	38	1 660 180	Abitibi-Price Inc. (Toronto)	1 700 418	15 000		Olympia & York Develop. 93%
38	44	1 605 696	Dofasco Inc. (Hamilton, Ont.)	2 175 145	11 400		Wide distribution
39	30	1 605 678	Alberta & Southern Gas Co. (Calgary)	561 748	145	100	Pacific Gas & Electric Co., San Francisco
40	45	1 528 451	British Columbia Hydro & Power Authority (Vancouver)	8 910 000	8 667		British Columbia government, 100%

Source: *The Financial Post 500*, June 1984, pp. 70, 71, 74.

Figure 1-1

Corporate Organization of Canadian Pacific Ltd., 1982

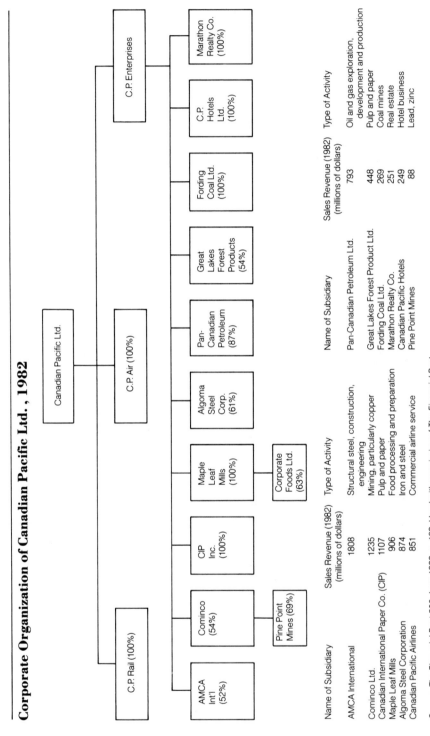

Name of Subsidiary	Sales Revenue (1982) (millions of dollars)	Type of Activity
AMCA International	1808	Structural steel, construction, engineering
Cominco Ltd.	1235	Mining, particularly copper
Canadian International Paper Co. (CIP)	1107	Pulp and paper
Maple Leaf Mills	906	Food processing and preparation
Algoma Steel Corporation	874	Iron and steel
Canadian Pacific Airlines	851	Commercial airline service

Name of Subsidiary	Sales Revenue (1982) (millions of dollars)	Type of Activity
Pan-Canadian Petroleum Ltd.	793	Oil and gas exploration, development and production
Great Lakes Forest Product Ltd.	448	Pulp and paper
Fording Coal Ltd.	269	Coal mines
Marathon Realty Co.	251	Real estate
Canadian Pacific Hotels	249	Hotel business
Pine Point Mines	88	Lead, zinc

Source: The Financial Post 500 June 1983, p. 109. Used with permission of The Financial Post.

there is no separation of ownership from control, although the phenomenon of separation of ownership from control may apply to the parent firm. In a recent study, Antoniou investigated the ownership patterns among the 247 largest Canadian-owned firms.[19] In contrast to the U.S., the great majority of the largest Canadian-owned firms had a major owner who held a significant percentage of the firm's shares. In 92 cases (or 37 percent), the major owner held more than 50 percent of the firm's shares. The distribution of the 247 firms by percentage of share categories is as follows:

Percentage of shares held by major owner

1-5	5-10	10-20	20-50	50-100	No reliable data	Total
1 (.4)	2 (.8)	21 (8.5)	77 (31.2)	92 (37.2)	54 (21.9)	247 (100%)

Antoniou does not provide any explanation for the apparent difference between the largest U.S. firms and Canadian-owned firms in the degree to which shares are widely distributed and ownership dispersed. Undoubtedly the smaller average size of Canada's largest firms as compared to the largest U.S. firms accounts for some of the differences, but certainly not all. What Antoniou's study does provide is a glimpse of the interesting and intricate patterns of ownership and control among many of Canada's largest firms. By tracing ownership links among the 247 largest firms, Antoniou identified twenty "shadow groups" comprising not only wholly owned and majority owned subsidiaries, but minority owned companies as well. Table 1-10 shows the sectoral composition of the companies owned by ten of the most important "shadow groups."

A. Supercorporate Controls

How widespread are the Power-Argus type of networks? How important to the functioning of individual firms are the "shadow groups" Antoniou found by tracing minority as well as majority ownership ties? Is our economy dominated by a few large networks of firms with the apex holding company exercising some sort of supercorporate control over the firms actually producing goods and services? The answer appears to be that the Power-Argus type complexes, or even that represented by Canadian Pacific Limited and other shadow groups, are still the exception rather than the rule, although they may be becoming more prevalent. Nevertheless, many if not most of the largest firms in Canada are connected through share ownership with numerous other, smaller firms. A study for the Royal Commission on Corporate Concentration found that the 361

---

19. The 247 firms were among the 500 largest Canadian enterprises for which *The Financial Post* compiled data in 1979. A. Antoniou, *Ownership and Control of the Largest Canadian-Owned Corporations, 1979*, Ph.D. Dissertation, McGill University, 1983.

Table 1-10

Sectoral Distribution of Companies Comprising Ten Identifiable "Shadow Groups": 1979

Name of Shadow Group	Primary	Manufacturing	Construction	Sector Utilities	Trade	Finance	Services	Total
Weston Group	1	13	—	1	4	3	3	26
Bentley-Price Group	2	10	1	3	4	6	3	29
Edward and Peter Bronfman Group	6	15	—	3	9	12	5	50
Paul Desmarais Group (Power Corp.)	3	15	3	7	5	17	7	57
K.R. Thomson Group	1	2	1	2	10	8	2	26
Canadian Pacific Group	5	8	—	9	3	7	4	36
Conrad Black Group (Argus Corp.)	10	18	1	4	10	6	5	54
Edgar and Charles Bronfman Group	1	3	—	1	6	6	3	20
Banque Nationale & Caisse de depot Group	1	15	1	1	11	13	3	45
Dome Petroleum Group	1	4	—	1	—	15	3	24

Source: A. Antoniou, op. cit.

Figure 1-2

Power and Argus Corporations

Power Corporation of Canada, Limited. Major Investments, March 25, 1975. Common shares.

[a]Imperial Life Assurance ownership in The Investors Group was 13.2%.

[a]subsequently sold
[b]interest disposed of July 5, 1976.

Argus Corporation Limited. Major Investments, March 25, 1975.

Source: *Report of Royal Commission Corporate Concentration*, March 1978, pp. 170, 172. Reproduced by permission of the Minister of Supply and Services Canada.

largest firms in Canada had ownership ties with 4944 other firms.[20] Moreover, shortly after the Royal Commission's report was issued, Canada experienced a wave of large mergers, in which ownership of a number of Canada's leading firms, some initially foreign-owned, changed hands. See Table 1-11. Invariably the purchaser was a Canadian family, corporation or government, a fact contributing to a decline in the incidence of foreign ownership (see below) as well as an increase in the number of Canadian "conglomerates."[21]

One reason for expecting a growth in conglomerate-type firms is that they not only reduce risks and the cost of capital through diversifying production activities, but create a quasi-financial market under one ultimate control capable of moving funds quickly into whichever activity appears to be most profitable at the moment. However, whatever benefits are conveyed, there are political costs associated with concentrated wealth holdings, and economic consequences if independent enterprise business decisions give way to the movement of "chess pieces" by super corporate managers.

B. Interlocking Directorships

A milder form of intercorporate link is the "interlocking directorate," where one person sits on the Boards of Directors of two or more corporations. In most cases interlocks are innocuous enough, reflecting the scarcity of individuals with exceptional business and financial capabilities and experience. However, when interlocks provide a basis for the conveyance of information between competing firms they may, in the event, facilitate collusion.[22] But, what little we know of interlocking directorates does not suggest that interlocks between competitors are very frequent. Dooley found that in 1965 one eighth of the interlocking directorships among the largest financial and non-financial firms in the United

---

20. Stephen D. Berkowitz, Yehuda Kotowitz and Leonard Waverman, *Enterprise Structure and Corporate Concentration: A Technical Report*. Study Number 17, Royal Commission on Corporate Concentration (Ottawa, 1977), p. 3. An "ownership tie" exists for Canadian companies when share ownership is 10 percent or more (for domestically controlled firms) or 5 percent or more (for foreign-controlled firms).

21. It was this merger wave that motivated Antoniou's ownership and control study. It is interesting to consider the examples of Noranda and Dome Petroleum, two leading Canadian-owned firms, both of which were heavily involved in acquisitions during 1978-81. In 1981, Noranda was acquired, in part, by Brascan, itself owned by a branch of the Bronfman family, and, in part, by an agent of the Quebec government. In contrast, Dome Petroleum, unable to digest all of the debt floated in its acquisition of resource-based firms, had to be bailed out by the Federal government in 1982 and to divest itself of some of its acquisitions.

22. They may also facilitate the takeover of one firm by another when a director of one company makes use of confidential financial information provided by another company on whose Board he sits. This was alleged to have happened in the attempt by American Express to take over McGraw-Hill publishing company. See *New York Times*, Jan. 18, 1979, p. D-1.

Table 1-11

Mergers and Acquisitions in Canada Where Transactions Exceeded $200 Million, 1978 to July 1981

Acquiring Firm	Acquired Firm	Millions of $
1978		
Hudson's Bay	Simpson's Ltd. & Simpson's minority interest in Simpsons-Sears	347
Dome Petroleum	Siebens Oil & Gas	355
Petro-Canada	Pacific Petroleum	1500
Noranda	Matagami Mines	207
1979		
Kaiser Resources	Ashland Oil Canada	485
Thomson Family	Hudson's Bay	641
Nova	Husky Oil	392
Dome Petroleum	TransCanada PipeLines	244
Dome Petroleum	Mesa Petroleum (Canadian Assets)	640
Edper Equities	Brascan Ltd.	335
Consumer's Gas	Home Oil	444
1980		
Rio Algom	Preston Mines	236
Dome Petroleum	Kaiser Resources (on share oil & gas)	701
Noranda Mines	McLaren Power and Paper	240
Consumer's Gas	Hiram Walker	1300
Atco Ltd.	Canadian Utilities	320
British Columbia Resources Investment (BRIC)	Kaiser Resources	665
B.C. Forest Products	Rayonier Canada (B.C. forest assets)	U.S. 365+
1981		
Petro-Canada	Petrofina	1460
Olympia and York	Abitibi-Price	618
Sulpetro Ltd.	Can Del Oil	546
Noranda Mines	MacMillan Bloedel (49.8%)	627
Dome Petroleum	Hudson's Bay Oil and Gas (54%)	U.S. 1700
Canadian Pacific Enterprises	Canadian International Paper	1100
Husky Oil	Shell Explorer Ltd. (some Canadian assets)	430
Hudson's Bay Oil and Gas	Cyprus-Anvil Mines	290+
Brascade Resources (70% Brascan, 30% Caisse de depot et placement du Quebec)	Noranda Mines	1600+
Husky Oil Ltd.	Uno-Tex Petroleum Corp.	371

Source: W.T. Stanbury, "Merger Activity in Canada," Faculty of Commerce, University of British Columbia. (Unpublished paper, mimeo.)

States involved interlocks between competing firms.[23] Around the same time, a Canadian study found that about 10 percent of interlocks were between large industrial· firms in the same (broadly defined) market and, of these, half involved a parent-subsidiary relationship. Having representatives from the financial community on the Boards of non-financial firms is a much more important source of interlocking directorship.

Table 1-12 indicates the extent of interlocking directorships in Canada and the United States for two periods; 1951 and 1970 for Canada, 1935 and 1965 for the United States. The two most notable facets of the figures in Table 1-12 are (i) an apparently modest decline in the incidence of interlocking directorships among the largest firms in Canada in the postwar period,[24] and (ii) the similarity between the incidence of interlocks in Canada and the United States. In Canada, in 1951, 22 percent of the directors of the 170 largest non-financial firms held two or more directorships accounting for 45 percent of all directorships in these firms. The comparable figures for 1970 (based on the 200 largest non-financial and 60 largest financial firms) were 19 percent and 39.5 percent respectively. For the 200 largest non-financial and 50 largest financial firms in the United States eighteen percent of the directors held more than one directorship, in both 1935 and 1965, accounting for 37 and 35 percent respectively of the directorships in the largest U.S. corporations. The extent of interlocks between financial and non-financial corporations in Canada is indicated by the fact that, in 1951, the 10 largest banks and 10 largest insurance companies had a total of 331 directors, 196 of whom held 485 (or 36 percent) of the directorships in the largest non-financial corporations. By 1970 the incidence of interlocks between banks and industrial corporations had declined somewhat, although interlocks between financial and non-financial firms continued to be quite prevalent.

During the 1970s there was little apparent change in the incidence of interlocking directorships in Canada. Antoniou found that, in 1979, the 3152 board of director positions of the largest 247 Canadian-owned firms were occupied by 2274 different persons. Eighteen hundred of these held a single directorship within the group of 247. 474 directors held 1352 board positions among the group of 247 firms. Thus 21% of the directors held 43 percent of

23. Peter Dooley, "The Interlocking Directorate," *American Economic Review*, 59 (June 1969), pp. 314-323.
24. However, the figures for 1951 and 1970 are not strictly comparable. They neither include the same number of nonfinancial corporations, and the former excludes financial corporations altogether. Since there is evidence that the directors of financial corporations are more likely to interlock with other firms than are the directors of nonfinancial corporations, the 1951 figures may understate (relative to 1970) the incidence of interlocks among the largest Canadian corporations.

Table 1-12

Extent of Interlocking Directorates Among Largest Firms

Number of Directorships Held by One Person	1951 Canada[a]		1970 Canada[c]		1935 U.S.[b]		1965 U.S.[b]	
	Number of Persons	Number of Directorships	Number of Persons	Number of Directorships	Number of Persons	Number of Directorships	Number of Persons	Number of Directorships
1	719	719	1892	1892	2234	2234	2603	2603
2	113	226	268	536	303	606	372	744
3	43	129	81	243	102	306	123	369
4	20	80	40	160	48	192	49 –18%	196 –35%
5	13	65	28	140	19	95	13	65
6	7 –22%	42 –45%	9 –19%	54 –39.5%	6 –18%	36 –37%	5	30
7	3	21	6	42	6	42		
8	2	16	5	40	3	24		
9	1	9	2	18	1	9		
10	1	10	0	0				
Total	922	1317	2331	3125	2722	3544	3165	4007

[a] 170 largest non-financial firms.
[b] 200 largest non-financial firms plus 50 largest financial firms.
[c] 200 largest and 60 largest financial corporations.

Sources: J. Porter, "Concentration of Economic Power & The Economic Elite in Canada," *CJEPS* (May 1956); P. Dooley, "The Interlocking Directorate," *AER* (June 1969); L. Waverman and R. Baldwin, "Determinants of Interlocking Directorates in Canada," Working Paper Number 7501, Institute for Quantitative Analysis of Social and Economic Policy, University of Toronto, April 1975.

directorships. Not surprisingly, these interlocking directorships were found most frequently among corporations belonging to the same "shadow group"— implying that interlocking directorships are often employed as a method of coordinating decision-making within complex ownership groupings.

C. Foreign Ownership and Control

The most distinctive aspect of non-financial asset ownership in Canada is the extent to which it is foreign. The incidence of foreign ownership and control of resident enterprises in Canada is uniquely high among the industrialized nations of the world, although it has declined in recent years. A review of Table 1-9 shows that 10 of the largest 40 industrial enterprises in Canada are more than 50 percent foreign owned—in 5 cases foreign ownership is total, 100 percent. Of the 200 largest industrials, in 1983, 50 were 100 percent owned by foreigners and another 22 were more than 50 to 99 percent foreign owned.[25] These figures, however, tend to overstate the extent of foreign ownership (FO) and foreign control (FC) of all Canadian enterprise since "industrials" includes the two sectors, manufacturing and mining, in which FO and FC are greatest. Table 1-13 shows how the incidence of FO and FC by industry and the overall extent of FO and FC have changed since 1926. The figures for FO indicate the degree to which a firm's (and by summation an industry's) outstanding securities are held by foreigners, while FC indicates the degree to which voting control (50 percent or more of common voting shares) is in foreign hands. In 1926, the railroads were largely foreign owned but domestically controlled. By 1973 FO and FC of railroads and other utilities had declined to the point of being negligible. In contrast, FO and FC of the manufacturing and mining sectors grew rapidly until the early 1960s, and reached a peak in the early 1970s, since which time they have declined substantially. Overall, foreign control of the Canadian economy fell from 33 percent to 25 percent of the assets of all nonfinancial industries between 1973 and 1981.

It is the FO and FC of Canada's non-renewable resource sector that has been most disconcerting to many Canadians. As we have already seen, Canada's comparative advantage lies in its resource sector. While, in law, our resources cannot be alienated by the provinces, which retain legal ownership over the subsurface, firms are given the right to mine the subsurface and obtain ownership of what is taken out of the ground. That these firms were in great part foreign owned and controlled suggested to some persons that if Canada's destiny is to continue as a resource producer, Canadian participation in

---

25. The *Financial Post 500*, June 1984. In 1977, 15 of the largest 40 industrials were foreign controlled (i.e. more than 50 percent foreign owned); and of the largest 200 industrials 91 were foreign controlled, 69 being 100 percent foreign owned.

Table 1-13

Foreign Ownership and Control of Canadian Industry

Sector	1926 FO	1926 FC	1948 FO	1948 FC	1967 FO	1967 FC	U.S. 1967 FO	U.S. 1967 FC	1973 FO	1973 FC	1977 FC	1981 FC
Manufacturing	38	35	42	43	52	57	44	45	53	58	53	45
Mining & smelting	37	38	39	40	61	65	51	56	51	56	43[a]	30[a]
Petroleum & natural gas	—	—	—	—	62	74	51	60	58	75	74	49
Railways	55	3	45	3	19	2	8	2	{10	6}	7	4
Public utilities	32	20	20	24	19	5	18	5				
All sectors	37	17	32	25	35	35	29	28	34	33	30	25

[a]Does not include smelting

FO: Foreign ownership ratio; which is defined as equity and debt capital owned by non residents, as a percent of total capital in industry.

FC: Foreign control ratio; which is defined as equity and debt capital owned by residents and non residents in firms whose voting stock is controlled (50% +) by non residents, as a percent of total capital in industry.

Source: Foreign Ownership and the Structure of Canadian Industry (Queen's Printer, 1968) p. 422; for 1926, 1948, 1963; *Foreign Direct Investment in Canada* (Gray Report) (Ottawa: Information Canada, 1972) Table 4, p. 20, for 1967; Statistics Canada, *Corporations and Labour Unions Return Act, Report for 1973; 1977; 1981; Cat. 61-210*, selected tables. Data on foreign ownership, of Canadian as well as non-resident controlled corporations, was not published by CALURA in 1977 and 1981.

resource activities ought to be substantially greater. In 1977 eight of the ten largest resource firms in Canada were more than 50 percent foreign owned as were six of the ten largest firms in the mining and petroleum industries. Then came a series of giant mergers and acquisitions (see Table 1-11), many of which involved a Canadian firm (either privately or government owned) purchasing a foreign controlled, resource sector, firm. As a result, foreign control of Canadian resource industries fell dramatically between 1977 and 1981.

The remarkable decline in foreign control during the late 1970s and early 1980s is indicated in greater detail in Tables 1-14 and 1-15. Table 1-14

Table 1-14

Foreign Control by Sector or Broad Industry Group: 1976 and 1981

	Percentage of Foreign Controlled Assets	
Sector or Industry Group	1976	1981
Agriculture, forestry, fishing	8	4
Metal mining	40	28
Other (nonmetal) mining	56	34
Mineral fuels production	61	43
Manufacturing		
Food	38	29
Tobacco products	100	100
Textile mills	58	51
Clothing industry	16	14
Wood industries	21	15
Furniture industries	25	15
Rubber products	93	90
Paper and allied products	40	29
Primary metals (includes smelting)	15	13
Metal fabricating	40	35
Transportation equipment	77	69
Machinery	65	48
Electrical products	69	54
Chemicals & chemical products	73	75
Petroleum and coal products	92	61
Transportation	12	6
Communications	15	13
Public utilities	2	a
Retail trade	16	13
Services	16	15

aLess than one half of one percent
Source: Statistics Canada, CALURA, Cat 61-210. For 1977, Statement 9 and Table 4, pp. 41 and 159. For 1981, Table IX and Table 4, pp. 47 and 147.

Table 1-15

Extent of Foreign Control Among Canada's Leading Firms: 1978, 1980, 1982, 1983

Size Class of Largest Canadian Firms	No. of Firms 50% or More Foreign Owned				No. of Firms 100% Foreign Owned			
	1978	1980	1982	1983	1978	1980	1982	1983
Top 50	18	17	14	12	6	6	6	6
51-100	32	19	20	20	17	8	11	12
101-150	28	25	20	20	22	17	12	14
151-200	31	24	22	20	26	22	19	18
201-250	21	27	23	24	12	20	21	20
251-300	25	24	23	20	18	18	16	15
301-350	NA	22	23	28	NA	12	18	21
351-400	NA	30	25	24	NA	23	18	20
Total: Top 300	155	136	122	116	101	91	85	85
Top 400	NA	188	170	168	NA	126	121	126

Source: *Financial Post 500*, 1979, 1981, 1983, 1984.

employs a finer breakdown of sectors and industry groupings than does Table 1-13. It shows that the decline in foreign control between 1976 and 1981 was widespread, and not confined to the primary, or resource, sector. Table 1-15 indicates that the number of foreign-controlled firms which are counted among the largest 300 or 400 Canadian-owned firms has also declined in recent years. While mergers and acquisitions of foreign firms by Canadian firms undoubtedly account for some of the general decline in foreign control of Canadian industry, they probably do not account for all of it. Presumably Canada's Foreign Investment Review Agency (FIRA), which screens all acquisitions by foreign-controlled firms and all (except very small) proposals by foreigners to get established in Canada, has had an impact too.[26] Since mergers and acquisitions foster conglomerate growth, legislation making it very difficult for foreign-controlled firms to take that route to enterprise growth was bound to enhance the relative (to foreign-controlled firms) size of large Canadian-owned firms. Whether these changes in the structure of ownership have improved (or worsened) economic performance is, of course, quite a different, and controversial, matter.

26. The operations of FIRA are discussed in Chapter 12.

D. Public Ownership

There is a final facet to the ownership aspect that remains to be discussed: public ownership. In Canada, public ownership is rather extensive and the Crown corporation is the device through which government-owned enterprise is conducted. Not all Crown corporations are engaged in producing goods and services, but some very important ones are. At the federal level the leading operating Crown corporations are Air Canada, Canadian Broadcasting Corporation, Canadian National Railway, Eldorado Nuclear, Petro-Canada, and the Polymer Corporation (until it was sold to the Canada Development Corporation in 1973 and renamed Polysar). There are also numerous Crown corporations at the provincial level and the reach of their activities is not quite as likely to be public utility-related as in the case of federal Crown corporations. In 1973, there were 74 provincially owned Crown corporations engaged in industrial and commercial activities including steel production, pulp and paper, sawmilling, shipbuilding, fish processing, petroleum exploration and development, potash mining and telephone service (see chapter 11).

In addition all but two provinces, Prince Edward Island and Alberta, own electric power production, transmission and distribution systems which supply most of the provincial electrical energy requirements. Almost all provinces have their own Housing Corporations and Liquor Control Boards. While public enterprise is still the exception, it is much more common and diversified in Canada than in the United States. Moreover, the largest Canadian Crown

Table 1-16

Industrial Crown Corporations

Rank	Crown corporation	Assets 1983 $000
1.	Hydro Quebec	25 190 000
2.	Ontario Hydro	23 193 894
3.	British Columbia Hydro	8 910 000
4.	Canadian National Railways	6 789 765
5.	Manitoba Hydro Electric Board Authority	2 884 475
6.	New Brunswick Power Commission	2 743 527
7.	Saskatchewan Power Corporation	2 355 976
8.	Alberta Government Telephone	2 311 043
9.	Air Canada	2 190 567
10.	Newfoundland and Labrador Hydro Company	1 962 546

corporations have very substantial assets, in large part because of the capital-intensive nature of energy and transportation utilities in which public enterprise flourishes. In fact, seven of the largest 40 industrial firms, in 1983, were owned by federal or provincial governments (see Table 1-9). The number would be even larger if rank were by assets. Table 1-16 shows the ranking industrial crown corporations. The asset figures suggest that the Canadian governments are very large borrowers on capital account, playing a leading role with giant private corporations on the demand side of capital finance markets.

The Financial Sector

In studies of economic structure and industrial organization the financial sector is often neglected. To some extent this is the result of attempts to avoid double counting since the majority of the assets held by the financial sector are the liabilities of the non-financial sector. Nevertheless, the structure of the financial community is a major facet of an economy, although hypotheses relating the structure of the non-financial sector to the structure of the financial sector have been meagre in number and difficult to test. Here we simply attempt to describe Canada's financial sector, first by briefly looking at the largest firms and then by tracing the changes in the relative importance of, and industry concentration ratios for, the various financial intermediaries.

Table 1-17 lists the twenty largest financial corporations. The first five are chartered banks. These "big five" control over 90 percent of chartered bank assets. Of the remaining 15 financial intermediaries in the top 20, most are life insurance and trust companies. Significantly, three of the 15 are government agencies, two of which were established to make funds available to home buyers (CMHC) and exporters (EDC), and the third to invest pension funds (the Caisse de depot). Table 1-18 shows how the relative shares of assets held by financial intermediaries have changed over the past century. In 1870, the chartered banks accounted for over 70 percent of financial intermediary assets in Canada. The first important rivals of the banks were the insurance companies and the home finance companies (formerly building societies, more recently the trust companies). In recent years the growth of public and private pension plans has further cut into the financial intermediary asset shares of the chartered banks.

The decline in the concentration of financial intermediary assets held by chartered banks has been matched by a rise in the concentration of chartered bank assets among the largest banks. As Table 1-19 indicates, the four leading banks accounted for 44 percent of chartered bank assets in 1870 (39 percent in 1900); and 81 percent in 1969. The number of chartered banks declined by

Table 1-17

20 Largest Financial Corporations: 1983

Rank	Corporation	Assets 1983 ($000)
1.	Royal Bank of Canada	84 681 823
2.	Canadian Imperial Bank of Commerce	68 112 030
3.	Bank of Montreal	63 194 231
4.	Bank of Nova Scotia	54 808 616
5.	Toronto Dominion Bank	42 800 100
6.	Caisse de depot et placement du Quebec	18 200 000
7.	National Bank of Canada	17 774 486
8.	Trilon Financial Corp.	16 029 000
9.	Sun Life Assurance Co. of Canada	11 358 768
10.	Royal Trustco Ltd.	10 615 000
11.	Canada Mortgage and Housing Corp. (CMHC)	10 500 000
12.	Canada Trustco Mortgage Co.	10 182 058
13.	Manufacturer's Life Insurance Co.	9 437 961
14.	Great-West Life Assurance Co.	7 823 635
15.	Canada Permanent Mortgage Co.	7 036 001
16.	Export Development Corporation (EDC)	6 063 000
17.	Canada Life Assurance Co.	5 314 829
18.	Mutual Life Assurance Co. of Canada	5 155 511
19.	Montreal City and District Savings Bank	5 096 510
20.	London Life Insurance Co.	5 093 206

Source: Financial Post 500, June 1984, pp. 146, 153.

75 percent between 1900 and 1970, undoubtedly a reflection, in part, of the greater facility of the leading banks to engage in branch banking as communications systems improved. The tendency to increased concentration is not, however, evident among the chartered banks' chief rivals: the insurance and trust companies. To increase competition in banking, recently enacted amendments to the Bank Act open the way to increased participation in the Canadian market by foreign banks and facilitate the conversion of an existing financial institution to a chartered bank.[27] In addition, some non-bank financial intermediaries (particularly the trust companies and caisses populaires) engage in traditional banking activities although they are not legally permitted to call themselves banks unless specifically chartered as such by the federal parliament.

27. Canada, Department of Finance, *Summary of Banking Legislation*, 1978. Also see the symposium on Bank Act revision in *Canadian Public Policy*, Summer 1976, pp. 368-410.

Table 1-18

Relative Shares of Canadian Assets Held by Canadian Financial Intermediaries, Selected Years 1870-1968

	1870	1890	1910	1930	1950	1968
I Chartered banks	72.6	49.5	59.6	45.9	41.9	28.9
II Private non-bank	18.9	39.5	31.9	46.1	37.2	47.7
Insurance companies	5.6	12.1	15.2	29.8	22.1	16.1
Home finance[a]	9.6	24.5	12.8	9.4	4.0	8.0
Consumer loan and finance[b]	—	—	—	.9	4.0	9.1
Pension funds	—	—	—	—	4.2	8.9
Other[c]	3.7	2.9	3.9	6.1	2.9	5.5
III Public	8.4	11.0	8.4	8.0	20.8	23.4
Dominion note issue and Bank of Canada	5.2	3.1	5.1	3.0	11.4	4.6
Annuity insurance & pension plan	—	—	.1	1.5	5.0	10.9
Other federal	3.2	7.9	3.2	3.5	4.4	7.9
IV Private as a percent of total (I + II)	91.5	89.0	91.5	92.0	79.2	76.6

[a]Building societies, mortgage loan companies and trust companies.
[b]Consumer loan and finance companies, credit unions and caisse populaires.
[c]Quebec savings banks, fraternal benefit societies, close-end funds, development companies, mutual funds.
Source: E.P. Neufeld, *The Financial System of Canada* (Toronto: Macmillan, 1972), Statistical Appendix. Dr. Edward P. Neufeld generously granted permission to reprint.

The attempt to increase competition in banking is probably the most contentious issue in Bank Act revision. It is interesting in this respect to contrast the structure of Canadian chartered and U.S. commercial banks. In Canada there were, in 1980, ten chartered banks established along branch banking lines. That is, each bank has branches in many cities and provinces. In the United States there are 14 000 commercial banks in what is described as a "unit banking" system. Most banks have a single branch and those with multiple branches are territorially limited to a given city, or at most a state. One can speculate on what difference this sharp contrast in banking structures makes to households and firms utilizing banking services. We may hazard a guess that for households there is little difference between the Canadian and U.S. systems since the relevant market is local, and except for large cities there

Table 1-19

**Concentration of Assets Among Various Private Sector
Financial Intermediaries**

	1870	1900	1930	1950	1969
Chartered banks					
2 largest (%)	37	30	53	50	47
4 largest (%)	44	39	81	77	81
(Total number)	(20)	(36)	(11)	(10)	(9)
Federally registered					
life insurance companies					
2 largest (%)	—	56	51	47[a]	36
4 largest (%)	—	77	68	64[a]	58
(Total number)	—	(17)	(25)	(27)[a]	(33)
Trust companies[b]					
2 largest (%)	—	—	62[c]	53	59
4 largest (%)	—	—	95[c]	71	75
Consumer loan					
companies					
2 largest (%)	—	—	—	—	47
4 largest (%)	—	—	—	—	68
(Total number)	—	—	—	—	(57)

[a]1945.
[b]Estate, trust, and agency funds only.
[c]1926.
Source: E.P. Neufeld, *The Financial System of Canada*, Tables 4-6; 8-2; 9-3; 10-8. Used by
generous permission of Dr. E.P. Neufeld.

are relatively few banking alternatives to choose from for most customers in
either country. However, for firms, particularly large ones, which can go far
afield to borrow, the differential structure of Canadian and U.S. banking can
make a difference. Until recently at least, there simply were fewer alternatives
within the Canadian banking industry, suggesting there was likely to be less
price (interest rate) competition and more conservatism in lending decisions
here. The increased role of foreign banks may be in the process of changing this
situation.

Public Sector Growth

Our description of the Canadian economy has concentrated so far on the
industrial *source* of Canadian output. When we turn to the *uses* or expenditure

side we note a very consequential change that has taken place in the last 40 years or so. Since the 1930s Canada, like all other Western nations, has experienced a tremendous growth in the absolute and relative size of the government sector. The share of "exhaustive" government expenditures on goods and services, as a percentage of GNP, has doubled since the 1930s, although it is down appreciably from the World War II high of approximately 38 percent. Exhaustive, i.e., real resource using, government expenditures on goods and services now make up approximately a quarter of our GNP. In addition, transfer payments to persons (e.g. old age pensions, unemployment insurance payments, family allowances, social assistance) have grown rapidly, particularly during the 1960s and early 1970s. When transfer payments are added to exhaustive expenditures, the total came to over 40 percent of GNP in 1975, a plateau at which it has remained since then. In 1965, the comparable figure was 30 percent, which means that there was an extraordinary growth in government expenditure (and tax burdens) during the intervening decade.

The rise in the share of GNP absorbed by the government has meant that the share of gross income over which consumer units have "individual sovereignty" in spending decisions has declined. This is due to the fact that most of the increase in government economic activity is financed by taxation rather than user charges. Thus, an increasing share of what is produced is determined by a political process in which there may be "collective sovereignty" in the sense that choices are influenced by voting majorities or organized pressure group minorities, but for which the individual consumer sovereignty of the market place is lacking. Moreover, as the government has grown so has its proclivity to write rules for, and legislate the behaviour of, firms in the private sector. This increasing tendency to "regulate" the private sector is partly attributable to the growing demands that private enterprise be socially responsible and conform to broadly accepted social goals such as environmental, consumer, and health and safety protection, and non-discrimination. The growth may also be attributable to the natural tendency of (government) bureaucracies to seek to extend or maintain their status or even to justify their existence against charges of "do nothing." Here we begin to tread on relatively new territory. Nevertheless, it seems certain that students of industrial organization cannot ignore the impact of government on the structure, behaviour and performance of firms and industries.

Structure of Canadian Industry Summarized

This chapter has attempted to paint a picture of the structure of the Canadian economic landscape. It is a landscape of contrasts. The human element is

Table 1-20

Growth of Government Expenditures, 1926-1980

Year	Total Government Expenditure (including transfer payments to persons) as a % of GNP	"Exhaustive" Government Expenditures on Goods and Services as a % of GNP
1926	15.7	9.6
1933	27.4	13.7
1939	21.4	12.7
1943	45.4	38.2
1950	22.1	13.1
1955	26.3	17.5
1960	29.7	17.7
1965	29.9	19.5
1970	36.3	23.1
1973	37.6	22.8
1975	41.3	24.0
1978	41.6	24.0
1980	41.1	22.7

Sources: The National Finances 1974-75, Canadian Tax Foundation, 1975. Tables 2-10, 2-12, pp. 17-19, for years 1926-73; Dept. of Finance, *Economic Review* April 1981 for 1975-1979; *Canadian Statistical Review*, Jan. 1983 for 1980.

increasingly engaged in white-collar occupations in industries belonging to the tertiary sector. At the same time the goods-producing industries in the primary and secondary sectors remain absolutely vital to the continued prosperity and productivity of the Canadian economy. Canada's industrialized economy continues to have a strong resource base, and its comparative advantage in this regard was reinforced in the 1970s as the terms of trade turned toward raw materials in a resource-scarce and hungry world.

It is a landscape of the big and the small. The largest firms are very big, although not so by U.S. standards. The federal and provincial governments have grown so that their share of total expenditures is relatively large, although their ability to control events appears to grow correspondingly smaller. The "small" is in the large number of owner-managed firms that continue to dot the economic landscape. Recalling Table 1-7 reminds us of the diversity of industry structures within each of the nine broad industry groups. No one word such as monopoly, oligopoly, giantism, corporatism can begin to sufficiently describe the Canadian economic landscape. Add to this the peculiarities of foreign ownership and control, the public firm-private firm duopolies in railroads, airlines and broadcasting, and the proclivities of federal and provincial governments to experiment with public production via Crown corporations, and it is then clear that ours is a very "mixed" system, even harder to define than it is to describe.

2

Market Structure in Canadian Industry

This chapter is concerned with industrial market structure in Canada. The most important unit in the study of industrial organization is the *industry*, composed of one or more firms capable of supplying a particular consumer with products which are close substitutes. Industrial organization theory has placed more emphasis on the industry and somewhat less emphasis on the individual firm than is the case with standard microeconomic theory.[1] One reason for the difference in emphasis is that most industrial markets are oligopolistic and the economic theory of the firm hits a snag when it comes to oligopoly or "competition among the few." For here the group (or industry) becomes important because of recognized interdependence among the members of the group. Even where the number of firms in an industry is relatively large, rivals are nevertheless recognized and some degree of behavioural interdependence is likely. It is hard to think of a manufacturing or mining industry in which membership is anywhere near as impersonal as it is for the individual firm in the Canadian wheat industry.

The Industrial Organization Framework

The study of industrial organization relates market structure to firm behaviour and industry performance. An industry's structure is usually described in terms

1. Recently, however, industrial organization economists have begun to give more attention to the individual firm in an attempt to explain the size of giant firms and their proclivity to diversify. As chapter one suggested large "enterprises" can be thought of as a collection of firms, connected by ownership ties, each firm having one or more plants or "establishments."

of (a) the size distribution of firms; (b) product differentiation; (c) entry barriers; and (d) industry growth rates. These aspects of industry structure are presumed to exercise some influence on the behaviour of firms and the economic "performance" of the industry.[2] How closely behaviour and performance relate to industry structure is a major theme of industrial organization, and is the subject of much empirical work, and not a little controversy. At the heart of the matter are the structural conditions favourable to competitive behaviour and performance on the one hand and those favourable to monopolistic behaviour and performance on the other.

The standard industrial organization paradigm relates market structure, behaviour and performance in the following way:

STRUCTURE → BEHAVIOUR → PERFORMANCE

Market structure is said to influence firm behaviour, and the behaviour of firms, taken together, is said to affect industry performance.[3] For example, a common hypothesis is that monopolistic behaviour (collusion, price leadership) is more easily facilitated where industry concentration (defined below) and barriers to entry are high, than where concentration and barriers are relatively low. Monopolistic behaviour, in turn, is presumed to have the aim, and if effective, the result, of yielding monopoly profits through the elevation of prices and the restriction of output.

Higher prices and lower output are signs of misallocated resources and, thereby, less than optimal industry performance. In chapters 2, 3 and 4 we consider the elements of market structure and their determinants. Firm

2. The structure-conduct-performance paradigm of industrial organization was developed in the classic, though not particularly readable, text of Joe S. Bain, *Industrial Organization* (New York: Wiley, 1959, 1968). However, it was the writing and teaching of Bain's mentor at Harvard University, E.S. Mason, to which the field of industrial organization owes its heritage. Many of Mason's essays are collected in *Economic Concentration and the Monopoly Problem* (Cambridge: Harvard University Press, 1959).

3. Bain concluded that both theoretically and empirically the strongest relationship was between structure and performance. Thus his writings, particularly his well-known textbook *Industrial Organization*, give very short shrift to the discussion (and models) of behaviour. Bain's view was that a wide variety of market behaviour was consistent with various industry structures and observed performance. However, subsequent writers have been more skeptical about the "tightness" of the structure-performance relationship and have looked to models and studies of firm and industry behaviour for further insights into the rich variety of market structures and performance actually observed. This approach is clearly taken by F.M. Scherer, *Industrial Market Structure and Economic Performance* (Chicago: Rand-McNally, 1980). A somewhat more intermediate position is taken by W.G. Shepherd, *The Economics of Industrial Organization* (Englewood Cliffs, New Jersey: Prentice Hall, 1979). One leading economist who has questioned whether there is a separate field of industrial organization, but who has nevertheless made seminal contributions to that field, is George Stigler. Many of his important papers have been included in *The Organization of Industry* (Homewood, Illinois: Irwin, 1968).

Table 2-1

Market Structure Taxonomy

| | Number of Sellers | | |
	One	A few	Many
Homogeneous Product	Pure monopoly (electricity)	Homogeneous oligopoly (e.g., aluminum, steel, tin cans)	Pure competition (wheat)
Differentiated Product	Pure monopoly (BBC 20 years ago, with its three channels)	Differentiated oligopoly (e.g., autos, typewriters, refrigerators)	Monopolistic competition (shoes, women's dresses, retail trades & services)
Conditions of Entry	Entry blocked	Some entry barriers ranging from high to moderate-low	Easy entry

---

behaviour is considered in chapter 5, and market performance in chapter 6.[4]

Several market structures are distinguished by economists. These are shown in Table 2-1 where classification is by number of sellers on the one hand and similarity of the product of competing sellers on the other hand. Entry conditions are also indicated. This is the taxonomy familiar to all students of economics. It has a major weakness, however. The gap between the "one" and the "many" is very large and most industrial markets fall into the intermediate group. Yet the firm predictions of economic theory are based on models of "one" (monopoly) or many (competition) sellers in a given market. Thus economists interested in the field of industrial organization have attempted in their models to enrich and quantify the structural characteristics of industrial

4. Because of the nature of this text, our review of the literature in industrial organization is necessarily limited. The interested student will find, in addition to the leading texts and monographs on industrial organization, a number of collections of essays on specific topics in the field. Two older collections are American Economic Association, *Readings in Industrial Organization and Public Policy* (Homewood, Illinois: Irwin, 1958); Universities National Bureau for Economic Research, *Business Concentration and Price Policy* (Princeton: Princeton University Press, 1955); more recent collections include J.W. Markham and G.F. Papanek (eds.) *Industrial Organization and Economic Development* (Boston: Houghton-Mifflin, 1970); C.K. Rowley, *Readings in Industrial Economics* Vol. I, II (Macmillan, 1972); D. Needham, *Readings in the Economics of Industrial Organization* (New York: Holt, Rinehart, Winston, 1970).

markets in order to yield improved predictions of firm behaviour and performance.[5]

Although the "real world" of observed market structures lies almost wholly between the polar cases of pure competition and pure monopoly, the economic theorist's polar case models have withstood, in certain important respects, the test of time. They have yielded predictions about price and output behaviour which have provided important bench marks for more detailed analysis. Students of industrial organization have not escaped the understandable tendency of relating more complex descriptions of industrial structure, behaviour, and performance to the highly simplified models of the classical economic theory of the firm. Thus, the terms "monopolistic" and "competitive" are used to characterize a much wider variety of structure, behaviour and performance than that which is specific to the concepts of "pure monopoly" and "pure competition."

What are the predictions of the economic theory of the firm under conditions of monopoly and pure competition which provide such useful benchmarks? Figure 2-1 presents the case of pure competition at the level of the industry and the firm respectively. Short-run equilibrium and long-run equilibrium positions are distinguished by the use of primes to denote the latter. In the short run $P = MR = MC$, but economic (or excess) profits (or losses) may exist. These are indicated by the shaded rectangle in the righthand part of Figure 2-1. In the long run, when the number or scale of firms has had a chance to adjust, changes in industry supply react on price and unit cost in such a way as to squeeze out excess profits (or losses).

Figure 2-2 presents the case of monopoly. The firm and industry demand curves are identical. The firm's marginal revenue curve lies below the downward-sloping demand curve, implying that when the monopolist maximizes profits, $MR = MC$ while $P > MC$. To remain a monopolist, barriers to entry must be sufficiently high to deter prospective entrants, thus allowing the monopolist to earn excess profits (the shaded rectangle in Figure 2-2) in the long run as well as the short run.

The state of long-run competitive equilibrium has three normative properties. First, the price paid for the last unit of output produced is just equal to the cost of producing the last unit—its marginal cost. This equality (between P and MC) implies that the condition for profit maximization under pure competition $(MR = P = MC)$ is consistent with the fundamental condition for welfare maximization: that the marginal social valuation (MSV) of the product by consumers is equal to the marginal social cost (MSC) of producing it. In the

---

5. An early study of one important element of market structure is Joe S. Bain, *Barriers to New Competition* (Cambridge: Harvard University Press, 1956).

Price and Output under Conditions of Pure Competition and Monopoly:

Figure 2-1

Pure Competition

where

AC = average cost   AR = average revenue   (MB) = marginal benefit
MC = marginal cost   MR = marginal revenue   (ΣMC) = sum of individual firm MC curves

Short run profits, indicated by the shaded area, induce entry of new firms, causing supply curve to shift to S¹S¹ and price falls to P¹; industry output rises to Q¹.

Figure 2-2

Pure Monopoly

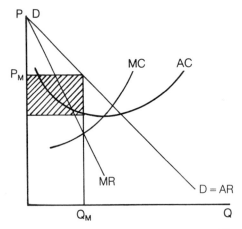

Profits indicated by shaded area will not be "competed" away in long run because entry is blocked. However if new (and superior) goods are created by other firms, and those new goods are substitutes for the monopolist's output, the monopolist may lose his market and his profits. [This underlies Schumpeter's "creative destruction" which was integral to his argument that monopoly may be better than competition in a long-run, dynamic sense.]

absence of externalities (divergencies between social and private benefits and costs), MSV is reflected in the price (P) which consumers are willing to pay for the product while MSC is equal to the marginal opportunity cost (MC) of producing it. When MSV=MSC for each good and service produced in the economy, the value of total output is maximized given available resources.[6] When competitive conditions assure that MSV = MSC, resources are allocated as efficiently as possible among their various uses.

The fundamental notion of allocative efficiency implied by MSV=MSC can be illustrated by looking again at the left hand part of Figure 2-1. In the absence of externalities, the market demand curve reflects the marginal benefit, i.e., the marginal valuation of a commodity by consumers. The market supply curve, the sum of individual firm marginal cost curves, reflects the marginal social cost of the resources required to produce the commodity. The intersection of the demand and supply curves is not only a point of equilibrium, but one which maximizes the net benefit (total benefit − total cost), as guided by society's preferences, from producing the commodity. At any *other* price than the long run equilibrium price, P^1, MSV>MSC or MSV<MSC. Society will gain by producing more of the commodity if MSV>MSC, less of the commodity if MSV<MSC. Only at P^1 is MSV=MSC; only at P^1 is the value of the output (marginal benefit) produced by an additional unit of resources used in this industry equal to the value of that unit of resources if it were used elsewhere (marginal opportunity cost). At P^1Q^1 nothing more can be gained by society from an increase or decrease in the output of the commodity.

The second facet of long-run competitive equilibrium with normative properties is the competition-induced equality between price and average cost. The equality between price and AC implies that supranormal profits are absent. Producers are earning enough to maintain the investment in the firm, but no more. Thus, the condition that $P = AC$ guarantees sufficient investment to produce equilibrium output, but requires no further transfer of income from consumers to producers. Third, in long-run competitive equilibrium each firm is forced to produce at the minimum point on its average cost curve. Firms that fail to operate at lowest unit cost will be driven out of business. Thus the pressure of competition ensures costs will be minimized, or, in other words, maximum production efficiency is achieved in the use of resources.

The welfare case for competition and against monopoly resides fundamentally in the first of the three normative properties of competitive equilibrium just described. In fact, the second and third properties do not necessarily distinguish monopoly from competition. A profit-maximizing monopolist will attempt to minimize production costs. A firm with monopoly power but facing weak

6. Another way of putting it is that when MSV = MSC, consumer surplus is maximized.

demand may earn zero excess profits—although if it does it will not be able to produce at the minimum point of its average cost curve. (The tangency point between a downward sloping demand curve and a U-shaped cost curve will be to the left of the minimum point of the latter.) What clearly distinguishes monopoly and competition is the differential relation between price and MC. Because the monopolist stops producing before price has fallen to the level of MC, the MSV of goods produced by monopolists will exceed their MSC. This means that there remain unsatisfied consumers who are willing to pay at least as much as it costs to produce additional units of output but who are unwilling to pay the monopoly price. Consumer surplus is thus sacrificed in the monopolist's drive for profit.[7]

The models of pure competition and monopoly can be brought together graphically to demonstrate the (static) economic welfare case against monopoly. In Figure 2-3 the subscripts m and c refer to the monopoly and purely competitive equilibrium price and quantity. The crucial difference between the purely competitive and monopoly cases is the relation between price and marginal cost in each. Figure 2-3 suggests the following comparison between competition and monopoly.

(a) *Ceteris paribus*, an industry's output will be higher and price lower if it is organized under structurally competitive rather than structurally monopolistic conditions. The higher price and lower output under monopoly results in a reallocation (and probably a misallocation) of resources away from the monopolized industry. If resources are optimally allocated under competitive conditions, the conversion to monopoly is said to result in "allocative inefficiency." The real or "deadweight" loss to society (the "welfare loss") is indicated by the triangle WL.[8]

(b) If the monopolist can maintain price persistently above opportunity cost, then, relative to the competitive case, there is a redistribution of income from consumers to producers (rectangle D).

(c) A lack of "competitive pressure" on monopolistic firms may result in a rise in costs as well as price. That is, the average cost curve may shift upward. This so-called "X-inefficiency" may arise if the slack afforded to the protected monopolist results in his failure to adopt least-cost methods of production, or if he fails to purchase inputs at lowest available prices.[9]

The analysis to this point has been carried out in "partial equilibrium" terms, focusing on the effects of monopoly in one industry. Cast in "general equilib-

---

7. As long as demand curves slope downward the sacrifice (or loss) of consumer surplus will exceed the monopolist's profit gain.
8. WL is the difference between the loss in consumer surplus PmPcCB and the rise in producer surplus PmPcFB.
9. Harvey Liebenstein, "Allocative Efficiency vs. X-Efficiency," *American Economic Review*, 56 (June 1966), pp. 392-415.

Figure 2-3

Simple (Static) Case Against Monopoly

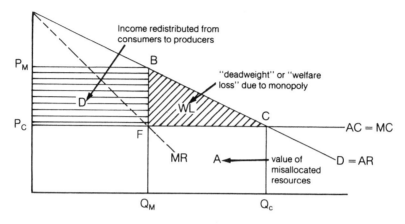

(a) the model indicates the *allocative inefficiency* criticism of monopoly.
(b) If monopolists also fail to keep costs down (because of the "slack" their profit margins allow) there is an "*X-inefficiency*" argument against monopoly. That is, lacking "competitive pressure," the monopolist may not use least-cost methods of production.
(c) Monopoly clearly produces a redistribution of income from consumers to producers.

rium" terms the loss to society due to monopoly pricing is not limited to triangle BFC in Figure 2-3. Monopoly pricing results in resources, whose value is indicated by rectangle A (equal to Q_mFCQ_c) in Figure 2-3, being released from, or remaining unused by, the monopolized sector. These resources will either lie idle, representing an additional deadweight loss to society or, as is usually assumed in general equilibrium analysis, they will be employed in competitively organized industries. As additional resources flow into competitive industries, output will increase, prices will decline and returns on investment will be reduced below what they could have earned had all of the industries in the economy been competitively organized. Thus, in addition to a "deadweight" loss of consumer surplus in the monopolized sector, monopoly pricing will, in a general equilibrium framework, produce a loss of producer surplus in the competitively organized sector.[10]

The basic model presented in Figure 2-3 must be modified to take account of economies of scale and technological change. Economies of scale, if they are to be exhausted, may require fewness of firms in a given industry (one in the case

10. The analysis here ignores externalities and "second best" problems. When in chapter 6 we again make use of the partial equilibrium analysis reflected in Figure 2-3, the student should keep in mind the results of general equilibrium analysis discussed here.

of "natural monopolies" such as the local telephone company). This is especially important in Canada where domestic markets are relatively small due to our small population. Where there are important economies of scale there is a "trade-off" between the monopolists' power to raise price above cost and the lower costs made possible by the exhaustion of economies of scale.[11] More on this in subsequent chapters.

Technological change is even more difficult to handle. Apart from the controversy over whether monopolistic or competitive conditions are more conducive to innovation and invention at the product and process level, there is a troublesome fact that adequate handling of technological change requires a more dynamic model than the intensely comparative static one employed here. Changes in technology take time, and time is ruinous to *ceteris paribus* assumptions. Over time demand curves shift in response to changing tastes and the introduction of new products, and so do cost curves as production techniques and input prices change. These developments are, of course, not independent of the pace of technological change nor is the latter independent of changes in demand and costs.

The Austrian, and later Harvard, economist, Joseph Schumpeter, rejected the comparative static models on which the predictions about monopoly and competitive behaviour and performance are based, and emphasized instead the "dynamic efficiency" resulting from the introduction of new products and processes.[12] For Schumpeter, the essence of competition was the replacement of the "old" by the "new." He argued that the inducement to innovate comes chiefly from the monopoly profits yielded up by successful introduction of new products and processes, while monopoly profits, in turn, provide the necessary funding for further research and development. Thus, for Schumpeter, monopoly power is to some degree both the cause and effect of innovation and invention. But monopoly power held by any one firm would be short lived as new products drive out the old. This is the essence of Schumpeter's theory of "creative destruction" in which one firm's monopoly in a given product line is destroyed by another firm's creativity in devising a better substitute. Here we may note that underlying Schumpeter's analysis is the implicit assumption that new products are introduced by new or different firms in a sufficient number of cases to ensure interfirm competition over time. If, as seems increasingly the case, large diversified firms introduce most new products and processes, replacing the old with the new in line with a carefully worked-out marketing

11. A classic statement of this problem is O.E. Williamson, "Economies as an Antitrust Defense," *American Economic Review* (March 1968). See the discussion of this model at the end of chapter 4.
12. Joseph Schumpeter, *Capitalism, Socialism, and Democracy* (New York: Harper, 1950), Chapters 7, 8.

strategy, there is some question as to the meaning of "creative destruction." Moreover, many economists who have studied the determinants of innovation and invention doubt high degrees of monopoly power are either necessary or even helpful.[13] We will return to this issue in chapter 6.

The juxtaposition of the price theory models and Schumpeter's hypotheses helps to highlight an underlying tension in the study of industrial organization. This tension inheres in the question of how much one can infer about competitive behaviour and performance from a study of industry structure. The "orthodox" view, which is largely followed here, is that industry structure has an important impact on behaviour and, particularly, performance. There are those who demur, pointing to the possibility that efficient performance (as indicated by price-cost relations) may be the cause, for example, of both high profitability and high market share, thereby reversing the lines of causation, or at least introducing a substantial bit of feedback from performance to structure.[14] These economists would argue that it is more accurate to show the line of causation as Behaviour→Performance→Structure.

Economists who argue that causation runs from behaviour to performance to structure emphasize cost differences between firms, cost differences that are unrelated to firm size or scale. They argue that these non-scale cost differences among firms in an industry are attributable primarily to differences in managerial efficiency. Differences in managerial efficiency are, in turn, attributable to interfirm differences in the ability to monitor team production and contractual relations with one's distributors and suppliers—i.e., to get the most out of one's resources and one's commercial relations.[15] Firms with "superior" managerial capabilities will, other things being equal, have lower costs than their competitors. They will be able to set lower prices and/or produce a superior product or service at the same price as their less efficient rivals. As a result, "superior" firms are likely to have *both* higher price-cost margins and larger market shares than their rivals. Although statistics will show a positive correlation between firm

13. Recently a "neo-Schumpeterian" school of thought is reflected in the approach to industrial organization taken by Richard Nelson and Sidney Winter. See, for example, "Forces Generating and Limiting Concentration under Schumpeterian Competition," *Bell Journal of Economics* (Autumn 1978), pp. 524-48, and, by the same authors, "The Schumpeterian Tradeoff Revisited," *American Economic Review* (March 1982) pp. 114-32.

14. The tension between the orthodox and what might loosely be termed the "Chicago" approach is clearly reflected in the pairs of essays by Scherer and McGee, Weiss and Demsetz, and Mann and Brozen in H. Goldschmid, H.M. Mann, and J. Fred Weston, *Industrial Concentration: The New Learning* (Boston: Little Brown, 1974). A somewhat different tack is taken by Almarin Phillips who has questioned the unidirectionality of interactions from structure through conduct to performance. A. Phillips, "Structure, Conduct, and Performance—and Performance, Conduct and Structure," in J.W. Markham and G.F. Papanek (eds.) *op. cit.*, Ch. 2.

15. See A. Alchian and H. Demsetz, "Production, Information Costs, and Economic Organization," *American Economic Review* 62 (Dec. 1972), pp. 777-795.

market share or industry concentration on the one hand and price cost margins or profitability on the other, the one is not the cause of the other. Rather, the argument runs, both large market shares and high profitability are the result of efficient conduct and superior performance by certain firms. Moreover, what appear to be monopoly profits earned by leading firms may only be "rents" warranted by superior managerial capabilities.

A further word on the distinction between monopoly profits and efficiency rents is required. When a firm has sufficient market power to raise price significantly above marginal cost, monopoly profits arise. When a scarce resource yields its owner an advantage not available to other firms, rents (which may look the same as profits to the layman) will be generated even though the rent-receiving firm is a price taker in the market (that is, it has no market power). Thus the appearance of returns substantially in excess of (opportunity) costs could be rents to relative efficiency, or "superiority", rather than monopoly profits owing to the exercise of market power. While the "orthodox" position in industrial organization has emphasized the latter explanation for supranormal returns, a growing number of industrial organization economists are inclined toward an alternative view (see the last section of Chapter 3) which emphasizes the former, "efficiency" rents, explanation for differential returns among firms and industries.

Non-scale cost differences between firms may also appear as a result of various constraints placed on the firm and the behaviour of its agents. Among the constraints are those posed by non-zero transactions, information, and adjustment costs; attenuated property rights due to public ownership; limits on profits and pricing behaviour attributable to regulation; and the existence of non-pecuniary sources of utility. While traditional neoclassical theory tended to assume away these additional constraints on profit and utility maximizing behaviour, there have been a number of recent attempts to generalize the neoclassical framework by taking explicitly into account transactions and information costs, non-pecuniary sources of utility, the consequences of limited transferability of property rights and the effects on managerial behaviour posed by profit constraints. One implication of the recent work is that it suggests that the X-efficiency construct and neoclassical analysis need not be in conflict. What appears to be non-maximizing behaviour in the form of a failure of firms to cost minimize (X-inefficiency) may in fact be cost minimization subject to a set of additional, cost-increasing, constraints.[16] If firms in an industry differ in the extent to which such additional constraints exist or are binding, one may expect to find cost differences among firms which are not attributable to scale

16. For a summary of the literature and an attempt to assess its implications for X-efficiency analysis, see Louis de Alessi, "Property Rights, Transactions Costs, and X-Efficiency: An Essay in Economic Theory," *American Economic Review*, 73 (March 1983), pp. 64-81.

differences. These non-scale cost differences not only may influence firm performance but may affect industry structure.

The issues raised by the two competing paradigms will not be resolved here. (The debate is reopened at the end of chapter 3.) Suffice it to say that both the structure-behaviour-performance and the behaviour-performance-structure paradigms contain important elements which must be kept in mind in any balanced study of industrial organization. In particular, it is crucial to keep both paradigms in mind when we evaluate structure-performance relations in chapter 6. In addition, the issues raised prompt some discussion here of the somewhat slippery concept of "competition."

The term "competition" can have two quite different meanings in economic parlance. First, there is "competition" in the sense of rivalrous behaviour. This appears to be what Adam Smith meant by competition. It also characterizes competition between oligopolists (when they are not engaged in collusion, tacit as well as explicit), although oligopolists have strong incentives to, and often do, compete in *non-price* ways. Second, there is competition in the "structural" sense of many sellers (or buyers), none of whom actually sees other sellers as rivals. Purely (or perfectly) competitive industries are characterized by "competition" in this sense. This is what economists usually mean when "competition" is used in the context of economic theory.[17] Almost four decades ago, J.M. Clark attempted to synthesize these two notions of competition in the concept of "workable competition." Clark argued that in an imperfect world "workable competition" would result if the following conditions are met: (i) there is rivalry among firms selling goods; (ii) sellers attempt to maximize net revenue (profits) and (iii) price discretion is limited by the option of buyers to purchase from rival sellers.[18] Taken together these three conditions apply to markets where there are several sellers of a "similar" product driven by the spur of profits, and where there are easy entry conditions into the industry for "new" sellers so that the established rivals are kept "honest." In such markets roughly competitive performance can be expected.

Recently, a new twist has been added in the form of "contestable" as opposed to perfectly, or workably, competitive markets.[19] Baumol *et al* argue that the welfare properties achieved under perfect competition can be achieved

17. Thus some writers argue that the conditions for perfect competition can be reduced to two: the firm is a price taker (rivalry is absent or negligible) and freedom of entry. R.L. Lipsey, G. Sparks, P. Steiner, *Economics*, 2nd ed. Ch. 14.
18. J.M. Clark, "Towards a Concept of Workable Competition," *American Economic Review* 30 (June 1940), pp. 241-56.
19. William J. Baumol, John C. Panzar and Robert D. Willig, *Contestable Markets and the Theory of Industry Structure* (New York: Harcourt Brace Jovanovich, Inc.) A useful dissection of contestability is by Michael Spense, "Contestable Markets and the Theory of Industry Structure: A Review Article," *Journal of Economic Literature*, 21 (September 1983), pp. 981-990.

in the case of oligopoly, even "natural monopoly" (see chapter 10), so long as there are no impediments to entry of new firms or exit by existing ones. A "contestable market" is defined "as one in which entry is absolutely free, and exit is absolutely costless."[20] That is, in a contestable market, entrants, potential or actual, do not suffer any cost advantage relative to incumbent firms, and any firm can quickly leave the industry without capital loss by either selling its plant and equipment or transferring it to another use. In contestable markets the threat of rapid entry forces established firms to set price equal to cost. Thus, "contestability" has important implications for oligopoly theory and the study of industrial organization. If markets are highly or perfectly contestable then the threat or check posed by potential entrants dominates more or less totally the mutual recognition of interdependence between the established rivals. In other words, in contestable markets, oligopolistic interdependence or "conjectural variation" are unimportant or do not exist. Similarly, strategic entry-deterring behaviour, which occupies an important place in industrial organization analysis (see chapter 3) is ineffective or irrelevant. In this book, however, we shall not so quickly set aside interdependent and strategic behaviour.[21]

The intention of this digression on "competition" and "contestability" is to suggest that claims that competition has been weakened by the disappearance of structurally competitive conditions may be misleading. Competitive behaviour in the rivalristic sense does not require perfectly competitive conditions or approximations thereto. In fact, duopolists may compete when they are not colluding, and, at least in principle, the competition can be quite vigorous. It is too simple to equate numbers with competition. Rivalry may be vigorous or weak; the determinants of one or the other are often complex. Certainly there are important incentives for rival firms to collude yet it is also clear that there are important deterrents to effective collusion, aside from the legal ones (see chapter 5). Competitive behaviour is a complex phenomenon that is neither wholly dependent on, nor independent of, industry structure. On this note we turn to the statistics of market structure in Canadian industry.

---

20. W.J. Baumol, "Contestable Markets: An Uprising in the Theory of Industry Structure," *American Economic Review*, 72, No. 1 (March 1982), pp. 1-15. For exit to be costless, sunk costs must be zero, or negligible.

21. Contestable market analysis also has implications for public policy—both antitrust policy and the regulation of "naturally monopolistic" industries, such as those sometimes found in the public utility field. Some of these issues are discussed in chapter 10. The public policy implications of contestability, particularly when taken in conjunction with the complementary analysis of cost conditions of firms experiencing some form of economies of scale, is perhaps the main contribution of the contestability analysis. For a critique of "contestability", see W.G. Shepherd "Contestability versus Competition" *American Economic Review* Vol. 74 (September, 1984), pp. 572-587.

Concentration Ratios in the Manufacturing and Mining Sectors

The most widely used summary statistic of market structure is the concentration ratio. The concentration ratio is the share of an industry's output, value added, employment or assets accounted for by a small number of the largest firms in the industry. The most widely used measure of concentration is the share of shipments, or, alternatively, value added accounted for by the largest four firms. Both assets and employment are somewhat defective measures because they are responsive to interfirm differences in capital and labour intensity and not simply to relative firm size in terms of market activity. Where the investigator is interested in the extent of vertical integration, value added is the preferred measure. However, data limitations do not always permit the investigator to be so choosy. For example, the concentration data available for the year 1948, the first date for which there is a comprehensive set of Canadian statistics, are only in terms of employment.

The statistics to be presented below are based on information compiled from censuses of manufacturing, mining and logging. The basic statistical unit is the establishment (equivalent to the plant in the manufacturing sector). Establishments are assigned to industries on the basis of their primary output. Each industry is given an industrial code. Once assigned, commonly controlled establishments are aggregated into "enterprises" or firms. Thus the data presented here are for the relevant decision-making unit, the enterprise or firm.[22]

The industrial code that is used is called the Standard Industrial Classification (SIC). The SIC has been revised from time to time, most recently in 1970. In the manufacturing sector there are 20 two-digit industry groups (see Table 1-6). These industry groups are subdivided into a number of "three-digit" and "four-digit" industries. The four-digit, and some three-digit industries are presumed to roughly approximate (though quite imperfectly so in many cases) the theoretical industry defined at the beginning of this chapter. Let us take, as

---

22. Alternatively, Berkowitz, et al. refer to "enterprises" as collections of companies under common control, where control depends on a combination of stock ownership and interlocking directorships and officerships. The "benchmark" enterprise involves majority ownership (50 percent or greater stock ownership) of component companies. Berkowitz, et al. then compare industry concentration ratios based on the benchmark definition of an enterprise with concentration ratios based on enterprises defined as collections of companies in which the former has at least 15 percent stock ownership in the latter plus three representatives on each company's board of directors (and/or three officers). The comparison indicates little difference in concentration ratios. See Berkowitz et al., *Enterprise Structure and Corporate Concentration*, Study No. 17, Royal Commission on Corporate Concentration, Ottawa, 1977.

Table 2-2

SIC Divisions of Transportation Equipment Industry

SIC Code	Industry	4-firm concentration ratio (Shipments 1980)
321	Aircraft and aircraft parts manufacturers	75
323	Motor vehicle manufacturers	94
324	Truck body and trailer manufacturers	
3241	Truck body manufacturers	36
3242	Non-commercial trailer manufacturers	40
3243	Commercial trailer manufacturers	53
325	Motor vehicle parts and accessories manufacturers	45
326	Railroad rolling stock industry	85
327	Shipbuilding and repair	56
328	Boatbuilding and repair	22
329	Miscellaneous vehicle manufacturers	87 (1972)

---

an example, the Transportation Equipment Industry group (SIC 32). It is subdivided as shown in Table 2-2.

Many three- and four-digit industries are too broadly defined, and a few too narrowly defined, to conform to the theoretical industry. For example SIC 321, aircraft and aircraft parts manufacturers, obviously covers products which are quite dissimilar. Commercial and military aircraft are lumped together as are private aircraft. Thus SIC 321 includes several theoretically distinct industries. When the SIC industry is too broad (relative to the theoretical industry) there is a tendency for the concentration ratio to be understated. That is, were establishments presently allocated to SIC 321, allocated among two or more distinct subgroups within 321, the resulting CR_4 for each product subgroup (e.g. commercial aircraft) would exceed the 75 percent figure in column 3. Much the same can be said for several other SIC industries (e.g. 324, 325, 326, 327) within the Transportation Equipment Industry group. On the whole, the Canadian SIC defines industries more broadly than does the SIC used in the United States. For example, there are 172 separately classified manufacturing industries in Canada, compared to about 450 in the United States. However the SIC is not always too broad relative to the theoretical industry. For example, producers of metal cans and glass containers are allocated to quite separate industry groups. Yet one can argue that there is a high degree of substitutability between these two products, particularly among beverage producers and distributors. Another example where potentially close substitutes are allocated

to different industry groups is wood (SIC 2541) and metal (SIC 3031) sash and
door manufacturers. When industries are defined too narrowly, the resultant
concentration ratios will tend to overstate the degree of market control of the
leading firms. That is, when effectively competing products are allocated to
different industries concentration ratios will be overstated relative to the one
which would apply if the products were allocated to the same (theoretically
correct) industry. On the whole, however, the three- and four-digit industries, in
both the U.S. and Canadian SIC, tend to be too broad rather than too narrow.
Examples are the lumping together of pharmaceuticals, soaps and detergents,
and farm machinery.

Two other factors that influence the meaning of the concentration ratios to be
presented below are geography and the competitive impact of imports. Concentration ratios refer to domestic production across the nation. Where markets are
geographically segmented, as quite a number are in a nation as large as
Canada, national concentration ratios tend to understate regional or local
concentration.[23] Good examples of industries with regional or local markets are
dairy products, bakeries, machine shops, cement and concrete products. In all,
at least 34 of 154 Canadian manufacturing industries were characterized as
regional in 1965. Some examples of industries where the relevant market is
substantially smaller than nationwide are given in Table 2-3. In some cases the
national concentration ratio exceeds the "local" one where the leading enterprises in the latter are relatively small compared to the leading firms at the
national level. Nevertheless, on the average, regional concentration ratios will
exceed the national one.

National concentration ratios tend to overstate the share of the market
controlled by the leading domestic firms when there is significant competition
from imports. Moreover, *potential* competition from imports can place important limitations on the monopoly power of leading firms in highly concentrated
industries. While international trade is very important to Canada (merchandise
imports account for about 25 percent of our GNP) the Canadian tariff offers
protection, up to a point, to most, though by no means all, manufacturing
industries. As we shall see, the tariff acts as a barrier to entry to competing
goods, thereby tending to protect a Canadian industry's structure from the
potential gales of market power destruction that a free trade policy would
stimulate. Nevertheless, potential and actual competition from abroad cannot
be ignored in drawing market power inferences from concentration ratios based
on domestic production. We shall return to the impact of the tariff on market
structure in chapter 4.

23. Of 154 manufacturing industries for which statistics were provided in 1965, 34 were
classified as regional. Department of Consumer and Corporate Affairs, *Concentration in the
Manufacturing Industries of Canada* (Ottawa, 1971), p. 37.

Table 2-3

Concentration Ratios for Regional Industries

Industry	National 4-firm CR (1965)	Highest Regional 4-firm CR (1965)	Lowest Regional 4-firm CR (1965)
		(percent)	
Dairy factories & process cheese mfrs.	25	88 (Sask.)	47 (Nova Scotia)
Commercial printing & publishing	13	55 (B.C)	19 (Ontario)
Machine shops	8	55 (Sask.)	8 (Ontario)
Concrete products & ready mix concrete mfrs.	21	66 (New Brunswick)	34 (Quebec, Ont.)
Petroleum refineries	80	92 (B.C., N.W.T.)	85 (Ontario)
Bakeries	32	76 (New Brunswick)	24 (Quebec)
Sawmills, & planing mills	16	23 (Prairie region)	8 (Atlantic, Que., Ont.)

Source: Department of Consumer and Corporate Affairs, *Concentration in the Manufacturing Industries of Canada*, Ottawa: Information Canada 1971, Table A-5.

Table 2-4 presents statistical information relating to concentration ratios in manufacturing, mining and logging industries in 1970 and 1980. About half of Canadian manufacturing industries in 1970 and 1980 had four-firm concentration ratios (CR_4) of 50 percent or more.[24] We can tentatively denote the concentration classes as shown in Table 2-5.

Approximately half of all manufacturing industries and shipments fall into the

24. A study by C. Marfels for the Royal Commission on Corporate Concentration reports that only 22 percent of 146 manufacturing industries in 1965 and 23 percent of 155 manufacturing industries in 1972 had four-firm concentration ratios in excess of 70 percent. However, Marfel's study excludes those industries for which no concentration ratios are published. Most such industries have very high concentration ratios and it is usually possible to determine whether the concentration level is above a given benchmark (say 75 or 80 percent) even if it is impossible to determine the precise number. Thus the figures in Table 2-4 include more industries than are included in Marfel's study, most of them with high CR4. See Christian Marfels, *Concentration Levels and Trends in the Canadian Economy, 1965-1973*, Study No. 31, Royal Commission on Corporate Concentration (Ottawa, 1977) p. 108.

Table 2-4

Industry Concentration Ratios, Canada 1970, 1980

Top 4 Enterprise Concentration Quartiles		Manufacturing Industries, Ranked by % of Factory Shipments Accounted for by Top 4 Enterprises			Mining and Logging Industries, Ranked by % of Shipments Accounted for by Top 4 Enterprises		
		Industries		Industry Value Added (% of Total)	Industries		Industry Value Added (% of Total)
		No.	% of Total		No.	% of Total	
75-100%	1980	29	17.1	17.3	10	66.7	50.0
	1970	39	22.7	24.6	13	59.1	53.4
50-74%	1980	49	29.0	24.0	2	13.3	29.3
	1970	43	25.0	18.2	4	18.2	19.9
25-49%	1980	64	37.9	37.7	2	13.3	2.0
	1970	63	36.6	37.7	5	22.7	26.7
Up to 25%	1980	27	16.0	21.0	1	6.7	18.7
	1970	27	15.7	19.5	0	0	0
Total	1980	169	100.0	100.0	15	100.0	100.0
	1970	172	100.0	100.0	22	100.0	100.0

Sources: Statistics Canada, *Industrial Organization and Concentration in the Manufacturing, Mining and Logging Industries*, Cat. 31-402, Biennial. For 1970, Table B, pp. 16-17; for 1980, Table 2.

Table 2-5

Industry Concentration Classes

CR4 (%)	Description of Level of Concentration		Percent of All Reported Manufacturing Industries		
			1965	1970	1980
75-100	Very high⎱	"tight"	25	23	17
50-75	High⎰	oligopoly	25	25	29
25-70	Moderate:	"loose" oligopoly	33	37	38
Below 25	Low:	atomistic	17	16	16
			100	100	100

top two concentration classes. These are industries which might be classified as "tight" oligopolies. However, the percentage of manufacturing industries which are highly concentrated (CR4 > 75%) has declined substantially in the last two decades. About a third of manufacturing industries are moderately concentrated ("loose" oligopolies) and a sixth have "low" concentration ratios, or are "atomistic." The small fraction of industries with "low" concentration is not, however, indicative of their importance in generating employment opportunities. About 40 percent of manufacturing employment is found in industries characterized by "low" concentration, especially in the labour-intensive food, clothing and leather goods industries.

Although many Canadian industries are concentrated, only 13 of the leading 40 Canadian manufacturing industries (measured in terms of shipments) had four-firm concentration ratios in excess of 50 percent in 1980. Table 2-6 provides shipment concentration ratios for 20 of the top 40 Canadian manufacturing industries in 1980 and 1970, and, where data is available, for 1965 and 1954. The 20 three- and four-digit industries include many "high profile" ones in the public consciousness. Among the industries included in the table no clear trend in industry concentration is observed. What is clear is that the word "oligopoly," to the extent it is used to apply to most of the industries included in the table, must cover a very wide spectrum of actual market structures.

An alternative method of classifying industries by level of concentration is the so-called "inverse index." The inverse index of concentration, in effect, asks how many firms (beginning with the largest) are required to account for 80 percent of industry shipments (or value added or employment). Professor Rosenbuth made wide use of this measure in the classic Canadian work on industry concentration. [25] The following characterization of concentration levels

25. G. Rosenbluth, *Concentration in Canadian Manufacturing,* National Bureau for Economic Research, 1957.

Table 2-6

Four-firm Concentration Ratios of 20 Leading Manufacturing Industries in Canada[a]

Rank[b]	Industry (SIC Code in Parentheses)	No. of firms in 1980	% of Shipments Accounted for by Leading Four Firms			
			1980	1970	1965	1954
1	Petroleum refining (3651)	16	61.7	79.0	84.8	86.4
2	Pulp and paper mills (271)	60	30.9	36.2	36.9	34.5 (1955)
3	Motor vehicle manufacturers (323)	15	93.7	93.3	93.3	95.4
4	Slaughtering and meat processors (1011)	490	43.3	54.8	61.8	60.9
5	Iron and steel mills (291)	39	77.9	76.2	78.8	—
6	Sawmills and planing mills (2513)	1180	19.2	20.9	16.8	—
9	Motor vehicle parts & accessories (325)	278	44.6	46.2	54.2	—
14	Mfrs. of industrial chemicals-organic (3783)	39	64.2	60.5	—	—
15	Communications equipment mfrs (335)	369	52.4	55.8	—	—
16	Aircraft and aircraft parts mfrs (321)	154	75.0	72.0	76.8	81.3[c]
17	Feed industry (106)	493	25.7	29.4	28.8	—
22	Electrical industrial equipment mfrs (336)	186	46.8	55.6	64.3	—
24	Men's clothing factories (2431)	440	20.6	12.0	11.1	10.5
26	Fish products industry (102)	283	44.7	39.2	35.6	—
27	Agricultural implement industry (311)	198	61.9	70.6	71.6	83.2
30	Women's clothing factories (2441)	533	6.4	8.0	6.4	4.1
32	Fruit and vegetable canner & preservers (1031)	155	39.0	41.7	—	—
33	Breweries (1093)	8	99.0	94.0	94.5	81.9
36	Household furniture mfr (2619)	873	17.6	13.1	—	—
38	Mfr's of pharmaceutical and medicines (374)	120	27.1	29.6	26.1	—

[a]Among 40 leading industries   [b]Rank by shipments   [c]1958

Source: Statistics Canada, *Industrial Organization and Concentration in the Manufacturing, Mining and Logging Industries*, 1980, Cat. 31-402, Table 1. Reproduced by permission of the Minister of Supply and Services Canada.

using the inverse index was employed by Rosenbluth and later by the Department of Consumer and Corporate Affairs.[26]

Number of Enterprises Accounting for 80% of Factory Shipments (or Employment) by a Specified Industry	Description of Level of Concentration
4 or fewer	Very high
Over 4 to 8	High
Over 8 to 20	Fairly high
Over 20 to 50	Fairly low
Over 50	Low

Table 2-7 presents industry concentration ratios for 1965 and 1970 using the inverse index. By this classification the percentage of manufacturing industries with "very high" concentration dropped from 20 to 14 percent between 1965 and 1970 (how much of this is attributable to the 1970 reclassification is unknown) while the fraction classified as "high" remained more or less constant at just below a fifth. At the other extreme there was a rise in the number and percentage of manufacturing industries whose inverse index indicated "low" concentration ratios. On the whole, however, there was not enough change between 1965 and 1970 to suggest any major structural shift or to warrant hedging one's description of concentration in Canadian manufacturing as generally "high."

Another index of industry concentration is the Herfindahl Index.[27] The Herfindahl Index (HI), unlike the concentration ratio and the inverse index, takes into consideration the market shares of *all* the firms in a given industry. Specifically, the HI is defined as the sum of the squares of each firm's share of total industry output. Algebraically, the formula is expressed as: $HI = \sum_{i=1}^{n} S_i^2$, where n is the number of firms in the industry and S_i is the market share of the ith firm. By squaring each market share, the weights given to each firm rapidly decline the smaller the firm's market share. This means that the HI is particularly useful in capturing *assymetries* in the sizes of the leading firms. For example, compare two industries A and B, each with six firms. Suppose that in industry A the largest four firms have market shares of 20% apiece, with the remaining two firms each having 10 percent shares. In contrast, suppose industry B is dominated by a single firm with a market share of 50 percent, the

26. Department of Consumer and Corporate Affairs, op. cit, p. 17. Statistics Canada, which has taken on the task of regularly publishing concentration statistics, no longer appears to make use of the inverse index.
27. It is sometimes, and more accurately, called the Herfindahl-Hirschman Index (or HHI for short).

Table 2-7

Industry Concentration Ratios Using Inverse Index, Canada 1965, 1970

	1965			1970	
Inverse Index[a]	No. of Industries	% of All Industries	% of Total Value Added in Mfg	No. of Industries	% of all Industries
1-4	31	20.1	22.8	24	14.4
5-8	29	18.8	10.9	33	19.8
9-12	13	8.4	8.1	16	9.6
13-16	16	10.4	10.5	18	10.8
17-20	8	5.2	6.8	14	8.4
21-50	31	20.1	17.3	29	17.4
51+	26	16.9	23.6	33	19.8
Total	154	100.0	100.0	167[b]	100.0

[a]Number of largest enterprises accounting for 80 percent of factory shipments in each industry.
[b]Out of a total 172 manufacturing industries, 5 could not be assigned due to data limitations.
Sources: Department of Consumer and Corporate Affairs, *op. cit.*, p. 17; Statistics Canada, "Industrial Organization" *op. cit.*, Table 1, pp. 29-53.

remaining five firms each having 10 percent shares. Both industries, A and B, have four-firm concentration ratios of 80 percent. However, their HI's are very different. For industry A, the HI is .18; for industry B it is .30. (Note that in a single-firm industry (pure monopoly) the HI is 1.0 while in perfect competition, with hundreds or thousands of firms none of which accounts for more than a negligible amount of industry output, the HI is approximately zero.[28]) The higher the HI, the more likely is it that one firm dominates the industry. The more dominant a single firm is in an industry, the greater the likelihood that it will behave as does a monopolist in standard theory, assuming there are at least some barriers to entry into the industry (see chapter 3). Although there is a high correlation between industries with high CR_4 and high HI, the HI is increasingly used alongside the standard concentration ratio because it helps throw additional light on the internal structure of oligopolies.[29]

28. Note, as well, that the HI declines rapidly as an industry's market structure moves away from single firm monopoly to oligopoly. An industry of three equal-sized firms would have an HI = .33. In fact if an industry is perfectly symmetrical, that is all firms have the same market shares, $HI = \frac{1}{n}$.
29. Another useful property of the HI is that it nicely captures the change in the size distribution of firms due to a horizontal merger. If two firms in the same industry, call them x and y, were to merge the change in the HI is equal to $\Delta H = (S_x + S_y)^2 - S_x{}^2 - S_y{}^2 = 2S_xS_y$.

Table 2-8

Concentration Levels for 116 Comparable Canadian and U.S. Manufacturing Industries

Number of Enterprises Required to Account for 80% of Shipments	Canada (1965) Industries No.	Canada (1965) Industries %	Canada (1965) Shipments %	U.S. (1963) Industries No.	U.S. (1963) Industries %	U.S. (1963) Shipments %
Up to 4	24	21	32.5	3	3	13.6
5-8	22	19	8.2	7	6	4.2
9-20	23	20	16.5	16	14	18.5
21-50	20	17	15.5	31	27	15.8
Over 50	27	23	27.3	59	51	47.9
Total	116	100	100.0	116	100	100.0

Source: Department of Consumer and Corporate Affairs, op. cit., p. 51.

How do Canadian concentration ratios compare with those of our chief trading partner, the United States? In 1977, 28.5 percent of the 445 U.S. manufacturing industries had four-firm concentration ratios in excess of 50 percent, compared to about one-half of all Canadian manufacturing industries. What about comparable U.S. and Canadian industries? The methods of measuring concentration in manufacturing in the two countries are similar, although the greater detail in defining manufacturing industries in the U.S. reduces the number of strictly comparable industries. The Department of Consumer and Corporate Affairs found in its concentration study that there were 116 Canadian industries (in a few cases these involved combining two 4-digit industries) which were sufficiently similar to a U.S. manufacturing industry (or combination thereof),[30] to afford useful comparisons. Of the 116 industries, 98 had four-firm concentration ratios that were significantly higher for the Canadian industry than for its U.S. counterpart. Some of the remaining 18 were also higher. The evidence overwhelmingly indicates that Canadian manufacturing industries are markedly more highly concentrated than those of the United States. (See Table 2-8). Similar conclusions were reached by Rosenbluth on the basis of statistics for 1948 and by Marfels for 1972.[31]

The Canadian-U.S. comparison of industry concentration ratios overlooks the fact that the Canadian economy is relatively more "open" than the U.S. economy. That is, while the ratio of exports or imports to GNP is approximately 30 percent in Canada, the comparable ratios for the U.S. are about 10 percent. Recently an attempt has been made, using newly available data for 140 Canadian manufacturing industries, to make consistent adjustments of concentration ratios to take account of imports—whose exclusion we have already noted tends to overstate concentration.[32] (See Table 2-9.) Once import competition is taken into account, average concentration in Canadian manufacturing industries is reduced by 10 percentage points—from 54 to 44 percent. In addition the *differential* in average concentration between Canadian and U.S. manufacturing industries declines by approximately 7 percentage points—from 20 to approximately 13 percent—after adjustments in each country for import competition.

Are manufacturing industries typically becoming more or less concentrated

30. Consumer and Corporate Affairs, op. cit, p. 48-49. The 116 U.S. industries or groups consisted of 231 four-digit industries. Where industries had to be grouped, maximum concentration ratios were estimated. The U.S. data are for 1963, Canada 1965.
31. Rosenbluth, op. cit, pp. 75-93. Marfels, op. cit., pp. 166-67.
32. J.R. Baldwin, P.K. Gorecki, and J.S. McVey, "Imports, Secondary Output, Price-Cost Margins and Measures of Concentration: Evidence for Canada, 1979," Economic Council of Canada, Discussion Paper No. 263, May 1984.

Table 2-9

Concentration Ratios Adjusted for Imports

CR$_4$ Group	Number of Manufacturing Industries, 1979	
	No adjustment for imports	Adjustment for imports
75-100	28	10
50-74	45	36
25-49	50	69
<25	17	25
Total	140	140

---

with the passage of time? Here we are faced with a lack of data for the pre-World War II period. A recent study provides evidence for the postwar period. Using a weighted (by industry employment) average of four-firm concentration ratios for 57 comparable (over time) Canadian manufacturing industries, Khemani found a 10 percentage point rise in weighted average concentration between 1948 and 1965 and a 3 point decline between 1965 and 1972, and almost no difference between the averages for 1958 and 1972 (see Table 2-10). When unweighted four-firm concentration ratios are used the overall rise in average concentration is more than halved. To what extent the exclusion of more than 100 industries is influential is not certain, but the distributions by concentration class of the 57 industries and all manufacturing industries are not dissimilar. Since 1970 the average level of concentration for all manufacturing industries has declined slightly or remained constant depending on which concentration index is used.[33]

The apparent rise in manufacturing industry concentration ratios in Canada in the first two decades following the end of World War II contrasts with the absence of any such general tendency among U.S. manufacturing industries. The remarkable facet of concentration in U.S. manufacturing industries is the rise in aggregate concentration (e.g. the share of all manufacturing assets accounted for by the 50, 100, and 200 largest manufacturing firms has increased markedly) while at the industry level no clear trend has been indicated. However, if one breaks U.S. manufacturing industries into producer goods and consumer goods industries there has been an apparent tendency for the concentration ratios of industries in the former group to fall and of those in

---

33. R.S. Khemani, op. cit.

Table 2-10

Average Levels of Concentration in Canadian Manufacturing Industries, 1948-1980

	1948	1954	1958	1965	1970	1972	1976	1978	1980
Average four-firm concentration ratio									
Simple average (1)[a]:					50.6	50.7	50.7	50.1	49.8
(2)[b]:	(44.4)	(47.6)	(47.5)	(47.3)	(47.6)	(48.3)			
Weighted average (1)[a]:					48.8	48.3	47.6	47.2	46.0
(2)[b]:	(44.3)	(48.7)	(50.2)	(53.9)	(52.9)	(51.1)			
Average Herfindahl Index									
Simple average (1)[a]:					0.114	0.115	0.115	0.115	0.116
Weighted average[c](1)[a]:					0.108	0.107	0.103	0.106	0.105

[a]Average concentration, based on shipments, of 167 manufacturing industries.
[b]Average concentration ratios, based on employment, of 57 comparable manufacturing industries studied by Khemani.
[c]Weighted by an industry's value added in manufacture.
Sources: Statistics Canada, *Industrial Organization and Concentration in the Manufacturing, Mining, and Logging Industries, 1980* Cat. 31-402, October 1983, Table I, p. 6; R.S. Khemani, *Concentration in the Manufacturing Industries of Canada: Analysis of Post War Changes*, Research Monograph No. 8, Consumer and Corporate Affairs Canada (Ottawa: 1980), Table 4-2, p. 54.

the latter group to rise since 1947.[34] There is also evidence of a tendency, in both Canada and the U.S., for industries with very high (low) concentration levels to experience a decline (rise) in concentration—a reflection of centripetal forces at work in the organization of industry.

Over a much longer period one interesting fact stands out. The meagre data suggests that the value of shipments accounted for by U.S. manufacturing industries with CR_4 greater than 50 percent has fluctuated in a relatively minor band between a quarter and a third in the period since 1900. The higher figure occurs around the turn of the century as a result of the great merger wave of 1898-1904 which produced a good deal of monopoly power in the U.S. economy. A similar, though relatively smaller, merger wave was experienced in Canada around 1911. One can only conjecture, however, whether Canadian industry concentration has experienced similar historical tendencies. Rosenbluth thought that industry concentration in 1948 was typically somewhat lower than it was in the 1920s. He also cites evidence that *plant* concentration had "increased substantially" between 1890 and 1922.[35]

Foreign Control and Concentration

Concentration is high in Canadian industry. So is the incidence of foreign ownership and control. Are these two phenomena related? Do foreign firms intentionally acquire firms in concentrated Canadian industries? Using CALURA (Corporations and Labour Unions Returns Act) data, Rosenbluth confirmed that firms subject to foreign control tend to be substantially larger than domestically controlled firms. This could be due to a tendency for foreign firms to seek out industries in which firms are typically large or because within any given industry foreign-controlled firms are typically larger than domestic firms. Rosenbluth found that both tendencies occur, but that the latter effect was much the more important of the two.[36] Further, using statistical techniques, Rosenbluth reached the conclusion on the basis of a sample of manufacturing

34. Willard F. Mueller and Larry G. Hamm, "Trends in Industrial Market Concentration, 1947 to 1970," *Review of Economics and Statistics* (November 1974), pp. 511-519. In contrast, Khemani, op. cit., found that CR4 for his sample of producer goods industries rose, on the average, more than that of consumer goods industries. However, Khemani, like Mueller and Hamm, found a centripetal force at work. Industries which initially had high concentration levels tended to experience a decline in concentration, while those with initially low levels of concentration tended to experience a rise.

35. Rosenbluth, op. cit., pp. 94 ff.

36. G. Rosenbluth, "The Relation Between Foreign Control and Concentration in Canadian Industry," *Canadian Journal of Economics* (Feb. 1970), pp. 16-17.

Table 2-11

Concentration in Canadian Industry and the Incidence of Foreign Control, 1964

8-Firm Concentration Class	Number of Industries	Average No. of Firms Among Leading 8 Which Are:		
		Foreign Controlled	U.S. Controlled	Overseas Controlled
90+	15	4.1	2.1	2.0
70-89	16	5.0	3.9	1.1
40-69	21	4.0	3.1	.9
Under 40	17	3.9	3.2	.7
Total	69			
Average		4.3	3.2	.9

Source: G. Rosenbluth, "The Relation Between Foreign Control and Concentration in Canadian Industry," *CJE* (Jan.1970), Table 2, p. 22.

industries in 1963-64 that "there is no evidence of a tendency to seek out the more concentrated industries."[37]

Table 2-11 summarizes the basic findings. It suggests that if there is any tendency for foreigners to seek out "concentrated industries" it is on the part of "overseas" nationals—European and Japanese firms. A reverse tendency is indicated where the parent firm is U.S. based. Table 2-12 cross-classifies 24 broad industry groups in several sectors of the economy by level of concentration and foreign control of the leading firms in the industry group. Again there is no indication that concentration and foreign control go together. One possible reason for this is that in three of the industries with high concentration and low foreign control (transport, telephone, and banks) foreign control is restricted by law—these being so-called "key sectors" of the economy in which public policy has sharply limited foreign entry and control. Finally, Rosenbluth could not find a *trend* toward increasing foreign control of leading firms in industries in which concentration had increased between 1954 and 1964. In fact just the opposite appeared to be the case. Of eight broad industry groups in which overall concentration increased between 1954 and 1964, foreign control of leading firms decreased in four, remained the same in three and increased in only one.

---

37. Ibid, p. 19.

Table 2-12

Distribution of 24 Broad Industries by Concentration and Foreign Control Among Leading Firms, 1964

Concentration[a]	Foreign Control[b]			
	High	Medium	Low	Total
High	Tobacco Automobiles Aircraft		Beverages Cotton textiles Iron & steel Transport Telephones Banks	9
Medium	Oil Rubber	Pipelines Agricultural machinery Mining & smelting	Structural steel Cement products Utilities	8
Low		Electrical products Food industries Trade Insurance Chemicals	Trust companies Pulp and paper	7
Total	5	8	11	24

Source: G. Rosenbluth, "The Relation Between Foreign Control and Concentration," op. cit., p. 28.

[a]Since the industry groups are very broad, the concentration figures are not those suitable for the discussion of market control. "High" concentration means the leading four firms account for 80 percent or more of assets and "low" concentration represents an asset share of 45 percent or less.

[b]Foreign control is "high" when all the leading firms are foreign controlled and it is low when the foreign-controlled firms account for less than 15 percent of the assets of the leading four (or fewer) firms.

Foreign control also declined in five of the eight broad industry groups experiencing a decrease in concentration during the same period.[38]

A little thought may suggest why there is little evidence of correlation, and less of causation, between foreign ownership and control and industry concentration. First, concentration ratios are high in many countries (e.g. England)

38. Ibid, p. 32.

where foreign control is quite limited. More important foreign firms usually invest in another country to (a) acquire direct access to needed raw materials or (b) to produce and market products more cheaply than tariff barriers allow. Since a foreigner usually incurs certain costs when directly investing in a foreign country (different language, laws, customs, etc.), he will usually only do so when he has something "distinctive" to sell.[39] In the case of many American firms selling consumer goods it is the name (or brand) which Canadians are usually familiar with since advertising over the airwaves knows few borders. In other industries what is distinctive may be "technological" in character. Thus we find many of the most foreign-controlled manufacturing industries in the consumer durables area (cars, tires, refrigerators and other electrical appliances). Some of these industries are highly concentrated on either side of the border (autos, tires) but others are not (electrical appliances). There are also numerous producer goods industries in which product homogeneity and relatively low tariff barriers have inhibited foreign control (iron and steel, cement, pulp and paper) where industry concentration ranges from very high to low. Interestingly, a number of these industries are, or are becoming, export oriented (pulp and paper, steel).

In short, the decision of foreign firms to invest in Canada is not primarily a function of the market power *per se* that leading firms in concentrated Canadian industries presumptively exercise. Rather foreign firms usually are seeking access to product markets or to raw material inputs. These markets may or may not have high levels of concentration, although most are concentrated by U.S. standards, as noted above. Foreign direct investment in Canada, leading to foreign control of substantial parts of our industrial sector, is too complex a phenomenon to be explained simply in terms of concentration ratios. Interestingly, as we shall see in chapter 4, one spur to foreign direct investment in Canada's manufacturing sector is Canada's high tariff walls. In turn, the tariff has protected many an inefficiently small producer, and may thereby have contributed to limiting rather than increasing concentration (measured on a domestic basis) in many Canadian manufacturing industries.

Aggregate Concentration

To this point we have focused on industry or market concentration. However, a concentration ratio can be applied to the economy as a whole, or to a major sector such as manufacturing. These "aggregate concentration" ratios do not tell us much about competition: however, they are one way of indicating the

39. The "distinctiveness" concept is discussed at length in Government of Canada, *Foreign Direct Investment in Canada* (Information Canada, 1972).

relative size of the largest firms in the economy. Some social scientists, a few economists among them, believe high aggregate concentration is a sign of the extent to which "power" (political as well as economic) is concentrated in a few hands. In chapter 1, we saw that a relatively few (100) giant corporations including a few very large government-owned enterprises account for about 49 percent of corporate assets and 28 percent of corporate sales.[40] In 1980, the 100 largest manufacturing and mining firms accounted for 49 percent of manufacturing value added and 51 percent of manufacturing shipments.[41]The Royal Commission on Corporate Concentration was primarily concerned with issues raised by corporate giantism and its causes, particularly mergers among and acquisitions by large firms.

As high as the share of assets and sales of the largest Canadian corporations is, that share was even higher in the first part of this century. The asset share of the 100 largest non-financial corporations was 48 percent in 1923 and rose to over 75 percent in 1933, before rapidly declining to just under 40 percent in the mid-1960s.[42] Since 1968 the asset share of the largest 25, 50, and 100 enterprises (including a few government-owned corporations) has risen a few percentage points. In the manufacturing sector the share of the top 100 firms rose slightly between 1970 and 1980.

In the United States the rise in aggregate concentration within the manufacturing sector is much more marked. The share of total value added in U.S. manufacturing accounted for by the largest 50 manufacturing firms rose from 17 percent to 25 percent between 1947 and 1966. The share of the largest 200 U.S. manufacturing firms rose from 30 to 42 percent over the same period, although market concentration in U.S. manufacturing has not trended upward.

The divergent trends between aggregate and market concentration, exhibited particularly in the United States, are explicable by reference to the increasing diversification of large firms. As the leading firms grow through diversification their size increases; however, since new fields are entered no inference may be drawn about the impact on market concentration. It is this sort of reasoning, incidentally, which has led some observers to argue that conglomerate mergers are not anti-competitive, and if anything tend to stimulate competition in the industry of the acquired firm by adding another "giant" to the list of firms active in that particular industry.

40. The largest corporations are relatively more capital intensive (have higher capital-labour ratios) than smaller ones. This is particularly true of the government-owned hydro corporations. If government-owned firms are excluded, the share of the largest 100 privately owned nonfinancial corporations is closer to 40 percent.
41. Statistics Canada, Cat. 31-402, 1980, op. cit., Table XI, p. 19.
42. Report of Royal Commission on Corporate Concentration, op. cit., p. 20. The decline is much less marked if transportation corporations are excluded, a fact which reflects how dominant were the railroads in the corporate structure of the Canadian economy earlier in this century.

Diversification

The growing diversification of large industrial firms is a fact of modern industrial life.[43] Work by Charles Berry for the United States shows that seventy percent of the 460 largest industrial firms in 1965 were engaged in producing activities across six or more 4-digit industries, and about half were active in ten or more 4-digit industries.[44] In most cases diversification appears to involve entry into the production of goods which are either horizontally or "vertically" related to one another—i.e. they are products that tend to complement one another in consumption (food-beverages-tobacco) or in production (petroleum-chemicals, chemicals-textiles). In most cases diversification occurs within a given 2-digit industry.

Until recently, the statistical evidence on diversification of Canadian firms was scanty. However, Statistics Canada has recently reported data indicating the degree of industrial homogeneity of enterprises classified to a given manufacturing industry, and studies for the Royal Commission on Corporate Concentration have provided some additional evidence. The picture that emerges in Canada is one in which most manufacturing firms are single-plant (95 percent) and single-industry (97 percent) firms. However, the 1430 multiplant and 849 multi-industry firms accounted for disproportionate shares (74 and 67 percent respectively) of manufacturing value added. The 849 multi-industry firms produced output assigned to an average of 3.2 different industries.[45] About 10 percent of multi-industry firms produced output assigned to six or more different industries, and these accounted for 30 percent of manufacturing value added. Clearly, then, it is a few relatively large firms which account for most diversification, but the trend toward diversification is continuing. (In 1965 only 31 manufacturing firms produced outputs assigned to six or more industries.)[46] Nevertheless, most (over 60 percent on average) of

43. Diversification is only one aspect of the economics of large firm size (vertical integration is another.) The modern approach to explaining the size and growth of large firms emphasizes the role of transaction costs: the costs associated with "internal" or intrafirm decision-making relative to the costs associated with market exchange. The leading advocate of the transactions cost approach is O.E. Williamson, *Markets and Hierarchies* (1975) and "The Modern Corporation: Origins, Evolution, Attributes," *Journal of Economic Literature*, 19 (December, 1981), pp. 1537-68.
44. Charles Berry, "Corporate Growth and Diversification," *The Journal of Law and Economics*, 14 (Oct. 1971), p. 372. K.D. George reports that the average number of 4-digit (2-digit) industries in which the 200 largest U.S. manufacturing corporations were active in 1968 was 20 (6). "The Changing Structure of Competitive Industry," *Economic Journal* (March 1972), Table II, p. 356.
45. The figures are for 1980 and found in Statistics Canada, cat. 31-402, pp. 12-15. The official statistics refer to plants as "establishments" and firms as "enterprises."
46. See C. Marfels, op. cit. Royal Commission on Corporate Concentration, p. 99. Various

the output of multi-industry firms is concentrated in the (primary) industry to which each firm is assigned. Thus, most diversified firms are *not* true conglomerates. Moreover, the trend toward diversification may have slowed in the 1970s. Between 1970 and 1980 the total number of multi-industry firms in the manufacturing, mining and logging industries of Canada actually declined, and evidence presented in chapter 4 suggests that in some industries, firms are moving toward greater specialization in production rather than the reverse.

Why the trend toward diversification by large firms? One view is that firms, like individual investors, will, if they are able, attempt to reduce risk by diversifying their portfolios—or, more prosaically, avoid putting all their chickens in one basket. There are good reasons for this. In an uncertain world with new products continually appearing to challenge the "old," a firm can never be sure when it will suddenly, and unexpectedly, lose its market for a given product. If it produces several products it is unlikely to suffer important losses in each at the same time. Even during business-cycle recessions there is likely to be some insurance in numbers. Reductions in consumer and business spending are usually not proportional across products and industries, so that diversified production provides something of a buffer against the full impact of sluggish or declining *aggregate* demand. Growth is another factor. The evidence indicates that diversification is usually out of slow growth into rapid growth industries.[47] Still another factor, of more importance in the United States than in Canada, are the anti-trust laws, especially where growth is by merger. For leading firms in the United States, the horizontal merger route to growth is now effectively blocked but conglomerate and product extension mergers have a much greater chance of passing judicial muster.

Of course, there are costs to diversification chiefly in the form of coordinating and controlling large diversified enterprises and in running the risk of spreading know-how too thin. However, modern communication has greatly increased the possibility of coordination and control of numerous, geographically differenti-

measures of diversification are discussed by Richard Caves, et al., *Studies in Canadian Industrial Organization*, Study No. 26, Royal Commission on Corporate Concentration (Ottawa, 1977), Ch. 4. Caves found a tendency for firms to diversify into industries with smaller establishments and lower seller concentration (p. 8). Another study for the RCCC indicated that of 312 large companies in Canada, in 1975, one third were not diversified, one third revealed at least some degree of conglomerate diversification, and one third were diversified, but only to the extent of producing goods which were horizontally or vertically related to their primary production. D.G. McFetridge and L.J. Weatherley, *Notes on the Economies of Large Firm Size*, Study No. 20, Royal Commission on Corporate Concentration (Ottawa, 1977), pp. 33-39. In still another study Caves found that the tobacco and pulp and paper industries are among the most diversified Canadian industries according to several measures of diversification. However, Caves was unable to determine empirically the causes of a particular industry's level of diversification. Caves et al., op. cit., Chapter 5.

47. Caves, et al, op. cit., Chapter 5, p. 113.

ated plants. Know-how is preserved by decentralizing decision making to the plant level. In addition, modern management training and the development of management teams has increased the likelihood that at any particular time a firm's senior management will have some "unused capacity"—both the time and initiative to spread its wings into some new field.

Determinants of Market Concentration

What are the causes of high market concentration in Canadian manufacturing? Leading potential candidates are (a) economies of scale; (b) market size; (c) mergers. We shall leave our discussion of economies of scale until chapter 3. [48] Suffice it to say here that the high proportion of manufacturing industry capacity which is either suboptimal or cannot be used to greatest efficiency raises important questions of the determinants of plant size and the length of production runs. Both high concentration and the failure to achieve scale efficiencies in production would appear to have an important common denominator: a small (population 25 million) domestic market. But is market size the only factor? What about mergers? Might not "horizontal" mergers (between firms engaged in similar production activities) obviate the constraints on efficient plant and firm size while having a tendency to increase concentration? While mergers have been numerous in Canada, and "merger waves" have been of some historical importance, it is not easy to credit mergers as the chief cause of high concentration in Canadian manufacturing. Nevertheless, mergers undoubtedly accounted for the formation of many leading firms earlier in this century and subsequently may have inhibited certain tendencies toward reduction in concentration. [49]

The great economist, Alfred Marshall, likened the life history of a firm to that of organic beings. [50] The firm has a birth, growth to maturity, old age, and death. Birth and death play the important roles of entry and exit in the neoclassical equilibrating process. The growth to maturity and old age stages reflect relative degrees of managerial dynamism and efficiency. Marshall's characterization pertained chiefly to unincorporated enterprises which tend to die with their owners (or the heirs). But Marshall did not fail to see that even for these types of

---

48. Scale economies are nonetheless important. Caves found that concentration levels in Canada were positively related to the size of the minimum efficient scale plants relative to market size. See Caves, et al., op. cit., p. 7.

49. Khemani's study of the determinants of the rise in average concentration of 57 comparable industries between 1948 and 1972 suggests horizontal mergers were one among a number of concentration-increasing factors. Khemani, op. cit., pp. 99-100.

50. Alfred Marshall, *Principles of Economics*, 8th ed. (New York: Macmillan, 1948), Book IV, Chap. 12.

firms death (or exit) is often via sale of the assets to other, typically larger, firms, usually organized along corporate lines. Corporations, because they are legal beings, have a life of their own, and short of bankruptcy almost always vanish through acquisition by other corporations. Thus mergers play a vital role in the life history of corporate enterprise, which is the most important form of industrial ownership. It is important, therefore, not to treat mergers as synonymous with anti-competitive, industrially concentrating processes. Mergers are just as likely to be the means whereby inefficient capacity and ineffective management are eliminated or replaced with little disturbance to effective competition. Moreover, the prospect of being able to "sell out" (merge) in the future is undoubtedly a crucial factor in many an entrepreneur's decision to start up a business in the first place. This view of mergers does not mean that all mergers are benign so far as market structure, behaviour, and performance are concerned. Some obviously are not, tending to substantially increase the market power of the acquiring firm without any offsetting cost advantages. However, even the hardest-nosed "trust buster" would surely exclude the majority of acquisitions from legal prohibitions or review.

As the economy has expanded and the number of industrial firms has grown so has the number of mergers. Table 2-13 indicates the number of Canadian firms acquired per decade since 1900.[51] The number of mergers has increased dramatically since the beginning of the century. The trend continued into the 1980s with almost 1500 mergers recorded in the three years 1980 through 1982.

Certain "merger waves" are discernible. These occurred between 1909-1912, again in the late 1920s with the peak in 1928-29, in the late 1960s with a peak in 1969, and in 1979-82, with a peak in 1982 before a severe recession struck the Canadian and world economies. All of the merger waves, except the last, are associated with stock market booms, presumably because conditions are then most favourable to the disposal of corporate shares. The tendency for mergers to be distributed unequally over time suggests that corporate death through merger is not always a "natural" phenomenon. For the acquired firm a merger *may* simply be a profitable means of capitalizing future earnings into present capital gains. For the acquiring firm a merger may increase overall profitability if monopoly or market power is thereby enhanced, or if the "new" management is more capable and efficient than the "old." Thus, especially during merger waves, one suspects that some mergers are little more than part

51. In a couple of instances the periods are not quite ten years in length due to the necessity of relying on several different sources of information. Since the definitions and coverage vary according to study, the figures for 1900-48, 1949-59 and 1960-75 are not strictly comparable. Especially in the early period, many mergers may not have been recorded.

Table 2-13

Number of Mergers 1900-79, by Decadal Periods

	1900-09	1910-19	1920-29	1930-39	1940-48	1949-59	1960-69	1970-79
Number of firms acquired	172	242	654	245	221	1135	2528	3824

Source: J.C. Weldon, "Consolidations in Canadian Industry, 1900-48," *Restrictive Trade Practices in Canada*, L.A. Skeoch, ed. (Toronto: McClelland and Stewart, 1966), p. 238; G. Rosenbluth, "The Relation Between Foreign Control and Concentration in Canadian Industry," *Canadian Journal of Economics* (Feb. 1970), p. 36, for 1949-59; *Consumer and Corporate Affairs, Annual Report*, Director of Investigation and Research, Combines Investigation Branch, 1983, p. 57 for 1960-79.

of a corporate "game" played with capitalized expected future earnings, sometimes producing negligible, or even negative, social benefits. To the extent that this is true, it is so, however, for only a small (although not inconsequential) proportion of all mergers that have actually taken place.

There are several different types of mergers, depending on the relationship between the acquired and acquiring firms. "Horizontal" mergers are those between competitors—between firms engaged in similar productive activities. Vertical mergers occur between purchasers and suppliers (vertical backward) and suppliers and distributors (vertical forward). Conglomerate mergers are those in which the acquiring and acquired firms are engaged in wholly unrelated activities. Product and geographic extension mergers are similar to horizontal mergers in that the acquired firm through its acquisition simply extends its territorial coverage or its product line. Table 2-14 shows how the composition of mergers has changed over time. In the early decades of the century mergers in Canada were overwhelmingly of a horizontal nature, a phenomenon similar to that experienced in the United States. The long-term trend, however, is a decline in the relative importance of horizontal mergers (also true of the United States). Until recently, vertical mergers increased as resource-oriented firms have brought together mining and processing activities under the same entrepreneurial umbrella and as large distributors have integrated backward into manufacturing and wholesaling.

More important has been the increasing diversification of industrial firms. Usually this takes the form of entry into a geographically distant market or into the production of products linked in some way to the firm's primary activity (e.g. detergents and bleach; petroleum and chemicals, electrical appliances of

Table 2-14

Percentage Distribution of Mergers by Type, 1900-1961, 1972-1977

	1900-09	1910-19	1920-29	1930-39	1940-48	1945-61	1972-74	1975-77
Horizontal	83	71	74	69	57	40	69[b]	59[b]
Vertical	4	9	12	6	18	23	11	11
Conglomerate	6	5	4	5	8	9	20	30
Other[a]	7	14	11	19	16	28	NA	NA
Total	100	100	100	100	100	100	100	100

[a]For 1900-48 includes Weldon's "complementary" (essentially product extension) category. For 1945-61 includes product and geographical extension mergers and "other horizontal."

[b]Horizontal includes geographic and product extension mergers and other mergers in the "other" category.

Source: J.C. Weldon, op. cit., p. 263; Economic Council of Canada, *Interim Report on Competition Policy*, (Ottawa, 1969), p. 212; Steven Globerman, *Mergers and Acquisitions in Canada*, Study No. 34, Royal Commission on Corporate Concentration, April 1977, Table 8, p. 62. D.N. Thompson, "Mergers, Effects, and Competition Policy: Some Empirical Evidence," in *Canadian Competition Policy: Essays in Law and Economics*, J.R.S. Prichard, W.T. Stanbury, and T.A Wilson, eds. (Toronto: Butterworth, 1979), p. 301.

various types). The result has been a rise in the number and importance of product and geographic extension mergers. Sometimes the diversification is "purely conglomerate" in character as, for example, Canadian Pacific Limited's acquisitions in the steel, paper, and mining industries, or the varied activities of firms owned by Power Corporation and Argus (see chapter 1). In the late 1960s, and again in the late 1970s, the United States experienced a wave of conglomerate mergers that for a short period of time created some popular concern that the American economy would be transformed into a few giant firms active across numerous industries. Each wave, and the concern they generated, largely subsided in the years that followed, although the phenomenon of enterprise diversification via merger remains important. Canada too experienced a rise in the relative importance of conglomerates in recent years (see Table 2-14 and by implication 2-16).[52]

Additional evidence on mergers in Canada is presented in Tables 2-15 and 2-16. The Department of Consumer and Corporate Affairs has compiled unpublished data on the sector or industry of the acquiring and acquired firms for almost all mergers of consequence. The data in the two tables cover the period 1980-1982, when there were not only numerous mergers, but also particularly close surveillance of foreign acquisitions by the Foreign Investment Review Agency (see chapter 12).[53] Table 2-15 indicates that during 1980-82, firms in the financial sector (including insurance and real estate firms) were particularly active in acquiring firms in other sectors. (The number of acquiring firms exceeds the number of acquired firms in the financial sector by a very wide margin in each year.) The table also indicates that firms in wholesale and retail trade were disproportionately targets for acquisitions in other sectors. (The number of acquired firms in the trade sector exceeds by a wide margin the number of acquiring firms.) Thus mergers of a conglomerate nature, reflecting the urge to diversify, were numerous in the early years of the present decade.

Table 2-15 also provides evidence on the importance of mergers in which the acquiring firm was foreign owned. Only in 1981, when the vigilance of the Foreign Investment Review Agency was at its height, were domestic acquisitions more numerous than ones which involved a foreign-owned firm. However,

52. In 1978-79, takeover bids, some successful, some not, included those by Domtar and Canadian Pacific Ltd. to take over MacMillan Bloedel; Hudson's Bay's successful takeover of Simpson's; Thomson's (successful) and George Weston's (unsuccessful) takeover of Hudson's Bay; and Brascan's abortive attempt to takeover Woolco followed by Edper Investment's (Bronfman family) successful takeover of Brascan. In the U.S. a spate of major conglomerate mergers led to pending legislation to limit mergers among the top 500 industrials. See *New York Times*, April 2, 1979, D4 and April 16, 1979, D1.

53. Surveillance was relaxed in 1982, with the result that the number of foreign acquisitions rose from 200 in 1981 to 371 in 1982, while domestic acquisitions declined from 291 in 1981 to 205 in 1982.

Table 2-15

Mergers in Canada: Acquiring and Acquired Firms by Sector and Ownership (1980-1982)

Sector	1980 Acquiring Firms	1980 Acquired Firms	1981 Acquiring Firms	1981 Acquired Firms	1982 Acquiring Firms	1982 Acquired Firms
Agriculture, forestry, fishing	2 (0)	4 (2)	1 (0)	2 (1)	4 (3)	4 (2)
Mining, quarrying and oil wells	27 (1)	26 (1)	54 (3)	52 (5)	40 (11)	40 (11)
Manufacturing	167 (117)	185 (121)	159 (74)	178 (72)	164 (118)	178 (116)
Construction	3 (2)	6 (3)	7 (5)	7 (5)	6 (1)	12 (7)
Transportation, communication & other utilities	25 (6)	24 (7)	18 (2)	12 (1)	25 (11)	27 (11)
Wholesale & retail trade	36 (17)	85 (62)	21 (12)	54 (35)	33 (20)	78 (63)
Finance, insurance and real estate	124 (74)	40 (14)	98 (51)	25 (8)	124 (74)	33 (17)
Community, business and personal services	20 (11)	48 (31)	31 (10)	62 (32)	49 (23)	91 (51)
TOTAL	404 (228)	418 (241)	389 (158)	392 (159)	445 (261)	463 (278)

Numbers in parentheses indicate foreign ownership.

Source: Figures taken from unpublished data from the Merger Register, Bureau of Competition Policy, Department of Consumer and Corporate Affairs, Ottawa. The Merger Register is compiled from published information but cannot be guaranteed as an authoritative listing.

it is significant that in the mining and petroleum sector there were almost no acquisitions by foreign-owned firms in 1980 and 1981 and relatively few in 1982. For a sector that has traditionally been dominated by foreign firms, the dearth of mergers involving foreign-owned firms undoubtedly is a reflection of the "Canadianization" program which comprised one component of the federal government's controversial energy policy, promulgated in 1980 (see chapter 10). One outcome is a decline in the incidence of foreign ownership in Canada's natural resource sector (see chapter 1).

The same body of data can be used to assess the degrees to which recent mergers are "horizontal" in nature. The term "horizontal" as it is used in Table

Table 2-16

All Mergers and Mergers Where Acquiring and Acquired Firms Are in Same Sector or Industry: 1980-82

	Total (1980-82)ᵃ		"Horizontal" (1980-82)ᵇ	
	(1)	(2)	(3)	(4)
	Acquiring Firms	Acquired Firms	Number	% of Total (3)/(1)
Agriculture, forestry, fishing	7	10	5	71.4
Mining, quarrying and oil wells	121	118	98	81.0
Manufacturing	490	541	311	63.5
Construction	16	25	11	68.7
Transportation, communications and other utilities	68	63	48	70.6
Wholesale & retail trade	90	217	67	74.4
Finance, insurance and real estate	346	98	88	25.4
Community, business and personal services	100	201	92	92.0
TOTAL	1238	1273	720	58.2

ᵃFrom Table 2-15.
ᵇIn the case of the manufacturing sector, these are mergers where the acquiring and acquired firm are in the *same* two-digit industry; for all other sectors, these are mergers where the acquiring and acquired firms are in the same sector.
Source: Same as Table 2-15.

2-16 must be interpreted carefully. Intrasector or intra-two-digit industry mergers (the bases for determining whether the merger was "horizontal") are not necessarily between competitors, since industrial sectors and two-digit industries are broadly defined.[54] Nevertheless, intrasector or intra-industry ("horizontal") mergers are not conglomerate—and involve limited, if any, diversification. Table 2-16 indicates that almost 60 percent of the mergers during 1980-82 were broadly "horizontal" in nature. The percentage of intrasector or intra-industry mergers ranged from 92 percent in non-financial services to 25 percent in the financial sector. More than a third of all acquisitions by manufacturing firms were outside the acquiring firm's own two-digit industry. A much smaller share were outside of the manufacturing sector altogether.

Mergers and Concentration

How have mergers affected industry concentration in Canada—particularly in the manufacturing sector? An answer to this question virtually requires a case-by-case study. Case studies of Canadian industries are few and far between. There are a few leading court cases (all lost by the Crown) indicating that in at least some instances mergers significantly increased the market share of the leading firms, and in two cases resulted in monopoly. Canadian Breweries acquired 37 firms in a three-decade period extending from 1930 and raised its share of the beer market from 11 percent to nearly 60 percent in Ontario and Quebec. Subsequently, Canadian Breweries' market share declined in the face of vigorous competition from its chief competitors, Molson's and Labatt's. The acquisition of Manitoba Sugar Refining Company by B.C. Sugar Refinery in the 1950s gave the latter virtually 100 percent of the refined sugar market west of Winnipeg. K.C. Irving's newspaper acquisitions between 1948 and 1970 gave him control of all English language dailies in New Brunswick. These, of course, are spectacular examples of monopoly gained via merger and are not at all representative of the typical outcome of mergers. In chapter 9, we will look at these three cases in greater depth since they represent the most obvious failings of Canadian anti-combines policy.

The evidence on the relation between mergers and concentration is weak. Some clues, however, are found in Table 2-17, where mergers between manufacturing firms are cross-classified by type and level of industry concentration. As Table 2-17 indicates, in the period 1945-61 most mergers occurred in the relatively less concentrated industries. However, it is also clear that in the

---

54. Mergers within the manufacturing sector were categorized within 20 two-digit industries.

Table 2-17

Types of Mergers and 1964 Concentration Levels of Manufacturing Industries Within Which Acquired Firms Were Operating, 1945-61

Level of Concentration[a]	Type of Merger				
	Horizontal	Vertical	Conglomerate	Other[b]	Total
1-4	28	2	7	16	53
	(4.3)[c]	(5.6)	(1.0)	(12.6)	(6.6)
4.1-8	36	18	11	12	83
	(3.5)	(26.4)	(2.0)	(2.1)	(8.1)
8.1-20	54	22	27	53	156
	(1.8)	(1.1)	(1.7)	(2.2)	(1.8)
20.1-60	73	16	23	39	151
	(3.1)	(1.3)	(7.2)	(1.0)	(3.0)
60.1 & more	101	22	27	84	234
	(.5)	(2.7)	(.7)	(1.4)	(1.1)
Total mergers	292	80	95	210	677
	(2.1)	(7.4)	(2.7)	(2.0)	(2.9)
Total assets acquired in millions of dollars	622.3	589.7	258.9	423.9	1993.1

[a]Inverse index; number of firms required to account for 80% of industry shipments.
[b]Product and geographical market extension mergers.
[c]Average asset size of acquired firm in millions of dollars.
Source: Economic Council of Canada, *Interim Report on Competition Policy* (Ottawa, 1969), Table A-4, pp. 214-15. Based on a questionnaire survey carried out by the Director of Investigation and Research, Combines Investigation Act.

case of "horizontal" and the quasi-horizontal "other" category the acquired firms were on the average much larger in the concentrated than in the unconcentrated industries. (Compare the number of mergers to the asset figures in parentheses.) It is among these cases that one is likely to find mergers which had a non-negligible impact on industry concentration as well as on the market power of the acquiring firm. In its *Interim Report on Competition Policy*, the Economic Council of Canada reported that after a case-by-case appraisal of 997 acquisitions by manufacturing firms (including some outside manufacturing) made between 1945 and 1961, it found that about 8 percent, accounting for 34 percent of total acquired assets, "might have qualified for a public interest examination" on the basis of their concentration and market power effects.[55]

If any conclusion can be safely reached it is that many leading firms got their start through a series of mergers in the early years of the twentieth century (e.g. Imperial Tobacco, Dominion Textiles, Seagrams, Eddy Match, Canada Cement). As had happened in the United States these multi-firm mergers sharply increased the market shares of the leading firm and consequently increased industry concentration to levels from which regression has been in some cases negligible. To this extent mergers can be said to have contributed to high concentration at the time in which national industries were formed out of the combination of numerous local, single-plant firms. What is much more difficult to discern is whether the subsequent history of mergers has materially influenced concentration in the manufacturing sector of the economy. Presumably, the merger wave of 1925-29 raised the level of concentration markedly in the textile, chemicals, and wood and paper products industries where so many of the mergers at the time were concentrated. However, the more likely impact of mergers on manufacturing industry concentration has been to inhibit concentration-reducing tendencies associated with market growth.

There is considerable evidence that the typical acquired firm is small, both absolutely and relative to the acquiring firm. Of 1534 consolidations between 1900 and 1948 studied by Weldon, half involved an acquiring firm at least seven times as large as the firm absorbed and in three out of four cases the ratio was at least two to one. Moreover, over the period 1900-1948 there was a sharply increasing trend in the percentage of mergers in which the absorbing firm was many times larger than the one absorbed.[56] While the size of the acquiring firm is not indicated in Table 2-17, a few mental calculations suggest that the typical acquired firm in the period 1945-61 had rather limited assets. The small size of the typical acquired firm in Canada suggests that in many (perhaps most) cases mergers have been the means of eliminating the most suboptimal of industry capacity, even though evidence is lacking that mergers have typically done much for the scale efficiency of the acquiring firm.[57] In other words, even if mergers have had only a limited impact in reducing the percentage of industry capacity which is suboptimal (see chapter 3), they may nevertheless have contributed in an important way to the elimination of the most

55. Economic Council of Canada, op. cit., p. 86.
56. Weldon, op. cit., pp. 268-69.
57. A questionnaire survey of the acquiring firms in the 1945-61 period yielded a surprisingly large percentage of replies that the merger yielded negligible or no economies, and where there were economies they were considered chiefly to have their source in administration and management, indicating firm rather than plant economies. Economic Council of Canada, *Interim Report*, op. cit., pp. 88, 213, 216-217.

inefficient capacity in the industry. A further conclusion is that in recent decades, mergers, often with the objective of diversifying a firm's activities, appear to have done more to increase firm size than to raise the level of concentration.

Vertical Integration

One characteristic of many firms, particularly large industrial ones, is that they are engaged in more than one potentially separable stage of production: that is, they are vertically integrated. Unfortunately the notion of "potentially separable" stages of production is rather ambiguous, because the feasibility of separating different stages of production depends in part on the cost and returns of such separation. What is separable under one set of conditions may not be separable under another. Nevertheless, it is easy to illustrate by example what is meant by vertical integration. The leading petroleum firms are fully integrated from the production stage through the pipeline and refining stages to the distribution or marketing stage. The leading steel firms often own iron ore mines, transport some of the ore in their own ships, convert the ore into pig iron and from there into steel. Pulp and paper firms harvest much of the timber they use in making paper and paper products. Alcan, and other world-scale aluminum firms, own bauxite deposits, produce alumina and aluminum and engage in the extrusion or fabrication of basic aluminum into shapes such as frames for windows, doors, etc. Sometimes large grocery chains are integrated "backward" into canning, while automobile firms are integrated "forward" into dealership networks. The number of examples is countless.

While examples of vertical integration are easy to cite, statistics are not. There are no government statistics on vertical integration analogous to the concentration data describing the size distribution of firms engaged at a given stage of production. In fact, there is no adequate or generally accepted *measure* of vertical integration. A crude measure is the ratio of value added (VA) to sales (S), with the higher ratios of VA to S suggesting greater degrees of vertical integration. But this measure is only useful for comparing differences in vertical integration among firms *within* an industry, since the ratio of VA to S varies from industry to industry, depending on the stage of production, technology, and the nature of the product.

A crucial question is why firms vertically integrate. The reasons that have been given are many, but certainly the most important one must be that it is efficient to do so. Efficiency gains from vertical integration may arise for technological reasons, as for example the prevention of heat loss between the pig iron producing and steel making stages in a steel plant. There may also be efficiency gains from reduced search, negotiation, and other transaction costs when arms length market exchange is side-stepped in favor of internal (to the firm) decision-making. (See footnote 43 *supra*.) Finally, when fluctuating input demand creates a high degree of uncertainty for a firm producing an intermediate product, vertical integration may reduce uncertainty, and generate efficiency gains associated with a reduction in market risk.

There are other reasons advanced as to why firms may vertically integrate. Three of the more important, or oft-mentioned, are to gain security of supply or distribution channels, extend market power, and to avoid some of the restrictions of regulation. A firm which is heavily dependent on certain raw materials may integrate backward to assure itself of adequate supplies—or at least to avoid the possibility of others gaining a monopoly over the supply of the essential input. A variant of the security rationale is backward integration to gain control of the cheapest or best quality inputs—an excellent example being Alcan's early development and ownership of hydroelectric sites. Firms may integrate forward to assure themselves distributional channels, particularly if their rivals are engaged in a similar form of integration. The acquisition of ready-mixed concrete firms by U.S. cement producers in the late 1950s and early 1960s is a case in point.

But an integrating firm may want more than security. It is sometimes argued that a firm with monopoly power will integrate forward to extend its monopoly power, although it is not clear how it can gain any greater market power than it has at the upstream stage. One possibility is that integration can thwart downstream substitutions away from the monopolized input. However, there are real profit gains from vertical integration by an input monopolist if it eliminates successive monopoly by acquiring a downstream monopolist. Finally, a regulated (natural) monopolist such as a telephone company can escape some of the profit limitations imposed by regulation of its final output price if it integrates backward and produces its own inputs (telephone equipment), assuming the prices of these are unregulated.

The effects attributed to vertical integration are almost as various as the rationales for integration. Three stand out. Whenever vertical integration is an efficient method of producing and doing business, it reduces costs and is welfare enhancing. But if vertical integration is an advantage to a firm, it may also make entry into an industry more difficult, by increasing the amount of capital a firm must raise in order to enter an industry in an integrated form. The result may be to produce an absolute cost advantage to established vertically integrated firms (see chapter 3). Vertical integration may also increase firm profitability. However, even where vertical integration increases the profits of a monopolist, as for example in the case of successive monopoly, it does so by increasing the amount of input used and final output produced. The result is an

2: Market Structure in Canadian Industry **91**

improvement in allocative efficiency as output is pushed somewhat closer to competitive levels. Thus, even where monopoly power is involved the welfare implications of vertical integration are often ambiguous. Finally, vertical integration by controlling input price fluctuations may enhance coordination among oligopolists, as Adams and Dirlam argued was the case in the U.S. steel industry when it came under pressure from increased imports in the 1950s. The varieties of effects produced by vertical integration make it a complex and little understood subject indeed.[58]

Extent of Monopoly or Market Power

This chapter has focused on one aspect of industrial structure: the size distribution of firms as reflected in some measure of concentration. The prominent place given to measures of concentration in the field of industrial organization is due to more than a simple desire to find a summary means of describing the organization of industry. Concentration measures are also employed because, appropriately interpreted, they may have analytical content as indicators of the existence of monopoly or market power. To the extent that concentration measures indicate the relative importance of one or a few firms in a given industry they provide some guidance to the extent of *potential* exercise of monopoly power or effective collusion by industrial firms.

The existence and exercise of market power depends on more than fewness of firms. Unless there are some barriers to entry of new firms or goods produced by foreign firms, existing firms will find their ability to raise price above cost severely limited. We have already seen that concentration is overstated when the domestic market is served by imports as well as by domestic production. In the next chapter we examine the role and importance of barriers to entry. Suffice it to say that increasing international trade and the increasing tendency of large established firms to enter new product markets when it is profitable to do so, may make concentration ratios a less dependable indicator of the existence of market power.

---

58. The barebones discussion of the causes and effects of vertical integration contained in the preceding paragraphs cannot begin to do justice to this exceedingly complex and analytically intricate subject. The interested reader is directed to two sources. F.M. Scherer *Industrial Market Structure and Economic Performance*, 1980; pp. 299-306, provides a neat, if not always easy to follow, analytic framework for evaluating the various conditions under which vertical integration may take place. Various theories of vertical integration are described and evaluated, and a vast literature cited, by David Kaserman "Theories of Vertical Integration: Implications for Antitrust Policy" *Antitrust Bulletin*, Autumn 1978, pp. 483-510. The steel industry example is found in W. Adams and J.B. Dirlam "Steel Imports and Vertical Oligopoly Power" *American Economic Review* vol. 54, September 1964: 626-655.

The issues raised here are of more than theoretical interest. In an important recent study of market power trends in the United States, Shepherd discovered a remarkable increase in the proportion of the U.S. economy which could be defined as "effectively competitive."[59] Using data on market structure (market shares of leading firms, concentration ratios, and entry barriers), behaviour (primarily pricing behaviour), and the extent of import competition, Shepherd found that effective competition had increased in virtually every sector of the U.S. economy. Overall, the share of U.S. national income produced in effectively competitive industries rose from 56 to 77 percent between 1958 and 1980—a remarkable rise. In the two decades prior to 1958, the estimated rise in effective competition was only 4 percentage points. By 1980, pure monopolies accounted for only 2.5 percent of national income and industries with dominant firms 2.8 percent—less than half their 1939 values. During the same period the share of "tight oligopoly" (in which Shepherd included markets where government regulation assisted collusion, such as milk markets) declined by about half—from 36 to 18 percent. Nevertheless, in some important markets, such as computers, photographic film, drugs, locomotives, newspapers and soups, market power remained high. Shepherd concluded that while, in 1958, the "neo-Chicago-school belief in a competitive economy was not really tenable," their view is now "more relevant," and that "the U.S. economy is now an enormous test case for the functioning of competition in a large-scale industrial economy."[60]

No analogous longitudinal study has been undertaken for the Canadian economy—and probably cannot be because of a lack of relevant data. However, in some unpublished work, Khemani has recently attempted to estimate the share of Canadian gross domestic product (GDP) contributed by effectively competitive industries in 1980.[61] He estimated that, in 1980, about 47 percent of GDP (not including public administration and defence) originated in effectively competitive markets. Of the remaining 53 percent of GDP, 19 percent originated in tightly oligopolistic markets, simply defined as non-regulated

59. W.G. Shepherd, "Causes of Increased Competition in the U.S. Economy, 1939-1980," *The Review of Economics and Statistics*, 64, No. 4 (November 1982), pp. 613-626. See especially Tables 2 and 3. Shepherd defines "effectively competitive" industries as those with four firm concentration ratios below 40 percent, with unstable market shares, and flexible pricing, or those with low entry barriers, little collusion and low profit rates.

60. Ibid., pp. 618, 620. Shepherd attributed the rise in effective competition to increased import competition, to deregulation of a number of industries, and most important of all to the economic effects of antitrust actions.

61. R.S. Khemani, "Extent and Evolution of Competition in the Canadian Economy," Bureau of Competition Policy, Ottawa, 1984 (mimeo). Khemani also provided figures for 1975, but the time period for comparison is too short, and the figures for 1975 and 1980 are too similar to allow any meaningful conclusions about trend.

markets with four-firm concentration ratios greater than 50 percent. The remaining 34 percent of GDP was produced in government supervised or regulated industries such as public utilities, transportation, and major parts of agriculture (see chapters 10 and 12).[62] While Khemani's study is not directly comparable with that of Shepherd, the estimated extent of effective competition in Canada relative to that in the U.S. is broadly what might be expected from the comparative concentration data discussed earlier in this chapter.[63]

Recapitulation

This chapter has introduced the student to the elements of industrial market structures in Canada. The symbiotic relationship between the economic theory of the firm and markets and the study of industrial organization was described at the beginning of the chapter. We then turned to an examination of the most widely used summary statistic of industrial market structure—the concentration ratio. We found that industry concentration ratios are systematically higher in Canada than in the United States—and for that matter above those in most western countries. Canada's huge expanse, small population, and tariff-protected markets undoubtedly contribute to high concentration levels here. Mergers are probably only a secondary factor contributing to observed concentration levels in Canada. The existence of large firms, growing primarily by diversifying their activities, is an important phenomenon in Canada as well as the United States. Industrial diversification has given new impetus to the study of the impact of firm investment behaviour on industry structure. Finally, the studies by Shepherd and Khemani suggest that the extent of competition and monopoly power is an evolving phenomenon subject to changes in world economic structure and domestic economic policy. These studies help motivate the further investigation of the elements of market structure in Canada, in chapter 3 and 4.

---

62. Ibid., Table I, p. 8.
63. Incidentally, both studies give no attention to the role of trade unions. Some labour unions, particularly in Canada, have effective monopoly power, the impact of which almost certainly overflows into product markets.

3

Determinants of Market Structure

In this chapter we continue our investigation of the determinants of market structure in Canadian industries. We begin with a discussion of economies of scale which, given market size, are potentially an important influence on firm size and the level of industry concentration. Then we turn to three additional elements of market structure: product differentiation, barriers to entry and market size and growth. At this point the interaction between industrial organization variables becomes more complex and problematic. There are four reasons for this added complexity. First, while barriers to entry and product differentiation are treated as separate elements of market structure, many industrial organization economists consider product differentiation, along with economies of scale and capital requirements, as a source of barriers to entry. Second, both product differentiation and entry barriers may be the outcome of strategic price and nonprice behaviour of firms including their decisions relating to promotional effort, scale of output and investments in plant capacity. This means that elements of market structure such as concentration and barriers to entry may depend not only on other structural elements such as economies of scale and product differentiation, but on firm behaviour. Thus the traditional structure-behaviour-performance paradigm is too simple: feedbacks from firm conduct or behaviour to industry structure clearly must be admitted.[1] Third,

1. For a fuller discussion see Richard E. Caves, Michael E. Porter, A. Michael Spense, with John T. Scott, *Competition in the Open Economy: A Model Applied to Canada* (Cambridge, Mass.: Harvard University Press, 1980), ch.1. Note that this partial reversal of causation is based on an argument quite different from the one in which high concentration and large market shares are said to be the result of nonscale differences in costs among firms owing to differences in managerial capabilities. See the last section of this chapter.

many industrial markets in Canada are dominated by foreign owned and controlled firms. Industrial organization analysis suggests that product differentiation is a part of the explanation for the important place of multinational enterprise (MNE) in Canada's manufacturing sector. Fourth, Canada is an "open," tariff-protected economy, a characterization which is justified by the approximately 25 percent of national output that moves in international trade and the high tariffs that protect many manufacturing industries. Canada's openness and its tariffs influence industry structure through their impact on industry concentration, the achievement of scale economies, intra-industry specialization and technology transfer. In addition, while tariffs may act as a barrier to the entry of goods, they may stimulate entry by foreign firms. Because the interaction of the tariff, foreign ownership, and industrial organization variables are sufficiently large and distinctive (to Canada) subjects, they are given separate treatment in chapter 4.

Economies of Scale

In microeconomic theory economies (and diseconomies) of scale are reflected in the shape of the long run average cost curve (LAC). The LAC is an "envelope" of short run average cost curves (SAC), each SAC representing a particular scale of plant. In the simplest case of the single-plant firm, the LAC represents the minimum costs associated with a set of options (plant sizes or scales) available to the firm at a particular time, given the "state of the arts" (technology) and input prices. Pictured in the textbooks, the LAC is usually U-shaped; empirical evidence, however, suggests it is "J-shaped."

There are several factors which at the plant level may give rise to economies of scale in production. These are (i) specialization of inputs made possible by large-scale production (mechanization); (ii) indivisibilities in plant size; (iii) the fact that in processing industries, such as petroleum refining, chemical production, cement making, glass manufacturing, where output tends to be proportional to the volume of the unit, the cost of construction of the surface area tends to rise as $2/3$ the power of output capacity; and (iv) the length of production runs. The last of these is particularly important in the Canadian context.

At the level of the firm there are also several factors which may give rise to economies of scale (including economies of multiplant operations). These include (i) the increased ability to incur risks via size-induced diversification; (ii) administrative economies associated with spreading the overhead cost of certain management services (e.g. accountants, financial planners, market researchers, etc.) over a larger output; (iii) economies of large scale in advertising and finance; (iv) the ability to spread the costs associated with research and development; (v) economies in distribution, including the establishment of dealer networks; and (vi) economies of massed reserves, in the form of stand-by machinery, inventories of replacement parts, etc.

In addition to the sources of firm economies mentioned above, the large enterprise with some monopolistic power may be able to obtain inputs at a lower per-unit price than its smaller competitors. Where such "economies" are obtained, they are said to be "pecuniary" economies of scale in contrast to "real" economies associated with reductions in input per unit of output as scale of plant or firm increases.

To this point we have confined ourselves to economies associated with the scale of output (essentially "horizontal" economies). There may also be "vertical" economies as technologically related processes are integrated within the plant or the firm, as, for example, the steel-making and steel-rolling processes within an iron and steel plant. On the other hand as an industry grows there may be vertical disintegration as market demand expands to levels sufficient to justify firms specializing in the production of particular inputs, including machinery.[2] To some extent there has been vertical disintegration within the computer industry as the use of computers expanded to the point that the provision of computer-related services by non-integrated specialty firms became profitable.

A. Plant Economies of Scale

The LAC curve in manufacturing industries appears to be J-shaped, rather than U-shaped. This was the conclusion reached by Joe Bain in his empirical study of the nature of plant LAC curves in U.S. manufacturing industries. Bain used data derived from engineering studies of plant output levels at which input per unit of output was minimized. Such studies have the defect of overlooking economic criteria such as input prices, but given the major defects of the two alternative methods of estimating scale economies (statistical cost analysis and the "survivor technique"—see below), engineering studies remain the most important and reliable source of information available to us on scale economies. In recent years, substantial use of the engineering technique has been made by Silbertson and Pratten for Great Britain and Scherer for the United States.[3] These studies

---

2. See G. Stigler, "The Division of Labour is Limited by the Extent of the Market," *Journal of Political Economy* (June 1951), pp. 134-138. Stigler credits Adam Smith with the idea that growing industries often experience vertical disintegration.

3. C. Pratten, *Economies of Scale in Manufacturing Industries* (London: Cambridge University Press, 1971); A Silbertson, "Economies of Scale in Theory and Practice," *Economic Journal* (March 1972, Supplement), pp. 369-391; F.M. Scherer, et al. *The Economies of Multi-Plant Operation: An International Comparisons Study* (Cambridge, Mass.: Harvard University Press, 1975). An excellent review of the literature and summary of the salient issues is contained in F.M. Scherer," Economies of Scale and Industrial Concentration," in *Industrial Concentration: The New Learning*, H. Goldschmid, H.M. Mann, and J. Fred Weston, eds. (Boston: Little Brown

Figure 3-1

Typical Plant LAC Curve

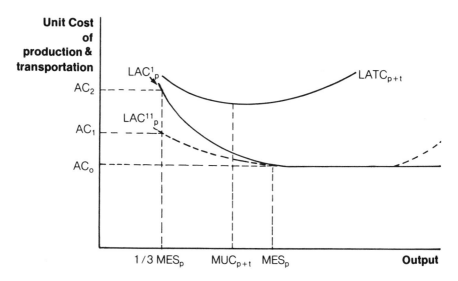

p = production costs
t = transportation costs
MUC = minimum unit cost

tend to confirm Bain's earlier findings on the shape of the LAC. In addition the more recent studies have provided statistical evidence on the cost disadvantage of building a plant at only a fraction of minimum efficient scale (MES).[4] MES is the smallest output at which scale economies are exhausted. Figure 3-1 presents a picture of the empirically estimated shape of the LAC along with the salient points along the LAC.

It is as important to know how steeply the LAC falls as MES is approached (or rises as scale is reduced below MES) as it is to know at what scale (in relation to market size) MES is reached. The latter is, of course, very important because it tells us the maximum number of (single plant) firms of efficient size market demand will support. In this respect, economies of scale, to the extent there are powerful forces tending to their exhaustion, constitute an extremely important

& Co., 1974), pp. 16-54 . Also see F.M. Scherer, *Industrial Market Structure and Economic Performance*, 2d ed. (Chicago: Rand-McNally, 1980), pp. 81-119. A skeptical view is presented by John S. McGee, "Efficiency and Economies of Scale," in Goldschmid, Mann, Weston, op. cit., pp. 55-97.
4. Some authors refer to minimum efficient size or minimum optimal scale (MOS).

determinant of the minimum levels of industry concentration. However, it is also important to know what cost disadvantage is incurred by plants at less than MES. For example, if plants with capacities of one-third MES incur 5 percent higher costs they will be better able to withstand competition from their larger rivals than if the cost disadvantage is 15 percent. In fact, if LAC curves are shaped like that of LAC''_p in Figure 3-1 we should expect to find numerous plants at substantially less than MES and, other things being equal, lower concentration than were the curve to be shaped as LAC'_p in Figure 3-1.

The link between economies of scale and actual levels of industry concentration is, however, weakened by the existence of (i) plant sizes in excess of MES, and (ii) multiplant firms. As Figure 3-1 shows, the LAC does not soon turn upward after MES is reached. The empirical evidence is that *observed* plant scales, though in many cases far greater than estimated MES, fail to exhibit the onset of diseconomies. But even if diseconomies were to set in shortly after MES is reached, the firm can sidestep these by building another plant (multiplant operations), unless of course there are diseconomies of firm size. Forty or fifty years ago economists generally hypothesized diseconomies of large firm size associated with managerial inefficiencies arising out of coordinating the far-flung operations of giant firms. However, the continuous growth in leading firm size, aided and abetted by diversification into numerous product fields, suggests that the constraints on firm size are, if anything, less binding than those on the plant (to be discussed below). That is, whatever diseconomies there may be in large-scale operation are apparently offset by economies of joint production (e.g. research and development, cost of finance, advertising packages) as well as the increased coordination and control made possible by computers and a high-speed communications system.

In spite of the theoretical (scale) efficiency gains of achieving at least MES, there is abundant evidence, in Canada, that production operations typically fall well below MES levels and that costs are significantly raised as a result. Before examining the empirical evidence on scale economies it might be useful to list the factors that may limit plant size (relative to MES levels). Scherer suggests there are three factors: (i) market size; (ii) transportation costs; and (iii) oligopolistic rivalry.[5] In addition, we might add a fourth—initial capital costs, which in, at least, a few activities, e.g. an integrated steel complex, may be prohibitive. Of the three factors noted by Scherer, market size and transportation costs are of undoubted importance in Canada. With a limited domestic market and a huge geographic expanse, it is not at all surprising that where markets are segmented geographically because of transportation costs, plant sizes will typically be

---

5. F.M. Scherer, "The Determinants of Industrial Plant Sizes in Six Nations," *Review of Economics and Statistics* (May 1973), pp. 135-145.

smaller than where MES is based solely on production costs. In fact, as the LAC_{p+t} curve in Figure 3-1 indicates, the inclusion of unit transportation costs substantially reduces the output rate at which lowest unit costs are reached. The shape of LAC_{p+t} reflects the fact that the decline in LAC_p is offset by rising unit costs of transportation as firms must expand the radius of their sales territories in order to market larger levels of plant output.

When rival firms are added to the picture, there may be further constraints on an individual plant achieving MES operation. For example, entering at MES may be viewed as a competitive attack on the market shares of established rivals, which can develop into the uncertainty and unprofitability of a price war. An alternate strategy is for inefficiently small firms to merge (assuming an acceptable selling price can be reached) with one plant undertaking production at MES levels, the remaining plants converted to some other form of activity, if possible, or left idle. However, the possibility that some plants would have to be idled suggests the merger route may not be a profitable one.

B. "Product Specific" or Production-Run Economies

Despite the market size and geographical constraints on MES-level operations, many Canadian plants are large enough to exhaust scale economies.[6] Yet in their operations they fall far short of achieving potential scale economies. Here we should distinguish between two facets of the achievement of scale economies: output per unit of time (mechanization) and the length of time over which production continues (length of production run). Many Canadian manufacturing plants achieve the scale economies associated with the former but not with the latter. That is, we often find that large Canadian plants produce several different outputs (e.g. refrigerators, ranges, washing machines, etc.) over a given period of time, the *production run* of each being sharply limited by the small Canadian market. This tendency is reinforced where Canadian subsidiaries of U.S. firms produce "miniature replicas" of the diverse product lines of large U.S. multiplant firms all within a single Canadian plant. When a production run ends there is a changeover from one production technique or assembly line to another. The shorter the production run, the more numerous the changeovers. Since changeovers take time during which no saleable output is produced, unit costs of production are raised. In addition, short production runs reduce the increases in efficiency gained by "learning from doing."

6. Moreover, some evidence indicates that once the lower end of the distribution of Canadian plant sizes is excluded, Canadian plants are not, in general, significantly smaller than those in other countries. *Report of the Royal Commission on Corporate Concentration* (Ottawa, 1978), p. 67.

Estimates of Minimum Efficient Scale

The first concerted effort to estimate scale efficiency in Canadian manufacturing industries was carried out by Eastman and Stykolt for 16 industries in the late 1950s. Eastman and Stykolt adopted the engineering method, modelling their analysis after that of Bain's study for the United States. They found that a high percentage of industry capacity (on the average somewhat above 50 percent) was of inefficient size, compared to an average of about 20 percent found by Bain for the 20 U.S. industries he studied.[7] In eight of the sixteen industries investigated the percentage of industry size accounted for by four plants of minimum efficient scale exceeded 50 percent (it exceeded 100 percent for electric refrigerators, electric ranges, primary steel, and fruit canning). Reported concentration ratios were generally considerably lower than the MES estimates would have dictated. The findings for Canada are in contrast to those for the United States, which indicate that MES is typically a small percentage of the market and that reported industry concentration ratios are generally much higher than MES would dictate. The difference between the U.S. and Canadian findings is mainly attributable to the tremendous (ten or eleven fold) differences in market sizes between the two countries.

A more recent study by Scherer supports the earlier findings. Scherer carried out an investigation of minimum efficient scale and the cost penalties associated with suboptimal scale for 12 industries in six countries, using the engineering method.[8] The basic findings for Canada and the United States are compared in Table 3-1. (Table 3-1 also includes four additional industries studied by Pratten and Silbertson.[9]) The first two columns compare the number of MES plants compatible with domestic consumption in Canada and the United States respectively. In six of the 16 industries the Canadian market, in 1967, could not have absorbed the output of four plants of MES; in one case, refrigerators and freezers, the domestic market was too small for even one firm. (The example of refrigerators and freezers is not exceptional. The Canadian market is too small to support the output of one MES plant producing agricultural machinery such as tractors or combines).[10] The contrast with the United States is stark. However, the cost penalty of operating at substantially less than MES is

---

7. H. Eastman and S. Stykolt, *The Tariff and Competition in Canada* (Toronto: Macmillan of Canada, 1967). Joe Bain, *Barriers to New Competition* (Yale University Press, 1956). Several of the industries studied by Eastman and Stykolt were the same as those included in Bain's sample.
8. Scherer, op. cit., Tables 2 and 4.
9. Paul Gorecki, *Economies of Scale and Efficient Plant Size in Canadian Manufacturing Industries*, Consumer and Corporate Affairs, Bureau of Competition Policy, Research Monograph No. 1 (Ottawa, 1976).
10. See David Schwartzman, *Oligopoly in the Farm Machinery Industry*, Study No. 12, Royal Commission on Farm Machinery (Ottawa, Information Canada, 1970), p. 83.

Table 3-1

International Evidence on Plant Economies of Scale, Canada and U.S., Circa 1967

Industry	No. of MES Plants Compatible with Domestic Consumption		% by Which Cost Rises Building at 1/3 MES	% of Canadian Consumption Accounted for by 4 MES-plants	Canadian Concentration Ratio (1970)	
	Canada	U.S.			Largest 4 firms	Largest 4 plants
Breweries	2.9	29.0	5.0	Over 100	94.0	41.6
Cigarettes	1.3	15.2	2.2	Over 100	96.8	63.2
Cotton and synthetic broad-winch fabrics	17.4	451.7	7.6	23.0	n.a.	n.a.
Paints and varnishes	6.3	69.8	4.4	63.5	39.7	18.9
Petroleum refining	6.0	51.6	4.8	66.7	79.0	28.9
Non-rubber shoes	59.2	523.0	1.5	6.8	24.6	19.4[b]
Glass bottles	7.2	65.5	11.0	55.6	73.6	72.2[b]
Portland cement	6.6	59.0	26.0	60.6	79.3	30.5
Integrated steel	2.6	38.9	11.0	Over 100	75.2	70.3
Anti-friction bearings	5.9	72.0	8.0	67.8	n.a.	n.a.
Refrigerators & freezers	0.7	7.1	6.5	Over 100	50.2[a]	n.a.
Automobile storage batteries	4.6	53.5	4.6	87.0	77.2	33.7
Sulphuric acid	2.7	n.a.	1.5	Over 100	57.6[a]	n.a.
Solid detergent	1.7	n.a.	3.8	Over 100	75.8	69.6
Bricks	32.0	n.a.	37.5	12.5	53.8[a]	n.a.
Bakeries	40.8	n.a.	11.3	9.8	31.4	12.5

Sources: Scherer, op. cit., Tables 2 and 4; Gorecki, op. cit., Table 6-4; Statistics Canada, *Industrial Organization*, op. cit.
[a]From Gorecki, Table 6-4, Col. 2.   [b]Largest 8.

quite variable. For a plant only 1/3 MES the penalty exceeded 5 percent in only half of the cases reported in Table 3-1. Evidently, in many industries the technology does not dictate steeply falling LAC curves. The last two columns of Table 3-1 provide firm and plant concentration ratios where available. Although the four-*firm* concentration ratios shown are generally high, they exceeded the percentage of domestic consumption accounted for by four MES plants in only six of the fourteen cases for which concentration ratios are reported in Table 3-1.

How representative are the samples of industries studied by Eastman and Stykolt and by Scherer? Most of the available evidence suggests that numerous manufacturing industries face much the same dilemma: the existence of scale efficiency and more than a handful of firms are inconsistent unless the industries are export oriented, as is the case in the paper industry. For example, in a study of 125 comparable Canadian and U.S. industries, Baldwin and Gorecki found that the ratio of the average size of larger Canadian plants to larger U.S. plants was substantially less than one (approximately .7).[11] The larger plants refer to the smallest number of the largest plants accounting for 50 percent of industry output or capacity. This measure has received increasing use as a proxy for MES.

There is one piece of evidence that suggests that the estimates discussed above may be too pessimistic. In a study carried out for the Bureau of Competition Policy of the Department of Consumer and Corporate Affairs, Gorecki found MES to be much smaller than is suggested by engineering studies. Estimates of MES plant sizes in 56 Canadian manufacturing industries were made using the so-called survivor technique. The survivor technique selects efficient size plants (or firms) on the basis of those plant (or firm) sizes which between two periods of time increase their *share* of industry sales. Specifically, the percentage share of industry sales accounted for by each of several establishment (plant) employment categories for the years 1961, 1966 and 1972 were examined. Those establishment size categories which experienced a rise in industry sales shares are considered to be of efficient size on the grounds that they have "passed" a crucial market test: survival.

Many criticisms have been levelled at the survivor technique: it indicates what "is" rather than what "ought" to, or could, be; it fails to differentiate between survival and efficiency, essentially equating the two; it overlooks the potential influences of market power and predatory conduct on the ability of firms to

11. J. Baldwin and P.K. Gorecki, "Trade, Tariffs and Relative Plant Scale in Canadian Manufacturing Industries: 1970-79," Discussion Paper No. 232, Economic Council of Canada, May 1983. The use of the largest plants accounting for 50 percent of industry output as a measure of MES was originated by W.S. Comanor and T.A. Wilson in *Advertising and Market Power* (Cambridge: Harvard University Press, 1974).

Table 3-2

A Comparison of Engineering and Survival Estimates of Minimum Efficient Plant Size as a Percentage of Industry Size, Seven Canadian Manufacturing Industries

Industry	Estimation Method		% of Industry Size Accounted for by 4 Largest Enterprises (1968)
	Survivor	Engineering	
	(percent)		
Petroleum refining	1.1	16.7	78
Non-rubber shoes	1.0	1.7	19
Integrated steel	0.2	38.5	77
Refrigerators & freezers	3.7	142.9	50
Automobile storage batteries	4.3	21.7	79
Bakeries	0.3	2.5	31
Bricks	1.4	3.1	54

Source: Paul K. Gorecki, op. cit., Table 6-1, p. 62. Reproduced by permission of the Minister of Supply and Services Canada.

survive. Yet the survivor technique nevertheless survives (the idea has been traced back to John Stuart Mill by its first applicator George Stigler, and has been employed by a number of economists).[12] Its attraction is its simplicity, relying on relatively easy-to-get data on changes in output over time compared to the relatively difficult-to-obtain data on which dependable engineering estimates of efficient size are based.

Minimum efficient plant size, using the survivor technique, is typically a small percentage of industry size. For 1972, 47 of the 56 manufacturing industries studied had minimum efficient plant sizes of less than 3 percent of industry size. These results are in sharp contrast to the findings from engineering studies and the picture painted by Table 3-1. When these results are compared with those of Eastman and Stykolt for seven industries studied in common (Table 3-2), the

---

12. G. Stigler, "The Economies of Scale," *Journal of Law and Economics* (October 1958), pp. 54-71; L. Weiss, "The Survival Technique and the Extent of Suboptimal Capacity," *Journal of Political Economy* (June 1964), pp. 246-61; T. Saving, "Estimation of Optimum Size of Plants by the Survivor Technique," *Quarterly Journal of Economics* (Nov. 1961), pp. 569-607. Stigler applied the survival technique to steel firms; Weiss and Saving to plants in several industries. A critical evaluation of the survivor technique is W.G. Shepherd, "What Does the Survivor Technique Show About Economies of Scale?" *Southern Economic Journal* (July 1967), pp. 113-122.

differences in the two indexes of MES are so great as to foreclose any acceptable compromise between the two. Given the oligopolistic structure of Canadian industry, tariff protection, a small domestic market, and limited opportunities to export, it is not surprising why:

> The introduction of plants of fully efficient size in terms of produc-
> tion costs (estimated using the engineering method) would lead to
> lower prices, might lead to losses and perhaps even to the oblivion of
> the initiating firm. In such circumstances competence consists of
> operating with as low costs as possible a plant too small to exhaust
> economies of scale. . . . If George Stigler's survival test had been
> used to determine the most efficient size of plant, much of the
> capacity which is found to be inefficiently small by the test
> (engineering estimates) used here would have been found of optimal
> size, because his test discovers the combination of attributes that
> makes for success, not simply minimizes average costs of produc-
> tion. (Eastman and Stykolt, op. cit., pp. vii-viii.)

Thus the cleavage between survival and efficiency, mentioned above, goes far to explain the conflicting results of engineering estimates and the survival test. In the United States, where oligopoly is generally "looser" and operates within a much larger market and behind lower tariff walls, "the estimates of MES based on survival data do seem to correspond reasonably well to engineering estimates in these industries."[13] But for Canada, the ingeniousness of the survivor technique cannot hide large and systematic differences between engineering and survivor estimates of MES, suggesting that attempts to estimate scale economies are "best pursued through the engineering technique."[14]

Suboptimal plant capacity is not the only factor that contributes to scale inefficiencies. Even optimally scaled plants in Canada tend to produce a much more diverse line of products than their U.S. counterparts as tariff-protected Canadian firms attempt to meet Canadian consumer demand and compete with imports.[15] There seems little doubt that a chief source of higher (relative to U.S.) cost production in many Canadian manufacturing industries is attributable to

13. Leonard Weiss, "The Survival Technique and the Extent of Suboptimal Capacity," *Journal of Political Economy* (June 1964), pp. 246-61. Weiss studied the automobile, steel, petroleum, refining, flour, and cement industries.
14. Gorecki, op. cit., p. 64. However, where markets are small and transportation costs are important, the engineering technique will tend to overstate MES estimated with respect to production costs only.
15. See J.R. Baldwin and P.K. Gorecki with J. McVey and J. Crysdale, "Trade, Tariffs, Product Diversity and Length of Production Run in Canadian Manufacturing Industries: 1970-79" (Discussion Paper No. 247, Economic Council of Canada, November 1983), pp. 13-15, for some evidence that product diversity is characteristic of Canadian plants but that there was some reduction in diversity during the 1970s, particularly in large plants.

short production runs due to small volumes dictated by a small domestic market. Evidence for, and examples of, this view are detailed in a study prepared almost two decades ago for the Economic Council of Canada.[16] That study found substantial productivity differences between Canada and U.S. manufacturing in the mid 1960s—differences on the order of 25 to 30 percent in favour of the United States. (There is no evidence that the productivity differential has disappeared, although it has been reduced particularly in the important automobile industry where the U.S.-Canada Auto Pact has "rationalized" automobile production through assembly plant specialization). Size of plant was not found to be a dominant factor behind the productivity differences. The length of production runs and the degree of specialization or diversification in production was much more important.[17]

The Economic Council study found that shortness of production runs created serious diseconomies of scale in the chemical, fine paper, rubber tire, consumer appliances and textile products industries. All of these are industries where a considerable amount of product differentiation exists. Consider the following industry statements quoted in the ECC study:

> We run more than five hundred sizes [tires] at our plant. Our change costs are tremendous, while some of our larger American plants may run only half a hundred sizes. . . . Then we have to shut down our machines and start them up again and get them running accurately to size and we have to pay our men during that period of time. . .
>
> This is brought about by the fact that Canadian consumers [of synthetic detergent] desire the same kind and type of products that are sold in the United States. . . This means constant shut downs for clean-out as we change from one brand to the other, whereas in the United States an item like 'Tide' will be blown six days a week 24 hours a day on one colour, thus getting the maximum efficiency and the lowest possible cost.

In the case of fine papers, industry representatives estimated a reduction of 12 to 15 percent in manufacturing costs if the paper machines could be run as continuously as is typical in the United States. Fortunately for the Canadian firms, they were protected by a 20-percent-plus tariff. Production runs of consumer appliances are ten times greater in the U.S. than production runs in

16. D.J. Daly, B.A. Keys, E.J. Spense, "Scale and Specialization in Canadian Manufacturing," Staff Study No. 21, Economic Council of Canada, Ottawa, 1968. These are the "product specific" as distinct from "plant specific" economies referred to above.
17. Ibid., Part II. The study indicated that among management analysts and engineers there was "widespread agreement that longer production runs would narrow the productivity differences between Canada and the United States to a significant degree."

Canada, and U.S. costs, in the 1960s, were about 85 percent of Canadian costs, even though Canadian wage levels were then substantially lower (a wage differential which is fast disappearing).[18] Finally, in the textile industry production efficiency requires longer runs of particular yarns and fabric types than was typical of most Canadian plants.[19] In contrast, the steel and wire cable industries are relatively efficient compared to their U.S. counterparts. Product differentiation is not a problem. The relative efficiency of these industries has allowed them to enter the export market, with 15 percent of Canadian steel production sold outside Canada.

The importance of inefficiently small plant scale and relatively high intraplant product diversity in Canada is beyond dispute. It is also beyond dispute that there exist substantial productivity differentials between individual Canadian industries and their U.S. counterparts that are not flattering to the Canadian side. An interesting question is how much of these productivity differentials can be explained by the scale (plant and product-specific) factor. A recent study by Baldwin and Gorecki suggests that suboptimal scale, whether due to inefficiently small plants or insufficiently long production runs, accounts for all of the productivity differentials between the manufacturing sectors of the two countries.[20] This is an important finding which in the main is likely to withstand the results of further research. It also has an important policy implication: tariff reductions will not necessarily leave Canada's manufacturing sector at a disadvantage. Existing productivity differentials can be wiped out by the specialization that would necessarily follow in the wake of free trade.

Economies of Large Firm Size

To this point we have focused on economies of scale associated with the *size* of plant ("plant-specific") or the length of production run within a plant ("product specific"). These are the scale economies to which economists have given most attention and for which they have accumulated the most evidence. However, there may also be multi-plant economies of scale and economies associated simply with large firm size. They are often associated with spreading overhead or economizing on marketing efforts. These economies are both less theoretically tractable and harder to measure, although in some cases they may be no less important than plant-related economies. In Canada, many leading busi-

18. The preceding examples are from Daly, Keys, Spense, op. cit., pp. 67, 74, 75, 82.
19. Textile and Clothing Board, *Textile and Clothing Inquiry*, June 30, 1980. Vol. 1 p. 37. However, in the early 1970s there was a degree of rationalization in the form of longer production runs of woven fabrics (p. 24).
20. J.R. Baldwin and P.K. Gorecki, "Canada-U.S. Productivity Differences in the Manufacturing Sector: 1970, 1979" (mimeo).

nessmen have argued that firms must be large in order to compete in export markets, acquire finance at lowest costs, attain lowest unit costs of advertising and other forms of promotion, and undertake meaningful R & D programs.[21] There seems little doubt that at least up to a point there are real economies in R & D and in large-scale finance.[22] Promotional (advertising) economies also exist, but there is a good deal of debate over whether they are real or pecuniary economies. Economies of scale in exporting and in administration are harder to verify and defend. Nevertheless, firm-level economies are crucial to the debate over the advantages and disadvantages to society of corporate giantism. The Royal Commission on Corporate Concentration stated that:

> It is our conclusion that in many industries firm-level economies in Canada justify larger-sized business than do plant-level economies. How large a firm is justified depends on the industry, but it may be sizeable. The major firm-level economy is probably found in risk-taking ability, in undertaking new investment, and in long-term R & D, with the largest firm-sizes probably justified in high-risk sectors such as energy exploration, aerospace and similar fields.[23]

These are views that are neither easily defended on the basis of existing research nor easily rejected on the basis of casual observation.

What little systematic evidence there is on multiplant and large firm economies of scale suggests the following:[24] managerial and central staff economies of multiplant operations are slight if they exist at all; large firm size, and market power, do produce cost advantage in raising equity capital; and economies of large-scale sales promotion and image differentiation (via advertising) are substantial in a number of consumer goods industries, and have contributed thereby to raising market concentration. Scherer concluded that multiplant economies of scale were sufficiently important in about a quarter of the twelve industries he studied in depth to require, in the U.S., an oligopolistic market structure. In Canada, with its much smaller domestic market, we can expect that in those industries where multiplant economies of scale are important, exhausting them would require a tight oligopoly or dominant-firm market structure.[25]

21. A number of industrial leaders presented briefs on this issue to the Royal Commission on Corporate Concentration. See the Commission's Report, op. cit. pp. 57-67. For an intensive and somewhat more skeptical examination see D.G. McFetridge and L.J. Weatherley, *Notes on the Economies of Large Firm Size*, Study No. 20, Royal Commission on Corporate Concentration (Ottawa, 1977).
22. The large firm can also diversify its activities and thereby spread risk—an advantage in a generally risk-averting world.
23. Royal Commission on Corporate Concentration, op. cit., p. 68.
24. Scherer, et al, *Economies of Multiplant Operation*, op. cit. is virtually the only systematic study of multiplant economies of sale.
25. Scherer, *Industrial Market Structure and Economic Performance*, 2d ed., 1980, pp. 101, 107, 116, 117-119.

Barriers to Entry

Another important element of industry structure is the height of barriers to entry faced by prospective entrants. The conditions of entry, along with product differentiation and the size distribution of firms summarized in the industry concentration ratio, are three chief structural characteristics of an industry. Bain has defined barriers to entry as the disadvantages of potential firms as compared to established firms. The height of the barriers is indicated by the extent to which, in the long run, established firms can elevate their selling price above minimum average costs of production and distribution without inducing entry.[26] Bain distinguishes three industrial sources of barriers to entry: (a) economies of scale or the "displacement barrier"; (b) absolute cost barriers, which can be subdivided into capital cost and "strategic" factors such as control over superior production techniques (via patents), raw materials, special skills, and distribution outlets; and (c) product differentiation, which to the extent it can be overcome simply by waging a sufficiently vigorous (and costly) advertising campaign is not conceptually different from a capital cost barrier. A fourth source of barriers is government regulations, quotas, licenses, and favourable sales and purchase policies.

The conditions of entry are extremely important in evaluating the degree to which competitive forces act upon an industry. Competitive forces can come from inside the industry—i.e. from established firms—or from "outside" the industry—i.e. from actual or potential entrants. The conditions of entry obviously relate to the external forces of competition. Unfortunately, however, the concept of barriers to entry is not without ambiguity and its behavioural and normative implications are subjects of increasing controversy. In addition, empirical evidence on the conditions of entry is scant. Moreover, it appears to be important to distinguish between the barriers in the way of entry by an established leading firm and that by a new or small established firm.

A. Theoretical and Conceptual Issues

There are several sources of controversy concerning barriers to entry. First there is disagreement over definition. Bain's definition focuses on the costs or advantages of established firms relative to those of potential entrants at a point in time. Stigler, in contrast, defines barriers "as a cost of producing (at some or

26. Joe S. Bain, *Barriers to New Competition* (New Haven: Yale University Press, 1956), and *Industrial Organization*, 2d ed. (Wiley, 1968), Chap. 8. Bain refers to this entry-deterring price as the "limit price." For an important theoretical contribution indicating how an established firm can set a price above Bain's "limit price" and still deter entry by threatening to cut price to marginal cost levels in the face of threatened entry see Michael Spence "Entry, Capacity, Investment and Oligopolistic Pricing," *Bell Journal of Economics* (Autumn 1977), pp. 534-44.

every rate of output) which must be borne by a firm which seeks to enter an industry but is not borne by firms already in the industry." Under Bain's definition product differentiation may constitute a barrier to entry if to overcome the differentiation advantage of established firms, potential entrants must engage in an expensive advertising campaign. However, under Stigler's definition, if established firms had to incur substantial advertising costs at some time in the past, say when they were getting established, potential entrants are under no special disadvantage in this respect. For this reason, Stigler rejects Bain's argument that product differentiation constitutes a barrier to entry. Stigler also rejects the idea that economies of scale are a barrier to entry so long as entrants have access to the same cost function as established firms.

Another source of disagreement concerning the barriers concept is its *normative* content. The problem arises chiefly because of Bain's reliance on profits as a test for the existence of barriers to entry. Under Bain's definition, the test of the existence of barriers is whether in the long run price exceeds long-run average costs. Since the existence of long-run supranormal profits is taken as *prima facie* evidence of a less than optimal allocation of resources, the existence of barriers to entry implies that something is wrong or amiss. Yet, clearly, if economies of scale are sufficiently important that MES is a sizeable fraction of market size, additional entry might be inefficient or suboptimal, because it may force costs and prices upward as each firm operates at a less than efficient scale. In this respect the scale barrier is efficient and desirable.[27] Moreover, a firm which profits from its investment in reputation may be acting in the general consumer interest, even if its reputation constitutes a costly hurdle or barrier that must be overcome by a successful entrant.[28] Thus, the existence of barriers to entry, even ones which generate profits for established firms, may be desirable or optimal.

B. Entry-Deterring Behaviour

A third area of controversy involves the behavioural implications of barriers to entry. What is the response of established firms to attempts by outsiders to enter the industry? Hold output and price constant? Aggressively increase output and lower price? Maintain, or raise, price and passively make way for the newco-

27. Thus C.C. von Weizsacker defines barriers to entry in terms of suboptimality arising when established firms are (overly) protected from entry. Thus, if in the economies of scale case entry would be socially suboptimal or inefficient, the failure to observe entry would not reflect a barrier to entry in Weizsacker's normative sense of the term. See "A Welfare Analysis of Barriers to Entry," *Bell Journal of Economics* (Autumn 1980).
28. See H. Demsetz, "Barriers to Entry," *American Economic Review*, 72 (March 1982), pp. 47–57. Demsetz also notes that sometimes real barriers exist even though established firms and entrants face the same costs and long-run profits are dissipated, as is the case with taxi medallions and quotas issued by supply management marketing boards (see ch. 12).

mers, as Canada Cement did between 1946 and 1970, which saw its share of the Canadian cement market decline from 80 percent to 34 percent.[29] The issue is perhaps clearest where economies of scale are important and the established firms—or at least the leading ones—have built optimally scaled plants.

Bain assumed that the rational response of the established firms would be to hold output constant in the face of threatened entry. If they did so—or at least if their threat to do so was credible to newcomers—the prospective entrants would be confronted with the following dilemma: if they enter small in order to avoid rocking the boat their costs will be higher than the costs of their already established competitors; if they enter by building an optimally scaled plant the addition to industry output will be sufficiently large that industry prices will have to fall in order for total output to be absorbed. Not only might the increase in capacity "rock the boat" sufficiently to spark a price war, but the new equilibrium industry price might be less than industry costs. The prospect of losses would be virtually assured if the established firms initially set what Bain termed the "limit price"—that price which just deters entry, precisely because if entry occurred, small or large, an entrant would not be able to cover its costs.[30]

A simple way in which to understand the concept of a "limit price" is to assume that the established firm(s) has some *absolute* cost advantage over potential entrants. For example, suppose that because of its access to a cheap source of some scarce but essential raw material input, or to patent-protected know how, the established firm's unit costs of production is 10.1 percent lower than the lowest costs of production that could be achieved by any newcomer (entrant) to the industry. The established firm can thereby deter entry to the industry by limiting its markup of price over unit cost to 10 percent—or less. In other words, the "limit price" is 110 percent of established firm average cost, because that is the highest price the established firm, or firms, can set and still foreclose an entering firm from being profitable.

Attempting to deter entry by limit pricing is not always an optimal strategy for established firms: whether it is or is not, depends on whether or not the present value of the prospective flow of profits from an entry-deterring strategy is

29. See F.M. Scherer, *The Economics of Multi-Plant Operation*, pp. 151-52. Another example is the International Nickel Co. (INCO) based in Sudbury, whose pricing policies helped spur entry into the industry by firms in other nations, causing INCO's share of the noncommunist world supply to decline from over 80 percent in 1950 to about 30 percent in 1977.

30. Bain's contention that the dominant strategy of the established firms would be to hold output constant and set a limit price in the face of large-scale entry was independently formalized by an Italian scholar, Paolo Sylos-Labini, and made familiar to English language economists by Franco Modigliani, "New Developments on the Oligopoly Front," *Journal of Political Economy* (June 1958). Since then the Bain-Sylos-Labini strategy has come to be known as the "Sylos Postulate."

greater or less than the present value of the profit flow from a short run profit maximization policy followed by entry and declining prices and profits. Where the threat of entry is from small scale (fringe) competitors, attempting to deter all new entry via a limit price or some other entry deterring strategy, is especially unlikely to be profitable. In this case the loss of profits from setting a price below the cost of the least disadvantaged (most efficient) fringe competitor is likely to exceed the loss of profits attributable to allowing some fringe entry.

The limit price analysis is relatively simple where there is an absolute cost advantage; the analysis is a good deal more complex where cost advantages are associated with economies of scale. Moreover, as the following discussion illustrates, it is not clear that setting the limit price in the face of large scale entry represents a "credible" threat to potential entrants. It is argued by some economists that there is a more potent strategy for deterring entry—one that is credible, and one which to some observers has the appearance of predatory pricing (see below).

The argument is illustrated in Figure 3-2. To begin with, focus on the solid lines and curves in the figure. DD is the industry demand curve facing a few, large established firms producing a homogeneous product. CC'C$_o$ is the long-run average cost curve facing the firms in the industry. The combined capacity of the established firms is represented by curve SAC. If industry output is Q$_o$,

Figure 3-2

Entry-Deterring Strategies

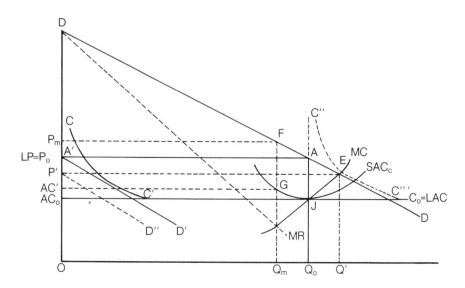

the "residual demand curve" facing prospective entrants is AD.[31] The residual demand curve can also be reproduced as A'D', which is drawn parallel to AD from a point on the ordinate, P_o, at the same height as A. P_o will be the "limit price," if there is no output level at which a new firm could *profitably* enter the industry. This will be the case if the residual demand curve is at all points to the left of the declining portion of the LAC curve, CC', as is the case in Figure 3-2.[32]

Assuming that established firms adopt a limit pricing strategy, entry to the industry will be deterred if prospective entrants believe that the established firms will hold their ground and refuse to reduce output in the face of entry. The implicit assumption of Bain's limit price analysis is that if such a strategy is adopted by the established firms it will represent a credible threat to outsiders. But some economists have questioned whether a strategy of maintaining output constant in the face of large-scale entry, and resultant industry-wide losses, is credible. It has been pointed out that if large-scale entry actually takes place, the established firms would do better, in the sense of reducing losses or increasing profits, by altering their strategy and reducing output somewhat. If this is so, the *threat* that the established firms will maintain output in the face of entry may not be a *credible* one, and therefore may not be the dominant strategy of oligopolists that Bain thought it would be.[33]

Recently there have been suggestions that a more credible entry-deterring threat is an increase in output accompanied by price cutting in the face of attempted entry.[34] Such a strategy requires that the established firm(s), when setting price above cost, hold in reserve excess capacity which would be brought into use should new firms attempt to enter the industry. While holding excess capacity is costly, the strategy may be more profitable than a limit price strategy if (a) it allows the established firms to set pre-entry prices higher than the limit price and (b) it is a more credible threat from the viewpoint of potential entrants.

Figure 3-2 can be used to illustrate the excess capacity strategy. When entry

31. The residual demand curve is that part of the market that is not supplied by existing sellers but could be by an efficient newcomer.

32. One or more of the points must be *just* to the left of CC' so that if the price set by established firms was a bit higher, part of the residual demand curve would be tangent to, or just to the right of, a portion of the cost curve CC'. Note that if the ordinate is moved rightward to AQ_o the LAC curve can be represented by a curve C"C''' which is at all times to the right of the residual demand curve AD.

33. On the credibility of threats, see T.C. Schelling, *The Strategy of Conflict* (Cambridge: Harvard University Press, 1960). B.C. Eaton and R.G. Lipsey, "Exit Barriers are Entry Barriers: The Durability of Capital as a Barrier to Entry," *Bell Journal of Economics*, 11, No. 2 (Autumn 1980), pp. 721-29, view investments in physical capacity and know-how as an irreversible commitment which makes entry-deterring threats credible.

34. Spence, supra, note 26.

is not threatened established firms would set the profit maximizing price, P_m, and output Q_m (where MR = MC). Assuming total capacity held by the established firms is represented, as before, by SAC_c, then industry excess capacity is Q_mQ_o when output is set at Q_m. Although selling price, P_m, exceeds the limit price P_o under this strategy, unit costs are also higher ($AC'>AC_o$). While the profitability rectangle P_mFGAC' under the excess capacity strategy may or may not be greater than the profitability rectangle P_oAJAC_o under the limit price strategy, the former is likely to be longer-lived if it is a more effective entry-deterring strategy.

There are two reasons why holding excess capacity is likely to be a more effective entry-deterring strategy than a simple limit pricing strategy. First, this strategy reduces the residual demand curve, making it even less likely that an entrant can find a profitable level of output. This can be illustrated by turning again to Figure 3-2. When entry is threatened the established firms will cut prices to the level of MC which means increasing output to Q', the output level at which P = MC. Such behaviour reduces the residual demand curve to ED, reproduced on the left hand side of the diagram as $P'D''$. Second, the price cutting-output increasing threat is *credible* since the firms by investing in costly excess capacity have made a largely irreversible commitment to its use.

Not surprisingly, the excess capacity strategy has generated a good deal of interest in a related topic: predatory pricing. The strategy suggests it is not necessary to drive price below cost in order to deter entry by potential rivals or expansion by established ones. However, as one of the case studies in chapter 5 shows, the combination of excess capacity and price cutting does not necessarily imply predatory pricing. On the contrary, it is just as likely, if not more likely, to reflect an attempt by a firm to minimize its losses in the face of a decline in industry demand or excessive entry into an industry. Alternatively, price cutting by a dominant firm(s) in the face of threatened entry or expansion by fringe rivals could simply reflect the absence of, or more likely the loss of, market power. If the dominant firm's costs are as low or slightly lower than those of their expansionist rivals, the latter may be driven from the market, their entry deterred, or their expansion curbed even if the price-cutting firm does not push price below cost. But if the dominant firm(s) is no longer able to raise prices substantially above costs without incurring entry, the price-cutting behaviour should be viewed as the result of competitive pressures rather than as an example of predation.[35]

35. For an excellent analysis, see F. Fisher, "Diagnosing Monopoly," *Quarterly Review of Economics and Business*, 19, No. 2 (1979), pp. 7-33. For further analysis of predation see chapter 9.

C. Empirical Evidence

The evidence on barriers to entry into Canadian manufacturing industries comes from two studies. Eastman and Stykolt[36] investigated the structure of 16 Canadian manufacturing industries. Table 3-3 lists the 16 industries and the conclusions the authors reached with respect to the height and source of barriers to entry into each. Their findings are reasonably consistent with those of Joe Bain in his classic study of barriers to entry into 20 U.S. manufacturing industries.[37] Economies of scale are a rather pervasive barrier (where barriers exist), and these tend to be of more consequence (greater height) than is indicated by Bain, presumably because of the much smaller size of the Canadian market. Bain found product differentiation to be the most important source of *high* barriers to entry into U.S. manufacturing industries. This is not as clearly indicated in the Canadian study, probably because Eastman and Stykolt did not include, as did Bain, such consumer-oriented industries as automobiles, typewriters, cigarettes, and fountain pens, in which product differentiation is the chief source of high barriers.[38]

The other Canadian study is by Orr. He examined 71 three-digit manufacturing industries using CALURA data for 1963-67. The 71 industries accounted for 80 percent of total manufacturing sales. Using advanced statistical techniques, Orr concluded that capital requirements (a proxy for absolute barriers), advertising intensity (a proxy for product differentiation), and high concentration were strong barriers to entry.[39] The extent of research and development (R & D) by established firms was a moderate barrier. Statistical problems prevented Orr's testing for the importance of scale barriers. However, *a priori*, one would expect that in many a Canadian manufacturing industry, attempting to enter at efficient scale would necessitate a substantial enough market share to suggest that this too is an important barrier—or would be if the Canadian tariff did not protect, and even stimulate, operations at well below efficient size.

36. H. Eastman and S. Stykolt, *The Tariff and Competition in Canada* (Toronto: Macmillan of Canada, 1967).
37. Joe S. Bain, *Barriers to New Competition* (Cambridge: Harvard University Press, 1956).
38. In the early 1970s it was argued, by the U.S. Federal Trade Commission in particular, that product differentiation was the chief source of barriers to entry into the tightly oligopolistic breakfast cereals industry. Apparently, the established firms were able to deter firm entry by product proliferation (introduction of new brands) in the face of changing consumer tastes: the "Big Three" cereal producers accounted for about 70 brands of cereal in 1972. See R. Schmalensee, "Entry Deterrence in the Ready-to-Eat Breakfast Cereal Industry," *The Bell Journal of Economics* (Autumn 1978), pp. 305-327.
39. Dale Orr, "The Determinants of Entry: A Study of the Canadian Manufacturing Industries," *Review of Economics and Statistics* (Feb. 1974), pp. 58-66. When Orr divided industries into "high barrier" and "low barrier" groups he found, as predicted, that entry rates were lower into the former than into the latter.

Table 3-3

Barriers to Entry into 16 Canadian Manufacturing Industries, Circa 1959

Industry	Year	Height of Barrier	Source of Barrier
Fruit canning	1958	Low	—
Vegetable canning	1958	Low to moderate	Product differentiation
Cement	1957	Low	—
Container board	1960	High	Economies of scale; difficulties of finding independent buyers for the output of mills of minimum efficient scale
Shipping containers	1958	Low	—
Synthetic detergent (solid)	1959	Very high	Product differentiation, economies of scale
Synthetic detergent (liquid)	1959	Low to moderate	Product differentiation
Electric refrigerators	1960	High for new non-established firms	Economies of scale; product differentiation, capital costs, technical knowledge
Electric ranges	1960	As above	As above
Wringer washing machines	1960	Moderate to high	Economies of scale, product differentiation
Newsprint	1958	Moderate	Capital requirements
Meatpacking (beef)	1959	Low	—
Meatpacking (pork)	1959	Low to moderate	Economies of scale
Petroleum refining	1956	Moderate to high	Economies of scale, capital requirements
Primary steel	1955	High	Economies of scale, capital requirements
Rubber tires	1959	High	Product differentiation, economies of scale

Source: Eastman and Stykolt, op. cit., various pages.

Entry into an industry may be by a newly-established firm (entry *de novo*) or by an already-established (*going*) firm which has decided to diversify its activities. The increasing diversification of large firms has, presumptively, reduced the role of entry *de novo*. Entry via diversification may also have some advantages in overcoming barriers to entry—the already established firm is able to draw on its funds from other activities, its experience, and any goodwill associated with its name. But the diversified firm may also create barriers to entry of its own. The diversified firm, capable of subsidizing losses in one industry from profits in other lines, is in a much better position to carry out a price-cutting strategy than is the single-product firm. One conjectures that such behaviour will tend to hinder entry by new firms (entry *de novo*), i.e. firms entering industrial activity for the first time. Thus one U.S. study finds evidence that diversification has on the one hand introduced competition in the form of "conglomerate entry" into concentrated industries (thereby tending to reduce concentration or disturb industrial "harmony") while on the other hand it has tended to protect the market position of leading firms from entry by other than established large firms.[40] Another study provided evidence that the consolidated balance sheets of diversified firms increased the difficulty of determining profitability in specific product lines.[41] Since profitability is the spur to entry, and entry is the ultimate means of keeping an industry "competitively honest," the resultant information loss may have important implications for industrial structure and performance if it, in fact, increases entry barriers.

The existence of barriers to entry, and barriers to exit, does not mean that entry and exit of firms into and from Canadian industries is an infrequent phenomenon. In fact, two recent studies indicate that there is a surprisingly high rate of both "births" and 'deaths" of plants and firms in Canada's industrial sector. One study of openings and closings in the manufacturing and mining sectors indicated that about a quarter of all plants (and firms too, since most firms have only a single plant) in existence in 1970, had disappeared by 1976. However, an approximately equal number were born during the same period, with the result that there was only a small decline in total numbers.[42]

A recent study of entry and exit into Canada's manufacturing sector during the decade of the 1970s provides additional evidence of the capitalist dynamic, in which winners and losers appear on and leave the economic stage in rapid succession.[43] From 1970 to 1979 new entries, via plant creation or acquisition, equalled 33 percent of the number of firms in existence in 1970. (See Table 3-4.) Firm exits, via plant scrapping and plant divestiture, equalled 43 percent.[44] As a result, the average numbers of firms in the 141 four-digit industries that

40. Charles Berry, "Corporate Diversification and Market Structure," *Bell Journal of Economics and Management Science* (Spring 1974), pp. 196-204.
41. Stephen Rhoades, "The Effect of Diversification on Industry Profit Performance in 241 Manufacturing Industries: 1963," *Review of Economics and Statistics* (May 1973), pp. 146-155.
42. Statistics Canada, *Mergers, Plant Openings and Closings of Large Transnational Firms and Other Enterprises*, Cat. 75-507 occ., Table I, p. 16.
43. J.R. Baldwin and P. Gorecki with J. McVey and J. Crysdale, "Entry and Exit to the Canadian Manufacturing Sector: 1970-1979," Economic Council of Canada, Discussion Paper 225, Ottawa Feb. 1983, Tables 3 and 4.
44. Plant creation and plant scrappings outweigh plant acquisition and plant divestitures by approximately 5 to 1.

Table 3-4

Average Number and Percentage Distribution of Firms and Establishments Entering and Exiting 141 Canadian Manufacturing Industries: 1970-1979

| | Number | | | | Percent Distribution | | | |
| | Firms | | Establishments | | Firms | | Establishments | |
Category	1970	1979	1970	1979	1970	1979	1970	1979
All Firms	88.1	74.6	105.3	93.3	100.0	100.0	100.0	100.0
Entrants[a]		24.6		28.2		32.5		29.9
Exits[b]	38.3		42.3		42.9		39.7	
Continuing firms[c]	50.3		63.5	65.4	57.1	67.4	60.3	70.1

[a]The number of firms (establishments) that entered between 1970 and 1979 by births and/or acquisitions.
[b]The number of firms (establishments) that exited between 1970 and 1979 by divestiture or scrapping.
[c]The number of firms (establishments) that existed in both 1970 and 1979.
Source: J. Baldwin and P. Gorecki, "Entry and Exit to the Canadian Manufacturing Sector: 1970-1979," Discussion Paper No. 225, Economic Council of Canada, Ottawa, Feb. 1983, Tables 3 and 4.

comprised the study fell from 88 to 75 between 1970 and 1979. On average, both entering and exiting firms were about half the size, whether measured in terms of shipments or employers, of continuing firms. An interesting finding is that declining birth rates rather than increasing death rates of firms characterized industries experiencing slow growth or contraction during the decade—thereby easing the difficulty of adjustment to continuing rapid economic change.[45]

Before leaving barriers to entry it is important to make reference to what appears to be an increasingly important source of entry barrier in Canada. Government restrictions and regulations appear to be an increasingly important factor in the entry picture, particularly outside the manufacturing sector. Degree requirements, certificates, licenses, etc. effectively exclude many potential entrants from professions and trades. Quotas limit entry into dairying, egg and poultry production, unless purchased at their capitalized value. More on this in chapter 12. Long-term electricity sales contracts by government-owned hydroelectric corporations have given established firms a substantial

---

45. On the implications of entry and exit experience for industrial adjustment, see Economic Council of Canada, *The Bottom Line* (Supply and Services Canada, 1983), pp. 115-122.

advantage over new entrants in a period of escalating energy prices.[46] Moreover, government purchase policies have a potential for favouring the established over the potential entrant, the large over the small. Even in its labour legislation government may be unintentionally raising barriers to entry to the unemployed, new labour market entrants, and the young. To the extent that the legislation has enhanced union powers to raise (real) wages, employment may be affected to some extent, and this will be the more so in periods when real output grows more slowly than the labour force. To some extent these observations are conjectural; however it would be an error to limit the barriers discussion to the "classic" types usually applicable to manufacturing industries when these may only be the "tip of the iceberg."

Product Differentiation

In economic theory one of the factors differentiating one market structure from another is product homogeneity or heterogeneity. When buyers can and do distinguish between the outputs of different sellers, each seller is said to have some control over the demand for his product. The source of the distinction between sellers may be location, brand name, quality of good or service, fashion, or individual idiosyncrasy. This differentiation of sellers, and thereby products, is termed product differentiation. Differentiation may be real or imagined, the latter in part due to persuasive advertising. The existence of product differentiation is presumably reflected in part, at least, in the slope of the seller's demand curve. The steepness of the slope, of course, indicates the degree to which the seller can raise prices without losing all of his customers. This ability reflects the seller's market power—i.e., his ability to raise price above MC, and profit (rather than lose) thereby. Thus product differentiation is not only a facet of market structure, it is also a reflection of the potential exercise of some degree of market power.

While most industrial organization economists include product differentiation among their list of structural variables, their treatment of this variable is more eclectic, for product differentiation not only defines one characteristic of a market condition but also connotes a form of non-price strategy. For example, where the benefits (additional revenue) exceed the advertising costs profit-maximizing firms have an incentive to attempt to differentiate their product in the minds of consumers. Alternatively, a given firm may find it profitable to

---

46. The province of Quebec has used its low cost hydroelectric power to attract investment in the highly electricity-intensive aluminum industry. An example of an absolute cost advantage is the cost of electricity to Alcan from its own hydroelectric generating capacity which is estimated to be about a third of what Hydro Quebec charges to other aluminum firms and one-ninth the cost of electricity to U.S. aluminum firms operating in the State of Washington.

cater to diverse tastes by increasing the number of similar, but slightly differentiated products it markets. Cereals, beer, and cigarettes come to mind, with the leading firms each marketing several brands. In fact, product proliferation may be profitable chiefly because it deters other firms from introducing a new brand and further subdividing industry profits.[47] Moreover, the inducement to engage in non-price behaviour such as product differentiation is heightened by the desire of highly interdependent members of an oligopoly to avoid price competition which could descend into price warfare. In any event, marketing strategies are now such an important part of the operation of most firms, and differentiating the product via advertising such an important part of marketing, that one can scarcely ignore product differentiation as a strategic behavioural variable.

It may, however, be useful to distinguish between real (intrinsic) differences between competing products (product differences) and attempts by firms to differentiate their own from their competitors' product (product differentiation). The former describes a facet of market structure while the latter emphasizes behaviour. The former raises questions about the proper definition of the product market, while the latter throws some doubt on the economic theorists' almost total emphasis on price behaviour. Moreover the two suggest different reactions so far as market performance is concerned. Given that tastes vary dramatically among people, real (intrinsic) differences are not only desirable but a basic indicator of good market performance. In servicing real (intrinsic) differences in tastes, advertising may be a relatively efficient means of disseminating information which is otherwise costly to acquire. This is particularly likely to apply in atomistic or otherwise "competitive" industries in which there is imperfect information about the goods and services a firm produces. On the other hand, to the extent that resources are used up to create imagined differences through advertising, there is some basis for arguing that there is some "waste," and, if so, something less than desirable or efficient market performance. Advertising is likely to exceed socially beneficial levels where oligopolistic rivalry is almost solely of a non-price sort. It has been estimated, for example, that as much as 50 percent of advertising expenditures are made primarily for persuasive purposes.[48]

47. See F.M. Scherer, "The Welfare Economics of Product Variety: An Application to the Ready-to-Eat Cereal Industry," *Journal of Industrial Economics* (Dec. 1979), pp. 113-134; R. Schmalensee, supra note 22.

48. F.M. Scherer, *Industrial Market Structure and Economic Performance* (Rand McNally, 1970), p. 326. For a good discussion of the economics of advertising, see Peter Doyle, "Economic Aspects of Advertising: A Survey," *Economic Journal* (Sept. 1968). For a survey of the impact of advertising on competition, see W. Comanor and T.A. Wilson, "The Effects of Advertising on Competition," *Journal of Economic Literature* (June 1979). A crucial but unresolved issue is the effect of advertising on the cross elasticity of demand.

Thus product differentiation impinges on all three of the basic parts of industrial organization analysis: structure, conduct or behaviour, and performance. It is therefore an important variable and yet one not easily dealt with. This is particularly so where empirical work is concerned. There is some evidence in support of the proposition that advertising intensity is both a barrier to entry by new (in contrast to going) firms and a factor in explaining exceptional profitability. However its relation to industry concentration is not clear. If product differentiation or advertising actually raise entry barriers, they could increase concentration. However, if product differentiation allows firms to survive at less than MES_p, it enlarges the potential number of sellers and may reduce concentration. But the direction of causation may be reversed. Presumably concentrated industries (oligopolists) prefer nonprice to price competition, suggesting that the line of causation runs from concentration to advertising.[49] Moreover, a monopolist or oligopolist may engage in socially excessive levels of advertising or product differentiation in an attempt to deter entry.[50] However, advertising is undoubtedly a competitive weapon and one which can just as easily erode as it can cement established market shares. Not surprisingly, then, it is often the case that the industries with the highest ratios of advertising to sales (a measure of advertising intensity) are moderately concentrated ones— those in which oligopolistic rivalry is likely to be quite intense.

A useful distinction in discussions of product differentiation is between producer goods and consumer goods.[51] Presumably the former are not only less

49. A recent study using matched industries from Canada and the U.S. to control for inter-industry differences in consumer behaviour, found that relative levels of advertising intensity could be substantially explained by relative levels of concentration and effective tariff protection. Michael Porter, "Comparative Advertising Behaviour in Canada and the United States," in R.E. Caves, et al., op. cit. pp. 66-70.

50. Scherer, supra note 46. A. Dixit and V. Norman, "Advertising and Welfare," *Bell Journal of Economics* (Spring 1978), pp. 1-17, show that even a pure monopolist (entry blockaded) may push advertising beyond socially desirable levels. Among other things the Dixit-Norman result depends on their view that advertising affects consumer tastes by increasing the marginal utility of the advertised goods, thereby shifting their demand curve to the right. For an alternative view of the role of advertising, one in which advertising affects the consumer's perception of the quality of goods by supplying information about product attributes, see Y. Kotowitz and F. Mathewson, "Advertising, Consumer Information, and Product Quality," *Bell Journal of Economics* (Autumn 1979), pp. 566-588.

51. Another useful distinction breaks down consumer goods into convenience and non-convenience goods. Convenience goods are sold through outlets providing little or no sales assistance and located close to the buyer. Obvious examples are cigarettes, beer, food and gasoline. Non-convenience goods involve relatively large, infrequent, postponable purchases, for which buyers "shop around" in selectively located outlets which provide substantial sales assistance. Obvious examples are furniture, appliances, and automobiles. Manufacturers of convenience goods usually attempt to differentiate their products through a strong brand image, while manufacturers of non-convenience goods must rely more heavily on the sales efforts of dealers and retailers. Clearly the role of advertising will differ in these two cases. See Michael Porter, *Interbrand Choice, Strategy and Bilateral Market Power*, (Cambridge: Harvard University

susceptible to differentiation than the latter, but producer-purchasers are more likely to be able to determine intrinsic vs. surface differences than are consumer-purchasers. This would, *ceteris paribus*, make it easier for the new or small established firm to challenge the leading firms in producer goods industries than in consumer goods industries. But the opposite may also be true, particularly in Canada. Product differentiation conveys "distinctiveness" which may make it easier for firms to cross borders and invade foreign territory. Thus, numerous U.S. consumer goods manufacturing firms have, with the aid of product differentiation, established Canadian subsidiaries, producing a so-called "miniature replica" effect. Examples are the automobile, tire, and consumer durables industries where similar numbers of leading firms flourish in a market one-tenth the size of the U.S. market.

Market Size and Growth

Undoubtedly one of the most important factors influencing manufacturing industry structure in Canada, including the degree of scale efficiency, is the small size of the Canadian market. With a population of 25 million persons Canadian consumption of most goods is about one third to one half the levels of the leading European nations and less than one tenth that of the Common Market and of the United States. Moreover, the population of Canada is spread over a huge area, suggesting that transportation costs further limit the number of firms servicing any particular customer. For these reasons some persons have advocated some form of economic integration with the United States—the most important step being substantial reductions in tariff barriers between the two countries.[52] Such a step is seen as a most important, if rather jarring, means of improving efficiency in Canadian industry and in reducing market concentration, if the latter is measured on a North American, rather than an American, basis.

Here, however, we are not interested in belabouring the free trade argument. Rather the issue is the way in which givens inevitably influence the variables—in this case market structure variables. Behind the tariff wall we are a numerically small but geographically very extensive nation. These are the givens that ultimately give Canadian market structure its distinctive flavour. No industrial policy short of abandoning tariffs is likely to radically change the relatively concentrated flavour of most Canadian manufacturing industries. True, a number of economists, particularly in the United States, have found the *rate of*

Press, 1976). Porter has applied his model to the Canadian scene in "The Comparative Structure of Retailing in Canada and the United States," in R.E. Caves, et al, op. cit., Chap.2.
52. Economic Council of Canada, *Looking Outwards* (Ottawa: Information Canada, 1975).

growth of an industry an important factor in determining levels of (or changes in) industry concentration. It is unlikely, however, that growth rates for Canadian manufacturing output will ever be great enough to offset other factors which tend to naturally stimulate growth in leading firm size. Thus an industrial growth policy is not by itself likely to affect the general nature of market structures in Canadian manufacturing industries. However, if export markets opened up to Canadian manufacturing firms growth could be sufficiently rapid to alter the structure of some domestic markets. But this requires increased efficiency and a reduction in foreign tariffs. Both are likely to wait upon a reduction in the Canadian tariffs.

An Alternative Paradigm

To this point in the chapter we have focused on elements of market structure, analyzing how these elements may influence other structural variables such as the industry concentration ratio. Thus, for example, we have seen how economies of scale or barriers to entry may influence the observed size distribution of firms. In addition, we have noted that certain types of behaviour employed by established firms, such as product differentiation or entry-deterring strategies, may influence market structure. Thus our analysis has enriched the standard industrial organization paradigm ($S \rightarrow C \rightarrow P$), by including feedbacks from conduct to structure (i.e., from $C \rightarrow S$). In the final section of this chapter we turn to an issue briefly raised at the beginning of chapter 2: the impact that superior firm performance, due to lower costs or a better product, may have on industry structure. Thus we will consider whether observed market structures might be at least partly a response to individual firm performance, in addition to the influence of structural or strategic conduct variables.

In chapter 2 we briefly alluded to a tug of war among industrial organization economists over the primacy and relevance of two basic paradigms: the standard one in which the main direction of "flow" is from $S \rightarrow C \rightarrow P$, and an "alternative" one, sometimes identified with economists at the University of Chicago and the University of California at Los Angeles (UCLA), in which the flow is from conduct and performance to structure, or more formally: $C \rightarrow P_F \rightarrow S$.[53] Essentially, the alternative paradigm maintains that differences in the ability of entrepreneurs or managers to conduct the affairs of a firm produce differences in *firm* performance. In turn, differences in firm performance produce a skewed distribution of firm sizes, with the "superior" firms naturally grabbing off the lion's share of the market.

The "alternative" I-O paradigm has several characteristics which distinguish

---

53. P_F stands for firm performance, as opposed to P, average industry performance.

it from the standard one on which the organization of this book is based. Not only is the size distribution of firms (summed up in the concentration ratio) made endogenous to performance of "superior" firms, but the role and importance given to other structural variables is different too. For example, the alternative paradigm plays down the importance of barriers to entry, strategic or otherwise. Any firm capable of "superior" performance will find it relatively easy to enter a particular market. One reason why barriers to entry faced by "superior" firms are viewed as minimal is that although scale economies may extend out to the very largest firms, *non-scale* differences in costs may dominate scale differences.[54] These non-scale differences in costs arise from interfirm differences in managing resources and monitoring team production. In effect, the scale (LRAC) curve is only a set of options in the *technological* sense. Cost minimization is not simply a result of choosing the correct factor proportions, given input prices and technology. There is a fourth factor of production, entrepreneurship, which consists in the "science," or better the "art," of getting the most out of resources whose productivities are *interdependent*, as is the case with all teams.[55] Thus smaller, "better managed" firms can survive alongside larger, more *technologically* efficient (in the scale economies sense) ones.

The "alternative" paradigm also views product differentiation and advertising in a wholly benign manner. First, product differentiation is viewed as an important means of being or becoming "superior," and advertising as the prime means of making this superiority known. Differentiated products which do not satisfy consumer wants, or are no better than other, lower-priced alternatives, will quickly vanish, and so will the firm that produces them if it doesn't come up with a product(s) that consumers do want. Thus product differentiation, far from being viewed as a barrier to entry, is a means by which a firm can successfully enter new markets, and advertising is the informational lubricant that facilitates new entry.[56] This view gives little credence to strategic entry deterrence via product proliferation or price cutting. The firm with a "superior" product or "superior" abilities in producing a product can't be beat out or undercut.

Thus the "alternative" paradigm, by playing down the importance of barriers to entry and making the size distribution of firms (concentration) endogenous to

54. This appears to be the view of John S. McGee, "Efficiency and Economics of Size," in H. Goldschmid, et al, eds., *Industrial Concentration: The New Learning* (Boston: Little, Brown, 1974), pp. 55-97.

55. The ability to effectively monitor team production and its role in the theory of the firm and, by extension, industrial organization is highlighted in A. Alchian and H. Demsetz, "Production, Information Costs and Economic Organization," *American Economic Review*, 62 (December 1972), pp. 777-795.

56. See for example Y. Brozen, "Entry Barriers, Advertising and Product Differentiation" in H. Goldschmid, et al., op. cit. pp. 114-137.

firm conduct and performance, leads to a very different set of predictions than the standard one. First, and of most importance, is its rejection of the view that performance can be predicted from knowledge of industry structure. If anything, it is the reverse that is regarded as true—although the real world is probably too complicated to make any simple relationship between the elements of structure and performance credible. Second, the alternative paradigm, by arguing that there are few or no barriers to entry (except those created by government) to efficient or "superior" firms, implies that the number of firms in an industry tells us little or nothing about the existence of market power. If market power consists in the ability to set price above cost, and keep it there, then this power will be infrequently found because of the asserted ease of entry into most markets. In other words, even one firm in a market will be forced to price competitively in the long run, if there are no significant barriers to entry.[57] To the observation that some firms do appear to persistently earn economic (pure) profit, the alternative paradigm answers that what actually may be observed are rents owing to superior capabilities, not excess profits flowing from the exercise of monopoly power.

For the student, it is probably very confusing to be presented with two apparently convincing, but seemingly opposed, paradigms. Which is the correct or better one? How does one choose? The economist's traditional answer is that we should choose the one which is more consistent with the evidence or predicts better. Unfortunately, attempts to test the paradigms in a way which would logically lead to acceptance of one and rejection of the other encounter difficulties, are few in number, and to date, are quite unconvincing. Moreover, casual empiricism, a powerful and pervasive tool in economics, provides numerous examples in support of one or the other of the two paradigms. In specified situations, each paradigm seems reasonable and is supported by some evidence. This suggest the desirability of a synthesis of the two paradigms. One possible synthesis is sketched here.

The "alternative" paradigm, by emphasizing the endogeneity of market structure to superior capabilities (conduct or performance) as well as to economies of scale, merits an important place in comprehending and explaining the observed size distribution of firms in a given market. Reinforcing the argument of the endogeneity of market structure to superior firm performance is the important role of new products and processes in giving firms a large share of a specific market.[58] In these circumstances large profits of leading firms may

57. Recently this view has received extensive analysis under the rubric of "contestable markets." See William J. Baumol, John C. Panzar, and Robert D. Willig, *Contestable Markets and the Theory of Industry Structure* (New York: Harcourt, Brace Jovanovich Inc., 1982).
58. For a fascinating analysis of how random successes in research and development can lead to highly concentrated markets in relatively short periods of time, see R. Nelson and S. Winter, "Forces Generating and Limiting the Growth of Concentration under Schumpeterian Competition," *Bell Journal of Economics* (Autumn 1978).

really be, in substantial part, rents reflecting a reward to innovation and superiority, rather than profits flowing from the exercise of monopoly power.

The "alternative" paradigm, however, may be too sanguine about the vulnerability of established "superior" firms to entry, or threats of entry, by new firms. Firms who have gained a large share of the market via superiority may well have real advantages over equally cost efficient potential entrants. These advantages may inhere in everything from reputation to large pools of cash which give the established firms more flexibility to respond to challenge by new firms. There is nothing wrong in this. However, their advantageous position may allow established firms to exercise market power. At least, one would expect that if a few firms dominate a market in which they have some advantage over potential entrants their interdependence will be recognized and their behaviour thereby influenced. Then, the standard paradigm comes into play with its theorems about the likelihood of cooperative behaviour (see chapter 5) and its impact on industry performance. In other words, while the alternative paradigm may be as important as, or even dominate, the standard one in explaining the size distribution of firms, the latter paradigm may play an important role in explaining the subsequent behaviour and performance of the leading firms. The synthesis of the two paradigms suggests that we may write $C \rightarrow P_F \rightarrow S \rightarrow C \rightarrow P$. We will return tangentially to the issues raised here when we examine the empirical evidence on market structure-performance relationships in chapter 6.

4

The Tariff, Foreign Ownership, and Canadian Industrial Organization

In chapters 2 and 3 we kept coming back to the tariff—almost as if we were a parrot for a Manchester School laissez-faire, free trade policy. The reasons are not hard to explain. We can hardly ignore the tariff since it is hard to believe that without it, the structure and ownership of Canada's manufacturing sector would be similar to that which presently exists. The same can *not* be said for the United States.

In this chapter we shall pursue the distinctive roles played by the Canadian tariff and foreign ownership and control. We shall try to relate, in somewhat more systematic fashion, such variables as profitability, cost efficiency, concentration, tariff protection, and foreign ownership and control. The relations between these variables are somewhat complex, and no simple model explains all cases. Nevertheless, something can be gained from the effort to more closely establish the lines of causation. At the end of the chapter we will look at a model demonstrating the trade-off between market power and scale economies because it would appear to be particularly applicable to the Canadian case.

The Tariff, Competition and Efficiency

The interactions between scale economies, concentration, and size of market are complicated by the Canadian tariff. There is no doubt that market size is an important factor in determining plant size and concentration levels. In chapter 2 we alluded to evidence suggesting an inverse relation between market size and concentration in Canada although numerous other factors also influence the latter. There is also convincing evidence of a direct relation between market and plant size.[1] The tariff complicates the analysis in several ways: (i) it protects Canadian firms from foreign competition, thereby reducing the competitive constraints on inefficiency, (ii) it induces foreign firms to "leap" the tariff wall through construction or purchase of a Canadian subsidiary, thereby contributing to the creation or maintenance of excessive suboptimal capacity; (iii) it provokes commercial retaliation against Canadian exports, thereby indirectly confining many Canadian firms to the Canadian (domestic) market by limiting their opportunities to export, at least those opportunities not already lost by tariff-induced higher costs of production.

The standard analysis of the impact of the Canadian tariff on the structure of Canada's manufacturing sector is that of Eastman and Stykolt.[2] They emphasize the incentives tariff protection gives to firms to produce limited (by domestic demand) volumes of a wide variety of consumer goods, and to the production inefficiencies that are thereby induced. The analysis tells us much more about the impact of the Canadian tariff on scale efficiencies than on industrial concentration.

Figure 4-1 is a version of the Eastman-Stykolt diagram of oligopoly pricing in a small market behind a tariff wall. Domestic consumer demand (dd) is only a fraction of the potential market available to efficient Canadian sellers. The demand curve facing Canadian firms is composed of three parts: DA, which is the price at which foreigners can sell in Canada after paying tariff duties (and transportation costs); AB is the relevant (to Canadian producers), section of the domestic demand curve, dd; BD' is the world price, at which efficient Canadian firms can sell all that it is profitable for them to produce. The reader should note the similarity between Figure 4-1 and Bain's limit price model.[3] In terms of Bain's model, DA is the highest price that just deters entry (or lowest price which can attract new entrants) in the long run. In Figure 4-1 a price of DA or more will attract imports in rather less time. Note that the curve which is marginal to DABD' is DAFGBD', the "kink" having implications similar to that of the well-known kinked-demand curve analysis in price theory.

Thus the Canadian tariff, protecting a small market adjacent to a very large and productive one (U.S.), substantially *alters* the relevant industry demand curve. It also affects the profit maximizing strategy of Canadian producers in a

1. Gorecki, op. cit., pp. 39-45.
2. Eastman and Stykolt, op. cit., Chap. 2. The following discussion also draws upon that of Harry Bloch, "Prices, Costs and Profits in Canadian Manufacturing: The Influence of Tariffs and Concentration," *Canadian Journal of Economics* (November, 1974).
3. See Chapter 3, pg. 108. The student who is interested in Bain's limit price model may want to read Joe Bain, *Industrial Organization*, 2d ed. (New York: Wiley, 1968), Chap. 8; F.M. Scherer, *Industrial Market Structure and Economic Performance* (Rand-McNally, 1980), Chap. 8.

Figure 4-1

The Tariff, Cost Curves, and Industrial Pricing

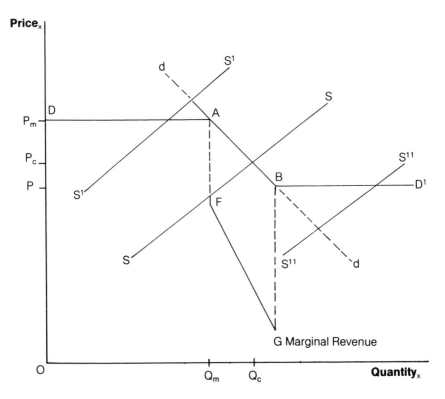

dd =   Domestic (Canadian) consumer demand for output x.
OP =   "World price" — price at which Canadian producers can sell in world market.
OD =   Price at which foreigners are willing to supply Canadian market. It is composed of foreign (or "world") price and transportation costs (assumed to be negligible) and tariff = PD.
DABD[1] =   Market demand curve facing Canadian producers.
SS =   The three curves, SS, S[1]S[1], S[11]S[11] represent three alternative Canadian industry supply curves, indicating three different assumptions about the efficiency of production.
DAFGBD[1] =   Curve which is marginal to demand curve DABD[1].

way which depends on the cost structure of the industry, as well as its market structure (concentrated or unconcentrated). The SS curves are, for given input prices, the industry supply curves, derived by a horizontal summation of the marginal cost curves of the individual firms in the industry. Three cases are considered:

(a) Industry supply curve SS. If the industry is unconcentrated and pricing is competitive, industry output and price are Q_c and P_c respectively. Price P_c does not attract imports. If the industry is concentrated, and firms jointly maximize profits, the profit maximizing output and price are Q_m and P_m, the latter held at a level just below that at which imports (foreign supply) are attracted. The similarity between this and the limit price analysis is close.

(b) Industry supply curve S'S'. Relative to SS, this industry cost curve indicates higher costs and lower efficiency, perhaps due to a higher fraction of suboptimal capacity. In this instance, industry output and selling price will be determined by the intersection of S'S' and DA, whether or not the industry structure is highly concentrated (monopolistic) or unconcentrated (competitive). (DA is, of course, the relevant section of the demand and marginal revenue curves).

(c) Industry supply curve S''S''. Relative to SS, this industry cost curve reflects lower costs and greater efficiency (presumably because most capacity is of MES). The domestic firms in this industry are not only able to meet domestic demand but can also competitively enter the export (world) market. Again the profit maximizing price and output is determined by the intersection of the demand (BD') and supply (S''S'') curves, whether or not the industry is concentrated.[4]

The preceding analysis is interesting, but is perhaps too static. For example, suppose initially the industry supply curve is SS and the industry is sufficiently concentrated to make monopolistic pricing possible. With price and output at P_m and Q_m respectively, the industry will be earning excess profits. If the profitability attracts entrants, then within the small and protected market, more firms (and plants) are competing for a limited domestic demand. This implies, other things being equal, more suboptimal plant capacity or shorter production runs. Both will tend to raise average costs of production and tend to squeeze profits. Thus the observation that tariffs not only protect existing inefficiency (due perhaps to too-small plant size), but also tend to promote further scale inefficiencies.[5]

But this is not all! The new entrants may be foreign firms; thus the allegation that the tariff promotes foreign ownership and control. In fact, there are two reasons to believe that, *ceteris paribus*, foreign entrants have more reason to enter than domestic firms. First, the foreign (U.S.) firm is already established and if it produces consumer goods, probably has a "brand name" (distinctiveness) with which Canadians are familiar. Second, the established foreign firm is

4. This statement must be modified if the industry is highly concentrated, tariff protected, and collusive. Then the leading firms could presumably agree to discriminate in price against domestic consumers. This case is, however, somewhat unrealistic since a high Canadian tariff is likely to be parried by a foreign tariff.

5. Theoretical and empirical support for a major implication of the Eastman-Stykolt analysis is provided in an important recent monograph by R.G. Harris with D. Cox, *Trade, Industrial Policy and Canadian Manufacturing* (Toronto: Ontario Economic Council, 1984). The implication, supported by the evidence, is that the Canadian manufacturing sector would gain, not lose, as a result of tariff reduction-induced improvements in scale efficiency (see below).

simply adding another establishment to its multiplant operations. Where advertising, R & D, central office expertise, and capital attraction costs are important, the foreign multiplant firm will have a cost advantage over a smaller, in most cases single plant, Canadian firm. In other words, if Canadian *plant* capacity is necessarily (due to market demand) suboptimal, then those firms which experience economies of scale at the *firm* level have an advantage over those which do not. This at least is the argument advanced by Eastman and Stykolt to explain observed levels of suboptimal capacity, product differentiation, and foreign ownership and control. Casual observation indicates why the hypothesis has withstood the test of time.

Some economists have questioned the theoretical underpinnings of the Eastman-Stykolt analysis, at least with respect to industries which produce homogeneous or undifferentiated products.[6] Why, so the argument runs, does not one of the suboptimally sized firms grab off the lion's share of the market by building an optimally scaled plant? By doing so the firm will be able to supply the market at substantially reduced costs and lower prices than can its slower moving, higher cost competitors. The answer that is sometimes given is that in oligopolistic industries firms are prevented or hindered from adopting such a strategy by their recognition of mutual interdependence. To some economists this answer lacks credibility, since the firm that moves first will increase its profits relative to those it could earn if each oligopolist were to retain its suboptimal size and jointly maximize much smaller industry profits. However, the first mover argument is not entirely convincing. It takes a good deal of time to build a new, more efficiently scaled plant, while it takes very little time for rivals to react to this threat by cutting prices. Thus prospective first movers do have reason to fear that their strategy may set off a price war with destructive effects on their own as well as industry profitability long before a more efficient plant can be brought into operation.

If products are differentiated or the firm is committed to producing a "full line" of products, the Eastman-Stykolt analysis is more convincing. Richard Caves has persuasively argued that the Eastman-Stykolt model is best appreciated by assuming an import competing differentiated oligopoly. The key here is product differentiation, since "differentiation causes each seller to be confronted with a downward-sloping demand curve." Its downward-sloping demand curve prevents any given seller from adopting a "winner take all" strategy via construction of the largest, most cost-efficient plant. Since many of the industries which best fit the Eastman-Stykolt model are heavily populated by

6. See for example Andrew Muller, "The Eastman-Stykolt Hypothesis Reconsidered," *Canadian Journal of Economics* (November 1982), pp. 757-765.

foreign-owned firms and since product differentiation (broadly defined) is typically the unique asset that assists foreign-owned firms in overcoming the disadvantage of producing in another nation's market (see below), Caves' method of rescuing the Eastman-Stykolt analysis has received a wide degree of acceptance among Canadian economists. Product differentiation is thus viewed as a crucial element in the Eastman-Stykolt model.

Recent studies of plant scale and specialization in Canada provide support for the Eastman-Stykolt hypothesis, particularly the interpretation of it that emphasizes the role of product "packing" or diversity in Canadian plants. One piece of evidence in favour of the Eastman-Stykolt hypothesis is that tariffs increase the prevalence of small plants, especially in consumer goods industries, and that they improve the economic viability of units smaller than MES.[7] Even more impressive evidence is provided in two studies undertaken for the Economic Council of Canada by J.R. Baldwin and P. Gorecki.[8] They found, just as the Eastman-Stykolt model predicts, that it is the *combination* of high tariffs and high concentration which negatively influences plant scale. Neither high tariffs alone nor foreign ownership appeared to separately influence plant scale. Moreover, the same two factors, high tariffs and high concentration, were also found to have an important influence on the degree to which plants specialize their production and the length of their production runs. Baldwin and Gorecki found that in high tariff, high concentration industries production runs are shorter and product diversity greater, for any given size plant, than where these conditions do not obtain. Again, foreign ownership *per se* had no independent impact on either product diversity or length of production run.

The Eastman-Stykolt analysis has an important implication. When in chapter 6 we discuss attempts to link market structure and performance we cannot, *a priori*, exclude the role of tariffs. For as the preceding discussion suggests simple attempts to relate concentration (market structure) and profit rates (performance), may be vitiated if tariffs, in fact, influence costs as well as prices. Theory and evidence indicate that the extent of suboptimal capacity is not a simple function of domestic market size. Behind tariff walls a large number of plants may inefficiently supply the domestic market. There is evidence that the extent of suboptimal capacity, measured by the ratio of actual to efficient plant

7. R.E. Caves, M.E. Porter, A.M. Spense with J.T. Scott (1980) *Competition in the Open Economy: A Model Applied to Canada* (Cambridge, Mass.: Harvard University Press), pp. 66, 376.

8. J.R. Baldwin and P. Gorecki with J. McVey and J. Crysdale (1983), "Trade, Tariffs and Relative Plant Scale in Canadian Manufacturing Industries: 1970-79," Discussion Paper No. 232 (Ottawa: Economic Council of Canada), and (1983) "Trade, Tariffs, Product Diversity and Length of Production Run in Canadian Manufacturing Industries: 1970-79," Discussion Paper No. 247 (Economic Council of Canada).

size, is found to be strongly related to tariff levels in Canada.[9] Thus the interaction between Canadian market structure, behaviour, and performance is more complex than standard textbook treatments, based as they usually are on U.S. circumstances, might suggest. This has policy implications running the gamut from tariff (commercial) policy, to merger policy, and to agreements among firms to specialize in production. To these we return later.

Tariffs, Foreign Ownership and Industrial Organization

We are now in a position to formally analyze the interrelationship between foreign ownership and other industrial organization variables. Clearly, any study of Canada's industrial structure requires that account be taken of the multinational firm. Multinational firms play a major role in many Canadian industries—a fact reflected in the high degree of foreign ownership and control in Canada's manufacturing and mining sectors. In addition, as we saw in chapter 2, multinational firms tend to be larger than their domestic counterparts, often playing the role of industry leaders. What explains the importance of multinational firms in Canada? What role does the Canadian tariff play? Do multinational firms influence the elements of industrial structure such as barriers to entry? What, if anything, does foreign ownership imply for industrial behaviour and market performance?

Until about a decade ago, most economists approached the phenomenon of foreign direct investment and the multinational enterprise within the framework of international economics. Thus foreign direct investment was viewed as a movement of capital (which it is) in response to differences in actual and expected rates of return between the capital-supplying and capital-receiving country. However, international differences in the profitability of specific kinds of investment do not by themselves explain why the investment is "direct" rather than "portfolio." Nor do they explain why differences in profitability

---

9. A study of 13 Canadian manufacturing industries in Canada by Gorecki revealed the following:

Level of Effective Tariff	Number of Industries	Average Value of Ratio of Actual to Efficient Plant Size[c]
High[a]	6	0.48
Low[b]	7	1.12

[a]29 percent or greater (1963)
[b]16 percent or less (1963)
[c]Actual plant size is the average size of the largest plants accounting for 50 percent of industry output. Efficient plant size is measured by the engineering method.
See P.K. Gorecki, op. cit., Table 5-5, p.54.

could not simply be exploited via arms-length trade rather than establishment of a subsidiary, unless factor (input) prices differ between the countries. Thus the international economics approach to understanding foreign direct investment brings trade barriers—particularly tariffs—into the picture. If trade is restricted by tariff, or nontariff, barriers, then capital flows become a substitute for arms-length trade. In effect the foreign firm with something to sell abroad "leaps" the tariff barrier by establishing a subsidiary in the host country. Thus tariffs have long been viewed as a factor in the foreign direct investment picture—particularly in Canada with its historic protectionist policies.

In recent years an increasing number of economists have adopted an alternative approach to explaining the incidence of foreign direct investment. The "modern" approach to the multinational firm starts from the proposition that the multinational firm must have certain advantages to compensate it for the disadvantage of being a "foreigner" in the host country—of having less innate knowledge of the commercial, legal, and cultural aspects of the local environment than does a domestic firm. The proposition of compensating advantages places the study of foreign direct investment within the field of industrial organization, where attention is given to the factors distinguishing one industry or firm from another.[10] What gives a foreign firm an advantage when it directly invests abroad is its ownership of certain unique assets not available to its domestic competitors. The unique assets may include a successfully differentiated product, patented knowledge, technical expertise, and managerial skills. Because of incomplete and imperfect markets for the sales of such "intangibles" as reputation, knowledge and skill, the cost to a firm contemplating an international transferral of these unique assets is generally lower when transfer is made *within* the firm than when the transfer is made through the market by an arms-length sale between firms. Thus firm-specific assets give their owner a degree of market power which it can often most profitably exploit through a foreign subsidiary. This inducement to multinational enterprise is enhanced if tariffs make the international transfer of goods, as opposed to assets, relatively costly.

The industrial organization approach to foreign direct investment brings the study of the multinational firm in close contact with two of the major elements of market structure: product differentiation and barriers to entry. Product differentiation is important because it is the unique asset which is probably most often the basis for the "horizontal" investments in a foreign subsidiary by a

---

10. The originator of this approach was Stephen Hymer in a 1961 Ph.D. dissertation that was not published until 1976: *The International Operation of National Firms: A Study of Direct Investment* (MIT Press, 1976). Also see R.E. Caves, "International Corporations: The Industrial Economics of Foreign Investment," *Economica*, 38 (1971).

multinational firm.[11] Barriers to entry come into the picture because the advantages accruing to a foreign subsidiary may become the basis for a disadvantage incurred by a potential *domestic* entrant into the industry. Thus, some recent empirical research has explored the hypothesis that differential barriers to entry face foreign and domestic firms, tending to reinforce the domination of many industries by foreign firms.

Before proceeding to the empirical evidence on the determinants of foreign investment, it is useful to sketch the hypothesized relationships between foreign ownership and the various industrial organization variables discussed in this and preceding chapters. Figure 4-2 indicates the general direction or flow of hypothesized relationships, with causation running from the variables on the left through foreign ownership in the middle to the variables on the right. In this analysis the left hand variables are treated as relatively exogenous, reflecting technological (economies of scale), political (tariffs) and demographic (market size) factors. In addition, product differentiation, although obviously dependent, in part, on strategic or tactical behaviour of firms, may reflect firm know-how or product-intrinsic qualities which can be taken as exogenous in the context of the foreign ownership relationship.

On the right hand side of Figure 4-2 are some of the hypothesized consequences of having small, tariff-protected markets for differentiated products. These include high concentration ratios, but not as high as they would be in the absence of tariffs; substantial suboptimal capacity; and barriers to entry by domestic firms into tariff-protected industries in which product differentiation and multiplant economies are important. Having a central place in several of the hypothesized relationships between left hand and right hand variables is the multinational firm, reflecting the extensive foreign ownership and control in Canada's manufacturing sector.

Although FDI is given centre stage in Figure 4-2, it is tariffs and product differentiation, the variables crucial to the Eastman-Stykolt model (as interpreted by Caves—see above), which play the major causative roles. High tariffs, by reducing the effective market size in which Canadian firms can sell, contribute to high concentration.[12] However, the tariff, to the extent that it induces FDI into small Canadian markets, tends to reduce concentration. The resultant overcrowding of firms and plants increases the incidence of suboptimal capacity, but this phenomenon should be viewed as the joint impact that product differentiation and tariffs have in inducing foreign subsidiaries to produce a wide diversity of products, each with relatively short production runs.

11. This analysis would not generally apply to "vertical" foreign direct investment, particularly backward integration into the production of raw materials located in another country.
12. In the absence of tariffs, the effective market would, in many instances, be North American, and properly computed, concentration ratios would be much lower.

Figure 4-2

The Industrial Organization Approach to FDI: Hypothesized Relationships

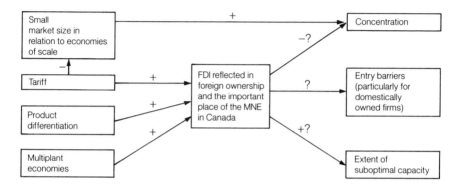

In addition, barriers to entry attributable to plant scale economies are partially mitigated by the protection tariffs give to suboptimal capacity. Thus the entry barriers faced by domestic firms are likely to owe in good part to product differentiation and multiplant economy advantages of foreign firms. In general, the scheme outlined in Figure 4-2 is a slightly modified version of the Eastman-Stykolt framework.

In recent years, a considerable amount of research has gone into testing the Eastman-Stykolt model and related hypotheses. Naturally, much attention has been given to the distinctive roles of product differentiation as a proxy for the unique assets owned by a firm which is considering making direct investments abroad, and to the role of effective tariff protection. Most of the current research takes the form of an analysis of the determinants of the extent of foreign direct investment (as an indicator of foreign ownership and control) in a *cross section* of Canadian manufacturing industries. Thus the empirical estimates provided by these studies purport to tell us which factors do and which factors do not account for differences among industries in the extent of foreign ownership and control.

The major studies to date appear unanimous in finding that product differentiation and other intangible assets are a major factor explaining the industrial distribution of foreign direct investment. The variables used to capture the role of product differentiation (broadly defined) include the relative (to industry sales) importance of advertising, research and development expenditures, and marketing expenditures.[13] These variables appear as statistically significantly

13. See Richard Caves, et al., op. cit., pp. 90-91; Ronald S. Saunders, "The Determinants of

related, at the industry level, to the importance of foreign ownership and control. These findings provide support for the industrial organization approach to explaining foreign direct investment which highlights the role of specific rent-earning assets that a firm may apply to foreign markets.

Somewhat surprisingly, most of these studies did not find tariffs to be an important explanatory variable.[14] That is, the level of tariff protection an industry receives is not clearly correlated with the incidence of foreign owner-ship in that industry. There are a number of possible explanations for this counter-intuitive result (aside from data problems and model specification). One factor is that, in the absence of intangible, rent-earning assets that might be applied by their owner to foreign markets, firms may view investment in a foreign subsidiary as too costly or dangerous to be worthwhile, even though tariffs provide substantial protection to the host country market. Second, as Saunders has noted, the cross section results are not inconsistent with the view that, historically, Canada's high tariffs were an inducement to foreign direct investment. However since 1960, many industries have experienced tariff reductions as a result of multinational negotiations (e.g. Kennedy and Tokyo Rounds), and it is not implausible that governments would be more inclined to reduce tariffs on industries populated by multinationals than by nationals. Finally, if lengthened production runs and intraindustry trade are viewed as increasingly important by firms thinking about investment in a foreign subsidi-ary, the height of the *export barriers* facing firms in the host country will be of major concern to the (foreign) investing firm. Clearly, the firm will prefer lower to higher export tariff barriers, but the actual height of the export tariff barrier is likely to be directly related to the height of import tariff barriers. Thus, the net impact of higher tariffs on FDI depends on whether the (foreign) investing firm is planning to produce only for the local market or, alternatively, is considering mandating its subsidiary to produce for the world market.[15] The cross-section studies referred to made no correction for this factor.

Interactions between foreign direct investment and other industrial organiza-tion variables have also been investigated in the studies referred to above. Caves et al. and Saunders found multiplant economies of scale to be a factor explaining the industrial distribution of FDI, as the Eastman-Stykolt analysis hypothesizes. Caves et al., Baldwin and Gorecki, and Shapiro have found that

Interindustry Variation of Foreign Ownership in Canadian Manufacturing," *Canadian Journal of Economics* (Feb. 1982), pp. 77-84; H. Edward English and Robert F. Owen, *The Role of Marketing in the Concentration and Multinational Control of Manufacturing Industries*, Research Monograph No. 11, Bureau of Competition Policy, Consumer and Corporate Affairs Canada, 1981, pp. 43-51.

14. See Saunders, op. cit.; English and Owen, op. cit.

15. For a discussion of world product mandate see B. Wolf, "World Product Mandating and Canada-United States Free Trade," York University (mimeo).

multinationals are undeterred by traditional entry barriers. An indication that multinationals are a significant source of market entrants is the finding of Caves et al. that concentration in Canadian industries is lower *relative* to their U.S. counterparts where foreign subsidiaries claim a large share of the market.[16] While traditional barriers to entry do deter domestic firms, these studies do not, however, tell us whether the very existence of multinationals in an industry is a deterrent to domestic entry.

Tariffs and Concentration

There is no single Canadian tariff in the sense of a percentage of duty applied to all goods. Tariff protection varies widely among industries both in terms of the legislated rate of duty (indicated by the term "nominal tariff") and the "effective" rate of tariff.[17] In addition, further protection is provided some industries by nontariff barriers (to imports) in the form of quota restriction and subsidies and tax concessions to domestic firms. Given the differentiated tariff structure protecting (in varying degrees) some but not all Canadian industries, can we find any market structure variable which is related to the level of protection? Since the concentration ratio is the most widely used proxy for, and summary statistic of, industrial market structure we examine the relation between tariff levels and concentration levels. Table 4-1 presents the relevant statistics for 1970. Most of the industries in Table 4-1 represent 2-digit industry groups. Thus the concentration (as well as the tariff) figures represent weighted averages of more narrowly defined industries composing each industry group.

16. Caves et al., op. cit., pp. 89-91; 377; John Baldwin and Paul Gorecki, "The Determinants of Entry and Exit to Canadian Manufacturing Industries in the 1970s" (Ottawa: Economic Council of Canada, Discussion Paper No. 225, 1983); Daniel Shapiro, "Entry, Exit and the Theory of the Multinational Corporation," Concordia University mimeo, February 1982.

17. A nominal tariff is the rate of duty on imported commodities listed in a country's tariff schedule. The "effective tariff" is a calculation of total tariff protection accorded an industry, taking account of the difference between tariff rates on purchased inputs and final output. When the tariff rate on purchased inputs differs from that on final output the nominal and effective tariff rates differ. In general, the latter will be greater (less) than the former when the rate of duty on final output is greater (less) than that on purchased inputs. The rate of effective protection (EP) given a firm is numerically equal to the final good duty (FD) minus the intermediate good duty (ID) (both in dollar terms) divided by the value added (VA) by the firm. $\left[EP = \dfrac{FD-ID}{VA} \right]$ Note that the rate of effective protection will be negative if ID > FD. For example, suppose the total cost of production of a commodity is $1.00 of which 50¢ is paid for intermediate goods plus a 10% tariff, or a total of 55¢. Suppose FD is 20% so that selling price of final output is 1.20. Then FD = $.20, ID = $.05, VA = $1.20 − $.55 = $.65. Thus, EP = .15/.65 = 23%.

Table 4-1

Concentration Levels & Tariff and Nontariff Protection Afforded Some Major Goods-producing Sectors of the Canadian Economy, 1970

	Nominal Tariffs[a]	Nontariff Barriers (Expressed as Tariff Equivalents)			Total Tariff and Nontariff Protection	Weighted Average (CR$_4$)	Tariff and Nontariff Protection (1976)[b]
		Quota Restrictions	Subsidies	Tax Concessions			
			(percent)				
All agriculture	2.82		4.18		7.00		6.6
Wheat			27.50		27.50		
Industrial milk			18.20		18.20		
All mining	0.04	4.11	0.61	8.88	13.64		13.7
Metals	0.01		1.28	8.15	9.44		
Mineral fuels	0	7.24	0.29	10.15	17.68		
Other mining (including asbestos, sand, gravel, etc.)	0.48			3.18	3.66		
All manufacturing	9.58	1.62	1.24		12.44		
Tobacco products	24.04				24.04	97	30.7
Food and beverages	10.00	2.53	1.66		14.19	47	14.3
Dairy products	16.92	14.84	9.75		41.51	29	
All textile mill production	16.99	9.74			26.73	59	17.1
Cotton yarn and cloth production	15.48	25.81			41.29	93	
Synthetic textile mill production	19.74	11.38			31.12		
Knitting mills	24.14	1.07			25.21	27	33.2
Clothing	22.01	4.08			26.09	14	32.4

4: The Tariff, Foreign Ownership and Industrial Organization **139**

Industry					
Wood industries	3.80		3.80	28	6.3
Furniture	17.20		17.20	18	15.8
Rubber products	14.88		14.88	53	9.9
Leather products	19.59		19.59	35	16.6
Paper and allied industries	9.12		9.12	38	10.1
Printing, publishing, and allied industries	5.65		5.65	26	5.6
Primary metals	4.13		4.13	75	5.6
Metal fabricating	12.17		12.17	31	8.7
Machinery	6.08		6.08	32	5.0
All transportation equipment	2.79	4.40	7.19	76	6.0
Aircraft and parts	0.02		0.02	72	
Motor vehicle manufacturing	2.95	6.13	9.08	93	
Vehicle parts manufacturing	0.88		0.88	46	
Ship construction	9.44	17.00	26.44	62	
Electrical equipment	13.71		13.71	60	10.4
Nonmetallic mineral products	7.44		7.44	60	7.6
Petroleum and coal products	7.63		7.63	79	2.8
Chemicals and chemical products	9.21		9.21	50	6.2
Miscellaneous manufacturing	11.80		11.80	44	9.1

[a]Nominal tariff rates were obtained by dividing customs duties in 1970 by the value of imports that year. When several items subject to tariff appear as one group—for example, "all agriculture" or "rubber products"—a representative tariff was obtained by weighting each nominal tariff by the item's importance in Canadian production.

[b]Nominal tariffs supplemented by *ad valorem* equivalents of nontariff barriers.

Sources: Economic Council of Canada, *Looking Outward: a New Trade Strategy for Canada* (Ottawa, 1975), p. 17; Statistics Canada, "Industrial Organization," op. cit., Table 2, Harris and Cox, op. cit. Table 19, pp. 112.

A moment's examination of Table 4-1 will confirm that there is no simple relationship between concentration and protection. Should we have expected one? And if so in what direction? If we believed, to begin with, that high concentration is a sign of a small domestic market and the latter a chief source of suboptimal capacity, then we might have hypothesized a direct relationship between protection and concentration. Presumably the rationale would be that tariffs are designed to offset the competitive disadvantage of producing with suboptimal capacity. If, on the other hand, we believed that low concentration was a sign of many inefficiently small firms (and plants), and that high concentration was the result of a few efficient plants (and firms) we might have hypothesized an inverse relation between tariff protection levels and concentration.

As a matter of fact neither conjecture can explain the alignment of protection levels and concentration shown in Table 4-1. Perhaps this is to be expected given the probable feedback from tariff protection to suboptimal capacity discussed in the preceding section. Of course, it is possible that the broad nature of the industry groups in Table 4-1 may hide some real connection between protection and our proxy for market structure, the concentration ratio. However, when statistics for 4-digit industries were examined there was no evident indication that the story told by Table 4-1 is misleading. However, this may not always have been the case. A study by Helleiner found that market concentration was directly related to the level of effective protection in 1961.[18] However, no such relation appeared in 1970. In fact, changes in tariffs between 1961 and 1970 were inversely (and inexplicably) *related* to industry concentration. Helleiner did find that by 1970 the degree to which the industry relied on unskilled labour was "far and away" the most significant explanatory variable in the Canadian tariff structure. . . ." In other words, low-wage, unskilled labour-intensive industries tend to receive the greatest protection. These tend to be the manufacturing industries exhibiting the lowest productivity levels (value added per worker). Thus the concentrated textile and tobacco products industries and the unconcentrated knitting mill, clothing and leather products industries all receive substantial protection. (Note that the rate of protection afforded the knitting and clothing industries rose sharply between 1970 and 1976 as a result of the imposition of quotas on clothing imports.[19]) Each is a relatively labour-intensive, low-wage (except tobacco) industry. In contrast the

18. G.K. Helleiner, "The Political Economy of Canada's Tariff Structure: An Alternative Model," *Canadian Journal of Economics* (May 1977), pp. 318-26.
19. While beneficial to employees in the clothing, knitting and textile industries, the protection afforded the clothing industry is estimated to have raised the annual cost to consumers of clothing purchases, in 1979, by an amount in excess of $100 per household. See G. Jenkins, "Costs and Consequences of the New Protectionism: The Case of Canada's Clothing Sector," *Canada in a Developing World Economy: Trade or Protection* (Oxford University Press, 1981).

relatively unconcentrated paper and machinery industries and the concentrated transportation equipment and primary metals industries receive relatively little protection, pay relatively high wages, and have relatively high productivity levels so far as Canadian manufacturing is concerned.[20]

Industrial Rationalization

Our account of inefficient scale and the consequent productivity differential between most Canadian and U.S. manufacturing industries suggests important gains to consumers if our industry structure were "rationalized." By rationalization we mean the efficient utilization of industrial capacity through specialization and consolidation of capacity and the idling of the most inefficient plants. Rationalization can be achieved through tariff reduction, specialization agreements, or mergers which result in the closing of inefficiently small plants and /or a rearrangement of production schedules among plants in order to achieve longer production runs in each. The advantage of tariff reduction is that it not only stimulates efficient production but in contrast to specialization agreements and mergers reduces the market power of the remaining firms. The drawback to tariff reduction is its supposed implications for employment. It is the employment dimension that makes rationalization via substantial tariff reduction so politically difficult to achieve. Nevertheless, an argument can be made that lowering tariffs would change the composition, not the level, of output and employment. In its pro- "free trade" report *Looking Outward: A New Trade Strategy for Canada,* the Economic Council of Canada states that: "The evidence of intra-industry specialization as the general response to free trade implies not a termination of operations, but a reorganization of production in subsidiaries, at least within certain limits of changing factor costs."

Several Canadian studies indicate that tariff reductions would lead to greater intra-industry specialization, longer production runs, reduced costs and a greater ability to compete in foreign markets. George Lermer studied the

20. Professor Caves has gone one step further and has attempted to test alternative hypotheses explaining the actual pattern of tariff protection of Canadian secondary manufacturing industries. Caves tested three models of political choice and found an interest group model to perform best. Briefly, the demand for tariff protection is directly related to the potential benefits (rents) generated by tariff protection. The supply (by Parliament) of tariff protection is directly related to an industry's exposure to economic adversity. The former but not the latter is likely to be directly related to industry concentration. The latter is likely to generate sufficient claims for equity where there are large numbers of low-skilled, low-wage workers. Richard E. Caves, "Economic Models of Political Choice: Canada's Tariff Structure," *Canadian Journal of Economics,* 9 (May 1976), pp. 278-300. But for some doubts see R. Saunders, "The Political Economy of Effective Tariff Protection in Canada's Manufacturing Sector," *Canadian Journal of Economics,* 13, No. 2 (May 1980), pp. 340-348.

impact on Canadian manufacturing industries of the tariff reductions agreed to by the Canadian government as a result of its participation in the 1963 "Kennedy Round" of tariff negotiations under the auspices of the General Agreement on Trade and Tariffs (GATT). He found that the industries affected by the tariff reductions, many of them in the two-digit machinery group, responded by specializing in the production of fewer products and exporting more of what they produced. There were increased imports of those goods Canadian manufacturers no longer produced. Thus tariff reductions appeared to stimulate greater specialization and increased trade.[21]

Even more dramatic results turn up in a simulation analysis carried out by Richard Harris and David Cox. Using data for 1976 they estimate that removing domestic tariffs on manufactured goods would substantially raise (a) real GNP (by 3.5 to 9 percent); (b) the output of most manufacturing industries; (c) manufacturing productivity (by 10 to 30 percent); (d) manufacturing wages (by 10 to 25 percent); (e) trade volume (by 50-80 percent); and thus (naturally) (f) economic welfare.[22] This amazing combination of desirable results for Canada is attributable to the nature of the cost functions employed in the general equilibrium model employed by Cox and Harris. Like Eastman and Stykolt and others, Harris and Cox assume that unit costs of production are sensitive to plant scale and specialization. Thus the model estimates that if domestic tariffs were removed competitive pressures would stimulate dramatic increases in production runs of those goods for which Canadian manufacturers choose to specialize. As a result, costs would fall sufficiently to allow Canadian firms to competitively penetrate many foreign markets.

A recent study by Baldwin and Gorecki finds that, on the average, plant product diversity declined and the average length of production runs increased during the 1970s.[23] Moreover they found, as the Eastman and Stykolt model predicts, that a combination of high tariffs and high concentration tend, for any given size plant, to be associated with a larger number of products and shorter production runs. Baldwin and Gorecki estimate that tariff reductions in the 1970s contributed to lengthened production runs and they conjecture that the

21. George Lermer, "Evidence from Trade Data Regarding the Rationalizing of Canadian Industry," *Canadian Journal of Economics*, 6 (May 1973), pp. 248-56.
22. Richard Harris with David Cox supra note 5. The gains in welfare, real GNP, manufacturing wages, and trade volume, are sensitive to whether the tariff reductions were unilateral or multilateral, with Canada gaining more if our trading partners simultaneously remove their tariff barriers against our goods. These findings provide clear support for the argument made by the Wonnacotts two decades ago. R.J. Wonnacott and P. Wonnacott, *Free Trade Between the United States and Canada: The Potential Economic Effects* (Cambridge, Mass: Harvard University Press, 1967).
23. J.R. Baldwin and P. Gorecki, "Trade, Tariffs, Product Diversity and Length of Production Run in Canadian Manufacturing Industries: 1970-79," Economic Council of Canada, Discussion Paper No. 247.

same will be true as the "Tokyo Round" tariff reductions, negotiated in the mid 1970s, are implemented in the 1980s.

Finally, Canadian manufacturing as a whole does not appear to have suffered as a result of a one-third decline in both nominal and effective tariff rates between 1966 and 1978. During the same period the percentage of manufacturing imports not subject to tariffs rose from 35 to 46 percent. However, a study by the Economic Council of Canada could find no indication that these substantial tariff reductions had produced manufacturing decline or "deindustrialization."[24] Rather, the evidence indicates that the increased interdependence between Canada and other manufacturing economies, induced in part by the tariff reductions, is leading to greater specialization within the manufacturing sector. Both import penetration and export penetration increased markedly. During the 1970s much of the increase in exports and imports occurred within the same industries, reflecting a tremendous growth in intra-industry trade. To the extent that tariff reduction had any observable impact on the manufacturing sector it was a slight reduction in the share of end products (clothing, radios, automobiles, etc.) relative to fabricated materials (steel, aluminum, etc.). The trend toward greater specialization is expected to continue during the 1980s as tariffs again decline by one-third, due to the implementation of the Tokyo Round tariff-reduction agreements.[25]

The argument that tariff reduction will stimulate greater intra-industry specialization and trade seems reasonable, but it is difficult to overcome the emotional reaction related to the inevitable loss of jobs in some locales, even though new jobs may open up elsewhere. In a country as large as Canada, transfer to new jobs can mean a move of thousands of miles, a change of culture, and the abandonment of relatives. Since many assets have limited portability and transferability (e.g. homes in single industry towns, private pension plans, seniority, tenure, spouse's job, pleasant surroundings and local reputation and friendships) those persons forced to move as a result of industrial rationalization may naturally view themselves as losers and fight to prevent the expected loss in wealth. The persons most affected are likely to be lower middle income non-professionals whose wealth is largely of the sort described and who stand to gain little or nothing from an occupational or locational change.[26] While the

24. Economic Council of Canada, *The Bottom Line* (Supply and Services Canada, 1983), pp. 101-102, 112. The weighted average of the nominal and effective tariffs in 167 four-digit manufacturing industries, in 1966, was 11.9 and 16.4 percent respectively. In 1978, average nominal and effective tariff rates were 7.8 and 11.7 percent respectively. However, effective protection has not declined as significantly because of increasing nontariff barriers. See Fred Lazar *The New Protectionism: Non Tariff Barriers and Their Effects on Canada* (Ottawa: Canadian Institute for Economic Policy, 1981).
25. The tariffs erected by our main trading partners are expected to decline by about 25 percent during the same period.
26. See C. Green, *Industrial Policy: The Fixities Hypothesis* (Toronto: Ontario Economic Council,

professionally-oriented are typically quite mobile, professional considerations are generally unimportant where factory workers are concerned. In short, there are high political and social barriers to rationalization via tariff reduction even though the great majority of persons, in their roles as consumers, would undoubtedly gain.

An alternative to tariff reduction is rationalization via merger of firms, with a consequent specialization in the use of the new or remaining firm's plant capacity. That is, a horizontal merger of multi-product firms may permit each plant to produce fewer products and thereby reduce unit costs by lengthened production runs. An example was the mid-1970s merger of the appliance divisions of GSW Ltd. and Canadian General Electric (CGE) and the purchase of the assets of Westinghouse Canada. The acquisitions gave the renamed firm, CAMCO, an estimated 36 percent of the Canadian appliance market. The creation of CAMCO transformed the major appliance industry in Canada from a stable oligopoly with six leading firms, each having market shares of 12 to 16 percent, into one with a dominant firm and two other viable firms, Inglis and White Consolidated industries. Since 1977, CAMCO has struggled to maintain its market share, while Inglis under much competitive pressure, and aided by its acquisition of Admiral in 1982, for which it received federal financial assistance, has substantially increased its market share.

In 1976 The Minister of Trade and Commerce gave strong backing to the CAMCO merger both on the grounds that it increased Canadian ownership and control, and that it would allow greater efficiency through specialization of production in each of GSW's plants. To gain approval the merger had to provide certain guarantees with regard to employment, at least in the short run.[27] In the event, internal disagreements between the management of GSW and CGE who ran CAMCO led, in 1983, to a purchase of a majority of CAMCO's shares by foreign-owned CGE.

More or less the same degree of rationalization can be achieved, at least in principle, by way of "specialization agreements." These involve agreements among competing firms, each producing a line of products, that each will specialize in one or a few items, thereby attaining longer production runs. The implicit cost of such a policy is the competition which is lost. The potential reduction in competition explains why specialization agreements are currently illegal under the Combines Act, at least where they would "unduly lessen competition." Recently proposed amendments to the Combines Act would make specialization agreements legal so long as some control were exercised

---

1984). The fact that there are some losers is no reason to give up the large gains from rationalization, but some form of compensation may be required.
27. *Montreal Star*, November 11, 1976.

over the parties to the agreement, in order to ensure that consumers as well as producers receive some of the benefits.

Reference to efficiency-increasing mergers is a reminder of the more general issue of the potential trade-off between efficiency and market power that mergers may create. In a classic paper, Williamson[28] developed the argument that mergers posed a trade-off between higher prices and profits on the one hand and lower costs through greater scale-efficiency on the other. Williamson's paper was directed at a controversy over whether economies of scale are a legitimate defence to a merger which would otherwise lessen competition sufficiently to run afoul of the merger provisions of the U.S. Antitrust Laws. Williamson showed the conditions under which scale efficiencies would be legitimate *economic* defence to market power creating mergers. For students of Canadian industrial organization the Williamson model is particularly apt, since the scale efficiency issue is far more critical here than in the United States.

The trade-off between power and efficiency is pictured in Figure 4-3, following the diagram employed by Williamson. DD is the total demand for the output of the firms prior to merger. AC_1 represents the level of average costs of the two (or more) firms prior to merger. For simplicity, price is assumed to just cover average cost ($P_1 = AC_1$), although more generally $P_1 = K\ AC_1$, where $K(\geq 1)$ is a measure of premerger market power. The effect of the merger is assumed to reduce average cost, through rationalization in the use of plant capacity, to AC_2, but also to raise price to $P_2(>P_1)$ as a result of the market power created by the joining of two (presumably important) competing firms. The result is that consumers pay higher prices for a smaller output which is produced using fewer inputs per unit of output. The merger has thereby produced a deadweight (welfare loss) shown by the shaded triangle, and at the same time a cost-saving shown by the shaded rectangle. Assuming that a dollar of cost saving equals a dollar of deadweight loss, one can compare the magnitude of the two areas and determine whether the *economic* benefits (cost savings) outweigh the economic cost (deadweight loss). Whether the former outweighs the latter depends on four factors: (i) the percentage reduction in average cost; (ii) the percentage rise in prices; (iii) the level of K; (iv) and, most important, the elasticity of demand. Williamson then demonstrates that on reasonable assumptions about the elasticity of demand (and assuming K = 1, for simplicity), it takes only modest average cost reductions (due to scale economies) to offset substantial price increases (due to the market power effects) associated with the merger. Hypothetical examples are shown in Table 4-2.

28. O.E. Williamson, "Economics as an Antitrust Defense," *American Economic Review*, 58 (March 1968).

Figure 4-3

Monopoly Power-Scale Efficiency Trade-Off

Table 4-2

Percentage Cost Reductions Sufficient To Offset Percentage Price Increase, for Selected Values of the Elasticity of Demand

Percentage Increase in Price	Elasticity of Demand		
	2	1	.5
	(percent)	(percent)	(percent)
5%	.25	.12	.06
10%	1.00	.50	.25
20%	4.00	2.00	1.00
30%	9.00	4.50	2.25

Source: Williamson, op. cit. p. 23.

This is the "naive" model. As Williamson explains, there are a number of qualifications to the estimates of benefits and costs if the model is to be a useful tool of policy. Among the factors that should be considered are: (1) whether market demand growth would have been sufficient to allow the firms to achieve the scale economies by internal growth rather than by merger within a reasonable period (say 5 years of time); (2) whether the merger will prompt a series of other mergers which lack compensating efficiency gains; (3) the possibility that the merger by raising industry concentration will increase the prices (but not reduce the costs) of some nonmerging firms; (4) whether the increased profitability of the merged firms is given a negative weight by the community; i.e., a dollar of producers' surplus may not be deemed to offset a dollar's loss of consumer surplus; (5) the possibility that the increase in profitability will incline the acquiring firm to be less vigilant in keeping costs at a minimum; in other words, the merger may lead to "X-inefficiency"; and (6) the effect of the merger on antitrust enforcement costs, concentration of political economic power, and research and development incentives.

The efficiency-market power trade-off model is potentially rich in its implications for, and applicability to, the Canadian industrial scene. Although there has been no effective legal barrier to mergers to date, consideration is being given to legislation that would increase the federal government's power to block mergers not deemed in the public interest. Williamson's model helps to define the factors relevant to the public interest and provides a basis for weighting the plusses and minuses; the benefits and costs. Further it demonstrates that most mergers are likely to have both positive and negative effects, and that a merger policy, where scale inefficiencies are substantial, cannot reasonably be based on a single economic criterion.[29]

We conclude this section with a schematic representation (Table 4-3) of the likely effects on prices, costs, profits, and employment of rationalization via tariff reduction on the one hand, and merger on the other. The two policies also differ in the degree to which rationalization is forced, and the degree of discretionary control once the policy is applied. If tariffs were lowered across the board, rationalization would be enforced by the strong market forces emanating from foreign (particularly U.S.) competition. The merger route originates with a voluntary decision among firms as to whether a merger is mutually profitable and then is subjected to the scrutiny of governmental authorities with regard to the relative benefits and costs. The tariff approach is

---

29. A decade later, Williamson reexamined the efficiencies defense, affirming its conceptual correctness, but treating somewhat more skeptically its operationality for policy purposes. O.E. Williamson, "Economies as an Antitrust Defense Revisited," *University of Pennsylvania Law Review*, 125 (April 1977), pp. 699-736.

Table 4-3

Impact of Tariff Reduction and Merger on Costs, Prices, Profits and Employment[a]

	Costs	Prices	Profits	Employment
Merger	(+)↓	?	(−)↑	?
Tariff Reduction	(+)↓	(+)↓	?	(−)↓

[a]The arrows indicate the likely direction of change. The (+) and (−) indicate whether the direction of change is "good" or "bad," respectively.

more impersonal, automatic, and unforgiving; the merger approach more personal, discretionary, and manipulable.[30]

The Legacy of Tariff Protection

The Canadian tariff initially contributed to the development of an important manufacturing sector in Canada. But there is a cost in terms of lack of specialization, inefficient capacity, lower productivity, and substantial foreign ownership and control. Whether the price we continue to pay by having high tariffs is worth the benefits is a political question related to important political and distributional as well as economic efficiency issues. However, there is no doubt that by reducing foreign competition, the tariff reduces Canadian competitiveness. For decades it was a barrier behind which monopoly power and pricing could flourish. In the 1970s it also became a barrier behind which rapidly rising wages contributed to further reduction in Canadian competitiveness. No study of Canadian industrial organization can ignore the past, present, and probable future role of tariffs.

30. For estimates of the impact on employment, productivity, and welfare of alternative rationalization and subsidy policies, see Harris and Cox, op. cit, Ch. 6.

5

Collusive and Competitive Behaviour in Canadian Industry

Behind tariff walls, Canadian firms in concentrated industries may enjoy the quiet life as long as no one "rocks the boat." The boat gets "rocked" when, for example, an established firm attempts to markedly increase its market share or where an important new entrant appears on the scene. In this chapter we focus on the market behaviour, particularly with respect to price and output, of industrial firms in oligopolistic industries. We shall do so, in part, by reference to history and in part by reference to what could be termed "case studies" arising out of actual and alleged collusive, discriminatory or predatory behaviour investigated by the Anti-Combines authorities. The reports of the Restrictive Trade Practices Commission (RTPC) and the often lengthy trial judgments provide an excellent basis for grasping the variety of competitive and anti-competitive behaviour of firms in markets characterized by "competition among the few." (Some readers may prefer, however, to delay reading the case studies until they have read Chapters 8 and 9 on Canadian anti-combines policy.)

Before turning to an historical overview of industrial behaviour and to the presentation of several case studies, it is useful to sketch a theoretical framework within which firm behaviour, in oligopolistic industries, can be analyzed. The framework sketched here draws heavily upon that developed by F.M. Scherer in *Industrial Market Structure and Economic Performance*, chapters 5-7.[1] The theoretical framework relates chiefly to price-output

---

1. Also see W.G. Shepherd, *The Economics of Industrial Organization* (Prentice-Hall, 1979), Chapters 14-16.

behaviour, including the avoidance of price competition, largely ignoring some other facets of industrial behaviour which deserve mention at the outset.

Industrial behaviour can be divided into at least four categories. First, and most important in economic theorizing, are the price-output decisions of firms. In oligopolistic industries these decisions are usually moulded by the firm's relation to its rivals. Second are a firm's sales promotion policies, the importance of which is enhanced by the fact that *independent* price output strategies are often non-optimal. Third are product design (quality) policies, which reflect recognized differences in consumer tastes and the exigencies of technological innovation. The final category is a firm's tactics toward its rivals. The tactics can be divided into three sub-categories: collusion, predation, and exclusion. By far the most common is collusion which is, as we shall see below, strongly motivated by the shortcomings (from the viewpoint of business) of independent pricing behaviour in oligopolistic industries. Actual predation is relatively rare, though often alleged, usually requiring a strong monopolistic position on the part of the predator and an unwillingness to tolerate the survival of smaller, sometimes energetic, rivals. Exclusion arises where a seller is able to capitalize on the monopoly power conveyed by a patented article, a brand name or some other advantage to carve out and maintain a share of the market relatively free from the competition of its rivals. Examples are exclusive dealing and tying contracts, which will be briefly discussed in chapter 9.

A Framework for Analyzing Industrial Behaviour

As all students of economics soon learn, oligopolistic behaviour is indeterminate with a vengeance. The ability, within limits, for an oligopolist to vary price and quantity obscures the firm's supply curve. The uncertain response of rivals to an oligopolist's own price and output behaviour makes indeterminate the firm's demand curve. Short of making strong assumptions about the response of rivals, it is not possible to postulate the profit maximizing price and output levels of an individual oligopolist. Worse, there is both theory and evidence suggesting the objectives of large, oligopolistic firms go beyond profit-maximization, at least of the short-run variety, to include sales maximization, (with a profit constraint) and various forms of "satisficing" behaviour. Thus the behaviour of large industrial firms is both variable and complex, subtle and pointed, predictable (in certain respects) and unpredictable (in others).

Despite these difficulties, economists have introduced theories of oligopoly price-output behaviour with determinate solutions. The better known include: (a) Cournot's duopoly model in which each firm chooses its profit-maximizing output on the assumption (both unrealistic and unfulfilled) that its rival's output will remain unchanged; (b) Chamberlin's small group, joint profit maximization model in which *each* firm not only recognizes mutual interdependence with its rivals but also realizes, and acts independently[2] upon that realization, that the only "sensible" and determinate price is the one a monopolist would set; (c) the game theory model where each risk-averting firm conservatively chooses strategies which minimize the losses or injury the response of its rivals will inflict (the so-called "minimax" strategy); (d) the kinked demand curve model in which the assumption that rivals will follow price reductions but not price increases leads each firm to avoid independent price changes, thus generating predictions of price rigidity even in the face of changing cost conditions; (e) Stigler's collusion model: because acting alone forces each oligopolist to act pessimistically, the classic Prisoner's Dilemma, Stigler builds his theory of oligopoly on the assumption that profit maximizing oligopolists will attempt to collude. The oligopoly problem then becomes the detection and prevention of cheating.

Although the student must look elsewhere for a systematic and formal presentation of oligopoly models, the following discussion and diagram may help the reader identify the salient characteristics of, and differences between, some of the theories of oligopoly identified in the preceding paragraph. Oligopoly models can be distinguished according to whether or not they assume each firm recognizes, and takes into account, that its behaviour will affect the decision of its rivals, and whether or not the models assume cooperative as opposed to non-cooperative, or independent, behaviour.

At one extreme is Cournot's model which assumes zero "conjectural variation", i.e., each firm assumes that its decision will not affect the decisions of its rivals (an assumption which, in fact, is repeatedly falsified, *ex post*.) The Cournot model also assumes non-cooperative behaviour: each firm independently acts in its own interest. At the other extreme is Stigler's model, which assumes that the leading firms recognize their interdependent and collective interests sufficiently to induce them to explicitly cooperate (collude). What limits cooperative behaviour in Stigler's model, aside from legal considerations, are the costs to the colluding firms of detecting and preventing cheating. Chamberlin's oligopoly model contrasts with the Cournot and Stigler models. In contrast to Cournot, Chamberlin assumes each firm fully takes into account the reactions of its rivals (one might say Chamberlin assumes "infinite" conjectural variation). But in contrast to Stigler, Chamberlin assumed that each firm recognizes its interdependence with its rivals so completely, that each *independently* chooses the price and output which jointly maximizes industry profits. No collusion is necessary.

The "optimism" (from the viewpoint of the individual firm) of the Chamberlin

2. Without collusion.

model contrasts strangely with the "pessimism" implied by the kinked demand curve and game theory (both zero and variable sum) models. In the kinked demand curve and game theory models, conjectural variation is non-zero (i.e. interdependence is recognized and strategies employed), but each firm is assumed to act non-cooperatively, in contrast to Chamberlin's model. In the kinked demand curve model the result is to produce inertia—or inaction. No firm will independently undertake to increase its price (even if it believes that a price increase by all firms would jointly maximize industry profits) because it believes the other firms will not follow its lead. Only if one of the firms is designated a price leader, is the perceived kink in the individual firm's demand curve, and the pessimism it implies, eliminated. Similarly, in the variable-sum, game theoretic models, independent, non-cooperative behaviour always produces worse results for each firm than would cooperative behaviour. But cooperative behaviour does not, in fact, dominate non-cooperative behaviour. Not only is achieving cooperation difficult, but once it is achieved the gains to an individual firm from cheating (i.e., secretly non-cooperating) are sufficiently great to cause many a cooperative effort to quickly dissolve.

The Cournot, Chamberlin, and kinked demand curve models can be illustrated with a single diagram, for which certain liberties are taken to simplify the exposition. The basic model used here follows the classic literature in making highly stylized assumptions about demand, cost, and entry conditions. Essentially, we assume a straightline market demand curve for an easily identified, homogeneous product, produced under similar, constant (average and marginal) cost conditions by two (or a very few) firms which face *no* threat of entry. The last assumption is especially important—and unrealistic. In effect, entry is assumed to be blockaded for one reason or another: there are *no external* forces of competition. Whatever "competition" exists is *internal* to the market.

In Figure 5-1, P_m and Q_m represent the profit maximizing price and output for the industry—the levels consistent with the intersection of the MR and MC curves. (For the moment concentrate on the heavily drawn revenue and cost curves.) Thus, P_m and Q_m are the price and industry output predicted by Chamberlin's model, in which each firm sets the price and output which jointly maximizes industry profits. P_m and Q_m contrast starkly with the competitive price and output, P_c and Q_c.

The Cournot equilibrium price and industry output are indicated by P_A and Q_A. The Cournot price is below and output above the joint profit maximizing (Chamberlin) levels because of independent, non-cooperative behaviour. The Cournot price and output combination is reached through an iterative procedure, in which each firm sequentially attempts to maximize its own profits, on the assumption that its rivals' output is fixed—an assumption which, as mentioned above, is *ex post* falsified. After a series of moves by each firm, industry equilibrium is reached at P_A and Q_A: here no firm has any incentive to

Figure 5-1

Models of Oligopoly

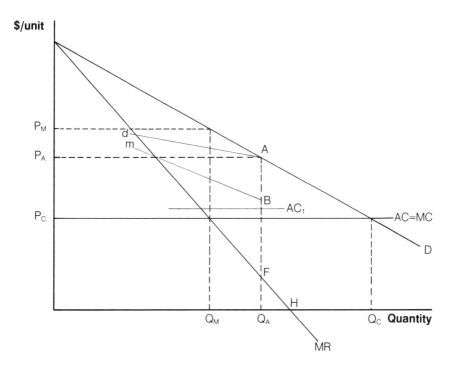

change its output (or price), again on the condition that it assumes its rivals' output (or price) is fixed (Cournot's assumption of zero conjectural variation).

Cournot was the first economist to show that as the number of firms (n) in the industry increases, the Cournot equilibrium output and price (Q_A and P_A) converge toward the competitive levels (Q_c and P_c). In fact, the relationship between Q_A and Q_c can be defined rather precisely. Industry output in Cournot equilibrium as a percentage of the competitive output is equal to ($\frac{n}{n+1}$), where n is the number of firms, each producing the same fraction of industry output at constant unit costs of production. Cournot equilibrium output and price will begin to approximate the competitive levels whenever n is more than a relatively smaller number. For example, if n is four, Q_A is 80 percent of Q_c.

The kinked demand curve model is also captured in Figure 5-1. Here the more lightly drawn lines come into play. Assume that the figure now represents the demand and cost conditions of any *one* of the rivals in an oligopolistic market. According to this theory each firm pessimistically presumes that its price increases will not be followed, while its price cuts will be matched by its rivals. Suppose, to begin with, that the firm's price and output are P_A and Q_A (chosen simply to avoid cluttering up the diagram). Then the individual oligopolist will perceive its demand curve to be dA for prices above P_A and AD for prices below P_A. The curve that is marginal to dAD is mBFH. Note that the kink at point A in the demand curve produces a gap, BF, in the marginal revenue curve.

The firm which *perceives* its demand curve in the manner described above (it is perception only: no economist to my knowledge has ever estimated a demand curve with a kink in it) will have little reason to *independently* alter its price and output (unless, of course demand shifts more or less permanently in one direction or another). Even an increase in costs would not provoke a change in price if, as is the case with average cost curve AC_1, in Figure 5-1, it falls within the gap in the MR curve.

Clearly, the kinked demand curve analysis describes a suboptimal situation from the standpoint of each rival oligopolist. It won't be long before each learns that designating one of its own as a price leader will largely erase the perceptions that generate the kink. A trustworthy price leader can be expected to lead on price increases or cuts which it believes are beneficial to the industry as well as itself. But whether the price leader can lead the way to the joint-profit maximizing price, P_m, depends on the ability and willingness of industry members to coordinate their behaviour—to say nothing about the condition of entry (external competition) which is (unrealistically) assumed to be blockaded. For, as will be explained below, coordination is not easy. Thus the limits on the exercise of price leadership are not unlike those which bear on explicit agreements (collusion) between individual firms. Each firm has an incentive to increase its output when price exceeds marginal cost (in more prosaic terms, an incentive to cheat), an incentive which increases as price increases and individual firm output (excess capacity) decreases (increases).

Each of these historically-important models of oligopoly yields some insights, but cannot begin to provide a useful basis for a general theory of oligopoly behaviour. And, in fact, it is doubtful that there will ever be a single theory of oligopoly price-output behaviour, given the nature of interdependence among a small number of competing rivals. It is instructive to note how easily each of the above-mentioned models, with their determinate solutions, founders in the face of small changes in their parameters. In the case of Cournot's model the simple fact of "learning" makes unrealistic the critical assumption by one firm that its rival's output will remain fixed, when in fact reaching the model's equilibrium solution requires continuous, iterative falsification of that assumption.[3]

---

3. However, assuming no entry into the market, the existence and stability of Cournot equilibrium are more compelling than the realism of the assumptions on which the Cournot model is based. That is, if the number of non-cooperating sellers of a homogeneous product produced under

Chamberlin's model assumes similar cost and demand functions facing each of the rivals, assumptions that efficiency differences (due to scale or other factors) and market share differences due to product differentiation readily upset. With differences in costs or market shares, the profit-maximizing price will, in general, no longer be the same for each firm, making it highly unlikely that firms can *independently*, jointly maximize profits. The minimax strategy is based on "zero sum" games in which one firm's gain is another's loss. Except where market shares are involved, the games played by oligopolists are usually variable sum (positive or negative) ones, as for example where each firm in the industry benefits by price increases, or incurs the costs of unrestrained selling efforts via advertising. The kinked demand curve model runs into problems when demand changes, providing neither an explanation for how prices will change, nor how prices come to be what they are in the first place. In fact, if independently acting oligopolists viewed their demand curve as if it were kinked, they would have a strong incentive to designate one of their number as a price leader, thereby eliminating the kink. Finally, Stigler's model, although it more realistically handles oligopoly motives, does not adequately handle non-price dimensions of competition, precisely the kinds of rivalry that are induced if collusion on price is effective.

The indeterminacy that is fed into the older (pre-Stiglerian) oligopoly models by the introduction of reasonable assumptions leads to an important conclusion. If rivals will respond to an individual firm's decision to alter price (and output), if costs and demand conditions vary among firms in a given industry, and if coordinated strategies can be mutually profitable, then there is likely to be a strong incentive for oligopolists to reach agreements among themselves. This implies that the realities of oligopoly generate powerful forces for collusion, as Stigler's model assumes, which may be overt or covert, tacit or explicit. Since agreements are generally illegal (because of antitrust or anti-combines laws), most attempts at agreement are covert rather than overt. However, agreements need not be explicit. If firms are few enough in number, entry barriers significant, and products are homogeneous, then "tacit agreement" is possible, each firm's behaviour "consciously paralleling" that of its chief rivals without

similar, constant cost conditions, is given, there is one (non-competitive) price at which none of the sellers has an incentive to alter its output (and price). Thus, even in the absence of collusion or cooperation between rivals, firms in an oligopolistic industry may earn supranormal profits. In general, however, the Cournot (or what is often called the Cournot-Nash) equilibrium price is below the joint profit maximizing price. The divergence between the Cournot-Nash equilibrium price and joint-profit maximizing price increases as the number of sellers (n) in the market increases. The larger is n, the closer is the Cournot-Nash equilibrium price to the competitive equilibrium price. Cournot provided a proof of these propositions assuming zero costs. More general proofs, couched generally in advanced mathematical terms, and probably of interest only to advanced students, can be found in J.W. Friedman, *Oligopoly and the Theory of Games* (Amsterdam: North-Holland, 1977), chapters 2 and 7.

prior agreement on the specifics. Nevertheless, the factors entering into price making are usually sufficiently complex, and the distribution of market shares among the leaders a sufficiently sensitive issue, that if some form of coordination is desired, explicit (though covert) agreement is typically required.

It was Adam Smith who observed that "People of the same trade seldom meet together, even for merriment and diversion, but the conversation ends in a conspiracy against the public, or in some contrivance to raise prices."[4] Smith's observation is an early recognition that however beneficial competition is to the community at large, competitors will do what they can to avoid it. In the 19th century conspiracies among firms were both widespread and legal, but often limited in duration and effect by the appearance of new firms, or "chiseling" by participants to the agreement. Easy entry and the internal breakdown in communications among participants to a conspiracy are strong forces undermining agreement and generating "competitive" behaviour. In some industries, however, entry conditions are sufficiently difficult and firms sufficiently few to make collusive agreements highly stable and profitable. Thus despite the strictures of the anticombines and antitrust laws, collusion may be widespread if one can assume that the number of court cases reflects only the proverbial "tip of the iceberg." In any event, collusion is the most obvious, and perhaps crudest, means of providing "oligopolistic coordination." Alleged collusion is the crux of the behaviour cited in most of the cases presented in the next-to-last section of this chapter.

Coordinated behaviour is not only important if oligopolists are to attain "monopolistic" prices, but is needed to *retain* them in a world of changing cost and demand conditions. As the kinked demand curve model so aptly demonstrates, the individual oligopolist will hesitate to act alone, unless, of course, he can expect a price increase to be followed. This expectation will usually be limited to price leaders. On the downside, firms will attempt to keep price cuts secret—"under the table." But secrecy is usually short run, so it is only a matter of time before price cuts become "gossip" among buyers, who will in turn demand similar treatment from their traditional suppliers.[5] Thus short of some agreement, tacit or explicit, as to how to coordinate price *changes*, shifting cost and demand conditions will tend to upset price agreements. In a full-fledged cartel, in which the suppliers as a group allocate output quotas and establish

4. Adam Smith, *The Wealth of Nations* (New York: Modern Library, 1937), p. 128. Reynolds has observed that "in economic writings the term 'competition' usually carries an overtone of beneficence. In business circles, however, 'cut throat' and 'competition' are regarded as virtually one word. Price reductions are termed 'ruinous', 'chaotic', 'insane', 'unethical'." Lloyd Reynolds, *The Control of Competition in Canada* (Cambridge: Harvard University Press, 1940), p. 94.

5. Stigler developed his theory of oligopoly around the information necessary to police (make effective) collusive agreements. George Stigler, "A Theory of Oligopoly," *Journal of Political Economy* (February 1964).

prices among themselves, agreement often can be maintained in the face of a changing environment. But cartels are illegal, and where firms are few enough may be unnecessary if there is a firm tradition of price leadership in the industry.

Economists have analyzed a variety of price leadership types, which the student is left to verify on his or her own.[6] It is sufficient to point out here that recognized leadership is an important means by which oligopolistic price behaviour is coordinated. Where the size distribution of the leading firms in an oligopolistic industry varies substantially, leadership will tend naturally to fall upon the largest firm. Where there is little variation in the size of the leading firms one is likely to be chosen leader, although leadership may change hands over time. Among the traditional price leaders in Canadian industry have been Imperial Tobacco, Imperial Oil, Canadian General Electric, Aluminum Company of Canada (Alcan), and Canada Cement Ltd. In the newsprint industry the identity of the price leader has tended to change over time.

The decisions of price leaders will be more easily foreseen and understood if common pricing formulas are used. This, perhaps, helps to explain the widespread use of "full cost pricing" in which prices or gross margins are set in relation to average (unit) costs (direct or total) at some "standard" level of output. While unit costs often vary among firms, similar changes in costs, in response to wage and raw material price changes, are likely to be experienced by each of the competing firms. If each of the firms employs the same pricing formula, similar cost changes will result in similar price changes.

In spite of the incentives for oligopolists to collude or follow parallel behaviour there are potentially powerful forces tending to undermine oligopolistic coordination. These include (a) the bargaining power of big buyers: *ceteris paribus*, cheating is much more likely where buyers are large; (b) easy-entry conditions: in the absence of entry barriers there is little or no market power; (c) the number of sellers, including the relative importance of the "competitive fringe"—the firms usually not included among the industry leaders; (d) cost differences among firms: low-cost firms may have little reason to reach agreements acceptable to high-cost firms; (e) a high degree of product heterogeneity: differentiation increases the incentives to, and likelihood of, non-price forms of competition; (f) a high ratio of fixed to total costs, which makes price cutting tempting when a cyclical decline in demand produces a substantial amount of unused capacity; (g) infrequent and "lumpy" orders, as for example,

---

6. George Stigler, "The Kinky Oligopoly Demand Curve and Rigid Prices," *Journal of Political Economy* (October 1947); Jesse Markham, "The Nature and Significance of Price Leadership," *American Economic Review*, 41 (December 1951); and F.M. Scherer, *Industrial Market Structure and Economic Performance* (Rand-McNally, 1980), pp. 176-184. Stigler identified "dominant" and "barometric" types of price leadership. Markham added a third type which Scherer denotes as "collusive" price leadership.

is the case with heavy electrical equipment: making a large and infrequent sale may mean more in profits to a firm than does "sharing" in a price fixing agreement; and (h) the ability to keep price cuts secret, a capability which will be influenced by the structure of the buyers' market, as Stigler's theory of oligopoly shows. The long list of factors making oligopolistic coordination difficult suggests that the view that concentrated industries will exhibit monopolistic behaviour is exaggerated. In fact, some students of oligopoly prefer to assume that in the absence of *enforceable* agreements between firms, oligopolistic behaviour is more accurately viewed as "non cooperative" rather than "cooperative".

An Historical Overview of Industrial Behaviour in Canada

Canada's small and tariff-protected markets are "ripe" for collusive behaviour by the leading firms in oligopolistic industries. Students of Canadian business history have had little trouble in documenting widespread attempts at market control. Prior to World War I employers' associations were the most important device for attempted cartelization.[7] Among the industries which experienced price agreements or attempted cartelization were the cotton textile, agricultural implement, binder twine and cordage, petroleum, salt, B.C. lumbering, sugar, flour, canning, iron and steel, furniture, and paper industries. When price agreements broke down, as they not infrequently did, especially where there were more than a few sellers, or where entry conditions were easy, industrial mergers often followed.[8] In addition to combines in manufacturing industries, Professor Naylor cites evidence of "mercantile cartels" in such trades as groceries, coal dealers, retail lumber, and livestock dealers. Although the first combines law was passed in 1889, in response to a parliamentary inquiry into, and finding of, widespread combinations in Canadian industry, the new law was so worded and administered as to assure it would have virtually no effect on the incidence of price agreements and combinations (see chapter 8).

Collusive activity remained a "way of life" in Canadian industry during the interwar period. Anti-combines legislation in 1910, 1919, and 1923 had little effect, although the 1923 legislation led to numerous investigations and the publication of several reports providing much-needed information about industrial behaviour. From these reports and those of Royal Commissions, Lloyd Reynolds was able to piece together a remarkable picture of collusion and other

7. Tom Naylor, *The History of Canadian Business 1867-1914*, Vol. II (Toronto: James Lorimer, 1975), p. 162.
8. Ibid., Chap. 14.

forms of anti-competitive behaviour. Writing in 1940, Reynolds could say:[9] "Anyone who reads through the investigations of the past decade must be impressed with the extent to which competition has been attenuated throughout Canadian industry. Price agreements have been formed at one time or another in nearly every industry listed in [Table 5-1]."

For price agreements to be sustaining, it is usually necessary for the combination to exercise some control over the output of its members. If there is no control, and the agreed price is set above marginal cost, individual firms are likely to produce more than can be sold at the agreed price, thereby tempting secret price cutting and an eventual breakdown in the price agreement. Thus Reynolds found that mature trade associations usually attempted to control production.[10] Typical of these agreements are two examples described by Reynolds.

1. The eight manufacturers of rubber footwear who had entered into informal price agreements as early as 1924 put the agreement in writing in 1932. The firms agreed to observe uniform list prices and discounts, standardization of the product, and allocated shares of the market. Fines were levied when quotas were exceeded and bonuses paid to firms selling less than their prescribed share. The association secretary held cash bonds posted by the companies and was empowered to examine each company's books and levy fines for breaches of agreement.[11]

2. In the cardboard box industry the conspiring firms established a single agency called Container Materials, Ltd. The board of directors of Container Materials was composed of one member of each of the 16 participating firms. Each firm agreed to nominally sell all its output to Container Materials and then to act as agent of the latter, selling at prices set by the selling agency. Container Materials never, in fact, handled any goods or performed any distributional functions. However, Container Materials set output quotas, collected fines and paid bonuses for over- and under-production, established discount structures, standardized credit and service terms, regulated quality, examined books, and, with the cash deposits placed by the member firms, bought out new firms or paid them to observe the fixed prices or not to produce at all.[12] In an important Anti-Combines case, that reached the Supreme Court of Canada in 1942, the participants in Container Materials Ltd. were convicted for violation of the Anti-Combines Act and paid $161 000 in fines. Twenty-four years later most of the

9. Lloyd Reynolds, *The Control of Competition in Canada*, (Harvard University Press, 1940), p. 11.
10. Ibid., p. 18.
11. Ibid., pp. 18-19.
12. Ibid., pp. 19-20. For more details see Department of Labour, *Report of Investigation into an Alleged Combine in the Manufacture of Paperboard Shipping Containers*, 1939.

Table 5-1

Classification of Canadian Manufacturing Industries by Extent of Competition, Circa 1930s

| Monopoly[a] | Price Agreement[b] | | Competition[b] | |
	Informal[c]	Formal[d]	Few Producers	Many Producers
Aluminum	Agricultural implements	Fertilizers	Flour	Bread
Cement	Brewing	Leather	Meat packing	Boots & shoes
Electrical equipment, heavy	Copper	Rubber footwear	Newsprint	Clothing
Explosives	Cotton cloth, yarn & thread	Tobacco products	Silk cloth	Furniture
Lead	Gasoline	Most paper products (except newsprint)	Silk hosiery	Jam
Nickel	Sugar	Most plumbing and heating equipment	Tires	
Rayon yarn	Some iron & steel products	Many hardware products	Woollen & worsted yarn & cloth	
Steel rails	Some textile products			
Some chemicals	Some canned foods			
Some iron & steel products				
Some non-ferrous metal products				

[a]Single firm control.

[b]The chief difference between the "price agreement" and "competition" groups is that "in the former the agreements have been well-observed, while in the latter they have broken down."

[c]"Informal" agreements: typically facilitated by price leadership.

[d]"Formal" agreements: typically facilitated by trade association.

Source: Lloyd Reynolds, op. cit., pp. 8, 11-12. Used by permission of Harvard University Press.

same firms (or their new owners) were convicted again for price fixing during the 1940s and 1950s and were fined a total of $391 500. There is no evidence that price fixing did not pay.[13]

According to Reynolds, Canadian trade associations of the pre-World War II era rarely performed the statistical gathering, cooperative research and institutional advertising that characterized trade associations in the United States. Canadian trade associations were judged primarily on their ability to maintain "fair prices," and Reynolds quotes one trade association secretary as saying that "manufacturers up here wouldn't be bothered with an association that couldn't control prices.[14] However, not all associations were able to control prices. Price agreements often broke down, were resurrected, only to collapse again in a number of industries. The reasons for collapse relate to one or more of the factors referred to above that make oligopolistic coordination difficult, if not impossible.[15]

Reynolds' survey of the control of competition in Canada in the pre-World War II years is an invaluable source of evidence that a combination of a small domestic market, high tariffs, and the natural proclivity of businessmen to avoid competition in price, collectively provide strong incentives to collusion— incentives that are not likely to be lost upon the great majority of businessmen. Thus the facts conform with the theory: oligopolistic interdependence generates powerful forces in the direction of price agreement and other collusive activities. But uniformity can be, and has been, undermined by cost and product differences, easy entry and excess capacity, strong independents and secrecy.[16]

13. (1942)/D.L.R. 529 and *R v. St. Lawrence Corporation Ltd. et al.*, (1966) 51 C.P.R. 170.
14. Reynolds, op. cit., p 21.
15. Ibid., pp. 21-28. Here are some examples cited by Reynolds. (1) A formal price agreement in 1932 among manufacturers of silk hosiery broke down because the makers of unbranded goods would not agree to set uniform prices with branded goods, while the makers of the latter would not agree to a price differential. Product differentiation was at the heart of the failure to maintain the agreement. (2) An agreement among woollen and worsted manufacturers, made in 1933, broke down in 1934 because the low-cost producer regarded the agreed-to-price as too high. It found it preferable to cut prices and expand sales. (3) In the newsprint industry, a doubling of capacity in the late 1920s led to such vast amounts of excess (unused) capacity in the depressed 1930s that price agreements quickly dissolved as firms secretly cut prices to attract business and spread heavy overhead costs over a larger output. (4) In the bakery industry agreements were common among the large bakers in most cities: their collapse was due to excess capacity, a large "competitive fringe" of small independent bakers, and the buying power of chain stores.
16. For example, when the newsprint industry, suffering from excess capacity, attempted to establish a joint selling agency in 1927, many firms, accounting for almost fifty percent of capacity, refused to join and the effort to fix prices failed. Even the attempt by the Ontario and Quebec governments to resurrect the cartel, and thereby lend support to one of their leading industries, failed when the leading and low-cost firm, International Paper, failed to go along. See T. Traves, *The State and Enterprise: Canadian Manufacturers and the Federal Government, 1917-1931* (Toronto: University of Toronto Press, 1979), pp. 77-78.

The legacy of business history provides a strong empirical basis of support for the theoretical framework developed at the beginning of this chapter in which forces promoting, and sources undermining, oligopolistic coordination tug at each other, the former apparently dominating the pre-World War II period.

No general study of industrial behaviour has been carried out for the postwar period. There are, however, four useful sources of information available. One of these is the numerous reports published by the combines authorities. A number of these reports (e.g. fine papers, metal culverts, rubber products, shipping containers) paint a picture of collusive behaviour stretching from the early 1930s into the 1950s. In some instances (e.g. sugar, metal culverts) the same group of firms has faced prosecution twice within the postwar period. Some industries cited for their collusive behaviour in both the pre-World War I and the interwar periods, also have been prosecuted in the post-World War II period (sugar, paper, shipping containers, gasoline). One is tempted to conclude that it is still "business as usual" so far as collusive behaviour is concerned. However, for certain reasons this viewpoint may be misleading. As the number of anticombines cases brought, prosecuted, and won has increased, there appears to be a tendency toward more subtle and complex forms of agreement. If so, it is probable that the "costs" of facilitating an agreement have risen, while there is no reason to believe that the benefits, already great, flowing from price agreements have increased. Thus at the margin, one would expect that collusion is not quite as widespread, not to say all-pervasive, as it once was. Added factors are the probable decline in market concentration from pre-War II levels, decreasing tariff protection for many industries, and the postwar growth of foreign entry into Canadian manufacturing industries. New entry always poses some problems for combinations and cartels since room must be made for the entrant, implying a reduction in market shares of existing firms. Moreover, if the entrant is unwilling to "play ball" the whole agreement may collapse. Thus while public knowledge of collusive behaviour has increased, the incidence of combination may have declined somewhat. Nevertheless, the evidence from combines reports and prosecutions, which in any event reflect only the tip of the iceberg, suggests it is still widespread, and a way of life in a number of industries.

A second source of evidence on postwar industrial behaviour is provided by Eastman and Stykolt for the 16 industries they studied in attempting to evaluate the effect of tariff protection on industry structure, behaviour, and performance. These industries (which have been combined into 11 by joining fruit and vegetable canning, beef and pork packing, liquid and solid detergents, and ranges, refrigerators and washing machines) and their respective behaviour, are reported in Table 5-2. This small sample, which includes some important Canadian manufacturing industries, suggests a variety of types of behaviour

Table 5-2

Industrial Behaviour in Eleven Industries: Postwar Period (Up to 1960)

Industry	Behaviour	Evidence of Collusion
Canning (fruit and vegetable)	Large firms selling branded goods exhibited oligopolistic behaviour, characterized by rigid prices, limit pricing, advertising; but easy entry and buying power of chains greatly weakened monopoly power. Competition strong among sellers of unbranded goods.	None cited
Cement	A transition from monopolistic to oligopolistic as Canada Cement Ltd.'s market share fell from over 80% in 1946 to about 50% in 1957. Canada Cement, the price leader; basing point pricing, originally as "Montreal Plus" and later a multiple-basing point system.	Basing point system
Container board	A long history of collusion and other means of suppressing competition (including market sharing) in this highly concentrated industry ($CR_4 = 85\%$ in 1950). Leading firms integrated forward by acquiring, via merger, the leading shipping container firms in 1945-60 period, thereby making entry difficult by eliminating independent container firms. Prices set at import-excluding levels—a form of limit pricing.	Abundant; a major investigation in early 1960s and prosecution in 1966
Shipping containers	Collusion via Container Materials Ltd. in 1930s and Container Statistics Ltd. in late 1940s and 1950s. Identical prices derived from printed manuals.	History of collusion dating back to 1931
Synthetic detergent	Aggresive non-price competition coupled with discounts to distributors to allow them to price cut with "Special Prices." Total promotional costs were between 20 and 30% of value of factory shipments. Tariff allowed higher prices but probably did not affect competitive behaviour.	None cited

Table 5-2 (continued)

Industry	Behaviour	Evidence of Collusion
Major electrical appliance (ranges, refrigerators, wringer washers)	Competition chiefly of a non-price sort, based on product differentiation related to both advertising and innovation.	None cited
Newsprint	Identical prices, under long-term contract; price leadership (possibly of a barometric variety) with identity of leader changing. Delivered pricing on sales to U.S. Industry discipline may have been helped by large number of interlocking directorships in mid-1950s. Trade Association an important source of statistical information.	No evidence of formal collusion in price setting
Meat packing (beef and pork)	Highly competitive; attempts at price leadership by Canada Packers generally ineffective; market shares varied substantially over time.	None between packers
Petroleum refining	A big 4 with 75 percent of market, led in mid 1950s by Imperial Oil with a 40 percent share. Price leadership which in times of excess capacity could break down into price wars. However new entry was at inefficiently small size so as to avoid price wars.	None cited; however, the leading firms used exclusive dealing & full requirement contracts to exclude independents
Primary steel	Price competition limited by application of a complex basing point system, centred at Hamilton. Rigid prices.	None cited
Rubber tire	Collusion in part (60%) of original equipment and replacement markets; price competition in sales to mass distributors and to Big Three auto makers. Thus, collusive arrangements were used to separate markets in which physically identical tires were sold at different prices. Goodyear a price leader.	Collusion established for period 1937-52. No dramatic change in behaviour 1952-60.

Source: H. Eastman and S. Stykolt, *The Tariff and Competition in Canada* (Toronto: Macmillan, 1968) Part II, various pages.

reflecting the particular circumstances in which individual members of the industry found themselves. As the third column of Table 5-2 indicates, formal collusion appears to have been important in only three of the industries, although evidence of identical prices and the use of basing points is indicated in four others. [17] Avoiding price competition, if possible, remains a major objective of business, but collusion may not be as common, (or as necessary ?), as it once appears to have been.

A third source of information on firm behaviour is the Report of the Royal Commission on Corporate Concentration and its 34 companion studies. Because of its mandate, the Royal Commission was primarily concerned with corporate history and development, corporate structure and intercorporate financial ties. Thus to the extent it examined behaviour, the Commission focused on the growth behaviour of Canada's largest enterprises. Few of the 16 company studies give much or any attention to pricing policies or to the other types of firm behaviour described earlier in this chapter.[18] However, the Commission's own report does indicate a concern about "conscious parallelism" and its treatment under the combines laws. The concern was motivated by recent anticombines cases involving parallel behaviour and by proposed amendments to the combines laws to deal with so-called "joint-monopolization," a euphemism for tacit collusion via consciously parallel pricing policies (see chapter 8). However, the Commission's report also reflects a belief that firms which are intent on fixing prices, or otherwise limiting competition, are apparently choosing more subtle means than hotel or trade association meetings to do so. The targets are tight oligopolies intent on joint profit maximization via parallel pricing policies (e.g. cement, sugar, some steel products, electrical equipment, agricultural implements, petroleum products, aluminum fabricators, cigarettes, etc.) All of these industries were characterized as dominant-firm monopolies or price-agreeing oligopolies in the 1930s by Reynolds (see Table 5-1). To deal with these and other tightly structured industries some persons have proposed deconcentration by government action. The Royal Commission opposed restructuring via deconcentration, recommending instead tariff reductions and more vigilance in combatting collusive-type activities. [19]

Fourth, a number of case studies of industrial pricing, particularly of industries producing, processing and fabricating basic materials, suggest that

17. Basing point systems are delivered pricing systems in which each firm (seller) in an industry quotes prices at any given location equal to the mill price at an agreed-on production point plus transportation costs from that production point to the point of delivery.
18. The exceptions are the studies of Alcan Aluminum Ltd. (No. 13) and the steel industry (No. 19) by Litvak and Maule, and the study of Macmillan Bloedel (No. 15) by Schwindt.
19. *Report of the Royal Commission on Corporate Concentration*, pp. 95-100. The Commission recommended that the basis for conviction for tacit collusion be "conscious parellelism plus," the "plus" factors being various devices or actions taken to facilitate the coordination of interfirm behaviour. See the light bulb and metal culvert case studies below.

pricing behaviour increasingly reflects the impingement of market forces. Choksi studied four Canadian industries in the primary metals group: copper, aluminum, nickel and steel. [20] She found that despite the dominance of these industries, in Canada, by one or a very few firms, pricing increasingly responded to short-run changes in demand in all but the Canadian steel industry. One reason is that these industries are not insulated from the world market. The Canadian copper, aluminum and nickel industries are large exporters, so that the prices of their products are subject to increasingly competitive world market conditions. In copper and nickel the responsiveness of price to short-run demand changes is accentuated by inelasticity of supply. The steel industry, a net importer over the postwar period studied by Choksi, was better able to administer prices independently of short-run demand changes. Nevertheless, its ability to price so as to achieve a target rate of return has been weakening. Moreover, by the late 1970s, the Canadian steel industry was increasingly coming under pressure from allegedly "dumped" imports of Japanese, Korean and European steel products. Finally, it bears repeating (see chapter 3) that monopolistic pricing in the early postwar period by such dominant firms as INCO and Canada Cement led to large-scale entry and sharp declines in market share. This, in turn, generated pricing behaviour which was either responsive to market forces or was at least more reflective of the fact that the once-dominant firm is now one among a number of "equals" hard pressed to maintain its customer share.

The Links Between Behaviour and Performance

Before turning to an examination of some actual cases of collusive and predatory behaviour, it is worthwhile asking what society actually loses when potential competitors enter price agreements. At the beginning of chapter 2 we showed that if an atomistic (and presumptively competitive) industry can be monopolized (either through merger into one dominant firm or by cartel agreement fixing prices and allocating output quotas) profits can be increased through the consequent reduction in output and increase in price. An alternative way of looking at it, is to say that price agreements are designed to eliminate price cutting (what businessmen self-servingly call "cut-throat competition") which would tend to reduce industry profits. However, a higher price and lower output are not the only costs to society associated with price-fixing agreements. For as noted above price agreements will tend to break down unless fortified by control over output. This is demonstrated in Figure 5-2 by the fact that so long

20. Shehrnaz Choksi, *Pricing Policies in the Canadian Copper, Aluminum, Nickel and Steel Industries*, Ph.D. Dissertation, Department of Economics, McGill University (unpublished).

Figure 5-2

Effect of Non-Price Competition

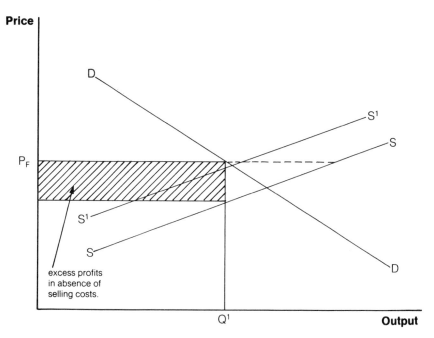

Price

P_F

D

S^1

S

S^1

S

D

excess profits
in absence of
selling costs.

Q^1 **Output**

as fixed price P_F exceeds industry supply price (indicated for each level of output by the curve SS), some, if not all, firms will have an incentive to increase output. If, however, output exceeds Q, then it can be sold only at a lower price, and price cutting, even if in secret and confined to the marginal (or additional) output, can quickly collapse the price structure. Thus the observation from both theory and experience that except in the most disciplined markets price agreements must be fortified with some form of output control.

Observations of social organizations indicate that when one form of behaviour is constrained, energies are diverted to some other form of behaviour. Thus when price decisions are constrained by group (industry) action, the individual firm is likely to engage in non-price behaviour. The usual form of non-price behaviour is sales promotion activity, unless, of course, each individual firm's output and selling costs are tightly controlled by the cartel as was the case in the rubber footwear and shipping container examples described above. Where, however, the cartel's control over individual firms is not so great, individual firms may expend substantial sums to differentiate the product, attract customers from rivals, all the while total industry output remaining consistent with the price fixed by the group. Thus, for example, during the 30 years the Civil

Aeronautics Board controlled both airline fares and entry into the U.S. commercial air service industry, it did not control the selling activities of the established firms. [21] Since sales promotion, on a large scale, is expensive, we can picture the effect of selling costs as an upward shift in the industry supply curve to S^1S^1. Thus, paradoxically, a price agreement which fails to control other facets of firm behaviour can lead, in time, to increased costs and a decline in profitability. Since increased profitability was presumably the *raison d'être* of the agreement in the first place, collusion may, in the long run, benefit neither consumer nor producer. The former pays higher prices, the latter earns only a normal profit, and resources which could have been used to produce more output desired by consumers are diverted into sales promotion activities which, by themselves, produce no utility.

Case Studies of Collusive and Predatory Behaviour

To the outsider the behaviour of industrial firms usually remains largely hidden. True, list prices often can be observed, and *sometimes* it is possible to learn the level of a firm's output, advertising expenditures, and the like. Normally, however, firms jealously guard their vital statistics, hesitating to make known any information that would be useful to rivals. Moreover, the student of industrial behaviour rarely has the opportunity to go behind the statistics to determine why a firm has acted in one way or another. Thus, for example, we normally must infer from the observation of similar selling prices the existence of some form of collusion or price leadership. But we are never certain.

There is, however, an important exception to the usual dearth of information about industrial behaviour. When the anticombines authorities have reason to believe that a firm or a group of firms has violated the anticombines laws, they can investigate and prosecute. In doing so, they may command the firms to make available their records, including statistics, letters and other correspondence, minutes of meetings, etc., and to answer questions under oath. From the information it is often possible to piece together a detailed picture of industry structure and behaviour over a period of years. Thus, the reports of the Combines Commissioner and his successor, the Restrictive Trade Practices

---

21. George W. Douglas and James C. Miller III, *Economic Regulation of Domestic Air Transport: Theory and Policy* (Washington: The Brookings Institution, 1974). For both a theoretical discussion and reference to relevant empirical studies see Richard Posner, "The Social Costs of Monopoly and Regulation," *Journal of Political Economy*, 83, No. 4 (1975), pp. 807-827. (Also see discussion in Chap. 12 of this text). In 1978, the U.S. Congress enacted a "sunset law" effectively deregulating the U.S. commercial airline industry. While the impact on the airlines non-price behaviour is hard to assess, deregulation has clearly increased the vigour of price competition and the variety of price-packages offered.

Commission (RTPC), some of them running to several hundred pages, are a virtually unparalleled source of information to the investigator. From these reports, and the trial judgements when prosecution followed, it is possible to discern some of the richness and variety of strategies and tactics firms adopt to avoid the uncertainties, the Prisoner's Dilemmas, inherent in oligopolistic rivalry. [22] If the student can avoid the understandable tendency to become self righteous in the face of palpable wrongdoing, he can learn much about small group behaviour, the strengths and weaknesses of competition, and even find some humour in the efforts of businessmen to avoid competition. The case studies presented below are brief summaries of some combines reports and trial judgements (and one Royal Commission Report) intended to highlight the variety of behaviour exhibited by oligopolistic industry. (Although the following case studies are designed to illustrate industrial behaviour, but not public policy, it bears repeating that those readers who find it disconcerting to read the case studies apart from the discussion of competition policy in Chapters 8 and 9, should proceed directly to Chapter 6 — picking up the thread of the discussion later on.)

A. Shipping Containers: A Case of Déjà Vu

When we last left the shipping container industry (on page 161) its members had just been convicted for participating in a price-fixing conspiracy which went under the name of Container Materials Limited. That was in 1940. As we look in again, it is early 1942. World War II is in full swing, and the Wartime Prices and Trade Board (WPTB) has just frozen the price of shipping containers at the price-fixing level set in 1940 by Container Materials Limited (CML). The CML pricing manual which had been condemned as contrary to the public interest in peacetime, was now adopted for the duration of the war by the WPTB. When the price controls ended in 1947, the somewhat modified pricing manual became the basis of a new price-fixing conspiracy which went under the name of Container Statistics. To make historical continuity complete, the wartime administrator, an industry official named F.C. Hayes, became the key figure in the establishment of Container Statistics, through which the next round of price fixing was facilitated. It was Hayes who developed the so-called "costing" manuals, and he was the intermediary through whom firms went when they wanted information about the costs of their competitors.[23]

---

22. Applied to oligopoly pricing the Prisoner's Dilemma implies there is a dominant strategy which if chosen by both (or all) parties acting independently will lead to an outcome in which all of the parties are worse off than they would be if they acted in concert. See Scherer op. cit., pp. 162-164.
23. Restrictive Trade Practices Commission, *Report Concerning the Manufacture, Distribution and Sale of Paperboard Shipping Containers and Related Products* (Ottawa, 1962), pp. 531-535.

Shipping containers are a custom-made product. They are made to order to meet the customer's requirements of size, style, weight to be carried, and printed information. One can thus imagine that the length of the "cost" manual would run into the hundreds of pages. It did. Moreover, it required continual upkeep, with a new edition appearing just prior to each industry price increase. Of course, what F.C. Hayes described as a cost manual was in fact a pricing manual. All that was required was that each firm add on to the cost information the manual provided, a common mark-up for profit margin, and price uniformity could thereby be maintained. [24] The Container Statistics system even allowed firms to make confidential discounts to purchasers who bought in particularly large quantities, owned shares or held a directorship in the shipping container company, or who were able and willing to import shipping containers. The last was obviously a minor concession as container board and shipping containers were protected by $22\frac{1}{2}$ percent and 20 percent tariffs respectively, imports never amounting to more than a few percentage points of total consumption. Between 1948 and 1954 the industry was one of the most profitable in Canada. [25]

Between 1945 and 1960 the structure of the shipping container industry changed markedly. In 1945, almost all shipping container firms were non-integrated, single-plant firms. By 1960, following a series of mergers, almost all firms were part of vertically integrated container board-shipping container complexes. Non-integrated shipping container firms now found it difficult to get the required supplies of container board. They were evidently victims of a supply "squeeze" not unlike the more common "price squeeze." Although the share of the market accounted for by the four largest container board firms declined from 92 percent to 75 percent between 1947 and 1960, vertical integration made entry at either the container board or shipping container levels very difficult. [26]

Not surprisingly, the Restrictive Trade Practices Commission found evidence that many of the mergers were consummated at inflated prices, no doubt reflecting the high profitability of shipping container firms made possible by their involvement in Container Statistics. Although the RTPC recommended the removal of customs duties on container board and shipping containers, thereby

24. Actually the costs, markups, and resultant prices varied between zones—or regions. The manual also supplied "costs" of transportation.
25. RTPC, pp. 492-95.
26. RTPC, pp. 50-60. In 1947, the Big Three container board firms were St. Lawrence, Bathurst, and Hinde and Dauch. Their market shares remained remarkably stable between 1947 and 1954, but declined somewhat when Canadian International Paper joined the industry in the late 1950s. By 1960, most container board output (at least that not destined for export) was destined for the firm's own shipping container "converter." As a result, the non-integrated firms accounted for only 11 percent of Canadian production.

opening the industry to foreign competition and supplies, the court, in finding the members of the industry guilty of a price-fixing conspiracy, did not see fit to accept the tariff removal remedy.[27]

B. Electric Large Lamps: Conscious Parallelism or Parallel Agreements

In September 1976, Canadian General Electric (CGE), Westinghouse Canada, and Sylvania Canada were convicted of price fixing in the sale of electric large lamps between 1959 and 1967.[28] "Large lamps," as distinct from "miniature lamps," are those used for residential, commercial, industrial, street or highway lighting. The three firms together supplied 95 percent of the Canadian market of which Canadian General Electric, the recognized price leader, supplied 45 percent. Imports were limited; customs duties were very high. No new entry occurred during the life of the alleged agreement. Given the market dominance of these three long-established firms, supplying an essentially homogeneous product (light bulbs of a particular specification are essentially the same), one might have thought that collusion was unnecessary, that recognized interdependence was so great that each firm would consciously follow parallel policies without actually *agreeing* to do so. In fact, the defendant firms made precisely this argument: their actions were those of rational, non-collusive oligopolists publishing parallel price lists in an industry in which price differentials could only result in profit-reducing price cutting.

The trial judge did not accept the conscious parallelism argument for reasons the RTPC report and the trial judgement make clear. The Big Three electric lamp producers were in constant contact with each other as part of their efforts to police identical sales plans. The sales plans had come into existence in 1959 and each were revised in 1961 as the three manufacturers attempted to control the prices set by their distribution systems. Unquestionably, price competition in the electric large lamp industry was the result of the rather complex system used in making sales to the large variety of users of lamps—residential consumers, industrial and commercial users, utilities, and governments. Some sales were made directly to final users (e.g. government, railroads), some to franchised retailers, and some to wholesalers and jobbers who then resold to commercial and industrial users, or to retailers before final resale to consumers. In some cases, distributors were on consignment, acting as agents of the

---

27. *Regina v. St. Lawrence Corporation, et. al,*(1966) 51 C.P.R. 170; (1969) 2 O.R.305.
28. *Regina v. Canadian General Electric Co. Ltd. et. al,* (1976) 34 C.C.C. (2d) 489. Also see Restrictive Trade Practices Commission, *Report in the Matter of an Inquiry Relating to the Production, Manufacture, Sale and Supply of Electric Large Lamps and Related Products,* Ottawa, 1971.

manufacturers who retained ownership of the goods until sold; in other cases the distributors took full possession of the goods. The upshot was a proliferating system of discounts, as competing distributional channels vied for business, in particular, for the commercial and industrial user markets. The impact of distributor discounts reached upward to the prices quoted by the three manufacturers. In the words of a CGE official speaking in February 1959:

> All of us lamp manufacturers have been contributing to lamp marketing conditions that are chaotic in almost every respect; where price cutting has largely replaced selling; where the growth and the breadth of our individual markets are being limited by runaway discounts, and where none of us is making the legitimate profits to which we are entitled.[29]

Soon thereafter, CGE put its 1959 large lamp sales plan into effect. It consisted of a detailed, 34-page document listing customer groups, prices, discount schedules and the like. The major aim of the plan was to eliminate competition between its agents serving the commercial and industrial market. Westinghouse and Sylvania followed suit with more or less similar plans. However, by 1960, it was clear that the sales plans had not assured price uniformity. Discounts continued to vary by size of order, volume of purchases and type of merchandising outlet. Thus all three manufacturers began to think about ways of revising their sales plans. The result was the introduction of the 1961 sales plans in which discounts from list prices were discontinued, to be replaced by a system of net prices. CGE issued its new price list in July 1961, and this was soon followed by the issuance of virtually identical lists by Westinghouse and Sylvania. Identical prices were also quoted in public tenders.

But maintaining price uniformity was not easy. From time to time distributors, or a low-level company official, broke from the sales plans, quoted lower prices, thereby initiating a flurry of correspondence or meetings between, and apologies from, senior company officials. For example, a Westinghouse bid of $8.55 per lamp on a contract to supply Northern Electric with 300 lamps brought the response that "it is a serious breach of the Lamp Sales programme": all the other bidders quoted $8.56 in line with the terms of the Sales Plans. Westinghouse cautioned its agents to calculate their quotes to three decimal places, and an executive of that company wrote "the jobber that breaks price without prior approval, is on the way out of the lamp business."[30] In another example, a CGE official apologized to Westinghouse for the actions of one of its agents who quoted a 5 percent cash discount instead of the normal 2

29. RTPC, p. 8.
30. *R v. Canadian General Electric Co. et. al*, p. 514.

percent. The CGE official promised to turn over the profits to charity.[31] Finally, when a service club in Moncton, N.B. decided to sell light bulbs as a means of raising funds, and had approached grocery wholesalers to secure a supply of bulbs, it set off a series of telephone calls between officials of CGE, Westinghouse and Sylvania.[32]

The evidence compiled by the RTPC and the prosecution makes it abundantly clear that maintaining price uniformity among the Big Three required much more than a simple recognition that parallel action is rational. The products of the three manufacturers had to be distributed and the distribution channels were more interested in sales than in maintaining price uniformity. If prices were to be kept uniform, more than the issuance of identical sales plans was necessary. The plans had to be policed, misunderstandings explained, and unexpected turns of event discussed by the three electric large lamp manufacturers. Thus competition in the distribution channels forced the manufacturers to collude extensively even though apparently none of the Big Three needed any prodding where identical pricing was concerned.

C. Ready-Mixed Concrete: The Merry Wives of Windsor

In 1966, four ready-mixed concrete firms based in Windsor, Ontario pleaded guilty to price fixing during 1963-64, and were fined a total of $13 500.[33] The case, while limited in time, space, and economic importance, illustrates well one of the motives for price agreements: the elimination of "special discounts" on which price competition in the ready-mixed concrete industry in Windsor had thrived. A rather humorous side to this case is evidence that the chief proponent of the pricing agreement may have been the first to break it.

Ready-mixed concrete markets are geographically limited to a radius of about 20 miles because of the time it takes the mixture to harden. The four Windsor builders' supplies firms which were parties to the agreement, Ryan, Sterling, Cross, and Woolatt, accounted for 94 percent of sales of Windsor-based plants, and 79 percent in Essex county. Ryan, the largest firm, and the driving force behind a price agreement, had a 42 percent market share in 1963. Prior to 1963, there had been a price agreement in 1959. From 1960 to 1963 list prices remained unchanged, but proliferating "special discounts" to customers eroded net prices.

Representatives of the four companies traditionally met over lunch on a social basis at what was called the "Glee Club." In November 1963, following a Glee

31. Ibid., p. 517-518.
32. RTPC, p. 58.
33. Restrictive Trade Practices Commission, *Report Relating to the Production, Manufacture, Sale and Supply of Ready-Mixed Concrete in Windsor, Ontario* (Ottawa, 1966). Also see *Regina v. Ryan Builders Supplies (Windsor) Ltd. et. al*, Supreme Court of Ontario, 1966.

Club meeting, executives of the four companies sat down to discuss the price-cutting problem. As a consequence, each firm drew up a list of special discounts from which a composite list was derived by Ryan to indicate, in the words of one participant, "the amount of money each company was throwing away through the forces of competition, and by the conniving of the customers of each individual firm." (The last clause is suggestive of the way in which buyers can limit the monopoly power of sellers by playing one off against the other.) The result was an agreement that each firm would: (a) phase out special discounts; (b) acknowledge (follow?) Ryan's published price list; (c) pay $1000 into a "trust fund," to be held in a safe deposit box. The precise use of the "trust fund" was apparently never determined, no system of fines having been agreed upon. When questioned, each member said that the money had been placed in the fund to show "good faith" in the effort to eliminate price cutting. As one participant said when questioned by the RTPC: "Well, nobody trusted each other and the one thousand dollars just flew out of the air, to keep everybody more or less free to speak up."[34]

The official beginning of the price agreement was January 1, 1964, at which time Ryan would cease making special discounts and quote prices from a published list dated January 18, 1960, to which federal sales tax would be tacked on. The others followed Ryan. Special discounts were greatly reduced and identical bids appeared in municipal tenders. One rather bizarre incident took place soon after the agreement went into effect. In February 1964, three of the firms, Ryan, Sterling, and Cross, submitted identical bids to the City of Windsor, to supply 1200 cubic yards of ready-mixed concrete, an amount that subsequently increased to 3500 cubic yards. Each bid included the usual 2 percent cash discount for prompt payment, usually before the 10th day of the month following delivery. Cross and Sterling quoted the 10th day. However, Ryan's bid quoted the 25th day, a fact which came to light when the *Windsor Star* reported that because of identical bids, the City had accepted Ryan's tender due to the extended payment term. Upon seeing the newspaper report (which naturally would have reached the eyes of his collaborators as well), Ryan called City Hall, claimed there had been a mistake, asked that the 25th be changed to the 10th, and when this was refused, withdrew his tender. The City of Windsor then rejected all three tenders, "by reason of similar bids," but subsequently purchased its requirements from Ryan.[35] The RTPC report does not indicate what Ryan's competitors and associates in the price agreement thought about the incident. However, identical tenders continued. On April 13, 1964, the Combines authorities moved in.

34. RTPC, op. cit., p 10.
35. Ibid., pp. 13-15.

D. Metal Culvert Manufacturers: Two-Time Losers

In September 1974, ten firms producing metal culverts for drainage were convicted before the Supreme Court of Ontario for violation of the price-fixing prohibition of the anticombines legislation and were fined a total of $515 000.[36] The heavy (by Canadian anticombine standards) fines were attributable to the fact that several of the conspirators were two-time losers, five having pleaded guilty, in 1959, to a charge of conspiring to fix and maintain uniform prices.[37] Thus culminated almost four decades of efforts to stifle price competition in the metal culvert industry.

The metal culvert industry was, until 1950, tightly oligopolistic. However, in the late 1950s and early 1960s, it loosened up somewhat primarily as a result of a combination of strong demand in the 1950s and 1960s as Canada's highway network rapidly expanded, and of easy entry conditions.[38] (It was stated by one defendant that around 1960 entry was possible with a capital investment of 40 to 50 thousand dollars, and that the required equipment could be housed in a barn). The metal culvert industry (and price) leader was Armco. Its market share in the early 1950s was about 40 percent of industry shipments; the next two largest firms together accounted for another 40 percent, and the fourth largest firm 10 percent. Imports were negligible, tariff barriers high. The main purchasers were governments: municipal, provincial and federal. Transportation costs were important, but a delivered price system was used to equalize the laydown prices of metal culverts charged by the various producers at any given locale.

In 1925, a Metal Culvert Council had been established with Eastern and Western sections. Price lists were distributed and, if the defendants' guilty plea is to be taken at face value, price fixing commenced immediately. There were repeated meetings at which prices were discussed. There were informal consultations between the firms about the various aspects of the pricing of their product, whose numerous dimensions, varieties of coatings, and transportation costs required a complex price list. Meetings of the Metal Culvert Council included resolutions on prices, as for example: "RESOLVED that prices to Steam Railway and Municipalities in all Western Provinces be increased a flat

---

36. *Regina v. Armco Canada Ltd. et al.* (1974) 21 C.C.C. (2d) 129; (1975) 24 C.C.C. (2d) 147.

37. *Regina v. Armco Drainage & Metal Products of Canada Ltd. et al*, Ontario Supreme Court, Nov. 13, 1959. Also see Restrictive Trade Practices Commission, *Report Concerning the Manufacture, Distribution and Sale of Metal Culverts and Related Products*, Ottawa, 1957. The fines for the first violation totaled $65,000.

38. While there is some competition between metal culverts and concrete pipe, the two products apparently occupy separate markets because the choice between the two depends on the size of pipe required, and underlying foundation, depth of fill, weight of traffic, installation costs, and anticipated life of culvert, as well as price. RTPC, pp 110-112.

2% all round, effective November 25th, 1949."[39] The price lists published by the various companies were identical, adherence to published prices was almost complete (though witnesses testified that from time to time prices varied by "the odd cent here and there"), and when governments began soliciting tenders in the mid 1950s, the bids were identical.

After their conviction for price fixing, in 1959, the metal culvert firms entered into stiff price competition with one another and with new entrants to the industry. (By 1962, there were 22 firms with 49 plants.)[40] Industry profits were reduced. Despite calls for an end to "cut-throat" competition, price-cutting continued as hungry firms vigorously bid for government contracts. In November 1961, five major producers formed a new association, the Canadian Steel Pipe Institute (CSPI), and were soon joined by several other culvert firms. The ostensible purpose of the association was to improve the position of metal vis-à-vis concrete pipe, but its real purpose was to stabilize prices and eliminate "cut-throat competition" in a manner that would not contravene the anticombines laws. The association was also joined by the two largest steel firms, STELCO and DOFASCO, who as suppliers of the basic input into the production of metal culverts, were to play a major role in getting each of the firms to adhere to an "Open Price Policy." (Apparently, tough competition in the metal culvert industry was putting downward pressure on the prices of the sheet steel used in culvert manufacture.)

The "Open Price Policy," which was first proposed by Robertsteel Canada, a major culvert producer, required that each firm independently and *openly* set out its prices, discounts, and credit terms in written and printed form and make them available to all customers and competitors. What in fact was really intended can be inferred from the following statement contained in a letter: "With the publication of individual price lists, which are arrived at by independent decision, it is expected that prices will adjust themselves, tending to reflect the true state of the market through the natural forces of *known* competition."[41] The "adjustment," of course, was meant to be in the direction of uniformity.

In June 1963, Robertsteel published an Open Price List, but the effort was unsuccessful as few firms were inclined to follow Robertsteel's lead. Armco as the low cost producer was especially reluctant. Shortly thereafter, representatives of STELCO and DOFASCO got into the act, publishing a report establishing the obvious; that price cutting was not in the best interests of the metal culvert industry. Robertsteel again published a price list, and this time, the other firms followed suit, including the "reluctant bride," Armco. Miraculously, identical

39. RTPC, p. 71.
40. *R v. Armco Canada Ltd.* (1974), p. 134. Also see Restrictive Trade Practices Commission, *The Metal Culvert Industry, Ontario and Quebec* (Ottawa, 1970), pp. 10-27.
41. *Regina v. Armco Canada Ltd. et al.*, 21 Canadian Criminal Cases (2d) 141.

bids appeared on tenders to the Department of Highways of Ontario (DHO) and to Ontario municipalities, where previously it was usual to have several tenders with no similar bids. Discounts to the DHO and to Ontario municipalities disappeared, and the percentage of contracts awarded to the low bidder sharply declined (because in so many cases there was no low bidder). A not uncommon occurrence is revealed in a letter written by the Clerk of Wentworth County who stated that nine tenders were opened but all bids were identical in the amount of $6,009.15.[42]

Despite some worries about the attitude of the anticombines authorities toward such tactics as sending one's price lists to one's competitors, the "agreement" held together until, in 1967, a new supplier of metal culverts refused to join CSPI and its "Open Price Policy." Then open price competition resumed, and so did the investigation of the industry by the Anti-Combines Branch. From an economist's view, however, what is perhaps most revealing is the timing of and ease with which the "Open Price Policy" disintegrated. It seems that competitive forces were potentially strong and never far below the surface. There is reason to believe that barring elaborate price-fixing schemes, metal culvert firms behave and perform in a manner not materially different from that of firms in an atomistic, competitive industry.

E. Western Fertilizers: A Case of Mistaken Identity

In early 1980, the Supreme Court of Alberta acquitted the six fertilizer-producing firms based in Western Canada of conspiring to fix identical prices.[43] The case is of interest because identity of list prices is not necessarily evidence, circumstantial or otherwise, of collusion, and list prices are not necessarily, or perhaps even usually, indications of actual or selling prices.

The Western Canadian fertilizer industry had its beginning in 1931 when Cominco, the mining giant, became the first firm to manufacture chemical fertilizer in Western Canada. Prior to this time fertilizer was not used by farmers in Canada's west. Cominco was induced to enter fertilizer production to make use of chemical byproducts of its metallurgical operations. Between 1931 and 1954 Cominco was the only producer of fertilizer in Western Canada. However, as the use of chemical fertilizers rapidly expanded in the postwar period, five other firms entered the industry between 1954 and 1969. Like Cominco, two of these entrants, Sheritt Gordon Mines Ltd. and Imperial Oil, are much better known for their activities in other industries.

The economic facts of the fertilizer industry in Western Canada are simple. After 1954 the industry became a classic oligopoly producing an essentially

---

42. Ibid., p. 168.
43. *R. v. Cominco Ltd. et al.* (1980) 2 W.W.R. 693; 46 C.P.R. (2d) 154.

homogeneous product. Except for Imperial Oil, none of the firms sold directly at retail. From the time Cominco entered the industry in 1931, industry capacity substantially exceeded the demand for fertilizer in Western Canada. As a result, the firms were continually attempting to find world, particularly U.S., markets for their excess production capacity.

In the mid 1970s the Anticombines Division began an investigation of the industry. On the basis of a massive sweep of the files of the six firms, the Crown built a case based on documentary evidence that the retail prices for any given formulation of fertilizer produced by each of the firms were identical, or so nearly so as to suggest a conspiracy to fix prices. In building its case the Crown was frank to admit that its evidence was purely circumstantial—it had no direct evidence of a conspiracy. Moreover, the pricing information disseminated by the manufacturers was sufficiently dissimilar and the timing sufficiently haphazard to make the government's case a difficult one. In fact, the very difficulty of building a legally convincing case might have suggested a quite different hypothesis: to wit, there was no conspiracy, and that the identity of prices was brought about as each firm adjusted its list prices to that set by the others in order not to place itself at a large disadvantage in the sale of an essentially homogeneous, heavily used, and well known to its users, product. Nevertheless, the Crown pressed on until its evidentiary balloon was punctured by the defence with abundant evidence not only of discounting but of a pervasive difference between apparent (list) and actual prices at which sales were made.

F. Wooden Matches: A Case Study in Predation

There is a school of economic thinking which argues that predatory pricing is economically irrational and consequently rare if not nonexistent.[44] If predation means something on the scale of the sordid activities engaged in by the swashbuckling Standard Oil empire of John D. Rockefeller in the late 19th century, then predation does, in fact, appear to be rare in modern Canadian business history. However, it is not non-existent, as is illustrated by the story of the Eddy Match Company in the period between 1927 and 1950.[45]

Prior to 1927, three Canadian firms supplied most of the wooden matches consumed in Canada. Two of these firms were foreign-owned by the three large international firms (Diamond of U.S., Bryant of Great Britain, and the Swedish Match Company) which had cartelized the wooden match industry in the western hemisphere. The third firm was the E.B. Eddy Co. In 1927, the three

---

44. A good discussion of this viewpoint and its shortcomings is found in Scherer, *Industrial Market Structure and Economic Performance*, pp. 335-340. Also see B.S. Yamey, "Predatory Price Cutting: Notes and Comments," *The Journal of Law and Economics* (April 1972) pp. 129-142.

45. *Rex v. Eddy Match Co. Ltd. et al*, (1952) 104 C.C.C. 39; (1954) 109 C.C.C. 1.

Canadian firms were merged into one with Bryant and Diamond holding 90 percent of the new corporation, the Eddy Match Co.

From its beginning the Eddy Match Co. did not like competition. This attitude was undoubtedly reinforced by the decision of its foreign owners, who dominated the industry internationally, to prevent any exports of matches to Canada. In return, all of Eddy's production had to be sold in Canada. Eddy's monopoly position did, however, give rise to sufficient profits to attract entry into an industry with few natural barriers. Between 1928 and 1949 four companies challenged Eddy's monopoly. (A fifth firm was established by Eddy's foreign owners as a "phony" competitor to conceal Eddy's monopolistic position.)[46] In each case Eddy eventually absorbed the challengers, but not before softening them up through such pricing devices as preferred prices and special discounts to customers wooed by the rival firm, "fighting brands," and flooding the rival's market with matches. These predatory practices may have been necessary to convince the rival firm to sell out; in any event they undoubtedly reduced the selling price of the established firms and dampened the enthusiasm of potential entrants.[47] Although all of the rival match firms eventually disappeared, two did so profitably. Before a further challenge could be made, the anticombines laws were applied and Eddy was convicted in 1951, for its monopolizing activities. In the meantime paper matches were establishing a more effective challenge to Eddy's monopoly.

G. Evaporated Milk: Meeting or Taming the Competition

While predatory pricing on the vicious scale once carried out by the Eddy Match Company is apparently rare, price cutting to tame one's actual or potential competitors is both more common and more likely to avoid legal sanctions. An interesting example is illustrated by the behaviour of the leading evaporated milk firm, the Carnation Company of Canada, which led to an RTPC investigation and report, a trial and an acquittal which was upheld on appeal.[48] What adds interest to the Carnation case is that at just about the same time, Carnation's U.S. parent was one of several firms that had to pay treble damages for what seems comparatively benign price-cutting behaviour, in a decision upheld by the U.S. Supreme Court.[49]

46. Ibid., (1952), p. 59.
47. In one case Eddy went far beyond predatory practices in its attempt to eliminate a rival. Eddy set up a comprehensive espionage and intelligence system in order to follow to the minutest detail the activities of the Federal Match Co. and its president, J.W. Charette.
48. Restrictive Trade Practices Commission, *Report Concerning the Manufacture, Distribution, and Sale of Evaporated Milk and Related Products*, Ottawa, 1962. *Regina v. Carnation Company of Canada Ltd.*, (1966) unreported; (1969) 4 D.L.R. (3d) 133.
49. *Utah Pie Co. v. Continental Baking Co. et al.* 386 U.S. 685 (1967).

Evaporated milk is not a particularly significant product. But it is, perhaps, representative of those nationally advertised, branded products whose sales depend in part on the promotional efforts of retailers, including displays, shelving, and special discounts. The scene of the drama that unfolded in 1959-1960 was Western Canada, primarily Alberta and British Columbia. Carnation, by far the largest supplier of evaporated milk in Canada, with a national market share slightly in excess of 60 percent, and 86 percent in central and eastern Canada, found itself pitted against two small but tough competitors, Alpha and Pacific, in the West. Carnation's overall Western share was approximately 25 percent; in Alberta where Alpha held sway it was 35 percent; in B.C. where Pacific held sway it was only 10 percent.[50]

Carnation's plants were located in Ontario and Quebec. It absorbed some of the freight costs of its shipments to the West from its profitable eastern sales, and maintained consumer goodwill through its own and the U.S. parent company's national advertising campaign. In contrast, Alpha and Pacific depended heavily on retailer efforts "purchased" through cooperative advertising, promotional allowances, secret rebates, consumer giveaways and the like. Late in 1959, Alpha, which until then had not made sales in B.C., attempted to get a foothold in B.C. with a 2¢-off promotional campaign limited to a small area in the eastern part of that province. Alpha advised Carnation and Pacific in advance of its plans, which were met by a "wait and see" attitude from Carnation. However, when the promotion began, Carnation retaliated by cutting price 2¢ per can across the whole of Alberta and B.C. In self-defence Pacific followed suit. Alpha was then forced to reduce its price 2¢ on its mainstay Alberta sales; a price war was in full swing.

What had happened? Unbeknownst to Alpha and Pacific, Carnation was spoiling for a fight. It had been losing ground in the West, losses it attributed to the retailer-oriented promotional efforts of Alpha and Pacific. Carnation's internal correspondence makes this clear:

> We feel that the time is getting close to when we will have a knock-down drag-out competitive situation in the West. This situation has been brewing ever since our spread between the eastern zone price and the western zone price became greater than ten cents. They have had more money to play with and are becoming increasingly liberal with their promotional programs.[51]

Alpha's 2¢-off sale triggered the inevitable "knock-down drag-out" fight. Alpha and Pacific soon found their position becoming untenable as they, unlike

---

50. Alpha held 45 percent of the Alberta market and Pacific 88 percent of the B.C. market in 1959.
51. RTPC, p.41.

Carnation, could not subsidize their price cutting with profits from Eastern Canada. However, Carnation would not relent until Alpha and Pacific promised to end cooperative advertising, retailer rebates and allowances, and specials. A number of top-level meetings between the three firms ensued, with Alpha and Pacific eventually caving in.

One inexplicable aspect of the case was the Government's decision to bring charges (which failed) under the price discrimination section of the anti-combines laws, rather than charges for attempting to eliminate competition. What is clear from the events is that Carnation was intent on ending price and other forms of competition, except that from general advertising. When questioned by the RTPC whether as part of the "agreement" to end the price war Carnation had forbidden future competition in price, an official of Pacific answered: "Forbidden is rather a strong word. I suppose there is a suggestion there. The suggestion is if you do it, the sky might fall on you."[52]

H. Plastic Lids: Or Tempest on a Coffee Cup

Sometimes competitive or "last resort" price cutting is mistaken for predatory pricing. A clear cut example is the behaviour of Portion Packaging, a division of Consumer's Glass of Toronto, which until 1975 was the only Canadian producer of small plastic lids to cover drink cups such as those found in most vending machines.[53] Portion was charged with predatory pricing after it engaged in price cutting following the entry into the lid market by a second Canadian firm, Amhil Enterprises. Entry into the plastic lid market is easy, requiring no more than the rental or purchase of approximately $200,000 worth of thermoforming equipment. Unfortunately Amhil's entry was not justified by existing market demand, since Portion had been operating at only 70 percent of capacity—a fraction which fell substantially after Amhil's appearance. However, Amhil, whose founders were former executives of Portion, anticipated, with some reason, that Portion would shortly withdraw from the lid market.

Portion, in fact, had decided to phase out its lid operations because its market share was declining in the face of foreign (U.S.) competition. Moreover, it appeared likely that some of Portion's five large customers would begin to produce lids in-house. However, Portion was not about to hasten its withdrawal in response to Amhil's entry. Portion reacted vigorously to what it probably viewed as "traitorous" behaviour by former executives who used the contacts they had forged in Portion's employment to lure business to their new firm, Amhil. Thus, Portion's response to an offer Amhil made to shave 2 to 3 percent

52. Ibid., p. 80.
53. See *R v. Consumer's Glass Co. Ltd. and Portion Packaging Ltd.* (1981) 33 O.R. (2d) 228.

off the price Portion quoted to its five large buyers was anything but friendly. Portion announced discounts averaging 16 percent which were subsequently enhanced another 5 percent. As it turned out Portion's price cut won back business lost to Amhil, placed Amhil in financial difficulty, and prompted Amhil to seek charges that Portion was engaged in a policy of predatory pricing in violation of section 34c of the Combines Investigation Act.

The predatory pricing charge lacked credibility, as the trial judge clearly grasped.[54] A necessary condition for predatory conduct is market power, something Portion lacked as a result of stiff foreign competition and the apparent willingness of large customers to make their own lids. Moreover, Portion's price cuts were necessary if the firm was to minimize losses produced as a result of sharing a limited domestic market with Amhil. Unable to raise prices due to foreign competition and the willingness of its customers to produce lids in-house, and faced with higher unit costs as capacity utilization dropped to 45 percent in 1976, Portion's only sensible strategy was to cut prices in order to regain market share and spread its fixed costs over a larger output. This policy was temporarily successful. But subsequent loss of a major customer, Continental Can, to Amhil led Portion to follow through on its earlier decision to withdraw from the market. This it did in 1979, leaving a financially distressed Amhil as the only Canadian supplier of plastic lids. The government, however, did not drop its charges of predation against Portion, even though that firm looked more like a victim of circumstances than a hard-bitten predator. It was left to the trial judge to apply the appropriate economic analysis and to finally put an end to the tempest over cup lids.

J. Farm Machinery: A Case of Multinational Price Discrimination

In popular parlance price discrimination is a "bad word." Yet price discrimination occurs whenever the prices of identical goods and services differ (to the same or different buyers) for reasons other than differences in cost of supply.[55] Thus we conjecture that price discrimination is a widespread phenomenon, that it is usually innocuous, and typically goes unnoticed. In some instances unsystematic, and temporary, price discrimination may be pro-competitive, and thus beneficial. For example, a firm which absorbs transportation costs in order to meet a competitor's price in another locale is technically engaged in a form of

---

54. Ibid., pp. 245–246.
55. Strictly speaking price discrimination occurs when transactions take place at different price-cost ratios for identical goods or services. Thus transactions at the same price entailing different costs involve price discrimination. An excellent discussion of price discrimination, particularly its geographical aspect, is F.M. Scherer, *Industrial Market Structure and Economic Performance*, Chap. 11.

geographic price discrimination, which no reasonable person should condemn. Price discrimination is, however, injurious when it is part of a campaign of predation. Eddy Match's sharpshooting practices (discussed above) provide one example. Another is the use by Zinc Oxide of Canada (ZOCO) of its position as a major buyer to extract discounts on refined zinc. The discounts were then used to finance a price cutting campaign aimed at "encouraging" ZOCO's zinc oxide producing competitors to merge with ZOCO.[56] Price discrimination is also injurious when it is systematic and long lived, resulting in the extraction of consumer surplus without providing any *quid pro quo* in the form of output level pushed to "competitive" (P = MC) levels.[57] An illustration of this objectionable form of price discrimination, which was carried out on a world scale, is provided by the farm machinery industry.

In 1970, a Royal Commission on Farm Machinery issued its report into the pricing practices of the multinational firms that dominate the agricultural machinery industry. The report confirmed a popular suspicion: Canadian farmers paid much more for tractors than their European counterparts, particularly those in England. The price differentials were much larger than transportation and related distribution costs. Tariffs were not the problem since the Canadian tariff on farm machinery had been removed in 1944. The crux of the problem was the market power of the world's leading farm equipment manufacturers (International Harvester, Deere, Ford, Massey-Ferguson) which permitted them to milk varying national demand elasticities, while at the same time effectively preventing Canadians from purchasing tractors directly from European dealers.[58]

The basic facts of the farm machinery case are these. Most of the world production of farm machinery is concentrated in the hands of the leading multinationals. Very substantial plant scale economies exist so that most of the firms at the competitive fringe operate at a cost disadvantage relative to the leading firms. In the 1960s no tractors were produced in Canada, although one of the leading firms, Massey-Ferguson, is located here, its Canadian plants specializing in the production of combines. In the first two decades after World War II a major shift in farm machinery *production* from North America to

---

56. The campaign was largely successful. Durham, the second largest producer, sold out to ZOCO giving the latter about 80% of the Canadian market. RTPC, *Report Concerning Production and Distribution of Zinc Oxide* (Ottawa, 1958).

57. The distinction here is between "third degree" price discrimination (always objectionable) and "first" and "second degree" price discrimination (with some redeeming features). See Scherer, op. cit., pp. 254-257.

58. Royal Commission on Farm Machinery, *Special Report on Prices of Tractors and Combines in Canada and Other Countries* (Ottawa, 1969). International Harvester and Deere *tractor* production was primarily in the U.S., while that of Ford and Massey-Ferguson was primarily in Europe.

Europe occurred—the former's share falling from 70 percent to 33 over the period.[59]

The pricing practices of the leading firms provided an umbrella for the competitive fringe. In addition the price structure was intentionally discriminatory with North American, particularly Canadian, consumers on the losing end. Since much of the production took place in lower-wage Europe while much of the demand was in North America, profit maximization on a world scale required high prices here and lower prices there. Canada, with no domestic production, was particularly vulnerable to the artificial transfer prices of the multinational firms. Evidence was amassed by the Royal Commission showing that Canadian farmers paid up to $1000 to $2000 more for small and medium-sized tractors than their English counterparts.[60] Yet ocean transportation and additional distribution costs were only about $500. However, when Canadian farmers tried to purchase tractors directly from English dealers they ran into difficulties. The manufacturers had included in the dealership agreements provisions prohibiting the sale of tractors for export—and these provisions were sharply enforced.[61] Failure to comply could mean a loss of dealership.

Large price differences, such as those that existed for tractors, would normally be "arbitraged" as products move from the low-price to the high-price market. It is for this reason that price discrimination is usually limited in time and degree. The farm machinery case is exceptional, although made somewhat more probable as a result of the oligopolistic and multinational features of the industry. It is not easy to combat. The Canadian market is much too small to support an efficient Canadian tractor plant, although Versatile, a Winnipeg-based manufacturer, began tractor production in the late 1960s. The Canadian anticombines laws do not extend to agreements between foreign firms and their dealers. However, the publicity generated by the Royal Commission may have led to pressures on the multinational firms to reduce price differences because the issue did not generate much heat in the 1970s.

Conclusion

The vignettes of oligopolistic behaviour chiefly illustrate the strength of the businessman's urge to avoid price competition. They also illustrate the fact that the economic environment is often not conducive to the maintenance of uniform prices. There are probably few industries in which uniform prices evolve

59. Ibid., p 7.
60. However the prices of large (75 + horsepower) tractors, primarily produced in the U.S., were often higher in Europe than in Canada.
61. The effective separation of markets by the farm machinery manufacturers is described in detail in Ibid., Chap. 7.

naturally and even fewer in which they can be maintained without some concerted joint efforts by the firms involved. Typically, both competitive forces *and* the desire for price uniformity are strong. (Presumably the former accentuates the desire for the latter.) Yet unless there are formal agreements, the latter is likely to be dominated by the former.

It exaggerates to attribute most oligopolistic price uniformity to conscious, but totally independent, parallelism. Usually something more is necessary, suggesting that a strong vigilant public policy against collusive agreements is perhaps the best guarantee of price competition. While high concentration might appear, on its face, to be a blueprint for monopolistic behaviour and performance, it is perhaps the greater ease of reaching agreement where numbers are very few, that makes high concentration most worrisome. In other words, fewness without formal collusion *may* spell more competition than most assumptions about oligopolistic behaviour imply. If so, the weight of "competitive" policies should fall on punishing collusion and keeping artificial barriers to entry low, rather than on policies designed to restructure concentrated industries. An exception perhaps are those industries dominated by a firm with a market share so large that the remaining firms are nothing but a passive fringe.

6

Canadian Industrial
Performance

The study of industrial organization usually culminates with an evaluation of industrial performance. Performance is evaluated not in terms of private advantage, but in terms of social benefit. Thus, for example, while a firm might well measure its own success in terms of its profitability, to an economist huge profitability, if it is the result of market power, suggests *social* inefficiency in the allocation of resources. A misallocation of resources is a burden on the community as a whole. Before we turn to a more detailed examination of the concept of market or industrial performance, as that term is used in the economics of industrial organization, it is useful to see how the discussion of performance relates to the elements of industry structure and behavior discussed in the three preceding chapters.

As we noted in chapter 2, the standard industrial organization paradigm has market structure influencing firm behaviour and affecting industry performance. For example, the highly concentrated shipping container industry, described in chapter 5, is a good illustration of the influence of industry structure on behaviour and performance. However, other industry vignettes presented in chapter 5 suggest that industry behaviour is not so predictable, and is, in addition, not easily quantifiable. For this reason most attempts to empirically test hypotheses about the influence of industry structure have related performance variables directly to structure. As we shall see, most of these studies have tested for the impact of such structural variables as the size distribution of firms (concentration ratio), economies of scale, product differentiation (advertising intensity) and entry barriers on average profit rates over a period of years. There are, however, some theoretical ambiguities or doubts about the hypothesized relationships.

Economic theory predicts that a profit-maximizing monopolist will restrict output and raise price relative to the output and price levels that would prevail in a competitively organized industry, assuming the cost conditions facing the monopolist and the competitors are similar. There are three potential problems with this widely understood and accepted prediction, so far as its application to the study of industrial organization is concerned. First, it is often remarked that few markets are monopolized, reducing the possible relevance (although not necessarily the usefulness) of the theoretical prediction. The relevance issue is more than a quibble if, as some economists argue, the theoretical grounds are weak for making the jump from the prediction that a monopolist will set a price above marginal cost (MC) to the hypothesis that concentrated industries will tend to enjoy supranormal profits.[1] The theoretical weakness resides in two factors. The monopoly model focuses on a single leading firm, while concentration refers to a group of firms where behaviour is much less predictable. In addition, monopoly and oligopoly theory make predictions about the relationship between price and MC, in contrast to the concentration-profitability hypothesis which refers to the relationship between price and average cost.

Second, even in those markets which are served by a single, or dominant firm, the exercise of market power is restrained unless there are high barriers to entry. In fact, most economists view the existence of substantial barriers to entry as an essential requisite to the *persistent* exercise of market power.[2] Moreover, in the absence of entry barriers it is questionable whether it is legitimate to speak of monopoly power even if a single, dominant, or small cluster of leading firms is capable of *temporarily* setting price above cost. Since the existence of high entry barriers is much less frequently found than is high concentration or monopoly, economists tend to be more skeptical about the existence of monopoly power than is the layman.

Third, if economies of scale do exist, the *ceteris paribus* assumption about similar cost conditions may be violated. As we have seen in chapter 3, the juxtaposition of technological conditions and Canada's small (domestic) market implies that in many industries there is room for only a few efficiently scaled firms. In these circumstances, it is possible for economic profits to persist in the long run, even in the absence of monopoly power (correctly defined). Here is an

1. For example, see Almarin Phillips, "A Critique of Empirical Studies of Relations Between Market Structure and Profitability," *Journal of Industrial Economics* (June 1976), pp. 241-43.
2. In fact, technically the monopoly concept presumes that entry is "blockaded." Entry is "blockaded" either when government limits sellers to those already in a market or when natural or strategic barriers to entry are so high that the price which would attract entry is above the profit maximizing price. See Joe Bain, *Barriers to New Competition* (Cambridge: Harvard University Press, 1956), chapter 1.

explanation why. Suppose that the market is only large enough for two and one-third minimum efficiently scaled, single plant, firms, and that in the range immediately above MES there are no diseconomies of scale. In this case, the market is not large enough for a third MES plant (firm) and can be efficiently supplied by two plants (firms). Economies of scale therefore constitute, in a real sense, a barrier to entry. However entry is otherwise assumed to be "free" in the sense that entry of newcomers is not impeded by legislation, ignorance, an imperfect capital market, or technological handicap.[3] Finally, let us assume that the two firms sufficiently recognize their interdependence that they are able to set price above cost and earn supranormal profits. These supranormal profits may continue to be earned in the long run if the industry could not profitably support a third firm, as is the case here, even though entry is otherwise "free." It would be an error, however, to employ this result as evidence of a concentration-profitability relationship as such. Rather, in the case described here, supranormal profitability in the presence of "free" entry is wholly explicable in terms of technological conditions, the size of the market, and oligopoly behaviour.[4]

There are additional causes for concern with the standard industrial paradigm. The one-way causation running from structure to performance, suggested by the I-O paradigm (see chapter 2) may mislead. For example, predatory and exclusive behaviour may influence industry structure. Alternatively, a firm's conduct (enterprising or lethargic) may influence its market performance and ultimately its market share (structure).[5] Thus a "superior" managerial or engineering team may initially give a firm non-scale-cost advantages which in turn are parlayed via lower prices or better services into larger market shares and rates of return. Or, it is possible that the direction of causation may be reversed. Poor industry performance may prompt government intervention, of a protectionist or regulatory nature. These may feedback upon industry behaviour and structure.[6] For example, tariff protection may make monopolistic *behaviour* easier, while regulation of entry or industry membership affects *market structure*.

3. See D. Dewey, "Industrial Concentration and the Rate of Profit: Some Neglected Theory," *Journal of Law and Economics* (April 1976), pp. 67-78.
4. Ibid., p. 78.
5. Phillips has labeled this C→P→S model the "Chicago School Approach." See Almarin Phillips,"Industrial Concentration and Public Policy: A Middle Ground," and "Commentary," *Industrial Concentration: The New Learning*, H.C. Goldschmid, et al. ed. (Boston: Little Brown, 1974) pp. 383-392 and especially 408-413. Alternatively, Phillips describes the "Chicago" approach as $G \nearrow^S_{\searrow C} \searrow_\nearrow P$ where government (G) plays an important "interventionist" or regulatory role.
6. Ibid., pp. 411-413. Phillips' model is much more complex than the orthodox or "Chicago" models. He employs extensive feedbacks from performance to structure and conduct by "affected parties" including government, regulators, potential entrants and existing firms.

Aspects of Industrial Performance

When industrial performance is evaluated the economic criteria on which judgements are based include (i) efficiency; (ii) technological progress; (iii) full utilization of resources (full employment) and (iv) income distribution effects. Most studies focus on various facets of economic efficiency, including its dynamic component, listed separately here as technological progress. The contribution (or lack of it) of specific forms of industrial structure and behaviour to the maintenance of full employment is highly uncertain, though not unimportant. The income distribution effects are more certain, but economists have tended to be leery of drawing value judgements, as is inevitable where distributional matters are concerned.

The efficiency criteria can be broken down into three subcategories (a) allocative efficiency, (b) scale or technical efficiency, and (c) "X"—or production at least cost—efficiency. Together with technological innovation and invention, "progressiveness" or (dynamic efficiency), the subcategories of efficiency have provided the most widely adopted bases for evaluating the influence of market structure on industrial performance.

Traditionally, economic theorists have been most concerned with allocative efficiency—the efficiency with which resources are allocated throughout the economy. The emphasis on allocative efficiency reflects the concern economists have had with the maximization of economic welfare. Welfare maximization requires that resources be allocated to the production of those goods and services that consumers want, which implies that production should be pushed to the point where the cost of producing an additional unit of a given output (marginal cost) equals the price that consumers (at the margin) are willing to pay for the last unit of output.

Economic *theorists* have given much less attention to X-inefficiency (because the profit maximization assumption implies cost minimization), to scale inefficiencies (by assuming constant returns to scale), and to dynamic inefficiency (by assuming technology is exogeneously determined). Yet the real costs to society of the latter types of inefficiency almost surely outweigh those of allocative inefficiency. While students of industrial organization have been more sensitive than pure theorists to the variety of types of inefficiency, and their relationships to market conditions, most empirical work, by focusing on profit rate–market structure relations, is implicitly related to the allocative efficiency issue. In the last decade or two, however, substantial work also has been done on the determinants of technological innovation and invention.[7]

7. For a recent comprehensive textual discussion of structure-performance relations see W.G. Shepherd, *The Economics of Industrial Organization* (Prentice-Hall, 1979), chapters 13, 20-22.

The logic of the profit rate–market structure relationship rests on the assumption that high rates of profits over extended (5 to 10 year) periods of time are an indication of the exercise of monopoly power rather than the reward for lower costs. Among the factors that convey market power are the market share(s) of the leading firm(s) and the height of barriers to entry. In particular, the hypothesis is that high industry concentration facilitates tacit or explicit collusion. If the level of industry profits is correlated with the statistical proxies of market structure (e.g. concentration ratios, advertising intensity) then, the argument runs, profitability is attributable to monopoly (market) power. Assuming a downward-sloping (industry) demand curve, and a dose of oligopolistic coordination, it is easy to infer from high profitability a misallocation of resources.

A pictoral presentation of the argument is given in Figure 6-1 (which is similar to Figure 2-2). "Excess" profitability implies that price is elevated substantially above marginal (and average) cost, AC_o (cost including normal profit). With a downward-sloping demand curve this implies that industry output is lower than would have prevailed had price been closer to marginal

Figure 6-1

The Welfare Loss Attributable to Monopolistic Resource Allocation and Waste

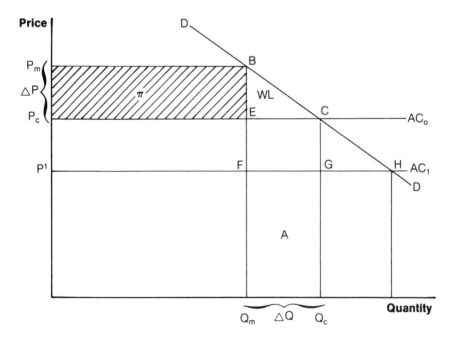

cost. Consumers pay for the smaller output at higher prices than is required to produce additional units of output, and they thereby transfer potential consumer surplus to producers who receive it in the form of profits π. However the smaller output ensures that the producer surplus (excess profits) is less than the consumer surplus lost (P_mBCP_c). The difference is the welfare loss due to the resources misallocated by monopoly pricing. If the released resources do not find a home in other employments, instead lying idle, there is an additional loss equal to rectangle A, i.e., ECQ_cQ_m.

The welfare loss (WL) due to the failure to achieve allocative efficiency is, in principle, measurable. It is $WL = \frac{1}{2}\Delta P\Delta Q = \frac{1}{2}\eta PQt^2$.[8] The welfare loss depends on the elasticity of demand and the percentage elevation in price.[9] Despite substantial evidence of excess profitability in a number of leading U.S. industries, some estimates of welfare loss have been very small, much less than one percentage point of GNP.[10] Estimates of monopoly-generated profitability are substantially greater, and quite impressive, when capitalized to determine net worth attributable to historical monopoly. Presumably, the distributional effects contribute to interest in, and concern about, the impact of monopoly power.

The link between monopoly power, profitability and efficiency is much more complicated than the preceding discussion might suggest. First, recall from chapters 2 and 3 that market structure and the achievement of scale efficiencies may be correlated. Where market size is small, achievement of scale efficiencies leaves room for fewer firms, each of which may have greater market power as a result of fewness. Second, it has been argued that the "excessive profitability" of leading firms may be due to their superior efficiency—that, in

8. Let $\dfrac{\Delta P}{P} = t$; $\eta = \dfrac{\Delta Q}{\Delta P} \cdot \dfrac{P}{Q}$; then $\Delta P = Pt$ and $\Delta Q = \eta\Delta P \dfrac{Q}{P} = \eta$ Qt, which may be substituted into the WL formula for ΔP and ΔQ respectively.

9. See the discussion in the final section of chapter 4. Note that it is incorrect to simply assume that the welfare loss necessarily increases as the elasticity of demand (η) increases. The reason is that the ability to exert market power, reflected in the size of $\Delta P/P$, declines as η increases. Landes and Posner show that, in fact, the WL will actually fall as η increases. See William Landes and Richard Posner, "Market Power in Antitrust Cases," *Harvard Law Review* 94, no. 5 (March 1981), pp. 991-95. Also, Stegemann shows that in an open economy (but not a "small" one) the exercise of market power may produce, in addition to the familiar WL, a loss due to "excessive importation." Excessive importation arises when monopolistic pricing induces some buyers to purchase imports when equivalent domestic goods could have been purchased at a lower social opportunity cost. See Klaus Stegemann, "The Social Costs of Monopoly in an Open Economy," *Canadian Journal of Economics* (November 1984). Because Stegemann's analysis does not apply to firms operating within a *small* open economy model, it may have limited application to Canada's manufacturing sector.

10. Early estimates placed it at less than .1 percent of GNP. See A. Harberger, "Monopoly and Resource Allocation," *American Economic Review*, 44, (May 1954), pp. 77-87. Other studies put the loss higher (see below). An excellent summary is Scherer, *Industrial Market Structure and Economic Performance*, Rand-McNally, 1980, ch. 17.

fact, their relative efficiency may be the chief cause of their relative size.[11] This possibility is a fundamental implication of the "alternative" industrial organization paradigm discussed in chapter 3. There, large market share is viewed as an indication of success in producing at a lower cost than one's competitors and/or producing a better product. Third, it is not clear that the exercise of monopoly power will ensure high profitability as costs may also become inflated. This may be particularly important in the Canadian context where tariffs protect high prices *and* production inefficiencies. Moreover, the X-inefficiency thesis maintains that firms which are not under competitive pressure to keep costs to a minimum may allow *some* of the "slack" created by monopoly profits to be eaten up by costs inflated by expenditures on perquisites (perks), higher factor payments, or failures to search out the least-cost combination of factor inputs. Where it exists, the welfare loss due to X-inefficiency is likely to be relatively large.[12] Presumably, the tendency to X-inefficiency, if it exists, is greater, or more probable, where firms are management-controlled than where firms are owner-controlled. The argument is that the former are less likely to be motivated chiefly by the goal of long-run profit maximization than are the latter, influenced as they are by "managerial" rather than ownership objectives.

Profitability Studies

A number of studies have shown a correlation between profitability, particularly the return to owner's equity, and the level of industry concentration. The leading and most suggestive studies are for the United States, so we will briefly summarize their findings before turning to the few Canadian studies available. It is important, at the outset, to keep in mind that profit rate studies are subject to measurement errors, particularly as a result of varying methods of handling the concept of profits. Economic profits, accounting profits, and profits for taxation purposes generally differ—sometimes considerably. Moreover, firms have incentives to overstate or understate reported profits depending on who they are trying to impress—or not impress.

Much of the data on profits comes from taxation statistics, but taxable profits

11. See Harold Demsetz, "Industry Structure, Market Rivalry, and Public Policy," *Journal of Law and Economics*, April 1973, pp. 1-9.
12. See discussion on pp. 131-132. Strictly speaking X-inefficiency applies to the failure to cost-minimize in real resource terms, and therefore should not include higher factor payments which only represent a transfer of income among economic groups. In this context, it is interesting that a recent U.S. study of the market structure-performance relationship found that unionized workers are the primary beneficiary of monopoly power—although evidence of actual monopoly power was weak. See Michael A. Salinger, "Tobin's q, Unionization, and the Concentration-Profits Relationship," *Rand Journal of Economics*, 15, no. 2 (Summer 1984), pp. 159-170.

Figure 6-2

Profitability-Concentration Relation

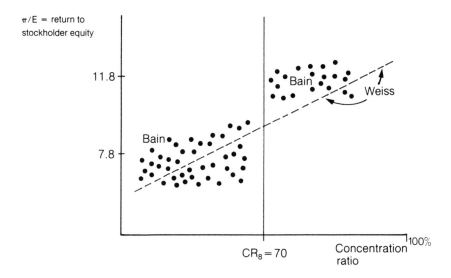

may not be—and usually are not—the "profits" of economic theory. Taxable profits include "normal profits," an opportunity cost from the viewpoint of economists, but they then understate profits by allowing for depreciation at rates more rapid than the economic life of the asset would imply. What about profits in the reports to stockholders? Profits may be overstated if the firm is attempting to hide a bad year or understated if the firm is planning to retain a large fraction of net earnings in a particularly profitable year. Also, during inflation profitability may be overstated if assets and equity are undervalued. In general, then, we have to be careful when using profit data because the accountant's concern is understandably not the economist's concern—and it is the accountant (or tax authority) who supplies the profit data.

Ever since the pioneering work of Joe Bain, numerous economists have found a persistent link between industry concentration and measures of profitability including price-cost margins.[13] Either the relationship is *dichotomous* as illustrated by the dots in Figure 6-2 (eg. Bain found for a sample of U.S. 4-digit

---

13. Joe S. Bain, "Relation of Profit Rates to Industry Concentration: American Manufacturing 1936-40," *Quarterly Journal of Economics* (August 1951), pp. 293-324; and *Barriers to New Competition* (Cambridge Mass.: Harvard University Press, 1956) pp. 195-197. The best summary and evaluation of the by-now vast literature on the concentration-profits relationship is Leonard Weiss, "The Concentration-Profits Relationship and Antitrust," *Industrial Concentration: The New Learning*, Goldschmid, et al., op. cit., pp. 184-233. Also see Scherer, *Industrial Market Structure and Economic Performance*, 1980, chapter 9.

manufacturing industries that (i) the rate of return to owners' equity was significantly higher in that group of industries in which the leading eight firms accounted for 70 percent or more of total industry shipments than in those industries in which the 8-firm concentration ratio was below 70 percent, and (ii) there was no systematic variation within the two groups); or it is *systematic* as illustrated by the dashed line in Figure 6-2 (e.g. Weiss).

There are, however, dissenters. Some studies failed to find a concentration-profits relation.[14] The relationship has been attacked on *statistical* grounds with the argument that if a longer time period (e.g. two or three decades) is used in computing the average profit rate variable, the positive relationship between rate of return and concentration disappears.[15] Others have attacked the theoretical underpinnings of the profit rate–concentration relation by suggesting that it probably reflects superior efficiency (technical and/or entrepreneurial) rather than the effects of market power *per se*.[16] In fact, a study by Demsetz concludes that the data favours the hypothesis that the concentration–profitability relationship is a reflection of the lower costs enjoyed by leading firms rather than any putative market power they may have. Some economists have worried about measurement errors in the profit variable and the specification of the direction of causation in the econometric studies of the relationship between market structure and profitability.[17]

Table 6-1 summarizes the results of some of the leading profit rate-concentration studies, including three Canadian studies to be discussed

14. For example, G. Stigler, *Capital and Rates of Return in Manufacturing Industries* (Princeton: Princeton University Press, 1963, pp. 54-70). Stigler argued that small firms were more likely to embed their profits in high owner-manager salaries than large firms. Since concentrated industries had fewer small firms than unconcentrated ones, Stigler adjusted his data in such a way that the initial differential between rates of return to concentrated and unconcentrated industries was nearly erased. An alternative adjustment of Stigler's data was made by Kilpatrick, which indicated a systematic, positive relationship between concentration and the return to stockholder equity. R.W. Kilpatrick, "Stigler on the Relationship Between Industry Profit Rates and Market Concentration," *JPE* (May-June 1968).
15. Yale Brozen, "Bain's Concentration and Rates of Return Revisited," *Journal of Law and Economics* (October 1971), pp. 351-370.
16. H. Demsetz, "Industry Structure, Market Rivalry, and Public Policy" *Journal of Law and Economics* (April 1973), pp. 1-10, and "Two Systems of Belief about Monopoly" in Goldschmid et al., op. cit., pp. 164-184; John S. McGee, *In Defense of Industrial Concentration* (Praeger, 1971).
17. A. Phillips, "A Critique of Empirical Studies of Relations Between Market Structure and Profitability," *The Journal of Industrial Economics* (June 1976), pp. 241-49. Phillips concluded we know very little from the empirical studies carried out to date. However, Weiss persuasively argues that, if anything, measurement errors would tend to reduce the observed concentration-profits relationship. L. Weiss, op. cit., pp. 193-200. But see Franklin Fisher and John McGowan "On the Misuse of Accounting Rates of Return To Infer Monopoly Profits" *American Economic Review* March 1983, 73, pp. 82-97, for a sweeping critique of the use of accounting profits in making inferences about monopoly profits.

Table 6-1

Summary of Findings of Concentration-Profitability Studies

Investigator	Country	Profit Variable[a] π/E	$\dfrac{\pi+i}{A}$	PCM	Type of Relation Continuous	Discontinuous	Strength of Relation Moderate to Strong	Weak
Bain-Mann	U.S.	X				X	X	
Weiss	U.S.	X			X		X	
Stigler	U.S.		X			X		X
Collins-Preston	U.S.			X	X		X	
Shepherd	U.S.	X			X			X[b]
McFetridge	Canada			X	X		X	
Jones-Laudadio-Percy	Canada		X		X		X	
Caves et al.	Canada	X		X	X		X	

[a]π/E = return to owner's equity; $\dfrac{\pi+i}{A}$ = rate of return on assets; PCM = price cost margin.

[b]Shepherd found a strong relation between market share of the leading firm and π/E.

below.[18] As Table 6-1 suggests, the empirical evidence indicates that concentration and profitability are associated or *correlated*. But is the relationship *causal* as well? One theoretical presumption is that the concentration–profitability relationship reflects the exercise of market power. However, the student should be aware that while many industrial organization economists accept this theoretical presumption, numerous economists do not. The alternative hypothesis is that the *correlation* between concentration and profitability actually reflects the rents received by relatively efficient leading firms which possess some advantage in production. To date no empirical study has convincingly discriminated between the two hypotheses, thereby tending to weaken support for the standard (market power) hypothesis without strengthening support for the alternative (efficient market structure) hypothesis. Moreover, as noted earlier in the chapter, the theoretical underpinnings of the concentration–profitability relationship are at least debatable.

Concentration is not the only market structure variable that appears to have an impact on profitability. The evidence suggest that high barriers to entry contribute to higher average rates of return on equity.[19] In Table 6-2 the rate-of-return estimates indicate that where both concentration *and* barriers are high (automobiles, cigarettes, distilled liquors, typewriters), return on equity is substantially higher than in industries where concentration is high but estimated barriers to entry are lower (farm machinery, steel, tires and tubes, tin cans). Note that the combination of very high barriers and "moderate" concentration appears to be an empty box. Also note that highly concentrated industries with moderate to low barriers to entry had, on the average, slightly higher rates of return to stockholders' equity than those with substantial barriers to entry.

18. Weiss reports in tabular form the results of 46 concentration-profit studies, 40 of which found a positive relationship between the two variables. Ibid., pp. 204-220. Although Table 6-1 is representative of the studies surveyed by Weiss, the table is somewhat dated and contains a bias. It is dated because almost all of the studies it lists are at least a decade old. Nevertheless, it remains representative of most concentration-profitability studies. The potential bias arises because the Table does not include any of the relatively few studies (Demsetz' being the best known) which purport to provide empirical support for the alternative hypotheses: that the profits of leading firms in concentrated industries are really Ricardian rents to "superior", cost-efficient firms rather than monopoly profits. Most of these studies, however, found at least a weak positive relationship between concentration and profitability: what they dispute is the causal relationship. A very recent study is noteworthy. Smirlock *et al* found that when their measure of profitability (Tobin's q) is regressed on a market share as well as a concentration variable only the market share (of the leading firm) variable is both positive and statistically significantly related to profitability. The authors argue, not altogether convincingly, in my view, that this reflects some production advantage of the leading firm, thereby providing supports for the alternative hypothesis. See Michael Smirlock, Thomas Gilligan, and William Marshall "Tobin's q and the Structure Performance Relationship" *American Economic Review* December 1984, pp. 1051-1060. But see Salinger, *supra* note 12, for a study, also using Tobin's q, which found no support for the alternative hypothesis and at least weak support for the standard, S→C→P, one.

19. Michael Mann, "Seller Concentration, Barriers to Entry, and Rates of Return in Thirty Industries," *Review of Economics and Statistics* (August 1966), pp. 296-307.

Table 6-2

Average Rates of Return on Equity of Leading Firms in a Sample of U.S. Manufacturing Industries, By Concentration and Barrier to Entry Levels

	Concentration	Barriers to Entry		
		Very High	Substantial	Moderate to Low
1947-51	High*	19.0	14.0	15.4
		(5)	(5)	(2)
	Moderate**	—	12.5	10.1
		(0)	(3)	(5)
1950-60	High*	16.4	11.1	11.9
		(8)	(8)	(5)
	Moderate**	—	12.2	8.6
		(0)	(1)	(8)

Source: Bain, *Barriers to New Competition*, pp. 192-200. Mann, op. cit., pp. 296-307.
*8 firm CR>70%
**8 firm CR<70%
( ) number of industries within sample.

According to Bain, product differentiation is an important barrier to entry (see chapter 3). Thus a number of economists have included advertising intensity (the ratio of advertising outlays to sales) among the elements of market structure presumed to influence profitability. The assumption is that advertising intensity is a good indicator of the effort made to "differentiate the product," and that, as a result, the level of advertising expenditures reflects a cost an entering firm will have to incur if it is to succeed against its established rivals. Many of the profitability studies that have included an advertising variable have found it influential. This may explain why some studies have found that a given level of concentration exerts a greater effect on rates of return or price-cost margins in consumer goods than in producer goods industries. A study of 41 three-digit consumer goods industries for the years 1954-57 showed that industries with high advertising outlays had rates of return on stockholder equity fifty percent greater (12 percent) than industries where advertising expenditures were much more modest (8 percent).[20] This and similar results have been

20. William S. Comanor and Thomas A. Wilson, "Advertising, Market Structure, and Performance," *Review of Economics and Statistics* (November 1967), pp. 423-40. However, Brozen challenges those who argue that an advertising-profits relation is an indicator that advertising is an important cause of concentration. He argues that, in fact, advertising enhances competition by facilitating entry, rather than reducing competition. See Yale Brozen, "Entry Barriers: Advertising and Product Differentiation" in Goldschmid, et al, op. cit., pp. 114-137.

questioned on the ground that if advertising expenditures are properly treated as investment expenditures to be amortized over their useful life, rather than as a current expenditure, the strength, and in some cases the statistical significance, of the advertising–profitability relationship disappears.[21]

Some economists have argued that because the economic theory of monopoly focuses on the individual firm, an individual firm's market share, not the industry concentration ratio, is the relevant market power variable.[22] The market share of the *leading* firm is, naturally, the most relevant one in a discussion of market power. When the market share of the leading firm is introduced alongside the four-firm concentration ratio in statistical analyses of the determinants of firm profitability, the former has appeared much the more important of the two variables as an influence on profitability. Shepherd found that each 10 percentage points of market share yield, on the average, 2.5 percentage points greater rate of return on equity. Another study found that both market share and concentration levels are important, the two variables interacting in their effect on profitability. For example, in two industries where the CR_4 equals 80 percent, profitability will be higher, *ceteris paribus*, in the industry where the leading firm has 40 percent of the market than in the industry where each of the four leading firms has about a 20 percent market share. Thus the market share variable captures the degree of asymmetry among the leading firms. It would seem that whether market share or the concentration ratio is more important would depend on whether one is attempting to explain the profitability of the leading firm (or firms) or the average profitability of the industry. An industry with a single dominant (and very profitable) firm may hold an umbrella over its much smaller, less efficient, and marginally profitable rivals. In contrast, the average profitability of an industry with several leading firms depends in good part on the degree of oligopolistic coordination attained among them—coordination which is facilitated the fewer the number of leading firms as well as the higher the barriers to entry and the degree of product homogeneity.

The evidence on the market structure-performance relationship in Canada is

21. Harry Bloch, "Advertising and Profitability: A Reappraisal," *Journal of Political Economy*, 82 (March-April 1984), pp. 276-84. But see Allyn D. Strickland and Leonard Weiss, "Advertising, Concentration and Price-Cost Margins," *Journal of Political Economy* 84 (October 1976), pp. 1009-21.

22. W.G. Shepherd, "The Elements of Market Structure," *Review of Economics and Statistics* (February 1972), pp. 25-37; and *The Treatment of Market Power: Antitrust Regulation and Public Enterprise* (Columbia University Press, 1975), Chapter 4. A recent U.S. study using data on 1080 lines of business found that concentration is not statistically significant in rate-of-return regressions when a market share variable is included. B. Gale and B. Branch, "Concentration versus Market Share: Which Determines Performance and Why Does It Matter," 27 *Antitrust Bulletin* 1982, pp. 83-106.

relatively meagre. What is available, however, tends generally to confirm, and conform to, that from the United States. The major difference is that effective tariff protection plays a relatively more important role in Canada than in the United States and it does so in a dual capacity. High tariffs may protect the monopoly and profitability of Canadian firms from the competitive gales of foreign competition. Tariffs can also protect suboptimal capacity and excessive cost so that protective tariffs may also be related to very marginal profitability. (See chapter 4.)

One study investigated the influence of various elements of market structure on price-cost margins in 43 three-digit Canadian industries for the period 1965-69.[23] It found seller concentration to be strongly related to the size of price cost margins, given the rate of growth of industry demand and the level of its capital intensity. A given level of concentration exerted a greater impact on price-cost margins in consumer goods than in producer goods industries. This, however, may simply reflect the impact of advertising intensity which was also found to be positively correlated with price-cost margins, but which raised margins by no more than the amount of the expenditure itself.[24] Of more consequence was the finding that tariff protection and price-cost margins were not correlated, suggesting that tariffs often protect both high-cost, marginally profitable industries with substantial amounts of acutely suboptimal capacity, as well as the profits of more efficient, concentrated industries.

Another study found a positive relationship between rates of return (on equity and assets) and concentration in 30 Canadian consumer goods manufacturing industries.[25] Perhaps more important was the result that when a variable representing the degree of import competition (imports as a percentage of industry output) was introduced, it produced a positive relationship between import competition and profitability. One possible explanation for the finding is that import competition stimulates domestic production efficiency and generates profitability through reduced costs. It is also consistent with the view that tariffs are mainly designed to protect high-cost industries, rather than increase the profits of more efficient and concentrated industries.

The interaction between tariff protection, concentration, prices, costs, and gross profits per unit is complicated. (The student should keep in mind the extended discussion in chapter 4 concerning the interaction of the Canadian

23. Donald McFetridge, "Market Structure and Price Cost Margins: An Analysis of the Canadian Manufacturing Sector," *Canadian Journal of Economics*, 6 (August 1973), pp. 345-54. The price cost margin (as a percent) is defined as price minus average variable cost, divided by value added per unit of output; which can be computed by subtracting wages and salaries from value added and dividing the difference by value added.
24. Ibid., p. 353.
25. J.C.H. Jones, L. Laudadio, and M. Percy, "Market Structure and Profitability in Canadian Manufacturing," *Canadian Journal of Economics* (August 1973).

tariff, pricing power, and factors affecting the cost of production in Canada's manufacturing sector.) A study of twenty Canadian manufacturing industries compared their selling prices, unit costs, and gross profits per unit with those of their counterpart industries in the United States.[26] The basic data are reproduced in Table 6-3. The three indexes simply indicate the ratio of the Canadian industry's prices, unit profits or costs to that of its U.S. counterpart. For example, a price index number of 100 indicates that the average industry selling price is the same in Canada as in the United States. If the price index exceeds 100, average industry selling prices are greater in Canada than in the United States, and vice-versa for index numbers less than 100.

From Table 6-3 it is clear that relative (to the United States) prices are greatest when Canadian industries are both concentrated and protected by high tariffs. Neither high tariffs nor high concentration alone appears capable of producing selling prices significantly higher than those in the United States, as a comparison of the two middle groupings in Table 6-3 indicates.[27] It is also clear that a combination of high concentration *and* high tariffs protects distinctly higher costs of production in the seven Canadian industries included in Table 6-3. In contrast, the existence of domestic competition (low concentration) *or* foreign competition (low tariffs) was sufficient to keep unit direct costs of Canadian industries more or less on a par with those of their U.S. counterparts. From the limited sample of industries included in the table, one can draw the tentative conclusion that in the mid 1960s (from which period the data is drawn) Canadian industry cost disadvantages, relative to the United States, were due in part, at least, to a lack of competition.

Table 6-3 also has something to say about relative profitability. It implies that concentration, but not tariffs, contribute to Canadian profitability—a conclusion supported by the evidence when the six industries where concentration is high in Canada and low in the United States are divided into a high and a low tariff group, and when the eight industries in which concentration is low in both the United States and Canada are divided into high and low tariff groups. Where Canadian concentration was high (relative to the United States), profitability was high, irrespective of the level of tariffs. Where Canadian concentration was low, relative profitability was low, irrespective of the level of tariffs. Presumably when concentration is high in Canada, low in the United States, and tariffs are low, the relative profitability of Canadian industries is due as much to the impact of foreign competition in keeping costs down as it is to the ability of Canadian firms to elevate price above cost due to a lack of domestic competition.

26. Harry Bloch, "Prices, Costs, and Profits in Canadian Manufacturing: The Influence of Tariffs and Concentration," *Canadian Journal of Economics*, 7 (November 1974), pp. 594-610.
27. Further support for this finding is provided by T. Hazeldine, "Testing Two Models of pricing and Protection with Canada/United States Data," *Journal of Industrial Economics*, 29 (December 1980), pp. 145-154.

Table 6-3

Concentration, Tariff Protection, and Price-Cost Data: Twenty Canadian Manufacturing Industries

Industry	(1) Canadian 4-Firm CR (1965)	(2) U.S. Concentration Classification	(3) Average Nominal Canadian Tariff (Percentage)	(4) Relative Price Index[a] (Group Average)	(5) Relative Direct Cost per Unit Index[a] (Group Average)	(6) Relative Gross Profit per Unit Index[a] (Group Average)
High concentration, high tariff industries						
1. Confectionery[b]	46	High	17.3			
2. Sugar refineries	NA	Low	24.2			
3. Tobacco products	91	High	30.0	111.6	119.3	117.3
4. Rubber industries	NA	High	20.1			
5. Battery manufacturers	84	High	17.4			
6. Paints-varnishes[b]	46	Low	16.7			
7. Soap & cleaning supplies	NA	High	19.5			
High concentration, low tariff industries						
8. Slaughtering & meatpacking	58	Low	5.2			
9. Fabricated structural metal	46	Low	8.0			
10. Motor vehicles & parts	83	High	10.2	104.4	100.3	121.6
11. Cement manufacturers	76	Low	3.4			
12. Petroleum refining	80	Low	5.3			

Table 6-3 (continued)

	(1) Canadian 4-Firm CR (1965)	(2) U.S. Concentration Classification	(3) Average Nominal Canadian Tariff (Percentage)	(4) Relative Price Index[a] (Group Average)	(5) Relative Direct Cost per Unit Index[a] (Group Average)	(6) Relative Gross Profit per Unit Index[a] (Group Average)
Low concentration, high tariff industries						
13. Hosiery mills	18	Low	25.2			
14. Other paper converters	29	Low	22.2			
15. Concrete products and ready-mix concrete	21	Low	18.3	99.8	102.8	91.2
Low concentration-low tariff industries						
16. Poultry processors	24	Low	12.7			
17. Dairy products	25	Low	7.1			
18. Food manufacturers	28	Low	7.2			
19. Bakeries	32	Low	8.0	101.6	105.9	79.9
20. Soft drinks	40	Low	4.9			

Source: Harry Bloch, "Prices, Costs, and Profits in Canadian Manufacturing: The Influence of Tariffs and Concentration," *Canadian Journal of Economics,* 7 (Nov. 1974), p. 604.

[a]Ratio of Canadian to U.S.

[b]High concentration is defined as $CR_4 > 50\%$ on a regionally adjusted basis. Both confectionery and paints-varnishes have regionally segmented markets in Canada.

The most thorough study to date of the factors that influence the market performance of Canadian manufacturing industries is that of Richard Caves and his associates.[28] Their research design involves the construction of a system of equations which is supposed to capture the complex interactions among such elements of market structure as industry concentration, scale economies, advertising intensity, foreign ownership, and imports' share of the domestic market, and between these variables and those acting as measures of market performance such as profitability and productivity. The model allows the testing of numerous hypotheses and produces a rich set of results. We focus on those related to the exercise of market power as reflected in industry profitability.

The analysis of profitability (an indicator of allocative inefficiency) in the study by Caves et al. is based on the assumption that high seller concentration, entry barriers and an absence of strong import competition are necessary to the exercise of market power. Their findings suggest that imports "act like a competitive fringe in limiting the market power of concentrated industries."[29] Industry concentration, particularly a form of this variable designed to capture size inequality among leading firms, is an important determinant of the profits of domestically owned firms. However, there was little evidence that profits were influenced by advertising intensity or economies of scale—proxies for barriers to entry. Thus, unlike Bain's earlier findings for the U.S., concentration and barriers to entry do not appear to interact in the determination of industry profitability in Canadian manufacturing industries. Of particular interest was the inability of any of the structural variables to explain the profits of Canadian subsidiaries of foreign-owned companies. This negative finding could be due to measured profitability being a poor indicator of actual profit streams. It could also reflect the role of the Eastman-Stykolt effect in which excessive entry by foreign firms results in suboptimal scale, short production runs, and low profitability (see chapter 4).

What conclusions can be drawn from the studies indicating a correlation between profitability and concentration, or other market structure variables? First, market power often pays off in the form of higher accounting profits.[30] This has income and wealth distribution effects to which we will briefly return later in this chapter. Second, there is undoubtedly some allocative ineffi-

28. Richard E. Caves, Michael E. Porter, A. Michael Spense, with John T. Scott, *Competition in the Open Economy: A Model Applied to Canada* (Cambridge: Harvard University Press, 1980). See in particular chapter 9.

29. Ibid., p. 254.

30. Strictly speaking only the owner at the time market power is initially exerted is assured a profit payoff. When the firm's ownership changes hands and the seller has capitalized the stream of extra profits in the sales price, the buyer—the new owner—will only reap normal returns. This is an issue to which we return in chapter 12.

ciency—misallocation of resources—due to the exercise of market power in Canada. However, initial estimates of the welfare loss due to monopoly (the triangle BEC in Figure 6-1) in the United States found it to be less than one tenth of one percent of national income.[31] Even after taking account of assumptions which tended to understate the welfare loss, more realistic, though more judgmental, estimates indicate a figure between one half and one percent.[32]

Critical to one's evaluation of the social cost of monopoly-induced allocative inefficiency, is whether monopoly power results in increased costs as well as increased prices. Traditionally, estimates have been based on the assumption that profit-maximizing firms would minimize costs, but recent literature has indicated the strong possibility that monopoly power may allow "X-inefficiency" to creep in. If it does, there are additional social costs in the form of increased allocative efficiency and "wasted" inputs. These increased costs are pictured in Figure 6-1, assuming that in the absence of monopoly power average cost (and price) would be AC_1. The full measure of allocative efficiency now becomes triangle BFH, which is four times the size of BEC if BE = EF— i.e., if the cost increase is of the same magnitude as the amount by which monopoly price exceeds actual average cost AC_o.[33] The loss due to outright waste of resources (assuming, perhaps unrealistically, that the higher costs are solely due to over-use of resources rather than inflated input prices) is equal to rectangle P_cEFP^1. Scherer suggested that taking X-inefficiency into account, total allocative inefficiency accounted for about 1.5 percent of U.S. GNP in 1966, and inefficiencies due to deficient cost control and wasteful promotion for another 3.6 percent of GNP[34] These estimates make the social costs of monopoly of more than academic interest. The costs of monopoly are unlikely to be proportionately smaller in Canada than in the United States, and may be greater as a result of the protection from competition yielded by high tariffs.

Technical Efficiency and Cost Competitiveness

For Canada, monopoly-induced inefficiencies may be only the tip of the inefficiency iceberg. This is so because, as we saw in chapter 3, there is

---

31. A. Harberger, op. cit., pp. 77-87; David Schwartzman, "The Burden of Monopoly," *Journal of Political Economy* (Dec. 1960), pp. 627-30.
32. See F.M. Scherer, *Industrial Market Structure and Economic Performance* (Rand-McNally, 1970), chap. 17.
33. William S. Comanor and Harvey Liebenstein, "Allocative Efficiency, X-Efficiency and the Measurement of Welfare Loss," *Economica*, 1969, pp. 304-309. The ratio of triangle BFH to BEC is equal to $(1 + X)^2$, where $X = EF \div BE$. If EF = BE, X = 1, and $(1 + X)^2 = 4$.
34. Scherer, op. cit., chapter 17. In his second edition, Scherer declines to give numbers.

widespread evidence that suboptimal capacity and short production runs may raise manufacturing production costs substantially. For the 16 industries studied by Eastman and Stykolt, suboptimal capacity averaged about 50 percent of total productive capacity. Efficient capacity as a percentage of total industry capacity ranged from a high of 100 percent (one case) to a low of zero (five cases). There is no indication that the extent of suboptimal capacity was correlated with market concentration ratios for the 16 industries in 1964.[35] Apparently either the average-size firm in concentrated industries was still too small to exhaust scale economies (achieve MES) or large firms were multiplant firms—each plant too small to be of MES. Of course, even where capacity is of efficient size, costs will be raised if production runs are short so that a single plant is forced to produce a line of different products, incurring substantial costs in the process of changeover from one to another.

While the Eastman-Stykolt findings are dated, the conclusion that scale inefficiencies, either because of inefficient plant size or insufficiently long production runs, are endemic in Canadian manufacturing has, unfortunately, held up rather well. Scherer's in-depth studies certainly support this view (see chapter 3). In addition, substantial evidence has recently been provided by Baldwin and Gorecki (see chapter 4) that relatively small (in relation to U.S.) plant scales, excessive product diversity within plants, and short production runs still contribute to technical inefficiency in many Canadian manufacturing industries. Moreover, productivity comparisons between Canadian industries and their U.S. counterparts remain embarrassing for the north side. In fact, evidence of a substantial productivity differential has been available for a number of decades.[36] In the mid-1960s the differential between average value added per worker in Canadian and U.S. manufacturing sectors was about thirty percent, or even somewhat higher. Limited evidence suggests an even higher differential prior to 1960. The rationalization of production in the automobile

---

35. For the U.S., Bain found no correlation between industry concentration and the percentage of an industry's output accounted for by suboptimal plants. However, the latter percentage ranged between 10 and 30 percent—averaging about 20 percent, in stark contrast to Canada. Weiss, using the survival technique to estimate the extent of suboptimal capacity, found a slight tendency for unconcentrated industries to have somewhat higher percentages of industry output produced by suboptimal plants. Joe S. Bain, *Barriers to New Competition*, 1956; Leonard Weiss, "The Survival Technique and the Extent of Suboptimal Capacity," *Journal of Political Economy* (June 1964), pp. 257-61. In a subsequent study, Weiss found even stronger indications of a negative relationship between concentration and suboptimal capacity. Using estimates of MES for plants in 33 industries, Weiss found that (a) suboptimal plants accounted for almost 50 percent of industry capacity, and (b) there was a systematic tendency for the suboptimal fringe to decrease as concentration increased—and the magnitude of this effect was important. L.W. Weiss, "Optimal Plant Size and the Extent of Suboptimal Capacity," Masson and Qualls, eds, *Essays on Industrial Organization in Honor of Joe S. Bain* (Cambridge: Ballinger, 1976), pp. 137-41.

industry made possible by the U.S.-Canada Auto Pact of 1965 and recent mergers in the consumer appliance field suggest that the productivity differential has declined somewhat in the last decade. Moreover, as the "Tokyo Round" reductions in tariffs are implemented during the course of the 1980s there are increasing pressures on firms and industries to reduce costs and increase productivity via specialization and rationalization.[37] Some of that rationalization has already taken place. Even so there is no doubt that a sizeable productivity differential continues, with scale and specialization at the heart of any reasonable explanation for it.[38]

In the mid 1960s a substantial fraction of the productivity differential between the United States and Canada was offset by a wage differential. In 1963, average hourly earnings in Canadian manufacturing were about 19 percent below average hourly earnings in U.S. manufacturing. Lower money wages in Canada thus offset a major part of the cost differences implied by the productivity differential. However, during the 1970s wages inflated much faster in Canada than in the United States. By 1976, the wage differential had been reversed, with the average manufacturing wage in Canada at a premium relative to that of the States.[39]

The change in the Canada-U.S. industrial wage ratio only made more obvious our underlying productivity disadvantage. Canadian industries found it increasingly difficult to compete in world markets or to stave off import competition. The Canadian dollar began to fall. As it did so, public awareness of the structural and commercial policy sources of our industrial difficulties increased. The following newspaper account from the *Montreal Star*, October 15, 1977, is suggestive.

> Running like a thread through the discussions of Canada's declining dollar is the question of this country's productivity. It seems that in the last analysis our currency is merely reflecting our inherent industrial inefficiency.

36. See D.J. Daly, B.A. Keys, and E.J. Spence, *"Scale and Specialization in Canadian Manufacturing,"* Staff Study No. 21, Economic Council of Canada, March 1968, pp. 9-15.
37. It is estimated that by 1990, the average tariff applicable to Canadian manufacturing industries will drop by a third from the levels of the late 1970s. The drop will be substantially more on wood products and certain types of machinery. For example, tariffs applicable to imports of major appliances are scheduled to decrease from the 20 percent level of the early 1980s to 12.5 percent in 1988.
38. For a detailed discussion of the Canadian-U.S. productivity (efficiency) differential and attempts to explain it using matched Canadian and U.S. industries see A. Michael Spence, "Efficiency, Scale and Trade in Canadian and U.S. Manufacturing Industries," *Studies in Canadian Industrial Organization*, Study No. 26, Royal Commission on Corporate Concentration, Ottawa, Chap. 11, pp. 240-277.
39. By 1977, average hourly earnings in the manufacturing sector were 7 percent higher in Canada than in the U.S., while the productivity gap was between 10 and 20 percent.

The argument is normally posed in terms of Canada's labour costs per unit of output, which are higher than those of its principal trading partner, the United States. In its most dramatic form it can be seen in the flight of what could be Canadian jobs south of the border as Canadian firms build plants in the more efficient U.S. environment.

There are any number of explanations of the phenomenon. Short production runs, militant labour (proportionately we have a higher degree of unionization than the U.S.), a small market which forbids economies of scale and so on. However, serious disagreement only comes when someone suggests doing something to improve the situation.

To many Canadians the most commonly suggested cure—free trade—is worse than the disease. . . .

Thus measured where it is most crucial to Canada—in the international trade arena—Canada's industrial performance worsened in the 1970s. The modest improvements in relative productivity in the 1960s were swamped by a cost-inflation which rendered Canada increasingly uncompetitive. Cries for protection increased, particularly in labour-intensive industries such as textile, shoes, clothing and furniture—many heavily represented in the Province of Quebec.[40] The federal government responded, in 1976, by imposing import quotas on shoes and clothing.[41] Nevertheless, those firms which did not decide to place their investments in new capacity beyond the Canadian border may have been tempted by the high price of labour to replace labour with more capital-intensive operations. Such a course only worsens Canada's unemployment problem and increases the taxpayer costs of providing for those out of work—costs that necessarily are ultimately born by those carrying out productive activities.

In short, then, Canada's industrial dilemma became starkly clear in the 1970s. During the first 90 of its 100 years of existence the National Policy allowed Canadian firms the luxury of significant cost inefficiencies—costs borne by Canadian consumers, many of whom laboured for those selfsame firms. Studies by Young, the Wonnacotts, and Harris and Cox have estimated the loss in real GNP due to the Canadian tariff at from 4 to 10 percent of GNP.[42] Then in

40. Helping to put upward pressure on manufacturing wages was the rapid rise in public sector wages and salaries as a result of the relative growth of the public sector and the increasing militancy of public sector unions. An additional factor was the rapid rise in minimum wages and the reservation wage-increasing impact of the generous and liberally-administered Unemployment Insurance Act of 1971.

41. Caroline Pestieau, *The Quebec Textile Industry in Canada* (Montreal: Howe Research Institute, 1978), pp. 37-53.

42. Daly, Keys, Spence, op. cit., pp. 4-5; Paul Wonnacott and R. J. Wonnacott, "Free Trade Between the United States and Canada: Fifteen Years Later," *Canadian Public Policy*, 8, Special Supplement, October 1982; Richard Harris with David Cox, *Trade, Industrial Policy and*

the next ten years (the 1970s) the National Policy protected workers as they attempted to extract their "pound of flesh" in the form of large wage increases. In reaction, the federal government resorted to monetarist policies in an attempt to reduce inflation and inflationary wage demands. The deflationary impact of this policy in conjunction with the deep world recession of 1982 moderated wage demands, but substantially raised the rate of unemployment as well. These short-sighted policies on the part of both the private sector and public authorities threaten unemployment for many and reduced real incomes for all of us. There are few better examples of the ultimate curse of private monopoly power and protection from competition in the economic arena.

Technological Progress

The fourth facet of efficiency is technological innovation, or "dynamic efficiency." By dynamic efficiency we do not simply mean the efficient allocation of resources at two different points in time. Rather we mean the optimal introduction of new, more efficient, productive processes and new products over time. New processes and products do not, however, grow on trees or appear as if from nowhere to be implemented with a minimum of effort, and a maximum of return. New, less costly (per unit of output) methods of production and new consumer products are usually the result of extensive innovative effort, and, in some cases, inventive genius. In most cases, innovation and invention involve intensive and time-consuming human effort. This means that most new processes and products (and here we exclude minor, essentially "cosmetic" changes in goods and services which are little more than an attempt to differentiate an essentially homogeneous product) have lengthy gestation periods and involve substantial uncertainty and expense. Thus an important facet of industrial performance involves investment in the research, design, development and introduction of new and better consumer and producer goods. In this sense, dynamic efficiency involves an evaluation of the effort expended on increasing knowledge (research) and the bringing to fruition (development) of better ways of satisfying human wants.

The issue which has long puzzled students of industrial organization is whether the elements of market structure influence in any systematic way the capacity and willingness of firms to undertake the necessary effort (ultimately measured in investment dollars) required to bring forth new processes and products. The Schumpeterian hypothesis provided a clear answer: monopoly power provided the required profits out of which research and development

Canadian Manufacturing (Toronto: Ontario Economic Council, 1984). The Wonnacotts and Harris and Cox place the gains from multilateral elimination of tariffs at 8 to 10 percent of GNP.

(R & D) investments would be financed, and prospective profits the incentive to carry out R & D activity. In Schumpeter's view, however, monopoly power would be short-lived, destroyed by the creativity of newly competing firms.[43] Later writers have found this view too simplistic. It does not answer the question of how much monopoly (or market) power is required to induce firms to innovate. And from what does power emanate: firm size? or market control? It leaves open the answer to the question whether innovation and invention "creatively destroy" as Schumpeter thought, or are the bases of the extended longevity of the modern corporation.

The determinants of technological progress are deemed important for public policy, especially in a country such as Canada where a small domestic market and large firms often imply market domination and control. If technological progress is correlated with firm size and market control, then there are important implications for competition policy. Technological progress has become, in some quarters, the "new defence of bigness," displacing the "old defence": economies of scale in production. (Of course the progressiveness argument is a variant of the economies of scale issue, tending however to justify large firms rather than large plants.) In his *The New Industrial State*, J.K. Galbraith advances the technological imperative as the *raison d'être* of the modern giant corporation. Drawing on a theme developed in Thorstein Veblen's *The Engineers and the Price System*, Galbraith focuses on the goals and incentives of the technological personnel (the "technostructure") within the giant firm. It is the technostructure that develops new products and processes. It is the job of the firms' managers to "plan" a market for new products by manipulating consumer (and government?) demand through various sales policies, including advertising. This caricature of the modern corporation has been attacked on a number of grounds, one of which is its apparent dependence on the argument that large size and market control are prerequisites for technological progress.

If there is an interaction between market structure and technological innovation it is surely not one-way. The race to innovate is a genuine form of competition in which success is reflected not only in higher short-run, if not long-run, profitability of the innovating firm, but increased market share as well. Nelson and Winter, using simulation techniques, have convincingly shown that technological competition can quickly transform an industry with firms of equal size into one which is highly concentrated—a few relatively successful firms accounting for the lion's share of industry sales.[44] This tendency is

43. "Newly competing firms" may be new firms or old firms with a new product which is competitive with or superior to the product or process which, for a time, gave its owner monopoly power.

44. R. Nelson and S. Winter, "Forces Generating and Limiting the Growth of Concentration Under Schumpeterian Competition," *Bell Journal of Economics*, 9 (Autumn 1978).

accentuated where "success breeds success," as appears to be the case in industries with a high degree of technological opportunity such as aircraft and electronics. Moreover, investment in R&D may create entry barriers to the extent that successful innovators are able to preempt subsequent competitors.[45] These "dynamic entry" barriers reinforce concentration-increasing tendencies and, in combination with patent rights, create substantial lags before the rents produced by innovation are competed away.

Successful introduction of a new technique (or product) will usually generate profitability. Suppose a firm introduces a new method of production which reduces unit costs from AC_0 to AC_1, in Figure 6-1. Suppose, further, price initially equalled AC_0 and that after the cost reduction there is no reduction in price. The value of resources saved by the new productive process is P_cCGP^1 while the "welfare loss" due to the failure of price to fall to AC_1 is CGH. But is this a true "welfare loss"? Does it arise as a result of monopoly? If in fact profits P_cCGP^1 are simply the reward for invention and innovation, and are the required rate of return on the investment in new techniques, there are no excess profits, and, therefore, there is no welfare loss due to monopoly. This suggests that it is important in profit rate-market structure studies to capitalize the expenditure on R & D in computing the "capital" base for estimating rates of return.[46]

In the industrial organization literature there are numerous studies investigating the relationship between market structure and such proxies for "progressiveness" as numbers of patents, R & D expenditures in relation to sales revenue, engineers and scientists as a proportion of the firm's work force, etc. One conclusion which has been drawn from the evidence for the United States is that, in many manufacturing industries, firm size, up to a point, appears to influence both the probability that a firm will undertake R & D, and, if it does do so, the relative (to sales) size of its R & D effort. But the apparent relationship does not extend beyond moderately sized industrial firms, and thus does not itself provide an "efficiency" justification for the existence of industrial giants.[47]

45. P. Dasgupta and J. Stiglitz, "Uncertainty, Industrial Structure, and the Speed of R & D," *Bell Journal of Economics*, 11, No. 1 (Spring 1980), pp. 1-28 and "Industrial Structure and the Nature of Innovative Activity," *Economic Journal* (June 1980), pp. 266-93.
46. The relationship between R and D and profitability, when R & D expenditures are capitalized, is treated in H.G. Grabowski and D.C. Mueller, "Industrial Research and Development, Intangible Capital Stocks, and Firm Profit Rates," *The Bell Journal of Economics*, 9 (Autumn 1978), pp. 328-343.
47. Scherer, op. cit., p. 420. The leading study is Edwin Mansfield, et al., *Research and Innovation in the Modern Corporation*, 1971. It undercuts the bigness claim pretty effectively. For a survey of the literature see M.I. Kamien and N.L. Schwartz, *Market Structure and Innovation* (Cambridge: Cambridge University Press, 1982). The literature, particularly as it relates to Canada is exhaustively discussed in Economic Council of Canada, *The Bottom Line: Technology, Trade and Income Growth* (Supply and Services Canada: 1983) Chs. 3-6.

Much the same conclusion can be drawn from studies of the relationship between industry concentration and innovative effort. A study by Scherer found a positive correlation between concentration and R & D as a percent of sales in industries with four-firm concentration ratios below 50 percent. For those industries with four-firm concentration ratios well above 50 percent, there was little indication of a relative R & D payoff accompanying increasing levels of industry concentration. Even this modest influence of size and concentration on relative R & D effort overlooks the fact that many of the most important inventions were made by small firms or by men and women working completely independently of industrial or governmental research organizations.[48] (Examples include xerography, DDT, insulin, the jet engine, FM radio, the helicopter, automatic transmission, and the Polaroid Land Camera). However, it often appears to be the case that it is the large firm, presumptively with market power, that is in the best position to *develop* the innovation for commercial purposes, and add refinements at a later stage of technological competition.[49]

Cutting across any market structure-technological change relationship is the fact that the opportunity for innovation and invention varies across industries. Presently, technological opportunity is especially high in the instrument, electronic, and aircraft industries. Arguably the existence of high technological opportunity may influence both market structure and innovation in such a way that an observed correlation between the two does not represent causation. At least, one could not infer a causal relationship running from market structure to innovation. For example, in industries where technological opportunity is great, success may "breed success', so that firms which succeed early ("first movers") may have a substantial advantage over those which succeed later, or late arrivals. In such cases, first movers may be observed to have both large market shares and be innovative. The observed positive relationship between the two would not, however, be causal, but rather the result of high technological opportunity. (Arguably, in this example, the relationship runs from innovation (performance) to market structure, as the alternative industrial organization paradigm suggests.)

Deciphering a market structure-progressiveness relationship for Canada, if one in fact exists, is difficult. Not only is the evidence scanty but the picture is confused by the fact that so many Canadian manufacturing firms, especially those in research-intensive industries, are subsidiaries of foreign-owned firms. This means that much of the new technology and product line may simply be transferred from the foreign parent to its Canadian subsidiary with little or no R & D effort undertaken by the latter. Thus indexes of progressiveness such as

---

48. John Jewkes, et al., *The Sources of Invention* (New York: Norton, 1959).
49. Dennis Mueller & John Tilton, "Research and Development Costs as a Barrier to Entry," *Canadian Journal of Economics* (November 1969).

a firm's R & D expenditures and scientific personnel may be meaningless in the Canadian context.[50] If the parent firm dictates that basic R & D activities will be centred in a home-country location, its foreign subsidiaries will appear to engage in little or no innovative activity. Yet this would be misleading since the subsidiary has access to new technology and may pay considerable sums to the parent to acquire new productive processes and products. This would seem to indicate that if R & D expenditures are used as an indicator of performance, some proportion of the parent firm's R & D expenditures should be credited to its subsidiaries. Alternatively, one might look at patents on the grounds that even if the invention or innovation is made elsewhere the foreign parent will have an incentive to protect its subsidiary's "monopoly" by acquiring a Canadian patent. As a matter of fact about 95 percent of all the patents granted by the Canadian government are granted to foreigners, a statistic which could be misleading if it is not read in conjunction with the theory of the multinational firm.[51] Among other things, this and similar statistics (such as the embarrassingly low ratio of Canadian R & D expenditures to GNP) have resulted in charges that Canada is essentially a technological parasite depending on the innovativeness of other countries, its own scientific genius withering at home, if it does not leave for foreign laboratories.

The limited evidence on the relationship between firm size and innovative activity in Canada can be briefly summarized. While there are some economies of scale within an R & D establishment, thereby giving some advantages to large firms, there is little evidence of a relationship between R & D *intensity* and firm size. A study undertaken for the Economic Council of Canada found no relationship between firm size and R & D expenditures as a percentage of sales. For 1965, 684 firms in 21 broadly defined (2-digit) industries were classified into three groups by size of firm. For each firm data on R & D outlays relative to sales was gathered. In nine broad industry groups the highest (relative to sales) R & D expenditures were made by the smallest firm-size class and in only five of the industry groups was the largest firm-size class the leader in relative

50. This view receives theoretical and empirical support in a paper by A. Rugman "Research and Development by Multinational and Domestic Firms in Canada," *Canadian Public Policy* (Autumn 1981), pp. 604-16. Rugman's analysis is based on the internalization view of the multinational enterprise which argues that a firm with a unique asset, in this case technological know how, is likely to find it easier to monitor its use "internally" via a foreign subsidiary, than externally via licensing of an independent firm located in the host country. Moreover, the MNE is likely to centralize its R & D activities, if for no other reason than to prevent dissipation of knowledge, with the result that little R & D is undertaken in the host country although a lot is available to it.
51. Economic Council of Canada, *Interim Report on Competition Policy* (Ottawa, 1969), p. 93. Also see Economic Council of Canada, *Report on Industrial and Intellectual Property* (Ottawa, 1971).

R & D expenditure.[52] The study, of course, indicated nothing about the relative benefits flowing from the R & D effort. Nor does the study indicate to what extent foreign-owned firms relied on the parent firm's R & D activity.

A study by McFetridge and Weatherly, directed at the issue of the economies of large firm size, investigated the relationship between size and innovation, using patents as a proxy for "progressiveness."[53] (There are pitfalls in using patents as an index of innovation: some patents may cover trivial "improvements," others may be "shelved" rather than used). They obtained data on patents originating with the largest 15 firms in both the electrical and chemical industries and the largest ten firms in the machinery industry. The authors found that while the largest three firms get the most patents, patent activity is otherwise independent of firm size. When the transportation equipment industry is included and smaller firms are added in each of the four industries there is a general pattern of increased patents per firm as firm size increases, except in the machinery industry. The results are shown in Table 6-4. However, it does not appear that the evidence supports the conclusion that the number of patents increases more than proportionately with firm size. Yet the justification of large firm size in terms of innovative activity requires not simply an increase in the absolute amount of activity, but an increase in activity *relative* to size. The McFetridge-Weatherly study is important because, though limited in scope, it focused on R & D intensive industries and failed to find support for the argument that progressiveness and size are directly related.[54]

A number of quantitative studies of the determinants of the level of industry or firm R & D expenditures in Canada have found government incentive grants or subsidies to be an important, often the only statistically significant, explanatory variable.[55] This result is not particularly surprising for two reasons. First the public good approach to technological innovation emphasizes the idea that an invention essentially consists of knowledge which, in principle, can be made available to all potential users at zero marginal cost. The patent grant, of course, is designed to restrict the *right to use* of the knowledge. Nevertheless, the innovator is typically unable to appropriate all of the potential gains from a new product or process and may need further inducement from a government

52. Economic Council of Canada, *Interim Report on Competition Policy*. For a more recent Economic Council of Canada study of R & D see, *The Bottom Line* (Ottawa: Minister of Supply and Services, 1983).
53. D.G. McFetridge and L.J. Weatherly, *Notes on the Economics of Large Firm Size*, Study No. 20, Royal Commission on Corporate Concentration, Ottawa, 1977, pp. 219 ff.
54. As the computer revolution, with the burgeoning numbers of small electronics firms, makes clear, it is the opportunities for innovation rather than firm size which is crucial.
55. See, for example, J.D. Howe and D.G. McFetridge, "The Determinants of R & D Expenditures," *Canadian Journal of Economics*, 9 (1976), and S. Globerman, "Market Structure and R & D in Canadian Industries," *Quarterly Review of Economics and Business* (1973), pp. 59-67.

Table 6-4

Firm Size and Patenting Activity: Patents per Firm by Size Class, 1972

Industry	SIC Codes	Size Class (1972 sales) in millions of dollars				
		0-1	1-10	10-50	50-100	over 100
Machinery	315,318	.42	.10	3.91	.50	3.00
		(12)	(31)	(11)	(2)	(1)
Transportation equipment	321,323,325	.29	.13	.14	.40	.67
		(7)	(16)	(7)	(5)	(3)
Electrical equipment	335,336	.30	.35	3.31	10.0	8.0
		(10)	(20)	(13)	(1)	(2)
Chemicals	374,376,377	.00	.28	.74	3.67	12.63
		(12)	(32)	(19)	(6)	(8)

Number of firms in the size class in brackets.
Source: McFetridge & Weatherly, op. cit., p. 226. Reproduced by permission of the Minister of Supply and Services Canada.

grant.[56] Second, the difficulty of appropriating the gains from innovation and invention is probably made more difficult for a small open economy such as Canada's. Not only are the possibilities of transnational "leakages" increased, but the concentration and barriers-to-entry-increasing-tendencies that innovation may generate (see above) mean relatively little in a small open-economy context in which the only effective bar to competition are tariffs. In addition, because in Canada so many likely innovators are foreign owned, it will often take government subsidies to generate adequate incentives for the subsidiary to innovate rather than leaving this activity up to the parent firm. Not surprisingly, then, an increasingly important subject of public policy is public subsidies to R & D type activities (see chapter 12). For these reasons many economists think it appropriate that Canada rely on inter-firm and intra-firm technology transfers from other countries such as the United States.

56. See D.G. McFetridge, *Government Support of Scientific Research and Development: An Economic Analysis* (Toronto: University of Toronto Press, 1977). For a nice statement and application to the Canadian electronics industry, see J.S. Cohen, J. Rubin and R.S. Saunders, "Chasing the Bandwagon: Government Policy for the Electronics Industry," *Canadian Public Policy* (March 1984), pp. 25-34.

Market Structure and Income Distribution

An important question is the impact of monopoly power on the distribution of income and wealth. The question is socially important; its economic answer elusive. To get a handle on the issue, we are talking about the added profits that firms with market power receive if they are able to raise price above cost, the latter term including, of course, a normal profit. In Figure 6-1 the "excess profitability" at issue is represented by the shaded rectangle labelled π. On the assumption that monopoly power raises prices but not costs (here we assume firms to be X-efficient), it is possible to make rough estimates of the amount of national income that is redistributed from consumers to firms and their stockholders in the form of monopoly profits. The usual assumption is that this redistribution increases income inequality because the great bulk of corporate stock is held by persons in upper income classes.[57]

For the United States, Schwartzman estimated monopoly profits at $3.6 billion in 1954—or one percent of GNP. However, his profit figures were confined to the manufacturing sector. Scherer has "guesstimated" that a figure between 2 and 3 percent of GNP is probable when other sectors of the economy are included and when capitalized profits "hidden" in corporate accounts are taken into consideration. Shepherd has also estimated monopoly profits at about 3 percent of U.S. national income. Moreover, he has estimated the capitalized value of profits generated by market power to be approximately 10 percent of the total value of all corporate stock.[58] Monopoly profits have obviously been the making of some family fortunes. These findings have received support in a study by Comanor and Smiley. They conclude that past and current monopoly in the United States has had a "major impact on the current degree of inequality in wealth distribution."[59]

No comparable studies have been carried out for Canada. One hazard any investigator will face is the fact, cited earlier, that the tariff and Canada's small market tend to raise costs as well as prices in many Canadian industries. It is quite conceivable that the main effect of monopoly power and commercial protection is to reduce all incomes in Canada, with perhaps little or no decisive redistribution of income in any particular direction. No doubt Canadian fortunes have been made in the past via the leverage exerted by monopoly power. It is less clear that this is still so. Unprotected (by tariff) Canadian industries often must face stiff competition from foreign sources of supply. Protected industries, and these are legion, have often become "overpopulated," with whatever

57. This may be changing as a result of the tremendous growth of private pension plans.
58. W.G. Shepherd, *Market Power and Economic Welfare*, 1970.
59. William S. Comanor and Robert H. Smiley, "Monopoly and the Distribution of Wealth," *Quarterly Journal of Economics* (May 1975), pp. 177-194.

monopoly rents protection might have afforded, having been "competed" away via the increased costs of added suboptimal capacity.[60] In short, it is unlikely that monopoly profits account for a higher percentage of Canadian national income than the 3 percent figure suggested by a number of U.S. studies. The reduction in national income emanating from our highly protective commercial policies has probably been a good deal more important in its effect on the income of the typical consumer.

Conclusion

This chapter has attempted to survey the evidence relating to market structure and economic performance in Canada. To provide some benchmarks, as well as insight, the often meagre Canadian evidence is compared to the more robust findings in U.S. studies. Generally, the evidence suggests that market structure affects profitability as economic theory suggests it will. Even this fact does not yield unambiguous conclusions about performance since in a "second best" world (which ours is at best) the violation of marginal rules (price equal to marginal cost) might be optimal. Moreover, profitability may, in many cases, be the result of "superiority" rather than market structure.

What is not optimal under any regime are cost-increasing tendencies, for which the Canadian tariff is perhaps most culpable. The price of protection has been high levels of suboptimal capacity, short production runs, and perhaps a strong dose of X-inefficiency. These "real" cost factors have been compounded by wage inflation that has further eroded Canada's competitive position in world markets. There is no apparent refuge in larger firm size where growth without specialization does not permit the attainment of greater scale economies. Nor is there evidence that size alone contributes to productivity growth via technological innovation.

---

60. Spence found evidence suggesting that when a combination of tariff protection and low costs generated rents, the rents were shared by production and nonproduction workers as well as capital. A. Michael Spence, op. cit., p. 265.

7

Public Policy Toward Business in Canada

Chapter seven, the first of six chapters forming the public policy half of the book, surveys an array of approaches toward the social control of business in Canada. These approaches, which include regulation, public ownership, competition policy, direct subsidization and protection, are briefly sketched in this chapter. Each is considered in more detail in subsequent chapters. The purpose of the present chapter is to highlight the alternative means of politically controlling business behaviour and performance and to place the approaches within the Canadian historical context. A subsidiary, though perhaps no less important objective, is to suggest a theory of politics or state activity which might explain the phenomenon of increasing social control in our mixed economy.

Before turning to specific government policies applied to the business sector we consider briefly the philosophical underpinnings of Western economic attitudes toward government intervention in the market place. These attitudes have their origins in the writings of classical economists, particularly Adam Smith who stated the case for a market economy in a manner that has not been equalled since. It is a short step from the subject of markets to the concept of competition, and from there to policies affecting competition.

Competition in Economic Thought

Economic thought about the proper role of government in the business arena has undergone a transformation in the two centuries since the appearance of Adam Smith's *Wealth of Nations*. Smith's classic work did not preclude an important role for government in the provision and maintenance of national defence, civil defence including the administration of justice, and public works, chiefly of a social infrastructure nature such as roads, bridges, harbours, canals, schools. However, Smith's anti-monopoly views made him an opponent of state intervention (the route by which most monopolies were created and sustained) in business affairs. Smith was, of course, well aware of the propensity for rival sellers to collude in order to raise prices, as his oft-quoted "People of the same trade..." statement indicates.[1] But Smith, and the classical economists in general, do not seem to have been much troubled by the possibility, or fact, of collusive agreements. Nor was the English common law, whose conspiracy doctrines were applied chiefly to labour unions, not businesses. An explanation lies in the tendency to assume that entry conditions were easy and that, therefore, potential or actual entrants were an effective constraint on monopoly behaviour in the long run. Thus while the common law generally would not enforce private contracts in restraint of trade, neither did it intervene where contracts or agreements were entered into with the express purpose of limiting or eliminating competition. The assumption was that there were always "third parties" (new entrants) waiting to compete away monopoly profits.

John Stuart Mill, who sympathized with the socialists of his day and looked forward to a time when the capital of firms would become "the joint property of all who participate in their productive employment," nevertheless castigated the socialists for their tendency to ascribe economic evils to competition.[2] In words which are music to modern proponents of antitrust or anticombines law("competition policy"), Mill stated:

> Instead of looking upon competition as the baneful and anti-social principle which it is held to be by the generality of Socialists, I conceive that, even in the present state of society and industry, every restriction of it is an evil, and every extension of it, even if for the time injuriously affecting some class of labourers, is always an ultimate good. To be protected against competition is to be protected in idleness, in mental dullness...[3]

Writing almost a century later the Chicagoan Henry Simons went even further and argued that competition was essential to democracy, as well as to an efficient capitalism ("the great enemy of democracy is monopoly in all its forms..."). Simons' sometime disciple, Milton Friedman, argues in somewhat analogous fashion that economic freedom, which implies freedom of individuals

---

1. Adam Smith, *The Wealth of Nations* (New York: Modern Library, 1937), p. 128. The full quote is given *infra* p. 156.
2. J.S. Mill, *Principles of Political Economy*, Vol. II, pp. 377-81.
3. Ibid., pp. 380-81.

to compete, is essential to political freedom.[4] But where Friedman and other modern Chicagoans tend to assume that in the absence of government intervention monopoly power is sufficiently limited that it can be kept in check by existing competitive pressure and forces, Simons had few illusions. He saw in gigantic corporations, trade associations and trade unions, "or, in general the organization and concentration of power within functional classes," the dead but destructive hand of monopoly. In his proposals for economic reform, put forth at the height of the Great Depression of the 1930s, Simons placed the abolition of private monopoly at the top of the list, arguing that his programme stood or fell on this condition. [5] If monopoly were inevitable, as in the case of some public utilities where scale economies made monopoly "natural," Simons called for public ownership, abjuring public regulation of private monopoly as the least palatable alternative. In his rejection of state regulation Simons was well ahead of his time. He saw that monopoly invited regulation, and regulation begat more regulation. According to Simons:

> . . .every suppression of competition gives rise to an apparent need for regulation; and every venture in regulation creates the necessity of more regulation; and every interference by government on behalf of one group necessitates, in the orderly routine of democratic corruption, additional interference on behalf of others. The outcome along these lines is: an accumulation of government regulation which yields, in many industries, all the afflictions of socialization and none of its possible benefits; an enterprise economy paralyzed by political control; the moral disintegration of representative government in the endless contest of innumerable pressure groups for special political favours; and dictatorship. (I omit inflation, calling it a symptom rather than a disease.)[6]

Numerous economists, of various political persuasions, have observed and lamented the great growth of regulation in the last half century, a growth which has accelerated in recent years with the onslaught of environmental, consumer, health and safety, and energy legislation. The crucial difference between Simons and the current critics of government intervention (and this is, as well, a difference between the classical economists of the 19th century and most modern economists) is the political context in which Simons analyzed the role of competition. The modern argument for competition is framed in essentially "efficiency" terms: thus when the market "fails" to produce "efficient results"

4. Milton Friedman, *Capitalism and Freedom* (Chicago: University of Chicago Press, 1962), Chap. 1.
5. Henry Simons, *Economic Policy for a Free Society* (Chicago: University of Chicago Press, 1948), pp. 57-58.
6. Simons, op. cit. pp. 87-88.

government intervention is often called for.[7] Until very recently, the political implications of that intervention were rarely considered explicitly by economists.[8]

The Theoretical Case for Government Intervention

Why should governments intervene in a market economy other than to stabilize it (through monetary and fiscal policies), redistribute income (through taxes and transfers), or provide for highly valued goods and services that the market will not supply (public goods provision)? The answer lies in the fact that sometimes the operation of markets does not come close to assuring equality between marginal social valuation (MSV) and marginal social cost (MSC) in the use of resources. (See the discussion on the optimality properties of MSV = MSC in the first section of Chapter 2.) Sometimes the problem is market imperfection in the form of monopoly power or information inadequacies. Sometimes the problem resides in market failures due to the existence of externalities or common property resources. Each of these is very briefly discussed below.

We have already seen that when markets are so structured that individual firms are in the position to exercise market power, or behave monopolistically, price (P) exceeds marginal cost (MC). When P > MC, then, in the absence of externalities, MSV > MSC. In these circumstances, too little output of the commodity in question is being produced, and society will gain from public policies which combat or prevent monopolistic behaviour by firms. (A special case is that of natural monopoly. See Chapter 10.)

Sometimes, however, the market imperfection is not due to market power, but rather to information inadequacies. These arise when economic agents (particularly consumers) are led astray because of ignorance, misjudgment or misinformation. The normative (welfare) properties of the competitive model are based on the assumption of consumer sovereignty. But consumers who are ignorant or misinformed are not fully sovereign. Consumers may make *errors of omission* when a lack of information leads them to consume too little of a

7. Where "market failure" is due to divergencies between social and private costs or benefits (so-called "externalities") negotiations between the (private) parties involved is, in principle, an alternative to government intervention (in the form of taxes and subsidies or direct regulation) as a means of eliminating the externalities. That is, if it is possible for the private parties to negotiate costlessly, the initial distribution of property rights and legal liability does not affect the optimal allocation of resources. For a full discussion of this interesting but difficult proposition, see Ronald Coase, "The Problem of Social Cost," *The Journal of Law and Economics* (Oct. 1960), pp. 1-44.
8. An important recent contribution is that of Dan Usher, who shows how dependent is the existence of democracy upon an impersonal market-oriented method of determining most of the income we receive. Usher shows how democracy would be eroded if most incomes were determined by the legislature or other government authority. See *The Economic Prerequisite to Democracy* (Oxford: Basil Blackwell, 1981).

product (MSV > MSC). Consumers may make *errors of commission* when they are mislead into purchasing more of a product than they would have had they been correctly informed. Public policies which improve information in the market place can contribute to making MSV more nearly equal to MSC.

Markets "fail" when, even if full information existed and competitive conditions were possible, market forces would not produce a socially desirable level of output. (This is a rather more narrow definition of market failure than is adopted by many economists or, in fact, is used elsewhere in this chapter.) The two chief sources of market failure, as defined here, are "externalities" and common property resources. Externalities exist when voluntary exchange between buyer and seller conveys benefits to (MSV > MSC) or costs upon (MSV < MSC) third parties—i.e. persons not a party to the exchange. For example, a major source of external costs is pollution. All production and consumption generate waste. When the price of a good does not fully reflect the costs of waste disposal, society as a whole bears the uncovered cost in one way or another—often in the form of despoiled air, water, and other natural assets. When important externalities exist, it usually takes some form of government intervention to force the parties to an exchange to fully account for all of the costs produced by their actions.

Some of our national heritage is owned by no one in particular—but is owned collectively, i.e., in common. The most important examples are bodies of water which yield up a harvest of fish or sea-bed minerals. Other examples include the radio spectrum and fugacious sub-surface mineral fuels such as oil and gas. Where common property resources exist, no individual exploiter of the resource has an incentive to limit his or her take—i.e., to conserve. For, in the absence of any collective restriction on the amount harvested, what person A does not "harvest" today, person B (or C, etc.) will. Thus government prorationing of oil in the 1950s and 1960s (see Ch. 10) and restrictions on ocean fishing in the 1970s and 1980s reflect the fact that in the absence of some form of government control, the existence of common property resources will result in excessive exploitation of the resource—i.e., a level of current output at which MSV < MSC.

The existence of market imperfections and market failures provide a theoretical case for government intervention in the market place. The practical problem is two-fold: (i) adopting the most efficient tool for intervening and (ii) restricting intervention to those cases which are theoretically defensible. The remaining chapters of this book suggest that coping with the practical problems is much more difficult than stating the ideal.

The Political Economy of Interventionism

Adam Smith's *Wealth of Nations* is widely viewed as providing a political-economic-social rationale for a market economy in which government intervention is limited to supplying what an unfettered private sector will not provide. Smith's insight did not, however, imply a theory of "perfect competition." As we noted in chapter 2, the classical economists' view of competition is better described in terms of rivalry. It was their "neoclassical" successors, with their penchant for neat mathematical results, who developed the theory of perfect competition, along with "proofs" of its "efficiency." Paradoxically, the concept of perfect competition has probably contributed to government intervention because, by implication, anything which is not "perfect" is "imperfect," and what is imperfect might be improved upon via some form of social intervention or control.[9] This, of course, is not what Adam Smith had in mind. Rivalry among sellers provided a form of social control, a set of incentives, and, in the long run, the most effective means of economic growth, in counter-distinction to the hamhanded interference and monopoly-creating activities of mercantilism. The failure to appreciate the role of competition in rivalristic terms, and the defence of competition by economists with a perfect competition model in mind, has probably contributed to a resurgence of interventionism, that might be described as a "new mercantilism."

What is the purpose of this discourse on competition? The answer is fairly obvious: most public policies toward business are in one way or another related to competition. Some policies promote competition, others prevent it, while still others supplant it by attempting to take an activity "out of the market place" (e.g. the public provision of primary and secondary education or medical care). Which policies are chosen depends in our economy on one's view of the benefits (or costs) flowing from competition. How widely one casts the net in looking for the beneficial results of competition depends in part on how competition is defined. "Perfect competition" focuses on efficiency, particularly allocative efficiency. Competition in the "classical" sense of the term was believed to contribute to much more than economic efficiency: as we have seen, various writers have credited competition with an influence on such widely disparate factors as individual character and political democracy, as well as economic growth.

In addition, our views on competition depend heavily upon *who* one believes

9. In fact, the existence of market failure is a necessary but not sufficient condition on which to build an economic case for government intervention. One must weigh against "market failure" the real possibility of "nonmarket (or government) failure." There is no assurance that government intervention will be efficient or effective: that the policies will be carried out at least cost and without unintended and expensive side effects. For example, government officials may not choose the most efficient or appropriate policies due to inadequate information or political pressures, while bureaucrats may use scarce resources to increase their own utility. See Charles Wolf, "A Theory of Nonmarket Failure: Framework for Implementation Analysis," *Journal of Law and Economics* (April 1979), pp. 107-139.

to be the appropriate beneficiaries from the organization of the economic system. Here we must distinguish between sellers and consumers and between individuals and the community at large. It is pretty clear from both economic theory and the observed behaviour of business that competition primarily benefits consumers at the expense of *existing* sellers. As we saw in chapter 5, Canadian business history is replete with attempts to stifle and "control" competition—evidencing a rational preference by established sellers for the "quiet life" accompanied by monopoly profits. It is consumers who are the real beneficiaries of the lower prices and greater product varieties that competition is presumed to stimulate. This is so, at least, for consumers taken as a group, since *ceteris paribus*, the efficiency contribution of competition increases the economic pie, thereby *raising* average real income per capita. However, for any given individual, competition may be disadvantageous to the extent that it reduces his or her income as a *seller* by more than it reduces the prices he or she must pay as a buyer. What applies here to a specific individual can be applied to specific groups who, nevertheless, comprise a tiny fraction of the total citizenry.

It is the diffusion of the benefits from competition and the concentration of its costs which is the Achilles' heel of public policies to promote competition. As a practical matter, democratic societies are susceptible to small group pressures which can be parlayed into minority-favouring legislation via the process of logrolling—vote trading. The problem is that benefits from competition that flow to the community at large are usually "shallow" relative to the "deep" benefits received by a specific seller group from the restriction of competition. Where benefits are diffuse and shallow, organized efforts to retain those benefits are unlikely—or certainly less likely that the organization of narrowly defined groups in quest of individually large payoffs. Thus the beneficiaries from competition are nowhere nearly as well-organized or as motivated as the beneficiaries from restricted competition. One of the hallmarks of the last half century of public sector growth is the increase in legislation designed to regulate or protect individuals or groups from the effects of the free operation of markets. The legislation takes many forms, including minimum or maximum prices or rates, control of entry, permission to collectively organize (form a monopoly), and self-regulation. We have seen a gradual alienation of the "police powers of the state" to private interest groups, not unlike the alienation of public real property (land) to private individuals or firms in the 19th century.

In sum, the great contest over appropriate public policies toward business encompasses far more than matters purely of economic efficiency. The classical economists recognized, as we should, the political elements inherent in government-business relations. The growth of the public sector in Western nations has not been neutral vis-à-vis government-business relations. This was not, in principle, inevitable. Governments could have confined themselves to stabilizing the economy, redistributing income through taxes and transfers, and the provision of (public) goods and services (e.g. national defence, primary education, roads), which the private sector would not supply, or would only supply in grossly inferior quantities. But modern governments have provided much more: they have sought to protect or augment the income and wealth of seller groups, including sellers of labour services, and in doing so have sharply curtailed, at points, the beneficial results of competition. In the words of Simons again:

> All the grosser mistakes in economic policy, if not most manifestations of democratic corruption, arise from focusing upon the interests of people as producers rather than upon their interests as consumers, that is, from acting on behalf of producer minorities rather than on behalf of the whole community as sellers of services and buyers of products. One gets the right answers usually by regarding simply the interests of consumers, since we are all consumers, and the answers reached by this approach are presumably the correct ones for laborers as a whole. But one does not get elected by approaching issues this way! People seldom vote in terms of their common interests, whether as sellers or buyers. There is no means for protecting the common interest save in terms of rules of policy; and it is only in terms of general rules or principles that democracy, which is government by free, intelligent discussion, can function tolerably or endure. Its nemesis is racketeering—tariffs, other subsidies, the patronage dispensations generally and, outside of government, monopoly, which in its basic aspect is impairment of the state's monopoly of coercive power.[10]

Thus the subject of public policies toward business encompasses much more than narrow economic concerns. It is a subject for philosophers and political theorists as well as economists and lawyers. As a *practical* matter it is as much concerned with issues of equity (income and wealth distribution) as with efficiency.

Competition Policy

The preceding section underlined the place of competition in a market economy. We have also seen that the benefits of competition flow chiefly to society in its capacity as consumers, while sellers, if given a chance, will attempt to avoid competition. Until about a century ago it was thought that sellers could not eliminate competition for longer than it took the lure of monopoly profits to attract new entrants. However, late nineteenth century industrial developments

10. Simons, op. cit., p. 123.

led many to question whether unrestricted business behaviour was necessarily efficacious. Large-scale enterprises, the result of changes in technology and financial institutions, created large size differentials among some competitors and between some buyers and sellers. The great differences in size were believed to weight bargaining power substantially in favour of the larger firm, a suspicion that was fueled by the alleged unsavoury tactics of the "robber barons." Once markets were dominated by a giant firm(s), competition, it was argued, would no longer be "fair," if it existed at all. Thus the spectre of monopoly, emanating from industrial developments, combined with Adam Smith's well-known views on collusion to provide the intellectual and political underpinnings for legislation defining the "rules of the game" in the business arena. These rules were aimed at curbing monopolizing behaviour in the form of predation or collusion or "trust."

Antimonopoly legislation in North America is almost a century old, the first Canadian legislation predating by one year the U.S. Sherman Antitrust Act of 1890. In 1889, following a House of Commons' Committee investigation into monopolistic activities in a number of Canadian industries, a section was added to the Criminal Code providing for sanctions against attempts to stifle competition. Although the first Anti-combines Act was not passed until 1910, and permanent administrative machinery not established until 1923, the legislation of 1889 is still the basis of section 32(1), the most frequently-used (except for misleading advertising) part of the present Combines Investigation Act. (This Act and the resultant jurisprudence are discussed in much greater detail in chapters 8 and 9).

An *economic* rationale for competition policy can be built around four propositions:

1. Firms will prefer the price and output levels that would occur under monopoly to those that would result under competitive conditions.

2. Left to themselves, firms will often attempt to achieve a monopolistic position (via collusive agreement, merger, predatory or other monopolizing or restrictive behaviour) if there are no legal prohibitions or limitations against such activities. (We may call this the "Adam Smith" postulate.)

3. These attempts will be successful in a sufficient number of cases to warrant legal prohibition or limitation.

4. Community (consumer) welfare is reduced by monopolistic distortion in the allocation of resources, the efficiency with which resources are used, and in the distribution of income.

Proposition (1) is predicated on standard, comparative-static, economic theory of the sort presented at the beginning of chapter 2. Proposition (2) follows logically from the assumption that firms prefer greater to lesser (or no) profits and from the more questionable assumption that entry barriers are sufficiently high, or the long run sufficiently long, to make the effort to achieve profits via "temporary" monopoly worthwhile. Certainly, Canadian business history is evidence in support of this proposition. The third proposition is more controversial, for there are schools of thought which appear to hold that most attempts to achieve monopoly results will be unsuccessful due to the competitive forces which remain, including the threat of entry by new firms or established firms (conglomerate entry). If monopoly attempted is rarely monopoly achieved, one might question whether the benefits of a formal competition policy exceed the costs of its administration and enforcement. This, however, has not been the general view, which has presumed, probably rightly so, that the incentive to avoid or restrict competition is sufficiently strong, and entry attempts sufficiently time consuming, or difficult, to warrant a positive programme for the preservation of competition.

The importance of the fourth proposition has been disputed following attempts to estimate the welfare loss due to monopoly (see chapter 6). The estimated welfare loss is very small, and the larger distributional effects too value laden for many economists. For this reason it has often been economists with a wider view of the role of competition, e.g. Henry Simons, who have been among the strongest advocates of competition (antitrust) policies. The relevance of the fourth proposition has also been disputed by Schumpeter and his followers, who have severely questioned the comparative-static framework from which the proposition is drawn. As we saw in chapter 2, a more dynamic view with innovation and technical change as its centre-piece, holds monopoly power to be a necessary and inevitable result of an efficient capitalism. Most antitrust advocates would not, however, dispute the acceptability of monopoly-creating inventions and innovations, but would argue that monopoly is often the result of attempts to achieve a "quiet life," and not simply the temporary outcome of creative efforts, as Schumpeter implied.

To this point we have considered competition policy at a high level of generality. When it comes to specific issues the problem of choosing appropriate policies becomes more difficult. To be sure, where behaviour is avoidable (collusion, exclusion, predation) *and* is hardly ever beneficial (price fixing, output control) it makes sense to write prohibitionary rules of the game. Penalties should be sufficiently great to achieve a modicum of prevention. But what about *existing* monopoly power held by dominant firms in highly concentrated industries? Or what about mergers which alter market structure and reduce the strength of competition? Many proponents of anticombines policies are unwilling to "restructure" tight oligopolies or dominant-firm industries through a process of enterprise dissolution. Some economists are also concerned that merger policy not be based on a single criterion: the preservation of competition.[11] Especially in Canada, where the domestic market is usually small and scale economies rarely exhausted, the efficiency gains, if any, from merger are thought to be a relevant policy criterion.

Beneath the surface of these issues is the question of appropriate standards for competition policy. Should policy be based on structural, behavioural, or performance standards—or some of each? Historically, the antitrust and anticombines laws have focused on undesirable and avoidable behaviour. This is understandable since lawyers and judges do not like to convict someone for what he *is*, but rather for what he *did*. In Canada, these sentiments have been reflected to an extreme in the so-called "abuse theory of detriment." In piloting the first Anti-combines Act through Parliament in 1910, then Labour Minister Mackenzie King stated that "the one end and purpose of the legislation is to prevent the mean man from profiting in virtue of his meanness."[12] A study of the administration and enforcement of the anticombines laws prior to 1960 termed it a "cops and robbers" effort, largely devoid of economic reasoning or criteria.[13]

One of the problems with behavioural standards for competition policy is that such standards do not fit nicely into economic analysis. The *economic* argument for competition policy is derived, in part, from theoretical welfare economics, and is therefore performance-oriented. Logically, competition policy ought to adopt performance standards—permitting those activities which improve economic performance (efficiency in its various dimensions, economic stability, income distributional effects) while thwarting those activities which are harmful to social welfare. But performance or welfare is notoriously difficult to assess or measure—and then typically only years after the fact, too late to undo the harm done, or to reverse any resultant change in market structure. Thus as a practical matter performance standards are suspect.[14] Nevertheless, where there are important trade-offs between competition and efficiency, as would appear to be the case in the Canadian manufacturing sector, it is easy to see the attractive-

11. For a nice statement of the trade-off between competition and scale efficiency see Oliver Williamson, "Economies as an Antitrust Defense," *American Economic Review* (March 1968), and the brief restatement of Williamson's argument at the end of chapter 4.

12. L.A. Skeoch, ed., *Restrictive Trade Practices in Canada* (Toronto: McClelland and Stewart, 1966), p. 22.

13. G. Rosenbluth and H.G. Thorburn, *Canadian Anti-Combines Administration 1952-60* (University of Toronto Press, 1963).

14. A strong argument for performance standards was made by Jesse Markham, "An Alternative Approach to the Concept of Workable Competition," *American Economic Review* 40 (1950), pp. 349-61. A strong counterargument is made by E.S. Mason, "The New Competition," *The Yale Review*, Autumn 1953. Reprinted in Mason, *Economic Concentration and the Monopoly Problem* (Cambridge: Harvard University Press, 1959), pp 371-81.

ness of performance criteria. Thus some of the most important proposed amendments to the Canadian Combines Investigation Act would give to the courts or a quasi-judicial tribunal powers to prohibit competition-reducing mergers and certain other practices or activities if their contribution to efficiency is not sufficient to offset their impact on competition (see chapter 9).

An alternative to performance criteria is structural standards. Two major arguments can be advanced in favour of market structure tests in the application of competition policy. First, if there are reasonably strong market structure-performance links, structural standards provide a potential basis for influencing or controlling performance. Thus, competition policy might focus on industries with a dominant firm or a few dominant firms. For example, in the late 1960s a White House Task Force on Antitrust Policy proposed that "tightly" oligopolistic industries in the United States be subjected to deconcentration via dissolution of the leading firms unless the latter could make a showing that their position was due to scale economies, superior efficiency, or innovativeness.[15] In other words, the task of proving "good works" would fall on the industrial giants under attack (rather than upon the government).

A second major argument for structural tests is that if competition policy is based solely on behavioural standards a "double standard" is created. The argument runs as follows: those highly concentrated industries in which monopoly power is already great, and overtly collusive or restrictive behaviour seemingly unnecessary, will escape the "bite" of competition policy if only "bad" behaviour is punished. In other words, under a conduct standard the laws are applied against those firms who must collude or "monopolize" to achieve monopoly power, but not against firms who already have, and can easily retain, monopoly powers. A fundamental presumption of this argument is that in tightly oligopolistic industries discipline and price uniformity are achieved via tacit understandings and price leadership, and do not require the type of agreement that can be proven beyond a reasonable doubt in a court of law. That is, "consciously parallel" behaviour requires nothing more than a recognition of mutual interdependence. However, there is reason to question the argument that in highly concentrated industries uniformity of behaviour does not require agreement among firms. There is growing evidence that much more than tacit understandings is required to maintain oligopolistic coordination even in highly concentrated industries. The examples of shipping containers, electric large lamps, and ready-mix concrete described in chapter 5 are illustrative. An important study of price-fixing cases in the United States suggests that the structure of the relevant markets where conspiracies were identified was

---

15. *White House Task Force on Anti Trust Policy*, Report 1 (in Trade Reg. Rep. supp. to no.415, May 26, 1969). Legislation along similar lines was also proposed by former Senator Phillip Hart.

typically concentrated.[16] Another U.S. study of price-fixing prosecutions indicates that defendant firms were not relatively profitable, suggesting that the colluding firms were restrained by either easy entry conditions or by their own proclivities to secretly honour their agreements in the breach.[17] These pieces of evidence suggest that a policy directed at inter-firm agreements and restrictive practices may be effective in promoting competition in concentrated as well as unconcentrated industries.

Economic Regulation

Regulation of the pricing, marketing and investment activities of firms has long been a well-used tool of governments—central and local. The *Wealth of Nations*, and the "laissez-faire" spirit for which Adam Smith's classic provided an intellectual base, can be seen as an attack on economic regulation of business, particularly where it took the form of franchised monopolies. Monarchs and parliaments had long used their sovereign powers to reward, protect, and promote particular individuals and their enterprises. This was done by granting them a monopoly over the production or distribution of a particular commodity within a particular area. A famous case was the grant by Queen Elizabeth I of a monopoly over the distribution of playing cards in England to a favourite courtier she desired to reward. The vigorous objection of Parliament led to a transferral of such powers to the House of Commons which in due course granted monopolies to the great companies trading in the Far East (East India) and the New World (Virginia, Hudson's Bay). The use of the sovereign's (government's) powers to protect specific enterprises is an old story, often forgotten, but still used.

As the 19th century wore on technological developments raised the spectre that, in some industries at least, monopoly would and must replace competitive rivalry between firms. "Cut-throat" competition among railroads led to bankruptcies, consolidations and ultimately regulation or public ownership. The budding electric power industry with its vast network of wires (tentacles), and a bit later the telephonic industry with somewhat similar characteristics, were granted franchises (positions of monopoly) in return for regulation of their rates. It was clear that duplication of networks by two or more competing firms was inefficient. Moreover, scale economies in railroading and in the production and transmission of electric power added to the status of these industries as natural

16. George A. Hay and Daniel Kelley, "An Empirical Survey of Price Fixing Conspiracies," *Journal of Law and Economics* (April 1974), pp. 13-38.
17. Peter Asch and J.J. Seneca, "Is Collusion Profitable?" *The Review of Economics and Statistics* (Feb. 1976), pp. 1-12.

monopolies. While the regulatory "hand" has been extended far beyond natural monopolies in the transportation, energy, and communication sectors (tariffs for example are one type of regulation—affecting the terms on which goods may enter a country) the economic analysis of regulation has until recently centred chiefly on the public utility sector.[18] (The industries making up this sector are dealt with in some detail in chapter 10.)

Direct regulation of economic activities in Canada is widespread. There is, of course, public utility type regulation of telecommunications, air transport, some rail transport (although non-statutory freight rates were deregulated in the 1960s), natural gas transmission and distribution, water and, in some cases, electricity rates (although most electricity is generated and transmitted by public enterprises usually not subject to regulatory board control). The provinces regulate both intraprovincial and interprovincial trucking. The Canadian Wheat Board regulates the marketing of Western grains. Provincial legislation has permitted the establishment of agricultural marketing boards, some of which exercise so-called "supply management" powers to control commodity output and thereby prices (e.g. eggs, broilers, turkeys, milk, flue-cured tobacco). Some marketing boards require that all produce of a given type produced in the province be channeled through it and in some cases this extends to all produce marketed in the province, wherever produced (for example, the Manitoba Vegetable Producers Marketing Board). The federal and provincial governments exercise substantial control over the Canadian dairy industry via systems of quotas. There is provincial regulation of professions from hairdressers to lawyers, morticians to doctors. The number of taxis is controlled in such cities as Toronto and Montreal, giving substantial value to the medallion conferring the right to operate a taxi. The province of Alberta regulates petroleum production; the federal government currently fixes the price of petroleum sold in Canada. Federal regulations limit the amount of shoes and clothing importers are allowed to purchase from foreign sources. Banks and other financial institutions are subject to certain kinds of regulation. The construction industry is subject to elaborate building codes and zoning laws. Labour legislation has given some unions control over the licensing or certification of their membership, particularly in the building trades. In Quebec, language legislation regulates the language of work and the language of schooling. From 1975 to 1978 the federal government exercised control over wages and prices through an Anti-Inflation Board.

The apparent attractiveness of regulation to governments bent on influencing the economy has given rise to some theories of economic regulation. These

18. The industries covered by the term "public utility" include electricity, gas, water, and telephone and railroads and local transit. See James C. Bonbright, *Principles of Public Utility Rates* (New York: Columbia University Press, 1961), pp. 3-5.

theories have focused on regulation at the industry rather than economy-wide level. Economists' interest in regulation has opened up fertile ground in the interfaces among economics, law, and politics. The new theories of regulation and detailed investigations of specific regulated industries have opened the doors to a "new" political economy in which theories of politics can play as large a role as economic theory.

In approaching the theory of economic regulation economists have asked two apparently similar, but, in fact, quite different questions. The older question is, Why regulate private enterprise? The other question which has been asked with increasing frequency is, Why are regulated enterprises regulated? The first question can be conveniently, but perhaps ambiguously, answered by reference to the term "market failure." Here "market failure" includes such problems as monopoly, "natural" or otherwise; externalities, particularly pollution damages to "third parties"; unstable market conditions due to inelastic demand, supply lags and supply shocks typical of certain agricultural commodities; and the existence of common property resources such as fisheries, grazing lands, or fugacious oil and gas pools. The ambiguity created by this litany derives from the fact that economists have shown that in many of the instances cited a system of taxes and subsidies is theoretically superior to regulation. Unfortunately, theoretical superiority does not necessarily mean practical superiority, including the political advantages of regulation relative to the popular distrust of specific taxes and cash subsidies. As a result, the main *economic* case for regulation arises out of "natural monopoly" (where it exists), although even here some writers have preferred no regulation to public regulation of private monopoly (see above).[19]

The logic of the second question, "Why are regulated industries regulated?" is traceable to the observation that many regulated industries fail to fit the categories of market failure which might have justified some form of government intervention. It is also traceable to a view that regulation, like "old soldiers," never dies (it doesn't "fade away" either), even though the conditions which may have justified some form of regulation in the past have long since vanished. (This view must be modified in the light of recent moves toward deregulation, particularly in the United States where the airlines, railroads, and highway trucking have been recently released from many, if not all, of their regulatory shackles.) So long as regulation was conceived as restraining, in the public's interest, enterprises from exercising monopoly power, the question of

19. One economist has argued that regulation of natural monopolies is unnecessary because there is a superior alternative: auctioning off to the highest bidder the franchise, or the right to be the sole supplier in a given market, for a utility service. See Harold Demsetz, "Why Regulate Utilities?" *Journal of Law and Economics*, 11 (April 1968), pp. 55-66. For a critique of the practicality of auctioning franchise monopolies, see O.E. Williamson, "Franchise Bidding for Natural Monopolies," *Bell Journal of Economics* (Spring 1976), pp. 73-104.

why certain industries were regulated (and others not) was rarely asked and never satisfactorily answered. It was the fundamental insight that firms or industries may actively seek regulation, in contrast to the popular view that firms avoid government regulations like the plague, that opened the doors to a new political economy of government intervention in the private sector of the economy.

The opening salvo was George Stigler's "The Theory of Economic Regulation."[20] Stigler attempted to explain the existence of regulation in demand and supply terms. Firms demand regulation to escape the rigours of competition, particularly regulation which restricts entry, even if this requires the firm to submit to some degree of control over the rates it charges. Politicians supply regulation in return for political support, both at the ballot box and in the pocket book. Underlying the *demand* for regulation is the theory of cartels. Cartels, especially if they are legally enforceable, are clearly capable of generating supranormal profits, at least for a time. Underlying the *supply* of regulation is a log-rolling view of the political process in which minority interests may be as well, or better, served than majority interests. Stigler's theory is perhaps simplistic, but it is also powerful. It shattered once-and-for-all the illusion that because regulation originates with legislation it must have been intended in the public interest. And even where the legislation is *intended* in the public (consumer) interest its *effect* is all too likely to be in the producer's interest.

Table 7-1 attempts to portray the relationship between various theories of regulation.[21] Much of the early regulation was proposed or supported by late 19th and early 20th century reformers who argued for government control over various forms of business as being in the public interest. The public interest theory held sway for several decades, by which time it was increasingly clear that the regulators were often the leading champions of the regulated. When someone asked "Who regulates the regulators?", the answer "the regulated" spawned the "capture theory," which implies that the regulatory agency is in the grasp of the industry it is supposed to regulate. This theory is consistent with the public interest theory so far as the *initial purpose* of the regulation is

20. G. Stigler, "The Theory of Economic Regulation," *Bell Journal of Economics and Management Science* (Spring 1971), pp. 3-21. A similar argument was made at about the same time by William Jordan, "Producer Protection, Prior Market Structure and the Effects of Government Regulation," *Journal of Law and Economics* (April 1972).
21. One theory which is not included because it does not fit nicely into any of the categories is Posner's view that much regulation is undertaken in order to cross-subsidize non-compensatory services with revenues from particularly profitable ones. Examples include the subsidization of local telephone service by long distance, short-haul by long-haul passenger air service. Richard Posner, "Taxation by Regulation," *Bell Journal of Economics and Management Science* (Spring 1971), pp. 22-50.

Table 7-1

A Taxonomy of Regulation Theories

Purpose of Regulation	Effect of Regulation	
	Consumer Protection	Producer Protection
Consumer Protection	1. "Naïve" public interest theory	2. "Capture" theory 3. Modified public interest theory
Producer Protection		4. Stigler's "Economic Theory of Regulation" and Jordan's "Producer Protection Theory" 5. Modern Marxist theory—powerful interest groups control government

concerned, but reaches different conclusions where *effects* are concerned. The reformer answer to the capture theory was that there was nothing wrong with the regulation that could not be remedied by improving the quality and independence of regulatory personnel. This view of regulatory reform has been placed on the defensive by the Stigler-Jordan "producer protection" theories of regulation. Interestingly, producer protection theories share the same quadrant with "Marxist" theories which argue that powerful interest groups (capitalists) control government and write regulations on their behalf. The Marxist theory fails, however, to contend with the fact that so much regulation is done on behalf of small business (pharmacists, barbers, truckers, taxi cab owners), farmers and union labour.[22]

The very brief survey of theories of regulation in the preceding paragraph suggests that many economists have moved away from viewing regulation as in the "public interest" to viewing it as a response to "private interest." While this interpretation is probably correct, it does not necessarily imply that regulatory limitations on competition either are intended to, or actually do, allow firms to earn supranormal profits. It has been argued that some regulation can be

---

22. It is possible to argue that labour legislation (industrial relations, regulations) has allowed many labour unions to amass substantial amounts of monopoly power (usually termed bargaining power), with the result unions may now be a major source of the "monopoly problem." This was foreseen by Henry Simons, "Some Reflections on Syndicalism," *Economic Policy for a Free Society* (Univ. of Chicago Press, 1948), Chap. 6.

viewed as a form of "economic due process" in which the weak and unsuspecting are protected from the "ruthless efficiency of the market."[23] In these cases the purpose of regulatory protection of producer groups (including, of course, producers of labour services), is to slow down the effects of unforeseen economic changes, such as technological change, which undermine as well as enhance investments in human and nonhuman capital. Thus some examples of producer-protection regulation may be viewed as a social response to inexorable economic change, in which government attempts to maintain *normal* returns on those private investments in human and non-human capital that, in the absence of intervention, would be unexpectedly eroded to subnormal or negative levels by an efficiently operating market. Of course, the actual effects of such regulations may be to produce the same sorts of rigidities and allocational inefficiencies as any other sort of protectionist regulation.

Even if producer protection regulation initially yields supranormal profits the gains may be transitory. If the regulation-induced monopoly profits are capitalized, the main beneficiaries from producer-protection type regulation are enterprises already established at the time the regulations were first implemented. That is, it is assumed that the beneficiaries of protective regulation will capitalize the benefits into the sale price of the enterprise. New entrants to the industry, who are forced by regulation to buy out an existing supplier (e.g. egg, dairy, and poultry farms in many provinces of Canada, taxi cabs in Toronto), will pay a price reflecting the value of the regulation-created profits. Thus in time, as the initial (at the time regulation was introduced) owners have disappeared, most firms will only be earning normal returns, in spite of the protections afforded by regulation. This makes eliminating the regulations difficult since it would create capital losses for existing suppliers. From this perspective it would appear that producer-protection regulations not only transfer income from consumers to producers, but from future generations of

---

23. Bruce Owen and Ronald Braeutigam, *The Regulation Game: The Strategic Use of the Administrative Process* (Cambridge: Ballinger, 1978), pp. 20-21. One could ask, who are the weak and unsuspecting? Arguably, in some cases, they include economic agents on both sides of the market: both buyers and sellers. Where, for example, shifting supply conditions, including those due to easy entry and exit, produce highly volatile prices and/or an uncertain supply, regulation of price or entry may be invoked to reduce what would otherwise be substantial risks or uncertainties for both buyers and sellers. (A possible case in point are nonstoreable services—see Ch. 10.) Here, it is argued, that regulation may represent an implicit and efficient "administered contract" when it is employed in situations where long term contracts could only be concluded with difficulty and under conditions of substantial risk, without the agency of government. Thus, in a dynamic context of fluctuating and uncertain demands and supplies, the case for regulation is stronger than is indicated by the essentially comparative static analysis underlying the private interest theories which became increasingly popular in the 1970s. See Victor Goldberg "Regulation and Administered Contracts" *Bell Journal of Economics* vol. 7, no. 2 (Autumn, 1976), pp. 426-448, and Robert D. Cairns *Rationales for Regulation*, Technical Report No. 2, Economic Council of Canada, Regulation Reference, October 1980, esp. pp. 50-72.

producers to the generation of producers around at the time the regulations are introduced.[24]

In this view regulation is a "trap," economically and politically. The gains, to anyone, are transient. Not only does regulation raise prices paid by consumers, it eventually increases the costs that must be carried by subsequent generations of producers. The profligacy of one generation of politicians in granting producer-protection legislation ties the hands of a subsequent generation of political leadership which must let the regulatory legislation stand so as not to produce unexpected and unfair capital losses for existing suppliers. If there is a permanent gainer, it is whatever bureaucracy is established to administer and enforce the regulations. Thus from one point of view, the issue of regulation is at the heart of some basic controversies over the nature of modern governments, who controls them, their impact on the distribution of income, and their contribution to inflationary pressure.

The view of regulation presented in this chapter is in sharp conflict with older views which regarded public regulation as a necessary offset to private monopoly or as an "institutional supplement" to competition.[25] The essence of the older views was that regulation was undertaken in the public interest to exercise social control over industries "clothed with the public interest," or to compensate for "market failures." To the extent that the regulation was applied to industries which were of the "natural monopoly" sort or where there were important externalities or common property resource characteristics the old view made sense, especially where countries, such as the United States, preferred private to public enterprise. Unfortunately, constitutions or constitutional decisions of courts have opened the door much wider. In Canada, there are no constitutional limits to regulatory legislation (parliaments are "sovereign"), although drawing the line between provincial and federal powers in this field still evokes legal controversy.[26] In the United States, there were judicial or constitutional limits to what a legislature could decide to regulate, until the landmark Supreme Court decision in *Nebbia v. New York* (1934). This case involved the power of the New York State legislature to set minimum retail

24. See Gordon Tullock, "The Transitional Gains Trap," *Bell Journal of Economics* (Autumn, 1975).

25. Morris Copeland, "Institutionalism and Welfare Economics," *American Economic Review*, 48 (March 1958), p. 10, articulates well the view that regulation is an institutional supplement to competition.

26. The Supreme Court of Canada decision in *MacDonald v. Vapour Canada Ltd.,(1976)* 66 DLR (3d) 1, bears on the jurisdictional issue. In addition to the federal-provincial question, there is also an issue of "due process" relating to the procedures under which a regulatory action proceeds. For a survey of issues raised by economic regulation in Canada, see G.B. Reschenthaler, "Direct Regulation in Canada: Some Policies and Problems," *Studies in Regulation in Canada*, W.T. Stanbury (ed.) (Institute for Research on Public Policy, 1978), pp. 37-112.

prices for milk.[27] In effect, the Supreme Court in a 5-4 decision held it was up to the legislature, not the courts, to decide what economic activities were "clothed," or affected, with the public interest. The *Nebbia* decision thereby opened the legislative door to broad-scale government intervention. One might wonder, however, whether the constitutional logic of the *Nebbia* decision can withstand the producer-protection thesis. If, in fact, most regulation is effectively to protect producers can it be justified on "affected with the public interest" grounds?

Paradoxically, with the appearance of the new theories of economic regulation in the early 1970s, came a new wave of regulations which do not fit neatly into the developing theoretical modes. Concerns with environment, energy, health and safety, and consumerism have generated massive amounts of new legislation, establishing new regulatory authorities and thousands of pages of new rules.[28] Many of these regulations have required firms to make cost-increasing investments and changes in production techniques, not to mention to incur added administrative costs to meet new "paper work" demands. While firms are sometimes able to pass the higher costs on to consumers in the form of higher prices, they are not always able to do so, particularly where the goods produced are in stiff competition with imported goods supplied by foreign firms not subject to cost-increasing regulations. Thus, it is the newer "social" regulations that have generated business opposition in the 1970s. The reasons are clear: the social regulations are designed to protect society from environmental, health and safety, and defective product hazards arising out of the production process. The regulations are, in effect, a tax on business activity, the incidence of which depends on the relevant demand and supply elasticities. It will be interesting to see whether established firms can turn the social regulations to their advantage vis-à-vis potential entrants to the industry.

Public Ownership

Governments sometimes choose outright public ownership in preference to public regulation of, or the promotion of competition among, privately owned enterprises. In North America, public ownership is thought of as somewhat

---

27. *Nebbia v. New York* 291 U.S. 502 (1934). A reading of the *Nebbia* decision suggests that the main thrust of the regulation of milk prices was to protect the large milk distributors from the price cutting by small retail outlets. The legislation was, of course, cast in a somewhat different light: to ensure an adequate supply of milk at a time of depressed prices.

28. It is still too early to tell whether these "social regulations" will be a permanent part of the scene or a passing fad, but the former seems the more likely. In certain respects, the concern evidenced by these "social" regulations is not so unlike the concerns during earlier phases of the industrial revolution with the use of child labour, hours of work and quality of working conditions. In each case the concern is with the *qualitative* impact of competitive and industrial processes, whether it be the quality of the good or service or the working or external environment.

exceptional, but there are many countries of the world where public ownership of business is widespread, and some where private ownership is truly exceptional. Since this book focuses on Canada, and most Canadians are committed, at least in principle, to private enterprise, we will examine the role of public ownership in the context of an otherwise private enterprise economy.

Canada is a particularly interesting country if one wants to examine the variety of uses of public enterprise in an essentially non-ideological context. There are a number of important federal government enterprises (Crown corporations are the typical instrument through which government enterprises are operated in Canada) and an even larger number chartered by the various provinces. The activities of these Crown corporations reflect a variety of rationales for public enterprises in Canada, some of which are listed below, and are treated in greater detail in chapter 11.

1. The "Public Utility" (or substitute for regulated private monopoly) rationale probably accounts for widespread government enterprise in the electric energy field, with provincial "hydro" companies responsible for electricity generation, transmission, and distribution in Newfoundland, Quebec, Ontario, Manitoba, Saskatchewan and B.C. The three prairie provinces also own the telephone companies operating within their borders. (In contrast, privately owned and publicly regulated telephone companies operate in the Maritimes, Quebec, Ontario and B.C.).

2. Public ownership as a spur to economic development accounts for such enterprises as Sidbec, Quebec's government-owned integrated steel operation, Nova Scotia's yet-to-be successful heavy water plant, Newfoundland's linerboard mill (which has recently been sold to a private firm after having been closed down), shipyards in Newfoundland and Prince Edward Island.

3. The production of vital goods prompted the federal government's creation during World War II of Polymer Corporation, which pioneered in plastics and related petrochemical products.

4. The creation of infrastructure explains, at least at their initiation, federal government enterprise in the airline industry and broadcasting.

5. Social capture of economic rents has been used to justify public enterprise in some of Canada's natural resource industries. To date, there are only a few examples, which include Saskatchewan's takeovers in the potash industry, petroleum and natural gas exploration companies in Quebec, Saskatchewan and British Columbia, and perhaps the parts of the federal government's National Energy Policy which gives preferences to the government-owned firm, Petrocan.[29] However, the idea received increasing attention during the 1970s,

29. One might be tempted to include the Quebec government's takeover of one of the major asbestos firms, if it were not so clear, even at the time of takeover, that there were no longer economic rents to be captured. On the contrary, prospective industry decline due to technological and environmental factors poses a real threat of large future losses.

particularly after the rapid rise in the prices of primary products, especially petroleum, in 1973-74. Nevertheless, most governments still prefer tax and royalty devices to ownership as a means of capturing economic rents.

6. Incomplete coverage of needy users and theoretically lower administrative costs have been used to explain government (to date B.C., Saskatchewan, Manitoba and Quebec) moves into the auto insurance field.

7. Bankruptcy and economic decline have motivated governments to take over private firms. The federal government's assumption of the debt of several bankrupt railroads around World War I led to the formation of the Canadian National Railway—one of the largest and most important Crown corporations in Canada. The decision by the federal government to take control of the Cape Breton coal industry and the decision by Nova Scotia to take control of the Dominion Steel Co. (DOSCO), were motivated by the inability of private enterprise to compete with more efficient and centrally located coal and steel firms in the United States and central Canada. The federal government's consolidation of several failing fish processing firms in Newfoundland into a single Crown-owned corporation is another example. (Under government ownership deficits are financed from general revenues.)

8. An important rationale for public enterprise is as a yardstick for "measuring" the efficiency of private enterprises. One of the features unique to the Canadian scene is the duopolistic competition between a large publicly owned and a large privately owned system in the fields of rail and air transportation and in broadcasting. In a number of other industries in which public firms now exist (e.g. steel, pulp and paper, petroleum production and refining, and retailing), yardstick competition between publicly and privately owned firms is a reality.

9. A combination of profit and public morality is reflected in provincially operated alcoholic beverage outlets.

In sum, the role of public enterprise in a mixed economy transcends ideological debates that so often have marred rational discussion of government ownership. The best assurance that government enterprise will efficiently produce what the public wants is the existence of privately owned competitors. In most industries where Canadian public enterprises are found this condition exists, in contrast to Great Britain where issues of public enterprise have usually involved nationalization of the whole industry as in steel, coal and shipbuilding.

Other Public Policies Toward Business

A variety of policies and programmes has been devised in Canada to promote economic development and self-sufficiency and to protect a diversified industrial establishment. These policies have been shaped by Canada's geography and history. As a nation of great geographical extent, small population, and close proximity to the United States, a major thrust of our economic policy has been to diversify Canadian industry beyond our historic comparative advantage as "hewers of wood and drawers of water." The goal was accomplished by the mid-twentieth century, primarily via tariff policy, although at a price of scale inefficiencies and a high degree of foreign ownership and control of many Canadian industries. In turn, Canadian policies became directed at limiting foreign control (Foreign Investment Review Act) promoting industrial rationalization (e.g. Canada-U.S. Auto Pact; the CAMCO merger of the assets of GE Canada, Westinghouse Canada and GSW Ltd.), and fostering homegrown research and development and product design through a variety of subsidy programmes administered by the Department of Industry, Trade and Commerce.

In addition, Canada's historical from-east-to-west development has left major economic backwaters in the Maritimes and parts of Quebec. (Despite the economic movement toward the "Sunbelt," the only comparable situation that has occurred in the United States, which, like Canada, developed on an east-to-west basis, is Appalachia.) As a result, Canadian policies have generally been economic development-minded, with huge subsidies paid to influence the location of industry. The Department of Regional Industrial Expansion (DRIE) and its predecessors have provided financial incentives for firms to locate in the more economically depressed areas of Canada, particularly the Atlantic provinces and Quebec. DRIE grants are only one of a number of important *industrial* subsidy schemes which have played a role in Canadian industrial development. In the late 19th century there was a "bonusing" system whereby municipalities competed for industry via tax concessions and outright "handouts" to firms. In this century, the federal government has provided funds in the form of firm-specific investment grants to influence their location, to save failing firms, and to spur industrial research and development; it has provided funds to bail out large established firms in deep financial trouble, such as Chrysler, Massey-Ferguson, Dome Petroleum, and ill-fated Maislin trucking; it has moulded the tax laws to include write-offs to spur the mining industry; a heavily subsidized higher-education system has provided a growing pool of talent to Canadian industry.

Both the federal and provincial governments have used their access to tax finance to stimulate enterprise. At one level these efforts are carried out through development corporations like the Canada Development Corporation, whose main objective appears to be to gain a "Canadian" interest in certain "strategic" industries (see chapter 12), and provincial development corporations whose primary aim is local industrial development. At another level some provinces have attempted to attract private entrepreneurship with public subsidies, often with disastrous results (e.g. Manitoba's Churchill Forests fiasco; Nova Scotia's heavy water plant) as Philip Mathias has documented.[30]

In short, Canadian public policies toward business have displayed a great deal of *ad hocery*, which is perhaps not surprising given the division of political powers and the piecemeal nature of our approach to industrial diversification and development. As a result, the sort of philosophical issues that underlie the tension between competition policy and regulation discussed earlier in this chapter have been all but ignored. Interventionism has been considered the natural and necessary result of Canada's peculiar geographic and demographic characteristics. Moreover, Canadian constitutional development has also played a role in moulding the particular character of public policies toward business. Under the British North America Act (B.N.A. Act), the federal parliament can enact criminal law, while powers to enact civil and property law were left to the provinces. At the time of its writing more than a century ago, it was probably thought that the "Commerce" and "Peace, Order, and Good Government" (POGG) clauses of the B.N.A. Act would give sufficient latitude to the federal government to "regulate" in the economic arena. However, the Commerce and POGG clauses have been rather narrowly construed, so that it is still not even clear whether non-criminal sanctions can be applied by the anticombines authorities.

Together with the jealous concern of the provinces for their powers, the constitutional limitations on the federal government's regulatory powers have meant that much economic legislation is enacted at the provincial level. Unfortunately, the provinces are much less likely to see the national implications of their economic legislation. To some extent each province is a "free rider" in the economic arena, expecting the benefits its legislation confers to be received locally while the costs are spread nationally. Thus, for example, marketing board legislation has eroded national marketing of farm products, even though it is unconstitutional for a province to block entry of goods from other provinces. In short, the protectionist spirit at the provincial level has mirrored a similar spirit at the national level.

A Final Note

In closing the chapter it is important to underline that the objectives of economic policies and programmes are usually multi-dimensional. Economists have naturally focused on the efficiency dimension. Politicians have focused on the

30. Philip Mathias, *Forced Growth: Five Studies of Government Involvement in the Development of Canada* (Toronto: James, Lewis and Samuel, 1971).

growth and equity dimensions, generally ignoring economists' arguments that there are better ways to promote growth and redistribute income than detailed intervention at the industry or firm level. Economists never tire of asking why we are ignored. The answer is usually that the politicians have a short time horizon, while the economists have a more distant one. Or perhaps it is that the two give a different weighting to socio-economic goals. But there may be another factor: economists and politicians may be using different *units* in evaluating the effect of a given policy. Economists focus on individuals as consumers, but politicians often focus on firms as producers in assaying the effectiveness of particular policies. The welfare economics which provides the theoretical basis for the economists' approach to measuring the benefits from, and effectiveness of, policy is not a part of the typical policy marker's parlance or mental framework. Organizations as well as individuals are considered by policy makers as politically relevant and deserving of benefits from public programmes. Unfortunately, if carried too far the power of organizations or "syndicates" can become an important threat to the very democratic process that provided them with some of that power in the first place.

8

Canadian Competition Policy: Part I

Competition policy is an important subject. The rationale for competition policy flows directly from the study of industrial organization—the subject of the first six chapters of this book. This chapter and the one that follows are designed to provide the student with a reasonably detailed understanding of the development, application, interpretation, economic sense, and sometimes, nonsense of Canadian anticombines policies, and attempts to reform those policies.

The description and assessment of Canadian competition policy is contained in this and the following chapter. The subject matter of this chapter includes the legislative background and development of anticombines law and policy, the government's enforcement activities, and the tangled jurisprudence relating to price fixing and other "horizontal" agreements. The next chapter covers the jurisprudence relating to monopoly and merger, price discrimination and predatory pricing, and "vertical" agreements such as resale price maintenance (RPM) and tying and exclusive dealing contracts. Chapter 9 concludes with an extended discussion and analysis of the efforts to reform the anticombines laws during the last fifteen years.

Background

Unless one's attachment to *laissez-faire* is without qualification, it is difficult to ignore attempts by sellers to collude or to "monopolize." In the 19th century the spirit of laissez faire and free trade was sufficient to stave off legislation against combinations and monopolies. However, the National Policy of 1879 erected high tariff barriers to international trade in commodities. Behind the Canadian tariff wall there was industrial growth, the appearance of new enterprises and local competition. But the tariff is the "mother of trusts."

Protected by tariffs, domestic competitors were often able to combine to avoid competition.

Earlier chapters have shown that the structure of Canadian manufacturing industries can be roughly characterized as ones where small domestic markets, high tariffs, and inefficiently short production runs and small plants stand in close geographic proximity to the markets and relative efficiency of the world's economic giant. Our industrial structure reflects a century of evolution from the watershed of 1879—the enactment of the National Policy Tariff. The first anticombines law was at least in part a response to the impact of the National Policy Tariff on industrial market structure and behaviour. The tariff, by substantially reducing or effectively eliminating competition from imports in many manufacturing industries, made Canada (or a regional subset thereof) rather than North America, the relevant market in most industries. Moreover, high tariff walls, by reducing the number of rival producers competing in the same market, enhanced the ability of firms to collude and to raise prices to levels just below those which would attract competition from imports. Because the tariff made collusion easier and more profitable, it is not surprising that in the 1880s there was a rash of combines.

By the end of the 1880s combinations and "monopoly" had become political issues. In 1888, a Select Committee of the House of Commons was appointed to investigate the nature and extent of certain combinations (in sugar and groceries, biscuits and confectionery, coal, binder twine, agricultural implements, stoves, coffin-makers, egg-dealers, fire insurance, etc.).[1] The Committee's report called for legislative action, which came in the next session, 1889. The proposed legislation, by criminalizing conspiratorial activity under certain circumstances, would have attempted to reduce the incentives to collude which the tariff walls had fostered. However, the legislation that was passed was an amended version of the legislation that was introduced. When final passage came, two words "unlawfully" and "unduly" reduced the effectiveness of the new law. Although the word "unlawfully" was dropped a decade later, "unduly" has played an important role in reducing, to this day, the effectiveness of Canadian anticombines legislation.

The Legislation

The law that passed in 1889 was consolidated into the Criminal Code in 1892 with minor amendments. It read as follows:[2]

516. A conspiracy in restraint of trade is an agreement between

---

1. See Maxwell Cohen, "The Canadian Antitrust Laws—Doctrinal and Legislative Beginnings," *Canadian Bar Review*, 1938, pp. 454-55.
2. In subsequent consolidations of the Criminal Code, Section 520 was renumbered 498 and eventually 411. The word "unlawfully" was deleted in 1901.

two or more persons to do or procure to be done by unlawful act in restraint of trade.

517. The purposes of a trade union are not, by reason merely that they are in restraint of trade, unlawful within the meaning of the next preceding section. R.S.C., c.131, s.22.

520. Every one is guilty of an indictable offence and liable to a penalty not exceeding four thousand dollars and not less than two hundred dollars, or to two years imprisonment, and if a corporation is liable to a penalty not exceeding ten thousand dollars and not less than one thousand dollars, who conspires, combines, agrees or arranges with any other person, or with any railway, steamship, steamboat or transportation company, unlawfully—

(a) to unduly limit the facilities for transporting, producing, manufacturing, supplying, storing or dealing in any article or commodity which may be a subject of trade or commerce; or—

(b) to restrain or injure trade or commerce in relation to any such article or commodity; or—

(c) to unduly prevent, limit, or lessen the manufacture or production of any such article or commodity, or to unreasonably enhance the price thereof; or—

(d) to unduly prevent or lessen competition in the production, manufacture, purchase, barter, sale, transportation or supply of any such article or commodity, or in the price of insurance upon person or property.

The courts interpreted "article" to refer to goods or physical commodities. It was not until 1976 that services were included under the provisions of the Combines Act.

In 1960, a slightly amended version of the original law was taken from the Criminal Code and placed in the Combines Investigation Act as section 32(1). Section 32(1) and its predecessors in the Criminal Code have been the most often applied (except for the provisions covering misleading advertising), and jurisprudentially most consequential, part of Canada's combines law.

Many of the members of Parliament at the time of the original law's passage, in 1889, thought they were "declaring the common law." That is, they thought that they were giving legislative voice to what had long been an offence under the English common law. This was an erroneous view for, in fact, the common law had lacked an explicit doctrine with respect to conspiracies among businessmen. Nevertheless, prior to 1889 there were common law doctrines regarding monopoly and restraint of trade. The "regulation" of competition was not something brand new in 1889 (or 1890 when the U.S. Sherman Antitrust Act was passed). For example, certain "middlemen offences" date from the later middle ages when townspeople were wholly dependent on the adjacent countryside for their food. Fear that merchants might "corner the market" in foodstuffs before they reached the final consumer led to the famous triumvirate of "forestalling," "regrating" and "engrossing"—the fine distinctions between the three depending on the place (field or market place) or the manner in which the monopolizing activity took place.[3] These early "monopoly laws," which were designed as prohibitions against interference with markets, were probably motivated by a desire to keep the price of foodstuffs, as well as wages, low. They were not a reflection of a philosophical prejudice against monopoly since both King and Parliament were quite willing to grant monopolies where it was thought advantageous, politically or economically, and to accept the existence of guilds—local monopolies of craftsmen.

There is another important strand of legal thought underlying modern anti-combines legislation. Although there was no settled common law doctrine of *conspiracy* with respect to restraint of trade (prosecutions of merchants for conspiring to monopolize or restrain trade were virtually unknown), there was a longstanding opposition by the courts to enforcing "contracts in restraint of trade." That is, the English courts did not prosecute businessmen for doing what Adam Smith said was typical when "people of the same trade...meet together"; but at the same time they usually refused to enforce *agreements* made by the combining or conspiring parties. This position of the courts dates back to the *Dyers* case (1415) in which an agreement between a master dyer and his workman that the latter would not engage in his trade within his town for six months was held legally void. The basic philosophy was that "no man should be restrained in the exercise of his calling." This view was later moderated in a series of cases involving contracts between sellers and buyers of a business, beginning with *Mitchell v. Reynolds* (1713). In that case the court upheld an agreement by a baker not to compete locally for five years after the sale of his bakery to the plaintiff, Mitchell, on the ground that the covenant was both reasonable (it was limited in time and space) and incidental (ancillary) to the principal transaction. As geographic markets grew so did the "space" over which a restrictive covenant might be reasonable, until it reached a world-wide scale in the *Maxim-Nordenfeldt* case (1894). What thus evolved was a sort of "rule of reason" in which contracts in restraint of trade might be reasonable if they were subordinate to a legal transaction. But general agreements, whose purpose was to restrain trade, were not enforceable.[4]

3. Donald Dewey, *Monopoly in Economics and Law* (Chicago: Rand McNally, 1959), p. 112. Also see Maxwell Cohen, op. cit., pp. 442-43. Adam Smith, however, was critical of these early anti-monopoly laws. *The Wealth of Nations*, pp. 499-501.
4. For an in-depth analysis of the common law position on monopoly and restraint of trade, see William Letwin, *Law and Economic Policy in America: The Origins of the Sherman Antitrust Act* (New York: Random House, 1965), Chap. 2. In his assessment of the legal foundations of the

The common law position on restraint of trade reflects the "classical" economic view that as long as government did not intervene to protect (or regulate) monopoly, competition could not long be stifled. It was not necessary, then, to prosecute colluding merchants, only to make sure that they could not legally enforce their collusive agreements. Together the common law refusal to enforce restraints on trade or to prosecute conspiracies in restraint of trade provided a legal foundation for "laissez faire." In a world of easy entry or widespread price chiselling there was a logic to this position. It was the late nineteenth century concern that tariffs and technology had stripped the laissez-faire position of its essentials, that gave rise to a reformist call for legislation against combination and monopoly.

Despite the initial urgency felt by its proponents, the Act of 1889 lay dormant for almost a decade. Amendments, which had been made to assure the legislation's passage, temporarily made it inoperative and left a legacy of ineffectiveness.[5] The word "unlawfully" robbed it of its force, since the object of the legislation had been to define what was henceforth to be illegal. While this defect was remedied in 1900, when the word "unlawfully" was dropped, other difficulties remained. The word "unduly" has, to this day, played havoc with judicial interpretations of the law. In addition, the legislation lacked any machinery for investigation. It omitted reference to mergers, which by the end of the first decade of the twentieth century were beginning to transform the Canadian industrial structure, and provide an apparently legal alternative to conspiracy as a means to monopoly. In principle, these defects were remedied by the Combines Act of 1910, which established a procedure whereby any six persons could apply to a judge for an order directing an investigation into an alleged "combine." A combine was defined to include trusts, monopoly, and merger, as well as horizontal agreements which operated or were likely to operate to the "detriment or against the interest of the public." In practice, the six persons rule was cumbersome, and though it is still a part of the Combines Investigation Act, it is not often used. The inclusion of "monopoly" and merger has had even less effect, there having been, to this day, only a few successful monopoly cases and no conviction (that was upheld on appeal) for merger.

The Act of 1910 was little used, in part because it failed to provide for continuity of administration, and was replaced, in 1919, by the Combines and

Sherman Act, Letwin argues that the common law did not always defend freedom of trade and oppose monopoly, and that by the end of the 19th century its opposition to monopoly was so weak and its position on restraint of trade so equivocal, that legislation was required if the law was going to protect competition.
5. An historian has suggested that even one of the law's chief proponents had helped emasculate it, for reasons better explained by the dominant conservative-protectionist philosophy of the time rather than duplicity. See Michael Bliss, "Another Antitrust Tradition: Canadian Anti-Combines Policy, 1889-1910," *Business History Review*, 47, no. 2 (Summer 1973), pp. 177-188.

Fair Prices Act. The 1919 Act established for the first time permanent investigative machinery in the form of a Board. It also attempted (unsuccessfully) to regulate prices and prohibit profiteering and the hoarding of necessities, a response to the shortages and inflation produced by World War I. However, these regulatory activities were declared *ultra vires* (unconstitutional) in 1922, as beyond the competence of the criminal powers given the federal government under the B.N.A. Act.[6] The Act of 1919 was replaced by the Combines Investigation Act of 1923 which, as subsequently amended, is the law today. The permanent investigative machinery was placed in the hands of a Registrar, renamed Commissioner in 1937 and Director in 1952. In the latter year a Restrictive Trade Practices Commission was added to undertake formal investigations and make reports. In 1935, a section on price discrimination was added to the Act and in 1952 Canada became the first country to prohibit, outright, resale price maintenance.

In 1960, the Combines Investigation Act was again amended. The Criminal Code section, embodying the original Act of 1889, was brought into the Combines Act as section 32(1). The term "combine," which dated from the Act of 1910, was dropped, but the prohibitions against "monopoly" and "merger" were retained in section 33, with legal definitions of these two terms provided in sections 2(e) and 2(f). Thus the substantive part of the Combines Investigation Act includes offences for collusive agreements (section 32); monopoly and merger (section 33); price discrimination (section 34); misleading advertising (sections 36 and 37) and resale price maintenance (section 38). The administrative machinery consists of a Director of Investigation and a three-person Restrictive Trade Practices Commission. The Director initiates actions and is responsible for seeing that the Act is enforced. The RTPC's role was solely investigatory until 1976 when it was empowered under a revised section 31 of the Act to issue prohibition orders where certain restrictive practices (exclusive dealing, tied selling) if adopted by "major suppliers" have the effect of substantially lessening competition.[7]

The remedies stipulated by the Combines Investigation Act include fines, loss of tariff protection, revocation of patent protection where exclusive patent rights have been used to stifle competition in other produce markets, and publicity.

6. In Canada, for reasons of constitutional interpretation, the only way in which the federal government could enact combines law was if it took the form of criminal law. This was so until 1976, when a still-to-be-fully-constitutionally tested section was added to the Combines Investigation Act, giving to the combines authorities civil law powers under which they can issue orders requiring firms to cease behaving in a manner injurious to competition. The heart of the 1984 reform proposals (see the final section of chapter 9) is a much broader application of civil law powers in combines cases.
7. This is the way the Act stood as of mid-1984 when a comprehensive set of amendments (Bill C-29) was tabled in the House of Commons.

The tariff protection and patent revocation remedies have on one or two occasions been threatened, but with one minor exception have never actually been used.[8] Fines are the typical remedy, but these are usually too small to either remedy or deter. Publicity has long been considered a deterrent and therefore an important weapon. Since 1923, reports of investigations of alleged illegal behaviour have been published, but these have probably contributed more to our knowledge of Canadian industrial organization than to the prevention of price fixing and related activities. However, the recent increase in fines, and an amendment to allow injured parties to sue for damages, may provide an "ounce of prevention."

Record of Enforcement

As we have seen, Canada, in 1889, became the first nation to enact an "antitrust law," beating out the U.S. Sherman Act by one year. But Canada quickly relinquished and never regained its lead. In the seven decades following the initial enactment in 1889, the only significant application of anticombines law was against a few long-lived price-fixing and/or market-sharing agreements, the members of which admitted to conspiratorial activity although they denied that they had either intended or done harm by their actions. In the 1960s, the pace of enforcement picked up with more government victories in conspiracy cases plus a number of triumphs as a result of the enactment, in 1952, of a tough law outlawing resale price maintenance (RPM). But the loss, in 1960, of the government's first two merger cases was both embarrassing and injurious to the application of anticombines law, and helped to stir, as we shall see in the next chapter, thoughts of fundamental reform in competition policy.

The 1970s were marked by accomplishment and failure. There were some important victories for the Crown, but also some signal failures before the Supreme Court of Canada. On the "plus" side the Crown continued to vigorously apply the conspiracy and RPM laws and to win in most instances. Among the price-fixing cases were four "conscious parallelism" cases. These were more difficult, but the Crown succeeded in winning two. The government won its first merger case at the trial court level, but lost on appeal.[9] Finally, the Crown won the first case it brought under the long-dormant predatory pricing section of the law (section 34(1)c). On the "minus" side the Crown lost all three of the major anticombines cases which were heard by the Supreme Court of

8. The one exception was the reduction, in 1901, of duties on newsprint, the impact of which was blunted because Canadian prices were lower than the other sources of supply. For greater detail on the use and magnitude of fines and other penalties in anticombines cases, see P.K. Gorecki and W.T. Stanbury, *The Objectives of Canadian Competition Policy, 1888-1983* (Montreal: Institute for Research on Public Policy, 1984).
9. *R v. K.C. Irving* (1974, 1975, 1977). See the extended discussion of this case in chapter 9.

Canada (*R. v. K.C. Irving*, 1977; *R. v. Aetna*, 1977; and *R. v. Atlantic Sugar Refineries Co. Ltd.*, 1980.) Not only have the decisions in these three cases established important precedents, but they set back enforcement of the conspiracy and merger sections of the law.

The accomplishments, or lack of them, in enforcing the anticombines laws can be given a quantitative dimension. One crude measure of anticombines enforcement is the number of investigations and prosecutions carried out, and convictions won, over time. A statistical picture of anticombines activities is presented in Tables 8-1 through 8-4. Table 8-1 shows that from 1890 to 1983 there were 256 prosecutions, or an average of 2.7 per year.[10] However 231, or 90 percent, of the prosecutions were brought during the last 27 years of the 93-year period covered by Table 8-1. Almost forty-five percent of the prosecutions were for conspiracy (section 32(1) cases) and forty-two percent were resale price maintenance cases. Only four percent of the cases were monopoly or merger cases. There were eleven prosecutions which included price discrimination or predatory pricing as a charge. In short, the overwhelming majority of cases involved horizontal or vertical agreements between independent parties. The arguably tougher cases—monopoly, merger, and price discrimination—are very few in number.

Table 8-2 shows that the government won most of the cases it brought before the courts. Between 1890 and 1983 the Crown won 182 of 255 completed cases for a "win" rate of 71.4 percent. However, the "win" rate varied considerably depending on the nature of the charge. The government won 77 percent of RPM cases and 75 percent of the conspiracy cases, but succeeded in only three price discrimination-predatory pricing prosecutions out of twelve. (However, as we shall see in chapter 9, the Crown recently won a major victory in a predatory pricing case.) Although the statistics in Table 8-2 indicate the government won five out of eleven monopoly or merger cases, they fail to show that the government has never won a contested merger case and only one major monopoly prosecution contested by the defendant.[11] The dismal record in prosecuting merger cases is reinforced by the fact that each year there are anywhere from 200 to 500 mergers in Canada, although admittedly most if not all of these are probably harmless or actually beneficial. For example, between 1977 and 1982 there were an average of over 450 mergers per year in Canada. The largest 55 mergers during the merger "wave" of 1978-81, involved a transactions value in excess of $100 million per acquisition. The acquisition cost of the largest ten mergers exceeded one billion dollars a piece.[12] Although

10. These statistics do not include the very numerous misleading advertising cases.
11. One of the five victories was overturned in 1977 by the Supreme Court of Canada: *R v. K.C. Irving Ltd. et al.* (1977) 25 CPR (2d) 223.
12. W.T. Stanbury, "The Merger Provisions of Bill C-29," *Canadian Competition Law* (Vancouver: Continuing Legal Education Society, 1984), chapter 2.

Table 8-1

Combines Cases and Activities: 1889/90-1982/83

Period[b]	Total Cases	Combines Prosecutions[a]				Discontinued Inquiries	Files Opened in Response to Complaints
		Conspiracy	Monopoly and/or Merger	RPM	Price Discrimination and Predatory Pricing		
1890-1910	8	8	—	—	—	n.a.	n.a.
1911-1923	1	1	—	—	—	n.a.	n.a.
1924-1940	14	11	1	—	—	n.a.	538
1941-1946	—	—	—	—	—	n.a.	66
1947-1955	12	9	1	2	—	25[d]	794
1956-1960	18	13	2	1	2	30	456
1961-1965	18	7	—	10	1	77	816
1966-1970	25	16	1	7	1	82	579
1971-1975	45	18	4	15	2	95	963
1976-1980	71	18	2	47	2	74	941
1981-1983	44	11	0	26	4	63	743
Total	256[c]	112	11	108	12	446	5986

n.a.: data not available

[a] Excludes three patent cases and all misleading advertising cases.

[b] Fiscal years, ending March 31.

[c] Includes 13 multiple offence cases.

[d] 1951-55 only.

Source: Adapted from P.K. Gorecki and W.T. Stanbury, "Canada's Combines Investigation Act: The Record of Public Law Enforcement 1889-1976," in J.R.S. Prichard, W.T. Stanbury and T.A. Wilson, editors, *Canadian Competition Policy: Essays in Law and Economics* (Toronto: Butterworth, 1979), Table 6, p. 187, plus updated material provided to me by Stanbury, which will appear in Gorecki and Stanbury, *The Objectives of Canadian Competition Policy, 1888-1983* (Halifax: Institute for Research on Public Policy, 1984), Table 2-B. Used by permission.

Table 8-2

Proportion of Combines Cases Won[a] by the Crown, by Offence, Fiscal Year Ending March 31

Offence	1890-1910	1911-1923	1924-1940	1941-1946	1947-1955	1956-1960	1961-1965	1966-1970	1971-1975	1976-1980	1981-1983	1890-1983
Conspiracy	5/8	0/1	11/12	—	8/9	13/13	7/7	15/16	11/17	10/18	4/11	84/112
RPM/Refusal to sell	—	—	—	—	2/2	1/1	9/10	7/7	13/15	36/47	15/26	83/108
Merger and/or monopoly	—	—	0/1	—	1/1	0/2	—	1/1	3/4	0/2	0/0	5/11
Price discrimination/ predatory pricing	—	—	—	—	—	0/2	0/1	0/1	1/2	0/2	2/4	3/12
Other (multiple offences)	—	—	1/1	—	—	—	—	—	4/6	1/2	1/3	7/12
Total cases	8	1	14	0	12	18	18	25	44	71	44	255
Total 'Win' rate[a]	5/8	0/1	12/14	—	11/12	14/18	16/18	23/25	32/44	47/71	22/44	182/255

[a]Includes granting of a prohibition order under S.30(2).
Source: Gorecki and Stanbury (1979), *op. cit.*, Table 9, p. 190, plus updated material provided to me by Stanbury which appears in Gorecki and Stanbury, *op. cit.*, Table 4-B.

many of these giant mergers were conglomerate mergers with presumptively little or no negative impact on competition, it is testimony to the passivity of merger law enforcement in Canada, that none of these mergers apparently generated an anticombines response.

A statistical picture of the work of the recently renamed Bureau of Competition Policy (formerly the Combines Branch) of the Department of Consumer and Corporate Affairs is presented in Table 8-3. The first row shows the number of complaints or inquiries received by the Bureau. Of these, only a handful were initiated by formal application of six persons to the Director of Investigation and Research (row 2). Many of the complaints apparently lack substance, and are therefore subjected to only limited inquiry. The number of complaints or inquiries which reach a serious, or actionable, stage is suggested by rows 3 and 4. Row 3 shows the number of reports published by the Restrictive Trade Practices Commission, following a formal and lengthy investigation into possible violations of the anticombines laws; these usually call for some sort of remedial action. The number of reports trailed off badly in the early 1970s—and since the mid 1970s are no longer a task of the RTPC. (This is unfortunate, if for no other reason than that RTPC reports are usually an excellent source of information on Canadian industrial behaviour). The fourth row indicates the number of instances where the Director of Investigation feels there is sufficient evidence to proceed directly to court action and the fifth row shows the number of prosecutions commenced. The number of these has risen in recent years, more than offsetting the decline in RTPC reports. The sixth row indicates the number of inquiries for which the files remained open at year's end.

The statistics in Table 8-3 understate the operations of the Bureau of Competition Policy because they do not include those for alleged misleading advertising or deceptive marketing practices. Table 8-4 gives a statistical picture of this facet of the Bureau's activity. What is striking is the growth in and absolute number of files opened and completed investigations (rows 1 and 2). Obviously, misleading advertising complaints are a time-consuming activity of the Bureau. Rows 3 through 6 indicate the number of cases for which legal action was attempted or taken. Evidently, the prosecution is usually successful in misleading advertising cases. There is a serious question whether the sort of "brush-fire-fighting" activity that misleading advertising usually involves is a sensible use of resources by the Bureau of Competition Policy.

Nor do the statistics in Tables 8-3 or 8-4 include the increasingly important and time-consuming representations of the Bureau of Competition Policy before federal and provincial regulatory boards and commissions. Since 1976, the Bureau has been charged with interventions in regulatory proceedings to protect the public interest in competition in those aspects of regulated firm

Table 8-3

Operations of the Bureau of Competition Policy, Excluding Misleading Advertising

	1970 -71	1971 -72	1972 -73	1973 -74	1974 -75	1975 -76	1976 -77	1977 -78	1978 -79	1979 -80	1980 -81	1981 -82
Number of files opened on receipt of complaints or inquiries in the nature of complaints	255	271	188	165	84	158	143	197	205	262	238	249
Formal application for inquiries by six persons	2	5	2	6	5	4	7	5	7	7	8	9
Reports to Minister by R.T.P.C.	5	0	1	0	0	0	1	—	—	—	—	—
Inquiries referred direct to the Attorney General of Canada under Section 15	9	16	9	14	11	18	26	22	14	24	21	34
Prosecutions or other proceedings commenced	8	6	14	8	7	12	16	24	11	21	6	24
Formal inquiries in progress at the end of year	83	86	76	77	81	71	73	76	73	78	69	67

Source: Annual Report, Director of Investigation and Research, Combines Investigation Act, March 1982, p. 10. (Years are fiscal years.)

Table 8-4

Operations Under Misleading Advertising and Deceptive Marketing Practices Provisions

	1972-73	1974-75	1976-77	1979-80	1981-82
Inquiries and Investigations					
1) Number of files opened	3470	5068	7850	9431	8557
2) Number of completed investigations	649	1047	1895	2234	2319
3) Number of referrals to Attorney General	84	126	117	132	142
Prosecutions					
4) Completed cases during the year					
a) Convictions	68	87	89	100	95
b) Acquittals, charges withdrawn	14	20	33	32	27
5) Cases before the courts at end of year (not including appeals)	44	75	89	82	141
6) Cases under appeal at end of year	5	8	4	17	15

Source: Annual Report, Director of Investigation and Research, Combines Investigation Act, March 31, 1982, pp. 84-85.

behaviour not directly controlled by a regulatory board. Thus, the Bureau of Competition Policy has intervened, for example, in numerous regulatory proceedings involving the telecommunications and transportation (particularly airline) industries. It has also intervened in the proceedings of agricultural marketing boards. Although it is difficult, if not impossible, to measure the Bureau's accomplishments as an intervener, it seems likely that its representations before regulatory agencies are one of the Bureau's most socially beneficial activities.

As with almost all bureaus, the staff of the Bureau of Competition Policy has grown substantially in recent years. Prior to 1950, there were only a handful of permanent staff. In 1980, the actual strength of the Bureau of Competition Policy was 185, 114 of whom were professionals and another 54 of whom occupied clerical and secretarial positions. The Bureau is divided into five enforcement branches (manufacturing, resources, services, regulated sector, and marketing practices), a legislative development and a research branch. It is clear that as an agency of government the Bureau of Competition Policy has come into its own.

The Jurisprudence

A major purpose of this and the succeeding chapter is to introduce the student to the law on competition—not so much as the legislators wrote it but as the judges have interpreted and applied it. The Combines Investigation Act is, to be sure, a lengthy document—and getting longer with each set of new amendments. By way of comparison, it is much longer and more detailed than the U.S. Sherman Antitrust and Clayton Acts combined. But despite the detail in the Combines Investigation Act one word ("unduly") and one clause ("to the detriment or against the interest of the public") have imbued the legislation with such ambiguity that at times the jurisprudence appears to reflect a sort of judicial gymnastics. For "unduly" and "public detriment" occupy strategic points in the law—and rare is the anticombines case that does not have to wrestle with one of these two terms. And yet the law regarding what is "undue" and what is "detrimental to the public" is still unsettled—although the two terms date from the legislation of 1889 and 1910 respectively. The difficulties these terms have posed for the courts require some immersion in the judicial opinions themselves. Only by comprehending the jurisprudence can one understand the thrust of the law itself.

A. Collusive Agreements

The law on agreements or conspiracies to fix prices and/or restrict output or entry presently reads as follows:

32. (1) Every one who conspires, combines, agrees or arranges with another person
    (a) to limit unduly the facilities for transporting, producing, manufacturing, supplying, storing or dealing in any product,
    (b) to prevent, limit or lessen, unduly, the manufacture or production of a product, or to enhance unreasonably the price thereof,
    (c) to prevent, or lessen, unduly, competition in the production, manufacture, purchase, barter, sale, storage, rental, transportation or supply of a product, or in the price of insurance upon persons or property, or
    (d) to otherwise restrain or injure competition unduly,
    is guilty of an indictable offence and is liable to imprisonment for five years or a fine of one million dollars or to both.

In 1960, the section was qualified by exempting agreements relating (i) to the exchange of statistics and credit information; (ii) to the definition of product standards and industrial or commercial terminology; (iii) to cooperation in research and development; or (iv) to the export of goods, so long as such agreements do not "lessen competition unduly" with respect to prices, output, etc. These exceptions have received little judicial attention. In 1976, section 32.1 was amended to include "bidrigging" and conspiracies relating to professional sport. It was amended further in order to clarify the meaning of the word "unduly."

32. (1.1) For greater certainty, in establishing that a conspiracy, combination, agreement or arrangement is in violation of subsection (1), it shall not be necessary to prove that the conspiracy, combination, agreement or arrangement, if carried into effect, would or would be likely to eliminate, completely or virtually, competition in the market to which it relates or that it was the object of any or all of the parties thereto to eliminate, completely or virtually, competition in that market.

The fact that Parliament saw fit to make this clarification goes to the heart of the difficulty of interpreting section 32 (1): when is competition lessened "unduly"?

It has long been established that the legal purpose of section 32(1) and its Criminal Code predecessors is to protect the public interest in "free competition."[13] In the first combines case to reach it (*Weidman v. Shragge*), the

---

13. Note that the word "competition" appears only in clauses (c) and (d) of section 32(1). The strength of section 32(1) lies in clause (c): there has been to our knowledge no conviction under

Supreme Court in 1912 held that an agreement between two Winnipeg junk
dealers to fix the maximum prices of the used goods they purchased and to
share the profits was illegal and unenforceable.[14] Because Weidman and
Shragge together accounted for 95 percent of the relevant market, the Supreme
Court concluded that the agreement suppressed competition and was thereby
undue.[15] That the public is entitled to the benefits of competition (except in so
far as competition is abrogated by constitutionally valid legislation—provincial
or federal) is stated most clearly in the Supreme Court decision in the *Container
Materials* (1942) case. The student will recall from chapter 5 that all of the
shipping container firms in Canada had established in the 1930s a common
selling agency, which they controlled, in order to fix prices and allocate output
quotas. Their conviction was upheld by the Supreme Court of Canada in an
opinion read by Chief Justice Duff who declared:

> The enactment before us, I have no doubt, was passed for the
> protection of the specific public interest in free competition. That, in
> effect, I think, is the view expressed in *Weidman v. Shragge*....
> Speaking broadly, the legislation is aimed at protecting the public
> interest in free competition.
>
> The lessening or prevention agreed upon will, in my opinion, be
> undue, within the meaning of the statute, if, when carried into effect,
> it will prejudice the public interest in free competition to a degree
> that the tribunal of fact finds to be undue...[16]

The view that the legislative purpose is to protect the public interest in

---

section 32(1), which did not include conviction under clause (c). Prior to 1960, section 32(1) was
section 411 of the Criminal Code (and before that sections 498 & 520) and clause (c) was then
clause (d).
14. In the first combines case of any judicial consequence, *Rex v. Eliot* (1905), which involved an
association of anthracite coal dealers in Ontario who had attempted to monopolize the trade in
coal, the court established that the offence at issue was conspiracy. There was no question of
"lawful" and "unlawful" conspiracies as such—a conspiracy or agreement was illegal if it was
undue: and it was undue when it suppressed competition.
15. The Supreme Court decision in *Weidman v. Shragge* makes repeated reference to an
important English case *The Mogul Steamship Co. v. McGregor, Gow and Co.* (1885, 1891).
There the Privy Council refused to allow damages against a league of steamship companies
trading between China and England which had refused admittance to plaintiff Mogul, and had
subsequently driven Mogul out of business via a rebate system and other allegedly "predatory
tactics." The *Mogul* case reflects the absence of an English common law position against
combinations and unsavoury "competitive tactics," and was used by the Supreme Court to
support their view that the purpose of the Canadian combines legislation was to establish
prohibitions against conspiracies and combinations which suppressed competition. The *Mogul*
case has been used as an interesting example of the impact of predatory pricing in an article by
Basil Yamey, "Predatory Price Cutting: Notes and Comments," *Journal of Law and Economics*
(April 1972), pp. 129-142.
16. *Container Materials Ltd. v The King* (1942) S.C.R. p. 148.

competition is still the view of Canadian courts. The problem has been one of deciding at what point an agreement limits competition sufficiently to regard it as an *undue* lessening of competition. Before pursuing this question of undueness (or "unduly") it is worth noting that the Chief Justice's statement, quoted above, might be interpreted as suggesting that competition is an end in itself, rather than a means to an end. What does one mean when one speaks of the "public interest in free competition"? Is it competition itself or the results of competition from which the public benefits? Most economists would presumably argue that competition is a means—not an end in itself—to achieving certain economic goals such as economic efficiency. This is certainly the view of the Economic Council of Canada in its *Interim Report on Competition Policy*—an important document in the annals of Canadian Combines reform. Canadian courts have been more ambiguous about the role of competition, tending to accept that the legislative purpose of the original legislation, and its successor 32(1), is to protect competition either because competition is good in itself or it leads to a "good."[17] The ambiguity about "the public interest in free competition" recalls the divergent views in the history of economic thought, over the role of competition (see chapter 7).

The outstanding issue in section 32(1) cases is the meaning of "unduly." When is a lessening of competition undue? In the early cases (*R v. Eliot, Weidman v. Shragge, R v. Container Materials*) the courts tended to clarify the meaning of undue by using synonyms such as improper, oppressive, excessive. As a matter of fact each of these cases had involved agreements among all or virtually all of the rival sellers in the industry. It is not surprising, then, that at some point "unduly" would be defined in quantitative terms relating to the extent of the market encompassed by the agreement. The leading judicial statement on "unduly" was made in an *obiter dictum* by Cartwright, J. (later Chief Justice) in the so-called "fine papers" case—*R v. Howard Smith Paper Mills Ltd. et al* (1957). This case is also important for the way it dealt with "effects" or alleged public benefits of price-fixing agreements.

The *Howard Smith Paper Mills* case involved the seven Canadian manufacturers and 21 wholesalers of fine papers (writing paper and printer's paper). The 28 firms belonged to the Canadian Pulp and Paper Association and through

---

17. The *Container Materials* case settled the issue of the kind of competition comprehended by the law. Competition from which everything that makes for success is eliminated except salesmanship is not the free competition that s. 498 is mainly designed to protect." In addition, the Court dealt with the question of intent (or *mens rea*). The defendant-appellants had argued that they had not intended that their arrangement have the *effect* of unduly lessening competition. (What other intention could it have had?) According to Chief Justice Duff, the government need not prove intent; the intent is embedded in the agreement. The government must prove there was an agreement and then show that the agreement lessened, or was likely to lessen, competition unduly.

that organization engaged in price-fixing activities over a period of 19 years, stretching from 1933 to 1952. This period included the Depression years when the market for "fine papers" was extremely weak and the War years when the industry was subject to price controls. On trial, the defendant firms argued that the Association and its pricing policies had helped to stabilize the industry in the 1930s, had helped the industry grow, and had charged "reasonable" prices. They argued that it was a defence to charges under s. 498(1)(d) that by charging "reasonable prices" and by obviating the "hardships of a depression by keeping all mills working part time—a real public advantage is gained."[18] In short, the firms implied that their actions were beneficial to the public and that the Crown had failed to show that the agreement had produced injurious effects or was "detrimental" to the public. The trial court, the Ontario Appeals Court, and the Supreme Court of Canada rejected these arguments. The Supreme Court held:

> It has been argued on behalf of the appellants that the offence is not complete, unless it has been established by the Crown beyond a reasonable doubt, that the agreement was detrimental to the public, in the sense that the manufacture or production was effectively lessened, limited or prevented, as a result of the agreements entered into. It has also been suggested that there is no offence, if it is shown that the acts complained of were beneficial to the public. With these submissions I entirely disagree. Conspiracy is a crime by itself, without the necessity of establishing the carrying out of an overt act. The public is entitled to the benefit of *free competition*, and the prohibitions of the Act cannot be evaded by good motives. Whether they be innocent and even commendable, they cannot alter the true character of the combine which the law forbids, and the wish to accomplish desirable purposes constitutes no defence and will not condone the undue restraint, which is the elimination of the free domestic markets.
>
> It is my strong view that traders, manufacturers and producers cannot, as the law now stands, monopolize a substantial part of the markets of the country in given industries, to promote their own business interests, and then set themselves up as public benefactors, by saying to the Courts that the conspiracy was organized in order to achieve the stabilization of prices and production.

In a concurring opinion, Cartwright J. focused on an issue that was not specifically under appeal—the meaning of "unduly." His opinion, the relevant portion of which is quoted below, has had a major impact on subsequent decisions, even beyond section 32 (1), as we shall see. According to Cartwright:

18. From the appellant firms' factum to the Supreme Court of Canada. Quoted by Kellock, J. in the *Howard Smith* case.

In essence the decisions referred to [Cartwright reviewed all earlier decisions involving the issue of undueness] appear to me to hold that an agreement to prevent or lessen competition in commercial activities of the sort described in the section becomes criminal when the prevention or lessening agreed upon reaches the point at which the participants in the agreement become free to carry on those activities virtually unaffected by the influence of competition, which influence Parliament is taken to regard as an indispensable protection of the public interest; that it is the arrogation to the members of the combination of the power to carry on their activities without competition which is rendered unlawful; that the question whether the power so obtained is in fact misused is treated as irrelevant; and that the Court, except I suppose on the question of sentence, is neither required nor permitted to inquire whether in the particular case the intended and actual results of the agreement have in fact benefited or harmed the public.

In other words, once it is established that there is an agreement to carry the prevention or lessening of competition to the point mentioned, injury to the public interest is conclusively presumed, and the parties to the agreement are liable to be convicted of the offence described in s. 498 (1) (d). The relevant question thus becomes the extent to which the prevention and limitation of competition are agreed to be carried and not the economic effect of the carrying out of the agreement. In each case which arises under the section the question whether the point described has been reached becomes one of fact.

The critical words in Cartwright's statement are that an agreement "becomes criminal when the prevention or lessening agreed upon reaches the point at which the participants in the agreement become free to carry on those activities *virtually unaffected* by the influence of competition. . ." (emphasis added). The words "virtually unaffected by the influence of competition" have been interpreted as requiring that no important segment of the market is not a party to the agreement, which presumably means that the agreeing sellers must account for at least 80 to 90 percent of industry output in the relevant market. But is a "virtual monopoly" a necessary condition for undueness? Or is it simply a sufficient, but not a necessary, condition for illegality? Or was Cartwright simply summarizing the facts of all previous opinions in which the word "unduly" loomed large, without any thought of binding future decisions? Unfortunately, judicial opinion has remained divided on these questions (which is one reason why, in 1976, an amendment to section 32(1) was added which attempts to clarify the meaning of "unduly.")[19]

19. In a 1960 judgement in a merger case the judge interpreted "virtual monopoly" as a necessary condition for conviction, and for this and other reasons acquitted the Canadian

There were, however, vigorous dissents from the narrow interpretation of Cartwright's *dictum*. In the *Abitibi* case, a 1960 decision in which seventeen paper companies were convicted for having joined together to fix the *maximum* price they would pay to pulpwood suppliers (many of them farmers and other small firms), Batshaw, J. held that:

Weighing the foregoing authorities, and having scrutinized all the other decisions on the point, I cannot accept the contention that the meaning of the word "undue" as hitherto defined by the Supreme Court of Canada has been substantially changed by the opinion expressed by Mr. Justice Cartwright in the *Fine Papers* case, which he prefaced by stating that he was merely interpreting in his own language the essence of the previous decisions.

I conclude, therefore, that it cannot be accepted as our law that only those conspiracies are illegal that completely eliminate or virtually eliminate all competition. To say that the prevention or lessening of competition must be carried to the point where there remains no competition, or virtually none, is tantamount to considering the words "prevent" or "lessen" as synonymous with "extinguish." Giving to words their ordinary meaning, it would seem that what the legislator intended by "prevent" or "lessen" is something less than "extinguish."

The accused firms accounted for between 70 and 75 percent of domestic consumption and for 55 to 65 percent of total consumption (including exports) of pulpwood during the period of agreement, 1947-54. Batshaw found this degree of control an undue lessening of competition in the purchase of pulpwood and fined the defendant firms a total of $240,000.[20] His opinion rested in good part on the unequal bargaining power between the large pulp and paper firms and the small, independent pulpwood suppliers.

Another combines case in which the judge held that "virtual monopoly" was a sufficient but not a necessary condition for undueness is that of *R v. Canadian Apron and Supply Ltd. et al.* (1967). This case is of particular interest because of the attempt by the judge (Gibson) to utilize some economic analysis in his judgement. Twenty-two firms on Montreal Island (the relevant geographical market), accounting for 85-90 percent of the business of supplying and servicing (cleaning) towels and uniforms for restaurants and other renderers of

Breweries, which had used the merger route to acquire somewhat more than 50 percent of the beer brewing market. In another case, in 1960, the judge in the *B.C. Sugar Refining* case made virtual monopoly a necessary, but not sufficient, condition for conviction on a merger charge (see below). Paradoxically, the same judge who had ruled in the *Breweries* case had expressed the view, in 1955 (two years before the Cartwright *obiter dictum*), that it was not essential for the Crown to prove a "virtual monopoly," in a conspiracy case. *R v. Northern Electric Company Ltd. et al* (1955) O.R. 431.

20. *Regina v Abitibi Power and Paper Co. Ltd. et al.* (1960), 131 CCC 201.

personal services, had organized the Montreal League of Linen Supply Owners. The firms used this organization to fix prices and enforce the prices agreed upon. The defendants admitted to price fixing, but argued that the commodity supplied was a *service* and not covered by the Combines Act which, until 1976, only covered "articles." The judge rejected the defence, arguing that the supply at issue were the linens, which are "articles." Since the defendants had a virtual monopoly in the linen supply business on Montreal Island, Gibson found them guilty. However, he attempted to distinguish between two classes of cases: those in which the facts indicate virtual monopoly so that a *per se* rule applies and those where there is something less than a virtual monopoly and a "rule of reason" must be applied. In the former case the agreement is, without further discussion, undue. In the latter case "unduly" must be resolved on a case-by-case basis, after evaluating the impact of the agreement. (*Canadian Apron, Howard Smith,* and *Container Materials* fit the former category, *Canadian Import* (1933) and *Abitibi* (1960) the latter.)

Most price-fixing cases that have come before the courts involve all or almost all of the important firms in the industry. If any large fraction of industry supply is outside the agreement, price cutting by non-members will generally undermine the price structure erected by the conspirators before the price fixing comes to public attention. The combines cases have typically involved agreements which stretched over several years, suggesting a high degree of discipline among the participating firms. Although the evidence is scanty, these agreements were surely profitable to the firms involved; if they weren't profitable, they would probably have broken down quickly. Thus the price-fixing agreements which are most likely to be harmful to the public are typically those which would lead to convictions even if Cartwright's *dictum* is construed narrowly: i.e. virtual monopoly is a necessary condition for undueness. Nevertheless, it is doubtful whether this fact can justify the time, expense, and uncertainty created by the term "unduly." Since attempted price fixing between would-be competitors is never beneficial, and is injurious on balance, it might be preferable to adopt the U.S. position and make price fixing and other conspiracies *per se* illegal: i.e. violations of the law once the agreement is proved.

The pitfalls created by "unduly" are illustrated in the *Aetna Insurance Co. et al.* (1977), and the *Atlantic Sugar Refineries Ltd. et al.* (1975, 1980) cases. In the *Aetna* case, a divided Nova Scotia Court of Appeals overturned the trial court decision of acquittal only to have its own decision reversed by a divided (5-3) Supreme Court of Canada. The basic, and undisputed, facts of the *Aetna* case were that 73 insurance companies writing fire insurance in Nova Scotia were members of the Nova Scotia Board of Insurance Underwriters. Membership bound the firms to follow a common set of rates, tariff rules and regulations, and policy forms, subject to penalties imposed by the Board for infractions. During the period covered by the indictment, 1960 to 1970, the share of total fire insurance premiums collected by Board members fell from 83 to 71 percent— a fact that may have coloured the decision. The trial judge concluded that "the members knew that they were agreeing to virtually eliminate competition among themselves when undertaking to abide by rates established by the Board." Based on the jurisprudence in earlier cases, particularly *Howard Smith,* this finding would have been sufficient for a verdict of guilty. Nevertheless, in what the Crown argued was the result of legal errors, the trial judge acquitted the defendant firms on the ground that: "...There is nothing in the evidence, however, that leads me to believe that the members of the Board ever *intended* its activities to *interfere* with the public's right to free competition in the purchase of insurance" (emphasis added). The trial judge arrived at this conclusion after admitting evidence by the Board Manager, Mr. Wilfred Shakespeare, that the activities of the Board were undertaken for "public benefit"—evidence that the judge used in evaluating whether the "lessening of competition" was undue.[21]

The Crown appealed, and in a 2-1 decision the Nova Scotia Court of Appeals held that the trial judge had erred, "Once the Crown established that the Board Companies...agreed, as the learned trial judge found, to virtually eliminate competition as to the price of fire insurance among themselves, then 'undueness' if not presumed was certainly established." The insurance firms reacted to this reversal by appealing to the Supreme Court of Canada. That Court sharply divided, with a majority holding that the trial judgement should be restored on the ground that "there is a substantial body of evidence to support the view of the trial judge that competition was not stifled by the Board's actions." The majority opinion thus put great weight on the segment of the Nova Scotia fire insurance industry which were not Board members. A scathing dissent read by the Chief Justice, Bora Laskin, argued that the trial judge had made important legal errors in applying the law to the evidence—particularly his admission of evidence relating to public benefit and his interpretation of undueness as requiring the Crown to prove that the accused *intended* their agreement to lessen competition unduly. Our account of previous combines cases would tend to support the Chief Justice's contention.

The most disturbing aspect of the *Aetna* decision was the apparent accept-ance by a majority of the Supreme Court justices that the Crown must prove that the defendant *intended* to lessen competition unduly. It is one thing to prove an intention to enter an agreement; it is quite another to prove beyond reasonable

---

21. Recall the opinion in the *Howard Smith* case that "public benefits" and "effects" were legally irrelevant in conspiracy cases. An extensive discussion of the issues raised by this and other recent cases is David Phillip Jones, "Trade Regulation," *Ottawa Law Review,* 10 (1978), pp. 167-213.

doubt the defendant's intention to act "unduly." In the absence of explicit documentation the Crown is rarely in a position to prove beyond reasonable doubt that the defendants intended their agreement to have an undue impact on competition. Thus it was no small matter whether this aspect of *Aetna* was the new law of the land or simply an aberration. An answer was not long in coming.

In the *Atlantic Sugar Refineries* (1975) case, the trial judge acquitted the big three sugar manufacturers, who accounted for 95 percent of the relevant market, of conspiring to maintain market shares and exclude competitors. (The facts of this case are discussed in more detail in the next section.) The trial judge, MacKay J., agreed that the evidence indicated the existence of a tacit agreement to maintain market shares. But like the trial judge in *Aetna*, he was not convinced that the defendants had *intended* to lessen competition unduly. In reaching his decision MacKay J. seemed to be formulating a "double-intent" requirement. On the one hand "the conspirators must have the intention of entering into an agreement" but on the other "it had not been shown that this agreement was arrived at with the *intention* of unduly preventing or lessening competition."[22] This questionable interpretation of the law prompted the Crown to appeal the decision. As in the *Aetna* case the Crown won a reversal in the Quebec Court of Appeals on grounds of judicial error, only to have that decision overruled, and the trial judgement reinstated, when the defendants appealed to the Supreme Court of Canada.

The Supreme Court *Sugar* decision, written by Pigeon J., is controversial in two respects. First it implicitly accepted the "double intent requirement" as Estey J., the only dissenting justice, was quick to point out. Second, and more explicitly, the Court majority seemed to say that a tacit agreement to maintain market shares is not necessarily an undue agreement. According to Pigeon J.[23]

> As I have already indicated, I cannot agree with the submission that this "tacit agreement" to maintain market shares involved the *elimination* of competition. On the contrary, as we have just seen the evidence is clear that it involved only a lessening of competition. (emphasis added)
>
> The decision to strive for stability on the basis of maintaining "historical market share" was therefore not a decision to forego *all* price competition. On the contrary, it meant that some price concessions would be made to the big buyers but that this would be adjusted so as to maintain the "historical market share" as close as possible without any increase or diminution. That this involved a *lessening of competition* is apparent. However it is equally clear that it did not involve a *suppression* of competition. (emphasis added)

22. 26 CPR(2d) 23, 103.
23. 16 CR(2d) 140.

The *Atlantic Sugar* decision raises all sorts of questions. Does not a tacit agreement to maintain traditional market shares imply an arrangement to avoid all significant rivalry, including price competition? When does a "lessening" of competition become its "elimination"? Can there be active competition if discounts to big buyers are meted out in such a way as to maintain traditional market shares? But above all, the really crucial question is whether the Crown is ever in a position to prove beyond reasonable doubt the defendants' intentions other than by proving that there was an agreement or arrangement to avoid competition among them. If as a result of *Aetna* and *Atlantic Sugar Refineries* the Crown must prove double intent (intention to agree *and* intention to lessen competition unduly) it is doubtful indeed that the Crown can continue to prosecute, with relative effectiveness, agreements among firms attempting to avoid competition among themselves.

The *Aetna* and *Sugar* cases have thrown the *jurisprudence* on price-fixing conspiracies into confusion, although only time will tell to what extent subsequent decisions will be affected. Some evidence that judicial opinion may return to earlier precedents is indicated in the *Albany Felt* (1982) case. There, the Quebec Court of Appeals upheld a trial court decision convicting the five manufacturers of wet felts, which are used by pulp and paper mills for their paper-making machines, of colluding on prices. The evidence clearly indicated that the wet felt manufacturers had engaged in price fixing agreements since the mid-1950s. When the defendants attempted to appeal to the Supreme Court of Canada that Court refused to hear the appeal, even though the defendants argued that the Crown had failed to prove they had *intended* to unduly lessen competition. One might infer from the *Albany Felt* case that where the evidence of agreement is overwhelming, the intent and object of the agreement coalesce so that the problems posed by the "double intent" doctrine of *Sugar* do not arise.

Even if the *Albany Felt* decision gets the conspiracy jurisprudence back on track, it is hard to see how either public interest or private safeguards are served by the continued use of the term "unduly." That term has played havoc with the jurisprudence, leading to a virtual breakdown in the law in recent years. A new perspective is needed. There is little dispute that price fixing is usually undesirable. There is even less dispute that Canada's small domestic markets mean that most manufacturing industries are relatively concentrated. Add to this the protection provided by tariff barriers, and one can only conclude that a more explicit prohibition of collusion is justified to ensure competitive behaviour in Canada. It makes more sense to thwart all collective attempts to lessen competition, not just those which are "undue."[24]

24. However, something less than a *per se* rule can be defended on the grounds that many price-fixing agreements probably create little harm and many collapse quite quickly in the face of

B. Conscious Parallelism

In the 1970s, a series of combines prosecutions revolved around whether the observed behaviour of the firms was evidence of a conspiracy. In *R. v. Canada Cement LaFarge Ltd.* (1973), *R. v. Armco Canada Ltd.* (1974), *R. v. Atlantic Sugar Refineries Ltd.* (1975, 1980), and *R. v. Canadian General Electric Ltd.* (1976) the contentious issue at trial was not whether there was a virtual elimination of competition, but whether there was sufficient evidence of agreement. The critical issue was not "unduly" but so-called "conscious parallelism."[25] "Conscious parallelism" is a lawyer's term which is supposed to characterize the rational economic behaviour of oligopolists selling relatively homogeneous products: to wit, match competitor prices, make few price changes, and, when you do, follow the leader. The basic reason for this "parallel" pricing behaviour is that non-established price differentials may induce retaliatory price cuts by the higher pricing firms, which if rematched by the lower pricing firms is an invitation to price war.[26] The preferred strategy is thus one of identical (quoted) prices or established (and accepted) differentials. In each of the four cases cited above the products were essentially homogeneous (Portland cement, metal culverts, refined sugar, and electric light bulbs) and in three of them the industries were highly concentrated (a big three in sugar and in electric large lamps, a big four in the cement industry), the industry leader accounting for from 33 to 45 percent of total output. The metal culvert industry was more loosely oligopolistic and it was the only one of the four in which barriers to entry were virtually nonexistent.

In each of the four cases the government brought charges of violation of section 32(1)(c): that the defendants had conspired or agreed or arranged to lessen competition unduly. In each of the cases the defendants, or their expert economic witnesses, argued that because of the oligopolistic nature of their industries, parallel pricing behaviour was inevitable, that the observed similarity of prices was the result of "conscious parallelism," not an agreement between the firms. The prosecution, for its part, compiled extensive evidence of attempts by the firms to avoid price competition, efforts which involved more than simply *recognizing* interdependence.

chiseling and threatened entry. In fact, Dewey has argued that where entry is easy and numbers of firms relatively large, collusion may even be socially beneficial. Here is why. Where entry is easy, collusion will not raise prices and profit rates but, by reducing uncertainty, price fixing may reduce the variability of prices and profits. Since the cost of capital includes a risk factor which usually increases with the *variability* of profits, a reduction in variability will, *ceteris paribus*, reduce the cost of capital. The reduced cost of capital, in turn, will tend to increase investment and output relative to non-collusive regimes. See Donald Dewey, "Information, Entry, and Welfare: The Case for Collusion," *American Economic Review*, 69 (September 1979), pp. 587-94.

25. A related case is *R. v. Aluminum Co. of Canada* (1976).

26. This presumes a basic similarity of cost conditions faced by oligopolists.

The government lost the *Cement* case for reasons which are worthy of mention. The *Cement* case involved the use of a basing point system in Ontario which had resulted in uniform delivered prices over the period 1959 to 1972. The basing point system included a base price for each cement plant of the accused firms and a variable transportation charge which resulted in identical prices at each destination regardless of the location of the plants of the four defendant firms. Even tenders on large government contracts were identical. In determining whether the uniform delivered pricing system employed by the cement firms constituted a violation of the law, the judge drew on an address delivered in 1962 by the then Director of Investigation and Research under the Combines Investigation Act, Mr. David Henry, who had noted:

> Conscious parallelism, if conducted without collusion among the members of the industry, is not an offense.
>
> ...In some circumstances the fact that a number of sellers have quoted identical prices raises a strong presumption of arrangements among them, while in other circumstances all suppliers are likely to quote identical prices whether the quotations are the subject of agreement or not.[27]

It seems doubtful, however, that if the tenders are by sealed bid, they would, in the absence of agreement, be identical, although admittedly the possibility of uniformity is increased when there are only three or four firms, a homogeneous product, a rule of thumb markup pricing formula is used, and the tenders are made to government bodies which make the winning bid public.[28] Nonetheless, the judge decided that because the similarity of prices was probably due to conscious parallelism the government had insufficient evidence of an agreement, and he discharged the defendant firms.

The government won convictions in the *Armco* and *Canadian General Electric* cases, the basic facts of which are described in chapter 5. The reader will recall the employment of an "open price policy" by the metal culvert producers as a means of avoiding competition on sealed bids to the Ontario Department of Highways, and the "sales plans" used by the large lamp suppliers to reduce or eliminate the price cutting and discounting of their distributors. Both of these cases illustrate the strengths of the factors undermin-

27. *R. v. Canada Cement LaFarge* (1974), 12 CPR 2d 14. "Conscious parallelism and nothing more" is not unlawful under either the U.S. or Canadian interpretation of their respective price-fixing laws.

28. If the individual market shares of the conspiring firms differ substantially, the firms with the largest market shares may prefer a *rotating* (low) bid system to identical bids since the latter could lead to a tendency for market share differentials to disappear if buyers *randomly* select among the identical bids. For this reason it may be mistaken to simply presume that agreements exist where bids are identical and that competition flourishes where there are non-identical bids. See W.S. Comanor and M.A. Schankerman, "Identical Bids and Cartel Behaviour," *The Bell Journal of Economics* (Spring 1976), pp. 281-86.

ing oligopolistic coordination (easy entry in one case, the nature of the distribution system in the other) and the extensive efforts (sometimes called "plus" factors) required to achieve parallel pricing policies.

Armco and *Canadian General Electric* can be viewed as the high watermark in Canadian prosecution of parallel behaviour. In each case the Crown was fortunate that the judges were willing to see the outline of an arrangement in the attempts by the firms in each industry to prop up pricing systems which would otherwise have tended to collapse. In effect, an implicit "conscious parallelism plus" doctrine was adopted, with the Crown willing to infer from evidence of "plus" actions that the parallel behaviour was based on an explicit agreement. In *Armco*, Lerner J. went so far as to say: "I fail to see on a common sense basis how conscious parallelism could be achieved without a conspiracy on the part of the accused to come to an agreement or arrangement beforehand." Thus Lerner J. pierced the veil of credibility which shrouds the conscious parallelism doctrine to find an *arrangement* among the defendants to act in parallel fashion. Similarly, Pennel J. in the *General Electric* case convicted the three leading manufacturers of large lamps by focusing on their efforts to enforce adherence to their identical Large Lamp Plans.

As we have seen the tide turned against the Crown in the *Atlantic Sugar Refineries* case, with the trial judge acquitting the three defendant firms.[29] The *Sugar* case was a complex one in which the prosecution's chief evidence consisted of several examples of parallel bahaviour, the alleged aim of which was to maintain constancy in the market shares of the three leading firms, Atlantic Sugar Refineries, Redpath Sugar, and St. Lawrence Sugar.[30] The examples of parallel behaviour included: (i) an ultimately unsuccessful attempt to prevent a new entrant, Cartier, from obtaining supplies of raw sugar from South Africa; (ii) a successful effort to keep a high quality raw sugar from India from being sold directly to confectionery and soft drink manufacturers; (iii) the maintenance of a 75¢ per hundred weight premium paid to members of the Commonwealth Sugar Association who supplied raw sugar to Canada under British Preference customs duties; (iv) a "Base Stock System" of inventory pricing which allowed each firm to daily set identical prices of *refined* sugar as a direct ratio of the world price (London Daily Price) of raw sugar; (v) a basing point system to assure uniform delivered prices; and (vi) posted price lists at Redpath headquarters which were reported each morning by agents of the "rival" firms. Not surprisingly, the market shares of the "Big Three" had remained virtually unchanged for over a decade.

In reaching his decision Mackay, J. seemed to consider each type of

29. On appeal the trial court decision was reversed in favour of the Crown but reinstated by the Supreme Court of Canada.
30. These firms were convicted of price fixing in 1962.

behaviour, or incident, in isolation. In each instance the judge decided that the Crown had failed to prove beyond a reasonable doubt that the defendants had engaged in a conspiracy to stifle competition. It is arguable, however, that the judge approached the case in the wrong way. Had he looked at the evidence as a whole, treating the various incidents as a related story, the outlines of an agreement to control the market and restrict entry would have been clear.

The line between conscious parallelism and an agreement to limit competition is a thin one. The more complex the history of industry behaviour, the more likely is parallel behaviour the result of an arrangement of some kind. In the *Armco* case the judge, as we have seen, rejected the defendant's argument that the "identical prices resulting from their 'Open Price Policy' " were nothing more than conscious parallelism of action. But, in the *Sugar* case, the judge explictly rejected the *Armco* view that conscious parallelism could only be achieved via a prior agreement or arrangement which transgressed the law. Yet in the *Sugar* case the judge's concluding remarks would seem to bear out a cause and effect relationship between agreement and parallelism of action.

> On the evidence, I found the maintenance of traditional market shares...was the result of a tacit agreement between the accused. But in my opinion, it has not been shown that this agreement was arrived at with the intention of unduly preventing or lessening competition. The reason for maintaining traditional market shares was to avoid a price war which would have resulted had the accused taken the only method of increasing them by price cutting through extensive discounts.[31]

In sum, "conscious parallelism" as such does not violate section 32(1). But there is some danger that the concept may become a widely used shield to protect otherwise prohibited conduct of oligopolists. Whether this danger is more apparent than real will depend on the willingness of judges to pierce the "veil of credibility" that shrouds parallel behaviour of rival firms. In the meantime, the dilemma posed by conscious parallelism has provoked efforts (as yet unsuccessful) to "radically" change the competition laws. Until relatively recently, the focus of reform proposals in the United States was on structural remedies which would deconcentrate tightly oligopolistic industries by breaking up leading firms which could provide no form of efficiency justification for their

---

31. *R v. Atlantic Sugar Refineries Ltd. et al.* (1976) C.S. 421 à 424. It was primarily this statement that led the Quebec Court of Appeal to reverse the trial court decision on grounds of judicial error in interpreting the law. The Appeals Court argued that it was not necessary for the Crown to prove the defendants *intended* to lessen competition; that once the trial court had concluded that the defendants, who supplied almost 100 percent of the Eastern Canadian market, had engaged in an agreement to maintain shares then, in law the trial judge should have found for the Crown. As we have seen, however, the Supreme Court of Canada, with the last word, did not agree.

dominant position. In Canada, the emphasis was on conduct-oriented approaches such as the proposal to give the combines authorities powers to issue prohibition orders against "joint monopolization" or "shared monopoly" behaviour.[32] Now there is a growing realization in both U.S. and Canadian antitrust circles that even in tightly oligopolistic industries, purely parallel behaviour and nothing more is unlikely to maintain a non-competitive price: complicating factors require specific or "plus" actions which make the behaviour culpable.

Conclusion

The prosecution of price fixing and other forms of collusive activity has historically been the most important contribution of Canada's anticombines laws. Until recently, price fixing cases substantially outnumbered all other types of cases (not including misleading advertising). However, the Crown's success rate in section 32 (1) cases has declined precipitously over the past 15 years as Table 8-5 indicates.[33] In part, this decline is attributable to the fact that the government has begun tackling the harder-to-win "conscious parallelism" cases. But part of the problem undoubtedly owes to a weakening of the jurisprudence as a result of the Supreme Court decisions in *Aetna* and *Atlantic Sugar*. One result is that in the late 1970s and the early 1980s much more of the government's prosecutorial effort has been redirected toward "vertical" price fixing in the form of resale price maintenance (RPM). As we shall see in the next chapter, the law on RPM approaches a *per se* rule, there being no issue of "undueness" in which to tangle the jurisprudence.

32. Joint monopolization is briefly discussed in the next chapter, in the section on reform of the combines laws. For a comprehensive discussion of conscious parallelism see W.T. Stanbury and G.B. Reschenthaler, "Oligopoly and Conscious Parallelism: Theory, Policy and Canadian Cases," *Osgoode Hall Law Journal*, (Dec. 1977), pp. 617-700. Also see George Hay, "Oligopoly, Shared Monopoly, and Antitrust Law," 1982 *Cornell Law Review*, 67, pp. 439-481.

33. The Quebec concrete case referred to in footnote 1 to Table 8-5 is of particular economic although not legal (the defendants plead guilty) interest. The case arose out of an·attempt by the major established concrete producers in Quebec City to impede the introduction of portable batching plants at construction sites. The innovation of automated on-site concrete-mixing rather than reliance on ready-mix trucks was introduced by Rocois Construction. It was estimated to reduce the cost of concrete at large construction sites by 25 percent. The established concrete producers attempted to deter proliferation of the new technology and to withhold supplies of concrete to Rocois on smaller construction sites where the portable plants were not economical. The case illustrates one way in which an attack on collusive activities can have large social benefits. Interestingly, the conviction was the first under the "residual" section (d) of 32 (1) which prohibits firms from "otherwise" restraining or injuring competition unduly. See *Annual Report*, Director of Investigation and Research, Combines Investigation Act, Year Ending March 31, 1983, pp. 15-16.

Table 8-5

The Disposition of Conspiracy Cases, 1970/71 to 1982/83

Disposition	1970/71-74/75	1975/76-79/80	1980/81-82/83
Total cases referred to Attorney General	19	28[b]	18[a]
Cases not prosecuted	4	8	6
Results of Prosecutions			
Non convictions	2	8	7
—charges dropped	0	1	1
—dismissed at preliminary hearing	2	1	1
—acquitted at trial	0	7	5
Convictions	13	11	5
—fine only	1	1	0
—prohibition order only	7	4	3
—fine and prohibition order	5	6	2
Conviction rate	87%	58%	42%

[a]Includes 1 case (Quebec concrete) in which a S. 33 charge was also laid but dropped when accused pleaded guilty to conspiracy charges.
[b]Includes 2 cases where accused was charged under *both* S. 32 and S. 33 (monopoly)—i.e., Large Lamps; Allied Chemical and Cominco.
Source: compiled by P.K. Gorecki and W.T. Stanbury from the *Annual Reports* of the Director of Investigation and Research, and generously made available to me by Professor Stanbury. From P.K. Gorecki and W.T. Stanbury, *The Objectives of Canadian Competition Policy, 1888-1983*. (Halifax: The Institute for Research on Public Policy, 1984.) Reprinted by permission.

9

Canadian Competition Policy: Part II

This chapter continues the analysis and assessment of anticombines jurisprudence begun in the preceding chapter. Whereas the conspiracy law received much of its jurisprudential development prior to 1960, the areas of law covered in this chapter (merger, monopoly, price discrimination, predatory pricing, resale price maintenance, and restrictive practices) have received virtually all of their development since 1960. As we shall see, the jurisprudence related to these matters is, in many respects, even less satisfying than that related to conspiracies. This fact, among others, has stimulated a search for a fundamental and acceptable reform of the anticombines law, the subject of the final sections of this chapter.

The Jurisprudence Continued

C. *Monopoly and Merger*

Section 33 of the Combines Investigation Act states that: "Every person who is a party or privy to or knowingly assists in, or in the formation of, a merger or monopoly is guilty of an indictable offence and is liable to imprisonment for two years." The Combines Act defines a merger as an "acquisition. . .of a competitor, supplier, customer, or any other person, whereby competition. . .is or is likely to be lessened to the detriment or against the interest of the public, whether consumers, producers, or others." A monopoly is defined as "a situation where one or more persons either substantially or completely controls throughout Canada...[a] species of business...and have operated such business or are likely to operate it to the detriment or against the interest of the public..."[1] Despite the broad language of the Act there have been very few convictions for monopoly and none for mergers.[2] Beyond a doubt the most unsatisfactory facet of Canadian competition policy is the law on mergers. Judicial decisions have virtually closed the door to successful prosecutions. There are two main reasons: the merger law is criminal law and the law has been interpreted by the courts to require that the Crown prove, beyond reasonable doubt, "detriment to the public." We shall begin by briefly describing the Canadian law on monopoly as it has developed to date and then turn to the more difficult and contentious merger decisions.

(i) Monopoly

Three cases in which monopoly was the primary charge illustrate the Canadian law on monopoly.[3] The Eddy Match Co. was convicted, in 1952, for its attempt to maintain its monopoly position in the wooden match industry, originally attained by way of merger in the 1920s through its successful use of predatory tactics (see chapter 5). In 1970, the Electric Reduction Company (ERCO) pleaded guilty to two counts of monopoly and one of merger after an RTPC report cited ERCO's use of price discrimination, its acquisition of a new competitor and its use of reciprocal arrangements with potential competitors, to maintain its monopoly position in the production of industrial phosphates behind a twenty percent Canadian tariff barrier. In 1976, Allied Chemical and Cominco were acquitted of having monopolized the British Columbia sulphuric acid market when Allied undertook to close its sulphuric acid plants and become the sole customer for Cominco's large supplies of acid, a by-product of Cominco's copper smelting operations. These three cases run from the easy (*Eddy Match*) to the difficult (*Allied Chemicals*) in law and economics.

Monopoly in Canadian law depends on a combination of market control and

1. Note that the "public" includes "producers" and "others" as well as "consumers."
2. However, the Electric Reduction Co. (ERCO) pleaded guilty in 1970 to a charge of merger in a case, the main element of which was monopoly.
3. There are only a few other monopoly cases. In 1973 Canada Safeway was convicted for monopolizing the supermarket trade in Edmonton ([1973], 1 WWR 210). The *Irving* case (see below) involved charges of both merger and monopoly. A sixth case, investigated by the RTPC, resulted in an agreement by CIL to supply ammunition to all sporting equipment wholesalers on demand. CIL had a monopoly over the non-military ammunition business in Canada, a monopoly due in part to economies of scale but one which was protected by high tariffs. The RTPC's report did not attack CIL's monopoly in production, but it did hit CIL's role as a distributor. CIL limited the number of distributors whenever additional outlets would increase competition but not sales. Between 1952-57 it had rejected applications from 46 potential outlets. CIL's policy thus restricted entry into the otherwise competitive market for the distribution of ammunition. The RTPC report thus recommended that CIL's continued tariff protection be conditional on its willingness to supply ammunition to all comers. CIL chose the latter route.

public detriment. In the *Eddy Match* case the judge concluded that:

> When a group of companies engaged in the same business are alone in the field; when they work together as a unit; when they are free to supply the market or to withhold their product; when there is no restriction on the prices which they charge, save their own self-interest; when their freedom to exclude individuals as customers, is restricted only by their interpretation of existing penal laws, then by all normal standards those companies are in control of the business in which they are engaged.[4]

Eddy Match and its subsidiaries had this degree of control.[5] The case then turned on whether Eddy's systematic elimination of competitors via "fighting brands," and other predatory tactics described in chapter 5, created public detriment. According to the Court ". . .when faced with facts which disclose the systematic elimination of competition, the presumption of public detriment becomes violent." *Eddy Match* is a classic monopolization case, somewhat akin to the famous *Standard Oil* and *American Tobacco* decisions rendered by the U.S. Supreme Court in 1911. There the Supreme Court enunciated a "rule of reason" under which the *behaviour* of monopolists determined the legality of monopoly. Eddy's monopoly position, when combined with predatory conduct, lent the "presumption of public detriment."

Like Eddy Match, the *Electric Reduction Company* ran afoul of Canadian law in its efforts to preserve a monopoly in the market for industrial phosphates. However, ERCO's tactics were somewhat more subtle. Its chief weapon was a discriminatory pricing policy which it employed to brilliant effect behind a 20 percent Canadian tariff barrier. ERCO's customers could be, and were, divided into two groups. On the one hand were three large foreign-owned soap manufacturers which purchased eighty percent of ERCO's industrial phosphates. These companies used their bargaining power (enhanced by their American parent's ability to purchase phosphates from U.S. producers at "deep discount" prices) to negotiate prices only slightly higher than U.S. mill price plus transportation costs. On the other hand were twenty smaller firms which purchased the balance of ERCO's output and were charged a price equal to the list price at the nearest U.S. mill, plus freight and the 20 percent Canadian tariff.[6] When in 1958 Dominion Fertilizers announced it was entering the industrial phosphate field, ERCO, desiring to preserve its monopoly, and fearing,

---

4. *Eddy Match Co. v. The Queen*, Quebec Court of Queen's Bench, Appeal Side (1954) 18 C.R. 371.
5. Eddy controlled other Canadian match companies via a holding company controlled by Eddy.
6. These and other facts in the case are well described by D.G. McFetridge, "The Emergence of a Canadian Merger Policy: The ERCO Case," *Antitrust Bulletin*, 1974, pp. 1-11. Also see Restrictive Trade Practices Commission, "Trade Practices in the Phosphorous Products and Sodium Chlorate Industries" (Ottawa, 1966).

with some justification, that there was not sufficient room in the industry for two firms of efficient scale, purchased Dominion. It also entered into reciprocal agreements with CIL and Cyanamid, both potential entrants, with respect to the division of production of industrial chemicals. This behaviour led to an RTPC investigation, a critical report, and a decision by the Justice Department to go to trial.

ERCO responded by pleading guilty to two counts of monopoly and one of merger. In doing so, it may have avoided divestiture of its holdings in Dominion Fertilizer. However, it had to accept a broad-scale prohibition order which (i) limited the spread between the prices negotiated with the major soap manufacturers and the prices paid by smaller purchasers; (ii) forbade arrangements with competitors or potential competitors regarding prices and market allocations; and (iii) prohibited attempts to deter new entry into the industry. Thus, what is perhaps most significant about the ERCO case is the scale of the prohibition order, and, through it, the government's attempt to control the behaviour of an admitted monopolist.

Where the ERCO case added nothing to the state of the *law* on monopoly and merger, the *Allied Chemical* decision, rendered by the Supreme Court of British Columbia in 1975, indicates something about the position of the dividing line between behaviour that is and is not "detrimental" to the public. The basic facts of the case are easily described. Prior to 1961, Allied Chemical Limited was the sole manufacturer of sulphuric acid in the western part of British Columbia, selling primarily to pulp and paper firms in the southwestern part of B.C., particularly Vancouver Island.[7] Around 1961, Cominco Limited, a major copper smelter, located at Trail, B.C., found itself with a huge over-supply of sulphuric acid, a by-product of its smelting operations.[8] At this point Allied and Cominco entered into an agreement whereby Allied would close its manufacturing plant and obtain its total requirements of sulphuric acid from Cominco. Cominco for its part made Allied its sole customer in western British Columbia, the two firms sharing equally the net revenues in excess of transportation costs. In effect, Allied, although it remained an independent company, became the marketing channel for Cominco. This profitable arrangement was still in force when, in 1974, the government brought monopoly charges against the two firms.[9]

7. There was however evidence that Allied had potential competitors in the northwestern U.S. and from Inland Chemicals located at Fort Saskatchewan (Alta.), and that Allied's pricing policy reflected this potential competition. See *Regina v. Allied Chemical Ltd. and Cominco Ltd.* (1975) 6 WWR 482-83.
8. In the 1950s Cominco disposed of its sulphuric acid by selling it to fertilizer producing firms, but by 1960 world competition and a surplus of fertilizer caused Cominco to look elsewhere to dispose of its acid.
9. It is interesting that during the period 1961-74 the Canadian price per ton of sulphuric acid rose little in absolute terms and fell substantially relative to U.S. prices of acid.

The Crown's argument was, in its essentials, that the arrangement between Allied and Cominco caused public detriment because it left the market with one supplier of sulphuric acid when there could have been two. In effect, the Crown contended that Cominco could have entered the market on a direct competitive basis, disposing of its acid at prices as low as $17 a ton (this figure was vigorously disputed by the defendants) compared to the actual price in the range of $29 per ton. It was argued that the arrangement between Allied and Cominco deprived the public of competition and lower prices, and this, the Crown argued, constituted public detriment. The Court rejected the Crown's argument on a number of grounds. One was that Allied met stiff competition from Inland Chemicals when Allied ventured into Northern and Eastern B.C. More important was evidence that had Cominco sold its acid at $17 a ton in direct competition with Allied, the "dog-eat-dog competition" would have resulted in the demise of Allied.[10] In fact, the Crown admitted as much. However, the $17 a ton figure was disputed as being far below the price necessary to cover transportation and distribution costs plus a return on capital. In the event, the Court held that the Crown had failed to provide sufficient evidence of public detriment and acquitted the defendant firms. One might gather from the *Allied Chemical* decision that the Courts are hesitant to conclude public detriment where a firm refused to do something which is not in its own interest. If this interpretation is correct the dividing line between acceptable and unacceptable monopoly behaviour lies between failure to compete (*Allied Chemicals*) and elimination of competitors (*Eddy Match*).

The Canadian law on monopoly (excluding specific charges of "predatory pricing," which is discussed below) may be summarized as follows:
1. If a monopolist maintains his monopoly by consistently driving out rivals via predatory tactics, public detriment is presumed, although it may be rebutted by the defence (*R.v. Eddy Match* (1954)).
2. A monopolist, even an efficient one, that exploits its position in the form of discriminatory pricing on an extensive and substantial scale will face prosecution and a strong probability of conviction (*R.v. Electric Reduction Company of Canada Ltd.* (1970)). ERCO avoided a trial and possibly dissolution by pleading guilty to two counts of monopoly and one of merger.
3. Firms who simply refuse to compete with each other will *not* be found guilty of monopoly. (*R.v. Allied Chemical* (1975)).
4. As a result of the *Irving* decision (see below) it is clear that simply gaining a monopoly, and to that extent lessening competition, is not in and of itself a violation of the monopoly law. The Crown must prove "public detriment," which in the absence of the type of predacious, exclusionary, or exploitative

10. The Judge also noted that Cominco might then have been charged under section 34(1)(c) of the Combines Investigation Act for selling at unreasonably low prices.

behaviour evidenced in *Eddy Match* and possibly in *ERCO*, would be difficult indeed.

In a real sense, it is a misnomer to label section 33 as dealing with "monopoly." Structural monopoly as such is not illegal, or at issue. The law deals with the act of monopolizing—or monopolization—and then only when the behaviour is particularly vicious. Canada is not alone in this regard; no other country has shown an interest in breaking up monopolies. Only in the 1970s did the U.S. indicate an interest in reducing the dominance of firms such as IBM by attacking the relatively subtle (and otherwise unobjectionable) forms of behaviour used to entrench their positions, and the IBM case has since been dropped.

(ii) Mergers

The difficulties with Canadian anticombines law and policy are best illustrated by the legal treatment of mergers. No firm has been convicted for merger in Canada. Prior to 1960 there were no merger cases worthy of the name, although two combines cases involved charges under the merger provisions of the law. In *R.v. Canadian Import* (1933) the accused were acquitted on a charge of merger, although convicted on two counts of conspiracy. In *R.v. Staples* (1940) the accused were acquitted of a merger charge in a case involving the question of the meaning of "control" of one business by another. In 1960, two important merger decisions were rendered by trial courts in Ontario and Manitoba, and these established the basic Canadian law on merger. However, because the Crown did not appeal the acquittals in the *Canadian Breweries* and *B.C. Sugar Refining* cases, a period of 16 years elapsed before the Supreme Court rendered its first decision in a merger case, this one involving the K.C. Irving newspaper interests in New Brunswick. The Supreme Court's decision in the *Irving* case may have ended any real possibility that the Crown could win, under existing law, a merger conviction.

Both the *Canadian Breweries* and *B.C. Sugar Refining* cases followed RTPC reports which indicated that competition in the beer and western sugar refining industries had been reduced as a result of mergers. In the *Breweries* case,[11] a long history of acquisitions (37 were included in the indictment) between the years 1930 and 1958 had propelled Canadian Breweries (CB) into a dominant position in the Canadian beer industry. In Ontario, CB's market share rose from 11 to 60 percent between 1930 and 1958; in Quebec from 13 to 52 percent. Except for the Maritimes, where local breweries received some degree of government protection, the Canadian beer industry became for all intents and purposes a triopoly, with a dominant firm (CB) and two smaller but vigorous rivals, Molson and Labatt.[12] In its defence, CB argued that its acquisition

11. *R v. Canadian Breweries Ltd.* (1960) 126 CCC 133.
12. As fate would have it CB's market share declined significantly after 1958, in the face of tough competition from Molson and Labatt.

program simply "rationalized" an industry (CB closed a number of the plants it acquired) whose structure would have inevitably changed in the face of evolving scale economies in production and marketing (including national advertising).[13] The scale economies argument was probably overstated. Since transportation costs are high relative to resale price the beer market tends to be a regional or local one. The scale advantage accrues mainly to multiplant firms where national brand names give rise to what some economists have argued is essentially a "pecuniary" rather than a "real" economy of scale. However, Canada is not the only country that has experienced a rapid decline in the number of beer firms. A similar process has taken place in the United States, though perhaps not on the same scale and not with the same domination by a single firm.

In his decision, McRuer J. placed great weight on the fact that beer, like other alcoholic beverages, is regulated by provincial Liquor Control Boards. He viewed regulation as both a limit on the application of the combines law and a constraint on monopoly pricing. However, the economic relevance of this regulation is, in fact, doubtful in as much as several provinces controlled retail beer prices simply by means of a mark-up over uncontrolled manufacturing prices.[14]

The Court also gave emphasis to the fact that CB still faced two tough competitors. In establishing whether or not the merger was detrimental to the public, McRuer J. considered the competition that remained more important than the competitors who were "extinguished."[15] This rather questionable approach was the result of the judge's attempt to determine the meaning of "public detriment" (recall this is the first bona fide merger case) by recourse to the jurisprudence on "unduly." Here McRuer J. had the "benefit" of Cartwright J.'s dictum on "undueness" in the *Howard Smith* case, and he proceeded to interpret it narrowly as requiring a "virtual elimination of competition." Armed with this "virtual monopoly" criterion, it was a relatively easy task to acquit Canadian Breweries which still yielded almost half the beer market to its competitors.

The application of a "virtual monopoly" doctrine in a merger case is not easy to accept. Does it make sense to let mergers proceed until monopoly is within reach and then attempt to undo the damage? In a nation with markets as large as

13. The alleged importance of scale economies has been questioned by J.C.H. Jones, "Mergers and Competition: The Brewing Case," *Canadian Journal of Economics*, (1967).
14. It is interesting that it was in the early 1960s that the U.S. courts made clear that government regulation of an industry was not a bar to the application of the merger provisions of the U.S. antitrust laws. See *U.S.v. Philadelphia National Bank* 374 U.S. 321 (1963) and *U.S. v. El Paso Natural Gas* 373 U.S. 930 (1964).
15. In an oft-quoted statement McRuer J. said "I do not think it is an offence against the Combines Act for one corporation to acquire the business of another merely because it wishes to *extinguish* a competitor." (Emphasis added.)

in the United States, a "virtual monopoly" doctrine makes little sense. However, in a nation with small domestic markets, such as those in Canada, it is easier to see the logic of the judge's position. Moreover the judge did acknowledge that the term "public detriment" and the criminal scope of the Canadian law prevented him from adopting the U.S. approach to mergers with its emphasis on "incipiency," that is "nipping monopoly in the bud." Nevertheless, it is hard to understand why he did not see fit to interpret a clearly substantial reduction in competition by way of merger as presumptively "detrimental" to the "public interest in competition." Against the presumption of public detriment can then be set evidence, if any, of benefits in the form of, say, cost reductions flowing from the achievement of economies of scale that the merger makes possible. (See chapter 4.) In any event, the *Breweries* decision established precedent and by doing so opened the way to a very narrow interpretation of the Canadian combines law on mergers.

Within months of the *Canadian Breweries* decision came an even more upsetting one (for the government), this time in the *B.C. Sugar Refining* case.[16] For here there was the "smoking pistol" of virtual monopoly, B.C. Sugar having acquired its only competitor in western Canada, the Manitoba Sugar Refining Company, in 1955. However, the judge argued that the Crown had nevertheless failed to establish "public detriment," and he rather contentiously placed great weight on the limited competitive impact in Manitoba of the Eastern sugar refineries, centred chiefly in Montreal.

Prior to the merger, B.C. Sugar Refining controlled 100 percent of the refined sugar market in B.C. and Alberta, 93 percent of the market in Saskatchewan, and had a 19 percent share in Manitoba. Manitoba Sugar, a relatively young and vigorous competitior, held a 7 percent market share in Saskatchewan and 51 percent in Manitoba. Eastern sugar refiners accounted for the remaining 30 percent market share in Manitoba. The industry was protected by high tariffs which it used as a form of limit price. Price competition, in the sugar refining industry, was constrained by a delivered price system with basing points in Vancouver, Montreal, and St. John's, Nfld. The basing point system explains, in part, the competitive overlap between the market of the Eastern and Western refiners in the province of Manitoba. Also, the Western refiners, unlike their Eastern counterparts, obtained some of their raw sugar from domestic sugar beet producers. An economic interpretation of these facts would suggest that the merger, by eliminating the one obviously competitive factor in the picture, gave B.C. Sugar substantial monopoly power. Yet the judge gave weight, instead, to the limits to that monopoly power posed by the eastern refiners and to the protection that the tariff gave to the sugar beet producers as well as to the sugar refiners. He rejected the Crown's argument

16. *R.v. B.C. Sugar Refining Co. Ltd.* (1961) 129 CCC 7.

that the monopsony power created by the merger was likely to reduce sugar beet prices to the detriment of the sugar beet producers.

In his decision, Williams C.J. referred extensively to the *Breweries* case. He adopted approvingly McRuer J.'s view that it is not a violation of the Combines Act for a firm to acquire another "merely because it wishes to extinguish a competitor," this despite the fact that in the case of B.C. Sugar the acquisition was of its sole competitor. He agreed that the Crown must also establish a "virtual stifling of competition," which he believed it had not done. But Williams C.J. went further and argued that the Crown must show public detriment:

> I should say here that in my opinion the Crown in this case must not only establish that as a result of the merger the accused acquired the "power" referred to in the cases decided under S.411 (S.498) of the Criminal Code: It must also establish excessive or exorbitant profits or prices. The Crown has not attempted to establish exorbitant profits, its attempt to establish exorbitant prices fails.

The legal implication of this ruling is that "public detriment" and "unduly" are not the same; the former requires more than the latter: that bad effects as well as the "virtual elimination" of competition be shown. The judgement implies that one is not allowed to infer from a merger's competitive effects its impact on economic welfare. Rather, the Crown would be forced to wait until well after a merger was consummated, and its ramifications apparent, before it could entertain a trial which it has any hope of winning. Even then, its chances of winning a conviction would be very slight given the elusiveness of agreement among experts about economic effects, and the difficulties of establishing "beyond a reasonable doubt" any particular impact on public or social welfare.

The Crown did not appeal either the *Breweries* or the *Sugar* cases. The failure to appeal the former is understandable because it to some degree turned on the regulation to which the beer industry was subjected. Failure to appeal the *B.C. Sugar* case is less easily explained, and was undoubtedly a more serious act of omission. It let stand a decision which made neither good economic nor legal sense. As a result no further cases were brought during the merger wave of the 1960s, presumably because the type of evidence demanded in the *B.C. Sugar* case was, understandably, lacking.[17] When, finally, the opportunity presented itself, so much time had elapsed that the principles of the *B.C Sugar* decision

---

17. For example, in 1960, the Department of Justice declined to prosecute Canada Packers which, in 1955, had acquired the fourth and tenth largest packing firms, even though the RTPC had recommended action be taken. Moreover, between 1960 and 1967 the RTPC published seven reports dealing with mergers, of which five brought no action, one resulted in a prosecution (ERCO—see above) and one resulted in a prohibition order. See G.B. Reschenthaler and W.T. Stanbury, "Benign Monopoly: Canadian Merger Policy and the K.C. Irving Case," *Canadian Business Law Journal* (August 1977) pp. 146-149.

had become accepted, and were employed by the Supreme Court in reversing the Crown's first trial court victory in a merger case.[18]

The three decisions in the *Irving* case (one at trial, two on appeal) illustrate well the pitfalls created by the *Breweries* and *Sugar* cases and the unsatisfactory language of the merger law. The facts of the case are these. K.C. Irving, a well-known industrialist, began in the 1950s to acquire newspapers in his home province of New Brunswick. By 1960, he had acquired control over four of the five English-language dailies in the province (two were in Moncton, two in St. John). In 1968, he completed the acquisition of the fifth (the Fredericton Gleaner), giving him a "monopoly," via merger, in the ownership of daily newspapers in New Brunswick. The Crown brought merger charges against K.C. Irving and the case went to trial in 1972. During the trial uncontradicted evidence was adduced that K.C. Irving (i) had given each newspaper complete editorial autonomy, and had never interfered in editorial policy; (ii) had invested heavily in improved plant and facilities of the newspapers, although he never received dividends from his investment; (iii) had made no attempt to block new entry into the newspaper field; and (iv) had made no attempt to restrict the circulation of the newspapers to specific areas. It was also argued by the defence that because the circulation area of four of the five newspapers was "local" the province of New Brunswick was not the relevant geographic market as the Crown insisted and the trial judge accepted.[19] Finally, it was noted that during the period of Irving ownership, circulation had not only increased but in some areas there was increased competition between English-language dailies.

In reaching his decision Robichaud, J. was influenced strongly by the judgement in the *Breweries* case. Like McRuer, he cited extensively the jurisprudence in conspiracy cases, and he related public detriment to the effect of the mergers on competition. He assumed that it was not necessary to consider economic advantages once there is "complete, virtual ownership." Since Robichaud, J. accepted that the relevant product and geographic markets were English language dailies in the province of New Brunswick respectively, Irving had a monopoly. This, according to the judge, was sufficient for conviction: "In my view, once a complete monopoly has been established, such as the evidence clearly discloses...detriment in Law, resulted."[20]

Irving appealed the conviction to the New Brunswick Court of Appeal which reversed the trial court judgement. Adopting the stance taken in the *B.C. Sugar Refining* decision, the Appeals Court decision rested heavily on the failure of

18. *R.v. K.C. Irving Ltd.* (1976) 25 CPR (2d) 223.
19. Only the St. John *Telegraph* was a "province-wide" newspaper, competing in the "North Shore" area with the Moncton *Times*, and elsewhere with the Fredericton *Gleaner*.
20. Robichaud, J. explicitly rejected the position taken by the judge in the *B.C. Sugar Refining* case, on the role of "public detriment."

the Crown to establish, and the trial judge to consider, "public detriment." It also questioned whether the mergers could have "lessened competition" if the dailies were not competing in the first place. In frustration, the Crown appealed to the Supreme Court of Canada, which, in 1976, rendered a unanimous decision, read by Chief Justice Laskin, dismissing the Crown's appeal, and holding for Irving. Agreeing with the New Brunswick Court of Appeals, the Supreme Court argued that no proof was shown of "detriment in fact." According to the Chief Justice:

> In light of the definition of "merger" in the present Combines Investigation Act it is impossible to say that acquisition of entire control over a business in a market area (as contrasted with acquisition of some control) must mean without more not only that competition therein was or was likely to be lessened but that by reason of such control the lessening or likely lessening is to the detriment or against the interest of the public. Even if the acquisition of entire control would be enough to support an inference of lessening or likely lessening of competition, that inference cannot be drawn here, in the face of evidence and the findings thereon by the trial judge and by the Court of Appeal that the pre-existing competition where it existed remained and was to some degree intensified by the takeover of the newspapers.

Thus, the Supreme Court's position is that since the law applies when "competition is lessened to the detriment of the public," the Crown must show not only that competition has been lessened, but that the lessening is detrimental to the public. In the *Irving* case the Supreme Court was even doubtful that there was any competition to be lessened. It also laid stress on the "good works" of K.C. Irving in supplying capital to the newspapers despite the long-term losses incurred by some of them. The Supreme Court decision explicitly laid to rest the simple analogy between "public detriment" and the "unduly" jurisprudence suggested by McRuer J. in the *Breweries* case. In doing so, the *Irving* decision appears to have enhanced the legal stature of the *B.C. Sugar Refining* case.[21] This is an unfortunate conclusion, because the *B.C. Sugar* decision

21. This position is reinforced by Laskin C.J.'s extensive reference to the *Morrey*(1957) case, which the Court in *B.C. Sugar* had heavily relied upon. The *Morrey* case, although it dealt with retail price fixing of gasoline, had wrestled with the meaning of "public detriment." The case had been brought under the section of the pre-1960 Combines Investigation Act dealing with combines which "lessen competition to the detriment of the public" rather than under the Criminal Code section with its long-established jurisprudence relating to the term "unduly." The British Columbia Appeals Court decision in *Morrey* made clear that "public detriment" must be shown in fact, and could not simply be inferred by references to the standards of undueness. Although the Supreme Court of Canada refused in 1957 to hear the *Morrey* case, Laskin C.J.'s decision would appear to enhance the legal standing of that case and the subsequent decisions, including *B.C. Sugar*, which relied upon it.

renders the Crown's position virtually impossible in merger cases under the existing law. The *Irving* case appears, then, to have hammered the last nail into the coffin of Canadian merger policy.[22]

The legal logic of the merger jurisprudence makes little economic sense. In effect, the Crown must show two bads (a lessening of competition *and* public detriment). One would have thought one "bad" was enough, that if there were a substantial lessening of competition, even though there was no *other* public detriment (or public benefit), that the merger would be deemed contrary to Canadian law and policy. In the *Irving* case the Supreme Court of Canada took a more extreme position and required that the Crown prove that there were two "bads"—one would not be enough. A more sensible approach, in my view, would have pitted a substantial lessening of competition (a "bad") against one or more "good" effects—say achievement of economies of scale or even the kinds of contributions that it is alleged K.C. Irving made to the modernization and survival of the newspapers he acquired. Operationally, this would place an onus on the Crown to prove that the merger substantially lessened competition, with a *prima facie* presumption of public detriment. The defendants would then be given the opportunity to rebut this presumption by providing evidence of offsetting "good" effects or public "benefits."

It is hard to escape the conclusion that the current legal treatment of mergers in Canada is basically unsound. In large part the difficulty is attributable to the criminal basis of the anticombines laws. Criminal law is particularly unsuited to merger cases because (a) the rules of evidence, (b) the requirement of proving beyond reasonable doubt, and (c) the implication of wrong doing, are simply inappropriate to the evaluation of the impact of mergers. Beyond this constitutional saddling with criminal law, difficulties are compounded by the requirement that both lessened competition and public detriment be found, as if the former did not imply the latter. What is overlooked entirely is the role a merger law should play: to prevent leading firms from further enhancing their market shares (and presumably their market power) the easy way—by acquiring competitors, suppliers or distributors. Nevertheless, it is important to keep in mind that Canada can less afford the luxury of condemning, as the United States very nearly has done, all market power-increasing mergers.[23] Canada's small

22. After the *Irving* case the Crown's decision to bring charges of merger and monopoly, as well as conspiracy, against the Southam and Thomson newspaper interests was an exercise in futility. The case was prompted by the closure, on the same day in 1980, of Thomson's Ottawa *Journal* and Southam's Winnipeg *Tribune*, and the sale to Southam of the Montreal *Star* (which it promptly closed) and the Vancouver *Sun*. The defendants were acquitted on all charges, in December 1983, and the Crown decided not to appeal the decision.

23. In 1982, the Antitrust Division of the U.S. Justice Department promulgated a new set of merger guidelines, raising the market power thresholds the antitrust authorities are willing to tolerate before bringing a case. The merger guidelines, whose unique features are the use of the Herfindahl index (see chapter 2) to set thresholds and the manner of defining the relevant market,

domestic market and the possibilities of achieving substantial scale economies via merger and plant specialization suggest there may be potential benefits to offset the costs of reduced competition due to merger. What is needed is some framework within which the benefits *and* the costs of mergers can be weighed, such as that suggested by Williamson (see chapter 4), and incorporated into recent competition policy reform proposals.[24]

D. Price Discrimination, and Predatory Pricing

Canadian Combines law includes sections applicable to price discrimination (sections 34(1) (a) and 34(1) (b)) and predatory pricing (34(1) (c)). Very few combines cases have been brought under section 34, although two recent cases dealing with alleged predatory pricing may indicate a new trend in enforcement. What is perhaps most surprising is that the subsection (34(1) (a)) dealing most specifically with price discrimination, has received very little application, a fact which is more easily explained after a study of its wording, to which we now turn.

(i) Price Discrimination

The law on price discrimination reads as follows:

> 34. (1) Everyone engaged in a business who:
>
> > (a) is a party to, or assists in, any sale that discriminates to his knowledge, directly or indirectly, against competitors of a purchaser of articles from him in that any discount, rebate, allowance, price concession or other advantage is granted to the purchaser over and above...that [which], at the time the articles are sold to such purchaser, is available to such competitors in respect of a sale of articles of like quality and quantity;
> >
> > (b) engages in a policy of selling products in any area of Canada at prices lower than those exacted by him elsewhere in Canada, having the effect or tendency of substantially lessening competition or eliminating a competitor in such part of Canada, or designed to have such effect;
>
> is guilty of an indictable offence and is liable to imprisonment for two years.

Section 34 (a) was supposed to prevent large distributors from securing price

are thoroughly analyzed by leading antitrust experts in a series of papers appearing in the *California Law Review*, 71 (March 1983). See especially Baker and Blumenthal, "The 1982 Guidelines and Preexisting Law," *infra* pp. 311-347.

24. However, for a skeptical view on the application of an efficiencies defence, see Alan A. Fisher and Robert H. Lande, "Efficiency Considerations in Merger Enforcement," *California Law Review*, 71 (September 1983), pp. 1582-1696.

advantages not available to their (presumably) smaller competitors. However, as the last four words of paragraph 34 (a) indicate, the section only applies where sales involve articles of "like quality and quantity." Since the law can be easily escaped by varying quantity or quality, the section is effectively unusable. It would not apply, for instance, to "big buyer" discounts even if not cost justified. Also note that the section applies to price discrimination as a "practice" and clearly does not apply to meeting competition on the spot.

Section 34 (b) applies to suppliers who use their geographic extent to tame local competitors in one market while maintaining higher prices in other locations where competition is less vigorous. It was this section that was applied in the *Carnation* case, the subject of one of the chapter 5 vignettes.

The only action under section 34 (a) followed an RTPC report into the pricing practices of Miss Mary Maxim Ltd., a manufacturer of knitting wool and patterns.[25] According to the RTPC report, Miss Mary Maxim gave discounts and rebates to some dealers and retailers and not to others, without any evidence that the distinction was based on differences in quantities purchased.[26] However, its discount on very large sales made to Eaton's, the department store chain, did not contravene the law.

The leading, and only contested, price discrimination case in Canada is the *Carnation* case. It will be recalled that Carnation had unexpectedly reduced its price on evaporated milk sold in Alberta and B.C. to "tame" the competition it was receiving from its local competitors, Alpha and Pacific. The Crown brought charges against Carnation for violating section 34 (b) of the Combines Investigation Act (see above), charges which were dismissed by the trial judge. The Crown's Appeal to the Alberta Supreme Court was rejected in a 2-1 decision.[27] The majority argued that the Crown had failed to prove that Carnation's price reductions in Alberta and B.C. were *intended* to "substantially lessen competition" rather than to meet competition. The Court appeared to give little consideration to the likelihood that while Carnation's price reductions might plausibly have been made simply to meet competition, its conditions (that Alpha

25. Restrictive Trade Practices Commission, *Pricing Practices of Miss Mary Maxim Ltd.*, RTPC No. 38, Ottawa, 1966. Other reports also examined the issue of price discrimination, but did not lead to legal action. See Canada, Dept. of Justice, *Discriminatory Pricing Policies in the Grocery Trade*, Ottawa, Queen's Printer, 1958; and three RTPC reports *Concerning The Distribution and Sale of Gasoline in the Toronto Area* (Alleged Price Discrimination by Texaco Canada Ltd., British American Oil Co. Ltd., Supertest Petroleum Corp. Ltd.) Ottawa, 1961.
26. A prohibition order under section 31(2) of the Combines Investigation Act was sought and granted.
27. The *Carnation* case contrasts vividly with the U.S. Supreme Court's decision in the *Utah Pie v. Continental Baking Co. et al.* case (386 U.S. 685 (1967)). In *Utah Pie*, the Court found the defendant firms, Pet, Carnation, and Continental Baking Co., had violated the price discrimination law and the Sherman Act by meeting and beating Utah Pie's low prices in the Salt Lake City area, and were thereby vulnerable to the treble damage suits brought against them by Utah Pie.

and Pacific end their competitive tactics—see chapter 5) for restoring prices indicated an attempt to stifle competition.

Before one condemns Canada's price discrimination law because of its ineffectiveness, it is worth considering whether an "effective" law would serve the goal of competition policy. Those who are familiar with the U.S. price discrimination law, the Robinson-Patman Act, and the literally thousands of investigations and cases which have arisen under it, will appreciate why it is perhaps desirable that section 34 (a) of our Combines Act is inoperative. To make it effective by deleting the words "like quality and quantity" opens the door to a possible flood of cases of a "cops and robbers" variety, with consequences more likely to stifle than promote competition. As we noted in chapter 5 (page 182) price discrimination is usually innocuous and in some cases beneficial when it promotes competition. When price discrimination serves a predatory purpose it should be attacked as monopolization (see below). When it takes the form of artificially separated markets (as in the farm machinery case described in chapter 5) it should be dealt with by attacking the sources of monopoly power or the artificial barriers to the free movement of goods and services.

(ii) Predatory Pricing

Section 34(1) c of the Combines Act deals specifically with predatory pricing. It reads:

> 34(1) Everyone engaged in a business who:
>> (c) engages in a policy of selling products at prices unrea- sonably low, having the effect or tendency of substan- tially lessening competition or eliminating a competitor, or designed to have such effect,
> is guilty of an indictable offense and is liable to imprisonment for two years.

In applying the law the courts must distinguish a "policy" of attempting to eliminate a competitor from temporarily low prices, or even giveaways, under- taken for promotional reasons. What is an "unreasonably low" price is left to the courts to decide, with no little advice from economists as to whether it implies price below average cost, marginal cost, or average variable cost. An "unreasonably low" price need not *actually* eliminate a competitor, or "sub- stantially lessen competition," in order for there to be a violation of the law. The Crown will succeed, if it can prove that the "unreasonably low" price was *intended* to have these effects.

Until recently, section 34(1) (c) had been used only once in an anticombines prosecution.[28] Why this is the case is a matter of conjecture. Part of the

---

28. The first application of what was then section 33a(1)c was in *R.v. Producers Dairy Ltd.* (1966, 50 C.P.R. (2d) 265). Producers Dairy was acquitted of charges that its reduction in prices to meet a small competitors' promotional price cut was predatory.

explanation probably lies in the fact that predatory price cutting may be viewed as "monopolization" and can be dealt with under section 33 (as was the case with *Eddy Match*), although this route may now be less reliable as a result of the blow dealt to monopoly and merger law by the *Irving* decision (see above). There was also at least one earlier missed opportunity for applying 34(1) (c). In that case, the Justice Department declined to follow up on a recommendation by the RTPC that the conduct of Zinc Oxide of Canada (ZOCO) be attacked. ZOCO had secured deep discounts from Hudson Bay Mining and Smelting in the mid 1950s and used them to launch a price war against ZOCO's zinc oxide producing competitors, with the ultimate aim of acquiring them via merger and gaining a monopoly position.[29] But the section could also be misapplied. In *The Allied Chemical* case, referred to above, had Cominco entered into direct competition with Allied in the sale of sulphuric acid, and if by doing so it had driven Allied out of business, Cominco might have been subjected (unreasonably) to charges of predatory pricing, as the trial judge in the case noted.

Finally, in the mid-1970s the anticombines authorities brought their second case under section 34(1) c. It was against the leading pharmaceutical firm, Hoffmann-Laroche, for selling the tranquilizer Valium at "unreasonably low" prices, allegedly for the purpose of driving its major rival, Horner, out of the lucrative tranquilizer market. During one six-month period, ultimately extended to a year, Hoffmann-LaRoche simply gave away Valium free to hospitals. Although Horner withdrew temporarily from the hospital market, it survived the Hoffman-LaRoche onslaught, experiencing large profit margins on non-hospital sales of its competing tranquilizer, Vivol. In a pathbreaking judgement, Linden J. of the Supreme Court of Ontario found Hoffmann-LaRoche guilty. The grounds for a guilty verdict were that the giveaway policy to hospitals was designed to eliminate the pesky competitor, Horner, and was not simply a promotional effort aimed at maximizing long-run profits. One indication of intent was the length of time Hoffmann-LaRoche was prepared to supply free all of the Valium Canadian hospitals needed. Moreover, the prosecution was able to provide written documentation from which intent could be inferred.[30] On appeal the trial court judgement was upheld.

---

29. See RTPC *Report Concerning Production and Distribution of Zinc Oxide* (1958). In its report the RTPC attacked ZOCO's conduct, but it did not seek a structural remedy (dissolution) to reduce ZOCO's 85 percent market share, partially achieved by merger. It recommended court orders to restrain discriminatory pricing and suggested consideration of reducing customs duties which had limited imports of zinc oxide to 11 percent of the Canadian market. The case was closed in 1959 after the Justice Department inexplicably decided not to prosecute.

30. Another piece of evidence of intent cited by the judge was that Hoffmann-LaRoche "was prepared to lose, and did lose, $2,600,000 in sales to prevent a forecasted loss of $600,000 in sales to Horner in that year." *R.v. Hoffmann-LaRoche Limited* (1980) 28 O.R. (2d) 164 at p. 210. Interestingly it is hard to find a victim in this case. Horner, although it withdrew from the hospital market for tranquilizers, remained a viable and highly competitive (in other pharmaceutical lines and markets) firm.

The *Hoffmann-LaRoche* case was a major and much-needed triumph for the Crown, following as it did on the disastrous decisions in *Irving*, *Aetna*, and *Atlantic Sugar*. In addition, the judgement helped settle some issues about the application of section 34c. In particular, the judge gave a good deal of attention to what is an "unreasonably low" price. He rejected the idea that any price below cost was unreasonable, arguing that the Court must consider all the circumstances involved in the case. He also distinguished between offensive and defensive price cutting, with the latter unlikely to sustain a charge of predatory design. Moreover, if a firm makes sales below cost to stay alive, the (low) price would be presumptively reasonable, a factor that played a role in the only other section 34 c case to reach the courts.

Flushed with its success in *Hoffmann-LaRoche*, the anticombines division brought charges of predatory pricing against Portion Packaging, a division of Consumers Glass Co., for allegedly attempting to drive its only domestic competitor, Amhil, from the plastic (coffee-cup and other container) lid market.[31] (See the vignette describing the behaviour of Portion and Amhil in chapter 5.) This time the Crown did not succeed. The judge, indicating a good deal more economic sophistication than Canadian judges are usually given credit for, saw through the prosecution's argument. Since high costs and large-scale imports left Portion with no market power, its price cutting in the face of Amhil's entry into the market was easily explicable as an attempt to minimize losses—hardly an offense under the combines act. The acquittal of Portion is likely to dampen but not terminate interest in the application of Canada's predatory pricing law—the "sleeping giant" of Canadian anticombines legislation.[32]

The *Hoffmann-LaRoche* and *Portion Packaging* cases illustrate some of the difficulties in detecting when a price cut or a "low" price is "unreasonable" or "predatory." A zero price on "sales" of a drug to hospitals might be aimed at eliminating a competitor or it might be an excellent form of promotion. The latter is quite plausible since there is a high likelihood that the drug will subsequently be prescribed by doctors, thereby stimulating sales in the retail market where demand is highly inelastic and price cost margins high. A cut in price below one's own and one's competitors' costs in the face of new entry may be evidence of predatory intent or it may be the only rational response when a

31. *Regina v. Consumers Glass Co. Ltd., et al.* (1982) 33 O.R. (2d) 228.
32. It will be interesting to see if the Crown proceeds to Court following the massive investigation of the petroleum industry by the Bureau of Competition Policy and the lengthy hearings on the Bureau's report before the RTPC. At issue is the behaviour, particularly at the marketing level, of the fully integrated petroleum firms. One of the main charges is that the industry leaders such as Imperial Oil, Texaco, and Shell engaged in exclusive and predatory conduct toward their non-integrated rivals—the independent refiners and distributors. See Director of Investigation and Research, *The State of Competition in the Petroleum Industry*, 7 volumes (Ottawa: Supply and Services Canada, 1981), especially volume 6 on Marketing.

market becomes "overcrowded" with each firm holding substantial excess capacity, experiencing high unit cost, and incurring losses. Or to take still another example, suppose a dominant firm which had been setting a monopoly price suddenly slashes its price in the face of new entry. Can we infer predatory behaviour? The answer is no. The dominant firm may simply be reacting to a change from monopolistic to competitive market conditions, due perhaps to the expiration of patent protection or loss of exclusive control over a specialized resource. Even if the dominant firm's price cut forces the entrant out of the market (e.g. the dominant firm's costs may be somewhat lower than those of the entrant), the former may no longer be able to set monopoly prices without quickly attracting entry. In this case, despite the elimination of its competitor, the dominant firm no longer has the market power (the ability to raise price without incurring entry) which is requisite to making any charge of "predatory pricing" credible.[33]

There does not seem to be any simple rule for detecting a predatory price. One rule, which has received much comment and some application in U.S. courts, is that a price below short-run marginal cost (SMC) is both a necessary and sufficient condition for predatory pricing. This rule has become known as the Areeda-Turner rule, after the two Harvard University law professors who framed it in a widely read law review article about a decade ago.[34] Unfortunately, the Areeda-Turner rule is not without its ambiguities even if the more easily calculable average variable cost (AVC) is substituted for SMC. As Figure 9-1 indicates, it is possible for P<SMC even though price is greater than average cost (see point α)—surely no basis for a charge of predatory pricing. It is also possible that P>SMC, while P<AVC (see point β)—a clear indication of predatory intent if not irrational behaviour.[35] In fairness to Areeda and Turner these two objections can perhaps be dismissed on the grounds that no profit-maximizing firms would set the price-quantity combinations represented by α and β in Figure 9-1.[36] Still, the logical possibilities do suggest that a rigid rule for defining predatory pricing may be counterproductive. Moreover, the two

33. For an important statement on this issue, see F.M. Fisher, "Diagnosing Monopoly." *Quarterly Review of Economics and Business*, 19 no.2 (1979), pp. 7-33.

34. Phillip Areeda and Donald Turner, "Predatory Pricing and Related Practices under Section 2 of the Sherman Act," 88 *Harvard Law Review* 697 (1975). For a good analysis of U.S. predatory pricing cases in which the Areeda-Turner rule has been applied, see Joel B. Dirlam, "Marginal Cost Pricing Tests for Predation: Naive Welfare Economics and Public Policy," *The Antitrust Bulletin*, 26 no. 4 (Winter 1981), pp. 769-814.

35. F.M. Scherer, "Predatory Pricing and the Sherman Act: A Comment," 89 *Harvard Law Review* 869 (1976).

36. Williamson has objected to the Areeda-Turner rule on the grounds that it is not necessary for P<SMC in order for a dominant firm to "predaciously" deter entry by an equally low cost firm. By holding excess capacity and then using that capacity by slashing prices to marginal cost levels in the face of new entry, a dominant firm can assure there is no room for profitable entry. This possibility is illustrated in Figure 3-2. See O.E. Williamson, "Predatory Pricing: A Strategic and Welfare Analysis," 87 *Yale Law Journal* 284 (1977).

Figure 9-1

Ambiguity of Cost-Based Rules for Predatory Pricing

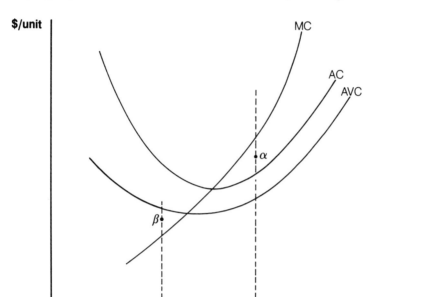

Canadian predatory pricing decisions to date suggest that a rigid rule is no substitute for judicial wisdom and common sense.[37]

E. Vertical Restrictions: Resale Price Maintenance and Restrictive Trade Practices

Two sections of the Canadian anticombines law deal explicitly with vertical, supplier-distributor, restrictions. Section 38, the resale price maintenance (RPM) law, prohibits a manufacturer from dictating a minimum resale price to retailers, or from refusing to deal with retailers who are not willing to set prices at the levels "suggested" by the manufacturer. The RPM law has been used often, particularly in recent years, and with a high degree of success. Section 31.4 applies to supplier-initiated contracts that limit a dealer's or distributor's freedom to purchase goods from other suppliers. These sections give the Restrictive Trade Practices Commission the power to prohibit agreements such

---

37. An excellent analysis of predatory pricing cases in Canada and how their decisions fit the various rules devised by economists to detect predatory pricing is D.G. McFetridge and S. Wong, "Predatory Pricing in Canada: The Law and the Economics," Number WSV1-17, Carleton University, 1984 (mimeo).

as exclusive dealing and tying contracts where they have a tendency to substantially lessen competition.[38] Since section 31 has only been in existence since 1976, its application to date has been limited. Moreover, its civil law character makes it sufficiently debatable on constitutional grounds that when the first case under the section reaches the Supreme Court, the chief issue will be whether the section is *ultra vires* the BNA Act.

(i) Resale Price Maintenance

The law on RPM reads in part as follows.

38 (1) No person who is engaged in the business of producing or supplying a product...shall directly or indirectly

(a) by agreement, threat, promise or any like means, attempt to influence upward, or to discourage the reduction of, the price at which any other person engaged in business in Canada supplies or offers to supply or advertises a product within Canada; or

(b) refuse to supply a product to or otherwise discriminate against any other person engaged in business in Canada because of the low pricing policy of that other person. . . .

(4) For the purposes of this section, the publication by a supplier of a product, other than a retailer, of an advertisement that mentions a retail price for the product is an attempt to influence upward the selling price to any person into whose hands the product comes for resale unless the price is so expressed as to make it clear to any person to whose attention the advertisement comes that the product may be sold at a lower price. . . .

(9) Where, in a prosecution under paragraph (1) (b), it is proved that the person charged refused or counselled the refusal to supply a product to any other person, no inference unfavourable to the person charged shall be drawn from such evidence if he satisfies the court that he and any one upon whose report he depended had reasonable cause to believe and did believe

(a) that the other person was making a practice of using products supplied by the person charged as loss-

---

38. Exclusive dealing contracts are ones in which a supplier stipulates to a distributor that supplies are conditional on the distributor dealing exclusively with the supplier. It is a widespread practice in the retail gasoline industry, and often occurs in the distribution of electrical appliances, farm machinery, and the like. Tying contracts are those whereby a supplier makes as a condition for supplying one product (the "tying" product) the requirement that customers purchase some other product (the tied product). Examples from the past include tying tin cans to the lease of can-closing machinery, *IBM* cards to *IBM* machines, grade D movies to first line movies, etc.

leaders, that is to say, not for the purpose of making a
profit thereon but for purposes of advertising;

Section 38 prohibits RPM essentially because it is a technique for "vertical"
price fixing, although it allows a supplier to withhold supplies (refuse to deal) if
he has good reason to believe his products are being used as "loss leaders."
When the RPM prohibition was first introduced in 1952 it did not include a loss
leader provision. However, the most popular defence of the RPM practice has
been that it prevents the alleged loss of "good will" and product credibility
associated with having one's product presented at low (below invoice cost)
prices by retailers seeking to attract customers to their outlets. Thus, in 1960,
the loss leader defence was added as a concession to business interests.

The leading cases under the RPM section are the *Moffat* (1957), *Sunbeam*
(1967), *Coutts* (1968), and *Phillips Electronics* (1981) cases.[39] Together they
give a reasonably good idea of the parameters of the law on RPM. The *Moffat*
case involved the use of a cooperative advertising plan to induce dealers to
advertise at prices at or above those stipulated by the supplier. Moffatt, a
manufacturer of electrical household appliances, principally stoves, refrigerators and television sets, was charged with attempting to maintain the retail prices
of its refrigerators by paying 50 percent of dealer advertising costs, on the
proviso that prices in the advertisement were not below levels fixed by Moffatt.
Beyond the inducement to maintain advertised prices, Moffatt apparently made
no other attempt to control resale prices, nor was it unusual for dealers to make
occasional sales at prices below those advertised. However, since RPM is
prohibited outright, or at least was between 1952 and 1960, Moffatt was found
guilty. Moffatt's appeal that the Crown had failed to show *intent* to control resale
prices was rejected by the Ontario Court of Appeals on the ground that intent
was adequately indicated by the cooperative advertising agreement, and that
such agreements fall within the prohibition of the RPM section of the anticombines law.

The *Sunbeam* case was essentially a test of the "loss leader" amendment,
introduced in 1960 into the section on RPM. Shortly after the amendment was
enacted Sunbeam established a "minimum profitable resale price plan" (MPRP)
designed to maintain retail prices on electric shavers. The MPRP was based on
alleged "cost" estimates made by Sunbeam of the "average operating costs" of
retailers to whom it sold.[40] It then established resale prices which would cover
costs plus a "reasonable profit." This information was sent to retailers along

---

39. *R.v. Moffat Limited* (1957) 25 C.R. 201; *R.v. Sunbeam* (1967) 1 O.R. 661 (Ont. C.A); *R.v.
William E. Coutts Co. Ltd.* (1968), 67 D.L.R. (2d) 87; 1 OR 549; *R.v. Phillips Electronics*
(1981), 30 O.R. (2d) 139.
40. Actually, no evidence was presented at trial as to the operating costs of retailers of Sunbeam's
appliances, nor would such estimates be credible if presented, given the insoluble problem of
allocating overhead expenses.

with a statement that lower prices would be considered "lossleadering" which could lead to a cutoff of supplies. Salesmen were then sent into the field to persuade dealers to adhere to the prices stipulated in the MPRP. Sunbeam was thereupon charged with violating the RPM prohibition. The defendant argued that it was simply attempting to prevent the loss-leadering of its shavers. Whatever the merits of the loss-leader allegation (there was no indication that, in fact, shavers were being "loss leadered"), the Court made clear that the loss leader amendment only comes into force after the product is loss leadered, at which point the supplier can "refuse to deal." The loss leader proviso does not apply to intimations of refusal to deal if resale price is below a stipulated level.

The applicability of the loss leader amendment is illustrated by the *Coutts* case. Coutts, a manufacturer of greeting cards, refused to supply a Halifax retailer after reading advertisements that the retailer was offering two cards at the price of one plus 1¢ (a "one cent sale"). Although the one-cent sale lasted only one week as part of the Halifax's retailer's grand opening, Coutts was acquitted of charges of attempted RPM.[41] The judge regarded the one cent sale a "practice" and Coutts' refusal to deal as based on good evidence available to the supplier that the average receipt per card was below invoice cost plus freight charges.

In 1976, the RPM law was amended to make it more difficult for a suggested retail price to become a minimum resale price. In order to deal with the possibility that an advertised price would be viewed as a minimum (and for that matter too, a maximum) resale price, section (4) was added. That section seems to indicate that a firm mentioning a resale price in its advertisement must also indicate that the product could be sold at a lower price. This interpretation was tested in the *Phillips Electronics* case which was not finally settled until the Supreme Court of Canada upheld, in 1982, two lower court verdicts of acquittal. The basic facts of the case were that Phillips Electronics in advertising television converters specified a resale price without making reference to the possibility that the product could be sold at a lower price. On these grounds the Crown brought charges of a violation of the amended RPM law. The case revolved around the meaning of the words "like means" in section 38(1) (a). A majority of the Ontario Court of Appeals ruled that an advertised price, in the absence of any evidence of an attempt via agreement, threat, or promise, to maintain that price, did not violate the law. The Court of Appeals rejected the idea that the simple failure to indicate any other price in the advertisement was "like means." Since the Crown conceded there was no evidence of an agreement, threat or promise (which distinguishes this case from the *Moffats* case) Phillips Electronics was acquitted.[42]

41. Coutts, however, was convicted on other counts of attempted RPM in Toronto.
42. *R.v. Phillips Electronics* (1981) 30 O.R. (2d) 139.

Before concluding our discussion of the jurisprudence relating to Canada's RPM law, the *H.D. Lee* (1981) case is worth noting.[43] This was an easy victory for the Crown. There was abundant evidence that H.D. Lee had refused to supply Lee jeans to Army and Navy Department stores because those stores persisted in reselling the jeans at a price lower than that specified by Lee. This, of course, is a clear cut violation of the law. What makes the case noteworthy is that Lee made an argument in its defence that has received increasing sympathy from antitrust economists, particularly in the United States where the RPM law has come under more criticism than it has here. Essentially, the argument is that a supplier-manufacturer may have a perfectly legitimate motive in specifying a minimum retail price if the product sold requires a certain amount of "point of sale service." In the absence of a minimum resale price, so the argument runs, customers could go into the higher-priced store, receive services in the form of knowledge about the product, and then, once that knowledge is acquired, go across the street and purchase the product from a discounter.[44] RPM is viewed as a welfare-enhancing method to eliminate this free rider problem. Thus, it is argued by some economists that RPM, where initiated by producers rather than a dealer cartel, should be viewed as part of an overall efficient system of distribution and should be presumed legal.[45] This kind of argument has contributed to an attempt by the U.S. Justice Department to relax the application of the RPM law in the U.S.A. In Canada, however persuasive this argument might be in economic terms, it cuts no legal ice, for here we have for all intents and purposes a *per se* rule against RPM.

In sum, the RPM law is a "success story." Canada was among the first countries to prohibit resale price maintenance, and although the law was watered down somewhat in 1960 by the "loss leader" amendment, it remains a relatively effective part of our anticombines statutes.

(ii) Restrictive Trade Practices

The addition, in 1976, of a civil law section (31) prohibiting certain trade practices and giving injured parties the right to sue for damages, reflects a maturing of combines policy in Canada, although the section is still constitutionally in doubt. The two most important practices covered by section 31 are

43. *Regina v. H.D. Lee of Canada Ltd.* (1981) 57 C.P.R. (2d) 186.

44. See, for example, Richard Posner, *Antitrust Law and Economic Perspective*, University of Chicago Press, 1976, chap. 6. The point of sales service argument was first made by L. Telser, "Why Should Manufacturers Want Fair Trade?" *Journal of Law and Economics*, 3 (1960), pp. 86-105.

45. For a rigorous presentation of this argument, see G. F. Mathewson and R. A. Winter, "An Economic Theory of Vertical Restraints," *Rand Journal of Economics* 1, no. 1 (1984). Mathewson and Winter apply their analysis to the Canadian scene and list 77 cases in which there were convictions for RPM and fines imposed in Canada through September 1983. "Competition Policy and the Nature of Vertical Exchange," University of Toronto (mimeo).

exclusive dealing and tied selling. Exclusive dealing involves an arrangement between a supplier and distributor-customer whereby the latter will only receive supplies of a product if it deals exclusively with the former. Tied selling is a practice whereby a supplier makes a condition of supply of a particular product that the distributor-customer also buy some other product from the supplier. Under section 31 the Director of Investigation and Research of the combines branch may apply to the Restrictive Trade Practices Commission (RTPC) for an order prohibiting exclusive dealing and tied selling. When such an application is made, the RTPC, after hearing both parties, may issue a prohibition order:

> 31.4(2) where...the Commission finds that exclusive dealing or tied selling, because it is engaged in by a major supplier of a product in a market or because it is widespread in a market, is likely to
> (a) impede entry into or expansion of a firm in the market,
> (b) impede introduction of a product into or expansion of sales of a product in the market or,
> (c) have any other exclusionary effect in the market, with the result that competition is or is likely to be lessened substantially....

Essentially section 31.4(2) allows the RTPC to order an end to exclusive dealing or tied selling where it is engaged in by a "major supplier" and has sufficient exclusionary effect that it lessens or is likely to lessen competition substantially.

To date, two cases have been heard before the Restrictive Trade Practices Commission involving alleged violations of section 31.4(2). One case dealt with exclusive dealing, the other with tied selling. In *Director of Investigation and Research v. Bombardier Ltd.* (1980), the RTPC ruled that Bombardier's policy of exclusive dealing did not substantially lessen competition. Bombardier, with 30 percent of North American and 50 percent of Eastern Canadian sales of snowmobiles in the early 1970s, was clearly a "major supplier" of snowmobiles and snowmobile accessories. In applying for a prohibition order the Director of the Combines branch argued that Bombardier's exclusive dealing agreements with local distributors helped maintain its dominant position in the market. Although there are no Canadian tariffs on snowmobiles, foreign competitors of Bombardier, particularly the Japanese firms Yamaha and Kawasaki, allegedly found entry into certain local markets difficult. Bombardier, it was argued, had tied to itself through the exclusive dealing agreements, the only, or most successful, enterpreneurs in many locales. Thus it often took some time for Bombardier's competitors to find and establish their own dealerships. The RTPC sensibly ruled, however, that since (a) entry into retailing is easy; (b) dealer turnover is substantial; (c) Bombardier's competitors usually did find dealers and their market share had been rising, that therefore Bombardier's exclusive dealing arrangements had not nor were likely to substantially lessen competition.[46]

The other restrictive practices case heard by the RTPC involved a tying arrangement. In *Director of Investigation and Research v. BBM Bureau of Measurement* (1981), the RTPC ruled that BBM's pricing scheme effectively tied the purchase of its radio audience data to the purchase of its television audience data. The tying arrangement was facilitated by a pricing policy in which purchasers of either radio *or* television audience data paid a relatively high basic price while purchasers of both paid only a marginal amount more than the price for one type of audience data.[47] As the sole supplier of local and national radio audience data, BBM was in a strong competitive position in the supply of television audience data to advertisers and other purchasers who needed both types of data. Not surprisingly, BBM held 85% of the Canadian market for television audience data in addition to 100% of the market for radio audience data. This clearly made BBM a "major supplier" of audience data. Thus the case revolved around the impact BBM's pricing policies had on competition. The Director of Investigation rejected BBM's argument that the structure of the price schedule was justified in terms of the fixed costs of operation. The Director argued that the effect of the price schedule was to prevent the expansion of BBM's only competitor in the supply of television audience data, thereby substantially lessening competition. The RTPC agreed. It issued an extensive prohibition order restraining BBM's pricing policies. BBM's initial appeal was rejected. It did not appeal further, so section 31.4 has yet to be constitutionally tested before the Supreme Court of Canada.

In sum, the current legislation dealing with non-price vertical agreements such as tying and exclusive dealing contracts properly uses a civil law approach and focuses on the use of these instruments by a major supplier. Restrictive practices are typically not harmful unless engaged in by firms with real economic power. Where restrictive practices clearly enhance market power and lessen competition substantially then the law should be applied.[48] The two cases decided, to date, under section 31.4(2) reflect a reasonably wise application of the law. However, the sections can only be applied appropriately if the test of substantiality is a tough and rigorous one and not a matter of rhetoric.

46. However, Professor Gideon Rosenbluth, an expert witness, pointed out that the refusal of Bombardier to allow its dealers to "dual" (i.e. to distribute more than one brand of snowmobile) may well have generated resource waste since, in the typical case, the turnover of a local distributorship was quite low—less than 20 units per year.

47. For example, advertisers with more than $25 000 000 of broadcast billings would pay $17 785 for either radio audience data *or* television audience data. If it bought both the total charge was $18 460 or only $675 more for the second type of audience data.

48. Some economists view all vertical restraints, if initiated by suppliers, as "efficient," and therefore to be presumed legal. For an analysis, see Mathewson and Winter, *supra* note 45.

Proposals for Reform

Our survey of Canadian anticombines law and jurisprudence highlights some of the difficulties with existing "competition policy." Two shortcomings are salient: (1) the wording of the legislation itself has produced lengthy, burdensome and sometimes contradictory judicial opinions which (2) typically skirt, or ignore altogether, important economic facets of the cases at issue. The result is that Canadian competition policy is neither effective nor logically sound. After 95 years Canadian combines law is almost rudderless, lacking a sense of purpose, except, perhaps, with respect to conspiracies under section 32(1) (and its Criminal Code predecessors) where the judicially declared aim is to protect the public interest in competition. But this objective can hardly be said to apply to other sections of the current law, particularly in the area of merger and monopoly. Nor do the opinions adequately reflect the peculiar facets of Canadian market structure which may limit, in some cases, the scope for the coexistence of both competition and economic efficiency.[49]

Three factors have contributed to the present weakness:

(1) The words "unduly" and "public detriment" are a continuing source of confusion and have tended to produce narrow constructions of the legal application of the Combines Investigation Act to horizontal agreements, monopoly and merger.

(2) The total reliance (until 1976) on criminal prohibitions (reflecting, in part, the narrow judicial interpretations of the commerce clause in the B.N.A. Act) is neither economically nor legally appropriate. Except perhaps in the case of conspiracies, clearcut predatory conduct, resale price maintenance, and misleading advertising, criminal law is both legally and economically restrictive. The Crown is forced to prove something "beyond reasonable doubt" which will almost always be in some doubt. Businessmen are treated as criminals in cases where reasonable men can disagree about appropriate behaviour. The criminal law leaves no scope for prohibiting certain activities not in the public interest without first finding the defendant guilty of a criminal act. Undertakings which in some cases are socially beneficial, and sometimes not, cannot be fairly or efficiently distinguished in a criminal setting.

(3) Political timidity, reinforced by pressure group opposition, has been a major stumbling block in the past to sensible and realistic changes in the anticombines laws. Although the Combines Investigation Act has undergone

---

49. For an early analysis of the shortcomings of Canada's competition policy see Irving Brecher, "Combines and Competition: A Reappraisal of Canadian Public Policy," *Canadian Bar Review* 38, no. 4 (December 1960). Two decades later, Brecher returned to his earlier theme in *Canada's Competition Policy Revisited: Some New Thoughts on an Old Story* (Montreal: Institute for Research on Public Policy, 1982).

faceliftings several times (1923, 1935, 1952, 1960, 1976) the main effect has been to make the Act more lengthy (the 1976 Office Consolidation which includes both the English and French versions runs to 63 pages) rather than to simplify and clarify. After 75 years the words "unduly" and "public detriment" remain. Their continuing importance is reflected in the fact that in 1976 (i) the Act was amended to clarify "unduly" by way of what it does not mean; and (ii) the Supreme Court announced its decision in the *Irving* merger case indicating that monopoly gained via merger is not itself a source of public detriment. Canada's protectionist spirit dating from the 19th century seems to carry over into the field of combines law. The fact that high tariffs make all the more important a domestic competition policy is acknowledged in principle and disregarded in fact. Even the sensible remedy of selectively reducing tariffs to correct a monopolistic problem, although legally available (section 28 of the Act), is rarely threatened and never applied. One imagines that the word "unduly" was thrust into the 1889 legislation just because the protectionist spirit made "too much" competition suspect. Combinations were acceptable so long as they did not become a total bar to competition. This mentality has not disappeared.

By the mid 1960s the need for a fundamental rethinking of competition policy was sufficiently evident to prompt the Liberal government of Lester Pearson to refer the issue of "combines, mergers, monopolies and restraint of trade" to the Economic Council of Canada (ECC) for study and recommendations for change. The immediate reason for the referral was the release, in 1962, of the so-called TBA (Tires, Batteries and Accessories) Report of the RTPC.[50] The TBA inquiry, which began in 1953, was concerned with the means used by the highly oligopolistic petroleum refining industry to tie their gasoline service station distributors to a full line of automotive products, either produced by them or by "favoured suppliers." The RTPC was chiefly concerned with the effect that exclusive dealing, tying, full line forcing, and directed buying contracts might have on the market access of independent suppliers of TBA. Unfortunately, there were no provisions in the Combines Investigation Act that could be used to prevent or arrest market foreclosure due to these restrictive practices. Thus the TBA report recommended that the Combines Act be amended to make these contracts offences if they were "likely to lessen competition substantially." Rather than simply amending the Combines Investigation Act to include exclusive dealing, tying contracts, etc., which, in any event, are ill-suited to the criminal law, the government turned the whole question of a rational competition policy over to the ECC.

50. Restrictive Trade Practices Commission, *Report on an Inquiry into the Distribution and Sale of Automotive Oils, Greases, Antifreeze, Additives, Tires, Batteries and Accessories and Related Products*, Queen's Printer, Ottawa, 1962.

The report which finally emanated from the ECC, in 1969, called for major changes in the anticombines law.[51] The title of the report itself is perhaps significant in that it refers not to "combines law," but to "competition policy." This reflects the ECC's concern that the legislation promote competition with the objective of achieving maximum economic efficiency. The report viewed competition essentially as a *means* towards achieving the *end* of economic efficiency. It rejected the idea that the distribution of income and the diffusion of political power be primary concerns of Canadian competition policy. These were to be dealt with by other means such as taxes and transfer payments. The ECC was optimistic that there was sufficient room in the Canadian economy for competitive forces, aided by an adequate competition policy, to make a major contribution toward efficient economic performance.[52] It also recommended that, wherever possible, competition policy be substituted for the direct regulation of rates and prices by regulatory boards.

The ECC recommended that the combines laws be divided into two parts. One part would retain certain broad prohibitions against collusive agreements to fix prices and allocate markets, resale price maintenance, and misleading advertising. The second part would represent an important innovation. The ECC recommended the creation of a "Competitive Practices Tribunal" (CPT) which would operate under civil law. (The ECC fully recognized the constitutional issues this recommendation raised. However it believed that the nonconstitutional grounds for the recommendation were strong enough, and the constitutional grounds against it sufficiently debatable, to press on). This tribunal would be made up of persons with a blend of experience and expertise. The CPT would be responsible for determining when mergers, specialization agreements, and "restrictive trade practices" (exclusive dealing, tying contracts, price discrimination, basing point systems, refusal to deal) were not in the public (consumer) interest. When they were not, the CPT, armed with the power to issue injunctions and prohibition orders, could step in and alter market structure (e.g. by dissolving a merger) or market behaviour (prohibiting a certain practice). There would be a right to appeal from the Tribunal to the Courts, but only on questions of law.

Two years after the appearance of the ECC's *Interim Report on Competition Policy* the Government acted. A "Competition Bill," which would have replaced the Combines Investigation Act, was tabled in the House of Commons in June 1971. It encompassed the recommendations of the ECC, and more, and had it

---

51. The Economic Council of Canada's *Interim Report on Competition Policy* is well worth reading by any student interested in the subject of competition policy.
52. ECC *Interim Report on Competition Policy*, p. 9. For a somewhat different view, see Milton Moore, *How Much Price Competition? The Prerequisites of an Effective Competition Policy* (Montreal: McGill—Queen's University Press, 1970).

been enacted essentially intact, it would have rocketed Canadian competition policy from the bottom to the top rank in terms of economic content and sophistication. Bill C-256, as the proposed Competition Act became known, essentially put into detailed legal form the proposals made by the Economic Council of Canada, including a *per se* rule in collusion cases and a Competitive Practice Tribunal to review mergers using criteria remarkably similar to those suggested by Williamson in his classic paper "Economies as an Antitrust Defense" (see chapter 4).

Bill C-256 was too much for the public to absorb and for businessmen to take. The latter flooded Parliament with briefs opposing the legislation, while groups representing the former provided, at most, lukewarm support. Bill C-256 never reached second reading and was not reintroduced in the next Parliamentary session. Instead the Government tried a new strategy: it introduced the reforms (i) in stages, and (ii) as amendments to the existing legislation. The first stage was introduced in 1973 but took more than two years to be enacted into law.[53] The "first stage" amendments clarified the meaning of "unduly," prohibited bid rigging, extended the Act's coverage to services, and made the misleading advertising sections unconscionably more lengthy and complex. A provision for civil damage suits was also enacted. The major innovation of the "first stage" amendments was the powers given to the RTPC to issue prohibition orders where restrictive practices such as exclusive dealing, tying contracts, directed buying or market restrictions are engaged in by "major suppliers" *and* have the effect of substantially lessening competition (s.31.2 to 31.4). The decision to deal with restrictive practices via civil law and procedures reflects a healthy recognition that there are many business activities that cannot be adequately and fairly dealt with under criminal law. It remains to be seen whether these new powers will be retained as a constitutional exercise of the federal powers.

In March 1977, the second stage amendments were introduced in Parliament.[54] Virtually all the important provisions were in the domain of civil law. The Stage II Bill (later known as Bill C-13) proposed that the Restrictive Trade Practices Commission be replaced by a Competition Board, the responsibilities of which would be purely quasi-judicial.[55] The Competition Board's

---

53. Canada, Department of Consumer and Corporate Affairs, *Proposals for a New Competition Policy for Canada* First Stage, Combines Investigation Act Amendments, November 1973.

54. Canada, Consumer and Corporate Affairs, *Proposals for a New Competition Policy for Canada* Second Stage, Combines Investigation Act Amendments, March 1977. Prior to the presentation of the Stage II amendments before Parliament, the Minister of Corporate and Consumer Affairs had established an independent committee to consider the Stage II revisions. Its report is widely known as the Skeoch-McDonald report after its principal authors. See *Dynamic Change and Accountability in a Canadian Market Economy, Proposals for a Further Revision of Canadian Competition Policy by an Independent Committee*, Department of Consumer and Corporate Affairs, Ottawa 1976.

55. The Competition Board would be relieved of tasks associated with criminal inquiries,

duties would be to review certain matters assigned to it under the amended legislation and issue "corrective orders" where need be. The matters reviewable by the Competition Board, in addition to the restrictive practices introduced in the First Stage Amendments, would be mergers, monopolization and "joint monopolization," patent abuse, interlocking directorates, specialization agreements, "price differentiation" and foreign conspiracies. A few of these require explanation.

(1) The second stage amendments provided that mergers which substantially lessen competition (in the case of horizontal mergers the combined market share must exceed 20 percent) may be dissolved by the Board unless it finds the merger produces "substantial gains in efficiency." An alternative to dissolution of a merger is a reduction in customs duties or a reduction in other international trade barriers.

(2) "Joint monopolization" refers to the parallel behaviour of firms in tightly oligopolistic industries. It was a scarcely veiled and hamhanded attack on the "conscious parallelism" problem. No agreement is necessary. If the parallel behaviour has the effect of restricting entry into the market, foreclosing markets to a competitor, coercing competitors or disciplining them for competitive conduct, or eliminating a competitor via a price squeeze, prohibition orders may be issued, and if these fail to remedy the problem, dissolution of one or more of the oligopolistic firms may be ordered.

(3) "Price differentiation," as it is defined in the second stage amendments, arises when a "major supplier" gives quantity discounts which cannot be cost justified and these discounts have the effect of impeding the expansion of an otherwise efficient competitor.

In addition to the civil law amendments, the second stage proposals included amendments to the criminal offence sections on monopoly and price discrimination, and a new section on delivered pricing. Taken as a whole the second stage amendments were so sweeping that they appeared to be Bill C-256 in disguise. The business community's reaction to the 1977 legislative proposals was no less abrupt than it was to those tabled six years earlier. Moreover, the proposals did not receive the support of professional economic and legal opinion that their authors had hoped for. Thus the "first phase" of the second stage amendments ended in failure. However, they set the stage for the subsequent proposals and ultimately the tabling of a reform bill in 1984 with the best chance so far of Parliamentary approval.

In 1981, after a three-year lull, the Minister of Consumer and Corporate

including the hearings into industry conduct which resulted in the RTPC reports repeatedly cited in this and the preceding chapters. An extensive analysis of Bill 13 is found in J.W. Rowley and W.T. Stanbury, eds., *Competition Policy in Canada* Stage II, Bill C-13 (Institute for Research on Public Policy, 1978).

Affairs, André Ouellet, rekindled the "second stage reform" effort.[56] The Ouellet Proposals, as they became known, are perhaps most notable because they represent the first major move away from reliance on a quasi-judicial tribunal as a pivotal part of competition policy reform. Instead of referring cases of merger, monopoly, joint monopolization, price differentiation, and restrictive practices to a tribunal as earlier reform proposals had suggested, they would be referred to civil law courts. Thus the fundamental idea that civil must replace criminal law in many areas of competition policy was retained, but courts would be substituted for a tribunal. This change reflected the concern of many in the business community that a tribunal would have too wide a discretion in exercising judgement, thereby engendering uncertainty about the application of the law.[57] Courts could be depended upon to exercise less latitude; presumably their decisions would be more predictable. To reduce uncertainty even further, it was proposed that thresholds be established to indicate when a merger, monopoly or "joint monopoly" presumptively violated the law. Finally, as a response to the Supreme Court decisions in *Aetna* and *Atlantic Sugar*, the problem of "undueness" would be exorcised by the adoption of a *per se* rule.

The Ouellet proposals did not curb business opposition, and they came in for a good deal of criticism from economists too. The business community was not attracted by a *per se* rule nor by the continued flirtation of the combines authorities with the "joint monopolization" concept. Economists were particularly critical of the attempt to define precise thresholds indicating when a merger becomes undesirable.[58] While the idea of relying on a test of "lessening competition significantly" was widely approved, it did not seem possible to indicate *ex ante* a market share at which such a point was reached, particularly in Canada's small tariff-protected markets. Moreover, the use of thresholds not only creates spurious precision, it generates a false sense of certainty. If thresholds are made all important then the determination of the relevant market becomes the new and shifting battleground.

The Ouellet proposals never made it to the floor of Parliament. The economic and political climate was not propitious. Instead, the 1981 proposals went through a further process of modification following intensive consultations with business groups. By April 1983 a proposed set of amendments was hammered out, and in early 1984 a bill (C-29) amending the Combines Investigation Act was tabled in the House of Commons. Bill C-29 adopts the Ouellet proposal of

56. Consumer and Corporate Affairs Canada, "Proposals for Amending the Combines Investigation Act: A Framework for Discussion," April 1981 (mimeo).
57. The tribunal approach also may have suffered from the impact of the regulatory reform effort which was then in full swing. There is legitimate concern that a quasi-judicial tribunal might soon begin to act like a regulatory agency, particularly where it is attempting to deal with complex economic behaviour such as is likely to be evidenced in merger and joint monopolization cases.
58. In fact, the Ouellet proposals would have dispensed with the efficiency tests that had been a part of earlier merger reform proposals.

relying on civil courts rather than the RTPC or some other quasi-judicial tribunal, but softens the rough edges in the earlier proposal. Gone is reference to "joint monopolization" and to a *per se* rule in conspiracy cases. Bill C-29 also dispenses with the term "monopoly," employing the concept of "abuse of a dominant position" in its place, thereby emphasizing behavioural rather than structural tests in market power cases.[59] Under Bill C-29 the matters that would be placed before civil courts include the restrictive practices (such as exclusive dealing and tied selling), which are currently reviewable by the RTPC (see above), plus abuse of dominant position, delivered pricing, and mergers.[60]

The most radical departure from the current law is the treatment of mergers. The merger section runs to 19 columns, including 13 columns devoted to the issue of notification of a proposed merger. Bill C-29 would require that the Director of Investigation be notified of all mergers where the combined assets or revenues of the merging firms exceed $500 million. Under section 31.72, a court which finds that a merger prevents or lessens competition significantly, or is likely to do so, may prohibit a proposed merger or direct that a completed merger be dissolved. (All references to "public detriment" have been removed.) However, no such order would be made if the Court finds that the proposed merger has or is likely to bring about efficiency gains that will result in a "substantial real net saving of resources for the Canadian economy"—gains that could not reasonably be expected to be attained in the absence of the merger. Moreover, even in the absence of cost savings, a merger which significantly lessens competition need not be dissolved if customs duties are reduced or removed thereby rendering the mergers' anti-competitive effects negligible.

Most of the other proposed amendments are relatively minor compared to the merger proposals. Four are worth mentioning. First, Bill C-20 would keep the existing conspiracy section 32(1) intact, including the word "unduly." However a new section 32(1.3) makes clear that there is no double intent requirement: all that needs to be shown is that the parties intended to and did enter into conspiracy or agreement. It is not necessary to prove that the agreeing parties intended to "unduly" lessen competition. Thus the confusion created by the *Aetna* and *Atlantic Sugar* decisions is clarified by amendment. Second, Bill C-29 would make the Combines Investigation Act applicable to Crown corporations, thereby avoiding the problem posed in the Uranium case.[61] Third, the

59. Examples of abuse of dominant position which are specified in Bill C-29 include vertical squeezes, preemption of scarce facilities, use of fighting brands, acquisition of a supplier in order to prevent entry by a competitor, etc. See section 31.41 (3) of Bill C-29.

60. These are included in subsections of section 31. Old section 33 dealing with monopoly and merger is repealed, and a new section 33, which brings banks under the jurisdiction of the Combines Investigation Act appears in its place.

61. As a result of the exposé in the 1970s of the operation of an international uranium cartel, with Canadian firms playing a leading role, a conspiracy case was brought. However, two of the

RTPC, which is stripped of its jurisdiction over restrictive practices, is given power to consider, register, and set the terms for specialization agreements (see chapter 4). Finally, and somewhat ominously, the new long title of the bill is "An Act to provide for the *general regulation* of trade and commerce in respect of combines, mergers, and trade practices affecting competition" (emphasis added). The phrase "general regulation of trade and commerce" has obviously been employed in order to increase the likelihood that the amendments will be *infra vires* (constitutional) the BNA Act.[62] Nevertheless, students of public policies toward business, well aware of the over-regulated nature of the Canadian economy, cannot but be uneasy about the use of the term "general regulation" in a statute which it is hoped will act as an alternative to the direct regulation of business.

Concluding Thoughts

After a decade and a half of reform effort it is time to take stock. Since the appearance of the Economic Council of Canada's *Interim Report on Competition Policy* it had been assumed that the centrepiece of reform would be the enactment of civil law enforced by a quasi-judicial tribunal or board. The tribunal's terms of reference had become increasingly complex as we proceeded from the *Interim Report* to Bill C-256 to the Second Stage Amendments. The increased complexity, epitomized by the "joint monopolization" section, might inadvertently have made the tribunal, had it ever been established, into a sort of regulatory agency or board. When one contemplates the issuance and enforcement of a potentially wide variety of prohibition orders governing conduct, the regulatory board comparison is not an unfair one. And yet it is an unfortunate comparison, for a major rationale of competition policy is that it is an alternative to regulation. Competition policy should be designed, as far as possible, to minimize interference with business conduct—striking only when that conduct is itself a barrier to competition. This is, to be sure, the spirit of the competition policy reform proposals of the 1970s. Yet there was abundant cause for concern whether the means of implementing that policy were consistent with the ultimate objectives of the policy.[63]

defendants, Uranium Canada Ltd. and Eldorado Nuclear Ltd. are Crown corporations which the Supreme Court of Canada found not to be subject to the Combines Investigation Act because their alleged conduct was within the scope of Crown purposes. See *Regina v. Uranium Canada Ltd.* (1982) 38 O.R. (2d) 130, and *Regina v. Eldorado Nuclear Ltd.* (1983) 39 O.R. (2d) 474. As a result charges were also dropped against four private uranium firms which had participated in the cartel.
62. See the opinion in *MacDonald v. Vapour Canada Ltd.* (1976) 66 DLR (3d) 1, and in *R.v. Hoffman-LaRoche Ltd.* (1980) 28 O.R. (2d) 164 and (1981) 33 O.R. (2d) 694.
63. See C. Green, "Canadian Competition Policy at a Crossroads," *Canadian Public Policy*, 7, no. 3 (Summer 1981), pp. 418-432.

An alternative to the tribunal approach is the enactment of civil law enforced within the court system, as is the case in much U.S. anti-trust law. This is the sensible direction in which the most recent reform proposals have moved, thereby making the proposed amendments in Bill C-29 the most appropriate to date.[64] The courts are likely to retain more public respect, and to be less bureaucratic than a quasi-judicial tribunal. Unfortunately, the constitutionality of this approach is still in doubt. If the constitutional barrier is compelling, what then? The proposal to use tariff reduction to offset the anti-competitive effects of mergers and specialization agreement is an excellent *structural* remedy. Since most North American markets are probably workably competitive, the elimination of tariff protection would provide sufficient competition to keep most Canadian industries competitively "honest."

Another way of looking at alternatives is to compare the Canadian approach to competition policy with that of other countries, particularly the United States and the United Kingdom. Broadly speaking Canada's anticombines laws occupy a middle ground between the U.S. and U.K. approaches. The United States tends to emphasize *per se* rules for collusive and restrictive (e.g. tying contracts) behaviour and preventive legislation to curb the growth of market power via mergers. Existing monopoly power goes largely untouched, so long as it is not exerted too strenuously. The United Kingdom looks primarily at the *effects* of business behaviour in determining whether they are permissible. Thus restrictive agreements may be allowed (historically not many have been) if they are believed to provide benefits such as increased employment, prevention of regional decline, increased exports, etc. which outweigh the market power "costs" of the agreement. Much the same sort of benefit-cost test is applied in reviewing merger proposals.

Neither the U.S. nor the U.K. approach is wholly suited to Canada. The application of a tough U.S.-type merger law to the Canadian scene is inconsistent with the facts of market size and industrial structure discussed in the first four chapters of the book. The application of a U.K.-type "effects" test to collusive agreements would open the door to an endless number of cases, particularly in tariff-protected industries, and to endless debate over the potential benefits particularly where industries are heavily represented in high unemployment—low income areas. A more sensible course is to follow the U.S. example in collusive and restrictive trade practices cases, while plying a course closer to the United Kingdom (than to the United States) when determining whether to allow market power-increasing mergers. In sum, the problem with Canadian competition policy to date is not that it is different from that of other countries, but rather that it has not been particularly appropriate to the circumstances at home.

64. Bill C-29 died with the Liberal government in the summer of 1984. As this text went to press, it was unclear whether the new government would reintroduce the proposed amendments.

10

Economic Regulation of
Public Utilities

This chapter is about the economic regulation of "public utilities" in the transportation, telecommunication, and energy fields.[1] Economic regulation applicable to other industries is considered in chapter 12. Although recent "theories" of regulation, discussed briefly in chapter 7, have tended to generalize across industries, the technological attributes of the traditional "public utilities" are sufficiently distinctive to warrant individual attention. In addition, the transportation, telecommunication, and energy (TTE) sector accounts for about 12 percent of Canadian GNP and 35 percent of total invested capital in Canada.

What is so distinctive about the TTE firms that they are traditionally given special treatment, either through public ownership or through regulatory control by a public board, commission, or agency? From a socio-economic point of view, a nation's transportation and telecommunications network and its energy system are essential parts of its infrastructure. The concept of infra-structure usually implies social benefits in excess of private benefits (external economies). Such externalities flowing from a regional or national network help to explain the use of direct subsidies (transportation), public ownership (electricity generation), and cross-subsidization via public control of rates and rate structures (telecommunications). The infrastructure role of the TTE industries is

---

1. "Public utility" is an old concept which may now be outmoded. In common parlance it refers to firms providing local gas, water, electric, telecommunications, and public mass transportation services. It is also stretched to include enterprises generating electricity, transmitting electricity and gas, and providing intercity telecommunications and public (or "common carrier") transportation services.

reflected in the legal view that they are sufficiently "clothed (or affected) with the public interest" to warrant public control of private capital invested in these industries, where there is not outright public ownership. But there is more to the "public utility" story than "externalities" and "public interest," for these attributes may characterize industries (e.g. education, milk supply) not usually considered public utilities. As we shall see, public utilities have certain technological characteristics which tend to differentiate them from enterprises in other industries. But we shall also see that parts of the utility sector are undergoing important changes calling into question the traditional regulatory model of assuring good performance.

Characteristics of Public Utilities

Most public utilities have certain characteristics in common. The one most often cited is that they are typically very capital intensive. Their capital intensity is reflected in capital to output ratios of three or four to one compared to ratios of unity or less for most manufacturing industries. Capital intensity gives rise to high fixed costs relative to total costs, and this in turn implies declining average costs over a considerable range of output. The capital intensive technology also creates indivisibilities in plant size, with the result that *optimum* plant size may be large relative to demand. It is this characteristic of public utilities that is usually credited with making them "natural monopolies."

The conditions of natural monopoly are pictured in Figure 10-1. The market demand curve DD cuts the LAC curve and the relevant SAC curve on their declining portions, indicating that market demand does not exhaust the capacity of a single efficient-size firm to supply the market. As a result the demand curve will also cut both the long-run marginal cost (LMC) and the short-run marginal cost curves (SMC) at points below the respective average cost curves.[2] Several price-output pairs are conceivable.

1. If the firm were an unregulated (as well as natural) profit maximizing but nondiscriminating, monopolist, it would, assuming entry was permanently blocked, set price at P_m and output at Q_m, in line with the point at which MR = MC.

2. If the firm were publicly owned and its managers were directed to set price and output at levels reflecting price equal to marginal cost, output would be pushed to level Q_o and consumers charged P_o per unit. However, the revenues raised from consumer charges would be JK per unit less than the unit costs of producing the service JQ_o. The public firm would thus run a deficit equal to the

2. Recall that the MC curve cuts the SAC curve at the latter's lowest point. Since the DD curve cuts the SAC while the latter is still declining, it must also cut the MC curve at a point where MC is below the SAC curve.

Figure 10-1

The Conditions of "Natural Monopoly"

shaded area in Figure 10-1.[3] (If the firm were privately owned it would require a per unit subsidy equal to JK, total subsidies equalling the area $CJKP_o$.)

3. If the firm were operated so as to cover all of its operating costs and to earn a "bare bones" return on capital, i.e. one just equal to the market cost of capital, the price-output pair would be P^1Q^1, in line with the point L where DD cuts the SAC curve. We may call this "strict" average cost pricing.

4. If the firm is privately owned and its regulators allow it to earn a "fair" rate of return on its undepreciated capital in excess of the market cost of capital, the price output pair (assuming a single type of output sold at the same price per unit to all consumers) would be P_R, Q_R. Price is higher and output is lower than in the "strict" average cost pricing case since under a "fair" return standard,

3. However by price discriminating, say by selling OQ_m at price P_m and Q_mQ_o at price P_o, the enterprise would more than cover all costs (see below).

profit above a "bare bones" level is typically allowed, reflecting "fairness" to investors as well as consumers.[4]

5. A regulated but discriminating monopolist might employ a two-part tariff selling, for example, OQ_M at P_M and Q_MQ_o at P_o, the profits on the former cross-subsidizing losses on the latter.

The fourth approach is the one typically adopted by regulatory agencies commissioned to regulate electric, telephone, and gas pipeline utilities.[5] It is called rate-of-return regulation. Although the practical problem facing regulatory agencies is establishing what is a fair rate of return, economists, in recent years, have pointed to a theoretical problem: the incentive for the firm to "overcapitalize." If the "fair" rate of return exceeds the cost to the firm of attracting capital, it will be motivated to use more capital and less of other factors than is required for cost minimization, given existing technology and factor prices.[6]

A second characteristic that most public utilities have in common is a physical network tying producer-distributor to customers. Public utilities are "tentacle" industries, with wires, pipes and roadbeds linking suppliers to users. Duplication of the network would be inefficient, not to say unsightly. It would also be very expensive, for it is the tentacle character of the railroads, of electric, gas and water distribution, and of local telecommunications systems that contributes mightily to their capital intensity. Thus the tentacle nature of the public utilities provides a double-barrelled reason for their treatment as natural monopolies.

A third characteristic of public utilities is that they provide important, non-storable services, for which there are effectively no close substitutes. The non-storability of electric, telephone and transportation services puts the buyer at the mercy of the unregulated supplier.[7] These services must be supplied when needed to have value. Consumers cannot hedge against the future by "stocking up now." This is obvious where electricity, gas, and telecommunications services are involved. It is also true, although to a lesser extent, for public transportation. Consumers pay not only for the service itself but for its "option demand"—the knowledge that the service will be available if and when they need it. The tentacle nature of the industries implies that for residential and

4. However, in the long run the higher profits will be capitalized into the price of the regulated firm's stock so that the return actually earned by new investors will approximate that of the market cost of capital.

5. Regulatory commissions, however, usually allow the firm some discretion in its rate structure, which may reflect a modified, and more modest, version of the fifth approach (see below).

6. The notion that rate of return regulation creates an inducement to utilities to overcapitalize is usually credited to an article by Harvey Averch and Leland Johnson, "Behavior of the Firm under Regulatory Constraint," *American Economic Review*, 52 (Dec. 1962), and it is widely termed the Averch-Johnson (A-J) effect.

7. The inability to store also puts the producer at risk.

commercial consumers there are effectively no close substitutes—at least in the short run. These consumers do not generally have the option that industrial consumers have of installing alternative sources of energy. In transportation, however, where there are usually alternative modes available (rail, air, road, water), the possibilities for substitutability are greater and competition is a reality.

The three characteristics, capital intensity, tentacle industry, and an essential, non-storable service combine to provide the classic case for government intervention either in the form of public ownership, or public control, through a regulatory device.[8] Enterprises with each of these three characteristics are clearly "natural monopolies" affected with the public interest. These enterprises typically are given a franchise (legal monopoly) to supply specified services to customers within a particular geographical area. In return, the utility must act as a "common carrier," providing services to all customers within its territory willing to pay the listed rates, charges, or tolls.[9]

Much regulatory theory, and practice, is based on this kind of description of public utilities. It is, however, a picture that is rapidly changing. Historical spadework has unearthed evidence that the causes of and motives for regulation were not nearly so pure as the natural monopoly model would suggest. More important are technological changes which are eroding the original technological bases for natural monopoly. In transportation, intermodal competition has virtually eliminated the monopoly position once held by the railroads. The newer modes of transportation, road and air, do not have the capital intensity of the railroads; moreover, the infrastructure network of roads and airports are publicly financed, in contrast to railway roadbeds. In telecommunications, rivalry already exists in certain intercity markets, and a technological revolution is threatening to further erode the monopoly of the regulated or government-owned carriers. Even energy *generation* is no longer naturally monopolistic, at least where large metropolitan markets are concerned. Energy demand has increased so substantially that several sources of electric power are now needed to meet customer demand in cities such as Montreal and Toronto. It is mainly at the transmission and local distribution levels with their physical tentacles that naturally monopolistic characteristics are retained.

There are other developments working to undermine the relevance, as a guide to regulation, of the natural monopoly model of public utility operations.

8. In addition, the possibility of discriminating is enhanced by the fact that the tentacle character of public utilities makes resale (arbitrage) of their services difficult or impossible. To the extent that consumer demands vary the unregulated utility is in an excellent position to "exploit" consumers via price discrimination.
9. However Demsetz has argued that at least in principle a system of auctioning off the monopoly franchise to the highest bidder is a welfare enhancing substitute for traditional regulation. See *supra* note 19 in Chapter 7.

The energy crunch and inflation have led to rising rather than falling unit costs of added energy-generating capacity. Even where scale economies are not yet exhausted (inputs per unit of output decline as capacity rises), rising construction and other input costs are producing rising supply prices for electricity. The contrast between the pre-1965 and the post-1970 experience is stark. In the earlier period productivity increases, due chiefly to the exhaustion of scale economies as demand expanded, offset increases in factor prices. There was no upward pressure on energy prices. Since 1970, rapidly rising fuel prices and general inflation have put strong upward pressure on the price of electricity.[10]

Regulatory Functions

What do regulatory boards regulate? Full regulation involves control over the prices, entry and, where necessary, quality of service. Full regulation is applied to telecommunications, oil and gas pipelines, and until very recently airlines in Canada. Sometimes only entry is regulated, as is the case with trucking in a number of provinces. Regulation of rates or prices without control of entry is rare—if entry is possible there is little need for the establishment of maximum prices, while the maintenance of minimum prices is economically unworkable in such cases. In some cases, for example broadcasting, an attempt is made to regulate the "quality" of service, but this is a difficult task and there is little evidence that it is particularly effective. Increasingly, the quality of the environment in which production (e.g. health and safety regulation) and consumption (e.g. consumer protection laws) take place, or the impact of economic activity on the environment, is now subject to regulation.

Rate-of-Return Regulation

The standard approach to regulating a capital intensive, naturally monopolistic public utility is to restrict the revenue raised to levels just covering the costs of services provided by the enterprise.[11] The regulatory constraint works in both directions, providing an assurance that investors are not expropriated as well as

10. John Helliwell, "Some Emerging Economic Issues in Utility Regulation and Rate-Making," *Studies in Economic Regulation*, W.T. Stanbury (ed.)(Institute for Research on Public Policy, 1978), pp. 113-130; Paul MacAvoy, *The Regulated Industries and the Economy* (New York: Norton, 1979), chapter 2.

11. For a full development of the economics of public utility rate making see A.E. Kahn, *The Economics of Regulation: Principles and Institutions* Vol. I (New York: Wiley, 1970). For an older "classic" see James C. Bonbright, *Principles of Public Utility Rates* (New York: Columbia University Press, 1961). At a more introductory level are the chapters on regulation in W.G. Shepherd and Clair Wilcox, *Public Policies Toward Business*, 6th edition (Homewood, Illinois: Irwin, 1979).

that consumers are not "exploited." There are two main costs of service that revenues must cover: operating costs which include fuel, maintenance, labour services, depreciation and taxes, and capital costs in the form of interest and dividend payments to bond and stock holders. The calculation of capital costs is a two-step procedure. First a rate base is established reflecting the value of the firm's assets minus depreciation. To avoid virtually insoluble valuation problems rate base values are now usually based on the "historical" cost, or purchase price, of the assets when originally acquired. Then a rate of return is applied to the rate base to determine the revenues the utility will be allowed to raise to cover its capital costs. The procedure is illustrated by the following formula:

$$R = O + (V-D)r$$

where R = the required level of revenues

O = operating costs

V = the acquisition "value" of the enterprise's "used and useful" assets

D = depreciation

(V-D) = rate base

r = allowed rate of return

The most controversial part of the procedure is the determination of the allowed rate of return, r.[12] It involves three steps, which essentially focus on the liability side of the utility's balance sheet. First, the regulatory commission must determine the utility's "capital structure," i.e. the division of the firm's liabilities between debt (bonds) and stockholder equity. Usually the commission chooses the capital structure actually indicated by the firm's books, but it may in some cases substitute a hypothetical one, especially where the Commission finds that the proportion of equity is unnecessarily, and expensively, high. Second, the firm's books are used to calculate the "embedded cost of the firm's debt," usually indicated by the weighted average of the utility's outstanding

---

12. At one time the most controversial facet of the procedure was the determination of the rate base (V-D), particularly V. The utilities argued that V ought to be determined on a reproduction or replacement cost basis: the cost of replacing the service at today's price of plant and machinery. During a period of rising prices this meant that replacement cost would exceed historical cost. But the former, because it is hypothetical, leads to endless debates about current costs. However, in the U.S. the utilities had the Courts on their side until 1944, when the doctrine of "fair value" stipulated in *Smyth v. Ames* (1898) was replaced by the functional approach taken in the *Hope Natural Gas* case (1944). *Smyth v. Ames* had required that in determining a fair and reasonable return evidence of both original or historical cost and reproduction cost had to be sought by the regulatory commission. With the *Hope* case regulatory commissions were allowed to bypass debate by adopting the easily obtainable historical cost figures and focus on the rate of return which attracted capital and was otherwise "fair" to consumers and investors alike. For Canada, the leading early case on rate-of-return regulation was *Northwestern Utilities Ltd. v. Edmonton*, Supreme Court of Canada (1929) 2 D.L.R. 4.

bonds and debentures. Finally, the Commission must determine a "fair" or "reasonable" rate of return on stockholder equity. Here controversy reaches a fever pitch, with expert witnesses for the utility suggesting a generous rate while the Commission is inclined to be somewhat more niggardly.

On what criteria should the rate of return on stockholder equity be based? If the utility is growing, it is clear that the rate of return should be sufficient to attract capital. While this answer is fine in theory, it does not, unfortunately, provide an answer to the basic problem facing the regulatory commission: the actual choice of a number to be used in calculating the required rate of return. There are two reasons why this is so:

1. In principle, a firm can attract new capital even when it is not allowed to earn a market rate of return on its invested capital. It can do so, however, only at the expense of its existing stockholders, by allowing the market value of its stock to fall. For example, suppose a utility wants to finance the purchase of $100,000,000 worth of new capital equipment. Suppose further that the market rate of return is 10 percent and the market value of its outstanding shares is $100. By selling 1,000,000 new shares the utility can raise the required capital. But suppose that the regulatory commission sets the allowed rate at 8 percent, i.e., it allows the utility to earn only an additional $8,000,000 (or $8 per share) on the $100,000,000 increment to its rate base. The utility can still attract capital if it is willing to sell the shares at $80 (8 ÷ 80 = 10%). But now it will have to sell 1,250,000 shares (at $80 each) to raise the needed $100,000,000. At $8 per share the 1,250,000 shares make claim to $10,000,000 of the utility earnings. This is $2,000,000 more than the additional earnings the regulatory commission has allowed the utility. The extra $2,000,000 can only come from the earnings the existing shareholders expected to receive. That is, a "dilution" of the earnings of existing stockholders is required if the utility is to attract capital at less than the market rate of return on its total invested capital. In the short run, attracting capital under these conditions produces capital losses to the initial stockholders. In the long run such an approach will be self-defeating since presumably stockholders will take into consideration (capitalize) the probability of the regulatory commission setting allowed rates of return below market rates. It is for these reasons that the term "fair" or "reasonable" is used in describing the rate of return regulatory commissions attempt to set. The return should both attract capital and be "reasonable" in that it should not "expropriate" existing investors.

2. There is no tried and true guide to determining just what is the capital-attracting rate of return for a given firm. Just as there is a structure of interest rates reflecting the different degrees of bond riskiness, there is a spectrum of capital attracting rates of return reflecting the varying degrees of risks among enterprises. It is traditional, then, in utility rate cases to place the utility into a

risk class, and to compare its earnings per share with that of similar enterprises in that risk class. This, of course, is not a foolproof procedure. It is likely that the comparisons are with other utilities. Their earnings experience will reflect in good part the degree of stringency with which they are regulated. If their regulation is lax or non-existent their earnings per share and return on equity may be well above what is required to attract capital. However, to the extent that this is recognized by the securities market, exceptional earnings per share ratios will tend to be reduced by increases in the market price of the shares. In other words, the earnings will be capitalized in the market price of the shares.

The determination of the allowed rate of return is capsulized in Table 10-1. A hypothetical firm's capital structure is shown in column (1). In column (2) the cost of capital is divided into the embedded cost of debt and the regulatory commission's estimate of the "cost of equity finance." The cost components that make up the allowed rate of return are simply the products of the first two columns. When added together they yield the allowed return on capital, in this case 10 percent.

The final step in rate-of-return regulation is to approve the means of raising sufficient revenue to cover operating and capital costs. Here the concern moves from the *rate level* (rate of return) to the *rate structure*. Historically, utility commissions employing rate of return regulation have paid relatively little attention to the rate structure, leaving the utility a wide latitude in choosing the rates it would charge to different classes of customers (residential, commercial, industrial) or for different quantities of service (e.g. kilowatt hours of electricity consumed per month). Commissions were mainly concerned that no consumer group was inordinately "exploited," often relying on public outcry to determine when this point was reached.[13]

Thus, over time rate structures evolved reflecting varying degrees of promotional designs, price discrimination and cross-subsidization. For example, electrical utilities have long employed a declining block rate structure. The first X kilowatt hours cost more per kilowatt than subsequent blocks, as indicated in Figure 10-2. In part, this structure reflects the attribution of "customer charges" and other fixed costs to the first block. However, the structure is clearly designed to promote the consumption of electricity. Promotional rate designs made sense when energy seemed inexhaustible and the main concern was to exhaust, to as great an extent as demand would allow, the economies of scale in the generation, transmission, and distribution system. In recent years, the exhaustion of scale economies at the generation level and the rising concern over energy shortages and environmental damage have made the declining

13. Kahn gives extended treatment to the economic principles underlying rate structure design, particularly marginal cost pricing and the issue of price discrimination. Kahn, op. cit., chapters 3-5.

Table 10-1

Calculation of the Allowed Rate of Return

	(1) Capital Structure	(2) Cost of Capital	(3) Cost Component (1) × (2)
	%	%	%
Long term debt	60	8.0	4.8
Common equity	40	13.0	5.2
	100		10%

Figure 10-2

Rate Structure, Electrical Utilities

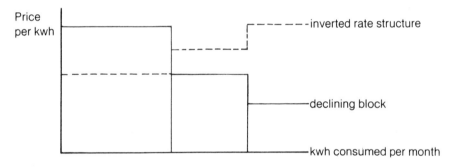

block structure both uneconomical (it causes average revenue to fall as consumption increases) and anti-social (it promotes consumption rather than providing inducement to conserve). Thus in recent years some regulatory commissions, often at the behest of environmental groups, have indicated interest in "inverted" rate structures—i.e., ones in which the incremental charge per kwh (or block of kwh's) rises rather than declines. (See dashed lines in Figure 10-2).[14] In other cases more attention is given to a form of marginal cost pricing in which "off peak" consumers pay only the cost of generating an extra kilowatt of electricity, while peak consumers are charged the full cost of supplying electricity including the cost of installing the required capacity.[15]

14. See Paul Joskow, "Inflation and Environmental Concern: Structural Change in the Process of Public Utility Regulation," *Journal of Law and Economics* (Oct. 1974). For example, Hydro Quebec uses a mildly inverted rate structure in supplying electricity to residential customers.
15. Ontario Hydro has proposed a rate structure in which the price of electricity would vary by time of day (TOD). However, substantial opposition to TOD rates exists and the proposal has yet to receive approval by the Ontario Energy Board. An early version of the proposal is evaluated in Ontario Energy Board, *Report to the Minister of Energy on Principles of Electricity Costing and*

Public utility rate structures often reflect wide variations in the ratio of price to marginal cost (the economist's criterion for price discrimination). In some cases the exceptional profitability of certain activities is required to offset losses on others. In telecommunications, charges for long-distance (toll) calls are usually far higher than the costs incurred in providing the service. These revenues are used to subsidize local service, especially in "skim" markets where revenues are often only a fraction of the full costs of providing telephone service. In transportation, airline fare structures used to, although no longer, reflect a subsidization of short-haul by long-haul passengers, while railroads at one time made their profits (before the trucks took it away) on high-valued, typically short-haul freight, barely covering out-of-pocket costs on much low-valued, long-distance freight.

Rate structures often reflect competition, where it exists.[16] In such regulated industries as airlines and trucking intramodal and intermodal competition exercises a restraint on rates charged. The "deregulation" of railroad freight rates after passage of the National Transportation Act, in 1967, provided the leeway needed by Canadian railroads to meet competition from air, road, and water carriers. Not surprisingly, intermodal competition has resulted in lower railroad freight rates per ton mile on traffic in the Windsor-Quebec corridor than on western routes where water carriage is nonexistent and over-the-road trucking a less economical alternative. In the telecommunications field, the CRTC, in 1979, approved CN/CP's application to interconnect its long distance system with Bell's local telephone system and a year later a similar application to interconnect with B.C. telephone was approved. Interconnection allows CN/CP to become a more effective competitor with Bell in long distance markets served by CN/CP, thereby increasing the downward pressure on long distance telephone rates, especially in "creamy" markets (see below). In fact, Bell Canada had argued that the resultant loss of revenue on toll calls in the "creamy" Montreal-Toronto market would undermine its ability to provide service in "skim" markets. Among other things, Bell Canada's argument provides evidence that existing rate structures reflect substantial cross-subsidization and price discrimination in the provision of telephone services.[17]

Pricing for Ontario Hydro, H.R. 5, December 20, 1979. The reaction to TOD proposals is discussed in R.P. Seth, "Load Management and Industrial Customers' Attitude towards TOD Pricing: A Case Study of Ontario Hydro," Mount Saint Vincent University, May 1984 (mimeo). On the application of peakload pricing see A.E. Kahn, *The Economics of Regulation*, Vol. I (New York: Wiley, 1971), pp. 87-103.
16. See Kahn, op. cit., chap. 6.
17. Lest the reader be misled, it should be noted that cross subsidization and price discrimination in the pricing of telecommunication services is widely popular with most consumers, is implicit in the pricing policies of the regulatory agencies (see below), and reflects popular views about fairness, if not economic efficiency. However, in North America, its incidence is likely to decline as a result of the breakup, in the U.S., of A.T. & T., which effectively divorces the provision of local and long distance telephone services.

Some Effects of Rate-of-Return Regulation

It is difficult to do justice to the richness and variety of problems encountered in public utility rate proceedings. However, before turning to an evaluation of the regulatory establishment in Canada and to public policies in the transportation, communications, and energy fields, it is important to briefly mention some of the implications of utility rate making.

A. Cream Skimming

As we noted earlier in this chapter, rate-of-return regulation focuses in principle on average cost (i.e. it is a sort of cost-plus device) and thus may produce results sharply different from those of marginal cost pricing. In practice, however, public utilities have been given wide scope in establishing the price structure for the various services they provide and for the different classes (e.g. residential, commercial, industrial) of customers whom they serve, so long as intragroup discrimination for a particular type of service is limited or non-existent. Thus it is likely that in some utility submarkets, for which competition from substitutes increases the elasticity of demand, prices of services may approximate marginal costs. Since $P = MC$ implies AR is less than AC under decreasing cost conditions, prices of some other services must substantially exceed MC in order for total revenues to equal or exceed total costs. Thus price discrimination is a fact of public utility life (just as it is endemic in almost all markets), even where utility commissions are devoted to "cost of service" as opposed to "value of service" principles.[18] Moreover, when utility commissions support or require area-wide pricing as in local telephone services, they are, in fact, fostering price

18. Price discrimination may reflect (a) varying degrees of competition in the provision of different utility services; (b) a genuine attempt to push services (in some markets) to levels at which P = MC, without necessitating public subsidy; or (c) an attempt to cover costs in situations where no single price would raise sufficient revenues to cover total costs—i.e. the demand curve is at all points to the left of the average cost curve. Of course, there are cases where public utility rate structures reflect "unjustified" price discrimination by milking certain customers to provide sufficient revenues to cover overly expanded rate bases. "Cost of service" implies that rates or charges are set so as to cover the average (?) opportunity costs of providing service, and do not reflect to any meaningful degree varying elasticities of demand. In contrast "value of service" pricing is responsive to demand elasticities, the producer charging "what the market will bear." *Ceteris paribus*, price cost margins will vary inversely with the elasticity of demand. In practice, under rate-of return regulation cost-of-service principles are used in setting the overall *rate level*, while *rate structures*, reflecting varying degrees of discrimination in response to competition and other factors influencing demand elasticities, indicate the application of value-of-service principles. While value-of-service pricing has a bad name, it can be shown that to maximize "welfare" (defined as the sum of consumer and producer surplus) the regulator of a *multiproduct* natural monopolist, charging a single (linear) price for each of the services it provides, should set the ratios of price to marginal cost so that they are *inversely* proportional to the elasticity of demand for each service. W. Baumol and D. Bradford, "Optimal Departures from Marginal Cost Pricing," *American Economic Review*, 60 (June 1970). These have become known as "Ramsey prices" after a British economist who, in 1929, discovered their "optimal" properties.

discrimination since the cost of serving a customer in a "skim" market exceeds that of a "creamy" market. Where area-wide averaging in the pricing of some services results in total revenues less than total costs, revenues will have to be made up on other services—as for example long distance telephone services cross-subsidizing local services.

B. X-inefficiency

Rate-of-return regulation, unless carried out with great care including specific incentives to efficiency, may lead to an overall rise in costs (an upward movement of the AC curve in Figure 10-1). The problem is the one commonly encountered in all cost-plus type schemes. If the return over cost is fixed, or limited to a certain maximum, there is little incentive for the producer to minimize costs, to bargain hard with input suppliers, to ride herd on employees, to cut out frills, etc. In short, one possible result of regulation is X-inefficiency, even where allocative inefficiency is squeezed out by the profit constraint.

C. The Rate Base Effect

Rate-of-return regulation, because it focuses on one input, capital, assuring it a minimum (as well as a maximum) return, may affect input combinations. If the allowed rate of return exceeds the actual cost of capital, there will be an implicit subsidy to capital, thereby creating an incentive for producers to overcapital-ize—i.e. use more capital and less labour than market prices would induce. This is the so-called A-J "rate-base" effect mentioned above.

The A-J effect can be illustrated rather simply. Assuming a single output q, two factors of production, labour (L) and capital (K), the firm's objective function is:

(1) $\pi = pq - wL - r^*K$ where π = economic (pure) profits; p = price of the output; w = wage rate; and r^* = the cost of (attracting) capital to the firm. We saw above that under rate-of-return regulation, revenues (R = pq) must equal the sum of operating cost (O) plus a return r, on the capital rate base, V-D, provided by investors. Now let us assume that the regulatory commission allows the regulated firm to earn a rate of return on capital, r, in excess of the market cost of capital, r^*. Using the assumptions and notation of equation (1), the regulatory constraint may be written as:

(2) $pq = wL + rK$,   where $r > r^*$, and where wL stands for operating costs; and K stands for the rate base

Substituting (2) into (1) for pq, yields:

(3) $\pi = wL + rK - wL - r^*K$

Cancelling and consolidating terms gives us:

(4) $\pi = (r - r^*)K$

This implies that if $r > r^*$, the firm can add to its economic (or pure) profits, π, by increasing the amount of capital, K, it uses relative to the amount of other factors of production it employs.

The A–J "rate base" effect is the basis of many normative analyses of rate-of-return regulation.[19] In addition, there are a few empirical studies providing some tentative support for the A-J hypothesis.[20] On the whole, however, the weight given to the A-J effect is probably wholly out of proportion to its actual impact, if any. For a number of reasons, the A-J effect may be of little practical importance. These include (a) "regulatory lag," in which there may be a substantial delay between the time when it is evident that a regulated firm needs a rate increase to cover increased costs and the time the rate increase is actually granted by the regulatory board; (b) the rising cost of capital in the 1970s and concerns that the regulatory boards would not raise rates sufficiently to cover capital costs, which led many firms to consider economizing on the amount of capital they used; and (c) limited substitutability among factors of production. In contrast to studies of the A-J effect, relatively less attention is given to the potentially more important welfare implications of regulation-induced X-inefficiency or to the role of price discrimination as a firm's response to meeting competition when it is under regulatory restraint.[21]

Deregulation and Economic Efficiency

It is now a widely held view among economists that utility regulation may induce a degree of economic inefficiency. We have briefly examined some ways in which rate-of-return regulation may result in a regulated firm employing an inefficient combination (rate base effect) or amount (X-inefficiency) of inputs in producing a given quantity of output. Moreover, the price structures of regulated firms often diverge substantially from what either the cost of producing the service and/or the elasticity of demand for the service would have dictated, thereby resulting in an inefficient allocation of resources. When

---

19. Averch and Johnson, op. cit.; William J. Baumol and Alvin K. Klevorick, "Input Choices and Rate of Return Regulation: An Overview of the Discussions," *Bell Journal of Economics and Management Science* (Autumn 1970), pp. 162-190.

20. L. Courville, "Regulation and Efficiency in the Electric Utilities Industry," *The Bell Journal of Economics and Management Science* (Spring 1974), pp. 53-74; R.M. Spann, "Rate of Return Regulation and Efficiency in Production: An Empirical Test of the Averch-Johnson Thesis," *Bell Journal of Economics and Management Science* (Spring 1974), pp. 38-52; H.C. Peterson, "An Empirical Test of Regulatory Effects," *The Bell Journal of Economics* (Spring 1975), pp. 111-126.

21. The implication here is that X-inefficiency, by increasing inputs per unit of output, can have a strong negative impact on economic welfare, while much-disparaged price discrimination, by contributing to more efficient pricing while obviating the need for subsidies, may have strong positive effects on economic welfare.

regulation of price and/or entry is applied to oligopolistic or atomistic industries, as in the case of transportation industries, petroleum, and agriculture, the
potential economic distortions are even greater.[22] As a result, many economists
have concluded that regulation should be used as little as possible, relying on
competition to serve, wherever possible, as an impersonal regulator. There have
been widespread calls for deregulation of many regulated industries and in
recent years some of these calls have been heeded, particularly the deregulation
of transport industries.[23]

However, not all economists are persuaded that economic efficiency will
always be served by replacing regulation with competition. These economists
argue that even if technology makes competition possible, as is now the case
with the provision of long distance telephone service, competition may raise, not
lower, the cost of production. The reasons lie in possible cost complementarities
in the provision of two or more services—e.g. local and long distance telephone
services. In other words, even if *economies of scale* are not sufficiently important
to preclude two or more firms providing a given service, *economies of scope* may
exist. *Economies of scope* exist when it is cheaper, or less costly, for one firm to
provide two (or more) services than to have the same level of services supplied
separately by two (or more) firms.[24] Thus if there are common overhead costs in
the provision of certain services (e.g., they may use some of the same capital
equipment), it may be more efficient to have *one* firm provide these services
rather than to have them provided by different firms. Yet in the absence of
regulation, nothing prevents a new firm from profitably entering and providing
one of the services.[25]

The concept of *economies of scope*, which helps us recognize that some public
utilities provide more than one output or service, has broadened the concept of
"natural monopoly." By natural monopoly we mean that one firm can serve a
particular public more efficiently (at less cost) than two or more firms. Thus
both economies of scale (decreasing unit cost associated with the amount of
output produced per unit time) and economies of scope (cost complementarities
in the production of two or more services) may contribute to making a firm

22. Greater detail on the regulation of these industries is provided below.
23. For example, between 1978 and 1981, the U.S. effectively deregulated the airline, railroad,
and highway trucking industries. As we shall see below, Canada deregulated railway freight rates
(except for grain) in the 1960s and has slowly but only partially loosened the reins over the airline
industry.
24. More formally, economies of scope exist where: $c(q_1,q_2) < c(q_1,0) + c(0, q_2)$, where c(.) are
the cost functions and q_1 and q_2 are the quantities of the two services. The inequality tells us that
the cost of producing q_1 and q_2 together is less than the cost of producing them separately, with
one firm producing only q_1 and the other producing only q_2.
25. This statement is not quite true. Under certain circumstances, "Ramsey prices" in
conjunction with economies of scale and scope can be used by an established firm (monopolist) to
preclude entry. Practically speaking, however, no monopolist would be allowed to set such prices.

naturally monopolistic. Yet recent theoretical analysis has shown that the existence of natural monopoly is not sufficient to prevent competitive and profitable, albeit globally inefficient, entry from occurring in the absence of regulation.[26] To use recently introduced terminology, natural monopoly may not be "sustainable" in the absence of regulation of entry. If so, regulation may be necessary to prevent inefficient entry, even though new technology may have broken down the scale barriers to effective competition.

The Regulatory Establishment in Canada

The regulation of TTE industries in Canada is divided between federal and provincial jurisdictions and, within the latter, between (a) independent regulatory agencies (boards/commissions/tribunals), (b) municipal governments and (c) government-owned energy corporations. The division of regulatory authority between the federal and provincial governments is related in part to constitutional provisions giving the federal government wide powers over transportation and communications in Canada. There are, however, anomalies or exceptions. Trucking, whether intra- or extra-provincial, is regulated by provincial highway transport boards, although the Canadian Transport Commission's (CTC) power to regulate extra-provincial trucking is explicitly set forth in the federal National Transportation Act (1967). While most communications are federally regulated (including all broadcasting activities and CATV), most telephone firms are provincially regulated (although the two most important ones, Bell Canada and B.C. Telephone, are regulated federally by the Canadian Radio-television and Telecommunications Commission (CRTC)). Three of the provincially regulated telephone companies are government owned, while the others are investor owned.

Energy utilities are subject to provincial regulation, except where electric power or gas is transmitted across provincial lines or international borders, in which case regulation is by the federal National Energy Board (NEB). At the provincial level the jurisdiction of independent regulatory boards is usually (but not always) limited to investor-owned electric and gas utilities. Provincially owned electric power corporations (e.g. B.C. Hydro, Manitoba Hydro, Saskatchewan Power Corp., Hydro Quebec, to name just a few) which at one time

---

26. A good discussion of these issues, particularly as they pertain to Canada's telecommunications industry, is contained in Melvyn Fuss and Leonard Waverman, *The Regulation of Telecommunications in Canada*, Economic Council of Canada, Technical Report No. 7, March 1981, Chap. 1. Also see J. Panzar and R.D. Willig, "Free Entry and the Sustainability of Natural Monopoly," *Bell Journal of Economics*, 8 (Spring 1977), pp. 1-22 and W.J. Baumol, E. Bailey and R.D. Willig, "Weak Invisible Hand Theorems on Pricing and Entry in a Multiproduct Natural Monopoly," *American Economic Review* 67 (June 1977), pp. 350-65.

were self-regulated with provincial cabinet review in some cases, are now almost universally subject to some degree of regulation by the provincial regulatory board. Municipally owned electric and gas utilities are usually "regulated" by municipal governments although there are variations on this theme, as for example in Ontario where Ontario Hydro regulates retail electricity rates of municipally owned and operated utilities.

The regulatory and industry structure of the TTE industries in Canada are presented in Table 10-2. The first two columns summarize the jurisdictional aspect discussed briefly in the preceding paragraph. The final column indicates, in capsulized form, the basic industry structure of the TTE industries. These vary from the "naturally monopolistic" electricity, gas and telephone utilities to the "atomistically" structured trucking, water carrier, and oil producing industries. In between are the distinctively Canadian public-private firm duopolies in the rail and air transportation fields and in broadcasting.

Tables 10-3 through 10-6 provide more detail on the regulatory structure of telecommunications, energy, trucking, and broadcasting respectively. These tables are presented in order to detail the richness and variety of regulatory and industrial organization within the TTE sectors of Canada. Tables 10-3 and 10-4 also indicate where, and how widely, rate-of-return regulation is applied in Canada, while Table 10-5 shows the variations in the breadth of control over trucking by provincial highway transport boards.[27]

Among the more notable facts indicated in Tables 10-2 through 10-4 are the following: (a) Most telephone companies are privately owned, except in the Prairies where in each province the telephone system is provincially owned; (b) Alberta is the only province where trucking is effectively unregulated; (c) electric power is primarily generated, transmitted, and distributed by publicly owned enterprises in all provinces except Alberta, where electric power is provided by the investor-owned Canadian Utilities Limited; (d) most gas utilities and telephone companies are regulated by public utility boards using rate-of-return regulation; and (e) all provinces have their share of both publicly owned and investor (privately) owned utilities, except Saskatchewan, where public ownership is almost universal in the energy and telecommunications fields.

At the federal level, three regulatory commissions play a major role in the regulation of the TTE industries. They are the CTC, CRTC and NEB. Each is independent of direct political control—at least in principle.[28] Each holds public

27. Almost all of the provinces have separate motor carrier transport commissions in addition to their public utility boards. Note, that despite the growing debate about deregulation, Table 10-5 is as applicable to 1982 as 1976, indicating that there has been no essential change in provincial regulation of highway transport in recent years.

28. In fact, however, Ministerial influence can be important in Transportation and Communications and major NEB decisions are subject to Cabinet approval. See Richard Schultz, *Federalism and the Regulatory Process* (Montreal: Institute for Research on Public Policy, 1979) and by the same author "Federal Provincial Relations and the Regulatory System," G. Bruce Doern, ed. *The Regulatory Process in Canada* (Toronto: Macmillan, 1978).

Table 10-2

**Regulatory and Industry Structure: Transportation,
Communications And Energy Sectors Of Canada**

Good or Service	Regulatory Authority Federal	Provincial	Industry Structure
Railroads	Canadian Transport Commission(CTC)		Public firms (CNR)— private firm (CPR) duopoly
Airlines	Canadian Transport Commission (CTC)		Public firm (Air-Canada)— private firm (CP Air) national network, plus four regional air carriers two of which (Pacific Western Airlines and Quebecair) are government (Alberta and Quebec) owned. A third regional carrier, Nordair, is about to be purchased from Air Canada by a private firm, Innocan, and the fourth, Eastern Provincial Airways, was purchased by Canadian Pacific in mid-1984. Both purchases are subject to CTC approval, which is expected. There are also commuter airlines such as AirWest and Time Air.
Water Carriers	CTC		Loosely oligopolistic
Trucking		Highway Transport Boards in each province	Atomistic—but subject to regulatory constraints
Telephone	Canadian Radio-television and Telecommunications Commission (CRTC) regulates Bell Canada and B.C. Telephone, which together account for about 70% of Canadian telephones.	Provincial Public Utility Regulatory Boards for all other carriers	Monopoly in public local and long distance calls; some competition from CN/CP in long-distance data transmittal and private long-distance service. The telecommunications equipment market, once monopolized by a subsidiary of Bell Canada, is now competitive.

Good or Service	Regulatory Authority Federal	Provincial	Industry Structure
Broadcasting (TV and Radio)	CRTC		Two national networks, one public (CBC), one private (CTV) in *television* broadcasting. Two privately owned/regional networks (Global and TVA) and a number of privately owned TV firms. In addition to CBC *radio* network there are many independently owned and operated radio stations.
Cable TV	CRTC		Each firm has a territorial monopoly, but there may be several cable TV firms serving a metropolis. However, the industry is becoming nationally concentrated with Canadian Cable systems accounting for more than a quarter of all CATV customers.
Pay TV	CRTC		Regional monopoly in general programming PAY-TV. Some specialized services may be licensed.
Pipelines	National Energy Bd. (NEB) regulates interprovincial and export transmission of natural gas and oil	In Alberta, local transmission is provincially regulated.	Monopoly in interprovincial transport of oil and natural gas. Transcanada Pipeline and the Interprovincial Pipeline transmit gas and oil respectively to Eastern Canada; Westcoast Transmission and Trans Mountain Pipelines, gas and oil to West Coast.
Gas Utilities		Provincial Regulatory Commissions or Municipal Governments	Monopoly

Good or Service	Regulatory Authority		Industry Structure
	Federal	Provincial	
Electricity	NEB must approve export of electricity	In most provinces the government-owned electricity supplier is now subject to some form of regulation by a provincial regulatory board. In the provincial exceptions there may be some form of cabinet review.	Monopoly
Oil production		In Alberta, the Energy Resources Conservation Board. Nationally, the Minister of Energy.	Atomistic, but traditionally subject to regulatory controls (prorationing) over production.

hearings at which contending parties and other intervenors may be heard. Each in exercising social control, is carrying out, with varying degrees of effectiveness, broad public policies. In the remainder of this chapter we discuss the role of these three important federal regulatory agencies and the issues and policies related to the domain for which each is responsible.

The Regulation of Transport in Canada

Transportation systems have played an important role in Canadian history and development. The St. Lawrence and Great Lakes waterways influenced westward expansion and the location of population centres. The railways were a key

Table 10-3

Regulation and Ownership of Major Telephone Companies in Canada

Name of Carrier (I=Investor Owned G=Government Owned)	Operating Area	Regulated By	Approach to Rate Setting
Bell Canada (I)	Quebec, Ontario	CRTC	Rate-of-return regulation
Northwest Tel (G)	Northwest Territories	CRTC	Rate-of-return regulation
British Columbia Telephone (I)	British Columbia	CRTC	Rate-of-return regulation
Alberta Government Telephone (G)	Alberta, except Edmonton	Alberta Public Utilities Board	Rate-of-return regulation
Edmonton Telephones (G-city of Edmonton)	Edmonton	City of Edmonton	Rate-of-return regulation
Saskatchewan Telecommunications (G)	Saskatchewan	Saskatchewan Public Utility Review Commission	Not known
Manitoba Telephone System (G)	Manitoba	Manitoba Public Utilities Board	Rate-of-return regulation
Newfoundland Telephone Co.	Southern Nfld. and Labrador	Newfoundland Board of Public Utility Commissioners	Rate-of-return regulation

Company	Area served	Regulatory body	Type of regulation
Quebec Telephone (1.57% by GT&E)	Some locales in Quebec	Public Service Board of Quebec	Not known
New Brunswick Telephone Co. Ltd. (I)	New Brunswick	New Brunswick Board of Commissioners of Public Utilities	Rate-of-return regulation
Maritime Telegraph and Telephone Co. Ltd. (I)	Nova Scotia	Nova Scotia Board of Commissioners of Public Utilities	Rate-of-return regulation
Island Telephone	PEI	PEI Public Utilities Commission	Rate-of-return regulation
CN/CP Telecommunications (G-I)	Long distance and Yukon, Nfld.	CRTC	
TCTS (a consortium of the major telephone companies both investor and government owned)	Nonadjacent, interprovincial (toll) calls	TCTS is not regulated, but its members' long distance rates are subject to CRTC approval	Negotiated rates between members, subject to regulatory review.
Teleglobe (G)	International, overseas	—	Wide freedom to set rates

Source: Canadian Radio-television and Telecommunications Commission, *Annual Report* 1982-83, Table 9; D. Hartle, "The Regulation of Communications in Canada," *Government Regulation*, Ontario Economic Council, 1978, pp. 146-148.

Table 10-4

Electricity and Gas Utilities and Their Regulators in Canada

Province	Regulatory Authority	Jurisdiction	Leading Utilities (I=Investor Owned G=Government Owned)	Approach to Rate Regulation[a]
Alberta	Alberta Public Utilities Board (APUB)	Most electricity and gas generation and distribution	Canadian Utilities Ltd. (I) Canadian and Western Gas (I) Northwestern Utilities (I)	*Rate-of-return regulation*
	Municipal Governments	Electricity and gas distributed by municipally owned and operated utilities		Not specified
	Alberta Gas Trunkline	Gathering and transmission of natural gas within Alberta	Alberta Gas Trunkline Co. (I)	Not specified
British Columbia	B.C. Hydro	Electricity and gas generated and distributed by B.C. Hydro	B.C. Hydro (G)	Not specified
	B.C. Energy Commission	Regulation of all energy utilities except B.C. Hydro and certain municipally owned and operated utilities	Inland Natural Gas (I) Pacific Northern Gas (I) Columbia Natural Gas (I) Great Northern Gas Utilities (I) Three small investor-owned electric utilities (I)	Rates must be "fair and reasonable"—but specific methodology not specified
	Municipal governments	Electric and gas utilities owned and operated by municipalities where service is limited to those municipalities.		

Manitoba	Manitoba Public Utilities Board	All investor owned utilities, and all publicly owned utilities	Greater Winnipeg Gas Co. (I) Intercity Gas Ltd. (I) Plains Western Gas Ltd. (I) Manitoba Hydro (G)	Not specified in legislation; but *rate of return regulation* is used in practice Price must cover "full cost" of power provided
New Brunswick	New Brunswick Board of Public Utilities Commissioners	Electric energy supplied by the New Brunswick Electric Power Commission Natural gas distribution	New Brunswick Electric Power Commission (G) Moncton Utility Gas Ltd. (I)	Cover all costs plus that of attracting capital Just and reasonable rates, but method for so arriving is not specified
Newfoundland (no natural gas is distributed in Nfld.)	Board of Commissioners of Public Utilities	Electricity supplied by Nfld. & Labrador Power Electricity distributed by investor-owned electric utilities.	Newfoundland and Labrador Power (G) Newfoundland Light and Power Co. (I)	Basis is not prescribed *Rate of return regulation*

Province	Regulatory Authority	Jurisdiction	Leading Utilities (I=Investor Owned G=Government Owned)	Approach to Rate Regulation[a]
Nova Scotia (no natural gas distrib. in N.S.)	Board of Commissioners of Public Utilities	Power supplied by Nova Scotia Power Corp.	Nova Scotia Power Corp. (G)	Cover "cost" of power supplied
		Municipal water and electric utilities (there are no investor-owned electric utilities in N.S.)		*rate of return regulation*
Ontario	Ontario Hydro	Electricity rates, regulate rates of municipally owned electric utilities	Ontario Hydro (G)	Supply power to municipal distributors "at cost"
	Ontario Energy Board	Regulates wholesale and retail rates for gas transmission and distribution, and storage	Union Gas Ltd. (I) Consumers Gas Co. (I) Northern and Central Gas Corp. (I)	*Rate of return regulation*
		Can examine changes in Ontario Hydro wholesale rates for electricity		
	Municipalities	Municipally owned gas utilities		
PEI (no natural gas distrib. in PEI.)	Public Utilities Commission	Electricity supplied and distributed on PEI	Maritime Electric Co. (I) Summerside Electric Dept. (G)	Just and reasonable rates on an "earnings base."

Quebec	Hydro Quebec Electricity and Gas Board	Electric energy supplied by Hydro Quebec Gas distribution, and electricity supplied by utilities other than Hydro Quebec and municipal corporations	Hydro Quebec (G) Gas Metropolitain (G)	Lowest rates consistent with covering all costs Something approximating rate of return regulation
Saskatchewan	Public Utilities Review Commission	Electricity and natural gas supplied by the Saskatchewan Power Corporation; Electricity and gas of investor-owned utilities; and electricity and gas distributed by municipally owned and operated gas utilities	Saskatchewan Power Corporation (G) No important ones	Not specified Just and reasonable rates, but what constitutes such rates not prescribed
Federal	National Energy Board	Interprovincial and export transmission of natural gas and oil Export of electricity	Transcanada Pipelines (I) Trans Quebec and Maritime Pipeline (I) Interprovincial Pipeline (I) Trans Mountain Pipeline (I) Westcoast Transmission (I) Provincial Electricity Suppliers (mainly G)	Approval of export contracts; rate-of-return regulation Approval of export contracts

aEither prescribed by Act or adopted as a practice by the regulatory authority

Source: Energy Regulation Study, Report One (Edmonton, Alberta, Feb. 1975). Appendices B and Cd. pp. 62-82

Table 10-5

Canadian Trucking Regulation 1976 and 1982

Province	Intraprovincial		Interprovincial	
	Entry Regulation	Rate Regulation	Entry Regulation	Rate Regulation
British Columbia	Yes	Yes[a]	Yes	No[b]
Alberta	No	No	Yes	No
Saskatchewan	Yes	Yes[b]	Yes	No
Manitoba	Yes	Yes[b]	Yes	No[c]
Ontario	Yes	No[c]	Yes	No[c]
Quebec	Yes	Yes[a]	Yes	Yes[a]
New Brunswick	Yes	No[c]	Yes	No[c]
Nova Scotia	Yes	No[c]	Yes	No[c]
Prince Edward Island	Yes	No[c]	Yes	No[c]
Newfoundland	Yes	Yes[d]	Yes	Yes[c]

[a]Filing of rates required, with approval necessary for all increases.
[b]On intraprovincial traffic, Saskatchewan and Manitoba prescribe rates.
[c]Filing of rates required.
[d]While Newfoundland's regulatory agency has the power to regulate rates on extraprovincial traffic, there is some doubt whether this power has ever been effectively applied. Even on intraprovincial operations, the power to disallow rate increases has rarely been exercised.

Source: David Maister, "Regulation and the Level of Trucking Rates in Canada," University of British Columbia (mimeo) January 1977, p. 4, for 1976. Garland Chow, "How Much Longer Can we Live with Regulation of Canada's Trucking Industry," *Canadian Business Review* (Spring, 1983), p. 46, for 1982.

Table 10-6

Broadcasting and Cable TV in Canada: Originating Stations by Province, Type 1982

Province	TV				AM				FM				Total: All Broadcast	CATV Systems[a]
	E	F	M	Total	E	F	M	Total	E	F	M	Total		
Newfoundland	6			6	22			22	3		2	5	33	10
PEI	1			1	4			4	1			1	6	5
Nova Scotia	4			4	22			22	7		1	8	34	20
New Brunswick	3	1		4	15	4		19	4	1		5	28	28
Quebec	3	20	4	27	8	70		78	4	42	15	61	166	180
Ontario	27	2	2	31	93	5	3	101	66	2	1	69	201	141
Manitoba	4	1		5	16	1	3	20	7			7	32	39
Saskatchewan	8			8	20	0		20	9	1	1	11	39	57
Alberta	11	1		12	40	3	1	44	13			13	69	53
BC	12	1		13	57		1	58	14	1		15	86	90
Yukon Territory	1			1	2			2					3	} 2
Northwest Terr.	4	2			2	2	2	6			3	3	9	
Canada	80	26		112	303	83	10	396	130	47	21	198	706	625

Originating Stations; (originates in whole or in part daily programme schedule)
E = English
F = French
M = Multilingual; all other languages except English or French (includes Native and bilingual)
[a] March 1983
Source: CRTC Annual Report, 1981-82 Table 8-11, pp. 54-57; 1982-83, Table 5, p. 55.

part of the Canadian government's nation-making policy in the latter half of the 19th century.

Regulation of transportation by independent agency dates from 1903 when the Board of Railway Commissioners was established. (Prior to 1903 the railways were regulated by a cabinet committee, the Railway Committee of the Privy Council, under Railway Acts passed in 1851, 1868, and 1888, the last asserting control over rates.) The Board consisted of three members with the primary duty of regulating passenger fares and freight rates. With the growth of trucking competition in the 1920s and 1930s, and the advent of air carriage, the Board's title was changed, in 1938, to the Board of Transport Commissioners for Canada. It was given jurisdiction over air and water transport, and, in 1949, over interprovincial and international pipelines. However trucking, which had been regulated by the provinces since the 1920s, remained under provincial regulatory control, even in its extraprovincial aspect. Despite the *Winner* case (1954),[29] in which the Privy Council held that the provinces had no legislative authority to regulate extraprovincial trucking, this mode of transport was not brought under federal authority. The federal government promptly enacted legislation delegating powers to the provincial regulatory boards to regulate extraprovincial trucking. And there the authority remains.[30] In the meantime, the Board of Transport Commissioners lost control over air transport when, in 1944, an independent Air Transport Board was established.

This was the state of federal regulation over transport when the Royal Commission on Transportation (the MacPherson Commission) issued its report in 1961. Despite its title, the MacPherson Commission was chiefly concerned with the railroads in the context of an increasingly competitive intermodal climate. The MacPherson Commission advocated that freight rates be freed up from regulation, leaving to the carriers broad limits within which to set rates and charges on commodities not subject to statutory freight rates.[31] This important declaration in favour of competition was imprinted in the National Transportation Act passed in 1967, and although it has been applied only to rail transport,

---

29. *Attorney-General for Ontario v. Winner* (1954) A.C. 541.
30. On regulation of trucking, see chapter 12. Important recent research on the impact of regulation on Canadian trucking is found in F.P. Nix, *et al.*, "Motor Carrier Regulation: Institutions and Practices," Economic Council of Canada Working Paper No. E/I 1, August 1980; *Studies of Trucking Regulation*, Economic Council of Canada, Working Paper No. 3; and N.C. Bonsor, *Transportation Economics: Theory and Canadian Policy* (Toronto: Butterworth, 1984), chapter 5.
31. As a matter of fact, the Board of Railway Commissioners and its successor, the Board of Transport Commissioners, had allowed the railways to charge "competitive rates" (with Board approval) and to establish "agreed charges" with shippers in order to meet competition from highway trucking and water transport. Thus, as progressive a step as deregulation of freight rates was, it was not as big a step as might at first seem apparent. See M.A. Prabhu, "Freight Rate Regulation in Canada," *McGill Law Journal*, June 1971, pp. 292-359.

provided a strong contrast between the policies of the CTC and the U.S. Interstate Commerce Commission (ICC), which until very recently exercised rigid control over railway freight rates in the U.S.[32]

The creation of the Canadian Transport Commission (CTC), in 1967, brought the regulation of each transport mode under one roof. Although the MacPherson Commission had emphasized intermodal rather than intramodal competition, it had specifically advised against unifying the regulatory authority over competing modes. However, Parliament rejected this advice in drawing up the National Transportation Act, although the actual regulation of transportation by the CTC is undertaken by separate transport committees: railway, air, water, highway trucking and commodity pipelines (the last two are largely inoperative because trucking regulation is carried out primarily by the provinces and there are no "commodity"—as opposed to oil and natural gas—pipelines). The existence of separate transport committees of the CTC means that there is a substantial degree of independence between the regulation of the various transport modes. However, since most of the seventeen CTC commissioners sit on more than one transport committee some interaction in the regulation of the different modes exists.[33]

Although the National Transportation Act nominally reflects the MacPherson Commission's view that competition was an important ingredient in establishing and maintaining an economic and efficient transportation system, the actual facts of intermodal competition are otherwise. The regulation of highway transport has restricted entry and controlled rates and, until recently, the same was true of airlines.[34] Economies of scale and other technological factors limit *intramodal* competition among railroads, except perhaps between Toronto and Montreal and on long haul, transnational traffic. Only water carriage of bulk commodities (90 percent of the tonnage carried by ships) is free of both rate regulation and high entry barriers.[35]

Thus the focus of the National Transportation Act and the CTC is on *intermodal* competition. There can be no doubt that, in the past half century, competition from "new" modes (air and highway) has eroded the once naturally

---

32. In the late 1970s the ICC began to loosen its control over freight rates and, in 1980, with the passage of the Staggers Act deregulated the railways altogether.

33. Hudson Janisch, *The Regulatory Process of the Canadian Transport Commission*, Administrative Law Series, Law Reform Commission of Canada (Ottawa: Minister of Supply and Services Canada, 1978).

34. In mid-1984 the Minister of Transport issued a policy statement substantially relaxing entry and price controls over airlines (see below).

35. However, the establishment of common rate schedules by "shipping conferences" (associations of ocean liner operators) is widespread in the industry, and is currently exempt under the combines laws. Consumer and Corporate Affairs, Combines Investigation Act, *Annual Report*, Director of Investigation and Research, for year ended March 31, 1978 (Minister of Supply and Services, 1978), pp. 21-23.

monopolistic position of the railways, while competition from an "old" mode has blossomed with the construction of the St. Lawrence Seaway. Nevertheless, technological and geographical constraints limit somewhat the possibilities for *intermodal* competition. The main competitive interfaces are between (i) railroads and water carriers for the transport of bulk goods (raw materials) between the Lakehead and Eastern Canada; (ii) trucks and railroads for intermediate and long hauls of manufactured goods—trucks dominate the short-haul market; (iii) highway and air carriers for valuable, low density goods; (iv) water and air for the supply of isolated (arctic) communities; (v) bus and rail for short-haul passenger service not captured by the private automobile. Air has a virtual stranglehold on long-haul passenger service; pipelines on the shipment of natural gas and crude oil, although railroads can provide some competition for the latter.

In sum, competition between transport modes is imperfect—necessarily so. Yet the strength of even imperfect competition is such that arbitrary restraints would produce major distortions in the allocation of resources and could result in the bankrupting of certain modes (e.g. railroads—as the U.S. example suggests). At this juncture, it would appear that further increases in competition in the transport field require loosening the restraints on *intramodal* competition, especially in the air and trucking fields. At present, rate and entry regulation in trucking is one of the better examples of producer protection legislation conforming to Stigler's economic theory of regulation in intent, and to either the Posner or Tullock theories of regulatory effect (see chapter 7 and chapter 12). Much the same argument can be made about the effect of airline regulation.[36] However, the picture is somewhat complicated by the fact that as a matter of policy air service is provided, whether economic or not, between low density points as a means of providing greater communication over Canada's huge and sparsely populated expanse. Moreover, on the high density routes there was, until recently, a conscious policy of protecting the market for the government-owned carrier, Air Canada—clearly a means of providing the revenues necessary for cross-subsidization of Air Canada's less profitable, or plainly unprofitable, routes. CP Air, Canada's only other trunk air carrier, was, until 1979, limited by the CTC to a maximum of 25 percent of passengers carried on trunkline routes served by Air Canada.[37] While the limitations on CP

---

36. See William Jordan, *Performance of Regulated Canadian Airlines in Domestic and Transborder Operations* (Ottawa: Bureau of Competition Policy, Consumer and Corporate Affairs Canada), Research Monograph No. 12, 1982. Jordan uses comparisons of the performance of regulated interstate air carriers in the U.S. and Canada with that of unregulated intrastate carriers (in California and Texas) to draw inferences about the consequences of airline regulation in Canada.

37. In 1979, the Canadian Transport Commission, perhaps reacting to deregulation of commercial airlines in the U.S., lifted its restriction on CP Air's share of domestic markets. For a good discussion of the roadblocks thrown up against deregulation of Canada's airlines in the early

Air's capacity and its right to enter into direct competition with Air Canada were relaxed in the late 1970s, airline policy remained largely protectionist until mid 1984 when the Minister of Transport announced a substantial liberalization of airline regulation (see below). Until now, the basic argument for a protectionist policy seems to have been that the size of the Canadian market is not sufficient to allow all-out competition between air carriers, even if rivalry is limited to two carriers.

The regulation, and deregulation, of transport in Canada has been complicated by at least three factors:

(i) It is stymied by the conflicting objectives of economic efficiency called for by the MacPherson Report and reflected, at least in part, in the National Transportation Act and the use of transportation as a tool for regional economic development.[38]

(ii) The use of the transportation system, primarily railways, to subsidize particular groups requires that more than compensatory charges must be levied on other traffic, thus distorting the allocation of transportation resources and inducing a "second-round" of redistributive effects. The best-known example is the so-called "Crow's Nest Pass rates," which until 1984 were fixed at 1897 levels, for the movement of grain between the Prairie provinces and the ports at the Lakehead, Churchill, and Vancouver.

(iii) The decisions in the United States to deregulate airlines, railroads, and trucking, have had transborder effects. Of these, U.S. deregulation of its airlines has had the highest profile in Canada, resulting in substantial pressure for deregulation here.

A. Freight Rates

Under provisions of the NTA, the railways are permitted to set "competitive" freight rates within a broad band. At one end the rates must be "compensatory" (i.e. they must cover variable costs) and, at the other end they must not be "monopolistic" (i.e. they must not exceed 250 percent of variable costs to so-called "captive shippers"—those with no other transport alternatives). Under the NTA, the CTC may be called upon by shippers, or other interested parties, to determine, in specific cases, variable cost, the existence of "captive shipper" status, or to otherwise determine whether a particular rate "prejudicially affects the public interest." In its first decade, there were only a handful of applications to the CTC's Rail-Transport Committee for investigation of specific rail freight rates. However, the CTC was continually forced to look over its shoulder at parliamentary critics who argued that Canada lacks a transportation policy

1980s, see G.B. Reschenthaler and W.T. Stanbury, "Deregulating Canada's Airlines: Grounded by False Assumptions" *Canadian Public Policy*, June 1983, pp. 210-222 and the reply by Pierre Jeanniot in *CPP* (forthcoming).
38. See Howard Darling, *The Politics of Freight Rates* (Toronto: McClelland and Stewart, 1980).

(apparently competition is not considered a policy), and at interest groups intent on amending the NTA to give government more direct control over the carriers.[39]

Despite the appearance of being without a transportation policy, the increased reliance on market forces and competition in establishing freight rates and allocating railway resources is a policy—and a very successful one at that. Just how successful, is revealed in a comparative study of U.S. and Canadian railroads covering the two decades from the mid 1950s to the mid 1970s, a period when Canada was progressively deregulating while the U.S. was holding onto a rigid system of regulation.[40] The study estimated the productivity growth rate of the CNR and CPR and of five U.S. railroads with networks similar to the transcontinental facilities of Canada's two main railways.[41] Using a total factor measure of productivity, estimating cost functions rather than production functions, and employing advanced statistical techniques, the study found that the productivity growth of the Canadian railroads was much more rapid than that of the U.S. counterparts. Moreover, the spread between productivity growth rates grew after full deregulation of Canadian freight rates in the mid to late 1960s. The productivity growth differential was so marked that Canadian railway productivity levels which had been 25 percent lower than those of comparable U.S. railroads in the 1950s were by the mid 1970s twenty percent higher than those of the U.S. railroads. The authors of the study estimated that the cost of producing railway services in the U.S. in 1974 alone was $6.7 billion higher than it would have been had the productivity performance of the U.S. railroads matched that of Canada's railroads. The $6.7 billion, which amounted to 40 percent of total expenses of U.S. railroads, was the estimated cost of railway regulation in the U.S.—and by extension an indicator of the success of deregulation of railroads in Canada.

There is, however, a cloud on the horizon. The belated deregulation of U.S. railroads following passage of the Staggers Act in 1980, has important implications for the behaviour as well as the performance of Canada's railroads. Prior to U.S. deregulation, the relative (to Canada) rise in railway transportation

39. Trevor D. Heaver and James C. Nelson, *Railway Pricing Under Commercial Freedom: The Canadian Experience* (Vancouver: University of British Columbia, Centre for Transportation Studies, 1977). For a somewhat different view on the degree of transportation competition exercised under the NTA, see John C. McManus, "On the 'New' Transportation Policy After Ten Years," *Studies in Regulation in Canada*, ed. W.T. Stanbury (Toronto: Butterworth, 1978), pp. 109-230.
40. Recall that in the 1950s Canadian railroads were given permission to negotiate rates ("agreed charges") with shippers, a decade before fuller deregulation of freight rates under the NTA.
41. See Douglas Caves, Laurits Christensen and Joseph Swanson, "The High Cost of Regulating U.S. Railroads," *Regulation* (January- February 1981), pp. 41-46; and by the same authors "Economic Performance in Regulated and Unregulated Environments: A Comparison of U.S. and Canadian Railroads," *Quarterly Journal of Economics*, November 1981, pp. 559-581.

costs led to some diversion of cross-country traffic from U.S. to Canadian railways. As competition replaces regulation in the U.S. and improved efficiency allows costs and prices to decline, at least relatively, the U.S. roads can be expected to win back some or all of the traffic lost prior to deregulation. Moreover, in certain respects deregulation in the U.S. went beyond its Canadian counterpart. For example, U.S. railroads are allowed to make rebates to shippers in competing for orders, something Canadian railroads are not permitted to do. Moreover, whereas the Canadian railways are allowed to get together (collude) in setting freight rates (so-called "collective rate making"), the U.S. railroads would be in violation of the U.S. antitrust laws if they did so.[42] Since collective rate making does not necessarily imply prices in excess of competitive levels, this difference between the U.S. and Canada would not mean much were it not for the "extraterritorial" application of the U.S. antitrust laws. That is, the Sherman Antitrust Act can be applied to foreigners so long as their culpable (under U.S. law) behaviour may affect U.S. commerce.[43] Since both CN and CP hold substantial railway properties in the U.S., these could be held "hostage" if the antitrust laws were applied against "collective" rate-making on the Canadian portion of transborder shipments. Reaching an amenable understanding with the U.S. on the extraterritorial issue will be a test of Canadian-U.S. relations and diplomacy.

Although the deregulation of freight rates under the NTA has, on the whole, been a success, there remain powerful forces favouring greater interventionism in the railway industry. At the core of the problem is Canada's historic reliance on transportation as a tool of national and regional economic development. Transport is still seen as such a tool by the provinces—which is one of the reasons they now jealously guard their constitutionally questionable regulatory control over extraprovincial trucking. As all politicians do know, and economists should know, the term "development tool" is usually a scarcely disguised term for cross-subsidization—or simply outright subsidies. Thus uneconomic activities will be supported by economic ones, or by the pocketbooks of taxpayers. Typically, "development-minded" criticisms of the CTC take the form of complaints about railway freight charges—which we have seen are "competitively" set within a wide band and over which the CTC has little or no control. Many of these complaints come from Westerners who believe that the structure of freight rates has hindered the economic development of their provinces.

42. See Anthony P. Ellison, "Regulatory Reform in Transport: A Canadian Perspective," *Transportation Journal* (Summer 1984).
43. See David Peippo, "Developments in American Antitrust Law: Deregulation under the Staggers Rail Act and the Implications for Canadian Railroad Rate-Making," *McGill Law Journal*, 27 (1981-82), pp. 504-26.

Not all western complaints about railway freight rate charges are without economic (as opposed to income–distributional) merit. An example is the *Rapeseed* case.[44] In 1970, the Saskatchewan Wheat Pool and three western processors of rapeseed meal and oil applied to the CTC, under the "public interest" section (s.23) of the NTA, for an investigation of comparative freight rates for raw rapeseed and for rapeseed meal and oil. Both raw rapeseed and rapeseed meal and oil moved under Crow's Nest Pass rates from western Canada to Thunder Bay. From Thunder Bay to eastern and export markets rail freight rates for meal and oil exceeded those of raw rapeseed. The processors argued that there was no significant differential on cost grounds and that the rate differential would make it more profitable to locate processing plants in eastern Canada, to the detriment of industrial development in the West. The arguments of the processors were supported by the western provinces. For their part, the railways argued that the rapeseed oil and meal moved to eastern Canada under agreed charges which (due to an apparent technicality) were not covered by section 23 of the NTA.[45] After clearing away numerous procedural issues, the CTC, in 1973, finally rendered its decision in the *Rapeseed* case by deciding in favour of the processors. It ordered the railways to reduce freight charges on transport of rapeseed meal, but not those on rapeseed oil, which were no higher than those of other vegetable oils.[46]

B. Subsidies

A closely related problem is the historic use of the transportation system, primarily the railways, to subsidize particular groups. The subsidies take the form of lower (than compensatory) freight charges and passenger fares, and the continued operation of little-used lines. These tend to distort the allocation of transportation resources, require higher (than compensatory) charges on other traffic and induce thereby a "second round" of (usually unintended) redistributive effects.

44. Canadian Transport Commission, Railway Transport Committee, "Decision in the Matter of the Application and Appeal of Saskatchewan Wheat Pool, Agra Industries Ltd., Co-op Vegetable Oils Ltd., and Western Canadian Seed Processors Ltd., pursuant to section 23 of the *National Transportation Act*," File No. 30637.2.

45. Agreed charges are rates negotiated between shippers and the railways as a method by which the railways could meet competition.

46. For a discussion of the *Rapeseed* and some other CTC cases see Martin W. Westmacott, "The Canadian Transport Commission, Freight Rates and the Public Interest," *Transportation Policy: Regulation, Competition, and the Public Interest*, ed. Karl M. Ruppenthal and W.T. Stanbury, Centre for Transportation Studies (Vancouver: University of British Columbia Press, 1976), pp. 62 ff. On some other cases see H.N. Janisch, *The Canadian Transport Commission, supra* note 33. One reason why freight rates for processed rapeseed exceeded those of raw rapeseed is that the latter moved under the statutory Crow's Nest Pass rates at only a fraction of the real cost of transport incurred by the railways.

An example of cross-subsidization, implanted until recently into Canada's regional fabric, was the freight rates that governed the transport of grain between the Prairie provinces and the ports at Lakehead, Churchill, and Vancouver. These rates, known as the Crow's Nest Pass rates, required the railroads to transport western grain at levels established in 1897.[47] Long regarded (at least by the railroads) as uncompensatory even on a short-run, out-of-pocket basis, the Crow's Nest Pass rates provided a classic form of cross-subsidization of persons engaged in grain production and marketing by those not so engaged. Ironically, the cross-subsidization may not have been mainly interregional (as is usually argued) but intraregional, owing to the tendency for the railroads to charge higher freight rates on raw materials and manufactured goods shipped in the West, where *intermodal* competition is less intense.[48]

Direct payments by the federal government to the railroads in lieu of branch line abandonment constitute another example of subsidies to the grain trade. Canadian taxpayers now absorb 80 percent of the estimated losses incurred by the railroads on branch lines (mainly located in the Prairies) which the railroads would otherwise abandon as uneconomic. The rationale for nonabandonment is that many Western communities would not be viable without rail transportation to carry the grain to market. This was once true, but that was before trucks came along. However, one problem with the trucking alternative was that the Crow's Nest Pass rates only applied to rail transport of grains. Thus the implicit subsidies to rail transport in the carriage of grain made alternative, and otherwise more economic, modes of transport less attractive to grain shippers and thereby less politically palatable to transportation policymakers.[49]

By the early 1980s, the inadequacies of clinging to the Crow Rate were abundantly clear. A decade of inflation had widened the gap between the non-compensatory Crow Rate and the variable costs incurred by the railways in transporting grain. Out-of-pocket in the amount of hundreds of millions of dollars annually as a result of their grain transport activities, the railroads had

47. Recently there have been reports on both the cost of grain transport and branchline abandonment. Canada, *Report of the Commission to Determine the Costs of Transportation of Grain by Rail* (Snavely) Vol. 1, (Ottawa, Transport Canada, Dec. 1976); and Canada, *The Grain Handling and Transportation Commission* (Hall), Vols. I-II, Ottawa, 1977.

48. Since railroads can, within a fairly wide range, set freight rates, one would expect rates to be lower where intermodal competition is greater (Windsor-Quebec corridor) than in the Prairies where intermodal competition is more limited. Under the provisions of the NTA freight rates must be "compensatory"—i.e. they must cover variable costs including certain depreciation and maintenance costs. The upper bound is a rate two-and-one-half times variable costs if a "captive shipper" requests the CTC to set a rate at this level and be continued for a period no less than one year in length.

49. For a masterful description and analysis of the Canadian grain transport industry and regulatory (including statutory grain rates) barriers to its rationalization see David H. Maister, "Technical and Organizational Change in a Regulated Industry: The Case of Canadian Grain Transport," *Studies on Regulation in Canada*, op. cit., pp. 153-207.

neither the incentive nor the financial wherewithal to invest in new rolling stock, maintain roadbeds, and modernize port facilities for grain export. Thus in the 1970s the federal government had begun to pour hundreds of millions of dollars into the acquisition of a fleet of 10,000 grain hopper cars, maintenance of branchlines, and upkeep of port facilities. Still, the grain transport system was nearing a breakdown with mainlines and port facilities unable to handle the amounts of grain that Prairie farmers were able to produce and that other nations were willing to purchase. Something had to give, and Ottawa decided that it was time for "the Crow" to go.

In February 1982, Ottawa commissioned J.C. Gilson, a University of Manitoba agricultural economist, to examine alternatives to the Crow rate.[50] At the same time, the Minister of Transport announced that the federal government was committing itself to compensating a major part of the losses that would be incurred by various groups from alterations of the Crow rate. With this guarantee as a basis for finding a solution, Gilson and his committee focused on three questions. These were: (a) what were the railways *currently* losing as a result of transporting grain?; (b) who should foot the cost of *future* increases in rates for grain transport? and (c) who should receive the federal subsidies for grain transport, the farmers or the railways? The answers that the Gilson Report provided to the first two questions were: (i) that the railways were out-of-pocket $644 million in the 1981/82 crop year as a result of their transport of grain, an annual shortfall the federal government obligated itself to finance in perpetuity; and (ii) that future increases in rail freight rates for grain should be shared by the shippers and the federal government, with the latter shouldering all annual increases in excess of 3 percent until 1986 after which the breakpoint would rise to 6 percent per annum. Again Ottawa acquiesced.

The third issue, to whom should the federal subsidies be paid, was the most controversial. The farmers argued adamantly that the "Crow Benefit" should be paid to the railways and the railways just as adamantly, but with less political punch, argued that it should be paid to the shippers. Why the disagreement? Apparently neither party wanted to appear to be the recipient of subsidies nor to risk the possibility that a spendthrift federal government under new political leadership might someday pull in its spending horns and cut its subsidies to grain transport. In addition, farmer groups felt that if the Crow Benefit were paid to the railways the latter might find it politically more difficult to jack up freight rates in the future. In any event, Gilson proposed that in the first two or three years the subsidy be paid in full to the railways after which it would be split

50. For an excellent analysis of the Crow Rate and the Gilson Report, see Kenneth Norrie, "Not Much to Crow About: A Primer on the Statutory Grain Freight Rate Issue," *Canadian Public Policy* (Dec. 1983), pp. 434-445. My discussion of the Gilson Report relies heavily on the Norrie article.

with the proportion received by the railways declining to 19 percent and the proportion received by the shippers rising to 81 percent by the mid-1990s. This recommendation was varied by the federal government to a 50-50 split. However when the Crow rate legislation passed through Parliament in the spring of 1983, the farm lobbies had prevailed. All of the Crow Benefit was to be paid to the railways indefinitely.

At this point, the student may ask whether it matters who receives the Crow Benefit. The answer is, emphatically, yes! If it is paid to the shippers, the quid pro quo is a rise to compensatory levels in the actual freight rates paid by growers. If, alternatively, the Crow Benefit is paid to the railways, the actual amount paid by shippers remains at Crow levels, except that portion of future cost increases the shippers are obliged to pay. Thus payment of the "Crow Benefit" to the railways means that the distortions created by the Crow rate will continue. It will still be cheaper, if less efficient, to make short-haul shipments by railroad rather than trucks. It will still be cheaper, if locationally less efficient, to ship the raw grain to processing plants in the East rather than processing it in the West and shipping the finished product at unregulated rates to the eastern markets. Thus on a crucial, to economic common sense, issue the government caved in to extraordinary political pressures which so often explain the form if not the logic of regulatory legislation.

Airline Policy

The deregulation of transport in the United States has begun to have an influence on Canadian transportation policy. One mode which has been under pressure to relax its regulation is airlines.

Until the mid-1970s the airline industry consisted of two trunk airlines (Air Canada and CP Air), one publicly owned and one privately owned, and five privately owned regional carriers.[51] In 1975, one of the regional carriers (Pacific Western Airlines [PWA]) was purchased by the Alberta government. Then, in 1977, PWA, which serves routes in Alberta, B.C. and some northern (arctic) routes as well, agreed to purchase the failing Transair Company with routes in northern Ontario, Manitoba, and the Canadian Arctic. If Transair's routes were linked to PWA via Winnipeg-Edmonton and Winnipeg-Calgary (a condition of purchase by PWA) the merger would have effectively resulted in a third trunk airline. However behind-the-scenes negotiations between PWA and Air Canada took place with PWA seeking Air Canada support for the western

---

51. Essentially, the trunk carriers serve East-West routes in Canada and the international market. The regional carriers operate more nearly on a North-South route basis and in some cases provide charter service. A case study of Air Canada's behaviour under regulatory constraint is John R. Baldwin, *The Regulatory Agency and the Public Corporation: The Canadian Air Transport Industry* (Cambridge: Ballinger, 1975).

links between PWA and Transair routes in return for lopping off some of Transair's Ontario routes in favour of Nordair. Air Canada went along with the proposal, in part because it intended to (and eventually did) purchase Nordair, one of the remaining regional carriers.[52] In 1982, government ownership increased further when the Quebec government's purchase of Quebecair, the fifth of the original regional carriers, saved that firm from bankruptcy.

As Canada entered the 1980s its airline industry retained its national-regional structure. It also remained subject to relatively tight federal regulatory control over entry, exit, and fares. The first steps toward less restrictive regulation involved giving the national carriers, Air Canada and CP Air, wider latitude in setting fares, especially promotional ones in the form of charter class and seat sales.[53] Restrictions on entry by CP Air into new city pairs in competition with Air Canada were also eliminated. One result of these policies was that the regional airlines had to endure increased competition from the national carriers, but were unable to retaliate by invading national routes. To some obervers, the result was the demise of CTC's policy of having a combination of healthy regional as well as national air carriers. In the meantime, as the result of developments south of the border, pressure was building for further deregulation of Canada's airline industry—pressure resisted by government policy makers. Particularly evident to Canadian consumers was the wide variety of service quality and discount packages available to U.S. travellers—and to many Canadian travellers too, who were willing to drive across the border to nearby U.S. airports.

In May 1984, the Minister of Transport, Lloyd Axworthy, announced a major liberalization of airline regulation.[54] The announcement took the form of a policy statement, which the Minister wants the CTC to take into account in its decision making, rather than new legislation. The new airline policy would: (i) repeal all existing policies defining air carrier rules, so that, for example, Wardair, a charter carrier and PWA, a regional airline, could with CTC approval, fly national routes previously reserved for Air Canada and CP Air; (ii) eliminate all restrictions on airline licences, such as those specifying the kind and size of equipment used and those prohibiting or limiting the frequency of non-stop

52. Subsequently, Air Canada agreed to sell Nordair, but held onto the profitable regional carrier until 1984 when a private firm, Innocan, made an acceptable offer.
53. This made them more competitive with Wardair. Wardair is allowed to provide *charter* service on national routes with all this implies about advanced booking, etc. However, the charter level fare, which must cover all of the costs (variable and overhead) of a flight, is easily met by the charter class fares of the national carriers, and undercut by their seat sales. At the same time economy and first class fares allow the national carriers to cover their overhead expense. In short, airline policy in the early 1980s allowed the national carriers but not Wardair to price discriminate.
54. Minister of Transport, *New Canadian Air Policy*, Ministry of Transport Canada, May 10, 1984.

service a carrier could provide; (iii) lower the barriers to new entry and provide freedom of exit into and out of city pair routes and the industry as a whole; (iv) reduce control over airline pricing by giving the carriers unlimited freedom to reduce fares while limiting fare increases to an objective measure such as the rise in their non-labour costs; (v) simplify and speed up the regulatory process. In addition, the policy calls for a liberalization of air transport relations with the U.S. to allow greater freedom of entry into the provision of, and the prices set for, transborder services. The policy also directs Air Canada to be profitable and abjure money-losing policies (that the taxpayer would eventually have to foot) aimed at maintaining its market share.[55]

However, the new airline policy does not call for complete deregulation, or an end to all niggling restrictions. Not only are there limits on fare increases, but CTC approval is needed if a new firm wants to enter the industry or an existing firm wants to provide service between city pairs not currently covered by its licences. Moreover, the policy does not allow carriers to provide *nonstop* services between points not on the same licence. Thus, for example, PWA could provide service between Vancouver and Toronto—but not nonstop service. The same is true for service provided by EPA between St. John's, Newfoundland and Toronto. In addition, the new policy does not apply to services to or within Canada's north. Nevertheless, the *New Canadian Air Policy* represents a major departure from previous thinking and regulatory methods. It remains to be seen how far the CTC will go in carrying out the liberalization, although early signs indicate it is generally receptive to the new policy.

The Regulation Of Communications In Canada

The Canadian Radio-television and Telecommunications Commission (CRTC) was established in 1968 to administer federal policy in the broadcasting field. Federal involvement in broadcasting began in the 1930s with the creation of the Canadian Broadcasting Corporation (CBC), Canada's government-owned radio-television network. For two decades the CBC also exercised regulatory functions over broadcasting. The Broadcasting Act of 1958, partly in response to the growth of private broadcasters, vested regulatory authority in a Board of Broadcast Governors. The Broadcasting Act of 1968 replaced the Board with the CRTC and gave the CRTC authority to supervise and regulate all facets of the Canadian broadcasting system. In 1976, telecommunications, which until then had been regulated by the CTC because of the historic connection between railroads and telegraphy, was transferred to the CRTC. As Table 10-3 indicates,

55. Ibid., pp. 14-15. Air Canada's competitors feared the government-owned carrier, backed by the taxpayer pocketbook, might enter into predatory pricing and service proliferation in an attempt to prevent equally efficient competitors from taking a share of its market.

the CRTC thereby gained responsibility for regulating the leading telecommunications carriers in Canada: Bell Canada, B.C. Telephone, and CN/CP Telecommunications.

A. Broadcasting

When the CBC was created in the 1930s the main objective of federal policy was to provide a broadcasting network which would tie together Canada's far-flung regions and peoples. With the growth of broadcasting, particularly television, in the postwar period, the thrust of federal communications policy became more subtle and debatable. Four areas deserve mention: (i) the application of "Canadian content" rules; (ii) the regulation of cable TV (CATV); (iii) the method of granting licences; (iv) the promotion (or lack of it) of diversity in television programming.

In the CRTC's first decade three of these issues, Canadian content, control of CATV, and licensing criteria played a central role in broadcasting regulation. The three issues are interwined. The licensing of broadcasters has generally been protective of their economic position, a policy which makes it easier to administer Canadian content rules which, *ceteris paribus*, reduce the profits of Canadian broadcasters.[56] In turn, the CRTC has found it necessary to control the incursions by CATV in order to protect the profitability of local (Canadian) broadcasters.

1. Canadian Content

The Broadcasting Act of 1968 enunciated the position that Canada's cultural integrity must be defended by assuring a certain degree of Canadian content in radio and TV broadcasting. Section 3 of the Broadcasting Act of 1968 states that "the Canadian broadcasting system should be effectively owned and controlled by Canadians so as to safeguard, enrich and strengthen the cultural, political, social and economic fabric of Canada." Further, "the programming provided by the Canadian broadcasting system should be varied and comprehensive" and "the programming provided by each broadcaster should be of high standard, *using predominantly Canadian creative and other resources*" (emphasis added). The Canadian content issue arises because of the perceived domination of Canadian airwaves by foreign (read U.S.) programming. The Canadian content rules are aimed primarily at prime time viewing, the evening hours when the "typical" viewer watches more or less the same fare as his American counterpart. Since the Canadian content rules are applied to private broadcasters who depend totally on advertising revenues, as well as to the CBC

---

56. Given audience tastes for U.S.-type programming, it is cheaper to buy than to imitate the U.S. product, and more profitable to cater to mass tastes than to provide a truly distinctive bill of fare. An excellent discussion of these and other issues is found in Robert E. Babe, "Regulation of Private Television Broadcasting by the Canadian Radio-Television Commission: A Critique of Ends and Means," *Canadian Public Administration* (Winter 1976), pp. 552-586.

which can count on government subsidies to cover deficits, the CRTC, as an offset, has been solicitous of the economic position of the broadcasters. Thus its policies have been largely protective when dealing with the competitive inroads of cable television and licensing.

2. Cable TV

The threat that U.S. programming can reach the final consumer without any role played by local broadcast stations has influenced CRTC regulation of cable television. At first, the CRTC attempted to severely restrict the availability of CATV, but in the face of public outcry implemented a less restrictive set of policies designed to make CATV provide implicit subsidies to local broadcasters. These policies include CATV (a) giving priority to Canadian stations; (b) deleting U.S. programming where it simultaneously duplicates the fare of a local station; (c) compensating local broadcasters, and (d) considering the deletion of Canadian advertising carried by American stations.[57] In addition, the CRTC establishes maximum rates charged by CATV licensees.

3. Licensing

In an important respect, broadcast regulation in Canada has followed a pattern similar to that in the United States. Both the U.S. Federal Communications Commission (FCC) and the CRTC have been quite content to turn over to private interests an important piece of public property, the broadcast spectrum, for virtually no monetary compensation. Since the broadcast spectrum is limited, those who receive a licence to broadcast (to use a portion of the spectrum) are granted a valuable property right (asset) for which they do not have to pay, although they are nominally required to follow certain rules such as local programming and the Canadian content regulations. Given the strong demand by advertisers to use the airwaves to transmit commercial messages, the limited supply of broadcasters, and the relatively low cost of broadcasting equipment, it is not surprising to find that most radio and TV stations are highly profitable.[58]

57. Ibid., pp. 561-62. Many of these, and other telecommunications issues, are discussed in a report by the Consultative Committee on the Implications of Telecommunications for Canadian Sovereignty (Clyne Report), *Telecommunications and Canada*, March 1979 (Ottawa: Minister of Supply and Services Canada, 1979). Among the more controversial recommendations of the report is one stating that "The CRTC, in authorizing the carriage of television stations by *cable*, should continue to give precedence to Canadian stations and *should not increase beyond four* the number of U.S. stations that may be distributed" (emphasis added), p. 4. More recent works on broadcasting policy, particularly the cultural content issue, are *Report of the Federal Cultural Policy Review Committee* (Applebaum-Hébert) (Ottawa: Department of Communications, 1982), Chap. 10, and Paul Audley, *Canada's Cultural Industries: Broadcasting, Publishing, Records and Film* (Ottawa: Canadian Institute for Economic Policy, 1983). For a critical review of cultural regulation, see Steven Globerman, *Cultural Regulation in Canada* (Montreal: Institute for Research on Public Policy, 1983).

58. Ibid. p. 562. Babe reports an average rate of return on assets of 34 percent, a figure which hides to some extent the extremely high returns to the owners of equity in the more profitable broadcasting operations. The pattern is similar in the U.S. Clair Wilcox and W.G. Shepherd,

The virtual giveaway of a limited and valuable property right yields huge economic rents for which the public's only compensation is a vague pledge by the licensee to act in the "public interest."

As a result some economists have argued that when licences come up for renewal, as they do every three to five years, there should be a public bidding for them, with the highest bidder, *ceteris paribus*, receiving the licence, the public coffers to that degree enriched.[59] In this way, those broadcasters now enjoying "excess" profitability due to the licence to use a scarce resource, the broadcast spectrum, will have the economic rents bid away at the time of licence renewal, thereby transferring the rents into public revenues. However, one problem with this approach is that in many cases the economic rents, or a substantial portion thereof, have already been capitalized. The capitalization will occur when one licensee sells his rights (licence) to another—subject, of course, to CRTC (or FCC) approval. The sale value of the licence will reflect the rents or profitability of the operation: the paid-for value of the assets to the buyer will be correspondingly higher, and will typically exceed, substantially, the replacement cost of the physical assets transferred.[60] It is not surprising, then, to find that on the average about half of the value of the assets of broadcasters is the "good will" inherent in the licence. However, it does not follow that a return need not be earned on the good will. It is true that no return on good will is required to compensate the initial licensee. But subsequent purchasers who effectively paid for the licence as well as the physical equipment need a return on the former, as well as the latter, in order to cover all costs—including capital outlay.[61]

4. Diversity

One of the most debated issues in broadcasting is the diversity, or lack of it, in programming. In the U.S., until the Public Broadcasting System came along, television programming, with a few exceptions, was widely termed a "wasteland." The introduction of educational, non-commercial TV provided a distinct alternative to the fare provided by the three commercial networks. In Canada, the existence of a publicly owned network, the CBC, has not prevented similar criticisms from being applied to the programming here, much of it a representation of U.S. programming. The concern for diversity exists despite the fact that

Public Policies Toward Business, 5th edition (Homewood, Illinois: Irwin, 1975), p. 455. Incidentally, broadcasting licences are almost always renewed. Revocations are extremely rare.
59. Richard Coase, "The Economics of Broadcasting and Government Policy," *American Economic Review* 56 (May 1966).
60. The capitalization issue arises in numerous other contexts and will be discussed in more detail in chapter 12—particularly with respect to agriculture.
61. This is a good example of the "transitional gains trap" (see chapters 7 and 12) in which an attempt by current policy makers to "right an economic wrong" may result in large capital losses, unrequited by any past gain, by current holders of property rights.

the Broadcasting Act of 1968 charged the CRTC with assuring that programming was to be "varied," "balanced," and "of high standard." The CRTC, as noted above, attempted to meet these criteria, primarily via Canadian content rules. However, even if such rules had been effectively applied there is no assurance that "Canadian content" would achieve any greater diversity or higher standards than those achieved by commercial TV in the United States.[62]

There are theoretical grounds for predicting that a commercially oriented, oligopolistically structured broadcasting industry will provide less variety than a single-firm monopoly transmitting over several channels or wavelengths.[63] If we may assume, realistically enough, that commercial success is achieved by maximizing the size of the audience (rather than the aggregate utility or satisfaction of the potential audience), each oligopolist will have an incentive to cater to the mass audience.[64] The result is that the mass audience is shared among the competing stations by the minor distinctions in the programming each of them offers. Groups with "minority" and "off beat" tastes will be largely excluded. In contrast, a monopolist with several channels will attempt to maximize its audience (and commercial success) by providing greater variety— a role long played by the British Broadcasting Corporation. The mass audience could be retained even if the programming on one (or two) of the channels were transferred from majority tastes to minority tastes, thereby increasing the aggregate audience.

The predictions of theory have been largely supported by the evidence. The commercial networks seek the largest audiences, as they must, if they want to maintain their advertising revenues. The CBC, however, has occupied a middle ground. Supported by public (tax) funding as well as advertising revenues, it has attempted to carry out national policy and cater to the diffuse tastes of Canadians. There is some doubt that it has done so successfully. When it comes to mass audiences the CBC cannot out-compete its Canadian rival or the U.S. networks. The CBC's special programming is too infrequently done and too subconsciously concerned with audience approval and size, to give it a clearly distinctive flavour in the minds of the viewing public. As an alternative, it has

---

62. Another instrument for increasing diversity is the introduction of Pay-TV. In 1982-83 the CRTC granted licences to six of fifty firms who had applied to provide Pay-TV services. Two of the firms promptly went bankrupt and others were in serious financial condition. This, however, did not prevent the CRTC from giving the go-ahead to an all-sports and an all pop-music channel in April 1984. The growing commercial interest in Pay-TV is due in part to being able to piggyback it on CATV.
63. Peter O. Steiner, "Programming Patterns and Preferences, and the Workability of Competition in Radio Broadcasting," *Quarterly Journal of Economics* (May 1952), pp. 194-223.
64. Suppose, the mass audience is 80 percent of the potential while the remaining 20 percent are equally divided into two groups with sharply divergent (from each other as well as the "mass") tastes. If there are three commercial networks (or for that matter less than eight) equal shares of the mass audience will exceed the shares of either of the two minority audience shares.

been proposed that the CBC drop all pretence of being commercially viable, become public TV, and cater to the varied, minority tastes of Canadian viewers.[65] In effect, it would become a Canadian version of the U.S. Public Broadcasting System, the main difference being that the former would be fully, while the latter is only partially, funded by taxpayers. It would be left to CTV and the CATV-carried U.S. commercial stations to cater to the mass audience in Canada.

B. Telecommunications

The transferral of telecommunications regulation from the CTC to the CRTC in 1976 relieved the former of, and handed to the latter, burdensome responsibilities. If it were simply a matter of establishing "just and reasonable rates" for the two federally regulated telephone companies, Bell Canada and B.C. Telephone, the CRTC's responsibilities would be mainly time consuming but straightforward enough. However, in the past quarter century, rapidly advancing telecommunications technology has eroded the natural monopoly status of the common carrier telephone companies and thereby has opened a Pandora's Box of issues and problems that the regulators can no longer ignore. These are:

1. The role of "private" (as opposed to common) telecommunications carriers.
2. The right of the private carriers to *interconnect* with the locally switched systems of the common carriers.
3. The competitive role of communication satellites.
4. The right of customers to attach "alien" equipment to the telephone receiver or otherwise hook into the telecommunications network.
5. The appropriate structure of rates, particularly the relationship between long distance rates and local charges.

The issues have their source in new *competition*, which itself is largely due to *technological changes* in telecommunications. Since each of these issues has occupied the U.S. Federal Communications Commission, a brief résumé of that Commission's decisions is instructive in comprehending the issues the CRTC is now, and will be, facing.[66]

---

65. Douglas Hartle, "The Regulation of Communications in Canada," *Government Regulation* (Ontario Economic Council, 1978), pp. 180-183, 196-98. An alternative strategy was enunciated by Communications Minister Francis Fox in *Towards a New National Broadcasting Policy* (Minister of Supply and Services, Canada, 1983).
66. Since space limitations prevent any but the briefest discussion of the FCC decisions, the interested student is directed to Alfred Kahn, *The Economics of Regulation: Principles and Institutions*, Vol. II, Chap. 4, pp. 126-146; John R. Meyer *et al.*, *The Economics of Competition in the Telecommunications Industry* (Cambridge, Mass.: Oelgeschlager, Gunn & Hain, 1980); and Gerald Brock, *The Telecommunications Industry: The Dynamics of Market Structure* (Cambridge, Mass.: Harvard University Press, 1981).

1. Private Carriers

In the late 1950s, the FCC was forced to face the issues raised by the development of microwave radio transmission, which made it possible for its users to enter into direct competition with the traditional telephone system. Many large firms with large telecommunications demands wanted to establish their own private systems, but needed permission from the FCC to use the required portions of the radio spectrum. In 1959, the FCC rendered its so-called Above-890 decision in which it permitted the applicants to use the radio spectrum above 890 megacycles for private telecommunications purposes, but it did not give in and permit common carrier entry into the telecommunications market. Unable to prevent entry by private telecommunications carriers, the common carriers, led by the Bell System, entered into stiff price competition by establishing special (low) rates for private line services (e.g. WATS, TELEPAC), one result of which were charges of predatory pricing by AT&T. These charges led to a major antitrust suit against AT&T for allegedly attempting to monopolize the market for long distance services and the manufacture of telecommunications equipment. The suit was settled when AT&T agreed to divest itself of its local operating (Bell system) telephone companies. At the same time, a suit against IBM was settled which would allow IBM to compete with AT&T in the provision of certain telecommunications services, while at the same time AT&T would be allowed to invade some of IBM's territory in the production of computers and computer-related services.

No such "revolution" has yet taken place in Canada. However, CN/CP Telecommunications' TELEX operations, the successor of the old telegraph system, competes with the telephone companies for certain kinds of long distance message and data transmittal. However, until 1979, when the CRTC ordered interconnection of CN/CP with Bell Canada for the provision of private line services (see below), CN/CP's potential market and ability to compete with the telephone companies in the provision of any long distance services was sharply limited.

2. Interconnection

The prevention by the FCC of common carrier entry into the U.S. telecommunications market could not be indefinitely maintained. When in the late 1960s a small firm, Microwave Communications Inc. (MCI), applied for certification to provide common carrier microwave radio-communications service between St. Louis and Chicago, the FCC acquiesced and went so far as to order the telephone companies to negotiate interconnection with MCI. The FCC decision in the MCI case clearly came down on the side of competitive entry, but side-stepped the major argument raised by the telephone companies; the new entrants would "skim cream," siphoning off demand in the richer markets thereby forcing the telephone companies to raise rates and/or reduce service to other customers.

With the divestiture of AT&T from the local (Bell) telephone companies, full interconnection has taken place in the U.S. New firms may now interconnect with AT&T's "long lines" in the provision of general public long distance telephone services. Two firms have already done so.

In Canada, we are witnessing similar, but not as far-reaching, developments. In the late 1970s CN/CP Telecommunications brought suit to require Bell Canada to permit CN/CP to interconnect (to have direct access) with its local switched telephone network. After lengthy hearings the CRTC ordered interconnection, thereby allowing telephone subscribers to directly use the CN/CP data and private line services, CN/CP paying a fee to Bell Canada for interconnection service. The CRTC concluded that some competition in long distance telecommunications was both inevitable and healthy.[67] However, in the CRTC hearings Bell Canada argued that interconnection would result in "cream skimming" by CN/CP, who by charging low rates will milk the "creamy" inter-metropolitan markets such as Montreal-Toronto. In order to compensate for lost revenues, Bell argued, it would have to raise rates to other customers, particularly on local residential telephone service and service in rural and other less populous areas.[68] While Bell undoubtedly overstated its case, interconnection does pose a

67. The CRTC accepted CN/CP's argument that unless it was granted dial access to its private and data communications services, its share of these markets would continue to decline (and by implication Bell's would rise). Thus, the CRTC saw its decision as helping to maintain the competitive status quo, rejecting almost totally Bell Canada's contention that interconnection would be a radical, and eventually costly (to Bell's local subscribers) step. Only time will tell who was right, but there is little evidence that interconnection has done any damage to date. Canadian Radio-Television and Telecommunications Commission, *CNCP Telecommunications: Interconnection with Bell Canada* Telecom Decision CRTC 79-11, Ottawa, May 17, 1979. See especially pp. 238 ff. A year later the CRTC ordered that B.C. Telephone permit CN/CP to interconnect with its local switched network.

68. Note that this is an implicit admission that the current rate structure is discriminatory, long distance and urban users subsidizing local calls and rural customers. The following example is instructive: In 1969, Newfoundland Telephone Co. Ltd. applied to the Newfoundland Board of Commissions of Public Utilities for a rate increase, part of which was to finance new construction and the upgrading of service in 33 communities. However, evidence indicated that even if the full construction program were approved and completed, 65 communities within Newfoundland Telephone's service area would still be without service at the end of 1973. Company witnesses testified that were service supplied to these communities at its proposed rates, operating revenues from the 65 communities would not cover the fixed and operating costs of supplying service to them. The Utility Board responded by ordering the telephone company to file a four-year programme for supplying service to the 65 communities, and the increases in the proposed schedule of rates which would maintain the approved rate of return on the company's rate base. Following compliance by the company, the Utility Board raised the schedule of rates 4 percent higher than that originally requested by the company, and stated in its reasons for decision: "It is realized that this decision will make it necessary for subscribers in compensatory areas to pay higher telephone rates in order to make service available [at the same schedule of rates] in non-compensatory areas. On the other hand, these subscribers will obtain the advantage of telephone service to areas which cannot be reached now." (Remarks made by C.W. Powell, Chairman, Newfoundland Board of Commissions of Public Utilities, Seminar on Regulatory Purpose and Policy, Chateau Montebello, April 20-22, 1978, pp. 2–4.)

potential challenge to some widely accepted practices of telephone pricing. If increased competition, facilitated by interconnection, substantially reduces revenues from long distance service, then the wherewithal to subsidize local residential usage and usage in sparsely populated areas will disappear. The reality of the interconnection challenge is indicated by the recent application by CN/CP for permission to supply general public long distance services.

The interconnect case goes to the heart of an important theoretical as well as public policy question: is telecommunications an example of a natural monopoly? The question cannot be answered with a flat "yes" or "no." The reason is that the communications carriers provide a variety, or package, of services, the provision of some of which, e.g. long-distance messages and data transmittal, are ripe for competition from carriers such as CN/CP Telecommunications using microwave (radio-spectrum) transmittal.[69] However, the core of telecommunications service, the local network and switching apparatus, remains naturally monopolistic. Duplication of the network would be expensive and essentially purposeless. The result is that the core of the package of telecommunications services that the telephone companies are obliged to provide to all willing to pay the common tariff is, and must remain, under existing technology, the domain of the franchised monopolists. But as telecommunication services multiply in the face of changing technology and demands, increased competition at the fringes of the industry is inevitable. The task of the regulatory commissions is to ensure that the new competition does not erode the economic foundations of the basic services the traditional carriers are required to provide. In the U.S., the response has been divestiture—the separation of the firms providing monopolistic and competitive services. Only the former are regulated. Canada has not taken the divestiture step. While the CRTC and some provincial regulatory boards have ruled in favour of applications for interconnection in the provision of non-public telephone services, regulatory control over the competitive services continues.[70] It will be interesting to compare the results of the U.S. and Canadian approaches to the interconnection and telecommunications challenges, a few years hence.

3. Communications Satellites

The advent of satellite technology opened up a new arena for long-distance telecommunications. In 1962, the U.S. Congress created the Communications Satellite Corporation whose ownership was to be divided, by law, between the telephone carriers and the investing public. This left open the issue of competition between Comsat and the telephone carriers, an issue which the FCC

69. The microwave medium is also used by the traditional telecommunications carriers in much of their long-distance message transmittal.
70. Among the recent CRTC decisions was one which permitted Colins to interconnect with Bell Canada for the provision of radio paging services. A similar decision was recently taken by the Nova Scotia Board of Public Utility Commissioners.

decided largely in favour of the latter by sharply restricting direct dealings between customers and Comsat.

Competition is at the core of the contentious issue of whether Telesat, the 50 percent government-owned Canadian communications satellite corporation, should have been allowed, in 1977, to join the Trans Canada Telephone System (TCTS). TCTS is a consortium of the major telephone companies, publicly and privately owned, established to provide facilities and set tariffs for long-distance telecommunications services in Canada. Telesat's management decided that its future role in telecommunications lay in joining TCTS, thereby becoming primarily an instrument for long-distance message and data transmittal by the carrier members of TCTS. Telesat's affiliation with TCTS was opposed by CN/CP Telecommunications, several provincial governments and others who believed that an independent, unaffiliated Telesat afforded a technologically advanced instrument for competition with the telephone companies. The opponents of the proposed agreement between Telesat and TCTS argued that affiliation would result in the latter dominating the former, dictating the rate of advance in telecommunications satellite technology and suppressing potential price competition between satellite and terrestrial systems for long-distance telecommunications.

It was left to the CRTC to initially (the ultimate power of decision lay with the federal cabinet and was eventually utilized) decide the issue. In a path-breaking decision CRTC opposed the agreement (between Telesat and TCTS).[71] The CRTC based its decision on two kinds of criteria: regulatory issues and those affecting the public interest. On both grounds the CRTC opposed the agreement whereby Telesat would associate with TCTS and thereby transfer, to a significant degree, its decision-making capacity to the Board of Management of TCTS. According to the CRTC the agreement between Telesat and TCTS would complicate future rate hearings before the Commission. Telesat would become a carrier's carrier and the rates it charged each of the carriers would be subject to the approval of the several regulatory agencies which oversee the various members of TCTS. More critically: "As a member of TCTS, decisions about satellite system design, capital costs and performance requirements as well as proposed terms, conditions and rates for satellite services would be subject to the unanimous approval of TCTS members and hence the veto of any one of them."

Telesat, it was argued, would be dominated by TCTS. Although the federal government had consented to the agreement on condition that non-TCTS carriers be able to utilize Telesat's facilities, the CRTC accepted the arguments of CN/CP Telecommunications, the major outsider, that the agreement would

71. Canadian Radio-Television and Telecommunications Commission, Telecom. Decision CRTC 77-10, *Telesat Canada, Proposed Agreement with Trans-Canada Telephone System*, reported in The Canada Gazette, Part I, Sept. 3, 1977, pp. 4838-4883.

put it at a competitive disadvantage. The CRTC thus concluded that "it is clear from the evidence that as a result of the Agreement instead of there being three separate alternative carriers for long-haul traffic across Canada there would be two, one of whom—CN/CP—would be under certain disadvantages.[72]

In the event, the federal cabinet, without substantive explanations, overturned the CRTC decision. Aside from the legal and constitutional niceties, the Telesat case is interesting for what it might suggest about the long-term role of government enterprises. In the 1960s with the development of satellite technology, the federal government entered the satellite field, forestalling private interests who had made proposals of their own. In 1969, Parliament passed the Telesat Canada Act, and in 1973 the first of three satellites went into operation. The original idea was that the corporation would be owned one third by the federal government, one third by the telecommunications carriers, and one third by the general public. However, the shares were split 50-50 between the government and the carriers, with the President and Chairman of Telesat each owning one and tie-breaking shares on behalf of the public. The effect of the agreement would not alter ownership, but it would clearly affect control in the sense of decision making concerning the future role and development of Telesat. The cynic might conclude that having precluded private interests from the satellite field in the 1960s the federal government, frightened by its potential competitive advantages in the telecommunications field, had decided to take it easy on the main competition by joining them. The CRTC, in response, struck a blow for competition in deciding against the agreement, but it did not have the last word.[73]

4. Foreign Attachments

There are two important facets to the so-called "foreign attachment" issue.[74] On the one hand, the refusal by the telephone companies to allow attachment to their network of any equipment not furnished by them historically provided the basis for the monopoly position, in the telecommunications equipment field, of Western Electric and Northern Telecom, the manufacturing subsidiaries of AT & T and Bell Canada, respectively. In the 1970s, the issue of monopoly power came under investigation in Canada as the result of a Restrictive Trade Practices Commission inquiry into whether the vertical tie between Bell Canada and its manufacturing subsidiary, Northern Telecom, should be broken. Ultimately, the RTPC decided that vertical divestiture was unnecessary so long

---

72. CRTC, Telesat Decision, op. cit., p. 4866.
73. However, the CRTC was not totally frustrated. In 1978 it decided for the first time to review the long distance rates set by TCTS members, and in 1981 it ruled that broadcasters could deal directly with Telesat in leasing satellite transponders. CRTC Telecom Decision 81-13, July 7, 1981.
74. The "foreign attachment" issue is also known as "terminal interconnection" as distinct from "network interconnection" requested by CN/CP Telecommunications (see above).

as customers are free to purchase equipment meeting minimum standards from any supplier, a position adopted by the CRTC and reluctantly accepted by the carriers.[75] In the United States the separation of the local telephone companies from AT&T means that the latter's manufacturing subsidiary, Western Electric, no longer has an assured market for much of the telecommunications equipment it produces.

On the other hand, the restrictions on foreign attachments are viewed, chiefly by the telephone companies, as their most important weapon in maintaining the high quality of telephone services. There can be no doubt that some "foreign" attachments could create externalities in the sense that they may affect the quality of service to third parties by impeding the operation of the highly complicated and sensitive telephone network.

In the United States, the FCC met the service quality argument in the important *Carterfone* case (1968)[76] by distinguishing between harmful (to the total telephone network) and harmless (Carterfones) devices. The *Carterfone* decision opened the way to interconnection with the basic telephone system of a wide variety of terminal devices. It also sharply restricted AT & T's freedom to set discriminatory charges to interconnectors. In Canada the CRTC did not face the issue head on until the late 1970s, by which time a number of attempts had been made to break Bell Canada's control over the telecommunications equipment used by its customers. Finally, in a case brought by Challenge Communications, a small manufacturer of electronic equipment, the CRTC moved to sharply curtail Bell Canada's right to limit the equipment its customers attach to Bell's telecommunications network. However, the service quality issue underlies Bell Canada's long standing argument that if the multifaceted attack on its monopoly position succeeds, service quality will deteriorate in the face of divided responsibility for maintenance of service.[77]

5. Rate Structures

One of the most important barriers to reduced regulation of telecommunications in Canada is the widely accepted practice of cross-subsidizing local exchange service with revenues from toll service. Bell Canada has estimated that the actual cost of local services yielding one dollar of revenue is $1.84. In contrast,

75. Restrictive Trade Practices Commission, *The Impact of Vertical Integration on the Telecommunications Equipment Industry*, Ottawa, 1983.
76. FCC, *In the Matter of Use of the Carterfone Device in Message Toll Telephone Service*, Decision, 13 FCC 2d 420 (1968). The Carterfone is a device which makes possible two-way conversations between ordinary telephones and the individual units of mobile radio systems. The interconnection with the telephone system is limited to the use of telephone receivers; no wire-to-wire connection is used; messages are transmitted automatically via the radio spectrum. See Kahn, op. cit., pp. 142-43.
77. In other words, the traditional telephone carriers have argued that the "integrity" of the communications network depends on treating the system as a whole with one carrier responsible for providing service and maintaining quality.

the actual cost of providing toll services which provide one dollar of revenue is 43 cents. The underpricing of local exchange services, which is based on a flat monthly charge, is estimated by Bell Canada to have generated, in 1980, a $710 million shortfall which was paid for by a $725 million excess of toll revenues over the cost of providing long-distance telephone services.[78] Had prices been set at marginal cost for each type of service, local service rates would have had to increase by 70 percent while long distance rates would have declined by a comparable amount.[79]

The existing rate structure for local and long distance service creates at least two types of problems. The lesser of the two is that the flat monthly charges result in overuse of local exchange service, in some instances generating congestion and reducing service quality. As a result, Bell Canada and B.C. Telephone have raised the possibility of experimenting with two-part rates consisting of a small monthly charge plus a charge per call in excess of some specified number of calls per month.[80] The more important problem posed by the existing structure of rates is that the possibilities for competition are greatest in the provision of those telecommunications services which are currently over-priced—long-distance services. If regulators allow competitive pressures to increase, long-distance rates must decline and so must their role as cross-subsidizers of local exchange service. This is the real challenge posed by the applications for full interconnection with the local telephone network of the established telephone companies by prospective competitors in the provision of long-distance telephone services. Obviously, the increased competition would require substantial and presumably unpopular increases in monthly charges—a factor that must account for the reluctance to reduce the regulatory restraints on entry into the provision of basic telecommunication services. Here again, however, the U.S. is leading the way. The breakup of AT & T requires the suppliers of local telephone service to raise their rates to compensatory levels since they can no longer rely on AT & T's profitable long-distance service to cover local service losses.

Energy Regulation and Policy in Canada

In 1959, the National Energy Board was established to take command of Canada's energy policies. The NEB emerged as one of the main proposals of the

78. See W.T. Stanbury and Fred Thompson, *Regulatory Reform in Canada* (Montreal: The Institute for Research on Public Policy, 1982) p. 57.
79. Melvyn Fuss and Leonard Waverman, *The Regulation of Telecommunications in Canada* (Ottawa: Economic Council of Canada, Regulation Reference, Technical Report No. 7, March 1981), p. 152.
80. There are, at present, a number of experiments in the U.S. with what is called "local measured service" (LMS). A number of Canadian telephone companies have also indicated interest in LMS. See R. Schultz and P. Barnes (eds.) *Local Telephone Pricing: Is There a Better Way?"* (Montreal: Centre for the Study of Regulated Industries, 1984).

Borden Royal Commission on Energy which had been set up by the Diefenbaker government, in 1957, to recommend policies which would further the development of Canada's budding oil and gas industry.[81] In a sense the title NEB is something of a misnomer since its authority was limited to interprovincial and international movements of oil and gas and exports of electricity. The National Energy Board Act did not give the NEB authority over energy sources such as coal, atomic energy and domestic uses of Canada's huge electricity supplies and potential. Despite these limitations the increasing importance of oil and gas, and the export potential of Canada's huge hydro electricity projects, has thrust the NEB into the centre of Canada's energy whirlpool. The NEB's powers are both advisory (to the Minister of Energy, Mines and Resources) and regulatory. In its regulatory capacity the NEB (a) grants certificates of "public convenience and necessity" on proposed interprovincial and international pipeline projects; (b) controls the export and import of oil, gas and electric power by issuing licences for the international movement of these energy sources; and (c) approves pipeline tariffs and tolls and establishes fair rates of return on pipeline investment.[82]

A. "Pre-OPEC" Energy Issues

Energy policy in Canada can be roughly divided into three periods: 1959-1973, 1973-1980, and 1980 until the present. The initial dividing line is at the point when the Organization of Petroleum Exporting Countries (OPEC) brought about a four-fold rise in the price of crude oil. In the pre-OPEC period, Canada's "National Oil Policy" (NOP), the main policy outcome of the Borden Royal Commission, was in full flower. The NOP called for the development of Canada's petroleum potential by capturing Ontario for Alberta petroleum output and by exporting as much oil and gas to the United States as that increasingly protective (so far as petroleum was concerned) country would take. Under the NOP, the so-called "Borden line" running along the Ottawa valley divided Canada into two parts with respect to the marketing of petroleum products. East of the line, Quebec and the Maritimes would be supplied by Venezuelan oil. West of the line, Ontario, the Prairies and B.C. would be supplied by Western, primarily Albertan, oil. In addition, half of Alberta's output in the 1960s was destined for U.S. markets as the U.S. government exempted, for most of the period, Canada from the quotas she imposed on oil imports. These developments, of course, required a major effort in pipeline building, which was overseen by the NEB.

In its first decade, the NEB concentrated mainly on authorizing and oversee-

81. The initial political impetus to the establishment of the Borden Commission was the debilitating Pipeline Debate in 1957 which led to the downfall of the Liberal Government of Louis St. Laurent. Prior to 1959, pipelines were regulated by the Board of Transport Commissioners.
82. For an interesting discussion of the NEB from an administrative point of view see Alastair R. Lucas and Trevor Bell, *The National Energy Board: Policy, Procedure, Practice*, prepared for the Law Reform Commission of Canada, Ottawa, 1977.

ing pipeline construction and the issuance of export licences. Canada's major oil and gas pipelines were built in the 1950s and 1960s.[83] As throughput increased due to expanded domestic and foreign demand the cost per barrel fell as the heavy fixed costs of the pipelines were spread over more barrels carried. The decline in unit costs is reflected in the fact that pipeline tolls and tariffs when they changed, fell rather than rose during this period. Since pipeline companies were not requesting rate or toll increases, but rather were reducing, over time, their tolls, the NEB made no attempt to hold rate hearings, although rates of return on pipeline rate bases were generally very high.[84] The NEB's first experience with rate hearings followed the request, in 1969, by Trans Canada Pipelines for a rate increase.[85] The Trans Canada case resulted in a decision, three years later, by the NEB to adopt standard rate-of-return regulation in controlling the rates of return earned and tolls charged by oil and gas pipelines.

The application of rate-of-return regulation to Canada's oil pipelines has not been as straightforward as might have been expected. One reason for this has been the drastic change in the world and Canadian energy scene since 1973. Whereas before 1973, the Canadian Government was attempting to spur production and exports and to maintain oil prices, since 1973 the Government has attempted to limit, and even phase out, petroleum exports and at the same time hold down domestic oil prices, while pushing the export of natural gas priced on a btu equivalent basis at the level of world oil prices. In short, the NOP of the 1960s became largely irrelevant after 1973. As a result at least one transnational oil pipeline company has found itself with capital invested in unused pipeline capacity, which the NEB has held cannot be included in the firm's rate base.[86] In another case, the Interprovincial Pipeline protested the

83. The major oil pipelines are the Interprovincial pipeline which carries Western (primarily Albertan) oil to the East via a route which dips south of the Great Lakes. The Transmountain pipeline carries Alberta oil to British Columbia. The major natural gas pipeline is Trans Canada Pipeline Ltd. which brings Alberta gas to the East via an all-Canadian route north of Lake Superior.
84. After-tax rates of return on equity in excess of twenty or even twenty-five percent do not seem to have been exceptional.
85. The NEB experience with rate regulation nicely fits the "Joskow view" of the actual process of rate-of-return regulation carried out by state regulatory commissions in the U.S. Joskow found that in periods such as the 1950s and early 1960s, when unit costs of production were declining for many utilities, there were very few rate cases heard by utility commissions. Only in the late 1960s when input costs began to rise faster than productivity increases, thereby necessitating utilities to request rate increases, did the number of rate cases rise precipitously. See Paul Joskow, "Inflation and Environmental Concern: Structural Change in the Process of Public Utility Regulation," *The Journal of Law and Economics*, October 1974, pp. 291-328, esp. pp. 305-311.
86. National Energy Board, Reasons for Decision. *In the matter of the Application under Part IV of the National Energy Board Act of Trans Mountain Pipeline Ltd.* 1977. On the grounds that it was neither "used nor useful," Trans Mountain's extension from British Columbia to the state of Washington was excluded from the company's rate base for rate-of-return regulation purposes.

NEB's use of physical life of pipelines for depreciation purposes (30 to 40 years) when the NEB in other contexts had warned of severe oil shortages within 15 years—severe enough to make the newly constructed extension of the oil pipeline from Toronto to Montreal uneconomic.[87]

The NEB rate cases of the 1970s are interesting for several reasons.

1. They reflect the Achilles' heel of rate-of-return regulation. In times of falling utility prices, regulatory life is easy, and utility profits flush. In times of rapidly rising input prices, regulatory life is rushed, neither consumers nor utility investors are happy, and difficult issues revolving around inflation accounting arise.[88]

2. When national policies change, certain investments undertaken in good faith by the utility (in this case pipeline) companies may no longer be "used and useful"—for reasons well beyond the control of the company. If "prudent investment," used and useful, is the basis for calculating utility rate bases, as it should be in the usual case, changes of the sort just described may result in an arbitrary reduction in the rate base of the utility at the expense of past investors.

3. The element of risk is an even more contentious issue than it usually is in rate cases, when the energy flows from a non-renewable, exhaustible resource such as oil and gas. The lifetime of pipelines in physical terms is very long, but economic life depends on the availability of sufficient supplies of oil and gas. Pronouncements by the NEB itself raised questions about the sufficiency of oil and gas supplies. At the same time, national policy called for making Canada as self-sufficient as possible in oil and gas. The federal government ordered, in 1974, that the Interprovincial oil pipeline be extended from Toronto to Montreal. In the late 1970s, work was begun on an extension of the Trans Canada natural gas pipeline to the Maritimes. On what basis should the heavy capital expenditures incurred in pipeline building be written off—physical life? or the shortest assured economic life of the pipeline? or something in between?

B. Post-OPEC Energy Policy: 1973-1980

The events of 1973, the Arab oil embargo, followed by the quadrupling of crude oil prices as OPEC exerted its cartel (monopoly) powers, radically changed the world energy picture. In Canada, those changes have tended to make us inward-looking, rather than export-oriented as in the pre-1973 period. From a concern

87. National Energy Board, Reason for Decision. *In the matter of the Application under Part IV of the National Energy Board Act of Interprovincial Pipelines Limited*, 1977. By the mid 1980s many of these issues appeared academic as the fear of oil shortages receded in the face of reductions in demand and increases in supply induced by rising domestic oil prices.

88. The problems of applying rate-of-return regulation in an inflationary environment, and an evaluation of tariff leveling proposals, was the subject of a conference sponsored by the NEB and the Centre for the Study of Regulated Industries, McGill University, in 1982. The proceedings of that conference are contained in R.N. Morrison and R.J. Schultz, *Pipeline Regulation and Inflation: An Evaluation of Tariff Leveling* (Montreal: McGill University, 1983).

with maintaining some sort of floor under petroleum prices, the concern became one of placing an adjustable upward ceiling on oil prices. Since 1974, Canada has maintained domestic oil prices below world prices (see below). Where, before 1973, confidence in Canada's long-run supplies of petroleum energy was unshaken, after 1973 concern about energy shortages existed. Government involvement in the oil and gas industry has increased, taking a number of forms.

The federal government provides subsidies to firms engaged in exploration and development in the Canadian north and offshore; it sets domestic oil prices; it is engaged in joint ventures such as the Syncrude (tar sands) oil project in Northern Alberta; and last but not least there is government ownership in the form of Petrocan, a fully integrated, from production to distribution, oil giant, which among other things took over the federal government's investment in the Panarctic Consortium engaged in Arctic exploration. (The growth of government enterprise in the energy sector is discussed in chapter 11. Here it is sufficient to note its growth, for it involves government in the oil and gas industry quite independent of the regulatory powers of the NEB.)

In some respects the NEB's regulatory concerns became more consequential. First, the granting of licences for the export of natural gas which were once routine, became the subject of media reports and national concern because of heightened awareness of potential limits on energy supply. However, by the early 1980s, the rise in natural gas prices had produced large increases in reserves, easing concern about shortages and prompting sales to the U.S. at premium prices. Second, the quest for oil and gas in the Arctic raised numerous environmental and other strategic as well as technical issues where pipeline construction is involved. In its three-volume report on a Northern Pipeline, the NEB sided with the Berger report in rejecting the Arctic Gas consortium's proposal for a MacKenzie River Pipeline and chose instead the Foothills proposals for an Alcan route through the Yukon and Northern B.C. to bring Alaskan North Slope Gas to the "lower 48" and the Canadian provinces.[89] The choice of the Alcan route over the Mackenzie Valley route involved a number of important considerations in addition to socioeconomic and environmental ones. It implicitly accepted that Canada's southern (Alberta and B.C.) supplies of natural gas are sufficient to meet domestic needs until the 1990s. Thus Canada can wait longer in order to determine whether natural gas reserves in the MacKenzie delta are sufficient to justify a pipeline. In contrast, the U.S. demand for natural gas appeared more pressing as did the problem of coping with the inventories of gas built up as a joint product with the production of Alaskan oil. However, by the 1980s, as energy shortages receded, and pipeline construction costs soared, the Alcan pipeline seemed less economic. As a result, the United

---

89. National Energy Board, *Reasons for Decision: Northern Pipelines*, 3 vols. (Minister of Supply and Services Canada, 1972).

States has yet to fulfil its commitment to the financing of the pipeline, a prerequisite to the commencement of its construction.

In any event, Canada's choice of the Alcan route involved stategic and political decisions of a high order. In reaching its decision the NEB was acutely aware of the fact that, on such matters, the federal cabinet will have the last say. (Canadian regulatory agencies are not fully independent, particularly so where issues involve the national interest in a major way.) This fact means that the nature of the NEB's report, its reasoning, its weighing of advantages and disadvantages of the proposal at hand, are quite as important, perhaps more so, as the decision itself.

C. The Era of the NEP: 1980-

The development of post-OPEC energy policy came to a head in 1980 when the federal government promulgated its National Energy Program (NEP). The October 1980 version of the NEP reflected the strains produced by the fact that world oil prices had doubled again in 1979-80, as a result of the Iranian crisis. With domestic oil prices less than half the world price, then about $40 Canadian, the federal government was forced to pay billions of dollars in subsidies to importers of foreign oil in order to maintain its ceiling on domestic oil prices. Moreover, the drain on the federal Treasury was made more acute by the failure of Ottawa to reach an agreement with the producing provinces on a formula for sharing the rents from conventional oil production among the two levels of government and the producing firms. At the time the federal government was receiving only 10 percent of the gross income from oil production; Alberta and the producing firms shared equally the remaining 90 percent.

With Alberta refusing to budge on the new sharing formula, at least until the federal government moved domestic prices much closer to world oil prices, Ottawa moved unilaterally. The October 1980 budget implemented a series of new taxes designed to raise the federal share in oil revenues to 24 percent— mainly at the expense of the oil companies, whose share would fall from 45 to 33 percent. Although, as a quid pro quo, the federal government would increase federal subsidies for exploration and development, the policy switch to higher federal tax and greater subsidies was generally viewed as an undesirable increase in government intervention in the petroleum industry. These fears were heightened by the "Canadianization" facet of the NEP in which preferences were given to domestically owned petroleum companies, particularly government-owned PetroCan. The upshot was capital flight from the Canadian oil industry and a sharp cut-back in oil production ordered by Alberta.

Having gone head to head over energy pricing policy and resource-revenue sharing, the federal government and the producing provinces sat down to negotiate a compromise.[90] In September 1981, a Memorandum of Agreement

90. See John Helliwell and Robert McRae, "Resolving the Energy Conflict: From the National Energy Program to the Energy Agreements," *Canadian Public Policy* (Winter 1982), pp. 14-23.

(MOA) was signed by all parties. Under the MOA, whose provisions were to apply for the five-year period 1981-86, the parties agreed to a set of federal taxes and to a set of semi-annual price increases for conventional crude oil. Moreover, the MOA specified that all nonconventional oils (e.g. tarsands and "frontier" oil) and all "new" conventional oil (i.e. oil from newly developed pools) would immediately be priced at world levels. Thus the domestic oil price would be a "blend" of "old" and "new" oil prices. In addition, natural gas prices would be set at 65 percent (btu parity) of domestic oil prices. Although world prices began to fall in early 1982, the MOA has remained essentially intact, although the federal government has had to bear much of the brunt of the revenue decline.[91] With world prices continuing to fall and federal budget deficit worries growing, the new Progressive Conservative government let Canadian oil prices rise to world levels by eliminating the "cap" on the conventional crude oil price.

D. Energy Issues of the 1980s

What are the energy (particularly oil and gas) related issues Canadians will face in the latter half of the 1980s?[92] It seems clear that most have their source in post-OPEC developments and the policies adopted by the Canadian government to deal with them. Our purpose here is to enumerate the major issues and their implications for further government intervention in, and regulation of, the oil and gas industry. These issues are:

1. The prospect for growth-limiting energy shortages.
2. The adoption of a "self-sufficiency" as opposed to an export-oriented energy policy.
3. The method of conserving energy resources.
4. The continuation of Canada's two-price system for oil.
5. The distribution of rents generated by high oil prices.
6. The prospects for new energy sources as a result of technological developments.

1. Energy Shortages?

Most economists do not believe we face energy shortages so critical as to place important limits on economic growth. Economists' optimism is based on the assumption that if energy prices are allowed to rise sufficiently they will induce exploration for and development of seemingly large potential energy supplies—

For an analysis of what was wrong under the first version of the NEP, see Brian Scarfe, "The Federal Budget and Energy Program, October 28, 1980: A Review," *Canadian Public Policy* (Winter 1981), pp. 1-14.

91. See John F. Helliwell, Mary E. MacGregor, and Andre Plourde, "The National Energy Program Meets Falling World Oil Prices," *Canadian Public Policy*, September 1983, pp. 284-296.

92. Most of these issues became important in the 1970s, but have yet to be resolved in any definitive fashion.

a prediction which appears to have been borne out by events in the last decade. For example, at the relatively low prices of crude oil which prevailed in the 1950s and 1960s exploitation of the oil-rich Alberta tar sands was out of the question. When the world price of oil quadrupled in 1973-74 and doubled again in 1979-80, the picture changed; it became economic to obtain a steadily rising supply of tar sands oil. By the early 1980s, several mega-projects were underway to exploit Canada's vast supplies of heavy and tar sands oil. In the meantime, exploration for and development of, oil and gas fields in the Canadian arctic and off the East Coast, particularly the Hibernia field off the coast of Newfoundland, had begun in earnest. While the fall in oil prices in 1982, reaching a plateau in 1983 about 15-20 percent below the apogee reached in early 1981, poses a threat to the economic viability of at least some of the mega-projects, there is no doubt that the oil price rise of the 1970s has led to increased availability of petroleum and has lessened the fear of shortage.

Even if economic growth is not sharply restrained by energy shortages, its course will, nevertheless, be affected by the change in the relative price of energy. During the three or four decades prior to the 1970s Western economic growth was predicated on the assumption of cheap energy. Cheap energy is no more, and this has implications for the production of highly energy-intensive outputs (e.g. aluminum, oil-fired electricity generating plants) and use of energy or energy-dependent inputs. For these reasons energy cannot be taken for granted and major efforts will probably continue, through the 1980s, to find alternative energy sources and new supplies of existing sources. It is to be hoped, however, that we will no longer witness misguided attempts to arbitrarily depress or restrain energy prices, either through direct subsidies, tax incentives, or price controls in the face of rising prices for energy.

2. Export Policy

Should Canada continue to export oil and gas to the United States? If so, at what prices? For the time being these questions have been given answers. In the mid-1970s, it was decided that oil exports to the United States were to be phased out. In the meantime, oil was exported to the States at world (OPEC) prices, the Canadian government garnishing a per barrel of oil export tax representing the difference between world prices and the ceiling placed on oil purchased for domestic consumption (see below).[93] Natural gas continues to be exported, although export licences became more difficult to come by in the 1970s, and the price per thousand cubic feet of gas exports was set at levels equivalent to oil prices using the B.T.U. as the common denominator. One result of these policies is a supply bubble of Canadian natural gas as a consequence of the increased (price) incentives to find and exploit natural gas. Thus in the 1970s

93. The net price to Canadian producers, of oil exported to the U.S. or consumed in Canada, is thereby the same. As the gap between world prices and the domestic price of crude oil, set by agreement between Ottawa and Alberta, narrowed the export tax naturally declined.

Canada may have been too hasty in deciding to phase out the oil flow and reduce the gas flow to the United States. If energy prices resume their rise, and result in the discovery of large new supplies, there may be good economic reasons for continuing to supply the U.S. market, at world level prices.

3. Energy Conservation

If either temporary or long-term shortages of oil and gas are in the offing, how should these resources be conserved? High prices? Rationing of supplies? As a result of the Arab oil embargo of 1973, Eastern Canada which was, and to some extent still is, dependent on foreign oil was threatened with severe shortages. The federal government responded by passage of an Energy Supplies Allocation Act establishing the basis of an "equitable" allocation (rationing) of petroleum products in the event of a severe shortage. The Act is a short-run palliative at best; and it was never put to the test as the embargo was lifted before the Act could take effect. For the longer term, the federal government moved to make Western oil accessible to Quebec by ordering an eastern extension of the Interprovincial Pipeline (see above). These moves, however, do not answer the question of what to do in the now unlikely event of severe long-term shortages of oil. The economists' natural inclination would be to advise letting prices ration demand, but for at least two important reasons such a course is not likely to be socially or politically acceptable. Letting (relative) prices of a necessity rise is always difficult to accept because of the distributional consequences, but it is particularly so if the price rise is *not* expected to substantially increase supplies, only restrain quantities demanded. That is, reliance on the price mechanism, rather than some other form of rationing, is even more difficult to accept if long-run supply elasticity is very low, although we should not ignore the allocative inefficiency arising from failure to allocate scarce supplies to their most valuable uses.

The present "optimism" of economists relative to their more futuristic colleagues in other social sciences, so far as energy is concerned, is due to a basic trust that economists have in the (long-run) elasticity of supply: let energy prices rise and in time more energy supplies will be forthcoming. The experience of the last few years clearly points to a relatively high long-run elasticity of supply. Thus, permitting oil and gas prices to rise will act as a necessary inducement to increase supplies of these resources, as well as act as a spur to development of substitutes—i.e. alternative energy sources.

4. The "Made in Canada" Oil Price Policy

The precipitous rise in world oil prices in the 1970s turned the tables on Canadian oil pricing policies. Prior to 1973, Alberta, Canada's main domestic source of petroleum, prorationed production of its oil wells for both efficiency and price maintenance reasons. Oil is a fugacious substance moving to maintain a common level in any given pool, ignoring the boundaries between the various owners of the surface above the pool. As a result, each independent owner will maximize his own take (although reduce the aggregate) by taking oil out of the ground as fast as possible—i.e., before his neighbours do. Too rapid production not only depresses prices and fails to conserve a scarce resource, it reduces the percentages of a pool which is recoverable, by allowing the gas pressures that push oil to the surface to subside too quickly. As a result, the main producing states (Texas and Louisiana) in the United States as well as Alberta established regulatory agencies with powers to allocate production quotas among wells.[94] In Alberta, the Energy Resources Conservation Board (ERCB) regulates oil and gas in the province. In the 1960s the ERCB set production quotas so as to maintain crude oil prices at a level that would keep the less efficient (less flush) wells in existence.[95] Thus, west of the Borden line, Ontario paid somewhat higher prices for crude oil and petroleum products than did Quebecers who received their oil from foreign suppliers.

When oil prices quadrupled in 1973-74 the tables were turned. Eastern Canada now was dependent on very expensive foreign oil. Westerners, with assured supplies of Alberta oil, could enjoy lower prices if Alberta could be prevented from raising prices to the world level. The federal government entered the scene using its powers to regulate interprovincial as well as international movements of oil to keep domestic prices well below the world price level, although almost double the prices that prevailed in 1971. With world prices at approximately $11.00 per barrel, in 1974, the federal government established a domestic price at about $6.00 and placed a tax of $5.00 on oil exported to the United States. The proceeds of the export tax were used to subsidize Eastern refiners who were paying the world price for their foreign oil supplies. The intent and result of the policy was to ensure more or less similar prices for petroleum products consumed domestically, prices well below those paid by Europeans, although more or less in line with prices in the United States, where price controls on oil remained in effect.

From 1974 to 1979, world prices rose, although no faster than the inflation rate, to around $17.00 per barrel at the beginning of 1979. During the same period, the federal government, partly in response to pressures from the chief producing province, Alberta, and partly in response to the resilience of the OPEC cartel and its ability to maintain oil prices, raised the domestic price of crude oil so that the gap between the domestic and world prices narrowed to about $3.00 in 1977 and appeared as if it would eventually disappear. Then in 1979-80, the

94. A more efficient alternative to prorationing is "unitization"—treating an oil field as a unit by requiring its owners to reach an agreement on the amount to be produced per unit time and sharing the revenues in proportion to each owner's production capacity (number of wells).

95. To a considerable extent the policy reflects the political strength of many small producers. The production end of the petroleum industry is much more atomistic than the better-known, and highly oligopolistic, refining end of the industry.

world price of oil doubled again. Within a year the domestic price of oil was barely half the world price. These developments threw into sharper relief than ever the question of whether the dual price system was desirable, and more important, whether it was desirable strategy for the future.

Before tracing developments, since 1980, it is useful to assess the consequences of a "dual price" (a domestic price which differs significantly from the world price) policy. The maintenance of a dual price for oil has potential efficiency and distributional consequences. In terms of economic efficiency the sale of oil to Canadians at a price less than it fetches in the world market has three likely effects:

a. Relative to the world price the lower domestic price induces over-consumption of a scarce resource, inhibiting the substitution of other energy sources for oil in consumption and production.

b. Lower prices for domestic use combined with an export tax on sales abroad reduce the incentives of producers to explore for and develop new sources of petroleum in Canada.

c. Because the revenues lost exceed the additional consumer surplus due to lower domestic prices, Canadians as a whole suffer a welfare loss.[96]

96. An important assumption of the welfare theoretic analysis underlying this statement is that the utility of a dollar is the same no matter who receives it: consumers, producers, or government on behalf of taxpayers. The diagrammatics, adopted from H.G. Grubel and S. Sydney Smith, "The Taxation of Windfall Gains on Stocks of Natural Resources," *Canadian Public Policy* (Winter 1975), pp. 27-29, are as follows:

1. Under dual price system Canadians consume OQ_0 barrels of oil at price P_D, Q_oS being exported at price P_W. Producers receive gross revenue equal to OP_DFS; the government collects export tax revenues of CEGF.

2. If all oil were sold at the single (world) price, P_W, Canadian consumers would consume OQ_1 barrels of oil, foreigners Q_1S (Canada as a relatively small petroleum producer is properly assumed to be able to sell all it wants at the world price, P_W). Producers receive OP_WGS in the absence of an excise tax on all oil produced; OP_DFS if the government places a tax equal to P_W-P_D on each barrel of oil. In either case total (producer plus government) revenue raised from producing OS is the same.

3. The difference in total revenue received by producers and the government in the two cases (dual price v. single world price) is indicated by rectangle P_DP_WEC. Of this difference, P_DP_WBC is offset by greater consumer surplus under the dual price system. The differences between the revenue loss and the consumer surplus gain produced by the dual price system is the shaded triangle BCE—the "deadweight loss" of standard welfare economics.

4. In the long run, the supply of oil, per period, which will be forthcoming, is indicated by LS, assuming no excise-type taxes are levied on each barrel of oil. In the long run, with price at P_W, supply will expand to OQ_2. However, if a tax of P_W-P_D is levied on each barrel the LS will shift to LS^1 and output will remain at OS.

Figure 10-3

P = world price
P_0 = domestic price
D_c = Canadian demand for oil
SS = maximum output from existing fields per time period
LS = Long run supply curve (in the absence of export tax)
LS^1 = Long run supply curve with an export, or some other excise, tax.

The importance of these effects depends on the elasticity of demand (a + c) and the elasticity of supply (b). While these elasticities are not known with any precision, and are often subject to debate and disagreement, it is an error to assume either of the elasticities is zero or close to it, particularly over periods of time long enough to allow consumers and producers to adjust to price changes and differentials.[97] Unless an input or output is technologically or naturally fixed in supply, the economic incentives of consumers and producers almost ensure a response to relative price differences and changes. Thus the dual price system, whatever its merits, is not conducive to either conserving petroleum or finding more of it.

The dual price system has distributional consequences, some obvious, some not so obvious. Clearly, one distributional effect of the dual price system is to transfer income from owners of oil companies to consumers of oil products. As it turns out, many of the former are foreigners (the petroleum industry is one of the most highly foreign-controlled industries in Canada) while most of the latter are Canadians. However, some large consumers of petroleum are themselves producers, particularly in the manufacturing sector, which is over 50 percent foreign controlled. If the lower price of domestically consumed oil increases the competitiveness and profitability of energy-intensive Canadian manufacturing industries, stockholders benefit—and many of these are foreigners. If lower oil prices lead to lower output prices consumers of these products benefit, and these include foreigners where the output is exported. In short, the dual price for oil results in a rather odd levy on some foreigners and a subsidy to others. Among Canadians, the distributional consequences are less clear. Waverman has attempted to determine whether a subsidy to oil consumption is a progressive or regressive subsidy. Overall, he found it to be mildly progressive, the lower middle class having the highest ratio of energy consumption to income, but these results vary to some extent across provinces and regions.[98]

In sum, the two-price system seemed like a sensible way in which to soften the shock produced by the quadrupling of crude oil prices in 1973-74. Had oil prices subsequently fallen, Canadians would have been saved from the resultant price fluctuations. Since crude oil prices did not fall, the dual price system could be justified as providing for a smoother transition to a single (world) price. The doubling of oil prices in 1979-80, however, made it difficult to defend, on

97. Scarfe reports "ball park" estimates of the elasticity of demand for crude oil over the longer term as 0.5 or more, in absolute terms. While the elasticity of supply of conventional crude from traditional producing areas is low, the overall elasticity of supply of all types of crude from all locations is considerably larger. B.L. Scarfe, "The Federal Budget and Energy Program, A Review," *Canadian Public Policy* 7, (Winter 1981), pp. 1-14. Also see W.R. Thirsk and R.A. Wright, "The Impact of the Crude Oil Subsidy on Economic Efficiency in Canada," *Canadian Public Policy*, 3 (Summer 1977), pp. 355-64.
98. Leonard Waverman, "The Two Price System in Energy: Subsidies Forgotten," *Canadian Public Policy* (Winter, 1975), pp. 78-88.

economic grounds at least, continuance over another decade of domestic prices that differed significantly from world oil prices. The stage was set for a new energy pricing policy, the NEP, which after eliciting an understandably hostile response from Alberta, was sufficiently modified to provide the basis for an acceptable domestic pricing policy (see above) and a resolution to the thorny issue of how the economic rents should be distributed, a subject to which we now turn. Nevertheless, the experience calls into question the continued regulation of energy prices.

5. The Distribution of Economic Rents

Who should receive the rents (profits) from high (and rising) prices of oil? The producers? consumers? governments?, and within the last, which level of government? The steep rise in oil prices has meant that low-cost producers of oil (those producing conventional crude from flush wells drilled years ago into easily accessible pools) will receive large economic rents. These are crudely pictured in Figure 10-4. The curve CS indicates the amount of oil, including non-conventional crude oils and conventional crude from harsh, difficult-to-reach environments, forthcoming at various prices.[99] The opportunity cost of

Figure 10-4

Economic Rents Received by Oil Producers

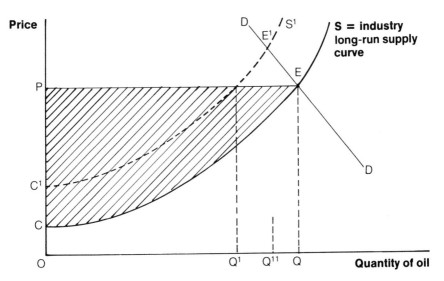

99. Actually the nature of the supply curve for petroleum and other exhaustible resources is much more complicated than Figure 10-4 suggests. Two modifications are crucial. One should recognize that there is a difference between (a) the supply price of new discoveries and (b) the

supplying oil from some wells is as low as OC; for some others, those at the margin, it approximates OP; for most of the operating wells something in between OC and OP. All of the inframarginal properties (wells) receive an economic rent varying from CP to approximately zero when the margin is reached. The shaded area PEC represents the total economic rent received by resource owners.

It is easy to see that a sudden upward shift in price, such as that which followed the oil embargo of 1973, will increase economic rents to resource owners. As a result the oil-producing provinces substantially increased the royalty payments oil producers must pay them for each barrel of oil produced. When the royalty takes the form of a payment per barrel produced, the effect is to shift the supply curve of oil upward (to C^1S^1 in Figure 10-4). An undesirable consequence is a decline in the oil supplied per unit time from OQ to OQ^1, if prices are fixed by the federal government (or by world market conditions) at OP.[100] The problem with a per barrel royalty fee is that it falls as heavily on marginal as it does on flush, high economic rent, properties. As a result Alberta began to use a flexible royalty scheme with higher royalties demanded from more profitable (higher rent) properties than from less profitable (lower rent) ones. Moreover, the current schemes for taxing income from oil production attempt to distinguish between "old," lower cost crude and "new" higher cost crude, a rough and ready way of distinguishing between inframarginal rents and marginal opportunity costs.

The huge economic rents believed to be received by resource owners following the rise in the price of many natural resources, including oil and gas, in the early 1970s, led to alternative schemes for extracting economic rents. These run the gamut from competitive bidding for prospective resource-yielding properties to outright government ownership, the whole of the eco-

supply price of oil from existing wells, once exploration and drilling costs have become sunk costs. The other is that owners of exhaustible, non-renewable resources will be influenced not only by the prevailing price at a point in time, but their expectations with respect to price changes. If for example prices are expected to rise substantially in the near future (at a rate per period of time in excess of the rate of interest), it will generally be more profitable to withhold supplies until the price rises. The converse holds when the price is expected to fall in the near future: producers will supply more now than they would, if today's "high" price is not expected to prevail in the foreseeable future. The effect of expected prices on supply reflects their *user cost* which Davidson, *et al.* define as "the highest present value of marginal future profits given up by producing that barrel of oil currently rather than in the future." See Paul Davidson, Lawrence Falk and Hoesung Lee, "Oil: Its Time Allocation and Project Independence," *Brookings Papers on Economic Activity* No. 2 1974, pp. 413-29, and Paul Davidson, "Public Policy Problems of the Domestic Crude Oil Industry," *American Economic Review*, 53 (March 1963), pp. 85-108. These papers provide a practical application of Keynes' discussion of "user cost." J.M. Keynes, *The General Theory of Employment, Interest and Money* (Harcourt-Brace, 1936) Chap. 4.
100. If the price of oil is able (and allowed) to rise, to where DD cuts C^1S^1, the royalty fee is thus shifted forward, in part, to consumers, and the fall in quantity supplied is less drastic, Q^1Q^{11}.

nomic rent being received by the government.[101] More modest proposals include more finely tuned tax schemes designed to capture a larger portion of the economic rents than does the flat, per unit, royalty.

While the argument that greater economic rents should be extracted and turned over to the "real" owners (the residents of the producing provinces) of the resources (in principle, subsurface rights cannot be alienated, only leased) is persuasive, there are certain factors that make the argument somewhat less attractive or convincing. First, is the fact that what goes up can, and sometimes does, go down—and this is precisely what happened in 1975-76 to the price of many natural resources (and in 1982-83 to the price of oil). The huge increase in economic rents of 1973 largely disappeared in 1975-76 for nickel, copper, and other minerals. Rent, as we know from Ricardo, is price-determined, not price-determining. A second consideration is that the existence of economic rents not only increases the incentive to further investment in exploration and development, it may also be necessary for such investment where high risks would make obtaining the finance in capital markets prohibitively expensive. This has often been argued as being important in the oil and gas industry, particularly as it moves to the "extensive margin" in Canada's hostile northern regions.

Indirectly related to the question of who is to receive the economic rents in a resource-scarce world, is foreign ownership of Canadian resource industries, including the oil and gas industry. Foreign control of the oil refining industry is high, although declining. The major firms are fully integrated firms with large stakes in the production, transmission and distribution of crude oil and petroleum products, as well as in refining activities. The fact that a large portion of economic rents goes to foreign owners of Canadian resources is obviously a political factor in whether to tax the rents more heavily or preempt them via government ownership. The issues are complicated and cannot be decided here, but they undoubtedly will continue to be a source of contention for years to come.

6. New Energy Sources

To what extent can we rely on future technological developments to provide us with new energy sources and thereby take the pressure off the oil and gas industry? How viable is nuclear technology? What about solar energy? Tidal

---

101. Professor Eric Kierans has been a leading proponent of the creation of Crown corporations to secure economic rents from the mining resources in Canada. See Eric Kierans, *Natural Resources Policy in Manitoba*, Manitoba, Planning and Priorities Committee of Cabinet Secretariat, 1973. For an analysis of the Kierans proposal and a suggestion that any Crown corporation should be a fully integrated firm established at the refining level, see J. Cohen and M. Krashinsky, "Capturing the Rents in Resource Land for the Public Landowners: The Case for a Crown Corporation," *Canadian Public Policy* (Summer 1976), pp. 411-22.

power from the Bay of Fundy? Here we can only speculate, and in a very superficial fashion. Nuclear energy is in trouble in the United States partly because of environmental opposition and partly due to technical problems which have led to a high rate of "down time" (non-operation) of nuclear reactors. Canada's nuclear power programme, using heavy water as a catalyst, has been more successful, or at least has generated less opposition. It is becoming an increasingly important source of energy in populous, industrial Ontario. Solar energy will probably remain a limited source of energy because of Canada's northern climes, but undoubtedly will be developed here more or less in tandem with its development in the United States.[102] Tidal power is also a limited option—limited to Canada's extremities. Moreover, the discovery of oil off Canada's East Coast makes the development of tidal power even more problematic since the energy-scarce Maritimes may no longer be so dependent on foreign sources of oil.

Related to the technological issues are environmental ones. Clearly, pushing the extensive margin in the quest for new supplies of oil and gas trespasses into ecologically more fragile territories such as the Canadian arctic and the oceans. Alternatively, nuclear power, so long as it depends on the fission process rather than fusion, requires finding means of disposing of deadly, long-lived (measured in thousands of years) residues or wastes. This fact, plus the safety issues surrounding the operation of nuclear reactors, has led the United States to place much more emphasis on its huge coal deposits. But these deposits can be mined cheaply only by strip mining with obvious ecological or environmental consequences, and burned cheaply only at the price of contaminating lakes and rivers with "acid rain."

In sum, resource-related issues are among the leading economic issues of the 1980s. In dealing with them, regulation will probably continue as an important tool. As a result the NEB may yet become Canada's best known, though not most revered, regulatory agency.

Conclusion

This overly long chapter has provided the student with a glimpse of the complicated issues surrounding the regulation of the transportation, telecommunications, and energy sectors of the Canadian economy. At both the theoretical and institutional levels there is much to learn, many issues with which to grapple. No one chapter can hope to do more than sketch the

---

102. Over a half century ago a civil engineer observed that the main impediment to the development of solar energy was economic rather than technical. Henry Lenschow, "Energy from the Sun," *The Wisconsin Engineer* (Jan. 1931), p. 109.

theoretical framework, describe the institutional environment, and briefly discuss some of the main issues of policy.

One of the overriding issues of policy is just how extensive economic regulation should be. For the better part of this century, it has been accepted by federal and provincial governments alike that they have an important, sometimes preeminent role to play in the public utility sector of the Canadian economy. Not only is public ownership extensive, but so has been economic regulation of the enterprises (public as well as private) which supply these important services. Now, however, for the first time in our history there is serious discussion about the appropriate role of government in the utility sector.[103] Serious questions have been posed about the desirability of extensive economic regulation as the possibilities for competition increase. We are much more aware today of the costs as well as the benefits of regulation. Moreover, advances in technology, particularly in the telecommunications industry, are breaking down industry lines, making regulation increasingly difficult if not impossible to apply in some fields. A reflection of these changes is the substantial deregulation of railroads two decades ago, the much more recent deregulation of the airlines, and the current whittling away at the monopoly enjoyed by the telephone companies. Pressure for further change is coming from developments in the U.S. which, in a brief span of 5 to 10 years, has substantially deregulated important industries once subject to tight economic regulation.

Students of the Canadian economy and public policy have much to learn from the developments now taking place in the utility sector of the economy. Until recently textbooks treated public utilities and regulation as part and parcel of the same subject. But a changing technological and institutional environment is creating pressures for divorce. This, however, should not be read as implying that regulation is on the decline. On the contrary! One of the ironies which so enlivens as well as enrages our complex social science is the apparent increase in regulation and other forms of direct intervention in sectors of the economy which, on their face, provide little or no justification for direct government intervention. Some of the issues raised by the new interventionism are treated in chapter 12.

103. One reflection of this was the Economic Council of Canada's "Regulation Reference."

11

Public Enterprise in Canada

The most direct form of government intervention in the market place is via the public corporation—a business enterprise owned and controlled by the government or its agents. In chapter 1 we noted that public enterprises—federal and provincial—in Canada are numerous. In chapter 7 we noted that the rationales for public ownership of business in Canada are also numerous—not moulded by any single or simple ideological viewpoint. In this chapter we (i) examine the public enterprise concept and its relation to the Crown corporation, the legal form under which public enterprise operates in Canada; (ii) explore the growth and extent of public enterprise in Canada; (iii) discuss the rationales for the existence of public enterprise in Canada; (iv) analyze certain economic issues related to the behaviour and performance of public enterprise; and (v) conclude with a few brief case studies of public (Crown) corporations in Canada.

The Concept of "Public Enterprise"

What is meant by the term "public enterprise"? Is it coterminous with "public ownership"? Are all Canadian Crown corporations public enterprises? Does the term "public enterprise" imply some degree of public finance or subsidy? Does it imply close public control by the government of the day? The answer to each of these questions (except, obviously, the first) is strictly speaking "no." Yet, it is probably impossible to provide a single unambiguous and generally accepted definition for the term "public enterprise" which can clearly differentiate among the numerous activities governments undertake.[1] Here we make no

1. The Dictionary of Social Sciences defines public enterprises as vehicles for "public services which are economic enterprises, i.e. ones which may be expected to pay for themselves. Education, the armed forces and the judiciary are public services which do not pay for themselves and are not therefore economic enterprises." UNESCO, *A Dictionary of Social Sciences*, 1964.

Table 11-1

Public-Private Activity Taxonomy

	Nature of Good or Service	
Ownership	Private (Marketable)	Public or Collective (publicly financed)
Private	Most business enter-prises in Canada	Government contracts out the supply of the service
	Major aim is profit making	Reliance on subsidies
Public	Public Enterprise— narrower (ordinary) meaning	Government Department or Public Enterprise— broad meaning
	Reliance on user charges	Reliance on public finance

---

attempt at formal definition; rather we begin by making some conceptual distinctions.

Table 11-1 presents a highly oversimplified, but nevertheless potentially useful, taxonomy, which distinguishes (horizontally) between the ownership of the enterprise (or department, as in the case of many government activities) providing the good or service and (vertically) between the nature of the good or service itself.[2]

As Table 11-1 suggests, government ownership, or lack of it, is *logically* unrelated to the question of whether the good or service can be provided via the market place (private goods) or must be provided collectively and financed publicly as in the case of "public" goods. Another way of putting the point is that there is an important distinction between public enterprise and public finance. The ordinary, and perhaps most useful, meaning of "public enter-prise" is that indicated by the lower left hand box where the good or service supplied can be, and is, marketed. Here the *choice* between public and private ownership is clear—there is nothing inherent in the good or service itself which

2. There is no universally accepted definition of a "public good." Here we emphasize the distinction between those goods which can be marketed privately and those which must be provided collectively and financed publicly if they are to be provided at all. The "collective" nature of the latter arises out of the technical characteristics of the good or service (usually the latter) which makes it impossible to *exclude* non-contributors from receiving the benefits. Examples of "pure public goods" are law and order, national defence, disease prevention programmes and externalities such as those associated with a basic minimum level of education or disease prevention. One of the most interesting discussions of the nature of public goods is contained in C.S. Shoup, *Public Finance* (Chicago: Aldine, 1969), Chaps. 3, 4.

prevents its supply by a non-subsidized profit-seeking private entrepreneur.

In contrast, some goods and services which must be consumed collectively such as national defence, police protection, the externalities emanating from basic, primary education, etc., could, in principle, be provided by a private firm under contract with the government. Either the government could provide subsidies to the private supplier or vouchers to the prospective consumers (or their parents), as Milton Friedman and others have suggested for primary and secondary education.[3] These are obviously potential examples of privately supplied, publicly subsidized or financed, public goods. Ordinarily, however, these public goods are publicly provided or supplied.

How should we treat collective consumption goods such as national defence, basic public education, etc., that are supplied by government? Are these examples of "public enterprise"? To so treat them would be to very broadly construe the meaning of public enterprise, making it more or less synonymous with "exhaustive" government expenditures. Given the tremendous growth in public expenditures in the last half century (see chapter 1), it would, perhaps, be unfortunate to equate that growth with the growth of "public enterprise"— which in its narrower sense has also been growing.

In the remainder of this chapter we will be concerned with public enterprise in the narrower sense of publicly owned enterprises producing generally marketable goods and services. This is not to suggest that externalities, in the sense of social benefits exceeding private benefits, do not exist. Surely one possible reason for opting for public enterprise is that a particular activity may generate strong external effects, in which case the good or service would be under-supplied by unhampered, unsupported (by subsidies) private enterprise.[4] However, the emphasis here is on alternative ownership forms, an issue which can be more sharply defined and analyzed by focusing on the supply of "private," marketable goods rather than the provision of public, collectively consumed ones.

Historical Background

Public enterprises are becoming more numerous in Canada. In the nineteenth century governments were generally disinclined to enter directly into commer-

3. Milton Friedman, *Capitalism and Freedom* (Chicago: University of Chicago Press, 1962), Chap. 6.
4. In the extreme, the good or service might not be provided at all by private enterprise if SB>SC=PC>PB for all levels of output, where SB=social benefits; SC=social costs assumed equal to private costs (PC); PB=private benefits. In this event, a public enterprise would require public subsidies to supplement user charges since the latter would not fully cover the costs of operation. It is, however, possible for a private or public firm with market power—an extreme but typical case is the natural monopolist—to cover losses on some activities from exceptional profitability on others (that is, by cross-subsidization, which is discussed in chapter 10).

cial activities. However, in order to tie together our rapidly growing but sparsely-populated expanse the Canadian government found itself the owner and operator of such infrastructures as canals, and the heavy subsidizer of the privately-owned railways. Beyond this the Canadian government was neither ideologically nor financially able to go. However, in the early twentieth century bankrupt railways and Ontario's budding hydroelectric industry were added to the list of Canadian public enterprises.[5]

It was during the 1930s and the war years of the 1940s that public enterprise, particularly that undertaken by the federal government, received its greatest impetus. In the 1930s a combination of depression-motivated criticisms of private enterprise and technological developments (in air travel and broadcasting) gave rise to several public enterprises. Perhaps the most important of these were the CBC and Trans Canada Airlines. Both public corporations were viewed as extensions of Canadian infrastructure with potentially important externalities, particularly so in the case of broadcasting. In both cases subsequent development was away from public enterprise monopoly to public/private enterprise duopoly (see chapter 10). In addition to broadcasting and air transport, public corporations in banking (Bank of Canada) and in wheat marketing (Canadian Wheat Board) came into existence in the 1930s.[6]

During World War II numerous Crown enterprises sprang up. Most were related to the war effort, and most of these were "Crown companies," incorporated under the Companies Act, like any private company. They were privately financed, but subject to Ministerial control including accounts open to public scrutiny. Most of the Crown companies disappeared with the war's end, disposed of by another Crown corporation, the War Assets (later Crown Assets Disposal) Corporation. However, two of the World War II public enterprises lived on: the well known Polymer Corporation (1942) in the synthetic rubber and plastic fields and Eldorado Mining and Refining (1944), an early source of uranium supply.[7] Since World War II there has been a steady increase in the number of Crown corporations, particularly public enterprises established at the provincial level.

5. The Canadian National Railway (CNR) was formed in 1919 out of three bankrupt roads: the Grand Trunk, the Grand Trunk Pacific and the Canadian Northern, in addition to some smaller government-owned roads. Thus was formed Canada's triumphant duopoly, pitting the epitome of private enterprise, The Canadian Pacific Railway, against Canada's largest Crown corporation, the CNR, in "friendly" competition.
6. A good discussion of federal Crown corporations in Canada is presented by J.E. Hodgetts, "The Public Corporation of Canada," in W. Friedmann, ed., *Government Enterprise* (New York: Columbia University Press, 1970), pp. 201-26. The best, most recent and comprehensive study is J.R.S. Prichard, ed., *Crown Corporations in Canada: The Calculus of Instrument Choice* (Toronto: Butterworth, 1983). For an early study see C.A. Ashley and R.G.H. Smails, *Canadian Crown Corporations* (Toronto: Macmillan, 1965).
7. In 1973, the ownership of Polymer Corporation was transferred to the Canadian Development Corporation (CDC).

The Crown (Public) Corporation

Before exploring the actual extent of public enterprise in Canada it is necessary to clarify the concept of the "Crown corporation." As suggested earlier in the chapter, not all Canadian Crown corporations are synonymous with the concept of public enterprise as that term is usually employed. Some Crown corporations are little more than government bureaus administering the provisions of certain statutes, such as the Veterans' Land Act, the Unemployment Insurance Commission, the Agriculture Stabilization Board, National Museums of Canada and the Atomic Energy Control Board. These have been classified as "departmental corporations" because their functions are administrative, supervisory or regulatory; they are financed by appropriations much the same as any ordinary government department.[8] A second type of Crown corporation is the "agency corporation" engaged in trading, service and procurement operations. Agency corporations are more financially independent than "departmental corporations" in that they can maintain revolving fund accounts based on receipts from their activities; however, they must submit an annual operating budget to the responsible Minister.[9] Most agency corporations only marginally fit the usual description of public enterprise. Examples of agency corporations include the Canadian Wheat Board, the Crown Assets Disposal Corporation, Atomic Energy of Canada Ltd., and Canadian Arsenals Ltd.

Finally, there are the "proprietary corporations." These Crown corporations fit the usual description of "public enterprises." Crown corporations of the "proprietary" sort engage in financial, commercial or industrial activities and are expected to be financially self-sustaining from the sale of goods and services. Nevertheless some of them, from time to time, must seek monies from parliament to cover operating deficits. The CBC, Air Canada, the Farm Credit Corporation, Central Mortgage and Housing Corporation, and Petro-Canada are examples of federally chartered proprietary Crown corporations. Quebec's

8. The Financial Administration Act of 1951 provided a three-tier classification of federal Crown corporations. It defined a departmental corporation as "a servant or agent of Her Majesty in right of Canada and is responsible for administrative, supervisory, or regulatory services of a government nature." See Ashley and Smails, op. cit., p. 99 ff. The other two types are the "agency" and "proprietrary" corporations.
9. Ibid., p. 113. Also see Hodgetts, op. cit., p. 204. Hodgetts makes an important point in his analysis of why the corporate firm is chosen where departments of government, on the face of it, could do just as well. According to Hodgetts, an important advantage of the Crown corporate form is in its personnel policies. Crown corporations are not limited to hiring persons who have been already hired by the Civil Service Commission. They also have greater flexibility in firing as well as hiring. In addition to flexibility in personnel policies, Crown corporations, particularly the agency and proprietary type, have greater financial autonomy than government departments which must grapple each year with the Treasury Board and Parliament over their budgetary estimates and requests.

integrated steel-making firm, Sidbec; Alberta-owned Pacific Western Airlines; British Columbia's Ocean Falls pulp and paper mill; Newfoundland's Labrador Linerboard Mill;[10] and the electric power corporations found in most provinces are provincially chartered examples.

Extent of Public Enterprise in Canada

Tables 11-2 and 11-3 summarize the basic information on public enterprise in Canada. Table 11-2 indicates that in 1980 there were 147 public enterprise firms in Canada of which 78, or fifty-three percent, were in the utility, manufacturing or mining sectors. The total assets of public enterprises are impressive, largely because of the electric energy corporations. Employment by

Table 11-2

Number of Public Enterprises, by Province 1980

	No.	Estimated No. of Employees[c]	No. of Utility, Industrial, Mining and Energy-related
Newfoundland	16	1,838	11
P.E.I.	3	199	1
Nova Scotia	5	2,335	3
New Brunswick	5	1,583	2
Quebec	16	20,496	10
Ontario	10	23,165	4
Manitoba	10	6,594	4
Saskatchewan	16	7,657	10
Alberta	13	12,810	6
British Columbia	15	15,187	10
Other[a]	6	78	0
Federal Government	34[b]	152,768	18
Total[d]	148	244,710	79

Sources: Statistics Canada, *Federal Government Enterprise Finance* 61-203; *Provincial Government Enterprise Finance* 61-204; *Federal Government Employment* Cat. 72-004; and *Provincial Government Employment* Cat. 72-007.
[a]Includes 2 Yukon, 2 N.W.T., and two regional public enterprises.
[b]Does not include any federal departmental corporations; also excludes 9 Harbour Commissions and 6 Bridge or Pilotage Authorities.
[c]Figures for October 1981, for public enterprises listed in Statistics Canada, *Provincial Government Employment*, Catalogue 72-007, and *Federal Government Employment*, Cat. 72-004.
[d]One enterprise (IPSCO) jointly owned by two provinces is counted twice.

10. Sold to private interests in the late 1970s.

government enterprises in 1981 is estimated at approximately 244,000, or 2.4 percent of the Canadian labour force. The major employer is the CNR.[11]

Table 11-3, at the end of this chapter, is more interesting and informative. It breaks down public enterprise, in Canada, by sector. The year in which the enterprise was established, and the major product or service it supplies, are also shown. Public enterprises, in Canada, are most frequently found in one of the utility sectors: transportation, communication or energy.[12] The relative importance of public enterprise in the utility sector is consistent with the picture painted in chapter 10. It is one of public enterprise monopolies in electric power (eight provinces) and telecommunications (three provinces); public-private enterprise duopoly in broadcasting, railroads and trunk airlines; and a smattering of provincial transport enterprises: railways in B.C. and Ontario, an airline and a natural gas pipeline in Alberta, highway transport in Saskatchewan.

The relative importance of public enterprise in the industrial sector (essentially mining and manufacturing) is not great—but it is growing. If energy development firms (shown separately) are included, the total number of industrial-and-related public firms has grown impressively in the last decade. Public enterprises of an industrial nature tend to evoke the most controversy since they are usually in direct competition with, rather than providing service to, private enterprise. At present, three industry groups stand out: steel, forest products, and petroleum exploration and production. Three of the four publicly owned steel firms, Sidbec, Sysco (Sydney Steel Corporation), and CANSTEEL, can be traced to the financial difficulties of Dominion Steel and Coal Co. (DOSCO). The fourth is Interprovincial Steel and Pipe Corporation (IPSCO), a joint public (40 percent)-private (60 percent) venture, the public portion shared equally by the Saskatchewan and Alberta governments. In Nova Scotia the purchase of DOSCO's works by the provincial government was primarily designed to maintain employment in depressed Cape Breton. In Quebec, the

11. A wealth of useful information on federal and provincial Crown corporations, many of which fit our definition of "public enterprises" (see above), is contained in the chapters by Langford and Huffman and Vining and Botterell in Prichard, *supra* note 6, chapters 4 and 5, pp. 219-368.
12. Totally excluded from Table 11-3 and, in general, from the discussion in this chapter, are municipally owned enterprises, typically utility in character such as water, gas, and electricity distributors. Largely excluded from Table 11-3, and from explicit consideration in this chapter, is a relatively new phenomenon: partial (less than 100 percent) government ownership of commercially oriented enterprises. A recent study by Elford and Stanbury has termed such firms "mixed enterprises" and estimates that there were 322 of them in 1983. Two thirds of these mixed enterprises involved less than 50 percent government ownership. In most cases, government minority interests took the form of portfolio investments, especially by Quebec's Caisse de Depot and Alberta's Heritage Fund. Whether most of these mixed enterprises reflect a new government-business relationship or simply a willingness to invest government pension and other funds in private sector equities is not altogether clear, but at the moment the latter seems the more likely. See E. Craig Elford and W.T. Stanbury, "Mixed Enterprises in Canada," University of British Columbia (mimeo), October 1984.

creation of Sidbec was a combination of "Quebec presence" and heavy industry development, not simply a "hold the employment line" policy, as in Nova Scotia. If Sidbec succeeds in developing a fully integrated and profitable steel complex, it must do so in stiff competition with the big three, privately owned, steel firms of Canada: Stelco, Dofasco, and Algoma (see last section of chapter).

Provincially owned forest products firms can be found in Newfoundland, Manitoba, Saskatchewan and B.C. These represent a mixture of economic developmental (Newfoundland, Manitoba, Saskatchewan) and employment maintenance (Newfoundland, B.C.) schemes. Among the government-owned forest product firms are several producing pulp and paper products. The pulp and paper industry, although oligopolistic in structure, is marked by strong competition, largely because it is export-oriented and success requires maintaining prices competitive in world markets. As a result several of the government-owned firms in this industry are dependent on public monies to keep them operating. Recently the linerboard mill at Stephenville, Newfoundland, was forced to close. The Manitoba complex is the fallout from the financially disastrous and scandalized Churchill Forests project.[13] The Ocean Falls mill in B.C. is dependent on provincial subsidies.

The sector that received the most attention from public enterprise in the 1970s was petroleum and natural gas. Crown corporations engaged in exploration, development and production of hydrocarbons have been established at the federal level (Petro-Canada); in Quebec (SOQUIP); in Ontario (The Ontario Energy Corporation); in Saskatchewan (Saskoil); in Alberta (Alberta Energy Company); and in British Columbia (British Columbia Petroleum Corporation). In large part, these public endeavours are a response to the oil crisis of the early 1970s, to the prospective rents accruing to producers, to the quest for greater security of energy supply, to the desire for greater Canadian control in an industry so heavily dominated by foreign ownership and control and perhaps, in some cases, to federal-provincial rivalry. To date, Petro-Canada (or PetroCan, for short) has had the highest profile of the public enterprises in the petroleum industry, with responsibility for the federal share in the Syncrude (tar sands) joint venture, exploratory activities and developmental projects in the Canadian Arctic, exploratory activities off the East Coast, and production of conventional and heavy oils in Alberta (see below).

Other fields in which government enterprises are frequently found are in housing, the sale of alcoholic beverages, and in finance and economic development. The first two of these reflect social priorities or views and are not particularly interesting from the standpoint of the study of public enterprise. More interesting, and surprising, are those which are broadly labelled as

13. See Philip Mathias, *Forced Growth* (Toronto: James, Lewis and Samuel, 1972).

financially or development oriented. Most of the purely lending and credit-type operations are at the federal level and need little discussion. Of more importance are the development corporations at the federal and provincial levels. The best known is the Canadian Development Corporation (which, in fact, is not a Crown corporation), created in 1971, primarily to (a) provide venture capital to certain technologically-oriented industries, and (b) to increase Canadian "presence" in certain strategic (e.g. natural resource) industries (see chapter 12). The best-known example of the latter was CDC's purchase of a controlling interest in previously U.S.-owned and controlled Texasgulf, Inc., which it eventually traded for outright ownership of Texasgulf's extensive mining properties in Northern Ontario.

In addition to the CDC several provinces have set up Crown corporations to promote regional (provincial) economic development. Most of these enterprises are rationalized on the grounds of (i) imperfections in capital markets, particularly with respect to the supply of risk capital, and (ii) regional shortages of managerial talent for establishing and operating domestically owned industrial firms. There is as yet little evidence of the impact these enterprises have had on the economic development of their respective regions. With so many in existence they may tend to cancel each other out. Nevertheless, their popularity reflects the (i) ever-present concern, in Canada, with economic disparities among regions; (ii) alleged conservatism of our financial institutions, particularly where the supply of venture capital is involved; and (iii) the historical reliance on government intervention (via tariffs, regulation, subsidy) in the process of Canadian economic development.

Rationales for the Creation of Public Enterprise

In chapter 7 we outlined several rationales for the existence of public enterprise. These include:

(a) publicly owned "public utilities" as a substitute for regulated private monopolies,

(b) public enterprise as a spur to regional economic development,

(c) bridging gaps—treading where private enterprise is unable or unwilling to go,

(d) the creation of infrastructure,

(e) capturing economic rents,

(f) rescuing and replacing a failing private firm,

(g) as a competitive yardstick to promote economic performance of private enterprise,

(h) social reasons, particularly the more equal distribution, via subsidization in kind, of "merit-type" goods such as housing, auto insurance, etc.,

(j) as part of a scheme of nationalization—either industry-wide as in coal and steel in Great Britain or economy-wide as in Eastern European countries,

(k) "nationalism"—the desire for political reasons to have a state "presence" in an industry.

Except for the nationalization rationale all of these potential justifications for public enterprise have played some role in the growth of public enterprise in Canada. Some, of course, are more important than others. For example, "bridging gaps" was undoubtedly a more powerful parliamentary motive than was "competitive yardstick." Moreover, in many cases more than one rationale applies to a particular public undertaking. For example, provincial public enterprises in the electricity generation and transmission field fit categories (a) and (d), and in some areas (b) and (c). Public enterprise in the resource field may be prompted chiefly by (e), but may also be justified by (c) and (g). Less credible are those public enterprises created for reason (f) but whose continued existence is sold on the basis of (b).[14]

Of the nine rationales listed above some are more compelling than others— and some are, at the very least, debatable. Among the more compelling rationales are the "bridging of gaps" and "competitive yardstick." Clearly, if there are economic activities which yield social benefits (SB) in excess of social costs (SC) economic analysis suggests that they should be undertaken. However, if $SB>SC=PC>PB$ the activities will not be undertaken by private entrepreneurs. Or, alternatively, if there are important absolute cost barriers to entry, such as very high capital costs, the project may not be undertaken privately. In these cases, economic welfare could be increased by government willingness to directly provide the services or to induce private enterprise to do so by compensating them through subsidies. Thus in the nineteenth century, the federal government heavily subsidized the building of the Canadian Pacific Railway. Some critics have argued, not altogether convincingly, that it would have been preferable for the government to have built, and owned, the railroad itself. Note however the key assumptions that $SB>SC$ and that $SC>PB$. Were $PB>SC$ the "filling the gap" justification would be much less convincing since presumably profit-maximizing entrepreneurs would be ready to do so.

An important, although a realistic enough, assumption also underlies the competitive yardstick rationale. That assumption is that competition is sufficiently weak, and market imperfections are sufficiently great, to create a presumption of substantially less than optimal performance from private agents alone. In this case the injection of an efficient public firm in competition with the private one(s) can improve economic performance. Of course, there is the subsidiary assumption that the public firm is efficient, and that its competition

---

14. For a somewhat different, although partially overlapping, set of rationales for public enterprise, see J.R.S. Prichard, *Crown Corporations in Canada: The Calculus of Instrument Choice* (Toronto: Butterworth, 1983), chapter 1.

with private firms will keep it so. An inefficient, public firm which must be subsidized in order to remain alive does not provide a useful yardstick for industrial performance. While "competitive yardstick" has not been an important basis for the creation of public enterprise in Canada, there are a number of major Canadian industries in which it is present, at least in principle: broadcasting, railroads, airlines, steel, petroleum exploration and production.

The yardstick rationale is, conceptually, at least, an important alternative to the tools of competition policy and economic regulation in dealing with monopoly power. On the one hand, competition policy has generally been unable to deal directly with market power arising from tight oligopoly. Even in the United States, the world leader in antitrust (competition) policy, there has been a long-standing reluctance to "break up the big boys." This is particularly so where a few firms rather than one firm dominate a market. As is evident from chapter 9, no thought is given to divestiture. On the other hand, few economists would favour direct regulation of prices of firms even in tightly oligopolistic industries. Economic regulation is not viewed as a substitute for competition, nor for the typical performance exhibited in otherwise monopolistic (high market power) industries. Regulation is about as likely to be successful in inducing good performance as were wartime cost-plus contracting or peacetime wage and price controls. In these circumstances, public enterprise represents an alternative tool for promoting competition and presumably improved economic performance at the industry level.[15] As noted above, however, this sort of reasoning has rarely, if ever, been adopted as the basis for the creation of public enterprise in Canada.

A related point is made by Shepherd with respect to the U.S. economy. He argues that "dominant firms in many industries are often able to retain their positions mainly because they are backed by major banks."[16] If this is true (and concrete evidence has yet to be presented one way or another), then public enterprise may have a more important yardstick role as a financier of efficient

15. The economic theory lying behind this view is presented in R. Harris and E. Wiens, "Government Enterprise: An Instrument for the Internal Regulation of Industry," *Canadian Journal of Economics*, Feb. 1980, pp. 125-131. An important issue not covered in the Harris-Wiens paper is whether it is preferable to ask the public firm competitor to achieve optimal performance goals or simply to provide rivalry by behaving as a competitor. In an oligopolistic industry the results of these two ways of acting need not be the same. A study of the oligopolistic potash industry found that the independent, generally noncooperative, behaviour of Saskatchewan and North American potash producers did not change after the Saskatchewan government, in the mid-1970s, created a dominant government enterprise, the Potash Corporation of Saskatchewan, with half of Saskatchewan capacity and a large share of the North American market. Frank Flatters and Nancy Olewiler, "Dominant Government Firms in an Oligopolistic Industry: The Case of Saskatchewan Potash," Queen's University, mimeo, May 1983.
16. W.G. Shepherd, "Objectives, Types and Accountability," in William G. Shepherd and Associates, *Public Enterprise: Economic Analysis of Theory and Practice*, Lexington Books, 1976, p. 35.

but struggling firms than as a direct competitor of non-financial firms. Perhaps the number of Crown corporations in Canada whose role is wholly, or essentially, financial is a reflection of the high concentration within the Canadian banking system (see chapter 1).

Another rationale for public enterprise is the public utility one. It obviously is important in Canada. Given the alternative of publicly regulating private enterprise in the utility field, the public utility rationale is almost as compelling as "fill the gap" or "competitive yardstick."[17] A combination of quasi-social objectives and huge capital requirements of the energy, telecommunications, and rail transportation utilities make public ownership tempting. Thus in Western Europe most utilities are publicly owned, in stark contrast to the United States where private ownership prevails. As we saw in chapter 10, Canada stands somewhere in between. While ideological factors may play some role in explaining the difference between the European and U.S. experience, practical matters undoubtedly have dominated in Canada. Moreover, in capital-hungry Canada there is undoubtedly an element of "fill the gap" in the decision by many provinces to "monopolize" the supply of electric energy in order to ensure the development of sufficient and efficient capacity to meet future as well as present needs.[18]

However, the very capital-intensity of public utilities may make them something less than the first choice for public ownership. In their initial stages they use huge amounts of what is in scarce supply to governments as well as private firms: capital. As a result, Canadian governments have come to rely on private financial markets, in Canada and the United States, to supply the requisite financial capital. There is, of course, nothing surprising in this; however, while the public are the nominal owners of the enterprise, it is the creditors who implicitly exercise the real control over these public enterprises. Whether or not the glow of public ownership is thereby dulled, the capital markets are an important force inducing efficient performance on the cost side by the publicly owned natural monopolies.[19] In many instances public enter-

17. In fact, the laissez-faire economist, Henry Simons, strongly advocated public ownership rather than economic regulation of natural monopolies. So does his sometime disciple, Milton Friedman, who not surprisingly prefers unregulated private enterprise monopoly to either. H. Simons, *Economic Policy for a Free Society* (Chicago: University of Chicago Press, 1948), M. Friedman, *Capitalism and Freedom* (Chicago: University of Chicago Press, 1962), p. 28.
18. The "creation of infrastructure" rationale may also apply.
19. However, on the price-setting side, full allocative efficiency may not be attained if utility rates do not cover the opportunity cost of capital to the enterprise, or, if there is a divergence from marginal cost pricing in order for revenues to cover all costs, the price of the service to different consumer groups is not inversely proportional to each group's elasticity of demand for the service. See J.T. Bernard, "Quebec Hydro: An Economic Analysis of a Public Enterprise," Laval University (mimeo) January 1980. The theory here is based on W.J. Baumol and D.F. Bradford, "Optimal Departures from Marginal Cost Pricing," *American Economic Review*, 60 (June 1970), pp. 265-283.

prises are not subject to economic regulation by regulatory commissions—and even if they were, there is no reason to believe that good performance would be thereby ensured. Moreover, there is no profit motive to induce efficient performance. But there is an almost insatiable demand for capital (at least in telecommunications and energy) and inefficient performance will increase the cost of capital, if not dry up its sources altogether. Thus the private (credit) financing of public enterprise may be the most effective control over its economic performance, at least in the absence of a (private) yardstick competitor.[20]

Among the least compelling economic grounds (other than nationalization of an oligopolistic or atomistic industry or "nationalism" (see below), which have little other than ideology to recommend them) for public enterprise are the "failing firm" and "economic development" ones. These two are often inter-twined; the rescue of a failing or bankrupt firm is often seen as vital to the continued economic growth and viability of a specific region. When it stands alone, the "failing firm" rationale is easy to puncture in economic terms, although it is often politically enticing and socially persuasive where large numbers of mature, long-tenured employees are involved. However, in Canada, at least, with its constant concern for regional disparities and regional growth, the failing firm rationale rarely stands alone. Typically, in the community of the rescued firm, employment opportunities are locally limited, or non-existent.

There are a number of examples of public enterprise in Canada replacing bankrupt or failing firms. Probably the most famous, and most successful, is the CNR. Here, the economic grounds were as compelling as the political: bank-ruptcy was due to financial excess; not, in general, to an otherwise uneconomic activity, or declining industry status. In some cases a public corporation has replaced an ill-conceived and heavily subsidized private one, as was the case with the Churchill Forests complex in Manitoba and the Nova Scotia heavy water plant, the latter eventually acquired by a federal Crown corporation, Atomic Energy of Canada Limited. In each case, there was an attempt to make good on some of the huge public investment (via subsidy) already undertaken. Then there are the outright failures—such as the DOSCO steel works on Cape Breton, which was sold to the Nova Scotia government and renamed the Sydney Steel Corporation, and which remains a persistent drain on both federal and

20. One naturally thinks of Hydro-Quebec, whose efficiency and credit worthiness is reflected in its good rating in the capital markets. One might say that given Hydro-Quebec's virtually insatiable demand for capital, chiefly supplied in foreign markets, it has little choice but to retain its image as a well-run enterprise. The very size of Hydro-Quebec and the economic weaknesses of Quebec make the provincial government's taxing powers a weak reed to rely on were Hydro-Quebec's efficiency to deteriorate sufficiently to create operating losses. If anything, the opposite is the case. There has been some wry comment that the provincial government could finance current government budget deficits more easily by selling bonds ostensibly to finance Hydro-Quebec.

provincial funds.[21] In British Columbia, a public enterprise replaced the retreating Crown Zellerbach operation at Ocean Falls. In Quebec, a slightly different scenario occurred when the textile firm known as Regent Knitting folded. It was taken over and managed by its workers as a cooperative under the name of Tricofil. However, the operation has not been able to survive without regular, and large, subsidies from the provincial government.[22]

The problem with the "failing firm" rationale is that unless there are special reasons why an enterprise which is unprofitable privately is yet capable of profitability under public ownership, then the investment made by the public sector will almost certainly represent a misallocation of scarce resources. Public funds must be used to cover operating deficits generated by the production of goods or services whose value in the market place is less than the opportunity costs associated with their production. Moreover, what might have been politically enticing in the short run due to the maintenance of employment opportunities becomes embarrassing in the long run as the subsidization of operating deficits adds up. Unfortunately, the short time horizons of most politicians lead to the placing of greater weight on the short-term benefits rather than on the long-term costs. Once "trapped" it is not easy for the government to extricate itself.[23] In an attempt to cut deficits and subsidies other forms of protection for the public firm are typically sought.

Much the same line of argument, though with somewhat less force, can be levelled against the "economic development" rationale for public enterprise. Unless there are some clearcut and substantial *external* benefits, there is the nagging question of why there is dependence on publicly owned firms rather than privately owned firms. Presumably, if privately owned firms are unwilling to invest, and there are no externalities to speak of, public investment will yield a return less than cost. In cost-benefit terms the investment (public enterprise) should not be undertaken. There is, however, an important (though probably infrequent) exception to this line of argument. If the government invests, via public enterprise, in an "infant industry," then the investment may prove profitable in the long run. This parallels the infant industry argument for protective tariffs, which occupies an important place in the international trade literature. In this case the public enterprise that receives subsidies over the short run is analogous to the private enterprise that is protected by tariffs until

21. The Federal Government took over the Cape Breton coal mines (originally owned by DOSCO), in 1967, placing them in the hands of the Cape Breton Development Corporation (DEVCO). A paper which argues that DEVCO'S raison d'être is largely "social" rather than economic is Alan Tupper, "Public Enterprise as Social Welfare: The Case of the Cape Breton Development Corporation," *Canadian Public Policy*, Autumn 1978, pp. 530-46.
22. A summary of Tricofil's trouble-filled history, including the suggestion that its troubles are due in large part to the non-entrepreneurial attitude and effort (or lack of it) of Tricofil's worker-management, is contained in *The Montreal Star*, Friday, June 9, 1978, p. A-5.
23. An example is the Georgetown Shipyard owned by the P.E.I. government (see below).

the industry has expanded sufficiently to achieve economies of scale and become profitable on its own. Unfortunately, just as experience indicates that infant-industry tariffs rarely vanish and ultimately are required to protect immature adults, subsidized public enterprise infants may go to the grave feeding from the public trough. Although it is perhaps still too early to tell, there is some concern that Quebec's Sidbec (steel) operation will never grow up economically. Of course, to the extent that the subsidized public enterprise provides much-needed (for economic development) infrastructure, the subsidies will be offset by external economies, reflected in the lower costs of other (usually private) firms.

Perhaps the most objectionable (on economic grounds) rationale for government ownership is the political desire to have a "presence" in an industry. Although on the whole Canadian governments have been pragmatic, if not always successful, in their use of the public enterprise instrument, we are not immune to a degree of "ornamentalism." Unhappily, the worst excesses are displayed in Quebec where nationalism in culture and politics has overflowed into the economic arena. As we shall see below, the ownership of chronically money-losing Sidbec is justified on the grounds of having a "Quebec presence" in the steel industry. Quebec's decision to purchase one of the leading firms in the declining asbestos industry has little other than political sentiment to recommend it. Most incomprehensible of all is Quebec's decision to pour tens of millions of dollars into the expansion of a small, money-losing, government-owned sugar refinery in Mont St. Hilaire so that all Quebecers can purchase government-produced sugar, with the brand name Marie Perle, from their local supermarket.[24] Coincidentally, the Quebec government agency that manages the pension funds of Quebecers now owns thirty percent of the province's largest food retailer, Provigo Inc.

Some Issues in Public Ownership

In the preceding section we attempted to evaluate some of the rationales for public enterprise. In this section we briefly consider some questions or issues that may arise when public enterprise is carried out in practice. These are:

(i) If government decides to enter an industry, what price should it pay the previous owners?

(ii) Should public ownership be complete or partial? Are joint ventures with the private sector to be sought, or avoided wherever possible?

(iii) Is public enterprise as efficient as private enterprise, *ceteris paribus*?

(iv) What sort of incentives for efficiency should be created? Profits? Budgetary?

24. *The Montreal Gazette*, Saturday June 25, 1983, p. H-1.

(v) What criteria should be employed in evaluating the economic performance of the public firm?

(vi) Related in part to (v), how autonomous should the public corporation be? To what extent should government or parliamentary controls be applied, with their potential for introducing noneconomic objectives and criteria?

(vii) If the public enterprise is saddled with some non-economic goals, to what extent should its losses on some activities be covered by *internal* cross-subsidization? or alternatively by direct government subsidies?

(viii) Should public enterprise be "privatized"?

It is easier to ask these questions than to answer them. Here we can only sketch tentative and brief answers. The economic literature on public enterprise (as opposed to socialist economies) is skimpy at best.

(i) What level of compensation should be paid to previous owners? Looked at from a narrow economic viewpoint (which, as a practical matter, probably is most sensible) the answer is simple: pay the market price of the firm, just as if a private firm were the purchaser. However, the politics of "public takeover" involve a much wider latitude for compensating previous owners. Since the state's police powers allow it to compel transfer of property, the price can range from zero (full expropriation) if there are no constitutional due process limits, to a price reflecting a fair or reasonable return to the sellers. In Canada, with its history of "due process" (which includes the rights of property ownership) an abhorrence of expropriation means past investors will be compensated; but if the market price reflects a capitalization of long-term monopoly profits or rents, the government's purchase price may be set substantially lower than the market price—allowing no more than a normal return on original owner's investment, although a potential capital loss to recent purchasers of the firm's shares.

(ii) Where public enterprise reflects ideological preferences, public control is almost certain to be complete. Even where other (than ideological) rationales dominate, the typical case has been for full public ownership of a given public enterprise. However, in recent years Canadian governments, both federal and provincial, have shown some interest in joint (public-private) ventures.[25] At present the major instances are in the resource sector, in particular the oil and gas industry. The federal government has, since 1970, been involved in a joint venture with major petroleum companies to explore for oil and gas in the Canadian Arctic.[26] The federal government and the governments of Ontario and

25. It is perhaps worth distinguishing "joint ventures" between government(s) and private corporations, and "joint ownership" where some of the shares are owned by the government, the remainder by numerous relatively small private investors. There are, of course, some mixed cases as well.

26. The federal government's interest in Panarctic Oils Ltd., the joint-venture exploratory effort in the arctic, was turned over to Petro-Canada in 1976. Some of the heavy and tar sands oil "mega-projects" are joint ventures in which federal and/or provincial governments have a share.

Alberta hold important shares in the formerly all-private Syncrude (tar sands) oil project. The federal government's vehicle for participation in these projects is the Crown corporation, PetroCan. Another example of what is effectively a joint venture is Telesat Canada, which although government-controlled, is approximately 50 percent owned by the major telecommunications carriers. Quebec has recently teamed up with the French-based aluminum giant, Pechiney, to build a 1.4 billion dollar aluminum smelter at Betancourt, near Trois Rivières. Quebec's stake is $470 million, not including the very favourable terms on which electricity will be supplied by government-owned Hydro-Quebec.[27]

Whether joint, public-private ventures are desirable depends upon the objective. If the purpose of public enterprise is (a) to assure a project is carried out by assisting in the provision of financial capital; (b) having some direct control over the project's or enterprise's direction; and (c) participating in whatever profits or rents are generated, then the joint-venture approach is both practical and capable of achieving the stated objectives. If, however, it is difficult to maintain co-operation between the partners, or if the involvement of both public and private interests adds nothing and is merely duplicative, then the joint-venture approach is to be avoided. There is also the argument that Canadian joint ventures to date are little more than privately controlled but partially government-financed (and owned) operations, which yield little benefit to the public. As with most issues it is hard to resolve conflicting views or to make across-the-board statements.

(iii) It is often argued that a publicly-owned enterprise will typically be less efficient than a similar privately-owned firm. Often, of course, there is a degree of political hyperbole underlying the assertion that government enterprise is relatively inefficient. However, the argument is not without some theoretical underpinnings. About twenty years ago Armen Alchian provided a classic statement based on a property rights analysis. According to Alchian, a crucial difference between public and private enterprise is that with the former there is no possibility of ownership exchange or specialization. In the case of public enterprise, everyone is compelled to be a part (a very small part) owner with little reason for any one person to monitor the firm's profitability or the behaviour of the firm's management. In the case of private enterprise, the transferability of ownership claims (shares) makes possible ownership specialization and thereby the stronger incentive for major shareholders to attempt to

27. *The Montreal Gazette*, Saturday, July 30, 1983, p. E-1. The joint venture is expected to create 2000 permanent jobs, or $700,000 per job. However, a dose of "nationalism" may also be a factor. Yves Duhaime, Quebec's Minister of Energy and Resources at the time, is quoted as saying the government "wanted a Quebecois presence in the decision-making process of the province's aluminum industry."

weed out inefficient management. The unsolicited takeover bid is perhaps the most radical manifestation of a shareholder interest in the efficiency of a firm's management.[28]

Alchian's property rights approach to the issue of public versus private enterprise efficiency is useful, but is not necessarily definitive. An alternative approach predicts efficiency differentials on the basis of market structure—on how competitive is the environment in which the firm operates. To test the competing hypotheses, one based on the nature of ownership claims, the other on the degree of competition, Caves and Christensen made a study of the productivity of Canadian railroads, an industry which pits publicly-owned CNR against privately-owned CPR.[29] Since the Second World War Canadian railroads have operated in an increasingly competitive environment as a result of increased intermodal competition and deregulation (see chapter 10). The study found that CNR's productivity was 14 percent below that of the CPR in the mid 1950s. However, following effective deregulation of Canada's railroads in the 1960s the productivity gap rapidly declined, disappearing altogether by the early 1970s.[30] Caves and Christensen conjecture that the reason other studies have found privately-owned firms to be relatively more efficient than publicly-owned ones is that they focused on firms in a noncompetitive (monopolistic and/or regulated) environment. In the Canadian railroad case the environment was increasingly competitive: CNR's survival in the absence of government subsidies depended on its being as cost-efficient as its privately owned competitors.[31] This view suggests that public ownership is not inherently less efficient than private ownership, especially if the government-owned enterprise is not isolated from effective competition.[32]

28. One of the best statements of Alchian's argument of which I am aware appears in D. Davies, "The Efficiency of Public v. Private Firms: The Case of Australia's Two Airlines," *Journal of Law and Economics* (April 1971), pp. 149-166. Also see T.E. Borcherding, "Toward a Positive Theory of Public Sector Supply Arrangements," and J. Palmer, J. Quinn and R. Resendes, "A Case Study of Public Enterprise: Gray Coach Lines Ltd." in Prichard (ed.), *supra* note 6, pp. 126-129 and Chapter 6. Palmer, *et al.* test the property rights theory in their study of inter-urban bus service in Ontario. They find that Gray Coach, the publicly owned firm, was less efficient than its private sector competitors, particularly because of satisficing behaviour on the part of Gray Coach's managers.

29. Douglas W. Caves and Laurits R. Christensen, "The Relative Efficiency of Public v. Private Firms in a Competitive Environment: The Case of Canada's Railroads," *Journal of Political Economy*, 88, no. 5 (September-October 1980), pp. 958-976.

30. Recall (from chapter 10) that both CNR and CPR experienced productivity growth much more rapid than that of the highly regulated U.S. railroads.

31. To the extent that CNR's capital formation was made possible without its having to pay, in full, the market cost of capital, the cost comparisons may be deficient. However this would not effect the differential rates of productivity growth that eliminated the measured productivity gap between CNR and CPR.

32. The property rights and structural environment hypotheses are examined in the context of a recent study of the efficiency of public enterprises in Canada. S.F. Borins and B.E.C. Boothman,

(iv) Should public enterprises attempt to maximize profits, or simply stay within budgetary projections, presumably by raising sufficient revenues to cover operating costs and debt retirement? It would seem that if the goals of the firm are strictly economic, the profit-maximizing objective is most likely to be consistent with economic efficiency in both production and in the allocation of resources. But suppose the government firm is a monopolist or has great market power in its particular industry. Then profit maximization not only "exploits" consumers, it will also result in a welfare loss, reflecting a misallocation of society's resources. Since many public enterprises, particularly in the utility fields, have monopoly or market power, a profit-maximizing rule is, in these cases, objectionable. A preferable goal is to set prices in order to cover all economic (opportunity) costs—including a "normal" or market rate of return on society's "equity" in the public enterprise. Erring by making too low a profit, or return on investment, is also to be avoided. A few years ago, an unpublished study by Jenkins indicated that the average rate of return on capital invested in provincially owned hydroelectric generating and transmitting facilities in Canada was 3.5 percent during the 1970s—a figure far below the market cost of capital.[33] When highly capital-intensive industries fail to earn a "normal" return on capital there will be an important misallocation of resources, especially in a country such as Canada which is chronically capital-hungry.

In sum, whether profit maximization or some other target should be employed depends on (a) the firm's objectives (see below) and (b) the market structure of the industry—if it is atomistic or oligopolistic and the public firm is a "yardstick," a profit-maximizing rule is an appropriate one. If it is a monopolist, a p = mc rule is preferable to a profit maximizing (MR = MC) one; if the monopoly is "natural," it may be desirable to demur from a strict p = mc rule, in order to avoid operating deficits requiring public subsidy.

(v) What performance criteria should be applied to the public firm? This question is obviously related to the previous one. If the public firm is a yardstick competitor, it has little choice but to minimize costs by adopting the means and objectives of private firms. If it is able to survive, to meet its competition, then in economically relevant respects, the public firm's performance is good. If instead, the public firm is a monopolist, or if it was established in order to achieve certain social, or distributional, as well as economic objectives, other standards of performance are required. As noted above profit maximization by a public enterprise monopolist is inappropriate. But does this imply that marginal

"Crown Corporations and Economic Efficiency." Paper prepared for the Royal Commission (Macdonald) on the Economic Union and Development Prospects for Canada, 1984.

33. G.P. Jenkins, "Public Utility Finance and Economic Waste", unpublished paper, Harvard University, 1980. As a basis of comparison the rate of return was about 10 percent in other industrial sectors.

cost pricing should be the rule? Alec Nove has argued that in the case of nationalized industries, where an effective (government) monopoly exists at the industry level, external economies and numerous interdependencies make standard marginal cost-pricing rules an inadequate, if not incorrect, criterion.[34] Nove is thinking, in particular, of nationalized industries (in Great Britian) that are of the network variety, such as transportation, where interdependencies between various local services make marginal cost pricing of each service inappropriate. But he presses his point further to include many enterprises whose overall demand is dependent on the goodwill it builds up from each of the products or services it supplies.[35]

If the public firm is expected to achieve certain social and redistributive objectives, it is clear that efficiency criteria alone will not suffice. Some other measure of goal attainment is needed, although economics enters when the analysis turns to the question of the cost incurred, or efficiency with which the objectives are attained. It is not unusual that such cost-benefit analyses often imply that the public firm should devote itself to economic objectives, and that other means, typically direct government expenditures and taxes and transfer payments, should be employed to meet the non-economic goals.

(vi) How autonomous is the public corporation? A much-debated issue is the degree to which management of public enterprises should be free from governmental and political influences and direction.[36] This issue is related to the preceding one, since the more numerous are the non-purely economic goals of the public firm, the greater is political control and direction of the enterprise likely to be. In Canada, few generalizations are possible. However, three points can be made: (i) in a basic legal or constitutional sense Crown corporations are "accountable" to a Minister or Parliament; (ii) managerial and financial autonomy is considered an important advantage of the Crown corporation, so that most public enterprises have been allowed a high degree of independence; (iii) since a number of Crown corporations were established to achieve certain social, as well as economic goals, e.g. CBC and Air Canada, political influence

34. Alec Nove, *Efficiency Criteria for Nationalized Industries* (Toronto: University of Toronto Press, 1973), Chap. 1. Nove has particularly in mind network industries such as transportation where the whole, in a sense, is more than the sum of its parts. The availability of service between points A and B may affect the demand for service between other points C,D...which are linked to A-B.

35. Nove makes an important point when he says that nationalized industry must maintain a sense of duty, purpose, obligation to the public (consumers) it serves. And it must do so on its own, for there is generally no regulatory agency to enforce upon the enterprise these values. These values are important if costs are to be kept down, service quality high. In their absence service quality falls and prices rise to cover higher costs. Nove, op. cit, chapter 6.

36. The accountability of Crown Corporations was a major concern of the recent (Lambert) Royal Commission on Financial Management and Accountability (Canadian Government Publishing Centre: Hull, Quebec, 1979).

will be no less (although perhaps more) than is necessary to assure that non-economic goals are not forgotten.

How autonomous public enterprises should be depends on what type of activity they are engaged in and one's view of the role of public enterprise. One suspects that much opposition to the concept of public enterprise arises from a suspicion that the enterprise will be used for political purposes (some of which may be objectionable) to the detriment of its economic tasks and financial self-efficiency (and thus at the expense of general economic welfare). Given the view of public enterprise presented in this chapter, more rather than less autonomy would be desirable. Yet there is room for some doubt. If a public enterprise is a big loser it may use its autonomy to hide its losses from Parliament until the day of reckoning with the government Treasury. Canadair appears to be an example, having incurred a $1.4 billion loss, mainly on the development and production of its highly touted Challenger jet. The astronomical losses did not become public until they were beyond repair and the federal government was forced to simply write them off.

(vii) Should the costs of achieving non-economic goals be met by direct subsidy or cross-subsidization? Many public enterprises are called upon to undertake activities which are not compensatory. Airlines may be required to fly routes whose traffic is so thin that no reasonable charges could cover out-of-pocket much less overhead costs. The CNR is asked to provide freight and passenger service in the Maritimes at rates which are not compensatory, and (like the CPR) it had to supply uneconomic (to the carriers) commuter services in the Montreal area until the transportation commission of Montreal took over the commuter services, with the aid of provincial subsidies. CBC programming to reflect the diversity of Canadian tastes is not expected to attract sufficient advertising revenues to cover all of its costs. In addition, some regulated *private* firms are required to carry out non-compensatory activities—e.g. until recently, CPR as well as CNR had to carry grain at 1897 Crow's Nest Pass rates and maintain uneconomic intercity passenger service; and private broadcasters are supposed to adhere to "Canadian content rules" even when it is not in their commercial interests to do so.

How are lost revenues made up? In some cases, such as private broadcasting, revenues lost only reduce large positive profits. In the case of public broadcasting, the CBC must seek subsidies from Parliament to cover operating losses arising out of their more diverse programming. But where an enterprise provides a variety of services or has a variety of customer classes each with its own set of charges, as is the case with airlines, rail transport, telecommunications, and energy companies, it is clearly possible to subsidize some services or customer classes by revenues from higher-than-compensatory charges levied on other services or classes. This is the internal cross-subsidization referred to in chapter 10. It is a widespread pricing technique used by public utilities, and is in fact fostered by the form of economic regulation to which some of these industries are subjected. Cross-subsidization is also an important phenomenon of, and issue in, public enterprises in socialist countries and in nationalized industries in countries such as Great Britain. Whether it is "good" or "bad" again depends on the enterprise's objectives. Where important social, non-economic goals are given the public firm, it may be preferable to directly subsidize them rather than make certain classes of customers with strong and inelastic demands pay for them. Where, however, the objectives are economic and there are strong bases for externalities and interdependencies as is the case with telecommunications services, local transportation, etc., cross-subsidization via area-wide rate averaging seems preferable to outright public subsidies.

(viii) Should publicly owned firms be "privatized"—sold off to the highest bidder?[37] In recent years, growing disenchantment with the losses piled up by many Crown corporations has led to calls for the government to get out. These calls translate into arguments that what the government obviously can't do profitably, the private sector may do better. Sometimes it is misleadingly inferred that if the government sold off losers it can only gain by obviating future losses to the public. But this overlooks the fact that if the enterprise would be a loser whether under public or private ownership, the only way to induce private ownership is by offering to sell the firm's assets at a (huge) loss to the original investor (government). This, of course, is not an argument against privatiza-tion—only a warning that the seller (government) doesn't gain something for nothing. Only if the private sector is genuinely able to manage the firm better than when it is under public ownership (see (iii) above) can one expect a real economic gain to government from selling off a public enterprise. Of course, there are many other than purely economic reasons to support "privatiza-tion"—and to oppose it too.[38]

Case Studies of Crown Corporations in Canada

A. Sidbec

Among Crown corporations, Sidbec is of obvious interest. It is an industrial firm, situated in the strategic Canadian steel industry. While Sidbec is Canada's fourth largest steel maker, it is considerably smaller than the "big three"—

---

37. A variant is for the government to dispose of its ownership by giving or selling to each citizen or resident a fixed number of shares. This was the course taken by the British Columbia Resources Investment Corporation as a means of disposing of investments made by the previous government.
38. The case against a rush to "privatization" should not be construed as a possible case for increasing the number of public enterprises. It isn't!

Stelco, Dofasco and Algoma.[39] At present Sidbec's share of industry capacity is between 8 and 9 percent, and its share of industry shipments is somewhat lower due to Sidbec's considerable excess capacity. However, Sidbec's obvious aim is to become a leading, fully integrated, steel producer.

Sidbec was created in the late 1960s from the Quebec remains of failing Dominion Steel and Coal Company (DOSCO), whose main works in Nova Scotia were also acquired by a Crown corporation, the Sydney Steel Corporation (SYSCO).[40] The avowed aim of the Quebec government was to gain a "Quebec presence" in the predominantly Ontario-based steel industry. Its main task has been to create an integrated steel complex with new capacity out of the aging plant it acquired from DOSCO. Sidbec apparently did not expect to show consistent profits in its first decade and a half of life, and it didn't. About the time when it might have been expected to move toward maturity (and profitability) the deep world recession of 1975-77 struck, producing large and damaging (to Sidbec's industrial credibility) losses, which have continued to this day.

One of Sidbec's problems is that it still relies on the older electric furnaces while the three industry leaders and SYSCO have generally converted to more modern and efficient oxygen furnaces. As a result, Sidbec is generally considered less efficient than the industry leaders and its costs proportionately higher. In 1977 Sidbec was reported to be selling steel at prices up to 20 percent below its production costs, a reflection of both external (recession) and internal (inefficiency) conditions. As a result, Sidbec is reported to have had operating losses of $28 million in 1977, despite government subsidies amounting to $11.6 million.[41] Losses have continued, rising to $59 million on steel making operations alone in the deep recession year of 1982, before dropping to $27 million in 1983.[42]

Another of Sidbec's problems is its partnership with the United States Steel Corporation and the British Steel Corporation in an iron ore mine and pelletizing operation, Sidbec-Normines Inc., located near Port Cartier.[43] When the partnership was formed in the mid 1970s the prospects for steel making, and by extension iron ore mining and pelletizing, appeared rosy. They seemed so rosy to Sidbec that the firm impulsively made expansion plans. These plans included contracting to purchase 3 million tons of pellets, even though the maximum needs of its steel making operations are for 1.5 million tons.[44] Since the contract

39. At present, Sidbec is one of six small Canadian steel producers (so-called "mini-mills") relying on electric furnaces in contrast to the more modern oxygen furnaces employed by the industry leaders.

40. As a result Sidbec is officially known as Sidbec-Dosco.

41. *The Montreal Gazette*, Thursday June 15, 1978, p. 17.

42. *The Montreal Gazette*, Saturday March 31, 1984, p. E-2.

43. Sidbec's holds a majority interest of 50.1 percent, while U.S. Steel and British Steel have 8 and 42 percent interests, respectively.

44. *The Montreal Gazette*, Saturday, July 17, 1982, p. H-1.

specified heavy penalties if Sidbec did not take the ore, it was forced to make the purchases at previously determined prices, and then dump the excess on a depressed world market. Not surprisingly it is the mining-pelletizing side of Sidbec's operation that is now the big money loser. For example, in 1981, when Sidbec actually made a small profit on its manufacturing operations, Sidbec-Normines cost the company $61.9 million.[45] The mining complex is now the major contributor to the $300 million in losses that Sidbec has accumulated since its purchase by the Quebec government in 1968.

The rationale for a publicly owned steel firm in Quebec evidently transcends the purely economic. Undoubtedly Sidbec plays a role in the industrial development of Quebec, and to the extent it does so, this is important. However, references by government officials to a "Quebec presence" in the steel industry suggest that nationalism has also played a role. (How much Quebecers are willing to pay for nationalism is a crucial—for Canada—and an, as yet, not fully decided issue. If one Parti Québécois minister is to be believed, it will cost plenty, since he is reported as having said that Sidbec was not intended as a money-maker.)[46] The problem with nationalism is that it is emotional, and hard to evaluate in economic terms. Suffice it to say that Sidbec has yet to be a real competitive threat to the privately owned Canadian steel industry. It has, however, become a threat to Quebec taxpayers as it continues to depend heavily on explicit subsidies, and on implicit ones such as a decision by a Quebec government to "buy Quebec" when it purchases steel for building and road construction.

B. Petro-Canada (PetroCan)

PetroCan was the federal government's response to the energy crisis of the 1970s. It is a federal Crown corporation, the first fully-integrated, Canadian-owned firm in the petroleum industry. Initially, PetroCan's main activities were largely of a joint-venture variety with various of the world leaders in the petroleum industry. But PetroCan was interested in more than cooperative exploratory ventures. Its expertise and entrepreneurial spirit were undoubtedly enhanced when it purchased the physical assets, and a large portion of the management, of Atlantic Richfield Canada Limited in 1976, for $330 million.

Petro-Canada was created in 1975, promptly set up headquarters in Calgary, and began operations. Upon its establishment the federal government transferred to PetroCan its 45 percent holdings in Panarctic Oils, its 15 percent holding in Syncrude Canada Limited, and its activities in the Polar Gas Projects. To these were soon added the production and exploration activities of Atlantic Richfield Canada.[47] It was not an inauspicious beginning; PetroCan has been in

45. Ibid. p. H-1.
46. *The Montreal Gazette* June 15, 1978, p. 17.
47. See Petro-Canada, Annual Report, 1976.

the newspapers ever since, and never more conspicuously than when its attempted bid to take over Husky Oil, with its huge investment in heavy-oil properties in Alberta and Saskatchewan, fell through at the last minute in the face of a counterattack by the privately and foreign owned petroleum industry. Six months later, however, PetroCan successfully acquired Pacific Petroleums, with extensive oil and gas producing properties in the West, for almost 1.5 billion dollars.

PetroCan's purchase of Pacific Petroleum gave it refining capacity and marketing channels in Western Canada. Desiring a nationwide network of retail outlets and the refining capacity to supply them, PetroCan purchased Belgian-owned Petrofina in 1981 and added the downstream operations of British Petroleum in 1983. By 1984 PetroCan owned 2976 gas stations located in every province, and was enjoying market share growth during a period of overall industry stagnation.

Despite the controversy it has generated from time to time, Petro-Canada has genuinely attempted to cooperate with the industry giants in the search for oil. It has done so via joint exploratory operations off Nova Scotia and Labrador, in the Arctic Islands, and in the Syncrude (tarsands) project. Petro-Canada played an instrumental role in the Mobil group which discovered and is now developing the rich Hibernia oil field off the coast of Newfoundland. But PetroCan is also a competitor at the development-production end—in good part because of its purchase of Atlantic Richfield Canada. This acquisition made PetroCan a producer as well as explorer and developer. Even in the latter activities, PetroCan may become a competitor of as well as cooperator with the petroleum giants, as some of the millions of acres of properties it has acquired begin to produce (earn) results.[48] Moreover, PetroCan originally expressed a longer-run concern in the development of alternative (to oil and gas) sources of energy. But, for the time being, PetroCan is primarily concerned with increasing the supply of oil and gas through a variety of largely cooperative, though sometimes competitive, activities.

It is still too early to evaluate Petro-Canada's performance. Whether the Canadian public (the effective owners of PetroCan) and the Canadian taxpayers (the ultimate "debtors" if PetroCan fails) will benefit, in net terms, from the billions of dollars invested by the federal government, is debatable. A few points

48. In addition to 23 million gross acreage acquired via the purchase of Atlantic Richfield, Petro-Canada's involvement in the arctic has three sides: (a) it is a major shareholder in Panarctic Oils, the exploratory and development consortium, or joint venture, first established in 1969; (b) it is a landholder in its own right, and (c) it is an 18 percent working interest partner in an exploration group which also includes Panarctic Oils, Gulf, and Imperial Oil. See Petro-Canada, *Annual Report*, pp. 9-11. In 1982, a fourth side was added when the Canada Lands legislation required that Petro-Canada hold a 25 percent interest in any consortium exploring for oil on lands not under provincial jurisdiction.

are worth noting: (i) PetroCan can and has acted as a catalyst to generate exploratory efforts when private entrepreneurial spirits have flagged. An example is the efforts to find oil off Canada's East Coast, an effort spurred by a PetroCan-initiated joint venture. (ii) PetroCan's acquisition of the federal government's share in Panarctic Oils has changed the public role in Panarctic from a "silent partner" to an "active" and energetic, partner;[49] (iii) PetroCan is now a formidable rival of the majors at the refining-marketing end, so that it virtually holds in its hands the power to assure effective competition in this phase of industry activity; (iv) PetroCan's exploratory efforts provide a new and independent source of information on oil and gas reserves which is at the disposal of the National Energy Board. The NEB has traditionally relied heavily on the petroleum industry for estimates of reserves. These estimates have fluctuated substantially from high, optimistic ones before 1973, as the industry attempted to justify exports of gas and oil, to low, pessimistic ones in the mid 1970s as the industry attempted to justify its arguments for higher domestic prices on the basis of limited supplies and future shortages.[50]

The other side of the coin is that PetroCan's "capitalization" has involved large outlays of public funds. Over $330 million went into the Atlantic Richfield purchase. At least $300 million, and probably much more, will go into the Syncrude project. (However, to be fair, the federal government's commitment to Syncrude, and that of the Ontario and Alberta governments, predates Petro-Canada). Pacific Petroleum represents a public outlay of $1.5 billion. Almost $2.1 billion has been invested in the properties formerly owned by Petrofina and B.P. In short, the federal government, in an attempt to spur energy development and to increase Canadian ownership in the petroleum industry has been, is, and will be, pouring hundreds of millions of dollars into investments which it hopes will have a big pay-off. (PetroCan also pays royalties and income taxes like any other petroleum firm). Whether the pay-off will be sufficient to offset benefits forgone from alternative uses of the funds is yet to be determined, and is a question that may never be answered, given the value judgements involved. The one thing that seems assured is that PetroCan does not plan to be a meek public firm, but rather has taken a leaf from the books of its giant, fully integrated, and swashbuckling competitors.

C. The Georgetown Shipyard

The Georgetown Shipyard is a Crown corporation of the government of Prince Edward Island. While the shipyard officially became a Crown corporation in 1971 it has been a virtual "ward" of the province since its christening, in 1964, as Bathurst Marine Limited. Unfortunately, the shipyard is an experience in

49. The Toronto *Globe and Mail*, April 16, 1976; *Oilweek* Dec. 12, 1983, p. 8.
50. "PetroCan's Progress," *Financial Post*, April 22, 1978, p. 6.

public subsidy to private enterprise, and then public enterprise itself, which the province would rather forget.

The story began in the mid-1960s when a Norwegian-born, Montreal-based entrepreneur sold the industry- and employment-hungry P.E.I. government on a shipyard-fish processing plant complex at Georgetown, P.E.I., which purportedly would employ 300 persons. The theory was that the boats built by the shipyard would supply fish to the processing plant. Within a few years the two operations were bankrupt; the province had poured in excess of $9 million into an enterprise valued at $3 million.[51] The publicly subsidized entrepreneur had, by then, disappeared. It took two years for the province to find a private buyer of the fish processing plant. The shipyard was turned over to the Fisherman's Loan Board, which in 1971 was amalgamated into the P.E.I. Lending Authority, a Crown corporation, which has managed the shipyard for the P.E.I. government ever since.

Two commissions of inquiry have investigated, in depth, the shipyard's activities. The first, the Trainor Commission, reported in 1969 that it found a history of profligate spending (with public funds) and mismanagement. Seven years later the second, the Large Commission, essentially found the same problems. Reporting on Georgetown Shipyard's first three years as a Crown corporation, Mr. Justice Frederic A. Large could only conclude that "the similarity which occurs in reading the 1969 Report and listening to the evidence of the witnesses today shows that one never learns from past mistakes."[52]

The grandiose design of the 1960s also seems to have imbued the managers of the public enterprise in the 1970s. Between 1973 and 1975 a rapid expansion of the shipyard was undertaken in order to turn it into a major East Coast shipyard. The enterprise was no longer content to build only fishing vessels, but aimed to construct any type of vessel the facilities would permit. This despite evidence on hand that other Atlantic coast shipyards were operating at losses. The problem, however, went beyond daydreaming. Internally the firm was found to be ill organized, financially mismanaged, and characterized by poor personnel policies reflected in overstaffing, low worker productivity and low morale.[53] Moreover, materials and labour time were squandered, often on personal undertakings.

> The Commission believes that many of the workers in the Georgetown Shipyard must have considered that the assets and resources

51. The sordid history of the venture is detailed in Philip Mathias, *Forced Growth* (James, Lewis and Samuel, 1971). The shipyard was known as Bathurst Marine Ltd. and the processing plant as Gulf Garden Foods Ltd.
52. Prince Edward Island, *Report of the Georgetown Shipyard Commission of Inquiry* (Charlottetown: Queen's Printer for P.E.I., Feb. 1976), p. 7.
53. Ibid., pp. 127-34.

of the Shipyard were limitless. Many displayed no concern for wasted effort, lack of intelligent oversight, the carrying on of practices which in an ordinary corporation would soon be discovered and the perpetrators fired. (Use of shipyard labour and labour [*sic*] [materials?] on private residences is one instance).[54]

Thus an employment-creating venture was being taken to the cleaners by its employees and mismanaged by the persons entrusted by the public with the job of reasonably operating a government enterprise. The Georgetown Shipyard is an example of the trap governments can fall into when they attempt to "force" industrialization. Even more scarce than capital may be managerial expertise. When expertise is lacking, failure or bankruptcy is almost certain. Having sunk large amounts of public funds, via subsidies, into an enterprise, the government is unlikely to "let bygones be bygones." Public takeover and additional outlays of funds result. However, unless market conditions are favourable and managerial talent is available to the public enterprise, the failing firm tends to sink further into financial difficulties. It is hard to see how the benefit from the local employment provided can offset the local impact of accumulated losses—unless of course subsidization is from "outside," i.e. from a more senior level of government. From this point of view the Georgetown Shipyard is an example of ill-considered public enterprise.

54. Ibid., p. 148.

Table 11-3

Federal and Provincial Public Enterprises, by Sector 1980[a]

Sector of Economy	Name of Enterprise	Gov't Responsible	Year of Origin	Product or Service
(a) Utilities:	1. Societés des Traversiers du Québec	Quebec	1974	Operation of ferry services
(i) transportation	2. Ontario Northland Transport Commission	Ontario	1902	Rail, highway & marine transport
	3. Urban Transportation Development Corp.	Ontario	1974	Research and development in transit systems
	4. Saskatchewan Transportation Company	Saskatchewan	1946	Operation of passenger and freight transport
	5. British Columbia Railway Company	B.C.	1924	Operation of passenger and freight railway service
	6. Pacific Western Airlines	Alberta	1974	Provision of passenger, air cargo, and trucking service
	7. Alberta Resources Railway Corp.	Alberta	1965	
	8. British Columbia Ferry Corp.	B.C.	1976	Operation of ferry services
	9. British Columbia Steamship Company	B.C.	1975	Operation of summer ferry between Victoria and Seattle, Washington
	10. Pacific Coach Lines Ltd.	B.C.	1978	Operation of intercity transit services
	11. Air Canada	Federal	1937	Domestic & international air service
	12. Eldorado Aviation Ltd.	Federal	1953	Passenger & freight air traffic for Eldorado Nuclear
	13. Canadian National Railway	Federal	1919	Land, water, air transportation and express, telecommunications & hotel services
	14. Northern Transportation Co. Ltd.	Federal	1947	Water transportation
	15. Via Rail	Federal	1977	Railway passenger service

Sector of Economy	Name of Enterprise	Gov't Responsible	Year of Origin	Product or Service
(ii) telecommunications and broadcasting	*1. Societe de Telecommunication de la Baie James	Quebec	1973	Establishment & operation of communications network in James Bay territory.
	2. Manitoba Telephone System	Manitoba	1908	Telephone service
	3. Saskatchewan Telecommunications	Saskatchewan	1947	Telephone, telegraph, radio network & microwave facilities
	4. Alberta Government Telephone Commission	Alberta	1958	Telephone service
	5. Canadian Broadcasting Corporation	Federal	1936	Radio & television services, domestic & international
	6. Teleglobe Canada	Federal	1949	Overseas telecommunications services
	*7. Telesat Canada	Federal	1969	Operation of domestic satellite telecommunications system
	*8. CN/CP Telecommunications	Federal		Long distance message and data transmittal
(iii) energy	1. Power Distribution District of Newfoundland & Labrador	Newfoundland	1966	Generation, transmission & distribution of electric power & energy
	2. Nfld. Labrador Power Corporation	Newfoundland	1954	
	3. Twin Falls Power Corporation	Newfoundland	1960	
	4. Nova Scotia Power Corporation	Nova Scotia	1919	
	5. New Brunswick Electric Power Commission	New Brunswick	1920	
	6. Quebec Hydro-Electric Commission	Quebec	1944	
	7. Ontario Hydro	Ontario	1907	
	8. Manitoba Hydro Electric Board	Manitoba	1921	

(Table 11-3 continued)

Sector of Economy	Name of Enterprise	Gov't Responsible	Year of Origin	Product or Service
	9. Saskatchewan Power Corporation	Saskatchewan	1929	Generation, transmission and distribution of electricity;
	10. B.C. Hydro and Power Authority	B.C.	1945	distribution of natural gas
(b) Energy Development:	1. Churchill Falls (Labrador) Corporation Ltd.	Newfoundland	1958	Generation of electric power & energy
	2. James Bay Development Corp.	Quebec	1971	Development of natural resources, particularly hydro-electric energy
	3. Quebec Petroleum Operations (SOQUIP)	Quebec	1969	Exploration, development, production, sale of hydrocarbons
	4. Ontario Energy Corp.	Ontario	1974	Exploration, development of energy sources
	5. Saskatchewan Oil & Gas Corporation (SASKOIL)	Saskatchewan	1973	Development & direction of, and participation in, the petroleum and natural gas industry in province
	6. Gas Alberta	Alberta	—	Purchases and sells natural gas, operates a pipeline and owns wells
	*7. Alberta Energy Co.	Alberta	1973	Participation in the Syncrude (tarsands) project
	8. B.C. Petroleum Corp.	B.C.	1973	Development of petroleum and natural gas industry
	9. Petro-Canada	Federal	1976	Oil and gas exploration, development, production, and marketing

(c) Industrial (including mining):

1. Burgeo Fish Industries Ltd.	Newfoundland	1954	Operation of fish processing plant
2. Labrador Linerboard Ltd.	Newfoundland	1972	Operation of linerboard mill & related wood harvesting facilities (inactive Dec. 1978)
3. Newfoundland Farm Products Corporation	Newfoundland	1963	Operation of meat packing plant
4. United Cotton Mills	Newfoundland	1962	Operation of textile mill
5. Marystown Shipyard Ltd.	Newfoundland	1966	Operation of a shipbuilding & repairyard & general engineering works
6. Newfoundland Fibroply Ltd.	Newfoundland	1959	Manufacture of wood panels and other wood products
7. Newfoundland Hardwoods Ltd.	Newfoundland	1950	Manufacture of furniture from local hardwood
8. Georgetown Shipyard Incorporated	P.E.I.	1973	Operation of shipyard
9. Sydney Steel Corp. (SYSCO)	Nova Scotia	1967	Operation of steelworks
10. CANSTEEL	Nova Scotia	1974	Provide the organization and vehicle for a new Cape Breton steel complex
11. New Brunswick Coal Ltd.	N.B.	N/A	Development and production of coal deposits
12. Quebec Sugar Refinery	Quebec	1943	Operation of beet sugar factory
13. Sidbec	Quebec	1964	Operation of an integrated steel complex
14. Quebec Mining Exploration Company (SOQUEM)	Quebec	1965	Mining exploration and participation in the development of discoveries and the bringing into production of mineral deposits
15. Societé Nationale de l'Amiante	Quebec	1978	Exploration, development and production of asbestos deposits

(Table 11-3 continued)

Sector of Economy	Name of Enterprise	Gov't Responsible	Year of Origin	Product or Service
	16. Rexfor	Quebec	N/A	Forestry and Sawmill operations
	17. Manitoba Forestry Resources	Manitoba	1973	Operation of pulp & paper mill & sawmill
	18. Flyer Industries Ltd.	Manitoba		Production and sale of transit buses
	19. Saskatchewan Forest Products Corp.	Saskatchewan	1949	Operations in woods, sawmills, lumber yards & planingmills
	20. Prairie malt	Saskatchewan	1974	Production of malt
	21. Interprovincial Steel & Pipe Corporation (IPSCO)	Saskatchewan & Alberta		Steel producer
	22. Saskatchewan Minerals	Saskatchewan	1944	Production and sale of sodium sulphate
	23. Saskatchewan Mining Development Corp.	Saskatchewan	1974	Searching for and developing all minerals in the province
	24. Potash Corporation of Saskatchewan	Saskatchewan	1975	Mining, production and sale of potash
	25. B.C. Cellulose Co.	B.C.	1973	Acquisition & holding of shares of forest product companies
	26. Ocean Falls Corp.	B.C.	1973	Operation of pulp & paper mill
	27. Plateau Mills Ltd.	B.C.	1973	Operation of sawmill
	28. Surrey Farm Products Ltd.	B.C.	1972	Production and processing of poultry meats (inactive)
	29. Canadair Ltd.	Federal	1944/ 1975	Manufacture of aircraft & parts

30. Cape Breton Dev. Corp.	Federal	1967	Coal mining, fish processing, marine farming, sawmill operator, industrial park, tourist development in Cape Breton, Nova Scotia
31. Canadian Arsenals Ltd.	Federal	1945	Manufacture and development of military equipment
32. De Havilland Aircraft of Canada Ltd.	Federal	1929/1974	Manufacture of aircraft
33. Eldorado Nuclear Ltd.	Federal	1944	Mining and milling of uranium ores
34. Polysar Ltd. (formerly Polymer)	Federal	1942	Production of synthetic rubber, chemicals & plastics. Now owned by CDC.
35. *Consolidated Computer	Federal		Manufacturing of computer-related machinery
36. Royal Canadian Mint	Federal	1969	Production of medals, plaques and other
(d) Finance Related, including insurance:			
1. Quebec Deposit and Investment Fund	Quebec	1965	Administration, as a trustee of assets of provincial bodies, principally the Quebec Pension Board, of long-term investments designed primarily to earn income but also to finance economic development
2. Société d'exploitation des loteries et courses de Québec (Loto Québec)	Quebec	1969	Organization and conduct of lottery schemes
3. Ontario Lottery Corp.	Ontario	1974	Organization and conduct of lottery schemes
4. Atlantic Lottery Corp		1976	Operates lotteries on behalf of Nfld., P.E.I., N.S., N.B.
5. Western Canada Lottery Corp.		1974	Operates lotteries on behalf of Man., Sask., Alta., and B.C.

(Table 11-3 continued)

Sector of Economy	Name of Enterprise	Gov't Responsible	Year of Origin	Product or Service
	6. Province of Ontario Savings Office	Ontario	1921	Operation of offices which receive interest-bearing deposits from public. Funds used according to Act.
	7. Quebec Automobile Insurance	Quebec	1977	Compulsory automobile liability insurance
	8. Manitoba Public Insurance Corp.	Manitoba	1970	Administration of comprehensive automobile accident insurance plan
	9. Sask. Gov. Insurance Office	Saskatchewan	1945	Provision of general insurance & administration of compulsory automobile insurance plan
	10. Alberta Investment Fund	Alberta	1965	Provision of funds to supply capital for investment in industrial and commercial development
	11. Alberta Home Mortgages Corp.	Alberta	1976	Provision of mortgage funds to assist Albertans
	12. Treasury Branches Deposit Funds	Alberta	1938	Provision of banking services
	13. Insurance Corp. of B.C.	B.C.	1973	Provision of general insurance & administration of compulsory automobile insurance
	14. Canada Deposit Insurance Corp.	Federal	1967	To provide protection for persons having deposits with member institutions; deposit insurance against loss of part or all of such deposits

15. Export Development Corp.	Federal	1969	To insure Canadian exports against non-payment by foreign buyers arising from credit & political risks
16. Farm Credit Corp.	Federal	1959	To provide longterm mortgage credit to Canadian farmers & make loans for purchase of farm machinery
17. Federal Business Development Bank	Federal	1975	To promote & assist in establishment of business enterprises, particularly small business
18. Loto Canada	Federal	1976	Administration and management of federal lottery
19. Federal Mortgage Exchange Corp.	Federal	1973	To develop a secondary mortgage market

(e) Marketing:

1. Handicraft Centre	Quebec	1961	Wholesale & retail sale of handicraft products
2. Ontario Food Terminal Board	Ontario	1954	Operation of wholesale fruit & market facilities to service metropolitan Toronto
3. Ontario Stock Yards Board	Ontario	1944	Operation of facilities for livestock market
4. Sask. Fur Marketing Service	Saskatchewan	1945	Marketing of pelts of fur-bearing animals
5. Alberta Terminals Ltd	Alberta	1979	Operation of grain terminal
6. Canadian Livestock Feed Board	Federal	1966	Subsidizing and marketing of feed
7. Canadian Saltfish Corp.	Federal	1970	Buying & selling of saltfish & preparation of fish
8. Canadian Wheat Board	Federal	1935	Management of interprovincial & export wheat trade

(Table 11-3 continued)

Sector of Economy	Name of Enterprise	Gov't Responsible	Year of Origin	Product or Service
	9. Crown Assets Disposal Corp.	Federal	1944	Marketing at home & abroad of Canadian and foreign government surplus equipment & material
	10. Freshwater Fish Marketing Corp.	Federal	1969	Marketing of freshwater fish products
	11. Uranium Canada Ltd.	Federal	1971	Agent on behalf of fed. govt. with right to acquisition & sale of uranium concentrate stockpiles
	12. Canadian Commercial Corp	Federal	1946	To assist in the development of trade between Canada and other nations
(f) Development Corporations:	1. Harman Corporation	Newfoundland	1966	Development of industry
	2. New Brunswick Development Corporation	N.B.	1959	Development of industry
	3. Industrial Estates Ltd.	Nova Scotia	1957	Development of industry
	4. General Investment Corp. of Quebec	Quebec	1973	Development of industry
	5. Manitoba Development Corp.	Manitoba	1958	Development of industry
	6. Saskatchewan Economic Development Corp.	Saskatchewan	1963	Provision of assistance to industry and specialized livestock enterprises

7. Alberta Opportunity Company (this is not the Alberta Heritage Fund but will receive some of its funding from the AHF)	Alberta	1972	Development of resources and promotion of diversification of Alberta's economy
8. British Columbia Development Corp.	B.C.	1974	Provide loans, investment, and technical assistance to industry
9. Canada Development Corporation[a]	Federal	1971	Publicly owned, multipurpose conglomerate

(g) Housing and Services:

1. St. John's Housing	Newfoundland	1949	Development of housing in St. John's, Nfld.
2. Hotel Buildings Ltd	Newfoundland	1966	Provision of hotel accommodation
3. Newfoundland and Labrador Housing Corp.	Newfoundland	1967	Development, control, & direction of housing
4. PEI Housing Corp	PEI	1975	Development and management of housing programmes
5. New Brunswick Housing Corp.	N.B.	1967	Development, direction, & control of housing
6. Ontario Housing Corp.	Ontario	1964	Development, direction, & control of housing
7. Leaf Rapids Development Corp. Ltd.	Manitoba	1971	Operation of townsite at Leaf Rapids
8. Manitoba Housing & Renewal Corp.	Manitoba	1967	Development, control, and direction of housing in province
9. Manitoba Water Services Board	Manitoba	1959	Supply of water to municipalities
10. Saskatchewan Housing Corp.	Saskatchewan	1973	Development, control, & direction of housing
11. Dunhill Development Corporation	B.C.	1974	Development and construction of housing projects
12. Saskatchewan Water Supply board	Saskatchewan	1966	Supply of water to municipalities and for wildlife projects

(Table 11-3 continued)

Sector of Economy	Name of Enterprise	Gov't Responsible	Year of Origin	Product or Service
	13. Alberta Housing Corp.	Alberta	1967	Development, control, & direction of housing
	14. British Columbia Housing Management Commission	B.C.	1975	Planning, constructing and management of housing in the province
	15. Northwest Territories Housing Corp		1975	Development and management of housing programmes
	16. Yukon Housing Corp		1972	Development and management of housing programmes
(h) Informational:	1. Canadian Patents & Development Ltd.	Federal	1948	Licensing of inventions arising from work of National Research Council
	2. International Development Research Centre	Federal	1970	Supports research into problems of developing regions of world, data bank

(i) Other:

1.	Newfoundland Liquor Corporation	1949
2.	Nova Scotia Liquor Corporation	1930
3.	New Brunswick Liquor Corporation	1927
4.	P.E.I. Liquor Control Commission	1948
5.	Quebec Liquor Corporation	1921
6.	Liquor Control Board of Ontario	1927
7.	Liquor Control Commission of Manitoba	1923
8.	Province of Saskatchewan Liquor Board	1925
9.	Alberta Liquor Control Board	1924
10.	Liquor Administration Branch (B.C.)	1921
11.	Liquor Control (Yukon)	1921
12.	Northwest Territories Liquor Control System	1939

Control & sale of alcoholic beverages

Explanation and Sources:

The above is a reasonably complete account of existing public enterprises in both the federal and provincial domain. The list, however, is not exhaustive owing both to the date of publication of the reference material and to the myriad of legalities which dictate government controlled enterprises' accounting practices, practices which ultimately determine how access to information concerning the very presence of these corporations is facilitated. Those enterprises which were purposely excluded from this list are:

1. corporations of a purely departmental nature (e.g. those set up for the maintenance of highways)
2. corporations classified by the *Financial Administration Act* as departmental
3. subsidiaries of other public enterprises unless they have been incorporated by an Act of Parliament and thus are suspected of acting autonomously vis-à-vis the parent company (e.g. Air Canada and CNR)

*joint public/private enterprises are indicated in the table by an asterisk(*).

^aThe CDC is not a Crown corporation.

Sources: Statistics Canada, Cat. 61-204; 61-203 (1980); J.W. Langford and K.J. Huffman, "The Uncharted Universe of Federal Public Corporations"; and A.R. Vining and R. Botterell, "An Interview of the Origins, Growth, Size and Functions of Provincial Crown Corporations," in Prichard, *supra* note 6, Chapter 4, Tables I and III, pp. 233-258, 291-95, chapter 5, Appendix Tables I and II, pp. 349-62.

12

Interventionist and Industrial Policies

Chapter 12 is divided into two parts. The first part is concerned with regulation outside the utility sector—particularly regulation of atomistic industries, where the purpose is to limit, or eliminate, competition. The second part is concerned with a variety of industrial policies designed to protect and promote industrial development and regional growth in Canada. The two parts of the chapter may seem somewhat at odds. There is a sense in which protective regulation (part I) and polices to promote growth and development (part II) are in conflict. The classical economists who decried government intervention in the economy, particularly where it was monopoly-creating or where it resulted in "wasteful" government expenditure, were preeminently concerned with economic growth. The tone was set by Adam Smith's *Wealth of Nations*, a book which attempted to set forth the mechanisms of economic growth and the gradual amelioration of the well-being of a nation's population. Rightly or wrongly, interference with market forces and intervention to protect favoured groups were believed to be the roadblocks to economic growth and to a rising standard of living. Rightly or wrongly, Canadian public policies of the last quarter century have combined a rising tide of protectionist legislation with increasingly desperate efforts to promote, almost bootstrap fashion, regional and industrial development. Little public thought is given to the possibility the policies are conflicting.

The first part of this chapter focuses on economic regulation designed to limit or suppress competition. Canadian agricultural policy is taken as the chief, and most important, illustration of this kind of regulation. It is not the only example: taxi medallions or "licences" limit the number of taxis in all major Canadian cities except Edmonton; entry into and tariffs charged by highway trucking are strictly controlled by most provinces; entry into certain personal services (e.g. barbers, beauticians, undertakers, etc.) is limited by licencing which requires, in some cases, completion of lengthy courses of study or apprenticeship; many professions (doctors, lawyers, academics, dentists, psychiatrists) have self-serving, self-regulating powers, including, in some cases, control over advertising and fees charged; craft unions run their own apprenticeship programmes, license journeymen, and thereby exercise control over the supply of certain kinds of skilled workers.[1]

The second part of the chapter examines some (but not all) of what might loosely be described as the "industrial policies" of the Canadian government. We include under this rubric policies to (a) increase efficiency by exhausting scale economies (e.g. Canada-U.S. Automotive Agreement); (b) promote industrial development, including R&D (Canada Development Corporation, Science Policy, Patent Policy, and various forms of direct industrial assistance); (c) promote regional economic development (DRIE grants); (d) promote domestic ownership (Foreign Investment Review Act); and (e) "regulate foreign competition" to limit (or increase) competitive pressures (anti-dumping laws; quotas on imports of shoes and textiles; Bank Act revisions concerning foreign banks).

I. Economic Regulation to Suppress Competition

The regulation of prices, output, and entry is not limited to the energy, communications and transportation industries that constitute the so-called "public utility" sector. As we noted in chapter 7, economic regulation has spread to many parts of the economy with little respect for the boundaries that distinguish "naturally monopolistic," "oligopolistic," and atomistic industries. In effect, the more structurally atomistic an industry the more likely it is that a regulatory scheme will be *sought* by the industry and supplied by the legislature. This, at least, is one of the predictions of Stigler's economic theory of regulation with its emphasis on control over entry. In atomistic industries regulation is viewed as a substitute for less formal, and illegal, devices such as

---

1. On the impact of professional licensing see T.R. Muzondo and B. Pazderka, *Professional Licensing and Competition Policy: Effects of Licensing on Earnings and Rates-of-Return Differentials*, Research Monograph No. 5, Bureau of Competition Policy (Ottawa: Minister of Supply and Services, 1979). Muzondo and Pazderka found that, on average, "individuals in professions which restrict advertising earn 32.8 per cent more than individuals in professions in which advertising is unrestricted. On average, individuals in professions in which fee competition is restricted earn 10.4 percent more than individuals in professions in which there is unrestricted fee competition, *ceteris paribus.*" "Occupational Licensing and Professional Incomes in Canada," *Canadian Journal of Economics* (November 1980), p. 666. Interprovincial differences in licensing restrictiveness permitted Muzondo and Pazderka to make their estimates of the effects of limits on advertising and fee competition on professional incomes.

price-fixing, output-allocating cartels. For even if such cartels were legal, they would tend to break down in the face of uncontrolled entry. The real purpose of sellers in seeking regulation is, then, to gain the legal power to exercise control of entry, and, where necessary, to allocate output shares. In these circumstances economic regulation may be viewed as a transfer, or "alienation" of the "police powers" of the state to producer groups. Protection is the name of the game. Just as industries have long sought tariff protection, industries today seek entry regulation. The impetus is the same, for tariffs and import quotas are a form of regulation.

A. Intervention in Agricultural Markets

Agriculture has long been an active arena for government policies. Intervention in agricultural industries has at least three sources; two economic in character, one political. As all beginning students of economics learn, the demand for basic commodities tends to be price inelastic while agricultural supply is notoriously vulnerable to exogenously determined shocks, usually associated with weather conditions. The combination of unstable supply and inelastic demand is a blueprint for sharp price fluctuations with equally acute effects on producer income. Since fixed costs make up a substantial fraction of farming production costs, income declines produce real hardships and tortuously slow exit of resources. Governments have reacted by providing easier access to loans through the creation of agricultural credit agencies. But this has done little to blunt the desire of farmers for some form of control over producer income.

Another factor which has contributed to interventionist policies in agriculture is the relative bargaining power of farmers on the one hand and those who transport, process, and distribute farm products on the other. Prior to the exercise of public control over freight rates that began with the Crow's Nest Pass Agreement in 1897, when the railway charges for grain shipments in the West were fixed by statute, it was the railroads which were the nemesis of farmers. The allegation that the railroads charged monopoly prices for the shipment of agricultural produce was a factor in the eventual regulation of the railroads. In this century, the farmer's nemesis has been the processors. In any given region of the country agricultural producers face an oligopolistic food processing industry. The early role of co-operatives and the original aim of some generally unsuccessful provincial marketing board schemes was to increase the bargaining power of farmers vis-à-vis processors and large wholesale-retail distribution chains.[2]

Although their very number is not an economic advantage to farmers, it

2. A rationale for the creation of the Royal Commission on Price Spreads in the mid 1930s was to investigate the reasons for the allegedly wide differential between the price received by agricultural producers and the price paid by final consumers.

proves to be a political one. Although the share of farmers in the total population has declined throughout this century, and precipitously since World War II, farmers, and those whose livelihoods depend on supplying the needs of farmers, are numerous enough, and sufficiently well placed geographically, to constitute an important voting block in many rural ridings. It is not easy for politicians to ignore the complaint of a group which is rightly viewed as hardworking, essential, and having real grievances. Unfortunately, in heeding the pleas of agriculturalists, governments have been relatively insensitive to the real costs of intervention. The popular view of agricultural policies is that they redistribute income from the more to the less well-to-do, from the strong to the weak. This somewhat oversimplified (because it ignores the income distribution among consumers) and somewhat misleading (because it ignores the fact that most programmes are more beneficial to large than to small operators) description of the distributive effects of agricultural programmes overlooks "real" effects on the efficiency of Canadian agriculture.[3] Present agriculture policies threaten to turn what were relatively efficient industries in one of the world's "bread baskets," into high-cost, increasingly uncompetitive, industries.

Agricultural programmes aimed at stabilizing and raising farm incomes have employed one or more of the following approaches:

(a) government price supports, with public purchase and storage of excess supply;

(b) deficiency payments;

(c) output restrictions, or what is today euphemistically termed "supply management";

(d) co-operative marketing organizations to improve farmer bargaining power with processors.

The first three approaches are represented in Figure 12-1 and described in the notes to the Figure. The first two approaches were treated as alternatives in the Agricultural Stabilization Act of 1958. This relatively enlightened piece of agricultural legislation was aimed at the primary economic woe: unstable producer income due to wide price fluctuations. It sought to place a floor under the prices of many basic commodities by guaranteeing producers 80 percent of the average price received during the previous ten years. Only wide fluctuations in price would bring the guarantee into effect. Once it came into effect farmers could receive a deficiency payment for the difference between the market price and the 80 percent of ten-year average, or the government could support prices at the floor level by purchasing any excess supplies at that price.[4]

3. On farm incomes, see G.L. Brinkman, *Farm Incomes in Canada* (Supply and Services Canada, 1981). On the impact of interventionist policies, see J.D. Forbes, R.D. Hughes, and T.K. Warley, *Economic Intervention and Regulation in Canadian Agriculture*, (Supply and Services Canada, 1982).
4. The Agricultural Stabilization Act also allowed for the payment of a fixed subsidy per unit of output. In terms of Figure 12-1 this implies a rightward shift in the SS curve.

Figure 12-1

Three Agricultural Income Support Programmes

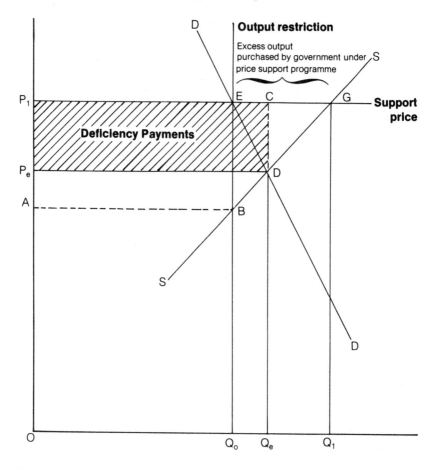

1. Price Support Programme: Government guarantees price P_1, purchasing excess supply Q_0Q_1. Government expenditures equal Q_0FGQ_1 plus storage costs minus revenues from sales of output "dumped" abroad.
2. Deficiency Payments: Government pays the difference between some guaranteed price (P_1) and the market clearing price, P_e. If the output is Q_e, total government payments to farmers equal P_eP_1CD, the shaded area in Figure 12-1.
3. Output Restriction: Either government can legislate output restriction, or, what is more common in Canada, government can give powers to agricultural marketing boards to curtail supply through a system of quotas. If price is to be maintained at P_1, total output quotas cannot exceed OQ_0. Assuming that the marketing board's administrative costs, plus any costs incurred in purchasing unexpected excess supplies, are financed by levies on producers, there are no direct government expenditures. However, if the quotas are saleable, they will be sold at a price that will reflect the monopoly profits (at a *maximum* AP_1FB) that are yielded by the quota system. The unit costs, including the purchase price of quotas, to new producers will approximate OP_1, with only "normal" profits being earned.

From the standpoint of stabilizing farm income, the Agricultural Stabilization Act has much to recommend it. It required government intervention only when prices fell suddenly and precipitously. However, the politics of agricultural policy apparently demand more than simply stabilizing farm incomes. To farmers, income support means higher as well as more stable income from farm production. With the added spectre of unequal bargaining power hovering over Parliamentary chambers, legislatures have progressively strengthened the hands of farmers with monopoly-power-creating legislation. The distinctive Canadian approach is the agricultural marketing board. There are now about one hundred provincially created marketing boards. Agricultural marketing boards are established by a majority vote of all the producers of a particular commodity, in a given province. The Board's membership consists of producers, although in a few cases there are token representatives of processors, distributors, and the consuming public.

1. Agricultural Marketing Boards

What exactly are agricultural marketing boards? They are "statutorily sanctioned, compulsory, horizontal cartels of the producers of agricultural products."[5] The compulsory feature is that all farms producing a given commodity in a specified province are compelled by statute to adhere to the regulations of a marketing plan once a majority of producers have voted to establish a marketing board. The horizontal feature refers to the marketing board's direct or indirect control over the total supply of a commodity via its control over the output of all the farmers who must participate in the marketing programme.

The activities and powers of marketing boards differ widely. At one end of the spectrum are marketing boards whose sole aim is educational and promotional (for example, those for potatoes in Alberta, Ontario, and PEI and for cattle in Alberta). The only influence over price exercised by these boards is via the effectiveness of their promotional efforts on the general demand for the commodity. Some boards negotiate prices with processors and other large buyers on behalf of individual producers. Here the board acts as a body which evens up the bargaining power between seller and buyer. Some marketing boards go beyond negotiation and fix the prices which must be paid by processors or distributors. Examples include Ontario's Asparagus Board and many provincial hog-marketing boards. Fixing prices involves, of course, a greater degree of power than does negotiation. It is not surprising, then, that to an increasing degree marketing boards have asked for and acquired price-fixing powers.[6] For example, whereas in 1960 all but two of Ontario's marketing boards were negotiating-type boards, in 1980 more than half of them had powers to set prices. In order to control prices effectively a marketing board must be able to exercise some control over supply. It may be able to do this by

5. Forbes et al, op. cit. p. 5.
6. See Prescott, *The Role of Marketing Boards in the Processed Tomato and Asparagus Industries*. Technical Report no. E/15 (Economic Council of Canada (ECC) and Institute for Research on Public Policy (IRPP), June 1981), p. 69.

requiring that all produce be channelled through the board acting as agent for producers, at which point it could limit, in an ad hoc fashion, the amount of produce purchased and marketed. Alternatively some marketing boards formally control supply through a quota system.

Marketing boards which control supply by assigning output quotas to individual producers have become known as "supply management" marketing boards. The leading examples of supply-managed commodities in Canada are dairy products, eggs, chickens, and turkeys in all or nearly all provinces, and flue-cured tobacco in Ontario. Marketing boards with supply-management powers control not only individual producer output but also entry into the industry by requiring that any new producer must purchase quota from an existing producer (if quotas can be traded, as they are in most provinces) or from the board (if quotas are legally untradable or if the board is expanding quota). The notoriety that agricultural marketing boards have gained is largely attributable to the activities and impact of supply management boards.

Table 12-1 provides some vital statistics about marketing boards in Canada. They are found in all provinces, their variation in number reflecting in large part the different opportunities for agricultural activity as determined by climate and soil. In 1979-80, 20 of the marketing boards were wood boards, attached to the forestry not the agricultural sector. Table 12-2 indicates the number of boards with price-fixing or price-negotiating powers (column 2). The capability of making monopolistic prices stick will usually depend on the power to set marketing or production limits. The ultimate power of marketing boards is reflected in column 3 indicating the number of boards which directly control output through production or marketing quotas. Column 5 indicates that almost a quarter of the value of agricultural produce is obtained through these supply-management boards.

The most interesting, and depressing, phenomenon is the growth in the number of marketing boards exercising supply management (quota-giving) powers. Until the early 1970s, the main examples were fluid milk marketing boards in most provinces and the flue-cured tobacco marketing board in Ontario. However, in the early and mid-1970s, egg, chicken, and turkey marketing boards adopted supply management powers following passage of federal legislation, the Farm Products Marketing Agencies Act of 1971. There has also been discussion of applying supply management principles to hogs and beef production.[7]

The coalescing of two factors led to the increase in the use of supply management powers by agricultural marketing boards. The first factor was recognition of the potential benefits to existing producers if a quota system

---

7. An ardent proponent of supply management powers for marketing boards was the federal minister for agriculture, Eugene Whelan, in the cabinet of Pierre Trudeau.

Table 12-1

Marketing Boards in Canada, 1979-80

	Nfld.	PEI	NS	NB	Que	Ont	Man	Sask	Alta	BC	Fed[a]	Canada
Grains						2	2				1	5
Oil seeds						1						1
Fruit				1	1	4				3		9
Vegetables			1	1	2	5	2		2	3		16
Tobacco			1	1	2	2						6
Hogs		2	3			1		1				7
Dairy products		2	1	1	4	2	1	1	1	1		14
Broilers				1	1	1	1	1	1	1		7
Turkeys		1	1	1		1		1	1	1		7
Broilers and turkeys								1	1			2
Eggs	1	1	1	1	1	1	1	1	1	1		10
Wood				6	14							20
Other[b]			1	1	1	2	1	1				7
Education and promotional[c]		2		1		1			3	1		8
TOTAL	1	8	9	15	26	23	8	7	10	11	1	119

[a] Canada Wheat Board

[b] Includes sheep and wool (Saskatchewan), honey (Manitoba), beans and seedling plants (Ontario), maple products (Quebec), greenhouse products (NB), and wool (NS).

[c] Includes sheep and wool (BC and Alberta), potatoes (Alberta, Ontario, PEI), cattle (Alberta), dairy cream (NB), and seed (PEI).

Source: Sullivan, *A Statistical Summary of Marketing Boards in Canada 1979-80*, Supply and Services Canada, 1981, table 2. Reprinted by permission of the Minister of Supply and Services Canada.

Table 12-2

Agricultural Marketing Boards, by Province and Powers

Province	(1) Number of marketing boards (1980)	(2) Number of boards which have the power to set prices by either formula, negotiation, or price fixing (1974)	(3) Products influenced by supply management (quota setting) boards (1978)[a]	(4) % of farm receipts obtained through marketing boards (1978)	(5) % of farm receipts obtained through supply management boards (1978)
Newfoundland	1	1	—	—	—
P.E.I.	8	5	2	42	21
Nova Scotia	9	5	4	62	54
New Brunswick	9[b]	7	4	53	38
Quebec	12[b]	11	4	62	58
Ontario	23	19	5	60	38
Manitoba	8	6	4	53	13
Saskatchewan	7	5	4	67	3
Alberta	10	5	4	42	8
B.C.	11	10	4	58	42
Total	99	74		57	24

[a]Quotas are actually used for eggs, milk, broilers, turkeys, tobacco, and hogs.
[b]In addition, there are 14 wood and pulpwood marketing boards or agencies in Quebec and 6 in New Brunswick
Sources: Sullivan, *A Statistical Summary of Marketing Boards in Canada 1979-80* (Supply and Services Canada 1981); J.D. Forbes et al. *Consumer Interest in Marketing Boards,* a report prepared for the Canadian Consumer Research Council, Study No. 1, September 1974, Appendix A; Economic Council of Canada *Reforming Regulation* (Supply and Services, Canada, 1981) Tables 6-4 and 6-5 pp. 56-57.

could be *effectively* applied. However, until 1971, the quota system of a provincial board could not be effective unless the province was the sole important supplier, in Canada, of the particular product (e.g. flue-cured tobacco in Ontario) or the product had to be consumed locally (fluid milk). The "fly in the ointment" is the provisions in the B.N.A. Act which prevent a province from interfering with imports from other provinces. Thus commodity flows across provincial boundaries would tend to effectively undercut a provincial marketing board's attempts to raise or maintain prices via supply restrictions on its own producers.

The second factor was the passage in 1972 of federal legislation providing for the establishment of federal marketing agencies which could allocate quotas to each province with a participating marketing board. The first federal board to be established was the Canadian Egg Marketing Agency (CEMA), whose early years of existence were checkered and scandalized. That eggs were the first product to be provided with effective federal controls over production was appropriate, for it was eggs that had prompted passage of the federal legislation. In the late 1960s, Quebec had attempted to protect its egg producers via a quota system, including a provision that all out-of-province eggs had to have a FEDCO (the initials of the Quebec egg board) stamp. FEDCO's attempt to limit "imports" from Ontario and Manitoba by allowing the eggs to sit in less-than-refrigerated circumstances for weeks on end was effectively circumvented by leading retail chains that simply carted the eggs into the province in truckload lots, delivering them directly to stores. FEDCO's move was also blunted when the Attorney General of Manitoba brought a reference case before the Supreme Court of Canada.[8] The Supreme Court found the proposed regulation *ultra vires* (unconstitutional) the B.N.A. Act, and, by extension, so were the provisions of Quebec's FEDCO.

The judicial victory for "free trade" and the operation of market forces was short-lived. The Liberal government of Pierre Trudeau reacted to complaints that the Supreme Court's decision undercut any real power that most marketing

8. *Attorney General of Manitoba v. Manitoba Egg and Poultry Association* (1971). Manitoba's egg producers were known to be relatively efficient at supplying eggs in numbers that far exceeded Manitoban demand. Concerned that FEDCO'S ploy would lead to similar ploys by other provinces, the Manitoba government decided to test the constitutionality of FEDCO'S plan. It did so by proposing a regulation under a supposed statute which would have made a proposed order of the Manitoba Egg and Poultry Board applicable to interprovincial as well as intraprovincial trade. The Attorney General of Manitoba then asked the Supreme Court of Canada to rule on the constitutionality of the proposed regulation.

Interestingly, in 1975, a Manitoba regulation applying to hog processors was ruled unconstitutional by the Supreme Court of Canada. In *Burns Food Ltd. v. Attorney General of Manitoba* (1975), the Court said that a regulation requiring that (a) hog processors purchase hogs only from the local producer board, and (b) hogs brought in from outside the province were to be deemed hogs produced in Manitoba and thereby subject to the Manitoba Natural Products Marketing Act and its regulation, was an unconstitutional interference with interprovincial trade.

boards might exercise. The federal government passed the Farm Products Marketing Agency Act (1972), permitting the establishment of federal marketing boards with province-wide quota setting powers. In doing so, the federal government has given the provinces the means to make output restrictions and resultant price hikes effective. The quotas that are assigned each province assure that one province will not be able to "flood" the market of provinces whose produce prices are higher. Each province's quota is a fraction of the total based on the previous five years' experience. Each year total supplies are allowed to grow slightly in line with population and demand growth.[9]

2. The Operation of a Marketing Board: The Case of Eggs

The operation of agricultural marketing boards has remained a mystery to most Canadians. Consumers rarely recognise the close association between the high prices of milk, eggs, and broilers, about which complaints are widespread, and the operation of marketing boards. However, a number of studies have begun to unravel some of the mysteries surrounding the marketing board phenomenon in Canada.[10] Here we present the salient facets of egg marketing boards in a rather analytical fashion, leaving to the student the responsibility for acquiring additional descriptive detail on his own.

Newspaper accounts, in 1974, that 28 million eggs were rotting while egg prices were skyrocketing focused public attention on the Canadian egg industry. The unsought notoriety was the direct consequence of the creation of the Canadian Egg Marketing Agency (CEMA) and the application of supply management powers by the member boards. The new system worked essentially as follows. CEMA allocated quotas to each of the provinces. (See Table 12-3.) Each province then allocated its quota among its producers according to a formula

9. The application of the federal legislation to the production and marketing of eggs was tested constitutionally and upheld in the Ontario Egg Reference, *Re Agricultural Products Marketing Act* [1978] 84 DLR (3d) 257. See C. Green, "Agricultural Marketing Boards in Canada: An Economic and Legal Analysis," (1983) 33 *University of Toronto Law Journal* 407-433.

10. The following studies deal with marketing boards utilizing the quota system. D.R. Campbell, "The Economics of Production Control: The Example of Tobacco," *Canadian Journal of Economics*, Feb. 1969; Food Prices Review Board, *Report on Egg Prices II*, Ottawa, August 1974; H. Grubel and R. Schwindt, *The Real Cost of the B.C. Milk Board: A Case Study in Canadian Agricultural Policy* (Fraser Institute, 1977); Broadwith, Hughes, and Associates, "The Ontario Milk Marketing Board: An Economic Analysis"; Ontario Economic Council, *Government Regulation* (Toronto, OEC, 1978), pp. 67-102; T. Borcherding (with G. Dorosh) *The Egg Marketing Board: A Case Study of Monopoly and its Social Costs*, Vancouver: Fraser Institute, 1981); Peter Arcus, *Broilers and Eggs*, Technical Report No. E/13, Economic Council of Canada and Institute for Research on Public Policy, March 1981; and Richard Barichello, *The Economics of Canadian Dairy Industry Regulation*, Technical Report No. E/12 (ECC and IRPP, March 1981). In addition, a good general analysis is presented in J.D. Forbes, et al., *A Report on Consumer's Interest in Marketing Boards*, prepared for the Canadian Consumer Council, Ottawa 1974, and the unpublished papers detailing the activities of marketing boards (hogs, vegetable growers, poultry, dairy, etc.) which form the basis of the Forbes study.

Table 12-3

Allocation of CEMA Quotas, 1973

Province	Millions of dozens	Percent of Total	Percent of Population
Newfoundland	8.5	1.8	2.5
P.E.I.	3.0	.6	.5
Nova Scotia	19.5	4.1	3.6
New Brunswick	8.7	1.8	2.9
Quebec	78.6	16.6	27.1
Ontario	181.3	38.2	36.2
Manitoba	54.2	11.4	4.4
Saskatchewan	22.6	4.7	4.0
Alberta	41.3	8.7	8.1
B.C.	57.3	12.1	10.7
	475.0	100.0	100.0

based on previous production. In order to enter the industry or to expand one's existing operation it was necessary to purchase quotas from present holders of quotas.

Given demand, the fixing of supply, along with the establishment of barriers to egg imports, should have been sufficient to maintain egg prices at a desired level. However, individual provinces not only allocated quotas but in some cases attempted to guarantee minimum prices higher than the CEMA price to producers selling within their assigned quotas. The result is pictured in Figure 12-2 where OQ is the quota allocated to the province and P_1 is the CEMA "intervention price," the price at which CEMA is prepared to step in and buy up any unsold eggs produced within assigned quotas.[11] (Note that, in reality, demand is not known, with certainty, beforehand. In Figure 12-2 the demand schedule, DD, is drawn on the assumption (a) that the demand curve facing a province's producers is identical with that province's consumer demand curve for eggs; (b) that the demand curve is independent of prices in neighbouring provinces; and (c) that it, by luck, intersects the fixed supply at the CEMA intervention price).

In most provinces (the exceptions were Ontario and Manitoba, the low-cost egg-producing provinces) the producer-controlled egg marketing boards set prices at levels higher than the CEMA intervention price. In Figure 12-2 the price is shown as P': at P' the quantity of eggs demanded is Q', leaving a surplus of $Q'Q$ of eggs produced within quota. Under the provisions of the CEMA

---

11. For each province there is an intervention price. In general, higher intervention prices are applied to those provinces where production costs tend to be higher.

Figure 12-2

The Operation of CEMA

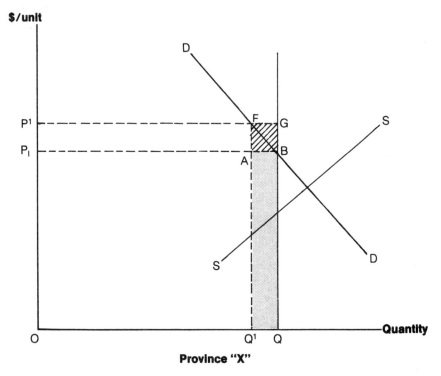

Province "X"

OQ   =   provincial quota awarded by CEMA.
DD   =   estimated demand for province "X" eggs, on assumption prices in all other provinces change in same proportion.
SS   =   unregulated supply curve of province's egg producers.
P_I =   CEMA's intervention price at which it stands ready to purchase any unsold eggs within quota and dispose of them on the "breaker" market.
P^1 =   province X's support price.
Q^1 =   quantity demanded at support price.
shaded area Q^1ABQ =   CEMA expenditure on unsold (Q^1Q) table eggs within quota. Expenditure is financed by a levy on producers.

plan, $Q'Q$ were purchased by CEMA at an expenditure represented by the shaded area $Q'ABQ$ and sold on the "breaker" market to processors producing cake mixes and the like, or were "dumped" abroad, chiefly in the U.S. market, at bargain prices to foreign processors and consumers. The remaining portion of the price guarantee, P_IP', was paid by the provincial board whose expenditure is represented by the shaded area AFGB. The expenditures of both CEMA and the provincial boards are financed by a levy of about 5¢ on each dozen eggs sold.[12]

12. In establishing the intervention price, CEMA treats the levy as a cost to be covered by the intervention price.

Where did the 28 million rotten eggs come from? As a matter of fact, the scandal was largely a result of the incentives created by the system to produce beyond the quotas—i.e. beyond the total provincial quota, OQ. (Tighter administration has evidently controlled these incentives in recent years.) Thus with a price of P' and cost conditions reflected in the supply curve SS it was obviously profitable to "overproduce" if CEMA was prepared to absorb the surplus. In its initial months CEMA did intervene and buy up all surplus eggs at the intervention price. The result was a huge excess supply which overtaxed storage facilities and disposal capabilities. While this horror story has evidently been laid to rest by better administration, Figure 12-2 indicates that egg prices are higher than market forces would set and that unsold "table eggs" must be sold on the "breaker" market or in foreign countries at highly subsidized prices.

The CEMA regulatory scheme was sufficient to raise the farm gate price of eggs from the 40-45¢ level to the 60-65¢ level in a short period of time, a price rise of approximately 50 percent. The student may wonder why such an increase did not lead to a flood of imports from the United States. It would have, had not the CEMA system been reinforced by import quotas with a "trigger" called the "indicative price." The indicative price was set at 60¢ a dozen (later reduced to 59¢). So long as the farm gate price in Ontario did not rise above 60¢ (plus 6¢ for transportation to market) the government-imposed quotas would be tightly applied. If Ontario prices rose above the indicative price, the quotas would be relaxed, imports would rise, and Ontario prices, and those of neighbouring provinces, would be reduced as the result of the increased supply.

3. Marketing Boards and Economic Efficiency

The operation of marketing boards may have important implications for economic efficiency. There are at least two ways in which efficiency is affected by a marketing board exercising supply management powers. First, output restriction creates allocative inefficiency by affecting the allocation of resources between their employment in the production of the output whose supply is restricted and all other agricultural and non-agricultural uses of those resources. Second, within the supply-controlled industry the apportioning of quotas among producers and the placing of limits on the amount of quota any one farmer may acquire affects the size distribution of producing units (farms), and as a result may create technical inefficiency by limiting the ability of the producing units to achieve scale efficiencies.

Studies of the operation of supply management marketing boards have found that both types of inefficiency exist.[13] Borcherding and Dorosh concluded, for example, that, in 1980, output restriction raised the price of a dozen eggs in British Columbia 23 cents above the price in the nearby state of Washington. In Figure 12-3 that might be equivalent to raising prices from P_e to P_m. The resulting allocative inefficiency is captured by the shaded "welfare loss"

13. See Grubel and Schwindt and Borcherding and Dorosh, *supra*, note 10.

Figure 12-3

Supply Restriction and Its Effects on Profits and Costs

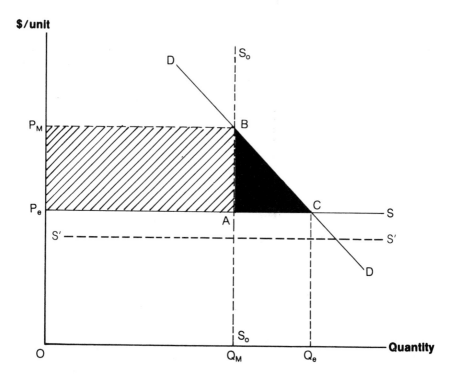

DD   =   demand curve
P_eS =   long run supply curve (constant cost industry)
S_oS_o =   supply fixed by quotas totaling OQ_M
ABC   =   deadweight loss due to supply restriction
P_MBAP_e =   transitory profits which get capitalized into quota values (Tullock); or the extra costs (of real
            resources used up) that are incurred by (a) the protected in order to keep outsiders out,
            and (b) the "outsiders" attempting to get in and have a piece of the "monopoly action"
            (Posner).

triangle ABC. Scale inefficiencies would exist if, in the absence of regulation,
the industry supply curve were $S'S'$ instead of P_eS.[14] In their study of the British
Columbia Egg Marketing Board, Borcherding and Dorosh found that egg
producers in that province were, on the average, considerably smaller than their
counterparts in the state of Washington. This they attributed to limits on
individual farm quotas set by the provincial marketing board. The smaller farm
size was estimated to have raised unit costs from 8 to 16 percent, helping to

---

14. The assumption underlying this analysis is that there is a constant cost of adding another firm
of average size to the industry, but that if firm size were raised unit costs would decline.

account for both higher costs of production and much higher prices for eggs in British Columbia than in Washington state.[15]

B. Effects of Regulation

Regulation which is essentially aimed at restricting supply has a number of other important economic and political-legal effects. The quotas applied to egg production, dairying, poultry farming, etc. are similar to taxi medallions which arbitrarily limit the supply of taxi services. It is well-known that the limitation in the supply of taxis has given the medallions (the licence to provide taxi services) value. In New York City, medallions sell for about $65,000. In Toronto, a medallion's value is nearly $40,000; in Montreal, $10,000.[16] The medallions are given value when their supply is restricted sufficiently to generate monopoly profits. The same applies to agricultural production or marketing quotas. The introduction of quotas in the dairy industry in the 1960s and in the egg and poultry industries in the 1970s has resulted in quota values of substantial magnitudes.

The process of quota value creation (or that of medallions or any other "licence" to supply whose quantity is restricted) is represented in Figure 12-3. Quotas OQm combined with demand DD result in a market clearing price of P_M. With constant costs represented by P_eS, monopoly profits of P_MBAP_e are created (see hatched area in Figure 12-3). These monopoly profits redistribute P_MBAP_e amount of income from consumers to producers, but reduce consumer surplus by even more, P_MBCP_e. The difference between the two, represented by triangle ABC, is the well-known welfare loss due to monopoly (see chapter 6).

The artificial creation of these monopoly profits gives that which created them value. The monopoly profits owe, of course, to the restriction in supply, enforced by means of the quota system.[17] Thus, the quotas become valuable to those who hold them. Because those without quotas cannot produce, and are thereby restricted from absorbing any of the monopoly profits, a market for quotas is created. Outsiders who want "in" will have to purchase quotas from those who hold them, and the price they will pay is the discounted (over future periods) value of the profits created by the quota system. Thus as the quotas

15. Borcherding and Dorosh, *supra* note 10, xvi, pp. 23, 39-42.
16. In Montreal, taxi permit owners narrowly voted in favour of a $30 million plan to buy back 2000 permits. Under the plan, taxi permit owners will be required to pay $1,500 a year for seven years—$10,500 in all. The ostensible rationale for the plan is to reduce excess capacity in the industry. Presumably, a majority of the taxi drivers believe that the 40 percent reduction in taxi permits (from 5,260 to 3,260) called for by the buy-back plan will raise the stream of future incomes, including the value of the permit, by substantially more than $10,500. *Montreal Gazette*, April 12, 1984, p. A-3.
17. In much the same way that a special talent or an especially efficient input commands a rent because of its scarcity value.

change hands the monopoly profits they create get capitalized into their selling price. The result is that the buyer of the quota incurs an extra cost when he enters into production, and this extra cost (the purchase price of the quota plus interest on the loan) will tend to approximate the profit area $P_M BAP_e$. Thus after the quota is exchanged the new producer only earns a normal return on his investment (including the investment in quota). Were the quota system to be abolished, supply to increase, and price to fall back to P_e, the producer would suffer a sizeable capital loss.

In Canada, the very right to produce fluid milk, eggs, poultry, and tobacco is now quite valuable. Table 12-4 provides estimates of the aggregate quota values of supply-managed commodities in 1978. In the aggregate, quota values exceeded two billion dollars in 1978 and are believed to have risen to three billion dollars in 1980. Here are some examples. A study of the Ontario Milk Marketing Board (OMMB) indicated that quota prices had risen to as high as $26.00 per pound of milk in the mid 1970s.[18] In 1976 the OMMB arbitrarily fixed the price at $16.00 and required that all sellers and buyers of quotas must deal directly with the Board. An average-sized dairy farm in Ontario produces about 2000 lb. of milk per day. Thus a person wanting to buy such a farm had to lay out $32,000 (2,000 × $16) just for the *right to produce*, before spending a cent on equipment, herd, buildings, etc.[19]

A study of the operation of the B.C. Milk Marketing Board indicated even more serious misallocation of resources and more valuable quotas.[20] In 1975, the estimated degree to which quotas raised price above cost in the area of the Fraser River Valley which supplies milk to Vancouver was $2.32 per hundred pounds of milk. This resulted in Vancouver consumers paying about $12 million more per year than was necessary to bring forth the required supply of milk.[21] The $12 million, when divided among the 1000 milk suppliers in the relevant section of the Fraser Valley, represented an average transfer from consumers to producers of $12,000 per year. At a discount rate of 12 percent, the capitalized value of the average amount of quota would be about $100,000 per farm ($\frac{$12,000}{.12}$). Quota values were said to be in the neighbourhood of $80 per

18. Broadwith, Hughes and Associates, "The Ontario Milk Marketing Board: An Economic Analysis," Ontario Economic Council, *Government Regulations* (Toronto, OEC, 1978), p. 79. The OMMB regulates the supply of "fluid" (drinking) milk. The supply of milk for "industrial" purposes (eg. cheese-making, ice-cream) is regulated federally by the Canadian Dairy Commission. The distinction between "fluid" and "industrial" milk is, of course, artificial; it is made for supply management purposes.
19. By arbitrarily restricting the value of quotas, the OMMB either reduced the incentive to sell quotas (but not the real flow of profits to which the quotas give rise) or induced a rise in the price of other assets which are complementary to the quotas (e.g. the physical assets of the farm itself), or both.
20. Grubel and Schwindt, op. cit.
21. Ibid., p. 39.

Table 12-4

Estimates of Aggregate Quota Values of Supply Managed Commodities in Canada in Mid-1978 (Millions of Dollars)

	PEI	NS	NB	Que	Ont	Man	Sask	Alta	BC	Canada
Fluid milk	1.0	14.6	9.2	171.7	98.4	20.6	18.9	41.0	262.4	637.8
Industrial milk	0	0	0	359.8	166.1	10.9	7.3	18.8	45.5	609.4
Eggs	0.7	4.9	3.1	30.2	87.9	10.8	3.1	7.0	49.7	197.4
Chickens	—	1.8	1.1	69.3	123.5	8.6	1.0	18.3	57.3	280.9
Turkeys	—	1.3	1.9	31.5	26.5	5.8	2.7	5.8	24.9	100.4
Tobacco	—				247.3					247.3
Total	1.8	22.6	15.3	662.5	749.7	56.7	33.0	90.9	440.8	2073.3

Source: George L. Brinkman, *Farm Incomes in Canada*, Economic Council of Canada and the Institute for Research on Public Policy, Table 3-21, p. 28, Supply and Services Canada (Ottawa: 1981). Reprinted by permission of the Minister of Supply and Services Canada.

Table 12-5

Capitalized Value of Broiler and Egg Quotas Fixed by Marketing Boards in February 1980

	Nfld.	PEI	NS	NB	Que	Ont	Man	Sask	Alta	BC	Canada
Broilers Capitalization											
(1) total ($ millions)	—	—	9	7	154	156	10	6	22	77	441
(2) per producer ($ thousands)[a]	—	—	67	159	166	218	83	100	138	405	193
Eggs Capitalization											
(5) total ($ millions)	2	1	5	5	35	124	13	4	8	85	282
(6) per producer ($ thousands)[a]	53	22	94	119	114	137	43	32	28	443	123

[a]Total capitalization or annual income equivalent divided by number of producers.
Source: Peter L. Arcus, *Broilers and Eggs*, Economic Council of Canada and the Institute for Research on Public Policy, (Ottawa: 1981), Tables 12 and 13, pp. 54 and 55.

lb. of milk in the mid 1970s. By the middle of 1978, fluid milk marketing quotas were selling for $150 per pound per day in British Columbia.

Table 12-5 provides evidence on what quota value means for individual producers of broilers and eggs in each province. Rows (2) and (6) in this table indicate the value in February 1980 of the average amount of quota for broilers and eggs respectively. These figures can be interpreted in two ways. For the purchaser of an average-sized broiler farm they indicate what he must invest in quota even before considering investment in land, building, chicks, etc. In British Columbia, this cost or investment would have required an outlay of $405,000 in February 1980. By the same token, the seller of an average-sized broiler farm in British Columbia would receive, in addition to whatever price his physical assets would fetch, a $405,000 windfall. The comparable figure for eggs in the province is $443,000. Although British Columbia quota values are substantially in excess of those in other provinces, the table indicates that to enter into the production of broilers or eggs in Canada can be a very expensive proposition. The value of the Canadian average quota for broilers was $193,000 and for eggs $123,000 in February 1980.

The evidence on quota values raises serious questions about the power that has been transferred by governments to producers through the medium of agricultural marketing boards. Many marketing boards have the power to create large property values for the relatively few, at the expense of consumers, and, perhaps more importantly, at the expense of the economic freedom of potential producers. The student might want to consider the implication of quota type systems applied across all industries. In such an event, three classes of persons would be created: (a) those who have sold their quotas and have "retired" (typically comfortably) on the capital sum received; (b) those who have purchased quotas and thereby have the right to produce (work) and (c) those without rights to produce (work), who are thereby dependent on the State for support. Fanciful, for the present, yes! But not an improbable outcome of the spread of interventionism to protect groups of suppliers, whether of final output or labour services.

The powers wielded by marketing boards have been viewed by some as a threat to civil liberties. Chief Justice McRuer in his report on Civil Liberties in Ontario worried about the wide delegation of powers to agricultural marketing boards.[22] Despite broad powers, the degree of accountability of marketing boards to the legislatures that gave them their powers is limited and weak. A frightening example of the misuse of power by an agricultural marketing board is the case of *Gershman v. Manitoba Vegetable Producers Marketing Board* (1975).[23] In the *Gershman* case the marketing board systematically harassed,

22. J.C. McRuer, *Royal Commission Inquiry into Civil Rights*, vol 5, (Province of Ontario, Toronto, 1971), Chapter 112.
23. (1976) 65 D.L.R. 3d. pp. 181-92.

and attempted to bankrupt, the owner of a Winnipeg wholesale fruit and vegetable company, who had opposed the creation of the marketing board five years earlier. The marketing board's harassment included two petitions for bankruptcy at a time when Gershman's firm was awaiting insurance payments following a fire which destroyed his warehouse and the produce therein. After Gershman went to work for another wholesaler, the Stella Company, and had made plans to become a partner in Stella, the marketing board withdrew its credit to Stella and threatened not to restore it until Gershman was dismissed. Gershman was dismissed and so was his sister who worked for another wholesaler which also found its credit threatened. The offer, to Gershman, of shares in the Stella Company was withdrawn. Gershman sued the marketing board for $35,000 and won a verdict for the full amount.[24] In concluding his judgement, Solomon J. had this to say:

> As the hearing progressed and the evidence disclosed more and more acts of vindictiveness by the Board against plaintiff, I found it difficult to believe that this drama was acted out in 1974 in Manitoba and was not from the pages of medieval history. Never in all my 16 years of public life and 18 years on the Bench have I come across a more flagrant abuse of power.

The judge went on to say that

> There are many Government-sanctioned boards in existence which now have exclusive jurisdictions to administer many facets of the economic life of our country, and as our life becomes more interdependent we will have even more such boards. These governmental boards are established to administer exclusively the many different economic programmes in our society. These are established with noble aims and for noble purposes. This most glaring abuse of powers by the Board, however, should not be allowed to pass without some assessment of punitive damages against it.[25]

One wonders just how noble are the aims and purposes of any supply-restricting policy. Such policies seem eminently self-serving and an almost perfect example of the "producer protection" hypothesis of regulation (see chapter 7). While the abuse of power reflected in the *Gershman* case is most unusual in its openness and vindictiveness there are undoubtedly more frequent, though more

24. Gershman's legal argument rested on what might appear to be a "technicality" so far as the real import of this case is concerned. By effectively forcing Stella Company to dismiss Gershman and withdraw the offer of shares to him, the marketing board was infringing on Gershman's contractual rights, even though in this case they were prospective so far as the purchase of shares was concerned. This issue is discussed at some length in The Appeals Court decision, upholding the trial court judgement. See *Gershman v. Manitoba Vegetable Producers Marketing Board* (1977) 69 D.L.R. (3d).
25. 1976 D.L.R. 3d, p. 191.

subtle, abuses produced by administrative boards brandishing the large powers turned over to them by governments.

Another possible consequence of supply-restricting regulation is that it will lead to a rise in the amount of real resources used by industry members or potential entrants to the industry. In chapter 5, we noted a well-known example of this tendency: the product differentiating activities of U.S. airlines in response to the control over prices and entry exercised by the U.S. Civil Aeronautics Board, prior to deregulation in 1978, resulted in the use of additional resources to wage non-price competition. Another example is that of trucking: in jurisdictions where new entry and rates are regulated, existing firms may then compete by providing more frequent service, thereby tending to raise costs.

Analytically, this process can be viewed as an upward shift in the supply (cost) curve P_eS shown in Figure 12-3. As the cost curve rises, profits originally represented by P_mBAP_e are squeezed out. The result is that, in the limit, the *long-term* effect of regulation is to increase real costs of supply rather than to increase profits.[26] This, of course, is an extreme view: in reality some middle ground is likely to be observed. However, the argument is an important one. It says, in brief, that regulation's chief *long-run* effect is to raise costs of production, resulting primarily in economic waste rather than a redistribution of wealth or income.[27] The increased costs (as more input is used per unit of output) may be due to:

(a) excess capacity created by supply restrictions, forcing firms to operate at higher unit costs than capacity production would allow.

(b) the failure of firms to exhaust economies of scale.

(c) real resources (legal, lobbying, etc.) used by industry members to prevent further entry.

(d) real resources used by outsiders in their attempt to convince the regulatory commission or board that they should be allowed to enter the industry.

(e) expensive non-price competition.

A good example of (c) and (d) is the trucking industry. In Canada all provinces except Alberta regulate entry into the trucking industry by issuing "certificates of convenience and necessity" (see chapter 10). One highway transport board

26. See Richard Posner, "The Social Costs of Monopoly and Regulation," *Journal of Political Economy*, Dec. 1975, pp. 807-26. Posner has argued that price fixing-output restricting cartels in unregulated industries will have much the same effect: short-run profits will be converted into higher costs in the long run as the result of non-price competition. *Antitrust Law: An Economic Perspective* (Chicago: The University of Chicago Press, 1976), Chap. 2.

27. This statement is perhaps too strong, for income undoubtedly is redistributed toward those professional groups (e.g. lawyers, accountants, etc.) who provide services before regulatory boards for potential entrants and for established producers.

that has been studied in some depth is that of Ontario.[28] Each year the Ontario Highway Transport Board holds literally thousands of hearings. Many involve attempts by existing firms to get additional routes, or by new firms to enter the industry. It is obvious that such hearings use up the (labour) resources of those directly involved, the applicants and the board members. But the regulatory process also involves intervention by established firms who attempt to limit or prevent new entry. One study reported that 5 percent of the labour costs (2.5 percent of the operating costs) of a large trucking firm were directly related to opposing licence applications.[29] As administrative tribunals and regulators proliferate, as the stakes for incumbents and potential entrants rise, one may expect an increasing amount of resources to be used up in the regulatory process. Predictably, there has been an increase in the number of "private" carriers (shippers who own and utilize their own trucks), truck leasing, and illegal trucking, as shippers and carriers alike attempt to avoid the red tape and high costs created by the regulatory environment.[30] If government is willing to create valuable monopolies it is to be expected that resources will be attracted toward attaining and maintaining a "piece of the action."

28. Norman Bonsor, "The Development of Regulation in the Highway Trucking Industry in Ontario," in Ontario Economic Council, *Government Regulation* (Toronto, OEC, 1978). Also see by the same author, *Transportation Rates and Economic Development in Northern Ontario*, University of Toronto Press for the Ontario Economic Council (OEC Research Study No. 7), Toronto 1977. Some of these issues were raised by John Palmer, "A Further Analysis of Provincial Trucking Regulation," *Bell Journal of Economics and Management Science* (Autumn 1973), pp. 655-64.

29. Bonsor, "The Development of Regulation," op. cit., p. 115. Nationally, $40 million was spent by established trucking firms applying for new licences, and opposing the applications of potential competitors. Economic Council of Canada, *Reforming Regulation*, p. 18. A study by Moore estimates that prior to deregulation in 1980, ICC regulation of trucking in the U.S. generated rents to teamster union members of between $1.0 and $1.3 billion, and rents to owners of certificates of public convenience of between $1.5 and $2.0 billion, in 1972. Moore predicted that were trucking to be deregulated in the U.S. *both* labour and capital would suffer a decline in income—which is one important reason why deregulation has been resisted by labour unions as well as the owners of trucking firms. Thomas Gale Moore, "The Beneficiaries of Trucking Regulation," Working Paper No. 77-17 Hoover Institution, Stanford University, August 1977 (mimeo). Moore's findings provide support for Peltzman's generalized theory of regulation in which the balance of political forces help to determine how the rents generated by regulation are distributed among various "interest" groups including "capital" and "labour." Sam Peltzman, "Toward a More General Theory of Regulation," *Journal of Law and Economics* (Autumn 1976), pp. 211-40.

30. Concern that highway trucking regulation is becoming too bureaucratic, costly, and in many cases unenforceable led to the establishment, in Ontario, of the Public Commercial Vehicles Act Review Committee in 1981. Although, predictably, the PCVA Review Committee did not follow the U.S. lead and call for the deregulation of highway trucking in Ontario, it did make a large number of recommendations aimed at streamlining the regulatory process and making it more enforceable. PCVA Review Committee, *Responsible Trucking: New Directions*, Ontario Ministry of Transportation and Communications, June 1983. The subject of illegal trucking has been dealt with by Michel Boucher, "Regulation of the Quebec Trucking Industry" *Studies of Trucking Regulation*, vol. II, Working Paper No. 3, Economic Council of Canada, Regulation Reference, August 1980, pp. 83-84.

The effects of regulation that we have just discussed are primarily due to controls over entry, output, or access to supplies of goods and services. In the absence of controls over entry and output, it is unlikely that other forms of regulation would have anything like the dramatic effects on economic efficiency and the distribution of income that quotas, licences, and medallions have had in some parts of the agricultural and transportation sectors. In general, as long as entry is both easy and "free" (of legal control), the establishment of price floors is likely to be ineffective as a means of generating rents—although it may generate economic "waste." Where entry and output are controlled, price floors are redundant. Thus studies of trucking regulation in Canada have generally found that charges are highest in provinces with entry control but no effective regulation of trucking tariffs—i.e. in Ontario, British Columbia and Quebec.[31] In the latter two provinces, rates are nominally regulated—see Table 10-5—but price control is ineffective.

The distinction made between the impact of entry/output regulation and effectiveness of price regulation has an important corollary. In the absence of regulation of any kind, it might not matter if the members of an industry collude, so long as they cannot force adherence to their agreement or membership in their cartel and entry into the industry is not difficult. This is the logic that underlies the present exemption of shipping conferences (associations of transocean carriers which set rates on the commodities they transport, but which cannot prevent non-members from entering the trade) and collective rate making by the railroads (see chapter 10), from the anticombines laws.[32] Competition from non-members, potential entrants, and suppliers of closely substitutable services severely limit the ability of the cartel or collective rate-makers to do anything more than "stabilize" prices at competitive levels.[33]

In the trucking industry, where entry but not volume of traffic is controlled, freight tariff bureaus (formal or informal bodies established by the carriers to publish and set rates) are believed to play an important role in making entry regulation an effective means of generating rents to those receiving licences from regulatory commissions.[34] While this view is not universally held,[35] it

31. It is interesting that in Manitoba and Saskatchewan, which take both rate and entry control seriously, regulated rates were below the level charged in Alberta which does not exercise any control over intraprovincial entry or rates. Economic Council of Canada, *Reforming Regulation*, pp. 19-20.

32. On shipping conferences, see I.A. Bryan and Y. Kotowitz, *Shipping Conferences in Canada*, Research Monograph No. 2, Consumer and Corporate Affairs (Ottawa: Minister of Supply and Services, 1978).

33. For this reason non-enforceable cartels may be a relatively innocuous means of eliminating alleged "destructive competition."

34. Boucher, op. cit., p. 90, reports that the market value of some Quebec permit clauses ranges from $3000 to $15 000; and some permits that change hands via merger or transfer may attain values of $25 000 and $125 000.

35. Doubts have been raised by J.J. McRae and D.M. Prescott, "Second Thoughts on Tariff Bureaus," *Canadian Public Policy*, 9, no. 2 (June 1983), pp. 200-209.

seems likely that in the absence of entry regulation, tariff bureaus could do little more than inform shippers about a common set of rates in the atomistic motor carrier industry. Thus if the highway trucking industry is "deregulated" (entry controls eliminated) in the future, it might be the better part of wisdom to permit tariff bureaus to operate, so long as no firm must belong to one or adhere to its rates.[36]

C. Macroeconomic Consequences of Economic Regulation

Until very recently the implications of economic regulation were considered in a totally microeconomic framework. However, the debate over the causes of inflation in the 1970s has tempted some writers to suggest that regulation is a contributor to cost-push inflation.[37] The basic argument is that regulation is cost- and price-increasing, and that higher prices require an increase in the money supply if falling demand and rising unemployment are to be prevented. (There is, of course, an implicit assumption that regulation is pervasive enough to affect the prices of many goods and services. In fact it is estimated that about 29.1 percent of Canadian gross domestic product was subject to some form of direct regulation in the late 1970s.[38] Regulation is thus viewed as having an impact on the price level similar to that of powerful unions. Note, however, that all we have described is a *once-over* rise in prices, which is not what economists mean by inflation (a *continuous* rise in the price level). As in all cost-push analyses, inflation is generated only if powerful groups continue to push up prices each time the government, or monetary authority, accommodates in order to prevent unemployment from rising.

There is another, and potentially more important, way in which regulation can have inflationary consequences. Most regulation includes control over entry. By erecting barriers to the free movement of economic resources, regulation may reduce supply elasticities. That is, if entry regulation is tight, an increase in aggregate demand may not call forth as large an increase in real output as it would if there were no regulation and resources (including previously idle ones) could move freely into industries experiencing an increase in demand. Put in rather grossly over-simplified terms, pervasive regulation may reduce the elasticity of aggregate supply. If the elasticity of supply is low, an increase in demand produces more price increase and less output increase than it would were supply elasticity high. The point seems important since a generation of

36. McRae and Prescott, op. cit., show that in some jurisdictions a substantial portion of freight is carried by non-members of tariff bureaus.
37. Some economists, mainly those who would describe themselves as "monetarists," reject the whole notion of cost-push inflation.
38. Economic Council of Canada, *Responsible Regulation*, An Interim Report of the Regulation Reference, Nov. 1979. Table B2-4, p. 124.

students, some of whom are now policy makers, were brought up on a (Keynesian) macroeconomic framework in which an autonomous increase in aggregate demand increased real output by an amount equal to the autonomous change in demand times some expenditure multiplier, so long as the economy has a substantial amount of unemployed resources. In its simplest form, the so-called "Keynesian Cross," an aggregate demand curve shifted up (or down) a $45°$ line. One of the tasks of teachers of introductory economics was to point out to students that (among other things) the $45°$ line implied a zero price response to aggregate demand change, until, of course, full employment was reached. In other words, the aggregate supply curve was assumed to be perfectly elastic. The suggestion here is that economic regulation may, by increasing artificial barriers to entry, reduce supply elasticities even when the economy is operating at substantially less than its potential.[39]

II. Intervention to Promote Industrial Growth, Regional Development and Canadian Control

At the end of chapter 7 we noted that Canadian governments have been obsessed with promoting industrial and regional development. A combination of regional disparities, a rapidly growing labour force, and proximity to the world's leading industrial power, the United States, are probable root factors. In any event, a Canadian study purporting to deal with public policies toward business cannot ignore what we shall here term, rather loosely, "industrial policies." Yet limitations of space, and reader tolerance, permit only a brief discussion of a variety of policies or tools used by Canadian governments, federal and provincial (but chiefly the former), to promote industrial development, regional growth and Canadian ownership and control. We shall deal with several policies singly, and where possible, emphasize the "statistical" record as an indicator of the breadth and depth of activity. This part of the chapter is necessarily disjointed (most of the subjects treated are not closely tied to one another) and incomplete (in the sense that it is clearly impossible in a single chapter—or even a book—to do justice to all of the industry-promoting schemes devised by the federal and provincial governments of Canada).

A. Patents

A patent is an exclusive right granted to an inventor for a specified period of time by the government. Most industrialized countries have patent systems. The Canadian system, which dates from 1823, was originally patterned on the

---

39. The reader should keep in mind that this is offered as a hypothesis rather than a validated statement.

British Statute of Monopolies (1624). During the last century the Canadian patent system has undergone a number of changes, some to bring it into conformity with international patent conventions, some to deal with potential patent abuse. During the last decade the Canadian patent system was the subject of intensive study by the Economic Council of Canada and the Department of Consumer and Corporate Affairs.[40]

In its report on the Canadian patent system, the Economic Council of Canada observed:[41] "In order for its economy to grow and develop satisfactorily, a society must be innovative; to be innovative, it must be well informed; to be well informed, it must be good at the production, distribution and use of knowledge." This statement suggests that from an economic standpoint, knowledge is a "public good." Knowledge is, in fact, a public good in two respects. First, as the above statement implies, more knowledge is better than less. Second, knowledge in the public domain is a classic example of a public good in the public finance sense: those who do not contribute to it still may not be excluded from it.[42] By protecting, for a limited period of time, the return on the investment in the production of technical knowledge, patents are assumed to encourage the development, public disclosure, and dissemination of innovations and inventions. Thus the benefits that a patent system confers are incentives to creation of new knowledge in the form of new products and processes; the "costs" (other than administrative) of a patent system are primarily those associated with the monopoly powers the patent confers on its recipient.

The Patent Act is administered by the Patent Office in the Department of Consumer and Corporate Affairs. Its 400-plus employees review upwards of 30 000 patent applications each year. In Canada, the patent is granted to the invention's originator. Except for the United States and the Philippines which also use the originator criteria, all other countries with patent systems use a "first-to-file" criterion. The latter, of course, is less open to conflicting claims. The life of the patent is 17 years (originally it was 14) extending from the date of the grant, which can be up to several years after date of application. The Canadian Patent Act includes provisions to insure that patents are "worked" within Canada within a three-year period following the patent grant. However, a high proportion of patents are apparently not worked—either in Canada or in other countries. This may reflect the fact that many patented innovations

40. Economic Council of Canada, *Report on Intellectual and Industrial Property* (Ottawa: Information Canada, 1971), Department of Consumer and Corporate Affairs, *Working Papers on Patent Law Revision and Proposed Patent Law* (Ottawa: Supply and Services Canada, 1976). The latter is reviewed by D.L. McQueen in *Canadian Public Policy* (Spring 1977), pp. 239-43.
41. Economic Council of Canada, op. cit., p. 9.
42. In addition, it can often be supplied to additional persons at zero marginal cost.

become obsolete shortly after the patent grant or are not economically feasible. Non-working of patents or any other patent "abuses" (to be discussed below) can result in revocation of the patent licence or compulsory licensing of those who wish to use the patented item. However, patent licences are rarely, if ever, revoked, and only 11 of a total of 53 compulsory licence applications, made between 1935 and 1970, were granted.[43]

One of the unique characteristics of the Canadian patent system is the very high proportion of patents granted to foreigners. Historically, only about 5 percent of Canadian patents have been granted to nationals, 95 percent to foreigners, two-thirds of whom are residents of the United States.[44] At the same time, Canada grants an inordinately large number of patents relative to its population. The explanation, of course, is Canada's close economic and technological relationships with the United States and the high proportion of foreign control of firms in the industrial sectors of the Canadian economy. Some argue that the high proportion of patents granted to foreigners is evidence that Canada is technologically "stunted,"—dependent on foreigners to supply us with new production techniques and processes, usually at high cost. For this reason a number of Canada's industrial assistance programmes (see below) are concerned with spurring R & D and other innovative efforts in Canada.[45]

Patents can be abused in several ways. When they are not "worked" they may suppress technological advances, although, as noted above, there are, in principle, provisions in the Canadian Patent Act to deal with non-working. Although it is not considered an abuse, patents may also be used as a non-tariff trade barrier, a particularly potent possibility in an economy as dependent on trade as Canada. The recipient of a Canadian patent can prevent Canadians from importing the patented good from abroad, since the patentee has the right to choose who, if anyone, should be licensed to manufacture and distribute his patented article. Moreover, the provisions for working the patented invention in Canada mean that production may take place under less efficient (shorter production run) conditions than if manufacture were in another country. The result is to raise prices to Canadian consumers. Patents may also be the basis for erecting a monopoly and restricting competition. Patent pools and tying

43. Economic Council of Canada, op. cit., pp. 61-63, 67-68.
44. Some unpublished data indicate that, in 1981, the ratio of patents for Canadian inventions to total patents granted in Canada was 10 percent. Successful applications for Canadian patents are concentrated—33 percent of the patents for Canadian inventions going to 8 percent of the applicants.
45. Official obsession with the statistics on Canadian patents and R & D spending prompted, in 1978, the Minister of State for Science and Technology to set a target for R & D expenditures at 1.5 percent of GNP. The idea of an economy-wide target for R & D expenditures has been attacked and so has the meaning of crude international comparisons of R & D expenditure intensity, by K.S. Palda and B. Pazderka, *Approaches to an International Comparison of Canada's R & D Expenditures*, Economic Council of Canada (Ottawa: Minister of Supply and Services Canada, 1982).

contracts are examples.[46] In addition, restrictions in patent licences may be used as the basis of a price-fixing conspiracy. Most of these actions are unlawful under the U.S. antitrust laws. In Canada section 29 of the Combines Investigation Act makes it an abuse of patent rights to attempt to extend the scope of the patent right to agreements to restrain trade or restrict competition. The section has been used only once (in 1970) resulting in a settlement between Union Carbide and its licensees of a process used in the manufacture of polyethylene resins.

An exception to the wide powers granted to patentees is the case of ethical drugs in Canada. Prior to 1970, the Canadian drug industry was a good example of the way in which patent protection in combination with a small domestic market may produce reliance on imports of high priced goods. The fact that drug prices in Canada were high in relation to both production costs and prices in many other advanced industrialized nations stimulated official concern in the 1960s.[47] In June 1969, Parliament amended the Patent Act to allow firms to be licensed to import and/or manufacture drugs for which patents were held in Canada. In effect, a policy of compulsory licenses for drugs was implemented under which a firm or individual, upon payment of an arbitrarily set royalty of 4 percent, can obtain a license to manufacture and/or sell a patented drug. The licensee thereby enters into direct competition with the patentee, by selling the same drug although under a different brand name. The idea is that by weakening patent protection and thereby stimulating competition from licensees, the goal of reducing drug prices could be achieved.[48]

Apparently, the compulsory licensing policy has succeeded in achieving its primary goal of reducing drug prices—at least at the manufacturing and wholesale levels.[49] A recent study found that, on average, the price of compulsorily licensed drugs sold to pharmacists fell from 86 percent of the U.S. price in 1968 to 45 percent in 1980—a finding consistent with other studies.[50] However, the compulsory licensing policy has its critics. Annoyed by the increased competition and the very low royalty rate, the Pharmaceutical Manufacturers Association of Canada (PMAC), representing the major drug firms in Canada, most of whom are foreign owned, has lobbied for changes in

46. There are numerous antitrust cases in the U.S. dealing with tying contracts where the monopoly element in the tying products owes to a patent. A classic case was *International Salt Co. Inc. v. United States* 332 U.S. 392 (1947).
47. But they were not high with respect to U.S. drug prices which were as high as, or higher than those in Canada.
48. During the 1970s most provinces established programmes aimed at increasing competition in the pharmaceutical industry and reducing drug prices.
49. There is less evidence and less optimism that consumer prices have been similarly affected, although presumably the important hospital market is able to take advantage of the reduced manufacturers' and wholesale price of drugs.
50. D.J. Fowler and M.J. Gordon, "The Effect of Public Policy Initiatives on Drug Prices in Canada," *Canadian Public Policy* 10, no. 1 (March 1984), pp. 64-73.

the policy. Recently, one of the major arguments of the PMAC, that the compulsory licensing policy has reduced R & D by the pharmaceutical industry, has been bought in Ottawa, which would like to stimulate both more manufacture of drugs in Canada and greater R & D spending.[51] (In real, inflation-corrected terms, R & D spending ceased to grow after 1973, but this was true in other countries, including the U.S., as well.) In early 1983, the Minister of Consumer and Corporate Affairs issued a report suggesting changes in the compulsory licensing and royalty rate provisions of the Patent Act which pertain to drugs. Interestingly, the Minister's own report provides evidence substantiating the relative decline in drug prices in Canada and, furthermore, casts doubt on the efficacy of attempts to raise R & D expenditures by altering the compulsory licensing provisions. But such is the national yearning for R & D in particular, and hi-tech in general, that one of Canada's more successful public policies may be gutted.

In summary, patent systems are viewed as instrumental to technological advance and ultimately to economic growth. However the patent creates a balancing act between the benefits from innovation and the costs of artificial monopoly. Some experts believe the give-away of monopoly power is too great for the benefits received. Believing this does not mean abandonment of the patent system. It can mean simply that it would be preferable if there were a shorter patent life (why 17 years?), sharper limitations on import restrictions demanded by patentees, more vigilance in dealing with anti-competitive extensions of the monopoly grant, and greater reliance on compulsory licensing. The Economic Council of Canada has recommended patent law revision in all of these areas plus a movement to a first-to-file basis for establishing patent rights.[52]

B. Automotive Agreement

The Canada-United States Automotive Products Agreement was signed, in 1965, by Prime Minister Pearson and President Johnson. The agreement eliminated tariffs, at the manufacturing level, on automotive vehicles and parts, and in doing so created an integrated North American market in automotive products. The agreement was also designed to increase, and in fact has had the effect of substantially increasing, the assembly of vehicles and the manufacture of parts in Canada—the lengthened production runs substantially reducing the

---

51. P. Gorecki and I. Henderson, "Compulsory Patent Licensing of Drugs in Canada: A Comment on the Debate," *Canadian Public Policy* 7, no. 4 (Autumn 1981), pp. 559-568; and Gorecki, "Changing Canada's Drug Patent Law: The Minister's Proposals," *Canadian Public Policy* 10, no. 1 (March 1984), pp. 77-80. Also see the notes by McRae and Tapan and by Hartle in the same issue. Gorecki reports that between 1969 and 1982 in excess of 290 licences were issued by the Commissioner of Patents for 62 drugs.

52. ECC, op. cit., pp. 88-92.

relative inefficiency of Canada's automotive industry.

Prior to the Automotive Agreement, Canadians, whose tastes in automobiles are similar to those of their neighbours to the South, paid from 10 to 17 percent more for comparable automobiles than their U.S. counterparts. Behind 17.5% tariff barriers, the subsidiaries of the U.S. "big three" (GM, Ford, and Chrysler) dominated the Canadian auto industry. Each produced a wide variety of makes for a population one-tenth the size of the U.S. population and with seven percent of its GNP. Exports to the United States were stymied by a 6.5 percent to 8.5 percent tariff erected by the U.S. The result was short production runs, substantially higher unit production costs, lower wages, and greater foreign car imports into Canada.[53] Most parts used in Canada were manufactured in the U.S. (despite high Canadian tariffs), greatly limiting the potential growth of automotive industry employment in Canada.

There were two components to the Automotive Agreement. First, there was the agreement between the United States and Canada permitting duty-free movement of most new vehicles and parts used as original equipment on automobiles. The elimination of duties, however, applies to manufacturers, not to Canadian consumers who continue to pay a 15 percent duty on automobiles purchased in the U.S. In eliminating duties at the manufacturing level the Canadian government imposed the condition that the 1964 ratio of Canadian production to Canadian sales be maintained. The United States also imposed conditions in order to prevent duty-free entry of "foreign" (overseas) automobiles into the United States via Canada. The second part of the agreement involved an understanding between Canada and the automakers themselves. The latter, in "letters of undertaking" agreed to expand, by 1968, Canadian production by substantially more than the intergovernmental agreement required. This part of the agreement was critical to Canada because she wanted to assure substantial growth of the domestic auto industry.

What has been the impact of the Automotive Agreement? On the statistical level the results have been impressive. Between 1964, the year before the agreement was signed, and 1973, the annual production of motor vehicles in Canada increased by 135 percent from 671 000 to 1 575 000. Canada's share of North American production rose from 7 to 11 percent between 1965 and 1973. Total automotive employment increased by 56 percent from 69.3 thousand to 108.5 thousand.[54] Trade in automobiles increased many times over. Canadian exports increased 1700 percent while U.S. exports to Canada

53. Measures of both productivity and wages indicated them to be 30 percent lower in Canada than in the U.S. In 1964, the 600,000 new car sales in Canada almost exactly matched Bain's estimate of the minimum efficient scale automobile manufacturers. Carl Beigie, *The Canada-U.S. Auto Agreement: An Evaluation* (Montreal: Private Planning Association, 1970), Chaps. 1,2.
54. Almost all of the employment increase came in parts manufacturing. David Wilton, *An Econometric Analysis of the Canada-U.S. Automotive Agreement: The First Seven Years* (Ottawa: Economic Council of Canada, 1976), pp. 84-85.

increased 1000 percent between 1965 and 1975, the huge increases reflecting the *rationalization* of the North American production of automobiles. As Canadian production runs lengthened, due to specialization in certain makes, the 30 percent productivity differential largely disappeared. In fact vehicle output per man hour was, in 1973, 10 percent higher in Canada than in the United States.[55] Auto industry wages have risen to U.S. levels. Some, but not all, of the price differential has disappeared. If the major aim of the Automotive Agreement was to increase the efficiency and relative share (in North American production) of the Canadian automotive industry, it appears to have done so admirably. It has, of course, done nothing to change the pattern of foreign ownership or the foreign location of design and R & D work, and little to alleviate annual concern over trade balance.[56]

In the late 1970s and 1980s a cloud appeared on the Auto Pact horizon. The failure of Detroit and its Canadian subsidiaries to respond sufficiently quickly to the change in energy costs opened the door to a flood of imported Japanese automobiles. As the share of the North American market supplied by North American producers fell, so did the implicit protection provided by the production commitments made by the automobile firms when the Auto Pact was signed in 1965. Added to these difficulties, the recessions of the early 1980s produced further setbacks to the integrated North American automobile industry, setbacks which some analysts prematurely took to be permanent. In response to pressures from the auto industry and the United Auto Workers, Ottawa imposed quotas on imports of Japanese automobiles and established, in 1981, a federal task force on the Canadian motor vehicle and automotive parts industries. The recommendations of the task force, which issued its report in 1983, reflect the auto industry-orientation of its co-chairmen.[57]

55. Department of Industry, Trade and Commerce, Automotive Task Force, *Review of the North American Automotive Industry* (Ottawa: April 1977), Table 9-4, p. 64 and Table A.2-4, p. 76. Also see Beigie, op. cit. pp. 101-2.

56. These issues, plus particular concern about the difficulties faced by independent Canadian parts manufacturers, prompted the Canadian government to commission an inquiry into the automotive industry known as the Reisman Report. *The Canadian Automotive Industry: Performance and Proposals for Progress*, Inquiry into the Automotive Industry, Simon Reisman, Commissioner (Ottawa: Supply and Services, October 1978). Perhaps the most important finding of the Reisman report is that while domestic production of original automotive parts has increased both absolutely and proportionately (to total North American production) since 1965, to an increasing degree auto parts manufacture is undertaken "in-house" by the Big-Three automakers. Also Canada has not done well in the aftermarket parts industry (which is not covered by the Auto Pact). The Report recommends that the Government make additional-loan finance available to independent parts manufacturers and proceed to "rationalize" the aftermarket parts industry (pp. 86, 246).

57. *An Automotive Strategy for Canada* (Ottawa: Ministry of Supply and Services Canada, 1983). The task force was co-chaired by Patrick Lavelle of the Automotive Parts Manufacturers' Association and Robert White of the United Auto Workers' Union. For an excellent evaluation of the Task Force Proposals and their welfare implications, see R. J. Wonnacott, "The Canadian

The Task Force Report's central recommendation is that *all* vehicle manufacturers who wish to sell in Canada make binding commitments analogous to the ones made by the signatories to the Auto Pact. Essentially this would impose compulsory Canadian content provisions on Japanese producers, forcing them to invest in automobile assembly and/or parts plants in Canada. The objective, of course, is to protect and promote domestic employment in the Canadian auto industry. To this politically attractive (but potentially economically damaging) feature of the proposal is the added appearance of equitable treatment as between U.S. and Japanese firms selling in the Canadian market. But this appearance is deceptive. At present both the Japanese and the U.S. face the same options: meet Canadian-content requirements and avoid tariff duties, or export to Canada and pay the tariff. The U.S. firms have chosen the former, the Japanese the latter option.[58] Making it compulsory for all (U.S., Japanese and other foreign) firms wishing to sell in Canada to meet content requirements would impose an extra burden on the Japanese, who, if they find meeting the requirements too costly might respond by suspending all sales of automobiles in the small Canadian market.[59] (Incidentally, the Task Force proposal might be viewed by the U.S. as a unilateral alteration in the Auto Pact, giving that government grounds for reviewing and eventually opting out of an agreement with which it has never been very happy). At the time of writing, the Canadian government had taken no action on the Task Force proposals. Happily, in mid-1984 the government was able to announce major expansions of operations in Canada by U.S. auto firms and at least one investment proposal by a Japanese automobile firm—each project, it would appear, aided by federal subsidies.

C. Industry Assistance Programme

Over the years the federal and provincial governments have enacted numerous programmes to assist industry to get established, improve productivity, undertake R & D, and increase export activity. In total, the federal programmes alone are too numerous to do more than mention.[60] Here we will briefly review the

Content Proposals of the Task Force on the Automobile Industry," *Canadian Public Policy* 10, no. 1 (March 1984), pp. 1-9.

58. That the Japanese haven't voluntarily chosen the Canadian content-no tariff option says something about the relative costs to them of producing in Canada vis-à-vis producing in Japan and paying transportation costs and tariff duties.

59. In this event, the content requirements would be equivalent to an infinite tariff resulting in a total loss of tariff revenues and consumer surplus. See Wonnacott, op. cit. pp. 2-3.

60. For a somewhat dated description, see *Canada Yearbook*, 1972 (Ottawa: Information Canada, 1972), pp. 779-92. The DREE programmes, designed to induce industry to locate in slow growth areas, are treated separately below. A number of the Department of Industry, Trade and Commerce Programmes (e.g. PEP, PAIT, IRDIA) were replaced, in 1977, by the Enterprise Development Program (EDP). For an in-depth description, evaluation and statistical summary of the major federal industrial assistance programmes (excluding the DREE programmes), see

major federal programmes. Table 12-6 lists the major federal programmes of direct federal assistance to business. In dollar terms most of the assistance is in the form of loans and loan guarantees, chiefly made by the Export Development Corporation (EDC). In recent years both direct subsidies and loans to business have increased rapidly. For example, in 1980, export financial assistance negotiated through the EDC totalled $3.5 billion in loans, insurance and guarantees. The Department of Industry, Trade and Commerce (ITC) administers a set of programmes which aid industry by providing financial assistance in the form of cash grants or loans, or by providing information, marketing and purchase services, or duty remissions. Table 12-7 lists the ITC programmes of financial assistance, and indicates the outlays in fiscal year 1981-82. The heavy emphasis in the cash grant programmes on productivity and R & D increasing activities is obvious, although ship construction subsidies accounted for about a sixth of the $423 million in expenditures under grant assistance programmes. Some of the provinces have similar programmes and almost all attempt to spur industry through development corporations.[61]

In addition to industry assistance programmes, there are outright subsidies for infrastructure (airports); government enterprises serving public purposes (CBC); staving off bankruptcy of high profile firms (e.g. Massey Ferguson, Chrysler, Maislin; Dome Petroleum); and for unprofitable firms or unprofitable activities (rail passenger services). The railroad and airline industries account for a substantial portion of federal subsidies to industry. In 1981-82, the federal government budget expenditures on rail transport totalled $966 million, of which $506 million was paid to Via Rail for providing non-remunerative passenger services. A substantial portion of the remaining $460 million was paid to the railroads in lieu of branchline abandonment and freight rate increases.[62] Subsidies to air transport, in 1981-82, totalled $702 million, $422 million of which were provided for "aviation infrastructure," including airports, meteorological services, and air traffic control operations.

D. Canada Development Corporation

The Canada Development Corporation (CDC) was established, in 1971, by an Act of Parliament. The creation of CDC brought to fruition an idea that began with the 1957 Royal Commission on Canada's Economic Prospects (Gordon

Economic Council of Canada, *The Bottom Line* (Ottawa: Supply and Services Canada, 1983), chapter 6 and Appendix A. Students interested in this subject should begin their inquiry with the E.C.C. study.
61. For a discussion of industrial assistance programmes in Ontario and Quebec, see P. Davenport, et al., *Industrial Policy in Ontario and Quebec* (Toronto: Ontario Economic Council, 1982), chapter 3.
62. Canadian Tax Foundation, *National Finances*, 1981-82, chapter 12.

Table 12-6

Major Programmes of Direct Federal Assistance to Business (Millions of Dollars in 1978-79 or Latest Year)

	Grants & contributions	Loans	Loan guarantees/ Insurance	Total
Financing				
Federal Business Development Bank		556		556
Regional Development Incentives	77			77
Small business loans			200	200
Farm improvement loans			232	232
Fisheries improvement loans			27	27
Farm Credit Corporation		513		513
Indian Economic Development Fund	32	3	3	38
Exports				
Export Development Corporation				
—Export loans and guarantees			(1071)	1071
—Export insurance (value of goods)			1299	1299
Program for Export Market Development	6			6
Promotional Projects Program	5			5

Research and development and innovation			
Industrial Energy R&D Program	2		2
Industrial Research Assistance Program	18		18
Enterprise Development Program	26		26
Defence Industry Productivity Program	40		46
Program for Industry Laboratory Projects		6	8
Scientific and Technology Employment Program	8		
Unsolicited Proposals Program	6		6
	14		14
Cooperative Projects with Industry	2		2
Labour force			
Canada Manpower Industrial Training	84		84
Job Experience Training	45		45
Adjustment assistance			
Enterprise Development Program		120	126
Canada Manpower Mobility Program	12	6	12
Canada Manpower Consultative Service	3		3
Adjustment Assistance Benefits	3		3
Total	383		4419

Source: Davenport, et al., *Industrial Policy in Ontario and Quebec* (Toronto: Ontario Economic Council, 1982), p. 52.

Table 12-7

Industrial Assistance Programmes Administered by the Department of Industry, Trade and Commerce

Name of Programme	Date Enacted	Purpose of Programme	Expenditure 1981/82 (000)
A. Enterprise Development Programs	1977	Coordinates seven programmes of assistance combining the basic features of the former programmes, four of which are described here	148 200
i. Industrial Research and Development Incentives Act (IRDIA)	1967	Provides cash grants, or tax credits, for capital and current expenditures on R&D by business	
ii. Programme for the Advancement of Industrial Technology (PAIT)	1965	Provides financial assistance (initially loans, now cash grants) for selected projects to improve or develop new products and processes involving advanced technology, in order to increase technical competitiveness of Canadian industry	
iii. Programme to Enhance Productivity (PEP)	—	Provides grants for feasibility studies of "significant and imaginative efficiency-improvement projects"	
iv. Industrial Design Assistance Programme	1971	Financial assistance to promote and expedite product improvement, including design training programmes	

B. Defence Industry Productivity Programme (DIPP)	1968	Provides financial assistance to industrial firms engaged in defence production in order to enhance the technological competence of Canadian defence industry, particularly where there is good export potential	102 100
C. Export Market Development		Provides financial assistance to enable Canadian firms to penetrate new export markets	36 000
D. Ship Construction Subsidy and Shipbuilding Temporary Assistance Programmes	1967 & 1970	Provides subsidies for construction of domestic and foreign flag ships in Canadian shipyards	75 000
E. Strategy for Technology Enhanced Productivity (STEP)	1982	Promotes the manufacture and use of electronic products in Canada	31 000[a]
F. Miscellaneous Programmes			30 900
Total			$423 200

[a] Annual estimates. The initial appropriation was $93 million over three years.
Source: *Canada Yearbook*, 1972, pp. 779-785; Canadian Tax Foundation, *National Finances*, 1981-82, Toronto 1982.

Report). That Commission was concerned with the extent of foreign ownership and control of the Canadian economy, and it had sought for ways in which greater Canadian participation in their own economy might be facilitated. The CDC therefore was to be a vehicle through which (a) Canadian investment in resident companies could be increased; (b) Canadian businesses could be created or developed; and (c) venture capital could be supplied to a variety of enterprises at reduced risk to investors.[63]

While the initial capitalization of CDC came from the federal government, the ultimate goal was for 90 percent equity ownership by the investing public. By 1976, the public held 32 percent of the voting stock, and by 1982 the government's share had declined to 49 percent. With the funds available to it, CDC has invested in a variety of enterprises. It has two basic criteria for choosing enterprises: one financial, one sectoral. First CDC looks for enterprises with high profit growth potential (in this it has not always succeeded). Second it concentrates its investments in the following areas: petroleum and natural gas; petrochemicals; mining; pipelines and related northern transportation; health care, including pharmaceuticals and medical equipment; venture capital enterprises. Only in pipelines has CDC failed to achieve a presence.

The CDC's holdings as of 1982 are shown in Table 12-8. Almost 90 percent of CDC's 1982 assets of 7.5 billion dollars are in three resource sectors: oil and gas, petrochemicals, and mining. CDC has come a long way since 1974 when its total assets were valued at $900 million. Its largest investment was then its 30.2 percent share in Texasgulf Inc.—an investment which through the controversy it stirred, particularly in the state of Texas where the company's headquarters was located, put CDC on the map. Although all of CDC's companies lost money in 1982, that year was the first in which CDC as a whole lost money. However, even during its profitable years, 1973-81, CDC's performance measured by return on assets, return on equity and price earnings ratios was below that of a sample of other comparable resource-based companies.[64] However, CDC's asset growth has been tremendous, reflecting its other goal of establishing a Canadian presence in certain sectors, particularly through a process of purchasing interests in, or the assets of, foreign-owned firms.

In the early 1980s, Ottawa began to interfere in the decisions of the CDC. It put pressure on the CDC to become involved in the bailout of Massey-Ferguson. It attempted to alter the composition of the Board of Directors in defiance of earlier pledges of non-interference. In each case, CDC successfully resisted. Exasperated, the federal government decided it would sell off its declining share

63. Michael R. Graham, *Canada Development Corporation*, Study No. 4, Royal Commission on Corporate Concentration, Ottawa, 1977.
64. See Anthony Boardman, "An Evaluation of Canada Development Corporation," University of British Columbia (mimeo).

Table 12-8

Canada Development Corporation Holdings, 1982

Sector (Company)	Assets	Sales Revenue ($ millions)	Net Income
Oil and gas (Canterra Energy)[a]	2918	597	−14.4
Mining (Kidd Creek)[b]	2272	2250	−38.6
Petrochemicals (Polysar, Petrosar)[c]	1415	324	−37.3
Fish products	25	—	−7.1
Office information (AES Data)[d]	690	650	−10.3
Industrial automation (Sentrol)[e]	39	30	−5.8
Life sciences (Conlab Holdings)	109	153	−3.9
Venture capital[f]	39	—	—
CDC Corporate	20	8	−16.2
Total	7527	4011	−125.8[g]

[a]Formed after CDC's purchase of the Acquitaine Company for $1.6 billion in 1981. Includes the former CDC Oil and Gas Company, the assets of which had been purchased from the major U.S. resource conglomerate, Tenneco, in 1975, for $111 million.
[b]In 1973, CDC had purchased a 30.2 percent (controlling) share in Texas Gulf Sulphur. In 1981 CDC purchased the Canadian assets of Texasgulf in exchange for its 30.2 percent share of Texasgulf plus $537 million. CDC's mining assets were then combined into a new subsidiary, Kidd Creek Mines.
[c]Petrosar provides petrochemical feeder stocks for Polysar (formerly the Crown corporation known as Polymer), a producer of synthetic rubber, and for other chemical companies.
[d]AES Data produces word processing equipment. CDC also has majority interests in three other office equipment producers.
[e]Sentrol is the largest Canadian supplier of process-control systems.
[f]Since 1973, CDC has included three venture capital companies: International, Ventures West Capital, and Innocan Investments, each of which has interests in several other companies.
[g]In 1980 and 1981 CDC's net income was $189 million and $85 million respectively. In fact, 1982, a year of deep recession when many major firms lost money, was CDC's first net income loss year. In its first 10 years of existence (1972-81), CDC had a cumulative net income of $598 million.
Source: Canada Development Corporation, *Annual Reports*; Anthony E. Boardman, "An Evaluation of Canada Development Corporation," University of British Columbia (mimeo), Tables 1 and 2.

in CDC. However, in the meantime, Ottawa turned over its 48 percent share of CDC to a new government-controlled firm, the Canada Development Investment Corporation (CDIC). The CDIC was also given responsibility for government-owned Canadair Ltd., de Havilland Aircraft, Teleglobe, Eldorado Nuclear Ltd. and the federal government's shares in Massey-Ferguson. One implication is that CDC's profits (at least the government's share of them) can now be used to support CDC's losing investments in Canadair and de Havilland. Thus the CDC's future is clouded. The government-created conglomerate may lose its identity and purpose if its original goals of profitability and Canadian presence are sacrificed for short-term financial expediencies. Thus fulfilling the government's original intention of turning over its shares to the public would appear to be the wisest course to follow, if undue interference in the operation of CDC is to be avoided. In late 1984, the new Progressive Conservative government of Brian Mulroney indicated its intention to "privatize" the holdings of the CDIC.

E. "DREE" Programmes

In 1969, the federal government created the Department of Regional Economic Expansion (DREE) to coordinate its efforts to reduce geographical income disparities across Canada. The new Department brought under one "roof" a number of disparate programmes implemented in the late 1950s and early 1960s to spur economic development and growth in rural areas and in the Atlantic Provinces.[65] In 1970, the federal government passed the Regional Development Incentives Act (RDIA) to be administered by DREE, and it phased out some of the older programmes.

RDIA gives to DREE the power and financial capability of subsidizing, on the basis of a "needs" formula, firms which invest in certain "designated" (less developed) areas.[66] The Act permits grants of *up to* 50 percent of capital employed or $30 000 per job, whichever is less.[67] In addition, DREE complements its investment incentives programme with a General Development Agreements (GDA) programme. Since it was held that the effectiveness of the industrial incentives programme depends on the development of "growth centres" in slow growth regions, DREE, under its GDA programme, aids provincial governments by supplying financial help for infrastructure and essential municipal services. Under the GDA programme, the federal government shares from 50 to 90 percent of the cost of a subsidiary agreement with the provinces. By mid-1981, over 100 subsidiary agreements had been signed with the provinces committing, through 1984, expenditures of $5 billion. The federal government's share of the total is $2.7 billion. Not all GDA subagreements are for infrastructure assistance. In June 1981, a subsidiary agreement was signed with Nova Scotia to rehabilitate the Sydney Steel Corporation's aged

65. These programmes, some of whose acronyms read like members of a family, were the Agricultural and Rural Development Act (ARDA); Fund for Rural Economic Development (FRED); the Area Development Agency (ADA); the Atlantic Development Board (ADB); Prairie Farm Rehabilitation Act (PFRA).
66. The designated areas include all of the Maritimes, Quebec, and parts of every other province.
67. The actual formula used for making RDIA grants is much more complicated than the text suggests.

Table 12-9

Expenditures by Department of Regional Economic Expansion, by Function: 1969-1982[a]

Purpose	Annual 1981/82	Cumulative 1969/70-1981/82
	(millions of dollars)	
Industrial incentives (primarily RDIA)	127.0	1092
Subsidiary agreements (primarily infrastructure assistance under General Development Agreements Program)	341.8	2134
Other (primarily Rural Development and Adjustment Programs)	83.3	2284[b]
Planning and administration	63.4	438
Total	615.6	5948

[a]In 1981 DREE was amalgamated into a new Department of Regional and Industrial Expansion.
[b]Prior to 1974 includes expenditures on a number of Special Area programmes which functionally were precursors of GDA programmes.
Source: Department of Regional Economic Expansion, *Annual Reports*.

and technically obsolete plant, with the federal government putting up $77 million of the $96 million sum committed to the project.[68]

Table 12-9 indicates the dollar magnitude of DREE's effort in 1981-82, and the distribution among various kinds of assistance. DREE's role in providing subsidies to industry and grants to locales is impressive. Since 1969-70 actual annual expenditures have risen from $220 million to $616 million. Cumulative expenditures over the 13 year period amounted to just under $6 billion with about 17 percent for industrial incentives (RDIA) and 60 percent for infrastructure assistance. Economists have been particularly interested in the RDIA grants with their potential for altering the geographical allocation of resources and affecting the way in which labour and capital are combined in production. Since its inception in 1969 until March 31, 1982, DREE has approved several thousand projects for the purpose of making industrial incentive (RDIA) grants. In doing so, DREE committed 1.092 billion dollars in subsidies to businesses who will make total investments (eligible for incentives) of nearly $6.5 billion. The new jobs created by this investment are estimated by DREE at 199 770. Of

68. Canadian Tax Foundation, *The National Finances* 1981-82, pp. 183-84.

the $1.092 billion, $532 million (or 49 percent) was destined for projects in Quebec. Another $260 million (or 24 percent) was for investment located in the Atlantic Provinces. One hundred and four million (or 9 percent) was destined for Ontario and $195 million (18 percent) for the western provinces.[69]

A number of economists have attempted to evaluate the RDIA programme.[70] They have raised questions about (i) the actual *net* increase in investment and jobs created by the incentive grants, (ii) their probable long-run contribution to economic growth in the "designated" regions, (iii) their contribution to national product, and (iv) their impact on the distribution of income. We can scarcely discuss each of these important, and controversial, issues in a short space. Instead we make a few points, leaving the interested reader to delve further.[71]

1. New investment associated with DREE grants may *displace*, in part, investments which would otherwise have been undertaken. For example, an already established firm in a "designated" area may decide against expansion or reinvestment if a competing firm is lured into the area as a result of DREE subsidies. Thus the *net* impact of DREE is surely less than the *gross* figures reported above.

2. Some grants may go to firms who would have invested in the designated area anyway. It seems unlikely that even a toughly administered needs criterion is sufficient to prevent some "windfall" payment to firms.

3. The estimated employment generated by DREE grants seems large given the substantial rise, rather than fall, in unemployment in the Maritimes and Quebec in the last decade. However, unemployment might have been even worse in the absence of DREE grants. Moreover, if the grants have in fact succeeded in promoting industrialization there would likely be "feedback" effects in the form of higher wage rates, higher labour force participation rates, reduced migration, all tending to increase the number of persons looking for employment.

4. Investments which require subsidies presumably yield a lower net return than those which do not. Thus DREE grants might reduce *national* income while increasing income in a particular region.

5. An investment incentives programme which reduces regional economic disparities does not *necessarily* reduce income inequalities between people. The grants could result in a transfer of income from upper-income taxpayers in richer regions to upper-income industrialists in poorer ones.

69. Department of Regional Economic Expansion, *Annual Report*, 1976-77, p. 127, and the annual reports of each succeeding year.
70. R.S. Woodward, "The Effectiveness of DREE's New Location Subsidies," *Canadian Public Policy*, Spring 1975, pp. 219-29; D. Usher, "Some Questions about the Regional Development Incentives Act," *Canadian Public Policy* (Autumn 1975), pp. 557-75. Both Woodward and Usher are concerned with a possible capital (relative to labour) bias in the RDIA subsidies.
71. I rely, here, heavily on the discussion by Usher, op. cit.

In short, the amount of RDIA-generated investment and employment which is "incremental" to the firm, the industry, and the economy, is surely far less than the figures provided in the reports of the Department of Regional Economic Expansion would have us believe.[72] In more prosaic terms, firm- and industry-specific subsidies make it more difficult for non-subsidized firms and industries to survive.

F. Foreign Investment Review Agency

The Foreign Investment Review Agency (FIRA) was established in 1973. It was the federal government's response to the Gray Report (1972) on foreign investment in Canada.[73] The Gray Report came at a time of heightened consciousness of the extent of foreign domination (control as well as ownership) of the industrial sectors of the Canadian economy (see chapter 1, Table 1-13). The Report not only documented the extent of foreign ownership and control, it also probed its apparent causes and effects. The Report suggested three possible policy alternatives, favouring the one actually adopted. The alternatives were (a) a "buy back" policy, regarded as neither economically beneficial nor financially possible; (b) a "key sector" policy in which certain important industries would be preserved for domestic ownership, just as the communications and banking sectors had been under earlier legislation; (c) a "screening agency" which would review all mergers in which the acquiring firm is "foreign," accepting those which will provide significant net benefits to Canadians, rejecting those which will not.

The federal government adopted the screening agency approach. However, it retained for the cabinet final decision-making powers.[74] FIRA reviewed all but the smallest (below $250 000 in assets) acquisitions and new investment proposals by foreigners, accepting or rejecting them on the basis of the ten criteria (see below).

Since its inception in April 1974 until March 31, 1983, the Foreign Investment Review Agency has received 5997 applications, of which 5230 were certified as reviewable.[75] Table 12-10 indicates that of the 5091 applications resolved by March 31, 1983, 4185 (82 percent) were accepted and 398

72. The issue of "incrementality," what is actually added net to the firm, industry, or economy, is analyzed in depth by Dan Usher, "The Benefits and Costs of Firm-Specific Investment Grants: A Study of Five Federal Programs," Queen's University (mimeo).
73. *Foreign Direct Investment in Canada* (Ottawa: Information Canada, 1972).
74. For a critical examination of the role of the cabinet in the review process, see Richard Schultz, Frank Swedlove and Katherine Swinton, "The Cabinet as a Regulatory Body: The Case of the Foreign Investment Review Act," Working Paper No. 6, Regulation Reference, Economic Council of Canada, 1980.
75. Over 500 of the original applications were withdrawn prior to certification and another 142 were returned as non-reviewable. Certification was pending on 84 applications.

Table 12-10

Activity of the Foreign Investment Review Agency: 1974/75-1982/83

	Year[a]									
	1974-1975	1975-1976	1976-1977	1977-1978	1978-1979	1979-1980	1980-1981	1981-1982	1982-1983	Total
(1) Applications Certified as Reviewable	150	170	424	632	713	784	731	739	887	5230
(2) Applications Resolved[b]	92	159	398	602	659	797	586	719	1079	5091
(3) —Allowed	63	114	319	541	576	687	448	513	924	4185
(4) —Disallowed	12	22	33	25	44	58	63	81	60	398
(5) —Withdrawn Prior to Final Decision	17	23	46	36	39	52	75	125	95	508
(6) Applications Under Assessment at Year's End	58	69	95	125	179	166	311	331	139	—
(7) % of resolved applications										
(a) allowed (3) ÷ (2)	68.5	71.7	80.1	89.9	87.4	86.2	76.4	71.3	85.6	82.2
(b) disallowed (4) ÷ (2)	13.0	13.8	8.3	4.1	6.7	7.3	10.8	11.3	5.6	7.8
(c) withdrawn (5) ÷ (2)	18.5	14.5	11.6	6.0	5.9	6.5	12.8	17.4	8.8	10.0
(d) Total	100.0	100.0	100.0	100.0	100.0	100.0	100.0	100.0	100.0	100.0

[a] April 1—March 31
[b] Resolved applications may exceed number of new applications certified when backlog of pending applications is reduced.
Source: Foreign Investment Review Agency, *Annual Reports* 1974/75—1982/83

(8 percent) disallowed. The remaining 10 percent of the applications were withdrawn before a final decision was made.

The percentage of applications accepted has not, however, remained constant. During the first two years of FIRA's operation about 70 percent of resolved applications were accepted. During the late 1970s, the percentage of accepted applications was in excess of 85 percent, while those disallowed hovered between 4 and 8 percent. When the Liberals returned to power in 1980, with Herb Gray the Minister responsible for the administration of FIRA, the signals given were that the Agency should adopt a tougher stance on foreign ownership. The percentage of applications accepted fell precipitously to 76 percent in 1980-81 and to 71 percent in 1981-82. While the number of applications disallowed rose to around 11 percent, it is the sharp rise in the number of applications eventually withdrawn which is particularly significant. Moreover, the number of certifiable applications in 1980-81 and 1981-82 fell well below the 1979-80 level, after having risen in every year since FIRA came into force, and in 1980-81 there was an even sharper decline (rise) in the number of applications resolved (pending at year's end). Clearly FIRA's impact on foreign investments is achieved not only through the applications disallowed, but through those withdrawn, those on which decisions are delayed, and those never made because of likelihood of rejection or costly terms for acceptance.[76]

FIRA's tougher stance in 1980 and 1981 evoked a strong, hostile response from foreign investors in particular and the business community in general. In 1982, Herb Gray was replaced, the review process was streamlined, and a number of ambiguities in the way the Act was interpreted were clarified.[77] The result was a sharp rise in new applications, applications revolved, and applications allowed, and a sharp decline in the inventory of outstanding cases. But FIRA had left its imprint. Its tougher stance in 1980 and 1981 coincided with a wave of large acquisitions of foreign-owned firms by Canadian firms (see Table 1-11). By restraining the merger activity of foreign controlled firms, FIRA probably contributed to the decline in the incidence of foreign control in the late 1970s and early 1980s.

Acceptance or rejection of foreign investment proposals is based on a set of ten criteria. These are indicated in Table 12-11. The right-hand side of Table 12-11 indicates the frequency with which each criterion is employed. The tenth, compatibility with national economic policy, seems to be a catchall since it is employed in virtually every positive decision.[78] Aside from this, most foreign

---

76. On many proposals, a bargaining process takes place between FIRA and the applicants with the former attempting to get the latter to increase its planned investment, employment, R&D expenditures, etc.

77. Foreign Investment Review Agency, *Annual Report* 1982-83, pp. 1-2.

78. FIRA does not provide published information on reasons for rejection.

Table 12-11

Foreign Investment Proposals and Reasons for Acceptance by FIRA, Selected Years[a]

Year	Number of Proposals Accepted	(1) Increased Employment	(2) New Investment	(3) Increased use of Canadian Products	(4) Additional Exports	(5) Canadian Participation	(6) Improved Productivity	(7) Enhanced Technology	(8) Improved Product Variety	(9) Impact on Competition	(10) Compatibility with National Economic Policy
				Reasons for Acceptance (number of times employed)[b]							
1975/76	114	99	92	70	50	53	90	35	59	41	114
1976/77	319	277	268	244	145	235	146	103	153	118	319
1978/79	576	474	469	359	200	326	251	111	265	210	574
1980/81	448	351	370	285	210	298	125	90	221	87	408
1982/83	924	752	775	774	437	742	237	182	329	179	913
Ranked importance		(3)	(2)	(4)	(6)	(5)	(8)	(10)	(7)	(9)	(1)

[a]Fiscal years, April 1–March 31
[b]Typically, several reasons are given when a proposal is accepted.
Source: Foreign Investment Review Agency, *Annual Reports*, selected years.

investment proposals were accepted because they were regarded as increasing both employment and investment. Least frequently are they regarded as enhancing technology or competition in Canadian markets. A casual reading of the table indicates little year-to-year change in each criterion's rank.

The economic impact of FIRA is problematic. The fact that the acceptance rate is high, albeit variable, and there is economic content in the criteria employed in choosing among applications might suggest few valuable foreign investments have been "lost" to Canada. On the other hand, it is probable that some desirable projects are not undertaken at all because of the review requirement. Thus FIRA might be viewed as a "tax" on foreign investment with a difficult-to-assess incidence.[79] By reducing the foreign demand for Canadian firms FIRA presumably reduces the overall demand for and price paid to Canadian firms which are up for sale. If so, FIRA transfers income from Canadian sellers to Canadian buyers of firms. In addition to influencing the *magnitude* of foreign investment, FIRA may affect its *distribution*. For example, FIRA guidelines would appear to favour existing vs. prospective foreign invest-ors, and probably tend to maintain the existing provincial distribution of foreign investment—a disadvantage from the standpoint of the industry-hungry Mari-times.

As this book went to press, the new Progressive Conservative government redeemed a campaign pledge to welcome increased foreign investment in Canada. On December 7, 1984, the government tabled legislation which would change the name of FIRA to Investment Canada. The renamed agency would be less menacing to foreign investors. Almost all new businesses would be exempt from review. Mergers and takeovers by foreign-owned firms would be subjected to review only where acquisitions exceeded 5 million dollars. However, any new business or acquisition in "culturally sensitive areas" could be subjected to review by Investment Canada. Finally for those foreign investment proposals subjected to review, the general criterion for acceptance would be changed from "significant benefit" to "net benefit." It will be interesting to see whether the proposed changes significantly alter the flow or composition of foreign invest-ment in Canada.

G. Anti-Dumping Tribunal (ADT)

"Dumping" is an old problem. It describes a situation where goods are sold in the producing country's external (foreign) market at a lower price than the one for which they are sold in the internal (home) market. "Dumping," then,

---

79. This view is held by Steven Globerman, *U.S. Ownership of Firms in Canada* (Montreal: C.D. Howe Institute, 1979).

involves price discrimination between two separate national markets.[80] Because it may be damaging to domestic producers, nations have long attempted to punish "dumpers" by levying "dumping duties" on dumped goods. But dumping can also benefit consumers by supplying them with goods at lower than the going market price.[81] Thus most analysts of dumping agree that before action is taken against it, "material injury" to domestic producers must be shown. This, of course, must be done on a case-by-case basis.

The Canadian anti-dumping system dates from 1904 when anti-dumping duties were introduced as an alternative to a more general increase in tariffs. The system of penalizing dumpers, whether or not they caused "material injury," remained essentially intact until the 1960s. However, after World War II, Canada, as a signatory of the General Agreement on Trade and Tariffs (GATT), began to feel pressures to bring its dumping system into line with the general principles of international trade on which GATT is based. These pressures could no longer be ignored in the 1960s when Canada, as a participant in the "Kennedy Round" of tariff negotiations, was obliged to draft a new anti-dumping code. This it did, and in 1968 Parliament enacted the Anti-Dumping Act and established the Anti-Dumping Tribunal (ADT).[82] In 1984, the ADT's name was changed and duties broadened as a result of new, more protective legislation (see below).

The antidumping procedures, which follow the United States pattern, work essentially as follows. Canadian producers who believe like goods are being dumped in Canada may complain to the Deputy Minister of National Revenue. The latter conducts initial inquiries to determine whether dumping has taken place, and if so, whether there is a basis for believing that the dumping may cause material injury.[83] The matter is then turned over to the ADT (or its successor) which conducts a thorough investigation. It then advises the Minister whether or not material injury is present or anticipated. If it finds material injury the minister levies dumping duties or threatens to levy them if future material injury is anticipated.

80. The "classic" work on dumping is Jacob Viner, *Dumping: a Problem in International Trade*, Reprints of Economic Classics (Kelley, New York, 1970). Dumping, of course, does not occur when the price of an imported good is below that of home-produced goods because of a comparative advantage in production enjoyed by the exporter.
81. However, if dumping is undertaken with predatory intent to eliminate a competitor in the importing country, after which dumping ceases and prices are raised, benefits are shortlived, to be followed by a net welfare loss.
82. A good discussion of the Canadian anti-dumping system is Rodney de C. Grey, *The Development of the Canadian Anti-Dumping System*, Montreal, Private Planning Association of Canada, 1973. Also see Philip Slayton, *The Anti-Dumping Tribunal*, Law Reform Commission of Canada (Ottawa: Supply and Services Canada, 1979).
83. It is also necessary that the "margin of dumping" (the *difference* between the price of the imported good and its "normal" price in the home market) be non-negligible.

Table 12-12 indicates the number of inquiries undertaken by the ADT to date. From 1969 to 1983 there were 150 inquiries, 50 of which ended with a finding of "no material injury." In eighty cases there was a finding of "material injury," and in another 20, a "likelihood of material injury." In 32 cases, these findings were subsequently rescinded. Table 12-12 also indicates some of the products and countries of origin for which decisions of "material injury" were found. These (and those for which no material injury was found) cover a wide spectrum of consumer and capital goods. From 1977 through 1983 21 ADT cases involved steel industry products, with material injury or its likelihood the finding in 17 of the cases.[84] While there is no clear evidence that the ADT has tended to become either more or less protectionist in its decisions, the number of cases is on the rise, and so is the proportion in which there is a finding of material injury. Moreover, there is pressure to make the antidumping law more protectionist.

During the 1970s, the antidumping procedures were, for the most part, sparingly and judiciously applied. However, pressure was building to provide greater protection from low-priced foreign goods, especially capital equipment. Since antidumping duties are not supposed to be applied retroactively foreign producers who dump in Canada receive what is called a "free bite"—i.e., an opportunity to make a sale at dumped prices before duties are levied. This does not pose much of a problem for consumer goods which are repetitively and frequently sold in Canada. However, many capital goods are custom designed, have a high unit cost, and are ordered rather infrequently. A "free bite" on a multimillion dollar generator or turbine may provide all the incentive that is needed for a foreign producer to risk later duties by dumping now.

The free bite issue was brought to a head in two antidumping cases involving Soviet-made hydraulic turbines and Japanese-made hydroelectric generators sold to B.C. Hydro, Newfoundland Hydro, and the New Brunswick Electric Power Commission.[85] Led by Dominion Engineering Works (a subsidiary of Canadian General Electric) and one of only two Canadian producers of generators and turbines, capital goods producers have put pressure on the federal government to put more protective teeth into the antidumping legislation. The federal government responded. In July 1980, it made proposals for

---

84. Nine of the steel industry-related cases were decided in 1983, eight of which produced a finding of material injury.

85. For a discussion and analysis of the turbines and generator cases see Klaus Stegemann, "The Net National Burden of Canadian Antidumping Policy: Turbines and Generators," *Cornell International Law Review*, 15, no. 2(Summer 1982), pp. 293-351. In both the turbines and generator cases the Deputy Minister found a substantial margin of dumping, but the ADT did not find that dumping had caused "material injury." In a third case, Newfoundland Hydro, fearing involvement in an antidumping case, sidestepped a low bid on hydroelectric generators by the Italian firm Ansaldo and paid 36 percent more for generators produced by CGE.

Table 12-12

Activities of Anti-Dumping Tribunal: 1969-1983

Year	Number of Findings	(1) Number of Inquiries which Resulted in a Finding of:[a]		(2) Past, Present & Future Injury Found & Anti-cipated[b]	(3) Likelihood of Future Injury	Some Products and Country(s) of Origin for which Material Injury Found (col. 2)
		Absence of Material Injury				
1969	3	3		—	—	Glace cherries (France)
1970	5	2		1	2	Electric can openers (Japan); syringes (U.S., Japan); TV sets (Japan, Taiwan)
1971	7	2		3	2	
1972	6	2		4	—	Fibreglass screening (U.S.A.); applejuice concentrates (Austria, Bulgaria, Greece, Hungary, Switzerland); circuit breakers (Japan, France)
1973	6	3		2	1	Double knit fabrics (U.K.)
1974	3	1		2	—	Zippers (Japan); tetanus globulin (U.S.A.); photo albums (Japan, Korea)
1975	7	3		3	1	Frozen dinners (U.S.A.); bricks (U.S.A.)
1976	13	6		5	2	Wood pommels (U.S.A.); hydraulic turbines (USSR)

Year					Products
1977	16	4	9	3	Polyester yarn (several countries); bicycles (Korea, Taiwan); wideflange steelshapes (U.K., France, Japan, South Africa, Luxembourg); hot rolled carbon steel (Japan)
1978	12	3	7	2	Stainless steel sheet (West Germany, Japan); canned tomatoes (Taiwan)
1979	14	6	7	1	Stainless steel pipe (Japan, U.K., Sweden); rubber footwear (Czechoslovakia, Poland, Korea, Taiwan)
1980	13	3	7	3	Hardboard panels (Poland); wheel rims (U.S.A.); sporting ammunition (U.S.A.)
1981	11	4	7	—	Brass-coated carbon steel wire (Belgium, Spain); telephone system intercoms (U.S.A.)
1982	15	4	9	2	Microwave ovens (Singapore, Korea); steel sheet piling (Luxembourg, France, U.K.)
1983	19	4	14	1	Stainless steel plate (Belgium, West Germany, France, Italy, Sweden, and U.K.); mold steel (West Germany); generators (Italy)
Total	150	50	80	20	

[a]Includes all inquiries where at least one country accused of "dumping" was found to have produced some degree of material injury.
[b]In 32 cases the findings of material injury have now been rescinded by the Tribunal. In another 4 cases the ADT decision was set aside by the Federal Court of Canada. In the remaining 64 cases, the decision of material injury was in effect as of December 31, 1983.
Source: Anti-Dumping Tribunal, Annual Reports 1969-1983.

amending the Anti-Dumping Act. The proposals were referred to a House of Commons Committee which, in 1982, issued its report supporting them. In essence, the proposals would allow formal investigations of dumping to begin at the time of tendering and before a contract is actually awarded. Moreover, end users rather than intermediate importers would be made responsible for paying antidumping duties. The intent of these proposals is to add to the deterrent effect of the antidumping laws. It is not clear, however, that Canadians as a whole stand to gain from implementing these proposals. Although they are likely to reduce the incidence of bids at dumped prices, they may not deter domestic buyers from making the purchase from foreign suppliers. (There is considerable evidence that this would have happened in the generator and turbine cases.) Thus consumers would pay more while domestic producers would gain nothing. Even when the deterrent is effective, causing domestic producers to win the contract, there may be a net welfare loss if the opportunity cost of domestic production is above that of foreign production. (See the analysis of deadweight loss in chapter 6).[86]

In January 1984, the government tabled, and in June 1984 Parliament enacted, a complex bill repealing the Anti-Dumping Act and replacing it with a Special Import Measures Act. Under the act, the ADT is replaced by a Canadian Import Tribunal (CIT) with broad powers to assess antidumping and countervailing duties—the latter where foreign governments are found to provide subsidies to persons or firms exporting to Canada. The material injury provision remains, but it is broadened to include "retardation" of the domestic industry. The act increases the flexibility of the Deputy Minister in initiating investigations and the Tribunal in imposing duties. Why did Parliament succumb to the protectionist urges which underlie the Special Import Measures Act? The government's decision to put more teeth into its antidumping legislation reflects the political reality associated with the economic reality of declining tariff barriers as the Tokyo Round of tariff negotiations are implemented in the 1980s. As tariff barriers decline, non-tariff barriers are going up, and the new legislation should be seen in this light. And Canada is not alone. The U.S. government is effectively imposing steel import quotas because American steel producers are being hurt by imports. The across-the-board nature of the steel import restrictions indicates that no attempt was made by the U.S. to determine on a case-by-case basis whether dumping had taken place.[87] It would be a tragedy if a "new protectionism" replaces the general faith in free trade that the GATT-initiated antidumping laws were designed to promote.

---

86. For a more detailed analysis of the welfare issues see Stegemann, op. cit., pp. 306-307. Also see Klaus Stegemann, "Special Measures Legislation: Deterring Dumping of Capital Goods," *Canadian Public Policy*, 8, no. 4 (Autumn 1982), pp. 573-585.
87. *Montreal Gazette*, June 16, 1984, p. E-5.

A Final Note

At the beginning of the chapter we suggested that there may be an inherent contradiction between protectionist policies on the one hand and attempts to spur economic growth and development on the other.[88] Classical liberal writers, with their faith in the invigorating forces of competition, recognized the conflict and etched their concern in the doctrine of free trade. Although many economists have drawn upon an "infant industry" argument to rationalize protectionist policies in an economic growth framework, the infant industry case was thought to be the exception "which proved the rule." The Canadian dilemma is that our geography has tempted us to believe that our whole economy is the exception to the rule. A three-thousand mile border with the United States has contributed to costly, and arguably unnecessary, efforts to maintain our economic "sovereignty" and, thereby, our political identity. Yet despite, or perhaps because of, our efforts, we still evince concern about the extent of foreign ownership, our resource-based economy, dependence on foreign technology, regional disparities, and the north-south lines of trade.

The programmes discussed in the preceding section only draw the main lines of the "industrial policies" employed by Canadian governments. We have focused on federal programmes, ignoring the too-numerous-to-mention ones undertaken at the provincial level.[89] However, the whole discussion of programmes, including the competition, regulatory, and public ownership policies discussed in chapters 8 to 11, should give the reader a feel for the richness and variety of public policies toward business behaviour and industrial growth in Canada. The very diversity which is Canada—geographically, culturally, linguistically, historically—is also reflected in our varied approaches to industrial problems. Yet for all our ingenuity in devising programmes, one may wonder whether, in the long run, they have helped or hindered.

The student who has come this far may also wonder whether economic sense can be made out of our seeming hodge-podge of public policies toward business. Further, he or she may even wonder whether economic "ties that bind" are any stronger than the political ties seem to be, threatened as they have been by strong regional tendencies. But this is too pessimistic a note on which to end. There are important threads of continuity in Canadian economic history and development. Natural resources and communications, which have played important roles in the development of the Canadian economy, continue to be

88. For an hypothesis linking an increasing demand for protectionist industrial policies to growing economic affluence, see Christopher Green, *Industrial Policy: The Fixities Hypotheses* (Toronto: Ontario Economic Council, 1984).
89. Hopefully, students, in choosing term paper subjects, will take the opportunity of investigating in some depth provincial public policies toward business.

important in a resource-hungry and communications-conscious world. Moreover, many of our institutions, such as the public firm-private firm duopolies in some of our regulated industries, reflect a healthy ingenuity and response to our unique environment.

In *Canadian Industrial Organization and Policy* our objective has been to comprehend Canada's industrial structure and the richness of our public policies toward business. What has often been lacking is an understanding and appreciation of our industrial landscape, its organization, behaviour and performance, and governments' responses to them. The second edition of this book will have served a useful purpose to the extent that it helps to fill that void..

Index

Subject Index

Rowell-Sirois Report, 2n
Royal Commission Inquiry into Civil Rights
(Ontario), 433n
Royal Commission on Canada's Economic
Prospects (Gordon Report), 447, 452
Royal Commission on Corporate Concentration,
20, 27, 29n, 30, 62n, 76, 77, 78n, 99n, 107,
165, 206n
Royal Commission on Energy (Borden), 358
Royal Commission on Farm Machinery, 183n,
184
Royal Commission on Financial Management and
Accountability (Lambert), 393n
Royal Commission on Price Spreads, 416n
Royal Commission on the Economic Union
and Development Prospects for Canada
(MacDonald), 392n
Royal Commission on Transportation
(MacPherson Commission), 334-335, 337
Royalties, 370, 399, 442
"Rule of reason," 245, 262, 274
*Ryan Building Supplies (Windsor) Ltd. et al,
Regina v.* (1964), 173n

St. Lawrence Corporation Ltd. et al, Regina v.
(1966, 1969), 161n, 171n
St. Lawrence Seaway, 336
Sales maximization, 150
"Sales plans," 171-172, 267
Science policy, 415
Second Stage Amendments, 300-301
Separation of ownership from control, 21, 27
Service sector, 4, 5, 9
Shadow groups, 27-28, 34
"Shared monopoly," 165, 270, 301, 302, 303,
304
Sherman Anti-trust Act, 225, 244, 248. *See also*
Antitrust laws, U.S.
Shipping Conferences, 335n, 437
Sidbec. *See* Public enterprise, Case studies of
Skeoch-McDonald Report, 300n
Smyth v. Ames (1898), 312n
Snavely Commission, 341n
Special Import Measures Act, 466. *See also*
Anti-Dumping Tribunal
Specialization agreements. *See* Industrial
rationalization
Staggers Act, 335n 338
Standard Industrial Classification (SIC), 59-61
Staples, Rex v. (1940), 277
Statute of monopolies (1624), 440
Strategic entry deterrence, 110-113, 119. *See
also* Barriers to entry, entry deterring behaviour·
Suboptimal capacity, 79, 100, 102-106,
129-131, 140, 205
Subsidiaries (Canadian), 3, 99, 121, 137, 211,
212, 214
Subsidies, 239, 337, 340-343, 362, 383, 427
exploration, 361

firm specific, 400, 455-457
implicit, 341
regional, 239
to public enterprise, 376, 387, 394-395, 397
to research and development, 213-214
to transport, 447
Sunbeam, Regina v. (1967), 292-293
"Sunset Law," 168n
Supercorporate controls, 27-30
"Supply management." *See* Marketing Boards
Supply restriction. *See* Quotas; Regulation, to limit
or suppress competition
Survivor technique, 102-104, 205n
Sustainability, 321
Syncrude (tar sands) project, 361, 390, 397, 398
"Syndicates," 241

Tacit collusion, 155, 156, 165n, 264, 269
Takeovers, 21, 30n, 83n, 391
Tariff Bureaus, 437-438
Tariffs, 1, 3, 61, 95, 121, 126-132, 136-144,
147, 149, 170, 207-208, 214, 446
and collusion, 162, 242-243
and commercial retaliation, 127
and competition, 127-129
and competition policy, 242-243, 298, 303
and concentration, 61, 127-129, 137-141
and efficiency, 127-130, 205-207
and foreign ownership and control, 75, 129,
132, 134-136
and inefficient scale, 104-105, 443-444
and models of political choice, 140-141
and pricing behaviour, 127-129
and profitability, 199-202, 215
and specialization, 141-143
as a barrier to entry, 61, 114, 274
effective rate of, 120n, 132n, 137-139
estimated cost of, 207
legacy of, 141, 216
nontariff barriers, 137, 441, 445-446, 466
reductions in, 106, 121-122, 141-144, 206,
466
selective reductions in, 303, 305
Taxes, 231, 299, 364, 371, 393
Taxi permits (value of), 429
TBA Report (of the RTPC), 298
Technical efficiency. *See* Efficiency, scale
Technological competition, 209-210, 270n
Technological opportunity, 210, 211
Technological progress, 53-54, 208-214,
371-372
structural determinants of, 208-211
in telecommunications, 351, 353, 373
Technology transfer, 95
"Technostructure," 209
Telecommunications, 316, 350-357
deregulation of, 316, 351-353, 357
network integrity of, 356

Name Index

483